THE BACKGROUND FOR COLLEGE TEACHING

Farrar & Rinehart Series in Education

Alvin C. Eurich, Editor

D0102470

In the
Farrar & Rinehart Series in Education

DEMOCRACY'S CHALLENGE TO EDUCATION
THE AMERICAN SCHOOL SYSTEM
THE BACKGROUND FOR COLLEGE TEACHING

THE
BACKGROUND
FOR
COLLEGE TEACHING

LUELLA COLE

FARRAR & RINEHART, INC.

PUBLISHERS   NEW YORK

To

E. E.

FOREWORD

The young man or woman who is preparing for teaching in college or university needs an understanding of the present situation in higher education.[1] The nature of the work given in colleges, the character of the student population, the methods of instruction, and the whole concept of education have recently changed and are still in the process of modification. It is the purpose of this book to give young people an overview of the problems they will almost certainly meet, plus such results of research as are now available on these various points. The presentation will be of somewhat uneven merit in the different chapters because in some fields there are far more data than in others. Naturally, I am not so naïve as to suppose that the information contained in this book is sufficient, in either amount or type, to solve all the problems of teaching in higher education. I have, however, tried to gather together what is actually known about college life, college students, and college instruction in such a way as to help the prospective teacher acquire the information he will need when he enters his profession.

At the moment the situation in colleges and universities is especially confusing. The change in the size and nature of the student population has precipitated one difficulty after another. During the last thirty years higher education has been

[1] This need has been voiced in a number of recent articles such as: W. C. Eells, "A University Course on the American College," *Journal of Higher Education,* 9: 141–44, 1938; B. L. Johnson, "Needed: A Doctor's Degree for General Education," *Journal of Higher Education,* 10: 75–78, 1939; and A. M. Palmer, "Courses in Higher Education," *Journal of Higher Education,* 9: 293–300, 1938.

a battlefield upon which several quite discrete engagements were in progress, without much relation to each other and certainly without a unifying command. The common bond among the various combatants seems to have been a conviction that the current situation was unsatisfactory. The reasons given, however, are almost as numerous as the critics. Struggles have arisen between the "new" and the "old" educational methods, between the scientist, who is determined to measure everything to the third decimal point, and the humanist, who believes the main values of education are intangible, between the defenders of advanced education for the common people and those who want it restricted to the select few, between the specialist and the general culturist, between those who want all education immediately applicable to daily life and those who think practicality less important, between the educational expert and the subject-matter expert. The objections and criticisms have come from research workers in education, from mental hygienists, from parents, from alumni, and—by reflection mainly—from administrators. Only a small portion of it arose within the teaching profession. Either college professors think they are competent, or else they are much better teachers than their critics suppose them to be. Since college instructors [2] have been on the receiving end of so much criticism it is only natural that they should respond, according to their individual dispositions, by being annoyed, resentful, defensive, bewildered, hurt, or discouraged. One typical attitude is expressed in the brief article quoted below:

I am a college teacher. I am forty years old and therefore grew up in what must have been old-fashioned schools. I went to an old-fashioned college which had entrance requirements. I have a Ph.D. from an old-fashioned graduate faculty. I once taught college-entrance requirements in an old-fashioned preparatory school before it went progressive and became a country-day school.

---

[2] Throughout the book I have used "teacher," "instructor," and "professor" as synonymous terms to avoid the monotony of repeating the single word "teacher." Unless otherwise indicated I mean merely a person, male or female, who gives instruction on the college level. Differences in academic rank are not intended.

I am therefore unhappily insulated against any knowledge of the new education.

I have been subscribing to *School and Society,* since the American Association of University Professors recommended it. Nearly every number gives me a jolt. I learn that scholars are harmful to education. I learn that the object of education is the creation of citizens. I learn that the worst teaching in the country is college teaching. I learn that college teachers will soon have to take courses in education. All this is news to my innocent ears.

My teaching (if I may still call it such) presents equal disturbances of mind. I note that the college requires all students to do over again most of the work they "took" in high school—one or two years of English, one or two years of natural science, one or two years of social science. In fact, the only high school studies that are accepted by the college as valid are foreign languages, and they are discounted up to 50 per cent of their face value. I note again that when I am asked to recommend college graduates for high school teaching, very little attention is paid to my idea of their scholarship. I hear of secondary school teachers who have never studied in college the subjects they teach. I hear strange things about relative grading and grading on effort, in the lower schools. And annually I observe the catastrophe of some 20 per cent of the freshman class in college, who are unable to do more than half their work, even under our present attenuated and repetitive curriculum.

Now I am fully aware of the beam in my own eye. I am not censuring or carping. What goes on in the lower schools is none of my business. But the effect on the college of the new theory and the present practice of the lower schools is a matter of some concern to me.

I have not yet heard it denied that the main object of higher education is knowledge and understanding. If the college is to achieve any such purpose, it cannot yield much more than it has done. It now devotes two years to work of high school grade. What will it do when the 6-6-4 plan is finally entrenched? Will the senior college then have to start where the junior college now starts—that is, with the teaching of the fundamentals six years too late, instead of only four years too late, as at present? Or are there no fundamentals any more? [3]

[3] G. B. Parks, *"Nos Morituri," School and Society,* 31:463–64, 1930. Used by permission of *School and Society* and the author. See also O. M. Johnston, "Academic Retrospect," *School and Society,* 38:329–32, 1933.

Most people who are now professors have, as reflected in
this excerpt, moments of nostalgia for the less complicated
academic life of years gone by. Any person who had an "old-
fashioned" education quite naturally finds the modern college
somewhat puzzling. The college teacher of today is beset by
many problems that his predecessors did not have to meet and
for which he often has no adequate preparation. It is only
human that many teachers should wish a return to the "good
old days" of long ago—which were not nearly as good at the
time as they seem in retrospect—and should resent the attacks
of those enthusiasts who want to throw away all educational
experience up to about 1920 and start higher education completely anew. However, the reactionist and the ultraprogressive
merely want two different kinds of utopia; education can
neither go back to its past nor escape from its own history.

Some of the criticisms made, either directly or by implication, against college teachers are disturbing. Many articles
describe present-day teachers as being either positively bad
influences or as generally footless and inept. The ideas in the
first type of article are well reflected in the titles: "The Hurt-
ful Influence of Scholars on Useful Educations,"[4] "Our Intellectual Graveyards,"[5] "The Dead Sea Fruits of Overspecializa-
tion,"[6] or "Is College Leadership Bankrupt?"[7] The titles of
the articles of the second type are milder, such as "The Auto-
biography of a College Professor,"[8] or "The Professor Goes
to Lunch."[9] In the former of these two articles the teacher is
portrayed as a failure in life; in the latter, he is presented as
a kindly person who has no understanding of modern youth
or of anything outside his narrow speciality. Every one of
the articles above listed has an element of caricature, melo-
drama, or farce, but all of them contain a kernel of unwelcome
truth.

[4] D. S. Snedden, *School and Society,* 31: 133–41, 1930.
[5] T. J. Wertenbaker, *American Scholar,* 3: 171–79, 1934.
[6] G. Frank, *Journal of Higher Education,* 7: 269–74, 1935.
[7] R. S. Uhrbrock, *Journal of Higher Education,* 6: 1–12, 1935.
[8] A. Hibbard, *School and Society,* 48: 368–71, 1938.
[9] W. P. Eaton, *Atlantic Monthly,* 155: 754–57, 1935.

Before leaving this topic I feel I should make my own position clear. For more than thirty-five years I have been either a student or a teacher in some educational institution. In this time I have known six faculties well and other groups less intimately. I not only have a degree in education but have spent the last twenty years in teaching professional subjects and doing educational research. And I still think college teachers as a group and regardless of the subject they teach are intelligent, sincere, stimulating, well-informed, entirely capable of managing their own affairs, and the most interesting people on earth. Faculties do not, it is true, fall in at once with every new idea. The members are too well disciplined by their own training to jump at conclusions, and they are too democratic to make a move until the great majority of them approve of it. I admit that many faculties have a Rock of Gibraltar quality. The few people who want to push teachers into a line of action for which they are not yet ready find this characteristic understandably annoying, but the many students who depend on their teachers find it an asset. If college faculties trimmed their sails to every passing breeze, higher education would be much worse off than even its most rabid assailants think it is. What I do believe to be true of college teachers is that they have too much work, too many students, too few facilities, and too little chance to develop their own minds.[10] Their teaching is often not as good as it could be, simply because human machines cannot operate at their highest efficiency when their vitality has been lowered by endless work and constant nervous strain. Within a generation the average teacher's actual load has doubled,[11] and his task of keeping up to date either in a single subject or on the world in general has become almost impossible. If administrators would cut the load in half, teaching would improve without any help from anyone. Naturally I do not regard college teachers as paragons, but I do not know who else in the community could do their work as well—or even do it at all.

Although I have great confidence in college faculties I have had too much training in the field of education to remain unaware of the average teacher's ignorance of many things he would want to know if only he knew where to learn them. The psychologist has much information about people and the educationalist knows many things about teaching that the graduate student of philology or

---

[10] See Wertenbaker, *op. cit.*
[11] See page 12.

ceramic engineering, for example, has no chance to learn. I am certainly as ignorant of other fields as experts in them are of mine. The difference is, however, that they have to use mine in their daily work, and I do not have to use theirs. They handle people—both individually and in groups—and they give instruction. They will do both better if they have more knowledge about human nature and teaching methods than they normally acquire in the course of their own preparation. It is therefore my purpose in writing this book to present educational and psychological data that are useful to college teachers. It is emphatically not my intention to draw anyone's conclusions for him or to tell him how to apply the facts to his own work. I have too much confidence in the intelligence of my colleagues for the former and too little knowledge of their specific problems for the latter. To be sure I sometimes express my own conclusions, but they are labeled as such—and I assume that any person with wit enough to be a college teacher is perfectly able to disagree with me if he wants to. This book does not, then, set forth any theory of education; it does not try to convert anyone to a new faith; it does not contain any panaceas for educational ills; it merely presents facts in a condensed and synthesized form and leaves the interpretation and application of them to the discretion of the reader.

One more point concerning the possible contribution of the present book to the development of an embryo college teacher should perhaps be mentioned, because of the criticisms which are sometimes expressed concerning the value of training in education for the production of better teaching. Nothing in this book will, in and of itself, make a good teacher out of a poor one. It seems to me that there are three main ingredients for successful teaching—knowledge of subject matter, information about all phases of teaching, and native talent. The first is supplied by a student's graduate years and his subsequent training as an assistant and instructor. The last is not learned; because of this element of talent, teaching remains an art rather than a science. The specialist in education can contribute only to the second element—information about teaching—and the most he can hope for is to help an already promising teacher to fulfill his promise.

The recent "revolution" in higher education has been accompanied by a vast literature. In the ten years between 1919 and

1929 no less than 735 books and articles [12] appeared, all of which dealt with some phase of college work—and the deluge still continues. In 222 of these publications curricular changes were described or recommended; in 256 some new procedure for handling students was discussed; there were 122 reports of experiments in methods of teaching and 135 descriptions of reorganization within some college or university.[13] During the last twenty-five years several new journals and yearbooks devoted to the presentation of college methods have been founded—the *Journal of Higher Education,* the *Bulletin of the American Association of Colleges,* the *Junior College Journal,* the *North Central Association Quarterly,* and the *Yearbooks* of the *American Association of Collegiate Registrars,* of the *Institute for Administrators of Higher Institutions,* of the *National Association of Deans of Women,* of the *Association of Urban Universities,* of the *Personnel Officers' Association,* of the *National Council of Religion in Higher Education,* of *College Teachers of Education.* In addition, many universities have started series of bulletins—of which those from Purdue and Oregon are good examples—while others have published whole volumes of reports—such as those from Chicago or Minnesota. The above list is only partial, but it indicates the immense amount of material that has appeared in recent years. All of this agitation should, in the course of time, lead to a fairly complete reorganization of higher education.[14]

[12] M. E. Haggerty, "Experimenting with the College Teacher's Problems," *Bulletin of the Association of American Colleges,* 15:99–110, 1929.

[13] This situation is brought out even more sharply by the record of publication within a single institution, as published in the *Bulletin of the Committee on Educational Research for the Biennium,* 1928–30, University of Minnesota Press, 1931, Vol. 34, No. 7, 148 pp. Beginning with 1914, when one member of the faculty published one article on some college problem, the number per year from the same group of teachers increased to 23 in 1920, to 29 in 1925, and to 68 in 1928. In the 17 years between 1914 and 1931 this one faculty had produced 430 books and articles, and the graduate students under their supervision had written 65 theses dealing with the problems of the college teacher.

[14] Good discussions of the general conclusions and trends of this interest can be found in C. S. Boucher, "Current Changes and Experiments in Liberal Arts Colleges," *Bulletin of the Association of American Colleges,* 17:178–95, 1931; K. W. Bigelow and M. S. MacLean, "Dominant Trends in General Education," *Thirty-eighth Yearbook of the National Society for the Study of Education,* 1939, pp. 351–80; in fact, this entire yearbook is devoted to a summary of the present developments.

Many of the articles in these periodicals and yearbooks have naturally been critical. One author [15] has summarized these criticisms by reading through all the issues of twelve general magazines and twenty-one educational periodicals for the years 1927, 1928, and 1929 and tabulating the objections found. There were thirty-seven different criticisms which occurred with some frequency between 1 and 32. The eight most common adverse comments are listed below, together with the number of times each was found:

(1) The college teacher does not receive proper recognition for good teaching 32
(2) College teaching ignores individual differences........... 32
(3) Methods of teaching are old fashioned, and there is not enough participation by the students................... 22
(4) Many teachers lack professional training............... 21
(5) College courses are poorly organized................... 16
(6) Students do not receive adequate guidance.............. 16
(7) Freshmen and sophomores are taught by inferior teachers 12
(8) There is too much class work and too little self-education by the student 11

It is interesting that almost all these major criticisms have to do with the same topic—the need for better teaching.[16]

From all the discussion, research, and publication about college problems, one might get the idea that higher education was at the moment hopelessly inadequate and that the recent

[15] C. W. Martin, "Adverse Criticisms of Higher Education," *Peabody Journal of Education,* 9: 3–8, 1931. Used by permission of the *Peabody Journal of Education* and the author.
[16] College alumni have also contributed their ideas by telling what they thought was wrong with their own education. In one sample study (G. R. Foster, *Social Change in Relation to Curricular Development in Collegiate Education for Women,* Colby College, Waterville, Maine, 1934, 203 pp.) the several hundred alumni were asked the following question:
In the light of your own experience have you any suggestions to offer for the reorganization of the curriculum in the college from which you were graduated?
The 373 suggestions made bring out four main points. These alumni wanted greater relevancy of the curriculum to life (42 per cent of the requests); more individualization (24 per cent); greater freedom from the beginning in a choice of courses (17 per cent); and more cultural courses (11 per cent). The first two motifs appear over and over again in the suggestions made by alumni groups. They want the curriculum to explain life, and they want the course of study so administered as to provide for individual differences among students in both ability and interests.

dissatisfaction was something quite new. Neither of these conclusions is true. Previous generations of students succeeded in getting an education and in growing into useful citizens. Their education could not have been as bad as the more ardent reformers seem to think. Nor is there anything new in complaints about education. They have existed since the beginning of history; in fact, they are almost the same complaints. Socrates objected to current methods of training Athenian youth, Roger Ascham raised his voice against both curriculum and methods in the time of Queen Elizabeth, Rousseau was violent in his criticism of all education in the latter half of the eighteenth century, Horace Mann was certainly dissatisfied with the American scene, and John Dewey has protested at length about schools and schoolwork from 1900 to the present. Lesser men by the hundreds have contributed their testimony as to the unsatisfactory work of colleges. The following excerpt appeared in 1911, but it is not distinguishable from many similar expressions of more recent date.

The present age is one of transition in higher education: the American college is on trial. Condemnation is heard on every hand. The capital charge is preferred that there is a general demoralization of college standards, expressing the fact that, as the college serves no particular educational purpose, it is immaterial whether the student takes the thing seriously or not. The college is said to retain traces of its English origin in the familiar twaddle about the college as a sort of gentleman factory—a gentleman being a youth free from the suspicion of thoroughness or definite purpose. The college is charged with failure in pedagogical insight at each of the critical junctures of the boy's education, so that a degree may be won with little or no systematic exertion, and as a result our college students are said to emerge flighty, superficial, and immature, lacking, as a class, concentration, seriousness, and thoroughness.

Mr. Charles Francis Adams says that the whole situation stands in crying need of reform. President Wilson observes that so far as colleges go, the side shows have swallowed up the circus, and we in the main tent do not know what is going on. Professor Cattell cannot understand why the public should pay a thousand dollars for the expenses of each boy who goes through college to enjoy the pleasures of drinking-clubs and betting on athletics. Professor Wendell declares that college education is to-day chiefly notable for its ineffectiveness. President Garfield deplores the weakening of intellectual stamina observed among undergraduates. President Pritchett bears witness that our schools, from the elementary school to the university, are inefficient, superficial, lacking in expert supervision.

The Nation summing up the testimony of many such witnesses, says that there is only too much concrete evidence to justify the complaint that college students are lacking in spontaneous and disinterested intellectual activity, and there is hardly a college in the country whose bachelor's degree is a genuine certificate of intellectual discipline. The *Dial* declares that modern society has thought to relieve itself of educational responsibility by multiplying the mere machinery of education, until many students nowadays get from their college life little but educational disadvantages. The *Columbia University Quarterly* concludes that the question really is not whether there should be radical changes in the American college, but what the changes should be. Thus there appear to be loud demands for scientific studies of all aspects of college administration. One of the most important of these is the administration of the curriculum.

Regarding the college curriculum of today President Hadley holds that there is something radically wrong about the principles under which we are working. Mr. Flexner says one can lay one's hands on nothing definite in the curriculum that is actually calculated to make for breadth, liberality, or citizenship. President W. L. Bryan finds that the excessive expansion of the course of study has cheapened the elementary college work. Professor Stephen Leacock declares that the American student's ignorance of all things except his own part of his subject has grown colossal. President Schurman deplores the fact that the college is without clear-cut notions of what a liberal education should be, and that this is not a local or special disability, but a paralysis affecting every College of Arts in America. The Glasgow *Herald* declares that in university matters, as in social and political affairs, America does not know where it is going, but it is determined to get there.

This confusion of ideas as to what should constitute the course of study for the Arts degree is revealed in the contradictory charges brought against the American college of today. President Eliot holds that freedom of choice has proved the only defensible

plan for administering the curriculum, while Professor Ladd declares that we must promptly and radically abandon the delusions
involved in the Elective System. Some critics condemn the college
for keeping its curriculum out of touch of the masses, and thus
harboring an indolent aristocracy; others condemn the college for
yielding weakly to the popular cry for more practical courses.
Some deplore the desertion of culture courses in favor of courses
of vocational trend; while others call the culture courses nothing
but soft, wishy-washy excuses for sloth, indifference, neglect, and
ill-concealed ridicule of the study and its teacher. Some critics
hold that the one thing necessary is to secure concentration of
each student's work in some department, while others enact complicated rules to enforce the scattering of electives among various
departments. And thus it goes. So great is the confusion of current discussions concerning the American college that an old negro
preacher seems unwittingly to have summed it up when he said,
"Education am de grand palladium ob our liberties and de pan-
demonium ob our civilization." [17]

Agitation over college work, college students, and college
teachers is merely a sign of a healthy interest in educational
matters. Fortunately there seems no likelihood that educators
will ever be satisfied. A genuine striving for perfection is
admirable, but if people ever arrived at this condition they
might find it quite uninteresting. Anyone who does not believe
this statement should read Dante's *Paradiso* and note the dead-
ening results of achieving an ideal. So long as the tumult and
the shouting continue, American education will develop and
prosper.

[17] W. T. Foster, *Administration of the College Curriculum*, Houghton
Mifflin Company, 1911, 390 pp. (pp. 159 ff.). Used by permission of Houghton Mifflin Company.

CONTENTS

II: THE COLLEGE STUDENT

CONTENTS   xix

LIST OF FIGURES

PAGE

LIST OF TABLES

I.

THE PRESENT-DAY SCENE

CHAPTER I

GENERAL SURVEY OF COLLEGES AND UNIVERSITIES

These United States are full of colleges and universities of all sizes and types. The smallest number in any single state is one and the largest nearly a hundred. In enrollments for the current year these institutions vary from 12 to 37,376 students.[1] The oldest was founded in 1638 and the youngest in 1937.[2] The grand total comes to 1,686 separate institutions among which there are 428 junior colleges, 66 normal schools, 166 teachers colleges, 259 professional schools, 661 colleges and universities, and 106 Negro schools.[3] Thus there is one college for every 5,352 persons in the country between the ages of 18 and 22.[4]

If one wishes to get an adequate view of modern higher education, one should begin with a survey of the objective facts about existing institutions. There are various points to be considered. What types of institution are represented? Where are these colleges and universities located? Who controls their policies? How many are private? How many are for members of one sex? What are the enrollments? How large is the teaching staff? How many students are there per teacher? What proportion of the nation's students go to colleges of different sizes? What proportion of teachers work in

---

[1] *The World Almanac,* 1940, *New York World-Telegram,* 1940, 960 pp.
[2] *Ibid.*
[3] *Biennial Survey of Education,* 1938–39, Part III, United States Department of the Interior, *Office of Education Bulletin,* No. 1, 1939.
[4] *Fifteenth Census,* Vol. 2, 1930.

NEW YORK } CALIFORNIA

PENNSYLVANIA

ILLINOIS

TEXAS

MICHIGAN

IOWA

OHIO

MASSACHUSETTS } WISCONSIN

MISSOURI

NORTH CAROLINA

GEORGIA

TENNESSEE

VIRGINIA

INDIANA } KANSAS

OKLAHOMA

MINNESOTA } MISSISSIPPI KENTUCKY

NEW JERSEY

SOUTH CAROLINA

WYOMING } NEVADA

DELAWARE

ARIZONA

RHODE ISLAND } NEW HAMPSHIRE

NEW MEXICO

IDAHO } UTAH

MONTANA } VERMONT NORTH DAKOTA

FLORIDA

MAINE

SOUTH DAKOTA

COLORADO

WEST VIRGINIA

OREGON } WASHINGTON DISTRICT OF COLUMBIA

LOUISIANA } CONNECTICUT

NEBRASKA } ARKANSAS

ALABAMA

MARYLAND

1 FIGURE = 10 COLLEGES
OR UNIVERSITIES

FIG. 1.—Geographical Distribution of Institutions.

4

small or large institutions? How long have the various colleges been in existence? Since the type of control, the type and number of students, the student load, and the age of an institution all have an effect upon teaching problems, and since these elements vary so markedly from place to place, these objective facts should be considered.

I. NUMBER, DISTRIBUTION, AND TYPES

1. Location: Figure 1 gives the information. The five states —New York, California, Pennsylvania, Illinois, and Texas— contribute 28 per cent of the total number of colleges in the United States. The twelve states at the top of the list—one-fourth the entire number—have 54 per cent of the colleges and universities in the country. The mere numbers should, however, be interpreted in terms of population. (Figure 2). The figures run from one institution per 31,000 people in Vermont to one for every 225,500 in Wyoming. Three states—Iowa, Wisconsin, and California—are among the first twelve on both lists, while four states—Delaware, Rhode Island, Wyoming, and Nevada—are among the lowest twelve on both. When population is considered, the five states that are outstanding as to mere number of colleges rank twelfth, twenty-fifth, thirty-fifth, fortieth, and forty-fifth from the top.

2. Control: What proportion of the institutions is private? What proportion is coeducational? What proportion is denominational? The data on these points are summarized in Figure 3. Higher education is predominantly public—even more so than appears in the diagram because most of the private colleges are small and most of the public ones large. Over 70 per cent of the colleges and universities are coeducational. Slightly more than 60 per cent are under nondenominational control. The typical institution for higher learning in this country is public, coeducational, and independent of religious affiliation.

3. Size: Data on size and on the points concerning the number of teachers and the age of institutions are difficult to obtain

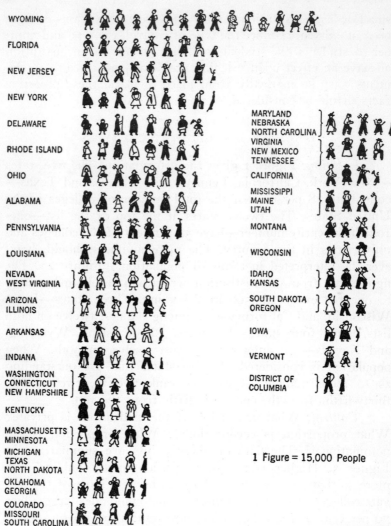

FIG. 2.—The Number of People per Institution for Each State.

because most published lists omit one or more of these items.[5] The best source I could find was the list published by the

[5] Thus the *Biennial Survey of Education* does not give either enrollments or the number of teachers. *The World Almanac* contains an incomplete list of colleges and only a smattering of technical schools or schools of education.

(a) PUBLIC OR PRIVATE

PRIVATE

PUBLIC

1 FIG. = 10%

(b) COEDUCATIONAL OR RESTRICTED

MEN ONLY

WOMEN ONLY

1 FIG. = 50 INSTITUTIONS

(c) DENOMINATIONAL OR NONDENOMINATIONAL

PROTESTANT

CATHOLIC

} AFFILIATED WITH SOME CHURCH

NONDENOM-INATIONAL

1 FIG. = 50 INSTITUTIONS

FIG. 3.—Proportion of Schools That Are (a) Public or Private; (b) Coeducational or for One Sex Only; and (c) Denominational or Nondenominational.

American Council on Education [6] which gives data for 667 accredited institutions. This total is less than half that to be found in the *Biennial Survey,* but the source contains a good sampling of schools of all types, and it gives all the information needed about each. From what data I collected about other colleges not on this list, I should judge that the distributions to be presented show a slightly more favorable situation than would be the case if all colleges were included. The difference would, however, not be large. For the remaining charts the total number of institutions is 667.

The size of the units in higher education covers a wide

[6] C. S. Marsh, *American Colleges and Universities,* American Council on Education, 1936, 1,129 pp.

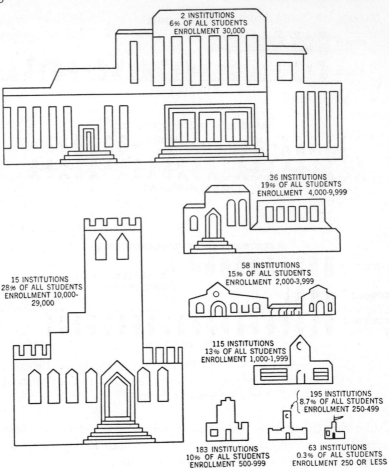

FIG. 4.—(a) The Relative Size of Institutions; (b) the Number of Schools of Each Size; and (c) the Proportion of All Students Attending Schools in Each Group.

range, the largest university being 3,114 times as large as the smallest college. The number of institutions of different sizes is not as important, however, as the proportions of students who attend each. Figure 4 gives information on both these points. Although there were only 17 schools that enrolled

10,000 or more students, the number of students attending them comes to more than a third of the total. Only 19 per cent of the students go to a college with an enrollment of less than a thousand and only 9 per cent to really small colleges—where there are not more than 500 students. One's conclusions about size of institutions are influenced by the way in which one summarizes the statistics. The brief table below is instructive.

ENROLLMENTS

	50–1,999	*2,000–9,999*	*10,000*
Per cent of students in each group..	32%	34%	34%
Number of colleges that contribute to each third	556	94	17

Two essential facts emerge from this table. First, one-third of American undergraduates attends schools with an enrollment of less than 2,000, one-third of them goes to institutions with enrollments between 2,000 and 10,000, and the remaining third attends schools where there are 10,000 or more students. Thus, second, there is a larger number of small colleges than of large, but their existence does not affect the lives of more than a fraction of the young people attending higher institutions. Smallness and intimacy are desirable, but not many students are getting them. One should never lose sight of these facts about size, because so many educational developments are the direct results of large enrollments. In the present book there will be more emphasis upon the problems of large than of small schools, because two-thirds of the students are enrolled in colleges having at least 1,000 students.

4. *Size of faculty:* The number of teachers per college varies from less than 10 to more than 1,500. The total distribution appears in Figure 5. Slightly more than half these teachers belong to faculties having 200 or more members. The proportions of young teachers in colleges of various sizes are not given. It is probable, however, that there are some recent Ph.D.'s on almost every faculty. Both the intellectual and the social life of a college faculty is to some extent influenced by the number of members. A young person who is preparing to enter college teaching can expect anything from

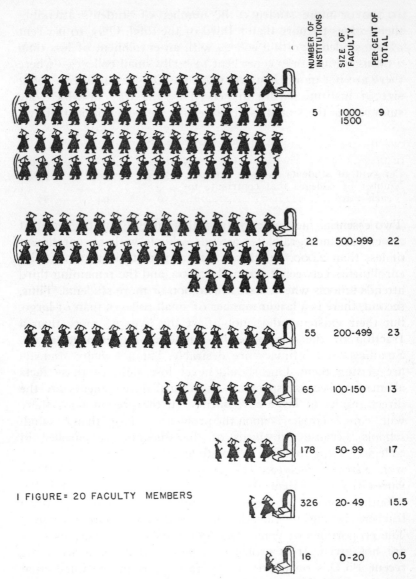

NUMBER OF INSTITUTIONS	SIZE OF FACULTY	PER CENT OF TOTAL
5	1000-1500	9
22	500-999	22
55	200-499	23
65	100-150	13
178	50-99	17
326	20-49	15.5
16	0-20	0.5

I FIGURE = 20 FACULTY MEMBERS

FIG. 5.—(a) The Relative Size of Faculties; (b) the Number of Schools with Each Size of Staff; and (c) the Percentage of All Teachers in Each Group.

the cozy interdependence of a small group in which everyone
knows everyone else to the relatively formal and distant relationships of a great university, in which a professor may teach
for forty years without so much as meeting many of his colleagues. Of the faculty members in the 667 institutions reported, about one-third—31 per cent—works in colleges having
a faculty personnel of at least 500, another third—36 per
cent—works in colleges having some number of teachers between 100 and 499, and the last third in colleges where the
faculty numbers less than 100 persons. The 520 smallest colleges together employ only 2 per cent more teachers than the
largest 27. Almost 75 per cent of college teachers work in
institutions in which the enrollment is at least 1,000. Here is
another reason for emphasizing the problem of the large college
more than those of the small—whenever the two are not the
same.

5. *Student load:* The term "student load" refers to the number of students per teacher and is calculated simply by dividing
the enrollment by the number on the faculty. The student load
thus reckoned for the 667 institutions studied is shown in
Figure 6. It varies from 3 to 95 students per teacher, with
a median of 12.1. The significance of this figure appears when
it is compared with similar medians for other years. At ten-
year intervals from 1899 through 1939 the number of students
per teacher in all kinds of higher institutions was, respectively,[7]
8, 8, 10, 13, and 15. Because the list used in constructing
Figure 6 contained only accredited colleges, the median of
12.1 is probably a little lower than that for the country as a
whole. In general, teachers of today have nearly twice as many
students as had those of 1909.

6. *Date of foundation:* The data on foundation present a
thumbnail sketch of growth in higher education. Of the 667
colleges for which the records are complete, only 16 were
founded before 1800. By 1820 there were 30. From then on
through 1935 at least one college was founded each year. The
period of greatest development was that from 1850 to 1900.

[7] Based on figures in the *Biennial Survey of Education,* 1932–34, for the
years 1899–1929 and upon *The World Almanac* for 1939.

Since the beginning of the present century the increase in number of schools has come chiefly from two sources. In the first twenty-five years most of the new colleges were teacher-training institutions; since then most of them have been experimental colleges. Although the additions are now being made more slowly, it would seem that the saturation point has not yet been reached.

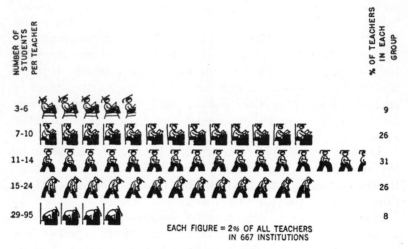

EACH FIGURE = 2% OF ALL TEACHERS
IN 667 INSTITUTIONS

FIG. 6.—Student Load.

II. SIGNIFICANCE OF THE FACTS

It would be pleasant if one could draw some tidy conclusions as to the location, nature, enrollments, size of faculty, and teaching load in the colleges of the United States. Such information would give a prospective teacher an idea of what kind of milieu he should be preparing to enter. One could, of course, compute medians or averages for the various distributions, but these calculations are helpful only to a limited degree. The fact is that American higher education has little uniformity. The schools are sprinkled, somewhat unevenly, all over the country. They may show any of numerous situations as regards type of control, nature of student body, or

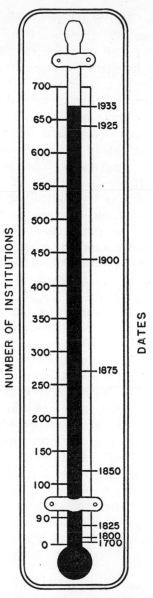

Fig. 7.—The Year of Foundation for 667 Institutions, Shown at Twenty-five-Year Intervals.

religious affiliation. The number of students and that of teachers vary enormously from place to place, as does the amount of work expected of teachers. The age of a school inevitably influences its character, since the presence or absence of tradition is largely a characteristic of age. Although there are colleges or universities that are typical of their class, there is essentially no such thing as a typical institution of higher learning for the entire country. It is difficult to find even two that match each other closely in all the points taken up in this chapter. In general, American colleges tend to adapt themselves to local situations—in the case of municipal and state schools; or to the bias of the controlling group—in the case of those that are private or denominational. Not all the possible combinations and permutations of the elements considered above exist, but a surprising proportion of them does.

Because of the great variations in these factors, plus further variations introduced by differences in objectives and types of subject matter, the problems of higher education are by no means the same in all colleges. In fact, the problems vary so much and the possible solutions are so dependent upon local situations that the presentation within a single book such as this must inevitably be incomplete and always restricted to those problems that are reported from the largest number of places. If in the following chapters it appears that work in large institutions is given more attention than work in the small ones, the reason is merely that two-thirds of the students and teachers work in colleges or universities with enrollments of 2,000 or more. Less than 20 per cent of teachers and students are to be found in really small schools. In a book of this kind it is necessary to put the major emphasis upon the outstanding problems of the greatest number. While the small college will not be neglected, it will receive less emphasis than the large university merely because it affects the lives of fewer people.

CHAPTER II

MODERN OBJECTIVES

There is no dearth of articles concerning the aims and objectives of a college education. These articles contain, however, material that is almost wholly subjective. The aims of education are, in their very nature, matters of opinion; they are not susceptible of objective proof. If they were, there would be no excuse for extended discussions about them. Since personal convictions do not constitute evidence, people can—and probably will—go on arguing about them without ever reaching a tenable conclusion. Like other beliefs, however, they can be studied objectively and their development traced. I have no intention in this chapter of being more than an impersonal recorder; in this role I shall merely summarize the opinions of others. Nor do I pretend to know who is right. All I can do—since there seems little sense in adding my own unprovable beliefs to an already large collection—is to present the data and let the reader make up his own mind. It is therefore the purpose of this chapter to show what the objectives of a college education—in so far as these are recorded in writing—have been at different times, by what means they have been determined, and in what direction they are now tending.

I. METHODS OF PROCEDURE

There are, in general, two methods by which educational leaders determine the objectives in which they believe. The older method is to draw them from one's inner consciousness, on the basis of one's own experiences and observations as to what training is most appropriate for producing an educated person. Such conclusions are, of course, wholly subjective. The other and more recently developed method is to assume that a college should fit its graduates for the life of an average person, and then to analyze "life" as objectively as possible. Thus, the investigator studies the daily activities of educated people, gathers information about their needs, and inquires into the difficulties they have had in adjusting to the world. With such evidence at hand he selects the most frequent activities, problems, and interests, and then assumes that higher education should train people in those matters of general value and of too complex a nature to be covered by the work of the public schools. The aims determined by this method have at least the virtue of objectivity. It should be noted that these two techniques—although different in actual procedures—have a common element. In both cases there is the intention of relating college to life. In the former the judgment of one or more experts is regarded as the best source of information; in the latter the compilation of facts becomes the point of departure. The intention remains, however, identical.

There are obvious limitations to both methods. The first rests upon unproved and largely unprovable beliefs. Those who think that a large enough collection of opinions from leading educators will somehow turn into proof should remember that the weight of opinion in the fifteenth century did not prove the world was flat. Even if one thousand outstanding thinkers say that the aim of education is to "train the mind," there is still no evidence to show that this objective is either correct or attainable. The second method has equally serious shortcomings. It cannot, for instance, deal with "imponderables." Moreover, it rests upon samplings of various kinds. It is impossible to analyze the activities of more than a small proportion of the college graduates in the population, and, since most people have no Boswell, the records kept are inevitably piecemeal and incomplete. In the third place, the compilation of items remains just raw data until someone interprets it and in so doing adds his own bias. The method is not as objective as it is sometimes supposed to be, because the meaning read into the statistics depends to such a great extent upon who does the reading. Finally, analysis of what people do from day to day does not reveal what they should do; that is, this technique does not include ideals. Neither of these methods [1] is, then, free from objection. Any intelligent person can criticize either, but thus far no one has found acceptable substitutes for them. Any given aim of education has the greatest degree of validity if it is deduced by one method and proved by the other.

To make clear the nature and end results of these two procedures in determining objectives, I want to give brief illustrations of each. The two specimens below could be duplicated a hundred times, with the same or with varying opinions. These selections consist merely of statements made by two individuals who set forth their concepts of the objectives to be reached through a college education.

You will ask me perhaps to suggest to you the particular intellectual benefit which I conceive students have a right to require of us, and which we engage by means of our classes to provide for them . . . Consider, for instance, what a discipline in accuracy of thought it is to have to construe a foreign language into your own; what a still severer and more improving exercise it is to translate from your own into a foreign language. Consider, again, what a lesson in memory and discrimination it is to get up, as it is called, any one chapter of history. Consider what a trial of acuteness, caution, and exactness it is to master, and still more to prove, a number of definitions. Again, what an exercise in logic is classification, what an exercise in logical precision it is to understand and enunciate the proof of any of the more difficult propositions of Euclid, or to master any one of the great arguments for Christianity so thoroughly as to bear examination upon it; or, again, to analyze sufficiently, yet in as few words as possible, a speech, or to draw up a critique upon a poem. And so of any other science,—chemistry, or comparative anatomy, or natural history; it does not matter what it is, if it be really studied and mastered, as far as it is taken up. The result is a formation of

---

[1] There is, of course, a number of variations of these two fundamental methods. Often they are used together in the same research.

mind,—that is, a habit of order and system, a habit of referring every accession of knowledge to what we already know, and of adjusting the one with the other; and, moreover, as such a habit implies, the actual acceptance and use of certain principles as centres of thought, around which our knowledge grows and is located.[2]

A second and more recent expression of the objectives of a college education is given below:

The liberal arts college not only provides a foundation for professional work, but increasingly emphasizes the aims of preparation for a worthy use of leisure and for an enlightened social cooperation. Perhaps the general aim that culture has always had in mind is the ennobling use of leisure time, but to-day the scope of this objective has gone far beyond its original limited application to artistic appreciation and enjoyment. It now includes all the desirable activities of the home and civic life in which one engages apart from his occupation or profession, as well as those which are usually thought of as recreational. In training for enlightened and morally guided social cooperation, the college finds its greatest opportunity and obligation. The knowledge of our physical environment and the ability to control it have far outrun our ability to direct this knowledge to the common good. The crowning event of education in the process of evolution has been the emergence of personality. The goal of education must be the ability and the desire of persons to cooperate in securing the highest social good. Scientific discoveries, inventions, and new uses of knowledge will surely continue to be made, but greater than the need of extending the limits of human knowledge is that of devising a way of applying the knowledge we already have to the improvement of human living.[3]

The above statements are well written, clearly expressed, and unexceptionable in all ways but one—neither author can demonstrate the truth of what he says. Each could get a host of others

[2] From J. H. C. Newman, *The Idea of a University,* Longmans, Green & Company, 1921 Edition, 527 pp. (pp. 501–2). Used by permission of Longmans, Green & Company.

[3] From F. W. Johnson, "The Liberal Arts College," *School and Society,* 35 : 168–70, 1932. Used by permission of *School and Society* and the author.

to agree with him, but he would be as far from proof as ever.

As a sample of objectives arrived at by the second method referred to above, I will give a brief résumé of work done at Stephens College, Missouri. This fundamental investigation is being used to determine both the aims and the curriculum for the college, but the present discussion will be limited to results on the former point.[4]

The administrative officers and the faculty of Stephens College felt that the traditional objectives in education and the traditional curriculum were not especially appropriate for the training of the average woman for an average life in the modern world. They decided, therefore, to make a careful study of the daily lives of women who were college graduates. The first step in this research was to locate, 1,000 college women graduates who were willing to keep a detailed diary over a period of time. These 1,000 women were graduates of 95 different colleges and were, at the time of the investigation, living in 37 different states. The majority of them were married; some were doing remunerative work, but most of them were not. Every effort was made to obtain a representative sampling of college graduates. Each of these women kept for a year a daily record of everything she did and every problem she had to meet. Analysis of these autobiographies revealed a total of 7,349 different activities, which were subsequently classified under 25 headings. The majority of the activities were concerned with the care of children, the maintenance of the home and family, the handling of money, various types of recreation, civic duties, and both formal and informal social relationships. The objectives based upon this study are as follows:

(1) Education in the practical management of a home
(2) Education in the care and understanding of children
(3) Education in the maintenance of a family
(4) Sex education
(5) Education in social relationships and activities
(6) Education for the development of acceptable personalities
(7) Education as a citizen

[4] J. M. Wood, "The College Curriculum for Women," in E. Hudelson, *Problems of College Education,* University of Minnesota Press, 1928, pp. 369–82. See also W. W. Charters, "Stephens College Program for the Education of Women," *Education Service Series,* No. 1, Columbia, Missouri, 1933, 62 pp.

It should be noted that these objectives are derived from data as to what women actually do. The fundamental objectives for the education of women are centered upon the development of personality, the maintenance of home life, and the development of social and civic capacities. These aims vary somewhat from those that would be derived from a similar study of 1,000 men college graduates. They differ also from many of the objectives expressed by individual writers on the subject. Conspicuously absent are the traditional academic aims of higher education. Women's activities, as they were revealed by this study, were not typically such as to furnish a basis for these aims.[5]

Even from this limited sampling it is clear that there are several possible aims of college work and more than one way of determining them. The philosopher prefers the first method, while the scientist puts his faith in the second. Both techniques have their virtues and their shortcomings. Fortunately they are supplementary, for one is strong precisely where the other is weak. A synthesis is naturally superior to either in isolation.

II. OBJECTIVES: PAST AND PRESENT

In the past some objectives have been more in vogue than others. Recent profound changes in social environment and in both the size and the nature of the student population have precipitated changes in objectives. A consideration of these modifications is of interest. Table 1 shows the results of an analysis of the literature on this subject, from about 1840 to the present time. The data in the first column rest upon a study of twenty-two books and articles that appeared between 1842 and 1876; those in the second column, upon forty articles published between 1909 and 1921; and those in the third, upon seventy-two articles and books between 1925 and the present. In so far as possible, the surveys here reported include the

[5] Although the aims may seem to exclude a good deal of the work usually thought of as being given in college, such is not actually the case. The curriculum is not limited to the topics enumerated above, although they furnish the basis for the fundamental, required courses. Since girls and women have many other interests which contribute to both the growth of personality and the preparation for leisure, there are many elective courses for the carrying out of these individual interests.

opinions of the outstanding leaders in education during the various periods indicated. Naturally most writers mentioned more than one aim, so the total number listed is far in excess of the number of articles. For purposes of comparison these numbers have been reduced to per cents.

TABLE I

Percentage of Mention for Various Objectives during Three Periods from 1842 to 1938

Objective	22 Books and Articles* 1842–76	40 Books and Articles* 1909–21	76 Books and Articles† 1925–39
1. Moral and religious development...........	*23*	*18*	4
2. Liberal education.........................	*21*	*14*	2
3. Mental discipline.........................	*19*	7	2
4. Civic and social responsibility.............	7	*14*	*10*
5. Good speech.............................	6	1	o
6. Preprofessional training...................	7	7	5
7. Professional training......................	3	*6*	1
8. Training for leisure and recreation.........	3	4	4
9. Development of leadership.................	2	5	1
10. Manners................................	2	o	o
11. Training for life's daily needs.............	2	5	*19*
12. Good health.............................	1	1	2
13. Training for domestic responsibility........	1	3	3
14. Knowledge for its own sake...............	1	2	o
15. Development of scholarly aims and ambitions.	2	5	*9*
16. Selection for graduate work...............	o	2	1
17. Co-ordination of students' work...........	o	2	1
18. Democratization of college education.......	o	1	o
19. Guidance and exploration.................	o	3	1
20. Development of a philosophy of life........	o	o	5
21. Training of the emotions..................	o	o	6
22. Adjustment to the modern world...........	o	o	*11*
23. Development of the individual as a person...	o	o	*13*
Total number of aims given:..................	118	213	271
Per cent mental discipline (3).................	19	7	2
Per cent scholarship (2, 14, 15, 16, 17, 19).......	24	28	14
Per cent vocational (6, 7).....................	10	13	6
Per cent moral and religious (1, 20)...........	23	18	9
Per cent leadership (9).......................	2	5	1
Per cent citizenship and life's needs (4, 8, 11, 13, 18, 22).....................................	13	27	47
Per cent development of individual (12, 21, 23)..	1	1	21
Per cent of others (5, 10)....................	8	1	o

* The percentages in these two columns come from L. V. Koos and C. C. Crawford, "The College Aims Past and Present," *School and Society*, 14:499–509, 1921. Used by permission of *School and Society* and the authors.

It is at once clear that objectives are by no means static. In the first period three aims—moral training, cultural background, and mental discipline—made up 63 per cent of the total. In the second period these constituted only 39 per cent, and in the more recent years they have shrunk to only 8 per cent. On the other hand, the social aims—as compared to the cultural —have been coming into greater popularity. Four objectives— civic responsibility, training for life's daily needs, adjustment to the modern world, and development of the individual— make up 53 per cent of those mentioned in the most recent period, as contrasted with only 9 per cent in the earliest. Those per cents that make up approximately two-thirds of each total have been italicized. The middle period is one of transition from the religious, cultural, and disciplinary to the largely social aims.

These changes reflect the social trends and philosophies of

Note to Table I, *continued*

† The percentages in the third column come from the following articles and books:

1. J. T. Anderson, "Improvement of Teaching in College," *Journal of Higher Education*, 7: 36–41, 1936.
2. W. W. Barlett, *Education for Humanity: The History of Otterbein College*, Westerville, Ohio, 1932, 285 pp.
3. M. E. Bennett, College and Life, McGraw-Hill Book Company, 1933, 456 pp.
4. C. E. Beury, "The Mission of the Modern University," *Journal of Higher Education*, 7: 469–74, 1936.
5. W. B. Bizzell, "The Social Inadequacy of Education," *Journal of Higher Education*, 8: 233–40, 1937.
6. K. Blunt, "What Constitutes a Good College for Women," *School and Society*, 32: 137–42, 1930.
7. B. H. Bode, "Aims in College Teaching," *Journal of Higher Education*, 3: 475–80, 1932.
8. H. A. Brown, "Curriculum Revision in a Teachers' College," *Journal of Higher Education*, 5: 490–96, 1934.
9. E. W. Burton, *Education in a Democratic World*, University of Chicago Press, 1927 166 pp.
10. S. P. Capen, "The University as a Social Institution," *Educational Record*, 18: 457–68, 1937.
11. H. R. Chidsey, "Culture in Education," *Journal of Higher Education*, 8: 175–84, 1937.
12. W. E. Clark, "A College Goal," *School and Society*, 37: 105–11, 1933.
13. L. D. Coffman, "The Obligation of the University to the Social Order," *School and Society*, 36: 641–47, 1932.
14. E. P. Conkle, "Some Higher Aims of the University," *Education*, 47: 28–31, 1926.
15. C. W. Coulter, "The Present Challenge," *Journal of Higher Education*, 5: 355–64, 1934.

the present time, and these in turn rest to some extent upon the great increases in enrollment. Until the last twenty years the number of students in college was small, and those who attended were of considerably more than average ability. For them the aim of mental discipline was by no means as absurd as some modern writers would have one think. All the experiments with the transfer of training show that the more intelligent a person is the more transfer he gets from one field to another. If college students are recruited from the highest 3 per cent of the population, one might expect some degree of general training in how to think. The further toward the average of the population one goes, the less transfer is likely to occur. As an objective at the present time it is impractical because the student group is not sufficiently selected. A similar argument holds for the gradual loss of the general cultural

Note to Table I, *continued*

16. P. W. L. Cox, C. C. Peters, and D. S. Snedden, "Objectives of Education," *Second Yearbook of the National Society for the Study of Educational Sociology*, Bureau of Publications, Columbia University, 1929, 174 pp.
17. W. F. Cunningham, "The Liberal College," *Journal of Higher Education*, 6: 253–60, 1935.
18. J. G. Darley and K. M. Darley, "The Keystone of Curricular Planning," *Journal of Higher Education*, 8: 18–26, 1937.
19. T. H. Eaton, "Mental Discipline," *Journal of Higher Education*, 2: 493–501, 1931.
20. R. C. Francis, "Blind Alley toward the Stars," *Education*, 48: 593–601, 1928.
21. W. S. Gray, "Recent Trends in American College Education," *Proceedings of the Institute for Administrative Officers of Higher Institutions*, Vol. 3, University of Chicago Press, 1931, 253 pp.
22. M. E. Haggerty, "The Educational Program," Chapter 2 in *The Evaluation of Higher Institutions*, University of Chicago Press, 1937, 335 pp.
23. R. F. Harlow, "Sociological Trends," *Journal of Higher Education*, 8: 403–12, 1937.
24. H. E. Hawkes, "The Function of the Liberal Arts College in a University," *School and Society*, 19: 203–09, 1924.
25. K. L. Heaton and C. R. Koopman, *A College Curriculum Based upon the Functional Needs of Students*, University of Chicago Press, 1936, 157 pp.
26. H. Holt, "Ideals for the Development of Rollins College," *School and Society*, 26: 153–56, 1927.
27. F. W. Johnson, "The Liberal Arts College," *School and Society*, 35: 168–70, 1932.
28. J. B. Johnston, *The Liberal College in a Changing Society*, The Century Company, 1930, 326 pp.
29. C. H. Judd, "Problems of Education in the United States," *Recent Social Trends in the United States*, McGraw-Hill Book Company, Inc., 1933, pp. 325–81.
30. F. J. Kelly, "The University in Prospect," *School and Society*, 28: 633–42, 1928.
31. F. J. Kelly, *The American Arts College*, The MacMillan Company, 1925, 198 pp.

aim. As long as the students came from the upper levels of the social scale one could hope that the chief result of their education would be the development of a cultural background. Culture implies some degree of leisure, and the students in earlier years were likely to have leisure. At present, college students come from all levels of society. If one continues to accept the cultural aim for higher education, one is automatically assuming that the typical culture of the upper groups can be successfully disseminated throughout the general population. If this assumption is true, there is no reason for abandoning the cultural ideal as an objective for all college graduates. If it is

Note to Table I, *continued*
32. R. L. Kelly (Ed.), *The Effective College*, Association of American Colleges, 1928, 302 pp.
33. R. A. Kent (Ed.), *Higher Education in America*, Ginn and Company, 1930, 689 pp.
34. W. H. Kilpatrick, *Education for a Changing Civilization*, The Macmillan Company, 1926, 144 pp.
35. W. H. Kilpatrick, "First Things in Education," *School and Society*, 34: 847–54, 1931.
36. J. C. Knode, "Implications of the General College," *Journal of Higher Education*, 7: 403–10, 1936.
37 G. J. Laing, "The Function of the University," *School and Society*, 27: 315–25, 1928.
38. M. S. MacLean, "The College of 1924," *Journal of Higher Education*, 5: 240–46, 314–22, 1934
39. H. N. MacCracken, "Notes on a Decade's Advance in Higher Education," *Progressive Education*, 6: 23–27, 1929.
40. D. D. McKean, "What a Freshman Expects of a Liberal Education," *School and Society*, 35: 57–60, 1932.
41. F. L. McVey, "Ways and Means," *Journal of Higher Education*, 6: 203–18, 1935.
42. E. D. Martin, *The Meaning of a Liberal Education*, W. W. Norton & Company, 1926, 319 pp.
43. W. J. Matherly, "A New General College," *Journal of Higher Education*, 6: 401–19, 1935.
44. S. E. Mezes, "The Passing of the Liberal Arts College," *School and Society*, 33: 577–81, 1931.
45. *National Student-Faculty Conference on Religion and Education*, "Educational Adequacy for Modern Times," Association Press, 1931, 276 pp.
46. A. J. Nock, *The Theory of Education in the United States*, Harcourt, Brace and Company, 1932, 160 pp.
47. J. Park, "The Philosophy of Curriculum Making," *Journal of Higher Education*, 3: 233–40, 1932.
48. A. S. Pease, "The Aims of a Liberal College," *School and Society*, 26: 695–705, 1927.
49. E. S. C. Percy, "A Policy of Higher Education," *School and Society*, 32: 305–313, 1930.
50. E. R. Prytle, "Vital Values in Education," *School and Society*, 32: 41–44, 1930.
51. H. P. Rainey, "Aims in College Teaching," *Journal of Higher Education*, 4: 165–68, 1933.

not true, then this objective is no longer sensible. Inevitably, the aims of education must have some reference to those to whom they are applied.

The social, vocational, and developmental objectives have increased in both importance and frequency. A glance at the catalogues of colleges forty years ago makes it clear that the vocational aim could hardly have been taken seriously, because there was not enough vocational work being offered in the undergraduate years. Today, a student can, if he wants, grad-

Note to Table I, *continued*

52. H. P. Rainey, "The Crisis in Liberal Education," *School and Society*, 28: 249–55, 1928.
53. F. W. Reeves, "Stated Aims of Liberal Arts Colleges," *School and Society*, 36: 283–85, 1932.
54. L. B. Richardson, *A Study of the Liberal College*, Dartmouth College, Hanover, New Hampshire, 1924, 282 pp.
55. B. A. W. R. Russell, *Education and the Modern World*, W. W. Norton & Company, 1932, 240 pp.
56. J. D. Russell, "General Education in the Liberal Arts Colleges," *38th Yearbook of the National Society for the Study of Education*, 1939, pp. 171–92.
57. W. T. Sanger, "The Shift of Emphasis in Higher Education," *School and Society*, 27: 743–45, 1928.
58. W. D. Scott, "The Rapid Development of Mechanical Power and Its Influence on American Education," *Journal of Educational Research*, 9: 133–49, 1928.
59. P. A. Schilpp, *Higher Education Faces the Future*, Liveright Publishing Corp., 1930, 408 pp.
60. C. E. Seashore, "A Job Analysis for Higher Education," *Journal of Higher Education*, 6: 173–78, 1935.
61. F. I. Sheeder, "Toward More Enlighted Educational Practices," *Journal of Higher Education*, 8: 123–28, 1937.
62. D. S. Snedden, "Colleges: For What Purposes?" *Journal of Higher Education*, 1: 365–72, 1930.
63. D. S. Snedden, "Functions of the University," *Journal of Higher Education*, 2: 384–89, 1931.
64. M. L. Spencer, "The Pathfinder in the Wilderness," *School and Society*, 27: 309–15, 1928.
65. S. M. Stoke, "Is the Game Worth the Candle?" *Journal of Higher Education*, 6: 295–99, 1935.
66. C. H. Thurber, "The Liberal Arts College," *Journal of Higher Education*, 5: 382–88, 1934.
67. W. E. Uphaus, "Bucknell's Question," *Journal of Higher Education*, 5: 485–89, 1934.
68. H. Walker, "Planning for the Future," *Journal of Higher Education*, 6: 287–94, 1935.
69. E. H. Wilkins, *The Changing College*, University of Chicago Press, 1927, 132 pp.
70. J. T. Williams, "The New College Degree, Bachelor of Citizenship," *School and Society*, 28: 383–86, 1928.
71. B. D. Wood, "The Major Strategy of Guidance," *Educational Record*, 15: 419–44, 1934.
72. H. M. Wriston, *The Nature of a Liberal College*, Lawrence College Press, Appleton, Wisconsin, 1937, 177 pp.

uate from many an institution without taking more than a few "cultural" courses—even if his high school work is included in the total. The notion that college courses should be designed primarily to prepare the average person for living intelligently in the modern world is also comparatively new. About twenty-five years ago, when the enrollments began to climb, educators realized what the elementary schools have known for a longer time: that the average person needs a different treatment from that which is appropriate for the embryo scholar and gentleman. Half the population may go to college, but half the population will not become scholars. What they could derive from their work would be a better understanding of themselves and their environment.

In recent years several excellent efforts have been made to determine objectives both for the large university and for the small college.[6] Among the smaller institutions Muskingum, Mt. Pleasant, Stephens, Black Mountain, St. John's, and Fenn have been especially active.[7] The objectives that have emerged from these studies are in the main social and developmental. Reduced to its simplest terms the aim is to develop all the capacities of each individual in such a way that he can grow into a normal, contented adult and can make the best possible adjustment to the world about him.

The objectives given by Heaton and Koopman are as follows:

(1) The student should be prepared for mature living in all areas of relationship

(2) Opportunity should be provided for a broad general education as well as specialization

[6] As examples see C. S. Boucher, *The Chicago College Plan,* University of Chicago Press, 1935, 344 pp.; C. R. Fish, "The Wisconsin Curriculum," *School and Society,* 33 : 242–45, 1931; M. E. Haggerty, "The Educational Program," *Evaluation of Higher Education,* Vol. 3, University of Chicago Press, 1937, 328 pp.; *Preliminary Report of the General College Adolescent and Adult Studies,* University of Minnesota Press, 1939, 258 pp. For the most recent discussion see R. F. Butts, *The College Charts Its Course,* McGraw-Hill Book Company, 1939, 464 pp.

[7] Anyone who is interested in the techniques used for the determination of objectives should consult the following references: Muskingum College Faculty, R. W. Ogan (Ed.), *A College Looks at Its Program,* New Concord, Ohio 1937, 326 pp. (Part IV); K. L. Heaton and G. R. Koopman, "A College Curriculum Based on the Functional Needs of Students," University of Chicago Press, 1936, 157 pp.; Charters, *op. cit.*

(3) There is need for individualization of instruction
(4) The student should gain skills in self-direction and self-appraisal
(5) The student should become proficient in the skills essential to participation in group action
(6) There is need for increasing the efficiency of learning
(7) There is need for integration of instruction which will increase the efficiency of a faculty of specialists
(8) There is need for such changes in the curriculum as will eventuate in changes in behavior [8]

Those college teachers who feel that they are wasting their talents in trying to instill into the minds of the average American student the typical ideas that interest the scholar might be more content if they would change their objectives and try merely to develop their students into good citizens. There is not much profit in trying to remake people; human beings are what they are, and, if one can believe history, they have not changed much in their fundamental traits since their appearance upon the earthly scene. If a student wastes his time in college trying to become what nature never intended him to be and if he does so because his college gives him no chance to do anything else, it is the college that is to blame—not the student. Teachers would save themselves a great deal of disillusionment if they would accept people as they are and give them the type of education from which they can most profit.

American in contrast to European education has always been aimed at the common man rather than at the scholar. It is therefore not surprising that it fails to stimulate adequately those with scholarly minds—whether they be teachers or students. Since Revolutionary days educators in this country have been trying to adapt schoolwork at all levels to the abilities and interests of the average person. American education has produced what it was designed to produce, an enlightened general public. This objective has always been clear so far as the lower schools were concerned. Now it has permeated higher education as well. The effect upon future scholars is perhaps detrimental, but America seems still firmly dedicated to the

[8] Used by permission of the University of Chicago Press.

principle of "the greatest good for the greatest number." The American college is unique among the higher institutions of the world. Its aims should therefore grow out of its nature, without too much reference to the objectives of other institutions that differ in essential characteristics.

Since there are so many different kinds of students in the colleges of today, one is justified in holding up more than one objective for them. The various aims are not mutually exclusive, except perhaps when applied to the same person. For some students the aim is largely vocational, both because of their work and the nature of their interests. For the largest number it is probably social. All students are complex human beings living in a complex social milieu. This situation will continue throughout their lives, no matter what kind of work they may do; they therefore need knowledge about themselves and about the modern world. For some, the objective can logically remain the development of a wide cultural background; and for the few with scholarly interests and abilities, no academic aim is too high. It seems to me more profitable to adjust the objective to the student than to develop a fanatic belief in any one aim.

Many heated discussions could be avoided if the participants were not so sure that objectives are immutable entities, separate from life. On the contrary, as indicated by Table 1, they come from life, and they change with the times.[9] It is only natural that many college teachers should cling emotionally to the objectives that stirred them in their youth. Such devotion is very human, but it does not make these aims either right or sensible. If people would only realize that time is a one-way street, they might waste less of it in useless operations on the clock.

III. OBJECTIVES FOR A SINGLE COURSE

It is of great value for a teacher to formulate objectives not only for higher education as a whole but for his own

---

[9] They change also with the educational level. For a good summary on this point, see L. V. Koos, "A Comparison of Aims from Elementary School to University," *Educational Review*, 69: 176–83, 1925.

courses. This idea, with samples of its practical application, has been well expressed in a recent publication.

The teacher who formulates his course objectives has taken the first important step in the improvement of his teaching. Especially is this true if the objectives are stated in terms of desired changes in the student rather than in terms of topics to be read, of time to be spent, or of other conventional requirements. When such objectives are made the constant center of reference in teaching activities, the needs of the learner become matters of prime importance. Inasmuch as student needs are both varied and variable, the curriculum so motivated develops a much needed flexibility. The instructor, also, is more likely to recognize the fact that each student should have his own individual goals, irrespective of those of the rest of the class.

One major problem in the formulation of objectives is that of determining their validity. How can the teacher be assured that he has not overlooked important objectives, that he has excluded trivial or inappropriate objectives, and that he has maintained the proper relative emphasis of elements? There can be no final validation of objectives just as there can be no final testing in the field of science. However, various methods of appraisal are open to the practical teacher, working as he usually does under the limitations of time and money. He may, for example, prepare his statement on the basis of objectives compatible with his teaching practice. Similarly, he may make another formulation on the basis of his judgment as a philosopher and scholar in his field. He may then compare the two statements and make any apparent disagreements matters for specific consideration and discussion. The examination of published statements relating to objectives in the subject constitutes still another essential means of validation. In addition, the teacher has, or should have, the benefit of his colleagues' criticisms and suggestions. The give and take of critical discussion about objectives and their implications is a means of validating them. Again, experience in using a statement of objectives is an essential means of discovering their validity. The science teacher may find, for example, that although in practice he considers it important to insist that the student write scientific reports in satisfactory English he has not listed the use of good English as one of his essential objectives. This experience leads him to consider whether he wishes to accept as one of his objectives the development of writing ability in his students. Thus experience may lead the teacher to add an important objective which he had inadvertently omitted. Experience in trying to attain a stated objective may demonstrate it to be unattainable, so far as any evidence shows. If under the practical working conditions necessarily involved the objective cannot be achieved with a reasonable effort, it is not valid. Perhaps the objective should be more adequately analyzed and stated; perhaps it is more appropriate to a related course. How to deal with such an objective, the teacher must judge. In the end he may discard the objective.

Finally, it may be well to emphasize that in the last analysis the formulation of objectives is a matter of judgment and critical thinking on the basis of available, pertinent information. He who states his objectives answers for present practical purposes the question, "What is good?" This question the honest teacher is obligated to answer.

In the statements of objectives that follow, the *procedures* of the various teachers who face the practical problem of formulating objectives may be more suggestive than the particular formulations they have thus far achieved. There is no thought that any particular statement, however adequate it may be for the author, is necessarily adequate if used by a different teacher in a different situation. The authors of the statements, furthermore, regard their statements as reports of progress and in no sense fixed or final.[10]

In the same volume there are a number of statements giving the objectives of various courses. Among the most interesting are the aims set forth for the first course in biology.

OBJECTIVES FOR GENERAL BIOLOGY STATED IN TERMS OF THE STUDENT'S GOALS

I. To procure certain biological knowledge including
  1. A basic working vocabulary: an ability to recall and recognize commonly used biological terms
  2. A comprehension of important biological facts and principles which should result in an increased ability to
      (a) Picture and understand the world in which we live

[10] Ogan, *op. cit.*, pp. 125–27. Used by permission of Muskingum College.

      (b) Deal more intelligently with everyday problems of a biological nature

      (c) Understand something about the biological background of child behavior

      (d) Understand the subject matter of the courses of a biological nature commonly offered in the elementary schools

II. To develop certain scientific skills, such as the ability to

1. Use a microscope and other essential biological tools
2. Read and construct graphs
3. Use keys for the identification of plants and animals
4. Express effectively biological facts and principles by means of the English language and diagrammatic sketches
5. Find facts in books and journals

III. To develop scientific methods of procedure and thinking, *e.g.,* the ability to

1. Formulate hypotheses, and locate and define problems
2. Plan and conduct experiments by which to test hypotheses
3. Make accurate observations and careful verifications
4. Arrange and classify data logically
5. Interpret and evaluate data: to draw valid conclusions and generalizations
6. Apply general principles to concrete situations
7. Distinguish between good and bad authority, fact, and theory

IV. To acquire certain desirable attitudes, *i.e.,*

1. A scientific attitude of mind, which the student may evidence by

      (a) Holding statements and conclusions tentative until adequate objective evidence is secured

      (b) Relying only on valid objective evidence, even though it may conflict with public opinion, tradition, external authority, prejudice, and superstition

      (c) Subjecting statements to constant criticism and accepting adequate new proofs

      (d) Refusing to fake facts or results, or to make overstatements or understatements

      (e) Retracting statements if evidence demands it, and always admitting ignorance

    2. Recognition and emotional apprehension of
        (a) The inadequacy of teleological explanations of bio-
           logical phenomena
        (b) The value of scientific method
        (c) The value of biology and the contributions of the
           great biologists in the modern social order
        (d) The importance of biology to the elementary-
           school teacher and its value in the elementary-school
           curriculum
        (e) The vastness of scientific knowledge, and the still
           greater vastness of the unknown
        (f) The wonder of life and the universe in which it
           exists
    3. Interests and desires including
        (a) An interest in discovering new facts, reasons, and
           relations: the spirit of inquiry
        (b) A desire for more biological and general scientific
           information
        (c) A desire to teach biological science
        (d) An interest in the further study of plants and ani-
           mals [11]

Although a teacher will probably not reach all these objectives in a single course, he is more likely to reach some of them if he has a clear formulation of them in his mind. His materials and methods will inevitably be influenced by his aims. Especially valuable in the above example is the principle of stating objectives in terms of the modifications in behavior, information, and attitudes of the student who completes the course.

IV. SUMMARY

Objectives, like other social and educational phenomena, develop and change. In the course of America's history they have shown certain clear tendencies, both in their nature and in the way they are determined. In establishing the aims of higher education leaders have become increasingly skeptical of objectives whose value cannot be more or less proved by re-

[11] V. A. Greulach, in Ogan, *op. cit.*, pp. 141–43. Used by permission of Muskingum College.

search. In their nature the aims have changed from a concentration upon the purely academic to a concentration upon the personal and social—that is, from the needs of the future scholar to the needs of the future citizen. The results of these modifications upon the content of the curriculum and the intellectual life of the college will become increasingly evident in the following chapters.[12]

[12] There is an interesting series of quotations concerning modern objectives in B. Amidon, *Democracy's Challenge to Education,* Farrar & Rinehart, 1940, 263 pp. (pp. 28–38).

CHAPTER III

THE CURRICULUM

The curriculum is the heart of the college. Without it colleges would not even exist as educational institutions; they would be merely social clubs. In some specific instances the curriculum has undoubtedly become so outmoded that it no longer interests the students, who promptly devote themselves to something else that promises more reality. They are at an age during which they insist upon learning about life, even if they have to bootleg it onto the campus. They had rather study it in class—but life they will have at all costs. If the alumni of a college testify that they derived little benefit from classwork and that the chief value of a college education lies in extracurricular activities, there is merely something wrong with the particular course of study to which they were exposed. Such statements are no proof that all curricula are necessarily futile. Although students should certainly develop in personality and social ability during their college years, their most marked gains should be intellectual. A young person will develop his individuality whether he is at college or not, and he will make lifelong friends during the years from eighteen to twenty-two because he is at the right age to make them. In college he may succeed in both respects better than he otherwise would, since his environment is especially appropriate for such developments, but neither result is brought about exclusively in an educational institution. What he can achieve only with difficulty outside the college is an education. The curricular offerings are therefore of paramount importance.

The view just expressed does not coincide with that upheld
by many people. One or two quotations of the opposing attitude
seem worth presenting. For instance: "Educators must come
more definitely to recognize that to the average undergraduate,
student life constitutes the real life of the college." [1] This
statement is probably true for certain colleges, but as an ideal
for educators it strikes me as nonsense. Over thirty years ago
President Wilson complained that the "side shows were more
important than the main tent." The answer to this situation
is to keep the main tent more interesting than the side shows—
not to abandon it. Another quotation expresses a somewhat
similar idea: "Broadly speaking, faculties tend to think in
terms of a subject-centered world and undergraduates in terms
of student activity." [2] Naturally. Subject matter is the faculty's
business, and colleges would not exist at all if someone did
not think about it. In some instances a particular teacher
undoubtedly thinks too much about his subject matter and too
little about either his students or the relation of his material
to life outside the classroom; but some degree of preoccupation
with subject matter on the part of the teacher is practically
unavoidable. The only teachers who do not think about their
material are lamentably poor members of the profession. The
two statements above are milder than many that could have
been quoted.

If in the past those students who are now alumni failed
to derive as much value as they should have from their studies
there may be several reasons. Perhaps they got the value but
do not know it, or perhaps the curriculum was inappropriate
and badly taught, or perhaps they simply did not study enough
to have profited by their courses, regardless of the content.
If the alumni feel that they developed their personalities
better on the football field or in college dramatics than they did
during class hours, this situation is proof only that they did
not have a course of study appropriate to their needs. I do
not defend all the curricula of all the colleges; I defend only

[1] W. H. Cowley and W. W. Waller, "A Study of Student Life," *Journal
of Higher Education,* 6: 132–42, 1935.
[2] R. H. Edwards, J. M. Artman, G. M. Fisher, *Undergraduates,* Double-
day, Doran & Company, 1928, 366 pp.

the principle that the curriculum is more important than anything else.

This chapter will be long, because there is so much to say
on the topics presented. It seems best to begin with a brief
history of curricular developments in American colleges, in
order that one may see the present-day situation in perspective.
The second section deals with the practical question of what
the curricular offerings now are in institutions of different
sizes; these data are based upon a detailed study of many
catalogues. Finally comes the highly debatable matter of what
the college curriculum of today should contain. These various
points will be taken up in order.

I. HISTORY OF CURRICULAR DEVELOPMENTS

In the history of the curriculum in American colleges and
universities one can discern five fairly definite periods, each
with its accompanying philosophy. The first (1), which was by
far the longest, may be called the period of the "uniform
curriculum." It began in the middle of the seventeenth century
with the study of Latin, Greek, Hebrew, logic, philosophy,
mathematics, and a small amount of natural science. The object
of this course of study was to train young men for the ministry. The basic assumption underlying it was that it contained
all the elements necessary for this purpose; there was therefore
no need for electives. This curriculum, which was a close
imitation of work in foreign universities, continued practically
unchanged until after the Revolutionary War. At that time,
as a part of the general desire for freedom from European
and English domination, there arose a demand for a course
of study more suited to American needs.

The change from this first period to the second (2) was
gradual. By slow stages the emphasis upon Greek, Hebrew,
and logic became less, and the curriculum broadened by the
inclusion of such subjects as chemistry (in 1820), history (in
1822), and the modern languages.[3] Under the democratic ideals

[3] W. T. Foster, *Administration of the Curriculum,* Houghton Mifflin Company, 1911, 390 pp.

of the Revolution a virtual renaissance in higher education developed in the decade from 1820 to 1830. The new curricula included more and more work in both natural and social science and had as their objective the training of leaders in a democracy. This idea of preparation for enlightened citizenship has become increasingly dominant with the passing of time and still continues as a main objective.

Until after the Civil War the curriculum was in the main prescribed, although in a few places, such as the University of Virginia, an elective system had already made its appearance. Throughout the nineteenth century the colleges added one subject after another to their offerings—sometimes not willingly, but because they were forced to do so, both by the growth of human knowledge and by the demands of an increasingly complex civilization. The American college is essentially a conservative and stable institution, but it has never, within the last hundred years at least, made more than sporadic efforts to resist the pressure of outside opinion. The American public has wanted its colleges to bring the advances in knowledge into vital relationship with current social, economic, political, and human needs. Americans are a practical people; the idea of cloistered halls wherein scholarship can develop for its own sake seems to them almost unintelligible. As soon as the colonies became an independent nation the national ideology found its way into education. The resulting curriculum was therefore more a response to the requirements of the American public than a formulation of any theory of what should constitute a liberal education. This second period, which extends roughly from 1820 to about 1870, is one of transition. It is characterized by a change in objectives and a development of the curriculum through the inclusion of new subjects. The element that remained generally unchanged was the tendency to prescription.

These various additions of subject matter were eventually and inevitably fatal to any prescribed course of study, because no student could conceivably take all the courses that were offered. In fact, knowledge grew at such a rate and courses multiplied so fast that college faculties and administrators could not keep pace with the situation. After a few efforts to cope with the rising tide they introduced the free elective system—or some one of its numerous modifications—which was fundamentally an admission that the curriculum had got completely out of control.[4] Modern knowledge had become an unmanageable mass, and educators simply retreated from it—leaving the student to get hold of any piece he could. The results remind one of the poem about the seven blind men and the elephant.

Not every college adopted a system of free electives between, roughly, 1870 and 1900, but enough of them did to make these years a somewhat distinct period (3) characterized by considerable confusion in both the courses of study and the objectives. Those colleges that did not institute an entirely elective system were sufficiently influenced to provide a much greater degree of choice than had been true until this period. In almost all cases the amount of prescribed work was reduced from between 80 to 90 per cent to some amount between 25 and 50 per cent. The end of prescription marked the end of uniformity in education. Freedom of choice among subjects is more in keeping with the American outlook on life, but it produces some curious results. Under a system of free electives it is entirely possible for two students to graduate in the same class from the same college without having had a single course in common. In spite of the many practical arguments in defense of the situation, I still think it an odd arrangement for handing down a common educational heritage.

The elective system in its original, untrammeled state was unsatisfactory largely because the ordinary student could not be sure of getting an education. In the course of time it simply collapsed under its own weight, especially in large institutions where the offerings were numerous and the guidance meager. Various efforts to salvage it by means of "group requirements" were made, some of which are still functioning. The main trouble with these arrangements is that they provide the student with a sampling of knowledge but without a synthesis of

---

[4] G. Frank, "The Revolt against Education," *School and Society,* 23:729–41, 1926.

it.[5] With or without the restrictions of a group system the plan of completely free electives proved unsatisfactory—although it has left its mark upon subsequent developments.

Only those who lived through the free elective system, either as a teacher or as a student, can realize the results from a personal angle. A few figures may, however, help one to appreciate the nature of student reactions to either unlimited or unguided choices. For instance, 640 graduates of 13 different liberal arts colleges took work during their four years in 7 to 23 departments, with an average of 15.[6] Since a high school graduate has usually made a start in only one or two fields, the average student among this number would have begun from 8 to 12 new subjects during his four years. With this number of elementary courses a student does not have time to make a dent on any field of knowledge. Certainly those students who elected work in as many as 23 departments must have had a severe case of mental indigestion.

At some time between 1890 and 1910 most colleges entered upon a fourth period (4) during which each student centered his work around a single "major subject" in a single department. This arrangement was intended to co-ordinate the student's efforts and to prevent him from having such a conglomerate mass of subjects as had often been the case under the system of free elections. It was a reflection also of the increasing need by society for highly trained specialists. At first this arrangement seemed a good solution to the scattering of effort that had previously been all too common, but soon another difficulty arose, especially in large universities where a student could concentrate in a very narrow field. I have known

[5] Another difficulty is purely practical. Few colleges have succeeded in wording their regulations so that the meaning was perfectly clear. The oftener one reads the statements about group electives in the average catalogue, the hazier one becomes as to what they mean. Moreover, there is the ever-present question of what exceptions can be allowed. I have watched many a faculty spend the valuable time of its members in deciding whether or not Mary Smith, who is otherwise ready to graduate, should be permitted to substitute one semester of botany and one of zoology for two in a single subject; or if John Doe, who is a chemistry major, may count four transferred hours in economics to satisfy the five-hour requirement in social science.

[6] C. Linton and F. B. O'Rear, "What Students in Certain Liberal Arts Colleges Take for a Bachelor's Degree," *Teachers College Record,* 30: 343–47, 1929.

students who majored in biochemistry, for instance, who—after satisfying the low general college requirements—had never taken a course outside the departments of chemistry and biology. In the reaction from too many electives and too much diversification college students tended to become extreme specialists who concentrated their work before they had developed an adequate general background. Upon the average college campus, trouble soon arose between departments, partly because of rivalry in the race for a sufficient number of majors and partly because—as time went on—the first generation of narrowly trained specialists became college teachers and proceeded to pass down to their students their own intolerance of other fields of learning.

One corollary of the "major" system was an even greater multiplication of courses. If a student were to major in medieval history, for instance, there had to be enough courses in the subject to fill at least a two-year schedule. Another student who wanted to major in comparative anatomy had to have enough courses. In short, every department had to maintain a sufficient supply of courses to satisfy any prospective specialist who might demand them. Because of the rapid advances in actual knowledge some of these additions to the already overloaded curriculum were justified, but one can hardly deny that in some cases the content became extremely thin.

This fourth period had a number of distinctive characteristics. The common requirements for all students were low.[7] The undergraduate was free to choose his major subject, but once he had made this decision his sequence of courses was in large measure prescribed. The practical object of the arrangement was to produce graduates who knew enough about some one thing to be employable after graduation. The curricular offerings in the catalogue were sufficiently wide to satisfy anyone, but for a given student they were often extremely narrow.

In many colleges and universities a combined system of major subjects and free electives continues to function. In others

[7] See page 62.

a fifth period (5) has appeared—beginning at some time between 1920 and the present. At first the movement was frankly
experimental, but it is rapidly spreading and shows all the
signs of becoming a stage in American education. This new
period has three outstanding characteristics—a return to general education, an emphasis upon the adjustment of work to the
individual, and the substitution of a "field of concentration"
for the "major" subject. This last change may seem to the
uninitiated only a quibbling with words, but the difference is
not one of mere terminology. The "field of concentration" is
not expected to produce specialization within one or two departments or even an increasing degree of advancement in the
knowledge of single subjects. It is intended to result in an
understanding of a given field through contact with many
related subjects, chosen from as many departments as may be
required.[8] There has not been time for a full appraisal of this
system of concentration, but to date it appears better than
either free electives or majors. For one thing, faculties saw at
once that students could not be left to work out such a plan
by themselves and therefore from the beginning arranged for
guidance. A given student's work is scattered among related
departments;[9] this constant crossing of departmental lines has
had its effect in breaking down existing antagonisms. Moreover, this system is usually accompanied by the adoption of the
comprehensive examination. These tests are of a nature that
require students to correlate and co-ordinate what knowledge
they have gained from various sources into a sensible interpretation of their work as a whole. The advantages of the "field
of concentration" over the "major" are essentially three: a
student gets a general rather than a technical education, he
has to integrate his own work, and he does not develop so
readily the petty antagonisms between a single corner of a
field and all the other corners.

[8] F. J. Kelly, *The American Arts College,* The Macmillan Company,
1925, 198 pp.
[9] Thus a student may major in "Spanish America," taking courses from
history, anthropology, and political science; or in "Greek Civilization,"
with courses from art, Greek, and history; or in "Modern House Design,"
with courses in physics, home economics, and architecture; or in "Child
Care," with courses from psychology, sociology, and home economics.

This development, because it is so flexible, permits the college curriculum to reflect the modern interest in individuals. A complete individualization of each student's schedule is a logical accompaniment of the "field of concentration." Since a student chooses—under guidance—not only his field but his courses, each schedule is different from every other. The plan of study is unified, not by external requirements but by the student's interests. Around them he and his advisor build a schedule, taking courses from any department that has something to contribute. The selections are naturally related to each other in their content, but the task of unifying them belongs to the student. This individualization is under way in only a few places as yet; it is therefore impossible to estimate the results.

A recent summary gives a good statement of the present-day trends in higher education. The list of developments is as follows:

(1) Increased emphasis upon general education, with the resultant distinct trend away from intense specialization at the undergraduate level.

(2) Separation of junior and senior colleges, with a general educational function for the former and a somewhat specialized function for the latter.

(3) Increase in the responsibility of the student in getting his education.

(4) Increase in the extent of individualization.

(5) Realization of the bad effects upon undergraduates of instruction by overspecialized teachers, with a resulting increased emphasis upon the need for more appropriate teaching.

(6) Extensive experimentation among all lines and in all fields.[10]

In the foregoing brief historical account certain ideas stand out. From the early part of the nineteenth century higher education has become more and more related to life outside the campus gates, increasingly practical—a fact reflected especially

[10] W. E. Peik, "Curriculum Investigations at the Teacher Training, College, and University Levels," *Review of Educational Research,* 4: 199–213, 1934. Used by permission of the *Review of Educational Research.*

by the growth of engineering colleges, business schools and schools of education—and more immediately preparatory for one's daily life. Especially notable is the application of scientific information to practical problems, with the establishment of such courses as psychology of advertising, agricultural chemistry, the writing of editorials, social case work, financial forecasts, applied optics, bridge stresses, power plant design, mental hygiene, household physics, or child care. Nowhere is the American genius for turning everything to practical use more clearly revealed than in the catalogue of a large state university.

The great increases in all fields of knowledge precipitated a series of changes in the undergraduate curriculum. First the course of study grew to such an extent as to become utterly unmanageable, and the faculty left to the student the job of sorting out the mess. The free elective system thus introduced was so unsatisfactory that a movement in the exactly opposite direction began, and students were required to specialize during their undergraduate years. This arrangement was no better, although for different reasons. When the disadvantages of both extremes had become apparent American colleges embarked upon compromise measures that preserved the best qualities of both the previous systems. The nature of these compromises was influenced to a considerable extent by the modern educational doctrines of individual differences and the paramount importance of individual interests.

The typical course of study found in the catalogues of today is characterized by the inclusion of everything under the sun, the preponderance of practical applications of knowledge to the problems of either daily life or daily occupations, and the introduction of a system of checks and balances through which the individual student can be guided into acquiring a general education within a limited field. Here the matter rests at the moment, but in no human endeavor is the pronunciamento of the Greek philosopher that "the only constant thing is continual change" any more true than in the case of the college curriculum.

II. THE PRESENT-DAY CURRICULUM

The method used for determining the nature of the modern curriculum was extremely simple. I analyzed catalogues. It was at once obvious that the offerings were affected by the size of an institution. It therefore seemed best to tabulate the results of this analysis according to the enrollments. For practical purposes I have disregarded those colleges with less than 500 students, mainly because such a small proportion—less than 10 per cent—of the total number of students in the country is in these schools. From the array of larger enrollments I took three samples—one from colleges having from 500 to 1,000 students, one from those having from 2,000 to 8,000 students, and one from those with an enrollment of 12,000 or more. I selected colleges from all parts of the country and maintained throughout the existing relation between private and public, denominational and nondenominational, coeducational and non-coeducational institutions.[11]

The procedure for determining curricular offerings in each group was wholly pragmatic in character. After assembling this large number of catalogues I first sorted into four piles those from colleges having an enrollment of 500 to 1,000 students. Each pile contained catalogues from a different part of the country—the Northeast, South, Middlewest, and West. Then I began to tabulate the courses given in each department

[11] Catalogues from the colleges listed below were used in this analysis. First group: Alfred, Arkansas State College, Beloit, Birmingham-Southern, Bowdoin, Centenary, Coe, Delaware, Denison, Furman, Goucher, Hamline, John B. Stetson, Illinois Wesleyan, Incarnate Word, Lafayette, Linfield, Middlebury, Mills, New Mexico State College, Occidental, Oglethorpe, Providence, Puget Sound, Reed, Russell Sage, Santa Clara, Simpson, Wesleyan, Whittier, University of South Dakota. Second group: University of Arizona, University of Arkansas, Baylor, Boston College, Cornell, Dartmouth, University of Denver, De Paul, Duke, University of Florida, George Washington University, University of Georgia, University of Idaho, Indiana University, University of Louisville, Marquette, University of Maryland, Miami (Ohio), Michigan State College, Mississippi State College, Montana University, University of North Carolina, Notre Dame, Pennsylvania State College, Saint Louis University, Smith College, Southern Methodist, Stanford, Washington University (Missouri), Western Reserve, University of Utah, University of Wyoming. Third group: University of California, University of Chicago, Columbia, Hunter College, University of Illinois, University of Minnesota, Ohio State University, University of Pittsburgh, University of Washington.

in each college. As I worked, I took the top catalogue from each pile in order—thus sampling offerings from all over the country. I had no preconceived idea of how many catalogues I should have to analyze before I had sufficient evidence, but the matter soon settled itself. By the time I had finished with the first department I worked on—mathematics—for five colleges it had become clear that I had reached a "saturation" point, because I was not finding any new courses. I decided therefore to analyze each department from as many colleges as necessary until the last three I added failed to contribute more than an average of one new course apiece. This saturation point came quickly in the older and more established departments—such as mathematics—and slowly in the newer subjects. The actual number of catalogues needed for getting an adequate idea of the curriculum in the smaller colleges varied from five in Greek to nineteen in music.

As I proceeded with this work I kept on taking catalogues off the piles, in order. Thus, if I used nine for French—two from each of the four piles and one extra from one of them— I did not put these nine back when I began the next department but continued until I got to the bottom of the piles. Then I started again at the top. The sampling is therefore quite random and is probably not exactly the same for any two departments. All catalogues were, however, used an equal number of times.

The great majority of the courses were found in the first catalogues studied. For history the first three catalogues listed twenty different courses, the fourth added two more, the fifth one course, the sixth two, and the seventh none. Since the last three together had contributed only three new courses, the saturation point as defined above had been reached. For mathematics this stage appeared even sooner. The first two catalogues listed seventeen courses, the third added none, the fourth one, and the fifth none. This procedure, upon which the statistics of this chapter rest, was identical for all remaining departments.

Sample tabulations for the departments of history and mathematics are shown in Table 2.

T A B L E 2

Analysis of Catalogues for Two Departments

Mathematics

	Algebra	Trigonometry	Analysis	Analytical Geometry	Differential Calculus	Integral Calculus	Solid Geometry	Finance	Statistics	Advanced Calculus	Differential Equations	Theory of Equations	Projective Geometry	Teaching of Mathematics	Survey of Mathematics	History of Mathematics	Mathematics of Astronomy	Engineering Drawing
First College	1	1	1	1	1	1	1	1	1	1	1	1	1	1	1	1		1
Second College	2		1	1	1	1	1	1	1		1	1	1	1				
Third College	1			1	1	1	1	1		1	1	1					1	
Fourth College	1	1	1	1	1	1												
Fifth College		1	1	1	1	1	1	1		1	1	1	1	1		1		1

History

	History of Europe	English History	American History	Europe, 19th Century	American Diplomacy	History of Greece	History of Rome	Ancient History	South America	History of France	French Revolution	Middle Ages	Renaissance	British Civilization	American Civilization	Modern World	China	Japan	Far East	Pacific	Near East	State History	Western Civilization	American Leaders	Teaching of History
First College		1	1	3	1	1	1	1	1		1	1				1	1	1	1		1	1		1	1
Second College	2	2	7	1	1											1						1			1
Third College	1	2	2	2	1	1	1	1	1																1
Fourth College	1		1	1	1			1	2																
Fifth College		1	1	1	1			1							1					1					1
Sixth College	1	1	1	1		1	1							1	1								1		
Seventh College	1		1	2			1			1			1		1							1			

46

When I had finished this work for the first group of colleges, I proceeded in exactly similar fashion with the second group—those with an enrollment of 2,000 to 8,000 students. The number of catalogues needed to establish the offerings in each department varied from five for Italian to eleven for sociology. In the case of the third group of institutions—those with an enrollment of 12,000 or more—I had to stop tabulating a few departments before I had quite finished adding courses for the excellent reason that I ran out of institutions of the necessary size. For over 85 per cent of the departments, however, the saturation point had already been reached.

1. Number of courses: The first method of summarizing this large amount of data about the curriculum consists merely in presenting the range and the number of courses offered in each department in the colleges of each size. These results appear in Table 3.[12] I have grouped related subjects together, since this arrangement seemed clearer than an alphabetical list.

The marked lack of uniformity from one college to another is clearly shown by this table. On this point I can make no more pertinent remark than to quote what someone else has already said about a somewhat similar compilation of data.

A mere glance at the table shows the wide diversity of practice which has resulted from the attempts of many groups of men in many states to decide what is the essential core of a liberal education. Indeed so great is the diversity that if any one of these institutions is exactly right all the rest must be wrong. . . . The vast amount of miscellaneous experimenting with the college curriculum that has produced the temporary results set forth gives point to the remark of Professor Cattell that the collective unwisdom of a college faculty is not often exceeded by the unwisdom of any individual student. Anyone who has watched a college faculty make a decision at one meeting and promptly reverse itself at the next, without a particle of new evidence on the issue, is not unreasonably skeptical concerning the stability or the worth of the facts summarized in these tables.[13]

[12] Any departments that did not appear in at least half the catalogues are not listed, because their median frequency was zero.
[13] W. T. Foster, *op. cit.* Used by permission of the Houghton Mifflin Company.

TABLE 3

Number and Range of Courses in Various Departments in Colleges of Different Sizes

Department	Small Colleges (500 to 599) Median		Medium-sized Colleges and Universities (2,000–7,999 Students) Median		Large Universities (12,000 Students or More) Median	
	Courses	Range	Courses	Range	Courses	Range
A. Languages						
1. French	10	6–23	21	5–30	29	26–32
2. German	9	5–19	16	6–36	34	28–38
3. Spanish	6	0–18	12	5–21	14	11–24
4. Italian			3	0–3	7	5–10
5. Oriental					4	0–12
6. Greek	4	0–12	7	0–15	10	6–26
7. Latin	10	1–15	16	0–25	17	12–29
B. English						
1. Literature and writing	17	13–39	33	20–81	42	36–68
2. Public speaking			22	0–59	4	0–11
3. Journalism					19	6–54
C. Social sciences						
1. History	11	7–25	29	6–54	35	29–38
2. Economics	15	7–29	25	9–59	38	32–57
3. Political science	12	2–13	19	6–39	23	19–31
4. Sociology	8	0–17	18	0–36	27	21–32
5. Business organization*			21	0–74	54	32–123
D. Physical sciences and mathematics						
1. Mathematics	14	9–22	23	13–49	25	21–29
2. Astronomy	2	0–12	3	0–13	12	7–19
3. Chemistry	9	5–21	33	17–66	36	27–58
4. Geology	4	0–27	24	6–34	17	14–21
5. Physics	10	9–23	17	14–44	28	22–35
6. Geography					11	6–15
7. Engineering						
a. mechanical			22	0–44	37	23–35
b. civil			18	0–49	34	31–43
c. electrics			24	0–45	37	32–46
d. chemical					13	0–25
e. mining					29	9–47
f. railway					19	0–26
g. ceramic					11	0–21
h. mechanics					3	0–19
i. mechanical drawing					27	23–35

* Some of these courses are duplicates from other departments.

TABLE 3 *continued*

Department	Small Colleges (500 to 599) *Median*		Medium-sized Colleges and Universities (2,000–7,999 Students) *Median*		Large Universities (12,000 Students or More) *Median*	
	Courses	Range	Courses	Range	Courses	Range
E. Biological sciences						
1. Botany† ⎱ Biology.....	8	2–21	21	4–28	21	16–29
2. Zoology ⎰	7	3–18	17	10–41	28	24–33
3. Anatomy..........			3	0–14	9	7–18
4. Bacteriology........			6	0–21	9	7–13
5. Physiology..........					5	0–11
6. Entomology........					14	0–22
7. Biochemistry.......					5	0–14
8. Hygiene............					2	0–5
9. Horticulture........					19	0–32
10. Agriculture.........					25	19–37
11. Agronomy.........					11	0–15
12. Animal husbandry...					21	17–27
13. Dairying...........					17	12–24
F. Physiology, philosophy, religion, and education						
1. Religion............	7	0–21				
2. Education.........	10	3–33	38	6–147	57	30–172
3. Philosophy.........	9	0–18	13	1–32	18	14–21
4. Psychology.........	8	4–13	21	5–27	26	22–37
G. Arts						
1. Art................	9	1–36	18	0–22	41	36–45
2. Dramatics‡.........	6	0–24				
3. Music..............	29	3–90	21	0–170	43	29–57
4. Architecture........					24	0–29
5. Landscape architecture.......					8	0–15
H. Physical education......	11	3–40	34	5–73	39	27–58
I. Home economics.......			18	0–64	39	27–58

† For colleges having a combined department of Biology, the individual courses were assigned to Botany or Zoology according to the catalogue description.

‡ This department is absorbed by Public Speaking in the larger universities.

Although the paragraph quoted on page 47 was written nearly thirty years ago and although it referred especially to the degree of prescription, the sentiments coincide with my own in regard to the great diversity of practice above revealed.

The correlation between the size of the colleges and the median size of the departments is practically perfect. The figures show only three exceptions. The size of the geology department appears to decrease for the universities, but only because the courses dealing with geography [14] have been put into a group by themselves. The department of religion does not exist as an entity in most large institutions, although the courses are given by either the department of philosophy or that of English. The music department is often unusually large in small colleges because many of them make a point of developing it as a specialty in order to attract students. With these exceptions, however, the median number of courses increases with the size of the institutions.

The range in the number of courses offered is quite wide. Thus, the smallest number for colleges of the middle group is usually less than the median for the small colleges and much less than the maximum. This situation reflects the customary lack of uniformity in American education. Some departments have so many courses that one feels skeptical about their content. I have no personal knowledge as to the need for 90 courses in music, or 123 in business organization, or of 47 in mining engineering, but I am certain that there are not enough known facts to fill 172 in education. The extreme degree of specialization indicated by the course offerings in large universities suggests strongly that these institutions are no place for an undergraduate to receive a general education, because he can hardly keep from getting into specialized courses before he is ready for them.

The table shows also that large departments tend to split when their size becomes too unwieldly for administration. For instance, small colleges have a department of biology; as the number of students becomes greater two departments—botany and zoology—appear. In the state universities the differentiation develops further, and there is the addition of such departmental units as anatomy, physiology, bacteriology, entomology, biochemistry, hygiene, and the applied sciences of horticulture, agriculture, agronomy, animal husbandry, and dairying. Similar specialization appears in other fields.

[14] Also paleontology, in a few instances.

From these figures it would appear that the average college with an enrollment between 500 and 1,000 has twenty-five departments. The median number of courses per department varies from two in astronomy to twenty-nine in music. For the colleges and universities with an enrollment of 2,000 to 8,000 the average number of departments has increased to thirty-two. The median number varies from three in Italian to thirty-eight in education. Further differentiation gives the largest institutions an average of fifty-two departments. The number of courses per group runs from two to fifty-seven.[15]

The number of courses in the largest institutions is simply staggering. This development is the direct result of two forces —the actual increases of human knowledge and the modern tendency to adapt college work to vocational demands. In general, the number of courses has increased 300 per cent in the last thirty years.[16] Even in such a nonvocational subject as English the six courses at Harvard University in 1869 developed into forty by 1896, into forty-nine by 1910, into sixty-five by 1924, and into seventy by 1938.[17]

Within the last fifteen years there has been a growing conviction that courses overlapped on each other,[18] especially when different departments studied essentially the same facts from slightly different points of view. In a few places a faculty committee has had the courage to attack this problem and the perseverance to carry the work to its logical conclusion of eliminating the duplicating courses.[19] In all such investigations one finds that the assign-

[15] For a similar study see T. M. Carter, "The Curriculum of Liberal Arts Colleges," *School and Society,* 45 : 893–96, 1937. This author gives semester hours rather than the number of courses from an analysis of twenty college catalogues. Also M. E. Haggerty, *The Evaluation of Higher Education,* III : "The Educational Program," University of Chicago Press, 1937, 328 pp. (Chap. 5), and, for junior colleges, W. W. Carpenter, "Curricular Offerings in Missouri," *Junior College Journal,* 2 : 16–23, 1931.

[16] S. M. Stoke, "Is the Game Worth the Candle?" *Journal of Higher Education,* 6 : 295–99, 1935.

[17] From Harvard catalogues for these years.

[18] See, for instance, A. Hibbard, "Why Not a Moratorium on New Courses?" *School and Society,* 36 : 225–29, 1932.

[19] See G. W. Eckelberry, "Faculty Control of Courses," *Journal of Higher Education,* 7 : 141–46, 1937; P. O. Johnson, *Curricular Problems in Science at the College Level,* 188 pp., University of Minnesota Press, 1930; and E. M. Freeman, "Procedures and Results of Efforts to Reorganize Science Instruction at Minnesota," *Peabody Journal of Education,* 6 : 204–18, 1929.

ment of material to one department or another is often mere historical accident. It is entirely possible for two or even three almost parallel courses to exist upon a large campus in different departments under different names at the same time without the instructor of any class even knowing about the presence of the others. Thus, the same material may be presented and the same books assigned in a course on "Home Life" in home economics, on "Child Development" in psychology, on "Supervision of Playgrounds" in physical education, on "The Elementary School Child" in principles of education, and on "The Family" in sociology. The catalogue of a big university is so complex and the course descriptions are so short that only the registrar, the deans, the official proofreader, and the college secretaries have ever read the catalogue or have more than a general idea of what is in it.

In spite of the multiplicity of courses, however, there are both "curricular gaps"[20] and curricular overlappings in the work of individual students. One investigation presents the obvious omissions and duplications in the case of 680 college students. The per cent who had failed, during either high school or college, to take any work at all in each subject is shown below:

1. *Languages*[20a]	*Per Cent*	3. *History*	*Per Cent*
Greek	93	European	23
Latin	17	American	5
German	70	Ancient	11
French	40	Medieval	16
2. *Sciences*		4. *Appreciation*	
Physics	35	Art	64
Chemistry	32	Music	63
Both	14		
Botany	59		

Although the necessary courses exist, it is by no means sure that students will get an adequate sampling of them. Many of the 680 students repeated sections of their high school work. The per cent who took such duplicating courses in college is shown below:

1. *Sciences*	*Per Cent*	2. *History*	*Per Cent*
Physics	14	American	42
Chemistry	19	Ancient	23
Zoology	5	European	21
Botany	10	English	9

[20] W. C. Ruediger, "Curricular Gaps," *School and Society,* 27:274–78, 1928.
[20a] Ruediger, *op. cit.* Used by permission of *School and Society* and the author.

It seems very silly that 21 per cent of these students should have repeated a course in European history while 23 per cent failed to have such a course in either high school or college, or that 33 per cent should repeat work in physics and chemistry together while 14 per cent never took either. Mere duplication of courses is not enough to insure an adequate schedule for individual students— the ultimate consumers.

2. The "core" of the curriculum: The next point to consider is the nature of the courses that are most widely offered. Certain courses are practically universal, while others appear in only one catalogue. I wanted to determine the "core" of each department in colleges of different sizes. For this purpose I listed those courses that were offered in half or more of the catalogues in each of the first two groups analyzed.[21] The lists are somewhat long, but without them one can hardly determine the essential content of the average undergraduate curriculum. I do not advise trying to read these lists through at one sitting. They are intended rather for reference. To save space I have omitted the course labeled "Special Problems" for the small colleges and those labeled "Research" or "Seminar" for the second group; these courses are almost universal. The departments have been listed in the same order as for the previous table.

A. *Foreign language*	*Small College*	*Medium-sized College*
1. French:	Elementary grammar	Elementary grammar
	Intermediate grammar	Intermediate grammar
	Advanced grammar	Advanced grammar
	Conversation	Conversation
	Survey of French literature	
	Contemporary literature	Contemporary literature
	Seventeenth century literature	Seventeenth century literature
	Eighteenth century literature	Eighteenth century literature
	Nineteenth century literature	Nineteenth century literature
	French drama	French drama
		Phonetics

[21] It was impossible, for lack of space, to list all the courses common to half or more of the large universities.

A. *Foreign language*	*Small College*	*Medium-sized College*
2. German:	Elementary grammar Intermediate grammar Advanced grammar Scientific German German classics German drama Modern authors Goethe	Elementary grammar Intermediate grammar Advanced grammar Scientific German Goethe History and geography of Germany German poetry Middle High German
3. Spanish:	Elementary grammar Advanced grammar History of literature Modern literature Golden Age	Elementary grammar Advanced grammar Modern literature Golden Age Spanish novel Spanish drama
4. Italian:		Elementary grammar
5. Oriental:		
6. Greek:	Elementary grammar Greek literature * Greek history * Greek civilization *	Elementary grammar Greek history * Greek comedy * Homer

* In English

7. Latin:	Elementary grammar Advanced grammar Prose and poetry Cicero Virgil Horace Satirists	Elementary grammar Advanced grammar Prose and poetry Cicero Virgil Historians Ovid Poetry Comedy Survey of literature

B. *English*

1. Literature and writing:	Required composition Creative writing Critical writing	Required composition Creative writing Critical writing

B. *English*	*Small College*	*Medium-sized College*
1. Literature and writing:	History of English literature	History of English literature
	American literature	American literature
	English romantic literature	English Romantic literature
	Contemporary literature	
	Nineteenth century prose and poetry	
	English novel	English novel
	Modern drama	Modern drama
	Shakespeare	Shakespeare
	Milton	Milton
	Chaucer	Chaucer
	English language	English language
		Victorian prose
		Contemporary poetry
		English Bible
		Renaissance literature
		Neoclassical literature
		Versification
		Criticism
		Old English
		Essay writing
		Teaching of English
2. Public speaking:	Principles	Principles
	Interpretative reading	Interpretative reading
	Debating	Debating
		Argumentation
		Parliamentary procedure
		Radio speech
		Drama
		Phonetics
		Speech defects
3. Journalism:		General principles
		Newspaper writing
		Editing

C. *Social science*		
1. History:	Development of European culture	Development of European culture
	English history	English history
	American history	American history
	Ancient history	Ancient history
	European history since 1914	European history since 1914
	American foreign relations	American foreign relations
	Teaching of history	Teaching of history
		Later Middle Ages
		Renaissance
		Modern imperialism
		Contemporary world
		South American history

C. *Social science*	*Small College*	*Medium-sized College*
1. History:		Social history of the United States Economic history of the United States American empire
2. Economics:	General principles Finance Markets History Money and banking Statistics Trade Accounting Theory	General principles Finance Markets History Money and banking Statistics Theory International trade Transportation Public finance Public utilities Economic problems
3. Political science:	American government American state government American municipal government American diplomacy International law International relations American constitutional law	American government American state government American municipal government American diplomacy International law International relations American constitutional law European governments Political parties Legislative organization Administration Governments of the Near East Governments of the Far East
4. Sociology:	Introductory Social	Introductory Social Rural Crime The family Social control
5. Business organization:		Accounting (6) Shorthand Secretarial practice Auditing Finance Corporation finance Banking Investments Business law

C. *Social science*	*Small College*	*Medium-sized College*
5. Business organization:		Real estate principles Organization and management Personnel administration Salesmanship Marketing Advertising Insurance Federal taxation

D. *Physical sciences and mathematics*

	Small College	*Medium-sized College*
1. Mathematics:	College algebra Trigonometry Analytical geometry Differential calculus Integral calculus Solid geometry Advanced calculus Theory of equations Differential equations Problems of finance	College algebra Trigonometry Analytical geometry Differential calculus Integral calculus Solid geometry Advanced calculus Theory of equations Differential equations Problems of finance History of mathematics Projective geometry
2. Astronomy:	General	General Practical
3. Chemistry:	Introduction Qualitative analysis Quantitative analysis Organic chemistry Physical chemistry	Introduction Qualitative analysis Quantitative analysis Organic chemistry (2) Physical chemistry Advanced inorganic History of chemistry Colloids Physiochemistry Thermodynamics
4. Geology:	General Economic geology	General Economic geology Historical Place Advanced Invertebrate paleontology Methods of mapping Structural geology Minerology Petroleum
5. Physics:	Introduction Modern physics Electricity Theoretical Mechanics	Introduction Modern physics Electricity Theoretical Measurement

58 THE PRESENT-DAY SCENE

D. *Physical sciences and mathematics*	*Small College*	*Medium-sized College*
5. Physics:		Molecular and anatomic theory
		Optics
		Dynamics
		Household physics
		Photography
		Analytics
		Magnetism
		Acoustics
		Light
6. Geography:		
7. Engineering: a. Mechanical:		Mechanisms
		Machine design
		Heat transfer
		Heat engines
		Heat power
		Industrial fuels
		Power plant design
		Heat and ventilation of buildings
		Materials and mechanics
		Mechanics laboratory
		Thermody
b. Civil:		Principles
		Bridge stresses
		Highway
		Railroad engineering
		Hydraulics
		Structural design
		Concrete construction
		Water supply
		Hydrology
c. Electrical:		Elements
		Direct currents
		Alternating currents
		Magnetic circuits
		Illumination
		Electrical design
		Power transmission
		Communications
		Radio
E. *Biological sciences* 1. Botany:	Introduction	Introduction
	Plant evolution	
	Plant ecology	Plant ecology
	Teaching of botany	
		Plant histology
		Plant physiology
		Plant pathology

E. *Biological sciences*	*Small College*	*Medium-sized College*
2. Zoology:	General Embryology Invertebrates Evolution Histology Comparative anatomy	General Embryology Invertebrates Evolution Histology Field work Mammalian anatomy Parasites Entomology Eugenics Ornithology Genetics, heredity
3. Anatomy:		General Embryology Histology Surgical
4. Bacteriology:		General
5. Psychology:	General Applied psychology Experimental psychology Child psychology Social psychology Tests and measurements	General Applied psychology Experimental psychology Child psychology Social psychology Tests and measurements Educational psychology Comparative psychology Clinical psychology Abnormal psychology Business psychology Statistics Psychology of adolescence Mental hygiene
F. *Philosophy and education*		
1. Religion and Bible:	History of religion Old Testament New Testament English Bible	
2. Education:	History of education General principles Teaching in high school Secondary education	History of education General principles Teaching in high school Secondary education American education Tests Children's literature Reading Social studies Elementary curriculum Practice teaching Administration

F. *Philosophy and education*	*Small College*	*Medium-sized College*
2. Education:		Vocational education Development of personality Citizenship Philosophy of education Educational sociology
3. Philosophy:	General History of philosophy Ethics Religion Logic	General History of philosophy Ethics Religion Logic Social ethics Currents of thought

G. *Arts*		
1. Art:	Drawing and painting Design and color Interior decorating Clay modeling Life class History of art	Drawing and painting Design and color Life class History of art Modern art Composition Commercial art
2. Dramatic art:	Acting Literary interpretation	
3. Music:	General Sight singing Harmony History of music Composition Counterpoint Conducting Teaching of music	General Sight singing Harmony History of music Composition Counterpoint Conducting Teaching of music Instrumentation Orchestration Glee club A capella Voice

H. *Physical education*	Required courses (2) Theory and practice	Required courses (2) Basketball Football Baseball Swimming Tennis Fundamentals of physical education Methods Principles

H. *Physical education*	*Small College*	*Medium-sized College*
		Administration
		First aid
		Teaching techniques
		Physiology of activity
		Hygiene
		Measurement
		Rhythm
		Health education
I. *Home economics*		General home economics
		Textiles
		Foods
		Household management
		Home decoration
		Costume design
		Dress construction
		Nutrition
		Social and economic problems of the family
		Teaching home economics
		Child care
		Problems of the consumer

Even in the smaller colleges a student can get a good general education. Most of the courses that appear in half or more of the catalogues are necessarily introductory in nature. They give, in short, typically undergraduate work. As the size of the institution increases, more and more work of an advanced character becomes common. Although most of the general introductory courses also remain, they make up a smaller per cent of the total. It seems to me that in the nature of its curriculum the small college has one distinct advantage over the large. It has a course of study that is intended for undergraduates and for no one else. This situation restricts the number of offerings, but it has the effect of creating an intellectual environment in which a boy or girl can live without strain. The curriculum is sufficiently varied to meet all tastes, it is sufficiently general to prevent students from too early a specialization, and it is sufficiently concentrated to afford the beginnings of specialization for the upperclassmen. The larger the institution, the less well adapted is its curriculum to the needs of undergraduates and the better is it arranged for advanced work and specialization. To be sure a freshman can find in a big university a good deal more equipment than he can get in a small college, but he is not yet ready to use most of it; the items he can use he will find almost anywhere. In the course of time universities may begin their work on the university level and leave the tasks of laying the general foundation and of providing general education to the colleges, where a restricted curriculum can provide appropriate mental pabulum for the young.

3. Graduation requirements: A third point of interest in the analysis of catalogues concerns the requirements for graduation. These vary less than the curriculum from one place to another. Approximately 120 semester hours of work are necessary. It is the usual custom to consider high school and college work together in deciding when a student has passed all his "required" subjects. The typical specific requirements are three years of any one foreign language, one year of college English, one year of social science in college, one year each of biological and nonbiological science in either college or high school, and both algebra and plane geometry. Recently the language and English requirements have been altered in many places. A student has to give evidence that he has a "reading knowledge" of one foreign language and the ability to write English acceptably; the number of courses he takes to reach this level and where he takes them do not in the least matter. Eventually, other requirements will undoubtedly be expressed in terms of performance rather than in hours of work.

The general academic level needed for admittance to the junior year in most colleges is a C average. The lowest level for graduation varies from a C to a C—. There is commonly a requirement that at least a fourth (sometimes a third) of the courses must be selected from those open only to juniors and seniors.

The concentration during the last two college years upon a major subject is almost universal. The exact number of hours is sometimes specified and sometimes not. In many of the colleges for which the catalogues were examined there are comprehensive examinations in the major subject. About a third of them specifically permit a student to concentrate in two allied fields if he wishes. In the larger places the basic courses within a department were listed as being required of all majors.

Just as a matter of interest I examined a considerable number of "courses of study" in the catalogues to find out how much purely elective work a student who followed any given course of study would be likely to have. The general requirements, as already discussed, are low. Thus, a freshman who has had three years of one language, a course in chemistry, and adequate mathematics in high school has, as general requirements, only one year each of social science, biological science, and English. This arrangement looks as if the entire curriculum were his to roam about in. Nothing, however, could be further from the truth. For instance, if a freshman decides to prepare himself for teaching physics in high school he will, in a typical university, have to complete thirty hours of professional work, thirty hours of physics, and thirty hours of mathematics, most of which will be specifically required. If he decides to major in economics, he will find a curriculum mapped out for him in which there are only a few electives. If he wants to become a social worker, public accountant, dietician, ceramic engineer, or a football coach he will have practically no electives. In short, one is left with the impression that a student "elects" actually only his major field and his occupational objective. From then on his schedule is fairly well planned for him if he attends a large institution. I still do not know whether this arrangement is better or worse than the largely elective system with which I was familiar thirty years ago. It is perhaps more practical, but it has certainly diminished the amount of initiative necessary for making out a schedule—although not the difficulty of the procedure.

In a few catalogues I found a statement to the effect that each student would be allowed to work out his own plan of study under the supervision of an advisor. His schedule could —in theory at least—vary from general to specific, from diversified to concentrated, from practical to impractical, according to his interests. The extent to which this scheme is actually carried out must depend upon the willingness of the advisors to let students do what they want and upon the willingness of a college to arrange its course offerings better than is commonly the case. From what I have seen of time schedules, con-

flicts of class hours, and the general unwillingness of adults
to let adolescents make mistakes I have a suspicion that the
individualization is not as complete in reality as it is on paper.[22]

III. NATURE OF CURRICULAR RESEARCH
AT THE PRESENT TIME

The basic research needed for an adaptation of the curriculum both to the modern student and to modern society has
been under way in a number of places for some years. The
results are only now being put into effect. It would seem as if
the newer type of curriculum would eventually supplant the
traditional kind already described. It is therefore worth while
to consider the various steps taken in the course of research
to date and the general philosophy upon which the investigations rest. For this purpose I am quoting a good summary of
the thinking and procedures involved.

INTRODUCTION AND BACKGROUND

A. General picture of recent developments in higher education
   1. Social factors affecting education
      a. Population changes
         Society is becoming increasingly an adult society. As
         a result the employment opportunities for young peo-
         ple under 21 are curtailed—thus flooding the schools
         with more students.
      b. Industrial developments
         Many such developments have tended to bar you from
         work—technological improvements.
      c. Increased complexity of living
         For living successfully in modern society more ex-
         tended preparation is desirable—social relations are
         more complex and democratic processes are increas-

[22] For further discussion see C. S. Boucher, "Curriculum Provisions for
the Individual in the University of Chicago," *Proceedings of the Institute
for Administrators of Higher Institutions,* 4:98–108, 1932; and J. B.
Johnston, "The Adjustment of the Curriculum to the Individual Students
Including Pre-Entrance Advising," *Thirty-first Yearbook of the National
Society for the Study of Education,* Part II, pp. 181–85, 1932; D. A.
Robertson, "Fitting the Curriculum to the Student," *Bulletin of the Asso-
ciation of American Colleges,* 22: 120–24, 1936; W. S. Grey (Ed.), "Recent
Trends in American College Education," *Proceedings of the Institute for
Administrators of Higher Institutions,* Vol. 3, 1931, 253 pp.

ingly difficult to follow without adequate training and understanding.

d. Expansion of knowledge

The organization of this knowledge into useful units is increasingly important. New knowledge—about science, society, human relations—needs to be synthesized to avoid the dangers of fragmentation.

2. Re-evaluations of the function of a college

a. The influx of students has strained the traditional concept of a college characterized by academic and professional curricula.

b. High student mortality—about 50% in most colleges—has led people to suspect that traditional academic and professional curricula are not suited to the abilities of many students now attending college, and to wonder just what useful knowledge and experience students are obtaining from these preliminary segments of professional education. The individual needs of each student should be considered more fully.

c. Studies have shown that there are wide variations in the characteristics of students in different colleges and even more striking variations in students at any one college—variations in abilities and needs and knowledge.

3. Attempts have been made to meet these problems of mortality, variability and fragmentation.

a. Personnel and guidance services have been expanded. This has led to more knowledge about students and to some success in helping students to distribute themselves among curricula appropriate to their aptitudes and interests.

b. Curricula have been unified. This drive toward unity has taken many forms—the establishment of junior and senior divisions in four-year colleges, the introduction of survey courses, the gradual breakdown of departmental and subject-matter boundaries.

c. Curricula have been made more functional. This is perhaps another aspect of the "drive toward unity"—between the life of the school and the life of the world outside, between students and the adults they will become.

B. The general development and philosophy of the General College at Minnesota

 1. Purpose of the General College

   a. To provide an opportunity to study the abilities and interests of a large group whose needs were not being met elsewhere in the University.

   b. To experiment with a new program of instruction.

 2. Philosophy of the General College

   a. Current trend in experimental education is essentially an attempt to apply a new formula which may be conceived as a triangle. Base of the triangle is the student, right side is the social environment, left side is the teaching environment.

   b. Ideally a new program would proceed from base to right side to left side. But in a practical situation one faces students who must be taught and thus some sort of program must be presented immediately.

 3. Development of the General College program

   a. The first curriculum was set up on best guesses as to the needs of students and society and adults. This program contained materials organized around 10 comprehensive areas: human biology, science and technology, psychology, euthenics, communication, general arts, contemporary affairs, social problems, economics, history and government.

   b. An extensive study of the entire student body was made by the counseling staff (the group in the college in 1935) and later with the Rockefeller grant an intensive study of 100 students and their parents was undertaken—the adolescent study. Thus the base of the triangle was constructed.

   c. As a result of staff conferences the curriculum was reorganized and co-ordinated in 1937–38 into four major areas of life need—personal, home and family, sociocivic, and vocational. Continually, too, new methods of instruction were being tried—conferences, visual aids, projects, etc. Thus the left side of the triangle was being developed.

 4. The Adult Study in relation to the philosophy and program of the General College

   a. There is considerable difference between serving the

needs and interests of the student as he is at the
present moment, and that of serving his needs and
interests both as they are at present and will be in the
future.

b. By projecting into the future to discover the needs,
interests, and wants likely to characterize the students
as adults it should be possible to balance the curricular
offerings more wisely.

c. This attempt to discover the needs and interests of
adults does not mean or imply that society is completely static, that the activities and interests of present
students as adults should be similar to the activities
and interests which former students have as adults.
Rather, by discovering the activities and interests of
present adults and by observing wherein those activities and interests are of a "lower order" than what
should be expected of former college students one
should be able to single out areas in which improvements might be made. Further, by discovering adults'
problems, students now in school might be helped to
anticipate their solution and thus avoid pitfalls, be
more effective individuals, family members, workers,
and citizens. The findings of the Adult Study will not
dictate the content of the curriculum, but they can
serve as a guide for the re-evaluation of it and for the
task of making it more useful to students.[23]

Research of this general type with a consequent reformula-
tion of the curriculum is in progress all over the country.
Sometimes those in charge of the investigations have attempted
chiefly to adapt college work to a local situation, as in the case
of Fenn College in Cleveland. The basic analysis in this instance consisted of the study of Cleveland and its vicinity.

[23] From the *Preliminary Report of the General College Adolescent and
Adult Studies,* University of Minnesota Press, 1939, pp. 176–78. Used by
permission of the General College of the University of Minnesota.
Other good formulations of the principles and methods of curricular
research may be found in J. M. Hughes, "Curricular Organization and
Integration," *Journal of Higher Education,* 10 : 268–72, 1939; D. Orton,
"The College Comes of Age," *Journal of Higher Education,* 8 : 289–96, 1937;
D. M. Keezer, "All Is Not Chaos That Confuses Mr. Hutchins," *Journal
of Higher Education,* 9 : 440–48, 1938; J. K. Norton and M. A. Norton,
Foundations of Curriculum Building, Ginn and Company, 1936, 599 pp

The courses established contain material drawn from life in Cleveland, and the students use the city as a large laboratory for their work. In other cases the research is on a larger scale. It may, as at Stephens College, center upon the life activities of adult women,[24] or it may cover the main developments of the entire life span,[25] or it may be concerned mainly with the adjustment of a single small college.[26] The scope varies, but the fundamental concept remains. The course of study comes from life and should explain life as much as possible; it is not thought of as a thing apart from daily experience but as a function of it. Consequently the curriculum is in constant need of change because life does not stand still.[27]

IV. A PROPOSED CURRICULUM

There is nothing new or heretical in the outline of work to be discussed in this section. Virtually this arrangement is

[24] See W. W. Charters, "Stephens College Program for the Education of Women," *Stephens College Bulletin,* 16: 14–176, 1935.

[25] S. L. Pressey, J. E. Janney, and R. G. Kuhlen, *Life: A Psychological Study,* Harper & Brothers, 1939, 654 pp.

[26] See, for instance, H. C. Binkley, "Design for a College Curriculum," *Journal of Higher Education,* 9: 409–16, 1938.

[27] For further references on the research that underlies curriculum construction see J. A. Hockett, "A Determination of the Major Social Problems of American Life," *Teachers College Contributions to Education,* No. 281, 1927, 102 pp.; *Recent Social Trends in the United States,* McGraw-Hill Book Company, 1933, pp. 325–81; R. G. Kuhlen, "Background data for the Study of the Psychology of Adult Life," Doctor's Thesis, Ohio State University, 1937, 214 pp.; K. L. Heaton and G. R. Koopman, *A College Curriculum Based on the Functional Needs of Students,* University of Chicago Press, 1936, 157 pp.; F. D. Watson, "What Some College Men Want to Know about Marriage and the Family," *Social Forces,* 11: 235–41, 1932; F. B. Sherbon and E. Ferris, "The Experiences and Opinions of 350 Married Women Graduates of the University of Kansas with Reference to the University Curriculum and Problems of the American Home," *University of Kansas Studies in Education,* Vol. 2, No. 2, 1931, 30 pp.; S. R. Powers, "The Choice of Materials for Advancing the Aims and Functions of General Education," *Thirty-eighth Yearbook of the National Society for the Study of Education,* 1929, pp. 325–50; "Modern Social and Economic Trends," *Research Bulletin of the National Education Association,* Vol. 12, No. 5, 1934; "Social Changes and Education," *Thirteenth Yearbook of the Department of Superintendence,* National Education Association, 1935; "The Use of Background in the Interpretation of Educational Issues," *Twenty-fifth Yearbook of the National Society of College Teachers of Education,* 1937, 256 pp.; G. R. Foster, *Social Changes in Relation to Curricular Development in College Education for Women,* Colby College, Waterville, Maine, 1934, 203 pp.

already in force in several places.[28] I include it here because
it seems to me the best kind of compromise thus far worked
out between the old type of curriculum for the scholar and
the new type for the average citizen.

This curriculum rests upon five practical assumptions in regard
to college entrance, required courses, individualization, credits,
and the amount of specialization. (1) Entrance to college work
should be based upon ability to write acceptable English, ability to
read both well enough and fast enough to keep up with college
assignments, ability to study with fair efficiency, ability to solve
simple problems in arithmetic and algebra, and ability to read—
with the aid of a dictionary, if necessary—simple prose in one
foreign language. Naturally, many students are not able to meet
all these requirements at entrance, and an institution would have
to continue giving courses on a precollege level [29] for those who
could not, but these courses should not carry college credit. The
noncredit, subcollege course in both mathematics and English is
already in existence in many places; the same type of work could
be extended to other fields. Until a freshman can demonstrate at
least four of the five abilities above listed, he should not be
allowed to take any college work at all but should put his whole
time into remedying his inadequate preparation. The curriculum
to be proposed assumes that these requirements have been met.
(2) The required courses should be concerned exclusively with
such topics as are necessary for an average person to know if he
is to adjust to the modern world. And the most essential of these
courses should come first, when the largest number of students
will take them. (3) Each student should proceed at his own rate,
his schedule depending upon his ability. I see no reason why the
load of classwork should not vary from a single three-hour course
for a dull student who has to support himself to eight such courses
for a well-prepared freshman with an I.Q. of 190. (4) Credit for
work should be given only upon evidence of mastery and never
for hours spent in a classroom. If a student does not learn enough
from a required course during his first attempt, let him take it
again until he does. In the case of an elective, let him drop it and

[28] As at the University of Chicago.
[29] Naturally, the greatest care has to be taken to prevent these precollege
courses from affecting the level of regular work. In some cases the existence
of prefreshman courses has actually lowered the standards, especially of the
freshman year.

take another, unless he prefers to repeat the same work. (5) A student should be able to specialize a little during his first two years and to whatever degree he wishes during his last two. In the proposed curriculum the required courses make up three-fifths of the first year schedule, two-fifths of the second year, one-fifth of the third year, and none of the fourth.[30] A student could therefore, so far as college requirements are concerned, vary the amount of concentration to suit himself.

The suggested curriculum appears below:

GENERALIZED SCHEDULE

First Year	Hours per Week	Second Year	Hours per Week
Survey, social science	3	Survey, physical science	3
Survey, biological science	3	Survey, world literature	3
Mental hygiene (first semester)	3	Electives	3–15*
Occupations (second semester)	3	Total—	9–21
Electives	0–9*		
Total—	12–21		

Third Year		Fourth Year	
Philosophy of life	3		3–24*
Electives	6–21*		
Total—	9–24		

* The number of elective hours is purposely left indefinite, with the intention that each student should take as many or as few courses as are appropriate for him. Naturally, anyone who took only a few hours of work each semester would need more than four years in which to complete his college career.

The four survey courses above listed, or others similar to them, already exist in a number of colleges and universities.[31]

[30] For a good summary of selection versus prescription see H. M. Wriston, H. W. Prescott, and L. Wirth, "Nature, Scope, and Essential Elements in General Education," *Proceedings of the Institute for Administrators of Higher Institutions,* 6: 1–35, 1934; A. J. Brumbaugh, "The Case for Prescription," *ibid.,* 9: 39–44, 1937; and E. J. McGrath, "The Case for Election," *ibid.,* 9: 45–60, 1937.

[31] Especially good are the following: Survey of the Humanities (Pasadena); Introduction to Social Sciences (Akron); Correlated Science (Idaho).

They are intended to provide students with a nontechnical over-view of the contributions from a given area of knowledge to the life of an ordinary person. The courses in mental hygiene and occupations are purely practical—the first to help the fresh-man with his personal problems and his adjustment to college life and the second to help him in finding a vocational objec-tive. The one remaining requirement on the list—the course called "Philosophy of Life"—is included because adolescents want it.[32] This class is not thought of as a history of philosophy but as a course in the integration of values in modern life. In bygone days youngsters were taught a definite code of morals upon which educated people had agreed. The standards were perhaps narrow and rigid, but they were at least known. During the last three or four decades, the force of traditional morality has become weaker and weaker. Christianity as a vital force in life seems to diminish steadily, and thus far man-kind has found nothing to take its place. One of the few principles of conduct that guide the boy or girl of today is the desire to be a "good sport." The normal adolescent interest in values is as alive as it ever was, but in the present-day cur-riculum in most colleges it finds only incidental nourishment. This course is suggested to fill the existing need for a syn-thesis of the discordant values in the modern world.[33]

[32] See page 124.
[33] The above schedule is simple and unpretentious. Other plans of work, some of them extensive, have appeared in the references given below:
J. A. Blaisdell, "Claremont Colleges: Some Educational Purposes and Results," *Bulletin of the Association of American Colleges,* 16: 63–74, 1930; C. S. Boucher, *The Chicago College Plan,* University of Chicago Press, 1935, 344 pp.; G. E. Carrothers, "Experiment at Rollins College," *School Review,* 35: 184–87, 1927; D. P. Cottrell, "General Education in Experi-mental Liberal Arts Colleges," *Thirty-eighth Yearbook of the National Society for the Study of Education,* 1929, pp. 193–218; S. C. Crawford, "New College Curriculum at Pittsburgh," *Pennsylvania School Journal,* 84: 352, 1936; J. H. Coffin, "The History of an Educational Adventure: The Whittier Idea," *Whittier College,* 1928, 34 pp.; A. C. Eurich, *The Effective General Curriculum,* University of Minnesota Press, 1936, 437 pp.; W. F. Cunningham, "The Liberal College," *Journal of Higher Education,* 6: 253–60, 1935; C. R. Fisher, "The Wisconsin Curriculum," *School and Society,* 33: 242–45, 1931; H. E. Hawkes, A. C. Hanford, R. Aydelotte, L. Hopkins, and C. S. Boucher, *Five College Plans,* Columbia University Press, 1931, 115 pp.; J. M. Gwynn, "Changes in the College Curriculum 1890–1934," Doctor's Thesis, Yale University, 1936; K. L. Heaton and

About half the work of the first two years is required; it is also different in character from the work of the last two. I would therefore decidedly favor the establishment of a definite stopping place at the end of the second year. This arrangement already exists in many colleges. A student gets a "Junior Certificate" for his work up to this point. The name strikes me as somewhat unfortunate, because it emphasizes the first two years as a preparatory stage for something further. Some such name as a "citizenship certificate" would be better, because it would emphasize the nature of the completed work. The real objective of these two years is the making of an intelligent citizen out of the young college student. Until this end has been reached, he has no business to start specializing. For the obtaining of a certificate—whatever its name—a student should give evidence that he has mastered the basic ideas of the six required courses and has passed his elective work. The second matter I would leave to the teachers of the classes elected, but the first I would delegate to an examining board, as is done at the University of Chicago.

For the graduation requirements I should want each student to pass a comprehensive examination in his major subject at the end of his junior and senior years and to write an acceptable senior topic or thesis. The actual number of hours spent in class seems to me unimportant. Since people are all different, some would have to spend more time than others in order to acquire a given amount of knowledge. The graduation requirements should—whatever the exact formulation—rest upon knowledge and not upon what one of my professors used to call "seat hours."

G. R. Koopman, *A College Curriculum Based on Functional Needs of Students,* University of Chicago Press, 1936, 157 pp.; R. H. Leigh, "The Bennington College Program," *Journal of Higher Education,* 1 : 520–24, 1930; A. Meikeljohn, *et al.,* "Reorganization of Content to Emphasize Fields of Learning," *Thirty-first Yearbook of the National Society for the Study of Education,* Part II, 1932, pp. 162–64; A. E. Morgan, "Transforming the American College System," *Current History,* 32 : 717–20, 1930; Oberlin College, *General Report of the Committee on the Curriculum,* 1930, 7 pp.; J. Park, "The New Curriculum of the University of Buffalo," *School and Society,* 33 : 832–35, 1931; R. Quintana, "The New Curriculum at Wisconsin," *Journal of Higher Education,* 2 : 233–38, 1931; H. P. Rainey, "Social Factors Affecting General Education," *Thirty-eighth Yearbook of the National Society for the Study of Education,* 1929, pp. 15–28; "The New Curriculum," *Rollins College Bulletin,* 1931, 40 pp.; "A Country College within an Urban University," *St. Stephens College Bulletin,* 1928, 32 pp.; E. O. Sisson, "An Experimental College in Its Twentieth Year," *School and Society,* 33 : 289–94, 1931. See also C. A. Boucher, "Curricula Designed for a Liberal Education," in *Curriculum Making in Current Practice,* Northwestern University, 1931, pp. 218–27.

Such a scheme as that outlined above would simplify the college credit system sufficiently to make it intelligible. Progress would depend more upon merit than it does now, but the amount of red tape would be mercifully reduced. A student who wanted to specialize could begin doing so as a freshman and continue with more and more concentration during his successive years; the program would not prevent the development—in so far as it can be done in the undergraduate years—of scholars for the next generation. But a specialist is also a citizen and needs the same comprehension of his world that anyone else does. A student who wished to concentrate less heavily could use his elective hours for sampling such fields of work as were not presented to him through his requirements. I see no reason why a capable student should not elect a year's work in each of three departments and a semester's work in each of four or five others before the end of his second year. The system is therefore flexible enough for various tastes.

V. SUMMARY

College faculties are always tinkering with the curriculum. No arrangement satisfies either students or teachers for long. This situation is normal and healthy; it is merely evidence that the course of study is dependent upon life and must consequently change with the times. The history of the curriculum shows clearly the influence of social change upon the courses in a college catalogue. From the beginning of the nineteenth century to the present the developments have all been in the direction of bringing togther life within and outside the college gates. The present offerings even in small colleges are adequate for a general education. The attitude at the moment—after a good many years of experience with free electives—is in favor of prescription of such material as will be useful to everyone.[34] There is also a strong current against too early specialization. The latest elements to appear upon the curricular scene are three: the survey course in which the facts from a given area

[34] The authorities at St. John's College have gone still further and have established a completely prescribed curriculum.

of knowledge are presented in such a way as to produce an enlightened citizen rather than a subject-matter expert, the "field of specialization" by which a student can correlate work from many departments into a unified whole, and the more or less complete individualizing of each student's program. All three of these elements represent efforts to restore the liberal education of former years—only along lines intimately connected with daily life and interests rather than remote from them.[35]

[35] For an excellent modern history of the curriculum in American colleges, see R. F. Butts, *The College Charts Its Course,* McGraw-Hill Book Company, 1939, 464 pp.

CHAPTER IV

COLLEGE POPULATIONS

Previous chapters have included data on the number and types of colleges in this country, the objectives of a college education, and the nature of the present-day curriculum. This chapter is concerned with such questions as the selection of freshmen from among high school graduates, the distribution of intelligence in typical classes, the home backgrounds of these freshmen, and the progress through college of the average entering class. A teacher's objectives give him an end toward which to work, and the curriculum gives him the means; the students are his human material. In recent years the nature of this student material has changed, and this change is fundamental to modern higher education. Because of it, colleges have increased in both number and size, the objectives have become different, and the curriculum has grown by leaps and bounds. Whether or not the changes in student personnel are desirable is not the question at this point; the fact is that they exist, and a teacher must take cognizance of them or he cannot adjust his teaching to the needs and abilities of his students.

I. STATISTICS OF COLLEGE ENROLLMENTS

The growth in the number of students attending both high school [1] and college has been phenomenal. This development for the colleges is shown in Figure 8.

[1] The increase from 1880 to 1930 for high school was 2,093 per cent.

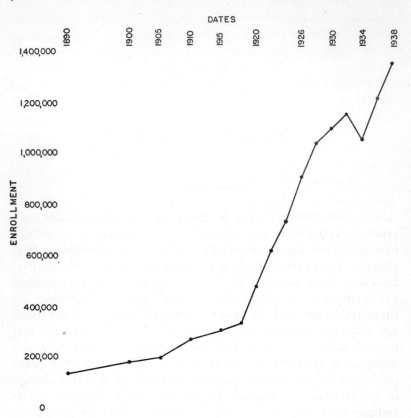

FIG. 8.—Total Enrollments since 1890.

Data for 1890 from the *Compendium of the Eleventh Census,* Vol. 2, 1934; for 1900–1936 from table quoted in *The World Almanac,* 1939, p. 395; for 1938, from the *Biennial Survey of Education,* 1938–39.

Since 1890 the total has increased nearly 900 per cent; from 1918 to 1938 alone the increase has been over 400 per cent. This development is still so new that higher education has had no time in which to adjust itself.[2] Of all the inhabitants who are between the ages of 19 and 22, 983 per

[2] A direct result of college growth is the development of the graduate schools. From 1900 to 1932 the number of graduate students in the entire country has increased from 5,831 to 76,953—or 1,150 per cent. (*Biennial Survey of Education,* 1930–32, Part I.)

100,000 were enrolled in 1934 in some kind of higher education, as compared with the 313 per 100,000 in 1900.[3] During the same period the proportion of those between the two ages who were in college rose from .3 per cent to 18 per cent.[4] As a result, the proportion of college graduates in the general population has also risen. In 1914 there were 27 graduates of colleges, universities, or higher technical schools per 10,000 inhabitants; in 1936 there were 71.[5] Every year sees an increase in this proportion. These figures take on added significance when they are compared with those of other countries. In England, for instance, there were 7 college graduates per 10,000 of the population in 1914—about a fourth the rate in this country. By 1936 the per cent had risen only to 11, as compared with 71 for the United States.[6]

The traditional occupations into which the college graduate goes are the professions. As long as colleges were producing only enough in each generation to replace those in the previous one and to supply a sufficient additional number for normal growth in population, the curriculum could remain appropriate for members of the learned professions only. At a liberal estimate, however, not more than 12 per cent of the population can be absorbed into any kind of "white-collar" job. In 1900 there were roughly 170,000 students in college, but in 1938 there were 1,350,000. Obviously the professions cannot absorb all these students, even if this number could be adequately educated to enter such work. It is this fundamental change in the number of students that has precipitated the same problems at the college level with which high school officials and teachers had to struggle two decades ago. The increases in enrollments are not due to growth in the general population. Between 1890 and 1930, for instance, the population increased only 236 per cent; during the same period college enrollments increased over 700 per cent.

---

[3] *Biennial Survey of Education,* 1934–36, United States Department of the Interior, *Office of Education Bulletin,* No. 2, 1937.
[4] *Ibid.*
[5] *Yearbook of Education,* Evans Brothers, London, 1934, pp. 178–79.
[6] *Yearbook of Education,* Evans Brothers, London, 1936.

78 THE PRESENT-DAY SCENE

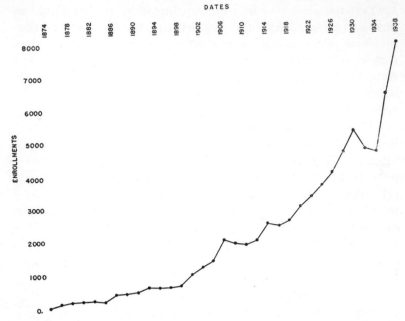

FIG. 9.—Enrollments at Purdue University, 1874–1938.

Hatt and McClusky, *op. cit.* "Report of the President," *Bulletin of Purdue University,* Vol. XXXIX, No. 2, 1939. Used by permission of Purdue University.

A specific example for a single college may make the situation clearer.[7] Purdue University was founded in 1874, with a total enrollment of 65 students. The curve of growth from that time to the present is shown in Figure 9. The increase from the beginning to 1938 is almost 13,000 per cent; the growth has been over 800 per cent since 1900. No sensible person can suppose that the education which was appropriate for 65 students in 1874 or 636 students in 1895 is equally suitable for the 8,243 in 1938. This example shows in miniature the essential changes in student population within the last fifty years.

[7] These data are from E. Hatt and F. D. McClusky, "A Study in Enrollment," *Purdue University Studies in Higher Education,* II, Vol. 27, No. 3, 1926, 49 pp. See also E. F. Potthoff, "Who Goes to College?" *Journal of Higher Education,* 2:294–97, 1931; M. E. Haggerty, "The Educational Program," in *The Evaluation of Higher Education,* III, University of Chicago Press, 1937, 328 pp. (Chap. 3); F. W. Reeves, E. C. Miller, and J. D. Russell, *Trends in University Growth,* University of Chicago Press, 1933, 242 pp.

With the development of enrollments there has been an increase in the average age of entering freshmen. They are now two years older than they were even twenty years ago [8]—nineteen as compared to seventeen. This difference may not have resulted in a greater average mental development because the present group is less selected, but it should have contributed something to emotional and social maturity. It is perhaps the fundamental reason why the "rah-rah" period of college life has mercifully waned.

There is only one indication that college enrollments may become somewhat smaller in about twelve years. For the last two or three seasons there has been a decrease in the size of entering elementary school classes. This situation was foretold when the strict immigration laws went into effect. Since there are fewer six-year-old children entering the first grade each year, there will perhaps be a smaller number of prospective college students. The reduction may, however, be entirely offset by changes in social conditions which make it desirable for more and more adolescents to remain in school as long as they can. It is even possible that, in spite of the smaller elementary school classes, college enrollments will continue to climb.

II. SELECTION OF COLLEGE FRESHMEN

In this section the word "selection" is used in the sense of "natural selection" rather than with reference to any artificial requirements for college entrance. Not all individuals in the world would go to college, no matter what the standards of admission might be. Various economic, social, and intellectual forces operate to set natural limits upon enrollments. One often hears the complaint that college students of today are a totally unselected group. This statement is sheer nonsense—as a few figures will show. What critics mean is, presumably, that freshmen are a less selected group than they used to be.

[8] L. V. Koos, "The Trend and Reorganization of Higher Education as Affecting the Junior College," in E. Hudelson, *Problems of College Education,* 1928, pp. 128–52, and J. M. Stalnaker, "A Statistical Study of Some Aspects of the Purdue Orientation Testing Program," *Purdue University Studies in Higher Education,* VIII, Vol. 28, No. 6, 44 pp.

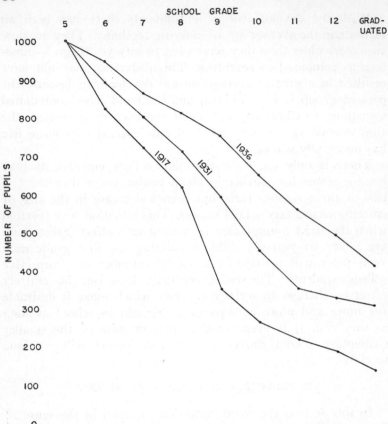

FIG. 10.—Elimination Rates at Three Different Times.

Foster, *op. cit.* Used by permission of *School Life.*

The simplest way to get a general understanding of the elimination that has already taken place before students reach college is to trace the educational careers of given groups of pupils. The chart above shows what happened to three different samples of 1,000 fifth-grade children.[9] The 160 children who

9 E. M. Foster, "School Survival Rates," *School Life,* 22: 13–14, 1936. See also L. V. Koos, *The American Secondary School,* Ginn and Company, 1927, 755 pp.; E. J. Kline, "Significant Changes in the Curve of Elimination Since 1900," *Journal of Education,* 26: 608–16, 1932; C. W. Odell, "Are College Students a Selected Group?" *University of Illinois Bureau of Educational Research Bulletin,* No. 34, 1927, 45 pp.

graduated from high school in 1917 were survivors of 1,000 fifth-graders seven years earlier. This group had lost 175 of its members even before the end of the sixth grade. In 1931 nearly twice as many of the 1,000 fifth-grade children from seven years before graduated from high school; in 1936, two and a half times as many. In spite of these increases in holding power, it is absurd to say that high school graduates are not a selected group. College freshmen are even more highly selected because less than half the high school graduates will go to college.[10] Freshmen may seem to offer an enormous range of abilities, but actually the range is far smaller than that with which the elementary school teacher has to cope. The college, of course, eliminates still further as time goes on; thus, every 62 graduating college seniors in 1934 were the survivors of 1,000 fifth-grade children eleven years earlier.[11]

One factor that influences entrance to college is, obviously, intelligence. An analysis of the test scores made by 5,304 high school seniors [12] illustrates this influence. The pupil's scores were first grouped by deciles; [13] then a record was kept of each pupil's career. The per cent from each decile who went to college is shown in Table 4.

[10] See Odell, *op. cit.*, also E. O. Holt, "Securing a More Highly Selected Student Body at the University of Wisconsin," *Proceedings of the Institute for Administrative Officers of Higher Institutions,* 4: 44–54, 1932.

[11] Foster, *op. cit.*

[12] R. A. Kent, *Higher Education in America,* Ginn and Company, 1930, 689 pp.

[13] For the sake of the reader without statistical training the following explanation of "decile" and "percentile" is presented. If one takes an entire distribution of scores from a test and divides it into tenths, the point at which one tenth ends and the next begins is a decile. If one divides an entire distribution into a hundred equal parts, the point at which one ends and the next begins is a percentile. The tenth percentile is therefore the first decile; the twentieth percentile is the second decile; and so on. If a student scores "at the fourth percentile" on a test, only 4 per cent of the other students in his group made a score lower than he did, and 96 per cent made higher scores. If he is "at the 68th percentile," 68 per cent of others scored below him and 32 per cent above. If he scored at the 99th percentile, only 1 per cent of the others made better scores and 99 per cent made lower. The students in the first decile are those scoring in the lowest 10 per cent; those in the seventh decile scored between the seventieth and eightieth percentiles—or in the seventh block of tens from the bottom. This explanation is purposely nontechnical; it would not do for a book on statistics, but to the general reader it may be more useful than a precise definition.

TABLE 4

Relation between Intelligence and College Entrance[13a]

Deciles in Intelligence	Per Cent Who Went to College	
	Men	*Women*
91–100	43	34
81–90	40	23
71–80	44	20
61–70	39	21
51–60	31	20
41–50	29	19
31–40	32	16
21–30	32	15
11–20	28	16
1–10	27	16
TOTAL............	2,345	2,961

The proportion of high school pupils going to college decreases with the mental level. This table shows again the amount of elimination that occurs between high school and college.[14]

The range of intellectual ability among freshmen is of importance in any consideration of the kind of work appropriate for them. According to results on the Ohio College Association Tests of Intelligence [15] 5 per cent of college freshmen score below the average for ninth-grade children,[16] 10 per cent below the average for the tenth grade, 15 per cent below that for the eleventh, and 25 per cent below that for high school seniors. The seventy-fifth percentile for the twelfth grade was two points above the median for college freshmen at entrance. Since only three months elapsed between these two measures

[13a] J. B. Johnston: "Selection of Students." From Kent's *Higher Education in America*. Boston, 1930. Used by permission of the publishers, Ginn and Company.

[14] Unfortunately the elimination does not always take place at the desired level. Thus, in one instance less than half the high school seniors in the highest decile went to college, whereas one-fourth of those in the lowest decile entered. (R. K. Byrns, "Scholastic Aptitude and Freshman Achievement," *School and Society*, 35: 714–18, 1932.)

[15] *Ohio College Association Bulletin*, No. 106, Mimeographed Report, 1937, Columbus, Ohio.

[16] Even lower figures are given by N. B. Cuff, "Prognosis and Diagnosis of Success in College," *Journal of Applied Psychology*, 14: 612–19, 1930.

it is evident that enough selection had taken place to raise the group a total of twenty-five percentiles. In actual scores on this particular test, entering freshmen vary from 28 to 150 points. This range corresponds to the difference between an average seventh-grade child and a good graduate student. Even though the college teacher does not have all possible levels of ability to deal with, he has more than he wants, especially if he teaches freshmen.

While this distribution is typical of freshman classes in public institutions, the average level of intelligence is by no means the same from one college to another. Thus, among the twenty-five colleges of the Ohio College Association the entering classes in a single year made average scores all the way from the twenty-fourth to the ninety-fifth percentile of the general norms.[17] This difference in average ability is equal to that between the low twelfth grade and the graduate school.[18]

There are differences of equal magnitude in the academic achievements of college students. The most conclusive data on this point comes from the Pennsylvania survey.[19] The investigators used objective tests that sample knowledge and judgment in all fields commonly studied by undergraduates. While these tests were by no means perfect, they were good enough to provide evidence as to average mastery along a number of lines. The forty-nine colleges from which results were obtained made scores as shown in Figure 11.

The college with the highest standing had an average score of 875 points, while the one with the lowest had an average of only 350. The difference between the best and poorest score within a single college was sometimes as great as 1,250 points —or more than twice that between the averages for the colleges as a whole. In short, students present as wide a variation in knowledge as they do in intelligence.

The college population consists, then, of students drawn for the most part from the upper third of the total distribution

---

[17] *Ohio College Association Bulletin*, No. 106, *op. cit.*
[18] Similar results have often been reported. See, for instance, E. Hudelson, *Problems of College Education*, University of Minnesota Press, 1928, 449 pp.
[19] W. S. Learned and B. D. Wood, *The Student and His Knowledge*, Carnegie Foundation for the Advancement of Teaching, 1938, 408 pp.

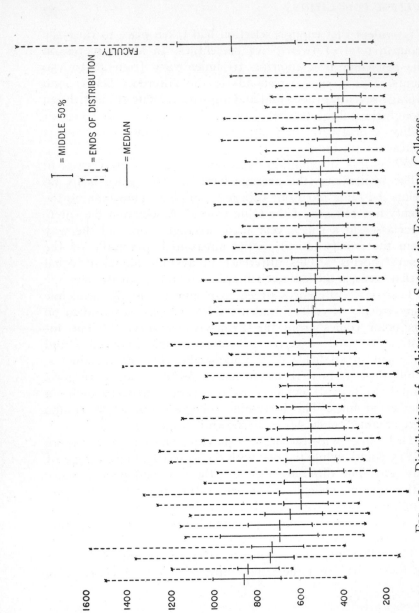

FIG. 11.—Distribution of Achievement Scores in Forty-nine Colleges.

Learned and Wood, *op. cit.*, p. 78. Used by permission of the Carnegie Foundation for the Advancement of Teaching.

84

of abilities. The successive eliminations from grade to grade have already operated to select the more capable individuals. Nevertheless, the amount of variation that remains is far too great to make the traditional curriculum suitable. No teacher can afford to forget this basic fact of wide individual differences among his students.

III. THE SOCIAL BACKGROUND OF COLLEGE STUDENTS

As pointed out in the first chapter, the great majority of college students are in public institutions. Although there are doubtless some private colleges in which the students come from a single social and economic level, this situation is not common. Usually all social classes are represented in the student group, although the proportions from each are different. Many studies have reported the occupational status of the fathers of college freshmen. Three of these [20] give typical results.

TABLE 5

Occupational Status of the Fathers of Freshmen

Occupation of Father	First Study	Second Study	Third Study
Industrial....................	19.5	4.3	8.6
Artisan....................	18.5	17.1	18.8
Mercantile....................	17.5	44.8	51.4
Professional....................	11.5	12.0	18.6
Agricultural....................	14.0	9.8	—
Clerical....................	6.5	3.2	2.6
Official....................	3.5	8.8	—
Miscellaneous....................	9.0	—	—

Usually the largest number of students comes from homes where the father is a businessman. The proportions of the various occupational groups in the general population are, however, somewhat different. In the second study quoted above,

[20] W. S. Hoffman, "Occupations of Parents of College Students," *School and Society*, 35: 25–26, 1932; E. F. Potthoff, "Who Goes to College?" *Journal of Higher Education*, 2: 294–97, 1931; J. B. Johnston, *The Liberal College in a Changing Society*, The Century Company, 1930, 326 pp.

the college enrollment was compared with the state census. For every student whose father was a professional man there were 21 professional men listed in the census. The ratio was thus 1 :21. Similar ratios for businessmen, farmers, artisans, and day laborers were respectively 1 :34, 1 :315, 1 :174, and 1 :1,583. From these percentages one can again see that, while there are representatives of all social classes in higher education, the students are a selected group socially and economically as well as intellectually, even when there are no artificial barriers to admission.[21]

One other study of this general matter seems worth quoting, since it covers other items besides occupational level. The students studied were engineers, but the situation is typical of any entering class in a large university.

TABLE 6

Social and Economic Background of a Typical Freshman Class[22]

Age, birthplace, and parentage
Median age of students............................. 18.9 years
Native-born students............................... 96.2 per cent
Native-born grandparents........................... 60.7 per cent

Geographical origin
Median distance, home to college.................... 107 miles
Students who do or could live at home............... 24.8 per cent
Students from within the state...................... 83.7 per cent
Students from foreign countries..................... 1.2 per cent
Students of rural origin............................ 15.0 per cent
Students from villages and small cities............. 24.2 per cent
Students from cities of more than 5,000............. 60.8 per cent

[21] For further data of similar character see "Analysis of the Occupations of Families of Freshmen in the University of Wisconsin," *School and Society,* 31: 11-12, 1930; A. J. Brumbaugh, "Characteristics of Pupil Population; Higher Education," *Review of Educational Research,* 6: 188–93, 1936; M. Moffet, "The Social Background and Activities of Teachers College Students," *Teachers College Contributions to Education,* No. 375, 1929, 133 pp.; O. E. Reynolds, "Social and Economic Status of College Students," *Teachers College Contributions to Education,* No. 272, 1927, 57 pp.
[22] Committee on Engineering Students and Graduates, "A Study of Engineering Students at the Time of Entrance to College," *Journal of Engineering Education,* 17 : 83–114, 1926. Used by permission of the *Journal of Engineering Education.*

T A B L E 6 *continued*

Father's occupation and position

Industrial . . . . 29.4 per cent
Mercantile or financial . . . . 22.4 per cent
Agricultural . . . . 17.1 per cent
Professional . . . . 15.8 per cent
Miscellaneous . . . . 15.4 per cent

Father's education

College or professional degree . . . . 12.9 per cent
Attended college, nongraduate . . . . 10.8 per cent
High school graduate . . . . 16.0 per cent
Attended high school, nongraduate . . . . 15.0 per cent
Grammar school graduate . . . . 26.9 per cent
All others . . . . 18.4 per cent

Scholastic origins of students

Graduates of public high schools . . . . 85.8 per cent
From private and parochial schools . . . . 9.3 per cent
College transfers, including graduates . . . . 15.1 per cent

Honor group in secondary school (highest tenth) . . . . 18.0 per cent
Total from upper third of preparatory class . . . . 60.6 per cent
Total from middle third . . . . 36.9 per cent
Total from lower third . . . . 2.6 per cent
Students admitted with entrance conditions . . . . 19.6 per cent

Most of the students in this class came from within the state, most of them were graduates of public schools, and more than half of them had superior high school records. They came from all kinds of homes and economic levels. Only 12.9 per cent of their fathers were college graduates,[23] while 18.4 per cent did not even complete grammar school.

So far as public institutions go, the student body is composed of young men and women from all classes in society, although the representation is very uneven. The business group furnishes the greatest actual number of students and the professional group the greatest proportion of its own number. It is not surprising that the student body of a university does not have any great social solidarity, since it is recruited from such a wide variation of social backgrounds. The com-

[23] In another study (Potthoff, *op. cit.*) it was pointed out that although only 18.6 per cent of the fathers in the group under consideration were college graduates, this fact did not indicate any inferiority. These men had received their degrees between 1890 and 1900, at which time about 4 per cent of the young men of their age were in college. The number holding college degrees is, then, about four and a half times as high as it would be if the fathers of college students were not a selected group educationally.

parative homogeneity of the small private college is the exception rather than the rule. Naturally, where it does exist, it acts as a force toward social cohesion and is thus an advantage.

IV. STUDENT SURVIVAL

As soon as colleges and universities began to grow at an abnormally rapid rate the number of eliminations became greater. By the middle of the decade that started in 1920 studies of student progress began to appear. There has been a steady stream of them even since. The figures given do not always agree, probably because eliminations and withdrawals actually are greater in some schools than in others, but even the most optimistic reports are bad enough. In ten different studies from large institutions [24] the per cent of entering freshmen who graduated in four years was given as 20, 30.1, 22.6, 33, 6.3, 40, 40.5, 34, 40, and 35. The greatest loss comes during the first year,[25] although the enrollment is reduced somewhat during the later years also. Naturally, there are some students who do not graduate within four years but do eventually get their degrees. Thus, at the end of nine years after entrance 52.4 per cent of one class had graduated from one university.[26] In another, 35 per cent finally graduated.[27] This

[24] M. S. MacLean, "A College of 1934," *Journal of Higher Education,* 5 : 240–46, 1934; R. M. West, "Student Mortality, Student Survival and Student Accounting," in Hudelson, *op. cit.,* pp. 199–209; R. A. Kent, *Higher Education in America,* Ginn and Company, 1930, 689 pp.; H. H. Remmers, "Purpose and Function of the Division of Educational Reference," *Purdue Studies in Higher Education,* I, Vol. 26, No. 10, 1926, 13 pp.; I. A. Booker, "Reducing Withdrawals," *Journal of Higher Education,* 4 : 249–54, 1933; F. P. O'Brien, "Mental Ability with Reference to Selection and Retention of College Students," *Journal of Educational Research,* 18 : 136–43, 1928; E. F. Potthoff and G. R. Noon, "Attendance and Scholastic Records of a Class at the University of Chicago," *Educational Administration and Supervision,* 12 : 549–60, 1926; H. A. Edgerton and H. A. Toops, *Academic Progress,* Ohio State University Press, 1929, 150 pp.; E. M. Pallett, "Studies of Student Mortality at the University of Oregon," *University of Oregon Publications, Studies in College Teaching,* 1933, Vol. 4, No. 2, 32 pp.; F. W. Reeves and J. D. Russell, "Admission and Retention of University Students," *University of Chicago Survey,* Vol. 5, 1933, 360 pp.

[25] The elimination during the freshman year is sometimes equal to half the original enrollment, see MacLean, *op. cit.*

[26] West, *op. cit.*

[27] MacLean, *op. cit.*

failure of so many students is not due to a lack of ability. It has been estimated [28] that 70 to 75 per cent of entering freshmen have enough intelligence to at least pass their work. However, between a third and a half of them get poorer marks than are necessary in view of their ability, and only 40 per cent—in this particular college—graduate. In one comprehensive study of twenty-five colleges and universities with a combined enrollment of over 15,000 freshmen, 45 per cent of the students left without a degree.[29] The fact is, then, that of a typical group of freshmen not many more than half can be expected to graduate at any time and not more than about 40 per cent within four years. Any observer who grew up in a small college where a group of students went through four years together and achieved a high degree of social solidarity in the process is likely to expect from university classes a homogeneity that simply does not exist. Only a third of the freshmen go straight through school; the remaining number straggle along, either not graduating at all or graduating from one year to twenty years after the expected date. Under such circumstances anything resembling "class spirit" is impossible.

Small colleges have some losses, but they are not nearly as large as those reported above, suggesting that a high elimination is chiefly a matter of size and of a failure to adapt work to ability. In a small place the teachers are acquainted with their students, and the students are able to make their desires and needs known. Perhaps without much conscious effort on anyone's part, the work load gets adapted to student capacity. It is not surprising, then, that a greater proportion of an entering freshman class remains than is the case in a big university. The typical situation is revealed in some figures sent me by the dean of a college that five years ago enrolled 196 freshmen. Of this number 178 graduated last year, and two others who dropped out are now back in college. Only 6 of the 14 students who left the college permanently were dismissed for poor work. When one examines the schedules and other records of students in a small college one finds clear evidence

[28] J. A. Starrak, "Matching Ability to Achievement," *Journal of Higher Education*, 8: 315–20, 1937.
[29] J. H. McNeeley, "College Student Mortality," *Office of Education Bulletin*, No. 11, 1937, 112 pp.

of the adjustment of work to individual interests and abilities and of the personal attention given to students. University professors often consider the continuity shown by classes in small colleges as a thing of the past, but it still exists.

The reasons for the high elimination in large institutions are numerous. Some proportion between 12 and 25 per cent of the students fail so much work that they have to leave.[30] In 1928 one freshman out of every four who entered a member college of the North Central Association failed during the first term of residence, and one in every three who entered a state university failed.[31] Students give a number of reasons other than poor work for leaving college—lack of money, lack of interest, illness, health, transfer to another school, marriage, or some crisis at home.[32] A very few students are expelled as a disciplinary measure.

It is of interest to follow a single group of freshmen through their college career and find out who survives. One such study is typical of all.[33] In this case 218 freshmen entered the same college together. Two years later there were 127; in another two years the total had shrunk to 50—or 22.9 per cent of the original number. All of these had either graduated or had completed four years of a five-year course. From the distribution one can easily see that the main reason for elimination—regardless of what the students themselves may have said—was poor marks. Thus, among B+ students, no one dropped out; among the B– students, about 25 per cent; among those with a C standing, about 45 per cent; among those with a high D average, 95 per cent; and at all levels below, 100 per cent. At the end of four years only 3 students remained who did not

---

[30] See for instance, A. E. Eurich, "College Failures," *School and Society,* 37 : 692–96, 1933; Reeves and Russell, *op. cit.*

[31] From an editorial in the *Journal of Higher Education,* 8 : 347, 1937.

[32] McNeely, *op. cit.;* G. R. Moon, "The Student Who Drops Out of College," *School and Society,* 27 : 576–8, 1928; A. L. Rogers, "A Study of the Causes of Elimination in a College of Liberal Arts for Women," *Fifteenth Yearbook of the National Society of College Teachers of Education,* 1926, pp. 172–80; L. M. Snyder, "Why Do They Leave?" *Journal of Higher Education,* 11 : 26–32, 1940.

[33] Reported in Kent, *op. cit.,* p. 433.

	AVERAGE GRADE								
SCORE	F–	F+	D–	D+	C–	C+	B–	B+	NO.
96-100							•	•	2
91-95						•	•	• •	4
86-90				⊘	⊘ •	○	•		5
81-85					⊘ ⊘ •	○ • •	○ ○		8
76-80				+	○	○ •	○	•	6
71-75					○ • • / • • •		⊘ • •		8
66-70	⊘	⊘	⊘ ○	○ ○	⊘ ○ • / • • •		• • •		15
61-65	⊘ ○		⊘	⊘ ○ ○	○ • / • •	•			11
56-60	⊘	⊘	⊘ ⊘	⊘ ⊘ ⊘ / ○ ⊘ ○ / ○	• • •				14
51-55			○	○ ○ ○ / ○ •	⊘ ○ • / • • •	•	•		14
46-50	⊘	⊘ ⊘	○ ○	○ ○ ○	⊘ ○ ○ / • •		•		14
41-45		⊘ ⊘ ⊘	○ ○ ○	⊘ ⊘ • / ○ ○ ○ / ○ ○ ○	○ • / • •				19
36-40	⊘		⊘	⊘ ○ • / ○ ○ ○ / ○ ○ ○	○ •		•		14
31-35	⊘ ○ ⊘	⊘ ⊘ / ⊘ ⊘	⊘ ○ / ⊘ ○	⊘ ⊘ ○ / ○ ○ ○ / ○	○				19
26-30	⊘ ⊘ / ⊘ ○	⊘	⊘ ⊘ ⊘ ⊘ / ⊘ ⊘ ⊘ ⊘ / ○ ○ ○ ○	○ ○ ○	⊘				20
21-25	○ ⊘	⊘ ⊘	○ ○ / ○ ○	○ ○ / ○ ○	○ ○				14
16-20	⊘ ⊘ / ⊘ ⊘	⊘ ⊘	○ ○	⊘ ○ ○ / ○ ○	○ ○				15
11-15	⊘ ⊘ / ⊘ ⊘	⊘ ⊘ ⊘ / ⊘ ⊘	○ ○	○					12
6-10	○ ○	⊘		○					4
0-5									
NO.	25	22	35	61	47	9	15	4	218

- • GRADUATED OR STILL IN COLLEGE
- ○ SIX QUARTERS' RESIDENCE
- ⊘ FOUR QUARTERS' RESIDENCE OR LESS
- + DECEASED

TABLE 7.—Progress of a Single Class for Four Years.

have a standing high enough for graduation, and they were just below the necessary level. The progress of these 218 freshmen is shown in relation to their combined intelligence and scholarship ratings at entrance. No one with a rating below the thirty-fifth percentile was left in college at the end of four years, and less than 8 per cent remained of those in the lower half of the distribution.

Such figures as emerge when one traces the academic history of any group of unselected freshmen suggest strongly either that the students are not able to profit by the curricular offerings or that the curriculum is so inappropriate to their needs and interests that they will not apply themselves. In any event the elimination is high and leads the observer to wonder what the great majority of these freshmen got out of their college experience and what permanent effect upon their lives their academic inferiority may have had.

V. SUMMARY

College students are a select group—the survivors of successive eliminations since elementary school days. Most of them are drawn from the upper third of the high school graduating class. They come from all levels of society, although the professional groups supply a larger proportion of their own numbers than any other. The largest actual number of students come from homes in which the father is a businessman. In spite of the fairly high selection, however, about a third of them are eliminated during the first year in college, and barely more than a half ever graduate. When one follows the progress of a typical entering class through four years of college, it becomes clear that the main reason for elimination is inability to do the work, although the reasons the students themselves give may often be contributing causes. Either the selection is too low for the work, or the work is too difficult for the selection.

CHAPTER V

PERSONNEL WORK

One other matter remains to be discussed concerning the general background against which the college teacher carries on his work. Each year more and more colleges are instituting what is known as "personnel work." It is not at all necessary for a teacher to know the details of this modern type of service to students, but he should understand why it exists, what its purposes are, what good it does, and what its relation is to his own work. For one thing, the personnel bureau is of great value to him if he is willing to make intelligent use of its material. Moreover, he is sure to receive communications of one kind or another from personnel workers, and he is more likely to be co-operative if he understands the problems involved. It is therefore the purpose of this chapter merely to present the main outlines of the situation so that the college teacher may see clearly the relation of the personnel bureau to his own work.

I. THE PERSONNEL MOVEMENT

As is the case with many other phenomena in the modern college, personnel work is an outgrowth of large enrollments. Forty years ago it was hardly needed. At that time there were eight students per teacher in American colleges as compared with fifteen students at present. The personal relationships between faculty members and students were fairly close, and

that between upper and lower classmen very close. If a freshman wanted information on any point he first asked an upper-
classman; if he did not get what he wanted, he asked a teacher.
Moreover, many of the problems that beset the freshmen of
today did not exist.

For instance, in a large college the mere matter of getting oneself properly registered is far from simple. When I entered college
this business was settled by mail. I took three required courses and
selected two electives from a list of about eight that were open to
freshmen. The whole process required about a half-hour of reading
the catalogue and five minutes of filling in a blank. When I arrived
at college the next fall my schedule was handed to me. In recent
years I have helped to register freshmen. It is no uncommon thing
for a boy or girl to keep steadily at work for three whole days before he or she is finally enrolled in class. The blanks are sometimes
so complicated that the faculty members themselves have to go
into a conference to decide what should be written on what line.
I even know of one university that cynically supplies every entrant
with duplicate copies of every blank, on the principle that no
human mind is intelligent enough to get the whole thing right the
first time. This assumption is well founded.

If a student were in doubt about what occupation to enter,
he talked the matter over with sundry teachers, whether he was
in their classes or not. The total range of occupations that a
college graduate was likely to enter was not large, and almost
any teacher had at least a superficial acquaintance with all of
them. Since the teachers knew both their students and the
demands of different professions, they were competent to give
advice and were usually willing to do so. If a student had some
emotional problem, he could seek the help of classmates, of
upperclassmen, or of teachers. Even though the first person he
asked might be unable to give him the desired information or
assistance, he could simply keep on asking—with reasonable
assurance that eventually he would find what he needed. As
long as classes were small and teachers were well acquainted
with their students, these matters could be and were settled
informally and incidentally. Perhaps the procedures were not
all that one might desire from a scientific point of view, but

they involved a human quality that is often lacking in the complicated system of tests and ratings now employed.

With the phenomenal growth in enrollments, three developments took place. First was the arrival in college of large numbers of freshmen who did not rightly belong there at all. Because of their inevitable maladjustment they presented not only more problems than former students but also new types of problems with which the average college teacher was not competent to deal. Secondly, the classes became so large that many teachers did not know even the names of their students. Finally, the dormitory system, quite universal in the small college, broke down so completely that the contacts among students were reduced to a minimum. It is a usual thing now for a student to attend the first sessions of all his classes without seeing more than one or two people he even recognizes— and often no one at all—although he may have been in attendance in the institution for two or three years. Under these circumstances, informal methods of counseling are impossible.

About 50 per cent of all the freshmen who entered a college or university last fall attended a school with a total enrollment of 4,000 or more. The average youngster went by himself, or with a friend or two, to a large campus on which he could and probably did get lost. He was confronted by a catalogue he could not read, entrance blanks he did not know what to do with, and a time schedule as complex as a railway guide. One good reason why a university class is never complete on the first day of the semester is simply that some of the students fail to find the room. In addition to any difficulties at the college, a freshman had to find a place to live and somewhere to eat. As guidance in this matter he probably had a list of approved rooming houses, with street addresses that were totally unfamiliar. If he wanted to work for part or all of his expenses, he had to locate the employment bureau, fill in another series of blanks, and wait more or less interminably for an interview. In the course of a week's hard work and confusion he probably got himself settled as to room, meals, schedule, work, books, and all the other stage properties needed for an education. Then his classes began. He knew no one in any of them and had no good means of getting acquainted. Neither his classmates nor his teachers paid much if any attention to him as an individual. The elements of an education were put in front of him, and he could take them or leave them. In the library there were not enough books to go around, and he soon found out that only by waiting with what patience he had could he get a book at all. At his rooming house he may have had a roommate with whom he could exchange views, but the group of students living there were selected merely on the basis of who happened to hire the rooms; as a group therefore there was little if any cohesion. The teaching he got was probably good enough of its kind. The professor lectured, while anywhere from 60 to 600 students took notes. One teacher presented facts and ideas about chemistry, another about history, another about French grammar. To his teachers he was simply a name in a class book; to his immediate neighbors in class, merely the student who sat beside or in front of them; to his landlady, the boy in the third-floor room; to the clerks in library, laboratory, or bookstore, just a general nuisance; and—in all probability—to any former acquaintances from the same town, more and more of a stranger. To no one was he a real human being with hopes and ambitions, loves and interests. Many a freshman gets tired of being a shadow and goes home defeated, and some of those who remain go through college without ever being known as real people. Others begin in their last two years to emerge from the common herd as majors in some department, but even here the interest of most teachers in them is only piece-meal. That is, the professor of physics is interested in a student's progress in physics, but he is not concerned with the boy's work in other fields, with his problems of self-support, or with his disastrous love affairs. As a major student most undergraduates get substantial help in the development of their minds but only casual and incidental aid in the growth of their personalities. In short, throughout his college career the student of today discovers over and over again that no one, except possibly one or two friends, really cares whether he lives or dies. A mature person can manage to bear the cold indifference of the world, but an individual in the later years of adolescence finds this lack of attention almost unendurable. Teachers are not to be blamed for this situation. They have altogether too many students to know more than a few of them well—and as long as the acquaintance remains superficial, the less advice given the better. Teachers may be forced through the sheer burden of huge enrollments to treat students as names in a class book, but human nature will have to change a great deal before any student will enjoy it.

The personnel movement came into existence primarily to supply the personal and individual treatment that students, especially freshmen, crave. It developed because there needed to be one place on a crowded campus where a student was considered as a person—one place where somebody really listened to him. The personnel officer gathers together all the data he can about each student. He gets reports on John Smith's physical condition, his voluntary participation in student activities, his ratings from the high school teachers who knew him, his scholastic record since his elementary school days, his own statement of interests and problems, his test results, and anything else that can be found. Then he talks with John Smith and subsequently looks into any complaints or difficulties. Work of this type exists fundamentally because adolescents need it and college teachers no longer have time for it with more than a small percentage of their students. The two outstanding characteristics of the modern college are its overwhelming size and its complete impersonality. Adolescents are confused by the former and hurt by the latter. The personnel bureau may not be the ideal solution to this situation, but it represents an earnest effort to infuse into higher education the humanness that was formerly such an outstanding element— and still is in the typical small college. In fact, many small colleges do not have personnel bureaus because they do not feel the need for them. Others maintain bureaus or some central committee to act as co-ordinator for the better development of students as individuals. Small colleges are just as likely as large ones to develop the point of view which underlies personnel work, but there are commonly certain differences in the history of and arrangements for the necessary activities. The development often originates in a desire to know students better and to co-ordinate all sorts of information about them into a coherent picture, rather than from the mere pressure of numbers. The procedures for making contacts are far less formal in a small than in a large college because the faculty members do most of the work. This arrangement has its undoubted advantages, but unfortunately only a few teachers and students out of the grand total in the country are affected by what happens in the small college.

II. WORK DONE BY PERSONNEL BUREAUS

When one tries to find out just who the personnel officers on a given campus are and just what they do, one is met by great confusion. There were, for instance, in 521 college catalogues the names of no fewer than 6,850 people who did some kind of work in this field.[1] In these same colleges were 77 faculty committees that were currently studying some phase of personnel work. The duties of the people chiefly involved are as confusing as their titles. In one college the people in the personnel bureau gather records for use by teachers and administrators; in another they interview failing students; in a third they give a course on vocational guidance; in a fourth they carry on an extensive testing program during freshman week and interview such freshmen as make unusual scores; in a fifth they maintain an employment bureau and give a course on mental hygiene. There is simply no uniformity from one place to another. In not more than a few universities does anything like an "ideal" bureau exist. In describing personnel work in any adequate way, then, I shall have to mention a number of functions, some of which are almost certain to be missing in any one college. For purposes of giving a comprehensive view—and by no other means can one get an understanding of the movement—I shall discuss all the activities that I have found reported in the literature.[2]

[1] R. C. Clothier, "College Personnel Principles and Functions," *Personnel Journal*, 10 : 9-17, 1931.
[2] For good general discussions of personnel problems and methods see American Council on Education, *Measurement and Guidance of College Students,* Williams and Wilkins, 1933, 199 pp.; H. M. Bell, *The Theory and Practice of Student Counseling,* Stanford University Press, 1935, 138 pp.; F. F. Bradshaw, "The Scope and Aim of a Personnel Program," *Educational Record,* 17 : 120–28, 1936; H. D. Bragdon, *Counseling the College Student,* Harvard University Press, 1929, 162 pp.; R. C. Clothier, "College Perosnnel: Principles and Functions," *Personnel Journal,* 10 : 9-17, 1931; W. H. Cowley, "The Nature of Student Personnel Work," *Educational*

The earliest point in a student's career at which the personnel bureau may function is in his selection and admission to the college or university.[3] In private colleges this type of work is quite common. In public institutions the personnel bureau collects the data about entering students, even though there is no real selection involved. The records thus accumulated give a picture of each student's development from childhood and are of great service in dealing with individuals. Thus one's attitude is tolerant toward a failing freshman if it turns out that he has a good previous record and excellent recommendations from his former teachers; on the other hand it is likely to be severe toward a freshman probationer with a record of scholastic difficulties that runs back to elementary school.

Upon his arrival at college the freshman is aided more or less systematically to find his way about according to the size of the place and its traditions. In a large university he usually arrives in time for Freshman Week—a period set aside for orienting the newcomers.[4] The personnel bureau is often directly responsible

Record, 18: 198–226, 1936; R. H. Edward and E. R. Hilgard, "Student Counseling," *National Committee on Religion in Higher Education Bulletin,* No. 7, Ithaca, 1928, 64 pp.; J. H. Estabrooks, "Modern Trends in College Personnel Work," *Personnel Journal,* 11: 86–92, 1932; D. H. Gardner, "Student Personnel Service," in *The Evaluation of Higher Institutions,* Part V, University of Chicago Press, 1936, 235 pp.; D. T. Howard, "The Personnel Department," in *Higher Education in America,* R. A. Kent (Ed.), Ginn and Company, 1930, pp. 488–501; L. Jones, "A Project in Student Personnel Service Designed to Facilitate Each Student's Achievement at the Level of His Ability," *University of Iowa Studies in Education,* Vol. 5, No. 1, 1928, 59 pp.; E. M. Lloyd-Jones and M. R. Smith, *A Student Personnel Program for Higher Education,* McGraw-Hill Book Company, 1938, 322 pp. (This is the best single reference.) D. G. Patterson, G. G. Schneidler, and E. G. Williamson, *Student Guidance Techniques,* McGraw-Hill Book Company, 1938, 316 pp.; M. E. Townsend, "Administration of Student Personnel Service in Teacher Training Institutions of the United States," *Teachers College Contributions to Education,* No. 536, 1932, 115 pp.; E. G. Williamson and J. B. Darley, *Student Personnel Work,* McGraw-Hill Book Company, 1936, 313 pp.; J. E. Walters, *Individualizing Education,* John Wiley & Sons, Inc., 1935, 278 pp.; E. G. Williamson and D. G. Patterson, "Co-ordinating Counseling Procedures," *Journal of Higher Education,* 5: 75–78, 1934; E. G. Williamson, *How to Counsel Students,* McGraw-Hill Book Company, 1939, 562 pp.

[3] See, for instance, A. J. Brumbaugh, "Selecting and Counseling of Students at the University of Chicago," *Proceedings of the Institute for Administrative Officers of Higher Institutions,* 4: 55–70, 1932; and J. B. Johnston, "Pre-Entrance Advising at the University of Minnesota," *ibid.,* 31–43.

[4] For sample descriptions see D. H. Gardner, "Freshman Week at the University of Akron," *School and Society,* 26: 591–92, 1927; J. C. Knode, "Orienting the Student in College with Special Reference to Freshman Week," *Teachers College Contributions to Education,* No. 415, 1930, 140 pp.;

---

for both the development and the administration of Freshman Week. During this period various tests are commonly given, and these records are added to what has already accumulated about each freshman. In many universities one feature of Freshman Week is an interview between each student and some member of the faculty. A report of this interview also goes into the files.

In colleges in which personnel work is well developed some official interviews at least all failing students, anyone who gets into disciplinary difficulties, or anyone who is reported as being queer. In other schools there is an effort to interview every student during his first few weeks in college. Sometimes a single person concentrates exclusively upon the brilliant freshmen or upon those who are not doing as good work as could be expected of them in view of their test records. If a personnel bureau exists at all, most freshmen can reasonably expect at least one interview sometime during their first year. In addition to those students who are included in some particular group—such as the probationers or those referred by members of the faculty—there are always many students who come voluntarily because they have some problem that they want to discuss. Under similar circumstances the student of thirty years ago sought out his favorite professor; the student of today goes to the personnel officer.

The general social program and the extracurricular activities are often under the general supervision of the personnel bureau, if for no other reason than that all such participation is entered in a student's record. What he does and how—in the opinion of other students—he does it are also recorded. Indeed, nothing about a student escapes the vigilant eye of a really good personnel bureau.

Students' living conditions and their adjustment to them are matters that sometimes interest personnel workers. In some places the entire housing problem is handled as an item of personnel service. House mothers turn in regular reports, as do the officers of fraternities and sororities. In all cases such materials are incorporated in the steadily growing record.

Another function of the personnel bureau is the giving of educational and vocational guidance. In the former, members of the

a series of reports about the meeting of freshmen needs at various colleges and universities in the *Ninth Yearbook of the National Educational Association,* 1931, and "Evaluation of Freshman Week," *Journal of Higher Education,* 1 : 224–25, 1930.

faculty can and do help; in the latter they can help very little, for reasons that are shortly to appear. Guidance within a department after a student has decided upon his major subject is relatively easy and is commonly left to a faculty advisor who has the necessary intimate knowledge of the courses; but for guidance in deciding upon a major one needs to know thoroughly the catalogue, the possible openings in various fields, and the student's entire history. Almost no teacher has all this information. The teacher's natural impulse in giving advice is to help students follow their interests. This idea is all right as far as it goes, but it does not take into consideration either the student's abilities or the possible demand for his services. No ordinary professor of Latin, for instance, has a clear notion of how many Latin teachers and scholars can be used by society. He can estimate both a student's interest and his ability, because both show so clearly in the classroom. The professor of sociology is not as well equipped, however, for judging whether or not a given student will make an acceptable social worker, for example. He has too many students to be really acquainted with most of them, his knowledge of supply and demand is probably inadequate, and he is not in a position to estimate a student's possession of the necessary abilities for doing case work because these do not appear in ordinary classroom situations. In the task of helping students select a major most faculty members are of little use because they know intimately only their own department and one or two others that are closely associated. What information they have about the many remaining departments is piecemeal and based on hearsay. They are also not immune from the temptation to keep an A student within their own bailiwick or to shunt an unpromising candidate into some other field of work. In fact, for the giving of sound advice upon the selection of a field for concentration, one needs to be totally outside the teaching situation and in such a position that it makes no difference whatever in what department a student concentrates.

The giving of good advice on vocational matters has become a complex business. One fundamental difficulty is that college work has been based in the past, and still is to some extent, upon the assumption that graduates would go exclusively into the professions. There is no longer room enough in the professions, however, for all the graduates who pour out of higher education every spring. The basic fact is that four-fifths of the 48,000,000 workers in the country are doing work that does not require a college education.[5] As the number of graduates increases, so also does the number who must go into some type of work of a nonprofessional character. College students certainly need assistance in their choice of a vocation. Thus in one study,[6] 95 per cent of the undergraduates wanted to enter one of the four already most overcrowded professions. About these the students had little information that was accurate; over 80 per cent of them expected to earn more than the actual average income. In another case [7] 83 per cent of the undergraduates of a single college were preparing to enter occupations in which only 47 per cent of the graduates from this college were employed. These two studies are typical of many others. To give the necessary guidance one has to have a sound and extensive knowledge of American industry, a reasonable amount of information about what qualities and skills are needed in specific kinds of work, and a clear picture of each student's abilities. An average personnel officer is a better advisor than an average teacher because he is more likely to have the needed information.[8]

More or less directly associated with vocational guidance are both the placement bureau and the student self-help service. As will be discussed in a later chapter, about half the students in American colleges are working to earn part or all of their expenses. The assignment of such work is reasonably regarded as a matter for some personnel officer, partly because of the effect the work may have upon the student's health and personality and partly because of the possibility that this temporary employment may be a step toward a permanent job. Thus, if a filling station owner wants a college boy to grease cars, the work had best be

[5] E. G. Williamson, *Students and Occupations,* Henry Holt and Company, 1937, 437 pp.
[6] E. J. Sparling, "Do College Students Choose Vocations Wisely?" *Teachers College Contributions to Education,* No. 561, 1933, 110 pp.; E. G. Williamson, "Scholastic Motivation and Choice of Vocation," *School and Society,* 46: 353–57, 1937.
[7] E. D. Sisson, "Vocational Choices of College Students," *School and Society,* 46: 765–68, 1937.
[8] For further discussion of vocational guidance see K. M. Cowdery, "An Interest Inventory in College Vocational Guidance," *Psychological Clinic,* 19: 59–62, 1930; L. B. Hopkins, "Personnel Work in College," *New Bulletin of the Bureau of Vocational Information,* No. 3, 1925, pp. 65–87; W. B. Pitkin, *New Careers for Youth,* Simon and Schuster, 1934, 236 pp.; E. G. Williamson and J. G. Darley, *Student Personnel Work,* McGraw-Hill Book Company, 1937, 313 pp.; E. G. Williamson, "A College Class in Occupational Information," *School Review,* 43: 273–80, 1935; C. G. Wrenn, "Career Information for College Students," *School and Society,* 31: 827–31, 1930.

given to a prospective mechanical engineer, since for him it will not be only a means of support but of practical education. The placement bureau is an almost inevitable outgrowth of vocational guidance. For one thing, the placement officer needs to use the records compiled by the personnel bureau. In fact, all work having to do with occupations—present or future—goes together.

As a result of their numerous activities, personnel workers found themselves saying the same things over and over in personal interviews with one student after another. The obvious inefficiency of this method soon became apparent. There were many ideas that could be presented just as well to a group of students as to each individually. For this reason one finds personnel officers giving a certain amount of class instruction. The most common course is that on vocations. The object of this teaching is to put before the students a complete survey of all kinds of work to which a college education could conceivably contribute. The course includes all available information about salaries, security, pensions and insurance, continuity of employment, trends in demand and supply, training needed, competition, total money investment before one begins to earn anything, nature of the work, capacities needed for it, and so on. The practical values of this course are too obvious to need comment. Three other courses are natural outgrowths of continual interviewing—one on mental hygiene, one on orientation to college life, and one on how to study. The first is usually better given by a doctor with a good grounding in psychology, but in many colleges such a person is not available; a clinical psychologist is the next best teacher for the mental hygiene class, but again one cannot always find the right person; *faute de mieux* a personnel worker often has the class. For the orientation course someone from the personnel bureau is probably the best-equipped person because the bureau collects automatically so much information on this situation. The course is essentially a continuation of "Freshman Week." The work on how to study is another type of instruction that most personnel officers are not eager to give, but they are often the only people who have enough contact with enough probationers to see the need. One element in such work—if it is to be successful—is the compiling of an adequate case history of each probationer. This the bureau already has. The course on how to study thus gravitates toward the personnel worker, whether he likes it or not.

It must be evident that many functions of personnel work grow directly out of the bureau's records. Since there is no sense in the duplication of such files, many types of activity for which the records are necessary fall into the hands of the personnel worker—in fact, more than he or she often desires. The one really essential function of all personnel bureaus is the constant accumulation and recording of information about students. Everything is grist for the mill. An objective record is not easy reading, but if one sits down and studies it, the student behind it soon emerges as a real person with unmistakable abilities, defects, ambitions, and interests. Any teacher with a dash of imagination gets better acquainted with a student in less time by reading a good personnel record than by any other method. Naturally, one expects to supplement the information thus obtained by one's own experiences and observation, but as a starting point the record is excellent.

Personnel work exists because students need it and because it covers gaps inevitably left by the division of instruction into departments. In any one place it develops according to the most pressing local needs. Consequently its functions differ from college to college, but its fundamental purpose of serving students in ways not covered by the academic curriculum remains unchanged.

III. OBJECTIVE RESULTS OF PERSONNEL WORK

The most common method of justifying any addition to the usual routine of teaching is to show that it produces higher marks and keeps more students in college. Two sample studies should suffice to bring out this point. In one case nineteen freshmen who received guidance were compared with twenty-nine of the same original standing who did not.[9] At the end

[9] P. W. Holaday, "The Long-Time Effects of Freshman Counseling," *School and Society,* 29: 234-36, 1929.

of each successive year for the first group there were nineteen, fourteen, twelve, and eight students still in college; of the last number, six graduated. The comparable figures for the second group were twenty-nine, twelve, six, and six students, with no graduates. The average level of grades was almost the same for the two groups. That is, approximately half of the students receiving advice were able to do as good work as the most successful one-fifth of those who were not counseled. In a second study [10] the freshmen who received advice made 23 per cent higher grades than would normally be expected of them in view of their entrance tests. It is probable that counseling, like any other individual treatment, does result in a greater persistence of students in college and in slightly higher marks.

However, such reports as the above, while interesting, seem to me somewhat irrelevant. Even if personnel work did not produce a single higher grade it might still be valuable. The personnel worker is not concerned with scholarship, except as it is one item of information about a student. His main business is the consideration of boys and girls as people and with their adjustment to their entire environment. One would prove the value of such work if one could show that students develop into adults with better balance, a better outlook on life in general, and a better adjustment to their occupations in a college with a personnel bureau than in a college without one. It would also be valuable to know if counseling makes students any happier while they are undergraduates or helps them to profit more from their college life. Thus far I can find no evidence on these matters.

There are, however, numerous estimates of the values obtained from personnel work. One of these, which is as good as any other, is quoted below. The writer listed the values he and other faculty members felt they had gained from the work at their institution:

[10] L. Jones, "Personnel Service and Freshman Scholarship," *Educational Record,* 12:71–83, 1931. See also J. B. Walters, "Measuring the Effectiveness of Personnel Counseling," *Personnel Journal,* 11:227–36, 1932; and E. G. Williamson and J. B. Darley, *Student Personnel Work,* McGraw-Hill Book Company, 1936, 313 pp. (Chap. 9).

(1) It has helped to give direction and purpose to our educational program.

(2) It is helping us to individualize our educational practices.

(3) It is supplying us with a large amount of information about our students.

(4) It is demonstrating rather effectively: first, that the college will have to shift its emphasis from formally prescribed standards to satisfying the individual needs of the students and secondly that the college program must fit into the broader picture, which includes the community, if maximal growth is to be achieved.

(5) It is developing some rather conclusive evidence: first that a student organizes and directs his activities in the degree that he visualizes the vocational objectives for which he is best qualified and in which he has the best chance of success and secondly that a college student can with proper guidance effectively plan, direct, criticize, analyze, and evaluate the experiences of his college years.[11]

This statement is temperate, balanced, and just a bit skeptical. For these reasons it carries more weight than a blindly enthusiastic recommendation.

In personnel work one is dealing with human values that are not reducible to an arithmetical evaluation. I find more justification for counseling in such statements as the one just quoted and in such case histories as those given below than in elaborate statistics.

Allen Monroe was a typical product of family dissension. His parents had been divorced, after much quarreling, and both of them had remarried. He was their only child and had, for ten or twelve years previous to his entrance into college, lived first with one parent and then with the other. In the meantime other children had been born in both families. These younger children absorbed most of the available time and attention from the adults of each group, with the result that Allen was decidedly neglected. By his own parents he was regarded as a distressing reminder of past difficulties which might have been forgotten had he not spent six months every year in each household.

[11] J. S. Kopas, "Evaluation of a Guidance Program," *Report of the Thirteenth Annual Meeting of the American College Personnel Association,* 1936, pp. 16–18. Used by permission of the American College Personnel Association.

The difficult situation was made somewhat more complex by the difference in standards between the two homes. In one home the parents were sober, repressed, strict, intolerant, narrow-minded, and strongly religious. The parents in the second home were easy-going, sophisticated, and casual. The boy was hopelessly confused in his own views because of the differences in his training in the two places. He had learned early that what he could do in one home he could often not do in the other, but he had also observed a considerable intolerance in the strictly moral home that he had not found where the views were more liberal.

Allen had not had many friends in either town, partly because he went from place to place and partly because children regarded him as rather queer in that he had two fathers and two mothers. As a result of this situation he experienced considerable social isolation and had come to feel that he was an outcast. In fact, he had developed a grudge against the world, because so many people treated him as if the irregularity of his family affairs were his fault.

Allen's college work had been erratic during his first six terms. His marks ranged all the way from A to E, with no apparent rhyme or reason. His own explanation of the failing grades was that his work went down whenever the family situation became unusually difficult. During the term when he got his worst grades he was trying to make up his mind whether he should quit school altogether and go to work somewhere away from both families, and (if he did follow this course) whether it might not be best to disappear and let no one know where he was. Usually a poor mark had been simply a reflection of some crisis in his emotional relationships.

The personnel officer who talked with Allen tried to make him see his situation objectively and unemotionally, especially from the point of view of his parents. It had evidently never occurred to the boy that he was as much of a problem to them as they were to him. Among other things Allen studied analytically the personalities of his father and mother and the characteristics of each home. This objective survey seemed to aid him a great deal in making a better adjustment to family conditions. Especially did it relieve his emotional pressure and reduce his feeling that all the world was against him.

This boy now has an intelligent grasp of the situation. He has succeeded in making at the University some friends who do not know or do not care about his home situation, has developed an interest in the subject in which he is majoring, and has achieved a somewhat more adult and tolerant attitude toward the difficulties of his parents. He has, however, and probably always will have an antagonistic and somewhat paranoid disposition, because he has never been able to develop that confidence in older people which the average child achieves without difficulty. He still has an intolerance of and resistance to advice as a result of his past experiences. It is quite evident that his difficulties of adjustment have left an indelible imprint upon his personality. It is however probable that he will be able to finish his college work and obtain a position where he can be happier than he has ever been before.

Dolores Seldon came to the personnel bureau to ask advice regarding certain misunderstandings which greatly troubled her between her mother and herself. The situation, as the writer came to know it from interviews with both Dolores and her mother, was so common that it may almost be called typical of the modern home.

Dolores was an attractive, vivacious girl who was decidedly popular with boys. She pursued the usual custom of going with first one boy and then another without concentrating her attention upon anyone, said she knew enough about sex to leave it alone, and seemed innocent of anything more than the usual good times; in short, she appeared generally to be a typical, self-sufficient, modern girl. Her objective, non-sentimental, easy-going, boy-and-girl friendships ought to have delighted the heart of any anxious mother. But quite the contrary was the case.

Her mother simply could not understand how Dolores could be so "promiscuous" in selecting her friends. She constantly feared the worst, and seemed quite unconscious of the fact that her daughter was well armored against sex excitement by the sophistication of the modern girl. The mother deplored modern dancing, would not allow cardplaying in her home, refused permission to her children to attend the movies, scolded constantly about filthy modern novels, and generally made herself incomprehensible to her children. She said she was willing that Dolores have her friends come to the house, but what, Dolores asked frankly, could they do when they got there? By the time Dolores had finished a year of college she and her mother had succeeded in coming to a complete misunderstanding. The mother argued that Dolores should not go out often with a boy unless she intended to marry him. She stated that when *she* was a girl anyone who behaved as Dolores did would be an outcast from nice society, as was probably true. She was sure it was time for her daughter to settle down and find herself a mate before she built up such a reputation for recklessness that no man would want her. The daughter's reply was, of course, that she was just an average girl, that she did nothing wrong, and that her mother was out of date.

The great difficulty about this misunderstanding was that both mother and daughter were right. The mother, talking about conditions of her own girlhood, could not realize that times had changed. Dolores, talking about conditions as she saw them, could not realize that her mother's youth was lived under different circumstances. The mother was trying desperately and sincerely to save her daughter from what she saw as frightful ruin, for she based her interpretation of Dolores' conduct upon the attitudes current in her own girlhood. Dolores was trying to live the active, straightforward, independent, and fundamentally more healthy life of the girl of today, a life in which many young men have a part. If either had been less sincere in her convictions there would have been less trouble.

The efforts of the writer, in dealing with this situation, were directed primarily toward bringing about some understanding between these excellent representatives of two generations. Several interviews with the mother soon made it clear, however, that she had become so thoroughly conventionalized, so shut in by her prejudices, that it was impossible to bring her to any glimpse of the changes in attitudes and points of view which had taken place since her girlhood. In fact, the very possibility of such changes seemed inconceivable to her; the manners and customs of rural Indiana thirty years ago seemed to her the one inspired, eternally-right-and-never-to-be-questioned mode of life. Dolores, however, soon came to an excellent understanding of the situation. She now tried to explain things whenever possible, to make allowance for differences in points of view, and to conduct herself so as to arouse as little antagonism as possible. It is probable that through her efforts any real disruption will be avoided. But as long as Dolores lives at home she will be subject to chronic criticism and nagging because she insists upon being a normal girl of her generation. Soon she will graduate, obtain a position elsewhere— and proceed to live her own life in her own way.

Dolores' difficulties are those faced by thousands of girls today. Of late years there has been added to the ever-present distrust of one generation for another the confusion and the conflict of attitudes inevitable in a society which is rapidly changing. *A priori,* it would seem that the parent should be the one most likely to have perspective and broad judgment in such a situation, since the parent has seen the change come about. But very often (as in the case of Dolores) it is the child only who comes to any understanding and who must bear the burden of adjustment if any adjustment is made.

Frank Pelotti was sent to the Dean of Men as a disciplinary case. The complaint was that Frank cut classes steadily. In fact, two of his three professors were on the point of failing him from mere nonattendance. In due course of time Frank arrived at the office. The Dean had expected a boy with a negative attitude and a tendency to argument. To his surprise he found Frank to be one of the nicest lads he had met in a long time. In the course of the preliminary conversational skirmishing the facts emerged that Frank was a farm boy and that he wanted to raise prize pigs. Once started on his hobby Frank undertook to give the Dean a résumé of hog culture that had all the enthusiasm—coupled with accuracy in this instance—of P. G. Wodehouse's Earl of Blandings. The Dean knew a one-track mind when he saw one. At the end of ten minutes he admitted willingly that Frank's métier was pig raising and eventually managed to slip in a question about why Frank had been cutting class so recklessly.

The gleam in the boy's eyes faded and the spate of words suddenly dried up. He began to hem and haw. Eventually he got out a copy of his schedule and passed it over to the Dean. There was, he asserted, no class he could stand—or even understand. The Dean looked at the schedule and saw one class each in elementary Spanish, physics, and English. What had all this to do with pigs, or even with life in the country? This question loosed Frank's tongue again. It seemed that his parents were Italian immigrants who had prospered in America sufficiently to own their farm. While they were not quite illiterate, their education had been of the slightest, and they were determined that their son should have the advantages they had missed. After much discussion they had picked out medicine as the proper vocation for their son. To Frank medicine meant doing something for sick pigs, so he acquiesced readily enough. He had therefore enrolled in the premedical curriculum. For about a month he had gone to class faithfully—apparently hoping that the work would eventually get around to some topic dealing with rural life. A day finally came when he could not stand the idea of being bored any longer, so he cut class. Having once found out what a relief it was to miss discussions which meant nothing to him, Frank simply forgot to go back.

In the spare time he had thus obtained Frank amused himself by taking a bus out into the country and wandering all day from farm to farm. Sometimes he did a day's work in return for a meal at noon. At no time did he do anything vicious or unwise. In spite of his disheartening experiences with his college education, Frank was still a bit loath to return home as a complete failure. The Dean therefore made an agreement with the boy. He would allow Frank to drop two of the three courses, if the work of the third were finished properly, and if Frank would follow advice about his future elections. Upon this arrangement they parted. Frank kept his promise, completing the course in physics with a C. The next semester he took a light schedule in the college of agriculture. The personnel bureau found him a job doing chores around the university farm. Besides doing his regular work faithfully he learned all anyone could tell him about the pigs. In June he passed his course, but by no very wide margin. It seemed wise to call a halt on the academic phase of Frank's education. He thought his parents would be satisfied with a single year of university work, and he had no desire to go further in the prescribed curriculum, but he was interested in some of the six-week courses given for farmers during the winter. In the following few years Frank attended four of these short courses, always taking work that dealt with the care or feeding of livestock, and always reporting his presence to the Dean—although there was no reason why he should do so. In the months that intervened between courses he continued to raise pigs and to get prizes at state fairs. At the university, that without personnel work would probably have expelled him, the Dean has framed behind his desk Frank's first blue ribbon. The Dean says the sight of it keeps him humble and reminds him that academic achievements are not necessarily the only goal in life.

Mabel Forsythe was a girl of about nineteen, with a stagy and affected manner, who professed great interest in nursing. It appeared at the first interview that she had always yearned to be a nurse, and had entered college with no other objective in mind. At first all had gone fairly well, as the curriculum in which she was enrolled demanded some work in such subjects as English, chemistry, history, and psychology before beginning the more technical work. But with the start of the third term the trouble began. She was enrolled in a course in anatomy, went to her first laboratory period, was told to watch the dissection of a cadaver, took one look at it, fled to her college office, and promptly withdrew from the course. Several days of thinking over the situation did not serve to help matters any. She discovered that she had an unalterable aversion to work with dead bodies and felt that she could never finish her course. In desperation she came for advice.

Apparently, Mabel had always thought of nursing as "smoothing the fevered brow," measuring out medicine, cheering the convalescent, and doing other pleasant things. She did not know that a nurse spent much of her practical training in scrubbing floors, sterilizing instruments, carrying bedpans, assisting at operations, and doing other such disagreeable tasks. Nor did she have the vaguest suspicion that one had to touch dead people. In her rosy dreams the patients always got well. She did not realize what courses in anatomy and physiology would be like, and apparently had no thoughts of dissecting even lower animals. She vowed emphatically that she could not possibly go on, but at the same time she insisted she could nurse if only she could be excused from the nauseating details in the laboratories. Assurance that work in the hospital would be even more nauseating did not shake her conviction in the matter—probably because she thought she knew all about nursing from reading stories, seeing movies, and watching nurses in clean uniforms going to and from a near-by hospital. In addition to her helplessness in the presence of a dead body, she admitted that she fainted at the sight of blood, became horror-stricken on the one occasion when she had witnessed seasickness, and could not bear the thought of being given a physical examination because she thought a nude body so "terrible."

As a candidate for nursing, Mabel seemed hopeless. She was told that she must do one of three things. She might set her teeth and go through the training. She might give up her ambition and settle upon some other objective, and forget about nursing. Or she could gain admission to a city hospital where the training was of the briefest, where there would be no laboratory courses, and where a certain amount of hardihood might come to her when she actually got down to work; that is, she might try practical work and see how she reacted, as she could be assured that nothing would be worse than her probation period. It was stressed on several occasions that she must make up her mind and get away from the emotional strain of her present indecision. Mabel would not even consider going back into her curriculum; she was sure she would "go crazy" if she so much as saw another dead body. As she learned more about the practical details of nursing from the experienced individuals to whom she was sent for conferences, she became convinced she could not stand nursing anyway. Finally she came to the conclusion that she must change her objective.

It should be noted that this girl was headed toward her idealized, sentimentalized idea of nursing, that she was quite ignorant of the facts and demands of the profession, and that she had already built up a series of reactions that made the possibility of success in such work very remote. It might perhaps have been possible, by long and tactful inquiry, to locate the sources of these emotional attitudes and modify them. Something of the sort was attempted, but it soon became evident that while she could be re-educated sufficiently to avoid hysteria on such critical occasions as might be involved in the average existence, she was hardly to be so made over as to enter a profession regularly involving acts that revolted her. As a matter of fact, Mabel had no interest in nursing; what she wanted was a white uniform, a position of authority (which nurses do not usually have), what looked like an easy existence—and is not.

Mabel is now in her last year of training as a prospective teacher of English. She has almost forgotten that she ever wanted to be a nurse. In this particular case no great harm was done by her initial mistake in vocational choice. Mabel was disillusioned before she had spent time and energy upon her training for nursing; in fact, all her work could be counted in another curriculum, so that she did not even lose any credits. She is now a fairly normal girl (although still somewhat squeamish), is satisfied, doing good work, and is looking forward with enthusism to a position as an English teacher—but she has her feet on the ground this time and is not expecting to find her path strewn with roses.[12]

[12] The second and fourth cases are from L. C. Pressey, *Some College Students and Their Problems,* Ohio State University, 1929, 98 pp.

Perhaps eventually someone will go through the records that accumulate in a personnel bureau and will publish some conclusions as to what good was done for different students by the procedures used. Data from case studies are a little hard to summarize, but it can be done. It is only in terms of student growth, in successful adjustment to difficulties, in development of good citizenship, and in the successful pursuit of a career that the efforts of the personnel bureau can properly be judged.

IV. THE RELATION OF COLLEGE TEACHERS
TO PERSONNEL WORK

There are two dominant points of view about the participation of teachers in the personnel activities of a college or university. Some people feel that college teachers need only a moderate amount of help to become the best available workers, while others are quite sure that only an occasional teacher has or is likely to develop the necessary abilities and attitudes. One group or the other must be wrong, but I have no clear idea which. Instead of agreeing with either I would prefer to add a third point of view based only on practicality and expediency. Until a college reduces teaching schedules sufficiently for faculty members to have the needed time for personnel work the question of whether or not they would do it well is beside the point. Since the Golden Age when a teacher will have time to meet his instructional obligations shows no immediate sign of arriving, I shall try to present the relation of the teacher to personnel work as it commonly develops—not as it might ideally be.

As far as the average teacher is concerned, his relations with the bureau are fourfold.[13] First, he can always use the records if he wants to—and he should want to. As soon as a teacher knows who is to be in his class he can spend a profitable afternoon reading through the appropriate records. In this way he can get a good picture of each student before he or she has

[13] With the actual techniques of personnel work and with its administration the college teacher usually has nothing whatever to do. I have therefore omitted all descriptions of how a bureau is organized, what tests it gives, how it selects which students to interview, and so on.

been in class more than a day or two. The knowledge thus gained puts the instructor several weeks ahead of his usual situation as regards acquaintance with his students' needs and interests. His second relationship consists in maintaining in his own dealings with students the personnel "point of view." [14] That is, he should also try to treat each student as an individual and should not become so engrossed in the minutiae of his own subject matter that he fails to notice the human needs of those in his class. Many an otherwise good teacher of the past has not had toward his students the attitude that is the essential characteristic of the personnel movement. One of my own teachers is an excellent example of this fact.

Mr. V was an agreeable and kindly man who undoubtedly found his specialty—the study of Homeric Greek—of absorbing interest. What entirely escaped him, however, was the nature of the adolescent minds and personalities with which he had to work. Each day he sent his students to the board to write out declensions or conjugations. As soon as we were in place he would tell us what word we were to inflect. Since he gave all members of the class the same word, we could always copy any form we did not know from someone else. He never seemed to notice this habit on the part of his students. After we had completed the work he went around the room looking at our productions on the board. There were few errors, because some student usually knew the required forms, and the others simply borrowed that knowledge. The practically perfect work always delighted Mr. V. While he was looking over the material on the board, the two students next to the door on either side usually availed themselves of the opportunity to slide unobtrusively out of the room. At the same time the others spread out a little to cover the empty spaces. I have known him to lose half his class by this method without ever apparently missing anyone. After about half an hour of work at the board we returned to our seats, and he began to ask us questions. The room had—providentially—five rows of chairs. He called on the first row Mondays, on the second row Tuesdays, and so on—by this means supposedly giving all members of the class an equal chance to recite. The only hitch in this simple system was

[14] A good statement of this point of view appears in G. W. Rightmire, *Communication to the University Faculty,* Ohio State University, Columbus, 1929, 23 pp.

that he did not know one student from another. Consequently, those who were prepared sat in the row that would be called on. This plan worked magnificently from Mr. V's point of view, because he always got reasonably correct answers. At no time during my two years of work with him did I see him treat any student as an individual. To him we were as alike as marbles in a box. To be sure, he talked willingly enough to any student, but he obviously neither knew nor cared with which one he was speaking. As far as actual instruction was concerned, Mr. V was really excellent. His explanations were clear, his organization of the material good, and his presentation interesting. From the personnel point of view, however, he was a definitely poor teacher because of his complete absorption in his subject and his complete obliviousness to the nature and needs of his students.

In addition to using records and to maintaining an alert interest in his students a college teacher should, in the third place, co-operate with the personnel bureau by sending to it any students who seem to be in need of the types of service it offers. Frequently a teacher has in his class a student who is obviously maladjusted to college life. Even if the instructor has adequate time for investigation, he usually does not know how to proceed. Under these circumstances he can ask the bureau to take over the job. Finally, a teacher can co-operate with personnel workers by making out as carefully and as accurately as possible any reports that are called for. These summaries will become a part of a student's permanent case history and will be used as evidence to decide matters that are, to the student at least, of considerable importance. Whatever a teacher says is almost certain to be read and used. Unanswered requests for information, inadequate reports, and snap judgments from faculty members are the bane of a personnel officer's life. Since a teacher can, if he wishes, get help from the personnel office, he should be willing in return to make out estimates as carefully as he can.

Some types of guidance are better given by teachers than by other people. In a few colleges members of the faculty have trained themselves for personnel work and have been markedly successful. Participation of the faculty in guidance is decidedly valuable.[15] There are, however, three important points to be considered. The first is that not all teachers are fitted by either temperament or training to do counseling. It is therefore not possible to spread out the work evenly among all members of a faculty, as has sometimes been done. The participation should always be restricted to those who do the work well and like to do it. The second point concerns the need for training. No person who lacks specific training—whether formal or not is unimportant—has any business giving advice to students. It is not enough merely to like helping people. One needs a great deal of specific information. Finally, no teacher who is working as a counselor should have a full schedule of classes. Unless the load is made lighter something will get neglected, or the teacher will become too tired to do anything well. When counseling has to be done on the wing between classes it had better be omitted altogether. If a college is willing to reduce the teaching load by one three-hour course for every twenty or thirty students for whom a teacher is to be the advisor, many faculty members will become excellent counselors. It is a type of work in which a young instructor may well develop an interest.

V. SUMMARY

Personnel work is a fairly new phenomenon which has come into existence largely because the old order of college life has broken down, and the personal contact between teachers and students has been greatly lessened—and sometimes completely lost. As more and more students crowded into higher education, a larger and larger proportion of the faculty became narrow specialists. At the same time the need of keeping some kind of academic record for each student precipitated the custom of reducing education to mathematical units. Somewhere during this entire shift in the nature of undergraduate work and life, many a college lost its soul. The personnel movement is primarily an effort to restore the vital flame

[15] See, for instance, E. S. Jones, "Faculty Advisors of Students and the Personnel Office," *School and Society,* 27 : 79–81, 1928; and R. G. Reynolds, "The Teacher's Part in Guidance," *Teachers College Record,* 37 : 691–97, 1936.

without which a person may be trained but not educated. This movement has developed in different ways in different places, but the essential point of view is the same. It exists for the purpose of treating students as individuals and of developing them into normal, useful human beings. The college teacher can get help in dealing with his students by consulting the extensive records kept by personnel workers and by sending to them for advice any students who need more help than he is equipped to give. The personnel office is a fixture upon the campus of the modern college or university. Since it is, teachers should understand its nature and functions, should carry its fundamental point of view into their own teaching, should co-operate with it, and should view its efforts with sympathy. Like everyone else, counselors make mistakes, but what they are trying to do is eminently worth doing.

II.

THE COLLEGE STUDENT

CHAPTER VI

THE LATER YEARS OF ADOLESCENCE
Physical, Mental, Social, and Emotional Development

The typical college student is a boy or girl in late adolescence. The boy is not yet a man, but he has outgrown most of his childishness; the girl is usually even nearer to maturity. Both have rather more independence than their elders commonly give them credit for, although both still disintegrate under pressure to the levels of behavior characteristic of the early adolescent period or even of childhood.

It is essential that a college teacher know the main facts about development during the years, roughly, from seventeen to twenty-four. Otherwise his work is likely to go badly because he is not able to adjust it adequately to the abilities and characteristics of his learners. Some of the points discussed in this chapter are more relevant than others to the work of the classroom, but all of them are needed for a balanced picture of the college student.

The total period of adolescence—from about twelve to twenty-five years of age—is usually divided into three parts. Early adolescence extends from twelve or thirteen to fourteen or fifteen; the middle period, from fifteen or sixteen to seventeen or eighteen; and late adolescence, from eighteen or nineteen to twenty-four or twenty-five. Chronological age alone places freshmen and sophomores on the dividing line between the last two stages. However, since each individual progresses at his own rate, many undergraduates still have a lower developmental age than one would expect, while others are as mature as the average adult. The psychology of adolescence is concerned primarily with the emotional and social growth that follows after the physical changes of pubescence have precipitated an individual from childhood into sexual maturity. The period has very definite objectives, by means of which one can tell when a given individual has "grown up." Many people, of course, never measure up to all these criteria and therefore remain, in some respects, adolescent to the end of their days. Most students have already reached some of these objectives before they enter college, but others they achieve during their college years. Teachers should be cognizant of these main goals of the period so that they can contribute their bit toward bringing about maturity as soon as possible.

Writers on the subject have mentioned more or less frequently seven criteria,[1] by which one can judge from a person's behavior whether or not he has become adult. In order of their usual development, these seven objectives are: the release from family supervision, the establishment of heterosexual interests, the preparation for a vocation, the narrowing of intellectual interests to those few that will be permanent, the concentration of emotional interest upon one person, the development of enough tolerance to live without too much friction, and the acquisition of a philosophy of life. The college contributes little to the first two problems, but much to the other five.

The first problem is generally solved either before a freshman comes to college or by the mere fact of his entrance. Unless he lives at home, the beginning of college automatically produces a still further degree of independence than he has already gained during high school. In a few instances, a

---

[1] See for instance, L. S. Hollingworth, *Psychology of the Adolescent*, D. Appleton-Century Company, 1928, 259 pp.; F. E. Williams, "Confronting the World: The Adjustments of Later Adolescence," in *Concerning Parents*, New Republic, Inc., 1926, pp. 137–59; D. A. Prescott, "Youth as Developing Organisms," *Thirty-eighth Yearbook of the National Society for the Study of Education*, 1939, pp. 29–48; A. C. Eurich, "Youth in the Colleges," *Ibid.*, pp. 73–96; A. J. Brumbaugh, "Youth as a Common Concern of High Schools and Colleges," *Ibid.*, pp. 97–112. See also the *Sixteenth Yearbook of the Department of Superintendence*, National Education Association, "Youth and Education To-day," 1938, 509 pp.

student's family tries to cling to him, but parents are generally forced to accept—willingly or otherwise—the escape of their offspring from their control. The second objective has also in most cases been reached long before a student arrives at his alma mater. Boys and girls first become interested in each other during the years of junior high and high school. All they apparently need for a normal development in this respect is the presence in their immediate environment of enough other people of the same age and the opposite sex. The public school supplies just such an environment. Almost 90 per cent of all secondary and college students are in coeducational schools or colleges; [2] even for the few who are not, the heterosexual interest is generally so well established during the early years of adolescence that it will survive four years of partial separation from members of the opposite sex.

Although the first two of these major problems are solved or on the way to solution, the average freshman has hardly made a beginning on the last five. He may have a vocational plan, but often he does not have even that; in any case, he has had little vocational training. His interests are likely to be catholic. There is sometimes almost nothing that a freshman does not want to do or be; frequently he has the firm intention of learning everything. During his college years he should select a vocation and at least start preparing for it; he should also narrow his interests enough to become something more than a dabbler. Otherwise he will remain *der ewige Student*— than whom in adult life there is no greater nuisance. Sometimes the selection of a vocation acts to narrow interests, and sometimes the concentration of interests acts as a basis for choosing a vocation. The two are obviously connected, although it is possible for one to take place without the other. A reflection of this narrowing of interests is seen in the number of purely play activities indulged in by children and adolescents. [3] The number of such activities per week among several thousand ten-year-olds is 36; the total becomes less with each year,

---

[2] See page 7.
[3] H. C. Lehman and P. A. Witty, *The Psychology of Play Activities*, A. S. Barnes, 1927, 242 pp.

until at twenty-two it is only 17. The seventy-fifth percentile of the distribution for seniors in college is below the twenty-fifth percentile for children. As far as play interests are concerned, this concentration is certainly voluntary and is presumably a function of maturity.

Concentration of emotional interest upon one person will often occur during college without any help from anyone. Mere biology is not, however, sufficient to insure happiness.

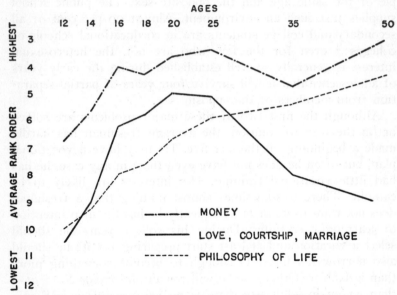

FIG. 12.—Changing Intensity of Three Problems.

Shuttleworth, *op. cit.* Used by permission of the National Research Council.

Instead of ignoring this phase of development, a college ought to offer definite help and guidance. As pointed out in the chapter on the curriculum, the problem is so universal, so relevant to the age of students, and so important that it should receive every consideration,[4] as is the case in the modern college.

The last two objectives—development of tolerance and of

[4] See pages 66–71.

a philosophy—are the undoubted business of the college. The average freshman still has many forms of adolescent prejudice and intolerance. He has them, not because he is stupid, but because he is young. One task of the college teacher is to widen horizons and bring about sympathetic understanding so that the opinionated boy can at least have a chance to grow into a tolerant man. If the seniors in a college are not more tolerant than the freshmen, then the institution has failed in one of its functions, and its students are being allowed to prolong their adolescence unduly. The beginnings of a philosophy of life should also appear during the later years of the adolescent period. Although many high schools make real efforts to develop general points of view toward the world, they are handicapped by the intellectual immaturity and restricted experiences of their pupils. The college has a better opportunity because the students are older. The senior's attitude toward life should be less incoherent, less piecemeal, and less superficial than the freshman's.

College students are really concerned in developing a philosophy of life. Figure 12 above summarizes an investigation on this point.[5] A large number of children, students, and adults were asked to list a series of topics in order from the one which presented the most problems to that which presented the fewest. For boys and men, "philosophy of life" rose from tenth place out of fifteen at the age of twelve to sixth place by the age of twenty-five, and fifth by the age of fifty. For girls it started at ninth place and rose to fifth by the age of twenty-five. By way of comparison, the corresponding curves for "money" and "courtship and marriage" are included on the chart. These results suggest that young people themselves feel the need of help in developing a philosophy.

One may, then, set up the following criteria for the college years:[6] some amount of vocational training, the narrowing of

[5] Based on unpublished data by P. M. Symonds, quoted in F. K. Shuttleworth, "The Adolescent Period," *Monographs of the Society for Research in Child Development,* Vol. 3, No. 3, 1938.

[6] For a good theoretical discussion of affective maturity and the contribution of education toward its development, see D. A. Prescott, *Emotion and the Educative Process,* American Council on Education, 1938, 323 pp.

interest, the development of tolerance, and the beginning of a philosophy of life. When an individual has met these objectives, plus the other three with which the college may or may not have to deal in individual cases, he is an adult—and until then he will merely grow older, not grow up.[7]

The college teacher needs in his mind a clear and consistent picture of American youth. In the course of his teaching career he is almost sure to develop such a picture on the basis of his own experience, but he can begin his work with fewer unnecessary errors if he has something more to draw upon than his casual observation of students and his own memories. To obtain this view of normal youth, one needs to consider the physical, mental, emotional, social, and moral developments that take place during the later years of adolescence, the typical attitudes of college students toward themselves and their world, the problems that commonly confront them during their four years, and their solutions—good or bad—to these problems. This and the following two chapters will be devoted to a discussion of these various points.

I. PHYSICAL DEVELOPMENT

The college does not have to struggle, as the high school does, with the problems that arise from mere physical growth and sexual maturing. Between the ages of thirteen and seventeen boys show an average increase in height of eleven inches and in weight of forty-one pounds; for girls the corresponding figures are seven inches and twenty-seven pounds.[8] The con-

[7] In spite of more precise and scientific statements of what constitutes emotional maturity, I still prefer the following formulation of adulthood (W. Lippmann, *A Preface to Morals,* The Macmillan Company, 1929, 349 pp.) : "A boy can take you into the open night and show you the stars; he might tell you no end of things about them, conceivably all that an astronomer could teach. But until and unless he feels the vast indifference of the universe to his own fate, and has placed himself in the perspective of cold and illimitable space, he has not looked maturely into the heavens. Until he has felt this, and unless he can endure it, he remains a child, and in his childishness he will resent the heavens when they are not accommodating. . . . The childish belief that each of us is the center of an adoring and solicitous universe becomes the source of endless disappointment because we cannot reconcile what we feel is due us with what we must resign ourselves to." Used by permission of The Macmillan Company.

[8] B. T. Baldwin, "The Physical Growth of Children from Birth to Maturity," *University of Iowa Studies in Child Welfare.* Vol. No. 1, 1923, 411 pp.

trast in growth rates between high school and college are illustrated by Figure 13 [9] which shows annual increments of body weight from birth to twenty-one years of age. From ten to sixteen years there are great gains in weight, especially among boys, but the annual increment for both sexes has become almost zero before the age of twenty-one. At fourteen about 80 per cent of the girls, but only 40 per cent of the boys,

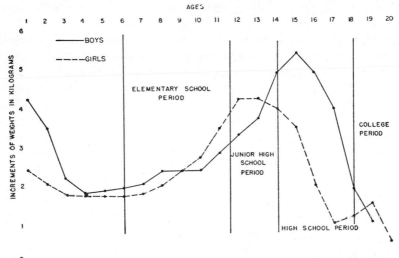

FIG. 13.—Increments of Weight from One to Twenty Years.

Used by permission of the *American Journal of Physical Anthropology*.

are sexually mature; by eighteen all members of both sexes are mature.[10] The high school years involve much stress and strain that arise merely from these abrupt changes in bodily size and function. Most college freshmen have not only reached their adult size, but they have had it long enough to get accustomed to it. Some of them are still awkward, and a few fall over their own feet, but the majority are quite well

[9] C. B. Davenport, "Human Metamorphosis," *American Journal of Physical Anthropology*, 9: 205–32, 1926.

[10] Baldwin, *op. cit.;* C. W. Crampton, "Physiological Growth," *American Physical Education Review*, 13: 141–54, 214–27, 268–83, 345–58, 1908; R. K. Atkinson, "A Study of Athletic Ability in High School Girls," *American Physical Education Review*, 30: 389–99, 1925.

organized on the adult level. Although an occasional student grows two or three inches or adds several pounds to his weight after entering college, the averages for students as a group remain almost stationary. The difference between freshmen and seniors in height is less than an inch and in weight less than two pounds.[11] The more serious emotional disturbances and embarrassments that arise from sexual maturing have for most students mercifully disappeared. It is therefore possible for college teachers to read Heine's poems, talk about Madame de Maintenon, discuss the puberty rites of primitive tribes, mention prostitution and venereal disease, or describe the development of the human embryo, without precipitating a scene of acute discomfort. Although in bodily development and proportions the college student is already an adult, he continues to increase in strength, as indicated in Figure 14.[12] Girls do not make such large gains as those shown for boys, but they are appreciably stronger at the end of college than at the beginning.[13]

The high school teacher needs to be very sensitive to the many personal problems that are precipitated by rapid growth. In college, however, the chief physical difficulties are those that arise from malfunctioning or defect. Although students are, as a group, healthy and vigorous, some of them have definite

[11] F. F. Gordon, "Physical Measurements of 1000 Smith College Students," *American Journal of Public Health,* 20: 963–68, 1930; C. M. Jackson, "Physical Measurements of the Female Students at the University of Minnesota," *American Journal of Physical Anthropology,* 12: 363–413, 1929; and C. M. Jackson, "The Physique of Male Students at the University of Minnesota," *American Journal of Anatomy,* 40: 59–126, 1927; J. S. Herriott, "Physical Development of College Women, 1904–1928," *Research Quarterly of the American Physical Education Association,* 1: 46–53, 1930; H. S. Diehl, "The Height and Weight of American College Men," *Human Biology,* 5: 445–79, 1933, and "The Height and Weight of American College Women," *Human Biology,* 5: 600–28, 1933.

[12] F. D. Brooks, *The Psychology of Adolescence,* Houghton Mifflin Company, 1929, 652 pp.

[13] There is also evidence to show that the modern college girl is taller, heavier, and better developed in every way than girls of the same ages and in the same colleges at any time since about 1880. (See M. Newcomer, "Physical Development of Vassar College Students from 1884 to 1920," *Quarterly Publication of the Statistical Association,* 17: 976–82, 1921; E. E. Jacobs, "The Physical Vigor of College Girls," *Social Science,* 6: 35–36, 1931; C. M. Jackson, "Changes in Stature and Weight of the Female Students at the University of Minnesota during the Past Eighteen Years," *American Journal of Physical Anthropology,* 14: 89, 1930.)

handicaps that interfere with classwork, some become over-fatigued, and some are chronically sick. A teacher is not supposed to be a doctor, but he should be able and willing to observe deviations from normal behavior on the part of his students. Some of these variations have clearly physical causes.

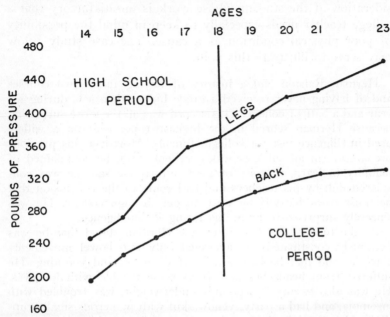

FIG. 14.—Increase for Boys in the Strength of Back and Legs.

Brooks, *op. cit.*, p. 48. Used by permission of Houghton Mifflin Company.

If these do not receive attention, the student will neither work at his maximum capacity nor develop into as normal a person as he could otherwise become.

First, as to specific conditions that influence personal development and classwork adversely. The most common of these are defects of vision,[14] (present and uncorrected in about 11 per cent of students), defects of posture (38 per cent), infected

[14] These figures are from H. S. Diehl, *The Health of College Students,* American Council on Education, 1939, 169 pp. Similar lists of figures that do not differ greatly may be found in W. E. Forsythe, "Health Service in American Colleges and Universities," *University of Michigan Bulletin,* New Series, Vol. 28, No. 11, 1926; E. A. Thacker, "A Study of Ocular Defects

tonsils (15 per cent), dental difficulties (58 per cent), more or less serious malfunctioning of the heart (8 per cent), anemia (19 per cent), and nasal abnormalities (32 per cent). Any one of these conditions lowers a student's vitality and sometimes causes academic failure. It is, in fact, in the consideration of the student whose work is unsatisfactory that a college teacher needs especially to keep in mind the possibility of poor physical condition as a cause. The case study below may serve to illustrate this point.

Herman Ralston had a history of having failed two courses and of having never received a grade higher than a C during his year and a half of college. This record was all the more surprising because Herman scored in the highest 1 per cent on a widely used intelligence test for college students. Moreover, his previous preparation in all subjects was excellent. Still, he complained of inability to learn, in spite of great effort. He said he was considered dull by his teachers and had come to the conclusion that he must work hard if he were to get through college. He was sincerely surprised to know his rating in intelligence.

At the time of his first interview Herman stated that he was extremely constipated—he averaged only two bowel movements a week—and that he had attacks of dizziness and vomiting. He suffered from headaches and from some trouble with his eyes. He was also twenty-five pounds underweight, was troubled with insomnia, and had a pasty, yellow skin with numerous small eruptions. He complained of fatigue but attributed this symptom to the work he was doing; he had a job on the night shift of a railroad office and often did not get enough sleep.

In addition to these physical defects, Herman showed quite marked emotional difficulties. He was unable to concentrate for more than a few minutes at a time. He was easily irritated and somewhat irresponsible and flighty. He felt that he was inferior to other students. He was easily discouraged if success did not immediately crown his efforts. He thought people disliked him. All told, he had a discouraged, unhappy attitude toward his college world.

The first efforts at correction of this boy's difficulties were directed toward remedying his physical condition. It seemed likely that his extreme constipation produced toxins which irritated the nerve centers. At least, the boy's toxic condition was serious and needed to be remedied. He was therefore given treatment by the college doctor to relieve the constipation, until a bowel movement every day was established. He was also put on a nonirritating diet, to which he adhered faithfully. His eyes were examined and corrected for astigmatism. His insomnia improved of itself as soon as he began to feel better. Since Herman had to do some work to stay in college, a place was found where he could work out of doors, in the daytime, at a florist's. As a result of these measures Herman has ceased to have vomiting attacks (two years have now elapsed since the last one), has gained fifteen pounds, and has developed a smooth, normal-looking skin.

With the physical conditions alleviated, something could be done in training this boy to study efficiently. He soon acquired systematic habits of work and became able to concentrate for any reasonable length of time. He was no longer jumpy and irritable. He lost his hangdog look, ceased to be discouraged, and began to consider himself as capable as other students. Soon he was competing on equal terms with others, both academically and socially. He has maintained an average only slightly below B for over two years since his period of adjustment. He also has a normal social life and as many friends as anyone else.[15]

Some students are definitely sick. Naturally their condition is not acute, or it would not remain unsuspected. As far as interfering with work is concerned, however, the unnoticed chronic illness is very serious. The effects upon both work and character are shown by the history below:

Ellen was a reasonably bright and industrious freshman. Her teachers noted, from almost her first day in class, that she was nervous and excitable. She wiggled and twisted continually, her facial muscles twitched, and she sometimes stammered. During class she was often so unable to inhibit her nervous impulses that she interrupted her teachers, laughed uproariously, or burst into tears. At first her work was good enough, but she was something of a problem in class, because of her restlessness and emotional instability. Although her teachers noticed her oddities, no one seemed to feel it a duty to report Ellen to the university physician.

[15] L. C. Pressey, *Some College Students and Their Problems,* Ohio State University Press, 1929, 97 pp.

As the semester wore on, Ellen's work became less and less acceptable. With each lowering of her grades she got more excitable, and with each access of excitement her work got worse. Quite by accident Ellen's difficulties were solved. One evening she had an acute attack of ptomaine poisoning. The university doctor who was called in was struck at once by Ellen's excessive nervousness and sent the girl to the hospital for observation. There she was found to have infected tonsils, infected teeth, infected sinuses, a chronic cystitis, and an infected gall bladder! Moreover her temperature was a degree above normal at all times and two degrees above during the afternoon and evening. Both her pulse and respiration were abnormally fast. In short, Ellen was sick. Upon advice of the physician she left college, spent a year in having her infections cleared up, returned to school an entirely different girl, and subsequently graduated without difficulty. Naturally Ellen's teachers could not be expected to know exactly what was the matter with her, but they should have realized she was in no condition to attend classes. They should also have suspected the connection between her misbehavior and her physical symptoms. Yet four instructors saw her almost daily for three months, complained about her to each other, scolded her for her outbursts—but did not report her to the doctor as a possibly sick student. It was sheer accident that she received attention before she was eliminated from college because of poor marks.

In general, the later years of adolescence are characterized by abounding health and a high resistance to disease. Statistics from fourteen leading colleges and universities [16] show an average of only eleven cases of infectious disease per thousand students. Further evidence on this point appears when one examines the incidence of illness at various ages. Figure 15 [17] shows the adolescent period to be the healthiest during a person's lifetime. Over half the persons between eighteen and

[16] Forsythe, *op. cit.* See also J. F. Rogers, "Student Health Services in Institutions of Higher Education," *Office of Education Bulletin,* No. 7, 1937, 61 pp., and "Instruction in Hygiene in Institutions of Higher Education," *Office of Education Bulletin,* No. 7, 1936, 47 pp.; D. F. Smiley, "Provisions for the Health of Students," *Proceedings of the Institute for Administrative Officers of Higher Institutions,* Vol. 4, 1932, p. 177–88. The best single reference is H. S. Diehl and C. E. Shepard, *op. cit.*

[17] S. D. Collins, "A General View of the Causes of Illness and Death at Specific Ages: Based on 9,000 Families in 18 States Visited Periodically for Twelve Months," *United States Public Health Reports,* 50: 237–55, 1935.

twenty-five are not sick at all. The number who were sick three or more times during a year was lowest at twenty years—less than 4 per cent of the population of that age. Most college students seem, in fact, to have a practically inexhaustible supply of vitality. Because adolescents normally have so much energy, they are inclined to burn the candle at both ends. As a result, the less vigorous among them are continually tired. The source of their fatigue may be too much social life, too much outside work, too many athletics, too much worry, too much respon-

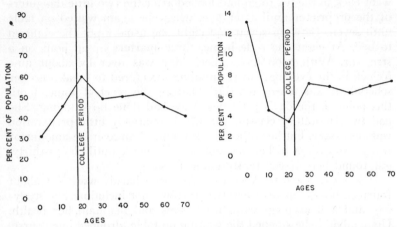

FIG. 15.—Vitality at Different Ages.

Collins, *op. cit.* Used by permission of the U. S. Public Health Service.

sibility, or even too much study. Freshmen are especially likely to wear themselves out in the course of their efforts to do everything, to know everyone, and to crowd a lifetime of experiences into a few weeks. A teacher of first-year classes therefore needs to be especially sensitive to the symptoms of exhaustion. Students cannot be trusted to stop when they are tired. If no one helps them with a word of advice they may easily get into the state described below:

Alice Smith was a tired, thin, nervous girl who was doing work far below the level of her ability. During her first interview she was asked, among other questions, what she did with her time.

Alice promptly gave a lucid and exact account of her activities for
the preceding three or four days. The average day ran something
like this:

She rose at six-thirty, got her breakfast, ate it, and washed her
dishes. She then rode on the street car for three-quarters of an
hour to get to the university in time for an eight o'clock class.
She was in class or laboratory continuously until twelve. At twelve
o'clock she went to a tea room where she waited on table until
one-thirty. She then had a class from two to three. After this
class she went to the gymnasium for an hour. At four o'clock she
went back to the tea room and looked after the two little daughters
of the proprietor until after five, when she again waited on table
until seven. Between seven and eight she usually put the children
to bed. At eight she rode home, three-quarters of an hour on a
streetcar. With good luck Alice's day was over by about nine
o'clock in the evening, but if anything interfered to break into her
schedule it was ten or ten-thirty before she reached home. Until
this point in the day's activities Alice had done no studying. She
had two laboratory classes, for which relatively little preparation
was necessary, but her other work required an average amount of
study. According to her account she did work until eleven-thirty,
but found herself constantly going to sleep.

It was explained to Alice that she could hardly work for about
fourteen hours out of every twenty-four, not including her studying, and still keep up with her lessons and maintain her health.
Upon advice, she stopped the waiting on table, dropped one course,
and slept for two hours every afternoon. She soon gained back
the weight she had lost, and her nervousness and chronic fatigue
disappeared.

As a result of these measures and of a continued observance of
ordinary hygiene, Alice has been able to complete her college
course and has graduated with a better than average record. She
is a good example of the overworked students who are trying to
earn their own way and carry a heavy schedule also. Because they
are young and energetic they seem to think they can work fourteen
to sixteen hours a day, eat hasty meals at irregular times, and still
do their studying in such spare moments as they may be able to
find.[18]

Only experienced college teachers realize the extremes to
which students will go to avoid having their work interrupted.

[18] Pressey, *op. cit.*

Adolescents will take the most terrible chances with their health rather than lose a few weeks of school. Most students still have enough of the child in them to be entirely reckless, but they are not very clever in their efforts to disguise an acute condition. Their friends usually notice the situation but often have no more sense than the student involved. Teachers should be both more observant and more sensible. It is amazing, however, what glaringly obvious symptoms they sometimes miss—presumably because they are not looking for them or else do not regard them as any of their business. The particular disease mentioned in the following illustration is relatively uncommon, but the picture of the student who keeps on going, long after he should be stopped, is a familiar one.

Mary was a senior in a small college. She had only three scheduled classes, no one of which enrolled more than fifteen students. Her other work was done by means of weekly individual conferences. Her teachers had, therefore, an adequate chance to observe her. All these teachers had had Mary in class at least once before, and from all of them she had received nothing but A's. Early in the second semester of her senior year this girl developed a bad case of shingles. The infection broke out in the nerves around her waist and made breathing extremely painful. Mary had had the disease before. She knew therefore that she would have to spend from two to six weeks in the college hospital, if she told the doctor about her condition. Since she had several relatives who were physicians she wrote to each and asked him to send her something to ease the pain. Shingles is an agonizing but not a serious disease. The doctors thus appealed to were willing to send the girl some codeine tablets. Because each thought he was the only one to whom she had written, each sent her enough to keep the pain under control during the probable course of the disease. The infection turned out to be very stubborn, and Mary, being supplied with adequate drugs, simply kept herself loaded with codeine. For a period of nearly three months she went about in a fog. She was unable to eat more than a few mouthfuls at once, she lost weight rapidly, and she could not learn anything because of her drugged condition. Mary tried to study, but she could remember hardly a word of what she read. As time went by, one assignment after another was left undone. About two weeks before the close of the semester the disease finally cleared up sufficiently to be bearable without drugs. Mary made what preparation she could for her examinations in the short time still remaining and managed to scrape past her courses. Throughout the entire period of her illness, no one of her teachers asked her if she were sick. One of the advantages of a small college is supposed to be the personal attention given to students by the faculty. This particular college allowed a girl to wander about the campus for three months in a drugged haze. If such a condition can escape notice, it is not surprising that the average teacher so often completely overlooks physical condition as a possible factor in causing unsatisfactory work.

Since most colleges have attendant physicians it seems inefficient in the extreme for students to be allowed to develop peculiarities of temperament or to fail in their work because of diseased conditions that are remediable. The doctors will do their part if teachers will send to them any students whose behavior in class suggests a chronic disease, an actual illness, or overfatigue. Even if students do not have the sense to go to a doctor voluntarily, teachers should have enough to report them.

II. MENTAL DEVELOPMENT

In the early days of intelligence testing, investigators made what seemed to be a vital discovery, namely, that intelligence reached its maximum development by the time a person was sixteen. This conclusion rested upon the objective fact that test scores did not increase perceptibly after this time. The assumption received further support during the World War as a result of the tests given to large numbers of recruits. The average mental age of the masculine half of the population turned out to be about thirteen and a half years, while the scores at the upper end of the scale were not over eighteen years and only a few of them over sixteen.[19] Subsequent tests of various adult groups yielded similar results. For more than a decade the matter was regarded as settled. In recent years, however, there has been a renewal of interest in this problem.

[19] C. S. Yoakum and R. M. Yerkes, *Army Mental Tests,* Henry Holt and Company, 1920, 303 pp.

Apparently some people simply did not believe that mental development stopped so early or at such a low level. Certainly it seems to the innocent bystander as if an individual had at thirty not only more knowledge but more mental ability than he had at sixteen. It seems also to most college teachers as if the same students were more intelligent as seniors than they had been as freshmen. There was obviously one possible source of error in the original measurements; perhaps the type of test which had been used measured only those mental traits that actually did reach full maturity in the middle years of adolescence. With tests of a different character it might be possible to measure mature kinds of mental growth. This supposition is rendered the more likely by analysis of scores made on the sub-tests of certain intelligence examinations. In one such study the older students showed almost no gains over the younger in tests of memory, of ability to comprehend simple ideas from reading matter, or of ability to carry out directions.[20] On any tests involving real thinking, however, there was a gain—and the more complex the reasoning required, the more gain occurred. This situation was not very evident in the total scores because most of the sub-tests meas ured relatively simple mental processes.

The most recent investigations bear out the common-sense view that college students do actually increase their mental stature during their four years. Not many students have thus far been examined at the beginning and end of their college careers with any test which gives them a chance to show development. In all cases investigated, however, the difference between the average score of the same students as freshmen and as seniors has been from five to eighteen times the probable error of the measurement and is, therefore, a true difference.[21]

[20] M. B. Wright, "The Development of Mental Ability at the College Adult Level," *Journal of Educational Psychology,* 22:610–28, 1931.
[21] O. B. Baldwin, "The Maturation of the College Student as Evidenced by Re-tests with the National Council Test," *Psychological Monographs,* Vol. 44, No. 1, Psychological Review Company, Princeton, New Jersey, 1933, pp. 233–62; F. D. Brooks, "Mental Development in Adolescence," *Review of Educational Research,* 6:85–101, 1936; T. R. McConnell, "Changes in Scores on the Psychological Examination of the American Council on Education from Freshman to Senior Year," *Journal of Educational Psychology,* 25:66–69, 1934; H. V. Masters and C. C. Upshall,

It is likely that the tests are not yet as good as they could be made. Eventually it should be possible to prove definitely that college students gain considerably in maturity and intellectual power.

There seems little doubt that the variability from the brightest to the dullest person of the same age increases as children grow older. Figure 16 [22] indicates the relative degrees of this variability. At ten years of age the range is twice as wide as that for five; at thirteen it is three and a half times as wide; at seventeen it is almost five times as wide. Since this development is so consistent from year to year there is no reason to suppose that students in college are not more unlike each other in mental capacity at the end of college than they were at the beginning.

It may be comforting for college professors to know that the level of freshman intelligence, as shown by test results, has been steadily rising during the past ten or fifteen years. Out of a total of 143 institutions, 112 have found a perceptible increase in average score since 1920; only 2 colleges reported a lower average.[23] The amount and nature of the increase is indicated by another study.[24] The university concerned had used the same test from 1926 through 1934. When all the scores were expressed in terms of the 1926 percentiles, it developed that the average score of entering students in 1934 was at the seventy-first percentile for the earliest year. In other words, in eight years the average level had risen twenty percentiles. The main cause for this increase lay

"Study of the Gains Made by Normal-School Students in Intelligence Test Scores," *Journal of Educational Research,* 27: 446–52, 1934; M. W. Moore, "A Study of Young High School Graduates," *Teachers College Contributions to Education,* No. 583, 1933, 78 pp.; F. M. Teagarden, "A Study of the Upper Limits of the Development of Intelligence," *Teachers College Contributions to Education,* No. 156, 1924, 112 pp.; M. J. Van Wagenen, "Has the College Student Reached His Mental Maturity When He Enters College?" *School and Society,* 9: 663–66, 1919; T. H. Weisenburg, A. Roe, and K. E. McBride, *Adult Intelligence,* Commonwealth Fund, 1936, 155 pp.

[22] L. L. Thurstone and L. Ackerson, "The Mental Growth Curve for the Binet Tests," *Journal of Educational Psychology,* 20: 569–83, 1929.

[23] W. H. Thompson, "Intelligence Tests in American Colleges," *School and Society,* 39: 790–92, 1934.

[24] E. G. Williamson, "Changes in College Freshman Intelligence," *School and Society,* 42: 547–51, 1935. See also C. D. Flory, "The Intellectual Growth of College Students," *Journal of Educational Research,* 33: 433–41, 1940; T. M. Liversay, "Does Tested Intelligence Increase at the College Level?" *Journal of Educational Psychology,* 30: 63–68, 1939; and T. R. McConnell, "Changes in Scores on the Psychological Examination of the American Council of Education from Freshman to Senior Years," *Journal of Educational Psychology,* 25: 66–69, 1934.

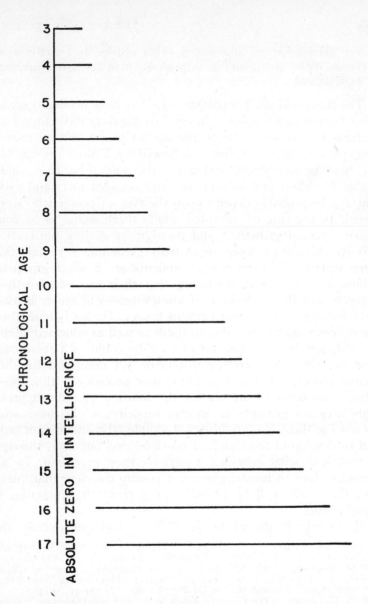

FIG. 16.—Variability in Intelligence from the Highest to the Lowest at Different Ages.

Thurstone and Ackerson, *op. cit.* Used by permission of the *Journal of Educational Psychology* and the authors.

in the elimination of low scores. This change is exactly what everyone most wants, and it is probably due to better guidance in high school.

The studies of adult intelligence to date have produced somewhat contradictory results. Many investigators have found an increase in test scores up to the age of about twenty, then a long plateau till about forty, followed by a slow decline for the next twenty years, and after the age of sixty a rapid decline.[25] Others find no decrease until between forty and fifty. The results probably depend upon the type of people who were tested. In the case of educated adults there seems to be continuous mental growth,[26] and no sign of decline until after seventy. All the evidence about truly great minds reveals this same situation.[27] Since college students are a select group of people, one is safe in assuming that their mental growth— regardless of the acquisition of knowledge—will go on at least until the age of forty and perhaps longer. If this is true, then the college senior is not able to think as well as educated adults do, although he can think better than he could as a freshman. Nor has the young college instructor yet developed his full mental power. The truth of the matter probably is that those adults who use their minds for the solution of difficult problems keep on growing in mental capacity, while those who do not use them for anything but simple adjustments not only fail to develop to their highest possible level but may, through disuse, lose what complex functions they ever had. In all considerations of mental growth it is only too clear that "unto him that hath shall be given"; the rest of the quotation is equally true.

Eventually it should be possible to find out exactly the

[25] See, for instance, H. E. Jones and H. S. Conrad, "The Growth and Decline of Intelligence," Genetic Psychology Monographs, 13: 223–98, 1933.
[26] H. Sorenson, "Adult Ages as a Factor in Learning," Journal of Educational Psychology, 21: 451–59, 1930, and "Mental Ability over a Wide Range of Adult Ages," Journal of Applied Psychology, 17: 729–41, 1933.
[27] H. C. Lehman, "The Creative Years in Science and Literature," Scientific Monthly, 43: 151–62, 1936; J. B. Heidler and H. C. Lehman, "Chronological Age and Productivity," English Journal, 26: 294–304, 1937; W. A. N. Dorland, "The Triumph of Maturity," Welfare Magazine, 18: 1,307–29, 1,444–65, 1927; S. C. Garrison, "Retests on Adults at Intervals of Ten Years," School and Society, 32: 326–28, 1930.

amount of intellectual development that takes place between the first and last years of college. Until this fact is known one cannot even hazard a guess as to how much harder a course for seniors can safely be as compared with a course for freshmen. It is, however, already clear that some increase in difficulty is not only possible but necessary, if teachers do not want to train upperclassmen in the gentle art of loafing.

III. THE SOCIAL LIFE OF LATE ADOLESCENCE

The attitudes of college professors toward the social life of the campus tend to cluster about two modes. At one extreme are those who feel that these activities absorb too much of a student's time and distract him from his only legitimate business in college—his classwork; these teachers feel quite sincerely that the side shows have become far too important. At the other extreme are those professors who believe, with equal sincerity, that the social life of the college is necessary for the development of normal personalities and that the extracurricular program therefore has a place parallel to the curricular offerings. The adoption of one attitude or the other depends chiefly upon one's notion as to the objectives of a college education. Those who want to produce scholars are understandably suspicious of the various social elements that distract students from study, while those who want to produce well-adjusted personalities appreciate the values of these same elements. Whatever one's attitude may be, the social life of the campus flows on, and students are influenced by it. A teacher simply cannot afford to disregard it; he should, on the contrary, try to understand it, to assess its values objectively, and to work with instead of against it.

Students show their social development in several ways, of which three have been studied more or less adequately. There are many reports on extracurricular activities and student self-support.[28] Recently a few studies of the more informal aspects

[28] See, for instance, R. C. Angell, *A Study in Undergraduate Adjustment,* University of Chicago Press, 1930, 173 pp.; A. Christensen, "Student Activities in Public Junior Colleges," *Junior College Journal,* 3: 251–54, 1933; B. W. Frazier *et al.,* "Health and Physical Education and Athletics: Extra-

of student life have appeared. These matters will be taken up in order.

1. Extracurricular activities: The first points to consider are the numbers and types of student organizations. One of the best studies [29] reports the situation at the University of Minnesota. Naturally, the number of organizations in a large university is larger than in any single college, but because the number in this institution is so complete, the report gives a good picture of what things interest the student mind. Since 1887, when records of student activities were first kept, there have been 533 different clubs or other organizations at this one university. Of these, 275 are still in existence. The most stable groups are the purely social organizations, the religious clubs, the honorary societies, and the various subdivisions of student government. The departmental clubs come next in point of stability, although 43 per cent of those once in existence have now disappeared. The groups that had the least permanence were those devoted to music, literature, publications, and dramatics. Of the 174 organizations in this last classification, 70 per cent have died a natural death—although some of them have been resurrected a number of times.

On most college campuses the formal activities of the students may be grouped under five main headings as being cultural, ethical, athletic, political, or purely social. All of these apparently serve the interests of students in their late adolescent years. The list of activities does not differ much from a similar one of the organizations in the large modern high school, except that it is usually shorter. The difference lies rather in the way in which the business of the group is carried on. In most colleges and universities there is an adequate diversity of student organizations to provide for the many interests of undergraduates.

curricular Activities," *National Survey of the Education of Teachers, Office of Education Bulletin,* No. 10, Vol. 5, pp. 188–214, 1933; H. C. Hand, *Campus Activities,* McGraw-Hill Book Company, 1938, 357 pp. This last reference is especially good. It presents an excellent plan for an activity program based upon a sound philosophy of higher education.

[29] F. Chapin, *Extra-Curricular Activities at the University of Minnesota,* University of Minnesota Press, 1929, 140 pp.

When it comes to the distribution of participation in these activities, however, the picture is somewhat different. In all investigations on this point two facts emerge: that approximately a third of the students take part in no activity whatever, while approximately 10 per cent carry on a third of all the activities. In Table 8 there is a summary of the degree of

TABLE 8

Distribution of Student Participation in Extracurricular Activities

Participants	Number of Activities								
	0	1	2	3	4	5	6	7	Total
Men..........	1,061	841	573	274	130	50	34	38	3,002
Women.......	490	440	333	169	107	49	26	21	1,635
Total.........	1,551	1,281	906	443	237	99	60	59	4,637
Total number of participations.......	0	1,281	1,812	1,332	948	495	360	413	6,641

participation on the part of 4,637 students in one university.[30] This table shows a total of 6,641 participations. Of this total, 455 students, or 9 per cent—those reporting 4 or more activities—account for 2,216 participations, or 32 per cent. Presumably these 455 are the boys and girls who are already most socialized and therefore most able to participate efficiently. No student who belongs to 6 or 7 organizations lacks the skill to make contacts or to get along with people. Presumably also the 1,551 nonparticipants are those who are too solitary to desire social relations or too inexperienced to know how such relations can be achieved. In either case they are the ones who need the experience for their own mental health. The real trouble with campus activities does not lie with their number, or their type, or their fascination for students, but with their dis-

[30] Chapin, *op. cit.*, p. 39. Used by permission of the University of Minnesota Press.

tribution.[31] Those that need them least get the lion's share, and those who need them most get no share at all.[32]

A more recent survey at the same university includes a summary of complaints by students about the social life of the campus and of the suggestions made for meeting these criticisms. Most students felt that they needed and wanted social training, but they pointed out a number of difficulties in getting it. They did not have the necessary time or money, they did not know which activities they could enter without a specific invitation, they did not know where to go in order to meet those interested in the same things they were, and they did not find enough opportunities to become acquainted with members of the opposite sex. Those who did not belong to any organization stated that there was no way for them to make the necessary contacts because the work was already distributed among others who were more experienced. These undergraduates made a number of practical suggestions for a better arrangement of campus activities. These appear below:

(1) Definite instruction in social conventions.

(2) Printing and distribution of a student handbook giving specific information about membership in each organization.

(3) Many entertainments that are open to all and for which the admission fee is not more than 10 cents per person.

(4) Discontinuance of most if not all of the large entertainments and substitution of a greater number of smaller ones.

(5) Arrangement for all students to live on or near the campus, so that they will have time for participation.

(6) Establishment of some permanent agency for helping students make the contacts they want and for locating those who need socialization.

[31] In another report (Angell, *op. cit.*) the distribution is even worse. In one group of 216 students, 115—or 53 per cent—took no part in any activity, while 22—or 10 per cent—carried on 46 per cent of all the activities of the entire group.

[32] This situation is not a problem of college and university only. It exists everywhere and perhaps more among older people than among adolescents and more among adolescents who are not in school than among those who are. For instance, in the Maryland survey (H. M. Bell, *Youth Tell Their Story,* American Council on Education, 1938, 261 pp.) 55 per cent of the adolescents in school or college belonged to no group of any kind, whereas 77 per cent of those out of school did not. If group activities are desirable for normal growth there should certainly be a more even distribution than is usually the case. For a report of a better distribution, see E. H. Wilkins, "On the Distribution of Extra-Curricular Activities," *School and Society,* 51 : 651–56, 1940.

(7) Definite restriction of activities on the part of the few people who would otherwise participate unduly. This arrangement is partly to prevent these students from exhausting themselves and partly to release enough activities for others.

(8) Careful restriction of fraternity and sorority members to keep them from dominating all campus life.

(9) More contacts between students and faculty and much greater participation of the latter in the social activities of the campus.[33]

These suggestions seem for the most part both sensible and feasible. Certainly if extracurricular activities are educational, there should be some arrangement by which they can best serve their purpose.

I would like to add one further suggestion. In many colleges there is a central committee to which the names for all teams, committees, or other activities must be submitted for approval. If a college really wants to pass around participation more evenly than is customary, all it has to do is to persuade or instruct this central committee to approve, for some stated interval, only names of students for whom they have as yet no record of participation. This restriction forces all chairmen or officers of student organizations to select only the people that most need socializing, because they cannot get permission to select anyone else. This plan does not work without protest, naturally, but it does work, if the central committee can stand pressure. Because of such a restriction, I was forced in my senior year to put on an entertainment with the help of girls who had no record of participation during their first three and a half years of college. Although I had the gloomiest forebodings, I had to admit later that I had never seen a more efficient or dependable group of workers. Why they had not had similar chances earlier remains a mystery; there was certainly nothing the matter with them.

The professors who complain most about the absorption of time and energy by campus activities should be comforted by the relationship between academic grades and participation in social life.[34] The students who are active always tend to get

[33] C. M. Brown, "The Social Activity Survey," *Journal of Higher Education*, 8: 257–64, 1937. Used by permission of the *Journal of Higher Education*.
[34] See for instance, J. E. Knox and R. A. Davis, "The Scholarship of University Students Participating in Extra-Curricular Activities," *Edu-*

better marks than those who are not. It may be that the socially active student knows he can afford the time he puts into such pursuits, or that he is unusually bright, or that his social contacts keep him contented and relaxed. Whatever the reason, it is only the occasional student with too much social life for his vitality who seems to suffer academically.

Many people feel that the chief value of campus activities lies in their "preparation for life." It is a familiar argument that the classwork does not have a socializing influence upon students, that the material learned in class is soon forgotten, and that academic chores are only an excuse for keeping students together long enough for them to develop a social life that will do them some real good in after years. This opinion of relative values seems exaggerated, but one hears it expressed. Cold facts make clearer the real situation. In one study [35] the subsequent, nonvocational activities of 241 prominent alumni were investigated; these people had all been leaders in student affairs during their college days. The summary below shows the relationship between participation during and after college in similar fields of interest.

During college, 65 per cent of these 241 adults belonged to literary or dramatic clubs, took part in plays, and so on, while 35 per cent did not. In later years, 70 per cent were active in similar adult organizations. Most of those who had been interested as students maintained their interest, while only 5 per cent of the remaining number took up such types of activity. There is, in all fields, some agreement between college and postcollege activities. To estimate the significance of this relation the investigators followed the records of 167 former students taken at random from the files; these graduates had not been prominent in any way during their college years. Here the agreement was not so high, but it was still appreciable. There seems, therefore, some reason to believe that campus activities do contribute to a person's later life, especially to his use of leisure time, and the more active he is in his partici-

cational Administration and Supervision, 15: 481–93, 1929; O. M. Mehus, "Extra-Curricular Activities and Academic Achievement," Journal of Educational Sociology, 6: 143–49, 1932; G. W. McMurtrey, "A Study of the Relationship between Some Factors Which Affect School Work," Journal of Educational Psychology, 23: 553–58, 1932; J. M. Stalnaker and R. C. Woellner, "Abilities of Employed Students at the University of Chicago," Journal of Higher Education, 7: 159–60, 1936.
[35] Chapin, op. cit.

pation the more is he influenced. The relation is not, however, so high as is sometimes claimed.

The more formal phases of social activity in college are, then, probably educative, but they could easily be more so. Campus life presents a rich variety of experience and a type of training that is often not given in class, although it could be given there, also. It supplements, rather than interferes with,

TABLE 9

Relation between Participation during College and Subsequently[35a]

Type of Organization	Per Cent Who Participated		Per Cent Who Did Not Participate	
	In College	AfterCollege	In College	AfterCollege
1. Literature, drama............	65	70	35	30
2. Fraternity, sorority..........	82	78	38	22
3. Student government..........	51	41	49	59
4. Social service...............	15	69	85	31
5. Religious.......	53	66	47	34
6. Publishing..................	46	32	54	68
7. Music......................	21	34	79	66
8. Athletics...................	45	56	55	44

the academic work of students. It is an element of college experience that prepares for the years to come. What it needs is regulation, so that it will not compete with the main business of college and so that the advantages may be felt by a larger proportion of the population. The program of classes and the program of extracurricular activities should form a coherent whole for the education of young people in all phases of their development.

2. Student self-support: It is a commonplace in most colleges and universities that many students will earn part or all of their expenses. About one third of the women and nearly two-thirds of the men have some kind of outside work for which they are paid. The working student used to be a special case upon the college campus, because in general only well-to-do families sent their children to college. The situation at

[35a] Chapin, *op. cit.,* p. 94. Used by permission of the University of Minnesota Press.

present is one more evidence of the extent to which colleges now draw from almost the total range of the population. One typical study [36] of self-help contains reports from 693 men and 679 women students. The per cent earning various proportions of their expenses appears below.

Proportion of Expenses Earned (Per Cent)	Men (Per Cent)	Women (Per Cent)
90–100	30 ⎫	17 ⎫
51–89	8 ⎬ 65	3 ⎬ 34
30–50	16	5
1–29	11 ⎭	9 ⎭
0	35	66

The girls tend to earn either all or none of their expenses; the men are about evenly divided into those who earn all, part, or none. These figures are typical of the situation in most large universities. In small colleges the proportion of working students is smaller, partly because the opportunities for employment are more limited. A university teacher can expect, however, that at least half the boys and a fourth of the girls in his classes will be doing some kind of remunerative work.[37]

The available statistics as to the effect of employment upon academic progress are somewhat contradictory.[38] I suspect that the results from any given group of working students depend in large measure upon whether or not their schedules have been adapted to take account of their employment. If students try

[36] E. H. Wilkins, *Report of the Faculty-Student Committee on the Distribution of Students' Time,* University of Chicago Press, 1925, p. 21. Used by permission of the University of Chicago Press.

[37] See, for instance, W. J. Greenleaf, "Self-Supporting Students in Colleges and Universities," *School Life,* 11: 188–89, 1926; Wilkins, *op. cit.;* T. G. Umstattd, *Student Self-Support at the University of Minnesota,* University of Minnesota Press, 1932, 205 pp.; A. J. Klein, "Survey of the Land-Grant Colleges and Universities," *Office of Education Bulletin,* Vol. 1, No. 9, 1930.

[38] F. E. Aden, "Some Facts Related to Student Life as Found in a Survey at the University of Colorado," *School and Society,* 39: 182–83, 1934; G. W. McMurtrey, "A Study of the Relationship between Some Factors Which Affect School Work," *Journal of Educational Psychology,* 23: 553–58, 1932; F. W. Reeves and J. D. Russell, "Some University Student Problems," *University of Chicago Survey,* Vol. 10, 1933, pp. 55–68; C. W. Reeder and S. C. Newman, "The Relationship of Employment to Scholarship," *Educational Research Bulletin,* 18: 203–14, 1937.

to carry a full academic load and to work at the same time, they need unusual ability if they are to get as good marks as those who have no extra chores. To some extent, self-supporting students compensate for their working hours by being unusually efficient in their studying and by participating less in the social life of the campus. So long as the working time does not interfere with the hours necesary for sleep or study, most students can get as good marks as they would if they had no remunerative employment. More and more students are discovering for themselves that they cannot carry a full schedule of courses and earn any considerable part of their expenses. They therefore enter college with the intention of remaining six years, and they take a reduced load. Under such circumstances their work acts as a steadying influence rather than as a handicap. If, however, a student takes the usual number of courses and works at some job from four to six hours a day, he must get this extra time from his sleep, his recreation, his meals, or his studying. Taking time from studying will certainly reduce his grades at once, and neglect of health will reduce them sooner or later. Even those students who can carry two loads at once should not do so, because they are likely to graduate from college in such poor physical condition [39] that they cannot make an efficient start on their adult lives.

3. Informal social activities: There have been comparatively few investigations of informal social activities, probably because of the difficulties involved. Two studies have, however, been made of informal conversation among college students,[40] four of the characteristics shown by student leaders,[41] and

[39] For the effect of outside work upon the health of students see R. W. Bradshaw, "Health of Self-supporting College Students," *Journal of the American Medical Association,* 90 : 1,775–76, 1928.

[40] S. M. Stoke and E. D. West, "The Conversational Interests of College Students," *School and Society,* 32 : 567–70, 1930 and "Sex Differences in Conversational Interests," *Journal of Social Psychology,* 2 : 120–26, 1931.

[41] F. S. Chapin, "Extra Curricular Activities of College Students: A Study of College Leadership," *School and Society,* 23 : 212–16, 1926; A. O. Bowden, "A Study of the Personality of Student Leaders in Colleges in the United States," *Journal of Abnormal and Social Psychology,* 21 : 149–60, 1926; L. H. Moore, "Leadership Traits of College Women," *Sociology and*

one of college friendships.[42] A summary of these studies follows.

The studies of adolescent conversation are based upon records kept by students of 498 relatively short periods of "just talk" among their friends. In all cases the members of each group were of one sex. The "reporters" were supposed by the others to be studying. The records should, then, reveal what students talk about when they are unsupervised. By the most generous interpretation, not more than 22 per cent of the men's conversation or more than 24 per cent of the women's could be regarded as being about academic or cultural matters. If students get their greatest mental stimulation from their friends—as many alumni affirm, in retrospect—it is a little hard to see how. The two main topics of conversation for both girls and boys were campus affairs and sex, with sports running a fairly close third. Approximately two-thirds of all the conversations concerned these three topics.

From one study of leadership among students only two facts emerged. The outstanding students in campus activities were superior in both physical condition and marks to those of average participation—and in an even greater degree to those of little or no participation. However, since there must have been many other healthy students with good grades who were not leaders, these two items do not seem especially vital. The second study contributes a bit more. Several student leaders were investigated with a series of tests, most of which concerned nonintellectual traits.

Figure 17 shows a profile of one leader. This student was far above average in intelligence, he had strong emotions, he was dominating, thoroughly expansive, and extraverted, he took part in many social activities, and he was a good judge of facial expressions. In insight and ability to evaluate himself he was about average. His self-interest was weaker than that shown by the ordinary student. The other leaders studied naturally varied somewhat from this particular one, but as a group they tended to have strong emotions, to be dominating, expansive, and extraverted, and to read facial expressions well. The leader has thus more than the ordinary amount of drive, he is so extraverted that his drives get into action, he is so expansive that he cannot let other people

Social Research, 17 : 44–54, 1932; N. E. Courtenay, "The Persistence of Leadership," *School Review,* 46 : 97–107, 1938.

[42] F. M. Vreeland and S. M. Corey, "A Study of College Friendships," *Journal of Abnormal and Social Psychology,* 30 : 229–36, 1935.

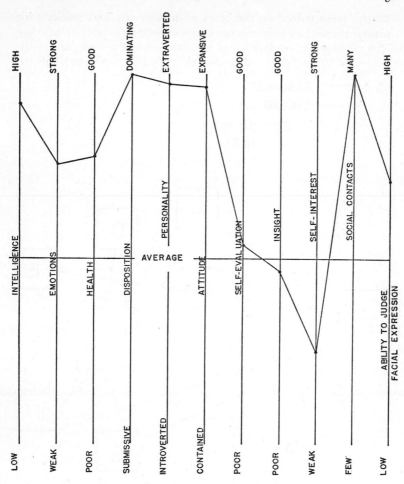

FIG. 17.—Profile of a Typical Student Leader.

Bowden, *op. cit.* Used by permission of the *Journal of Abnormal and Social Psychology* and the author.

alone, and, although he likes to dominate, he is unusually sensitive to what other people are feeling and thinking. The individual whose picture emerges from this study rings true to life.

The third article contributed little not brought out by the first two, but the last one added some information about persistence of the phenomenon of leadership. One hundred leaders in high school activities were paired on the basis of intelligence and marks with a similar number of nonleaders. The former group held an average of 7.9 positions of responsibility in school affairs as compared with 0.9 for the latter. Of the 100 leaders, 72 went to college; only 28

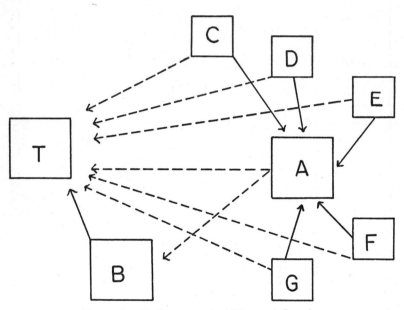

FIG. 18.—Influence of a Natural Leader.

Based upon a chart in J. L. Moreno, *Who Shall Survive?* Nervous and Mental Disease Publishing Company, 1934, 437 pp. Used by permission of the author.

of the nonleaders entered. In college the high school leaders held an average of 5.5 offices while the nonleaders had an average of 1.5. The comparison continued into life after school days were over. The entire group of leaders averaged 4.7 positions of responsibility in the community as compared with 1.1 for the nonleaders. Whatever social dominance may consist of, it appears to be a persistent trait of those who possess it. The development of this trait so that it may be as socially valuable as possible is eminently worth while.

The influence exerted by a leader, especially in a small group, is of great importance in the establishment of harmony among the members. The situation illustrated in Figure 18 is a case in point. Here Girl A was a natural leader who was antagonistic to the teacher. She had enlisted the sympathies of Girls C, D, E, F, and G. These five were not only attached to her, but they had caught her antagonism toward the teacher. The leader had had a quarrel with Girl B, and from then on rejected her. The others had taken up this attitude also. Girl B then made an effort to attach herself to the teacher and became the "teacher's pet," thus further emphasizing her isolation from her age-mates. A teacher cannot make much headway with such a group because the entire situation is unfavorable to learning. If she could win over Girl A this leader would bring her adherents with her, and the group would be far more harmonious than it is now. This study in miniature shows the strategic importance of educating natural leaders to use their influence for the good of the group rather than in antagonism to it.[43]

The one article on student friendships is not very enlightening. Between the two members of thirty different pairs of friends there was no appreciable similarity in level of intelligence, scholastic standing, or in attitude toward various social problems. If one friend of a pair was neurotic, there was a slight tendency for the other to be neurotic also. It was only in social interests and backgrounds that any real similarity between friends appeared, and even in this respect the likenesses were not great. It is safe to say that no one has yet discovered why who likes whom.

IV. EMOTIONAL DEVELOPMENTS OF LATE ADOLESCENCE

College students are less susceptible to emotional stimuli than are high school pupils, but they are more easily stimulated than adults. Their immaturity is, of course, more marked during their first year, when most of them are learning to live

[43] See also E. C. Hunter and A. M. Jordan, "An Analysis of Qualities Associated with Leadership among College Students," *Journal of Educational Psychology,* 30: 497–509, 1939.

away from home. Even the student who is developing in a perfectly normal way is somewhat overemotional by adult standards, and many students have occasional outbursts such as characterize the earlier years of adolescence. A college teacher should therefore expect to find some degree of instability and should not let himself be unduly disturbed by it. If he learns to recognize some of the more common manifestations and to assess them at their true importance, he will not only save himself a great deal of trouble, but he will be more helpful in bringing about greater maturity on the part of the students.

An emotional experience consists of three discernible parts.[44] There is, first, the stimulus that causes the emotion, then the internal bodily changes of which the emotion consists, and finally the overt reaction to the situation. The second of these parts appears to be practically invariable from birth to death, but there are great variations at different age levels in the stimuli which produce emotional responses and in the reactions which are made. A "life history" of an emotion would, then, show what stimuli affected people at different ages and what reactions they made to these stimuli. Although it is theoretically possible to write such a biography for any emotion, there are only three that have been studied in sufficient detail for this treatment; these three are anger, fear, and love. Most of the present discussion will be concerned with the manifestations of these emotions on the college level. A brief history of earlier development is, however, included, since it is easier to understand the emotional reactions of late adolescence if they are considered in the light of their genesis from early childhood.

1. *Anger:* The situations that cause anger in small children are relatively few and quite simple. Three-fourths of the outbursts arise because something has been snatched out of the child's hands, or because he resents being dressed, undressed, sent to the toilet, or washed.[45] As children grow older, they

---

[44] For an excellent discussion of the nature and development of emotional states, see Prescott, *op. cit.*

[45] See, for instance, A. F. Ricketts, "A Study of the Behavior of Young Children in Anger," *University of Iowa Studies in Child Welfare,* 9: 159–71, 1934.

begin to react to social stimuli. They get angry when other children call them bad names or borrow their property without asking for it. By the early years of adolescence social situations are the most powerful of all in precipitating emotional reactions. Naturally, some of the childish stimuli continue to affect individuals—in some cases throughout life. Below there appears a list of the typical stimuli that cause anger in college students.

"A professor's daughter acted like she owned the place." (B) [46]

"I was bawled out for talking in the library." (B)

"A kid in an old Ford cut in in front of me." (B)

"I was trying to study and three students came in and hung around and wouldn't let me." (B)

"The hostess of our sorority gave me the poorest cut of meat." (G)

"Somebody told me the boys were circulating an ugly snapshot of me." (G)

"A friend of mine turned back my alarm clock, making me late; she thought this was a joke." (G)

"The professor explained everyone else's paper but left out mine." (G)

"I was to meet two friends at the theater and they kept me waiting nearly an hour." (B)

"I went to a meeting that was supposed to last only half an hour and it lasted three, and I was sitting in a front seat and couldn't get out." (B)

"I washed my hair after a permanent and it wouldn't set right." (G)

"I spilled a bottle of ink on a paper and had to copy it over." (G)

"The oil from my car leaked out on my new clothes." (B)

"I smeared ink on a drawing, on which I had already spent several hours." (B)

"I broke a shoestring." (B)

"I stumbled and fell down in the mud." (G) [47]

It should be noted that most of these situations made the adolescent feel embarrassed or ridiculous. The application to

---

[46] (B) stands for boy and (G) for girl.

[47] H. Meltzer, "Student Adjustments in Anger," *Journal of Social Psychology,* 4: 285–308, 1933. Used by permission of the *Journal of Abnormal and Social Psychology* and the author. See also G. S. Gates, "An Observational Study of Anger," *Journal of Experimental Psychology,* 9: 325–36, 1936.

classwork is fairly obvious. A teacher who wants unruffled peace in his classroom would do well to avoid any situation that causes embarrassment. As people grow older, such stimuli as those listed above have less power to precipitate a crisis. The adult gets angry if his work is interfered with or if his family is injured in any way, and he may become enraged over abstract injustice or impersonal social conditions. The typical college student is a thorough mixture of child, adolescent, and adult. He can get angry because he pounds his thumb, because his teacher scolds him in front of his age mates, or because Austrian Jews are being treated with intolerance.

One investigator [48] asked ninety-three students to keep "anger diaries" for the period of one week. The students noted the cause of the anger, its duration, its effect upon themselves, and the reactions they made to it. The total number of anger situations was 393, or slightly more than 4 per person. The average duration was only 15 minutes, although the range was from one minute to 48 hours. Purely verbal responses were made to half the situations. All the typically childish responses together made up only 4 per cent of the total. In most cases—63 per cent—the effect upon the student was definitely dissociative; that is, he was too upset to continue efficiently with what he was doing. Moreover, half the responses made were of the nonadaptive type. This experimental picture of anger among students suggests that the experience is sufficiently disturbing to be avoided whenever possible.

The reactions one makes to anger also depend upon one's stage of development. The baby screams and turns red. The small child also screams, stamps his feet, bites, scratches, kicks, jumps up and down, and throws himself on the floor. As the years go by, he begins to substitute scolding, talking back, and shouting for his more overt behavior. Unless a college student is very angry indeed he will merely talk. He sometimes strikes his age mates, but he has outgrown most of the other infantile forms of response. Among girls the childish crying reaction persists, since it does not meet with the ridicule that has long since caused the boys to substitute swearing. The more mature students have learned to take a long walk, play

[48] Meltzer, *op. cit.*

a game, or do some hard work in order to get rid of their anger. It does not take a teacher long to find out that the talking reactions of college students include such forms as swearing, shouting, vulgarity, quite inexcusable rudeness, and "talking back." The trouble with all these responses is that they immediately evoke similar reactions in other people. When a student gets angry, a teacher has to watch himself or he will automatically become annoyed too. Since he is an adult, he should have better control than his pupils; if he loses his temper, he is likely to make matters very bad indeed.

Some years ago I was asked to investigate the case of an otherwise A student who had failed his course in English. The cause was not hard to find. One Friday afternoon in the middle of the previous semester the boy had arrived at class a little before the second bell rang and was leaning out of the window watching other students go past. While thus innocently engaged he spied a friend, to whom he "yoo-hoo-ed" and with whom he exchanged a number of more or less ribald remarks—decidedly *à haute voix*. During this interchange the instructor had entered the room, and the bell had rung. The boy's behavior was, of course, impolite and could hardly go unreproved, but the teacher completely lost his temper. After calling the student away from the window, he made him stand up in front of the class during an acrimonious reprimand—that showed no better manners than those revealed by the boy's activities—and then sent him out of class. As a parting shot, he told the boy he would not be allowed in class again until he had made a public apology. The student was a bright but somewhat immature lad—as indicated by his high school behavior—and he could not bring himself to make the apology. He therefore received an F from absence. I do not, of course, defend the boy's actions at any time in this narrative, but the teacher behaved about as badly. Such a scene is wholly unnecessary and certainly uneducative. A teacher does not teach an adolescent to control his temper by losing his own.

In general, the normal development of anger shows a change in the nature of the stimuli from the personal to the social and in the reactions from overt behavior to verbalism. In fact, for adults the talking responses have almost completely taken the place of all the others, although women still cry and men still kick things.

2. *Fear:* Of all the emotions, fear is the most disruptive. Anger gives unusual strength, and love produces new insights, but fear simply paralyzes. There is nothing about it that can be turned into an educational advantage. Although it is an innate response to relatively few stimuli, it can, unfortunately, be attached to anything or anybody; it is therefore ubiquitous.

Like anger, it has a typical development. The baby shows fear only when he is dropped or the bedclothes are pulled out from under him. From this simple beginning, a child of ten has usually developed a large assortment of fears.[49] Most of these relate to physical violence—fire, murder, accidents, burglars, knives, lightning, fights, guns, dogs, floods, poison, and so on. By the middle of adolescence most of these anxieties have given away to such stimuli as accidents, examinations, helplessness, money, sins, disease, germs, cheating, teachers, appearance, self-consciousness, and the like. Seniors in college admit only a few worries: money, ability, examinations, clothes, work, love, and marriage. These are precisely the things about which children do not worry at all. Adults have only three real concerns: money, family, and work. College students begin their four years with a number of typically adolescent fears, but by the time they graduate they are reacting chiefly to the situations that concern adults. Of course in individual cases the fears of childhood persist.[50] A college girl who is afraid of mice is showing the same immaturity that she would if she scratched a person with whom she was angry.

The reactions to fear are not varied. The first response is a rigidity and immobility of the entire body. The running-away behavior is usually secondary to this complete congealing. Any given person's reactions consist of more or less subtle variations upon these two central patterns. The most common

---

[49] The data in this paragraph comes from S. L. Pressey and L. C. Pressey, "Development of the Interest-Attitude Tests," *Journal of Applied Psychology,* 17: 1–16, 1933.

[50] Anyone interested in this topic can find a long list of fears mentioned by individual students in M. H. Means "Fears of 1,000 College Women," *Journal of Abnormal and Social Psychology,* 31: 291–311, 1936.

of these variations is the habit of running away before the stimulus appears. Thus the student who knows he will be called on to read a paper may develop a spurious toothache and be unable to attend class. However subtle or refined or circuitous the reactions may become, the primitive forms of terror are always lurking close behind one's defenses. Prolonged strain breaks down even the sanest student to the childish level of rigidity and flight. Fear is destructive to learning because its modes of expression are never useful for anything but escape; it merely disorganizes the person who experiences it. A teacher should, therefore, always avoid every situation in class or out that is likely to cause fear. This point will be discussed further presently.

3. Love: As in the case of fear and anger, there is a definite development from infancy to adulthood in the stimuli that cause this emotion. The reactions also change somewhat, though not as much. The first stimulus to love in any child's life is his mother, or someone who takes the mother's place. This "love-object" remains unchanged for most boys and for many girls until the middle years of childhood. In most families, the father will not caress his sons because he does not want them to become "sissies," but there is no social inhibition to prevent him from being as affectionate as he likes with his daughters. It does not take a small girl long to discover that her father will give her more affection when he comes home in the evening than she can get from a harassed mother at the end of several hours of her daughter's all too constant company. Many girls therefore substitute their fathers as their main love-object during the early years of childhood. It is something of an insult to the law of parsimony if one brings in an Oedipus complex to explain this phenomenon. In the first or second grades of school a teacher often takes first place in a child's affections; the primary teacher is, however, only a mother-substitute. Throughout the early years of childhood the typical love-object is an older person.

Before the end of elementary school most children have become more attached to some age mate of their own sex than they are to any adult. This period of development has often been called the "homosexual" stage, but the name is unfortunate since it implies abnormality where none exists. These attachments are normal and are an apparently necessary step in the gradual emancipation of a child from the emotional ties that originally bind him to his home. Children usually like members of their own sex so intensely during this period that boys and girls will have nothing to do with each other. At the beginning of adolescence, a third type of love-object becomes the norm—some person of about the same age but the opposite sex. This is an adult type of stimulus, but the adolescent does not confine himself or herself to a single person. For several years there is a period of experimentation and adjustment until, at some time usually between eighteen and twenty-five, an individual's choice narrows down to one relatively permanent love-object.

At entrance to college, students should have outgrown both their infantile and their childish love interests and should already have made the transfer to an adult type of stimulus. Most of them actually have. They are, however, for the most part still in the experimental stage. Most students remain at this level throughout their college days, but a few of them, at some time before graduation, settle upon what they expect to be their final object of devotion. As in other ways, the college student is part adolescent and part adult.

The overt love reactions are pretty much the same at all ages, except that they tend to become more subtle as one grows older. The small child normally pesters anyone who catches his fancy; later on, he is almost inseparable from his chum. In his earliest attachments to girls he is about as obvious. The ability to let a loved person alone is not usually acquired before the adult years—and not by some people at any age. Indirect evidences of affection begin to appear even in childhood and are quite in evidence by the time individuals reach college. The reactions of students toward the teachers of whom they are fond vary all the way from the pestiferousness of the small child to the stable, friendly affection of adults. For the most part, however, they tend to become disorganized under the stimulus of any love interest and to regress to early adolescent and even childish levels. A really experienced college professor cannot be surprised by any idiocy on the part of a student who is in love.

4. Common classroom situations that cause emotional disturbances among students: There are a number of definite and recurring emotional problems that arise in the classroom. Perhaps most common (1) are the fears generated by schoolwork. Of these, three are especially important—fear of examinations, fear of reciting, and fear of teachers as individuals. These three typically school worries interfere with learning and with the peaceful conduct of class discussions. Too many teachers are not willing to bring fears out into the daylight and discuss them with the class, yet this procedure is more effective than any other. The usual method of pretending that the worries are not there is of no value whatever. The most appropriate time for discussing fear of examinations is just before the first test takes place. The main element in the necessary mental hygiene is the teacher's ability to convince his students that the examination will be fair and that they have nothing to be afraid of, but too often the students bring with them from secondary school the notion that an instructor will always trick them if he can. Since most of them know he can if he wants to, they have an understandable fear of the consequences. Once they develop confidence in a professor this particular emotional difficulty is less in evidence.

The excitement over examinations is not pure imagination. The students generally have an increased blood pressure,[51] faster pulse and respiration rates, and an abnormal amount of blood sugar. The extent of these changes depends somewhat upon the individual but also upon the difficulty and importance of the test. Seniors who were taking their comprehensive examinations showed the greatest amount of disturbance. These facts are presented to indicate the reality of a student's anxiety and not to suggest a discontinuance of examinations. Actually students are sufficiently mature to control their emotions well

[51] C. H. Brown, "Emotional Reactions before Examinations: I. Physiological Changes," *Journal of Psychology*, 5: 1–9, 1938; II. "Results of a Questionnaire," *Journal of Psychology*, 5: 11–26, 1938.

enough to do their work. Even upon their own testimony the excitement does not interfere with their writing, except during the first few minutes and at the very end of the examination, in case they have not yet finished. Most of the anxiety is simply the same nervousness that a race horse shows as he dances up to the starting line; there is little if any nervousness left as soon as the race begins, and he can get on with his job.

Any teacher should be able to recognize the student who is afraid to recite or is afraid of him. Often the same person suffers from both conditions. In a class of thirty students there are almost certain to be two or three who cannot recite without stammering, blushing, or showing other signs of emotional perturbation, and at least one who is really afraid of any teacher. These conditions are more frequent than most teachers realize. In typical groups of students from a third to a half [52] report that they feel too timid to recite in class. Even if one discounts such evidence, one can hardly disregard so lightly the reports based upon clinical interviews. Such results usually show from half to 85 per cent [53] of unselected students to be nervous and apprehensive about reciting.

In dealing with those students who are afraid of teachers, one has to remember that fear produces a paralysis, which cannot possibly be cured by more fear. Scolding, reprimands, sarcasm, and impatience are therefore completely disastrous. It is admittedly unpleasant for a teacher when his students are afraid of him. In fact, a sensitive person is often so hurt by this attitude that he becomes angry, simply to cover his own distress, and thus produces more tension than before. There is only one constructive way in which a teacher can get rid of the discomfort caused by this situation, and that is by convincing a student that, whatever treatment he may have received from other teachers, he has nothing to fear from him. Since the worry comes largely from ignorance as to the kind

[52] See, for instance, E. Reinhardt, "Freshman Difficulties," *Journal of Higher Education,* 4: 307–9, 1933; or G. E. Garner and H. D. Pierce, "Inferiority Feelings of College Students," *Journal of Abnormal and Social Psychology,* 24: 8–13, 1929.

[53] See, for instance, S. Blanton, "Mental Hygiene Programs for Colleges," *Mental Hygiene,* 9: 478–88, 1925; or H. D. Palmer, "Mental Hygiene Problems in a University," *Mental Hygiene,* 18: 233–44, 1934.

of person the teacher is and the kind of treatment that can be expected in class, the student needs reassurance on both these points.

My own procedure is to keep after class any student who seems afraid and ask him to explain to me just what worries him. If it is only the class situation, I make an agreement with him to call on him frequently during the next few weeks, but always to propound easy questions, until he has discovered for himself that he can recite without embarrassment. If he "sticks," I agree to prompt him. This re-education takes time, but the results are worth it. All that most students need in order to get over their anxiety about reciting is a modicum of kindness and some individual help during class for a short period. Soon the student feels that he and I have a secret, and that I am his friend; then he can relax. If, however, a student is afraid of a teacher as a person the situation is not so easy, chiefly because of one's own tendency to run away from what is unpleasant; but if the instructor can be honest, unemotional, and objective, he can often change the student's attitude from fear to liking, simply by letting him get acquainted. In this matter the teacher must take the initiative; the student cannot because the social distance between him and a teacher is too great, especially if the difference in ages is more than ten years. A student who is afraid is precisely the one to select for every conceivable errand, every message to be sent, every personal service, every assistance during class. He can be asked to carry books, to collect or distribute papers, to keep an attendance record, to move charts about, to get or return books from the library, and so on. As he gets really acquainted by means of such services he loses his anxiety.

These three fears—about examinations, reciting, and teachers—are so important and so common that all instructors should develop some method of dealing with them. The suggestions made above are presumably not appropriate for all professional temperaments; they are merely one person's way of meeting these annoyances. The vital thing is to *meet them somehow* instead of avoiding them. Each teacher can work out whatever technique is possible for him, but he cannot afford to disregard the existence of fear in his classroom.

Some students manifest (2) more or less permanent aber-

rations in their love affairs. There are always a few who have
never outgrown their infantile fixation upon their parents.
They are therefore inclined to attach themselves to some
teacher, especially to a woman teacher, who can be regarded
as a mother-substitute. This relation is extremely hard for
most teachers to bear, because the student is such a nuisance.
Both boys and girls show behavior of this type. For the student there is no question that the feeling, though usually temporary, is entirely real. It does not, therefore, do at all to
sneer at the attachment, to laugh at it, or to make an effort
to stamp it out. Aside from the obvious unkindness involved,
such reactions are worse than useless because they generate
more emotion than already existed. These attachments indicate
merely that a student is emotionally childish and does not feel
secure in his college environment. Correct treatment will result
in a greater emotional maturity; incorrect treatment will produce a retreat to even lower levels of childishness.

There are at least two precautions that a teacher needs to take
when she—it is usually a woman—finds herself the recipient of
a youngster's devotion. The first principle is to make sure that
she is never alone with the student, especially behind a closed
door. This simple precaution will prevent most, if not all, of the
scenes that are so distressing. A second general principle of treatment is that the teacher give the student as many objective, routine things to do as she can think of. At the moment a student
who is in love with his or her teacher is burning up with a long-
ing to be of some use. If this feeling is given no normal means
of expression, it will sooner or later burst out in some way that
may be most embarrassing. If one keeps a student busy running
errands, he has less time to get into emotional scenes and he has
an acceptable method of expression for his feelings. It is undesirable to allow any intimacy at all, but it is essential to use up
as much of the student's time and energy as possible. An especially useful task is to let him or her do some reading of articles
in the library; the resulting notes may be of little value, but the
work reduces the emotional pressure considerably.

The particular attachment between a girl and a woman teacher
can usually be kept under control by these same means. In time
it will die a natural death, but it is most desirable that there be

no unpleasant episodes to trouble the memory of either person. It is no easy task for a teacher to deal wisely with a girl student who is violently in love with her. In the first place she has to recover from her own acute embarrassment. Some teachers simply cannot do so and must therefore resort to the "stamping out" technique, even though they know it is both heartless and inefficient. If a teacher can achieve a sufficient degree of objectivity, she can talk with the student and explain the childishness of the attachment. Students do not know that they are being merely immature; they usually suspect they are abnormal. Once they realize that the attachment to an older person is characteristic of children between the ages of two and eight they will generally make a real effort to grow up and will—incidentally—recover from their infatuation. Avoidance and secrecy on the part of a teacher produce chiefly heartbreak and greater childishness in the student. Honesty is not merely the best, but the only, policy.

There are also, especially in schools exclusively for members of one sex, some students who have not outgrown their childhood fixation upon their chums. They therefore soon fall in love with another student of the same sex. While this relationship does not directly affect classroom work, as the "crush" does, it is a situation that influences the behavior of those involved. If anything is to be done about such a relationship, it is the business of the doctor rather than the teacher, but the latter sometimes has opportunities for observing the symptoms and can report them to the proper person. The one time that a homosexual interest affects classwork—more than any other love affair—is when both members of a devoted pair take the same course, presumably because they cannot bear being separated for an hour. Their behavior is likely to be disconcerting to others, and they themselves will certainly be unable to give any serious consideration to what is going on. A teacher who sees two such devoted students can either keep them after class and warn them they will be separated if they do not show more self-control, or he can separate them without warning. In any case the lovemaking should be stopped at the first possible moment, for the benefit of all concerned. The same procedure holds for a boy and girl who are too obviously in love.

Finally, there are the perfectly normal, healthy affairs that sometimes develop when a young man stirs the emotions of a girl in his class or a young woman fires the imagination of a boy. The difference in age between a young Ph.D and his or her oldest students is often not more than three or four years. The young instructor cannot hide behind his dignity, because he does not have a great deal, nor can he remain at any considerable social distance, because he is not old enough. Most young teachers have a few such affairs to deal with. The chief precautions are the same as those already suggested—not to be alone with the student, especially behind a closed door.[54] In addition to any embarrassment that may result when a student of the opposite sex falls in love with a teacher, there is the very real danger that the affair—if not met with great discretion—will cost the instructor his or her job. College and university administrations are extremely sensitive to scandal of this sort. During an instructor's first year or two of work he usually teaches only sections of large classes. If one of his students begins to make trouble, he can and should ask to have him or her transferred to another section. There are likely to be some hurt feelings over this exchange, but unless the teacher happens to return the student's affection, this distress is going to happen sooner or later, and it had better be as soon as possible. These attractions between students and the younger members of a college faculty are normal enough—but they are loaded with dynamite.

Most of the emotional outbursts in class are caused by some maladjustment on the part of one or more students, but instructors sometimes precipitate trouble by their own behavior.

The most common bad habit is, perhaps, (1) the needless discrimination that one sees all too often. Teachers are human, and they naturally do not like all students equally well. Regardless of personal attitudes, however, one can *treat all students alike*. A teacher who is swayed by his personal attitudes arouses much unnecessary resentment among those he likes least and too much attachment among those he likes most. I have been in classes in which the teacher spent the hour in pleasant conversation with two or three favorites, whom he excused from many assignments. Some teachers declare openly to their colleagues that they would never give a Negro, Oriental, or a Jew any mark better than a C, no matter how good his work was. Behavior of this kind does

---

[54] This point may sound too obvious to mention, but rarely does a year go by without the dismissal of some young man or woman who has failed to take this simple precaution.

nothing to teach students tolerance. No matter how much an instructor may talk about being tolerant, his students will draw their own conclusions from his behavior. If a teacher wants to avoid the resentment and active dislike that are so disruptive to classwork he should learn to treat everyone alike.

A second bad habit (2) on the part of certain teachers is sarcasm. It reveals not only bad manners but also bad mental hygiene. A sarcastic teacher is an unhappy and poorly adjusted person, who is passing along his own discontent to the students. The emotions generally aroused by sarcasm are perhaps out of proportion to the stimulus. Students are likely to get into a paralysis of fear or a paroxysm of rage; either condition makes learning impossible. A really sarcastic teacher can reduce a group of freshmen to such a state of nerves that practically nothing is learned—except a further fear of teachers. Another and very practical objection to using sarcasm is the danger of real trouble from the occasional student who is able to defend himself. A disagreeable teacher expects a student to wilt under the strain; if he does not, there is likely to be a magnificent emotional display. When sarcasm backfires—as it inevitably does sooner or later—the teacher is in real difficulty. In mere self-protection, then, one should refrain from the use of this dreaded weapon.

(3) College students do not require much in the way of discipline, but there are usually some who are not yet entirely able to conduct themselves in a polite and sufficiently restrained manner. Most of the disturbances come from thoughtlessness and youthful exuberance rather than from intention. Use of any other restrictive influence than the mere presence of the teacher in the room is undesirable in a college class, but at times—especially with freshmen who have not yet adapted themselves to their new surroundings—something more is needed. Since only an occasional student requires controlling, one should try hard not to upset the rest of the class by the methods he uses. Even though a student may act like a child, he is one no longer and he will resent bitterly being treated in public as if he were. What is worse, the others in the group also resent it; even when they admit that their classmate is in the wrong, they still side with him against the teacher, if the disciplinary methods used are childish. The exact procedures vary, of course, according to the circumstances in which they are needed, but the best types of discipline I have seen have in common three characteristics—dignity, politeness, and a complete absence of emotion on the teacher's part.

Any college teacher can reduce the amount of emotional tension in his rooms and can thus provide a much better atmosphere for learning if he will avoid discrimination, sarcasm, and childish forms of discipline. Incidentally, his work will be far easier for him. While controlled emotion has its place in the schoolroom, because it is an integral element in both appreciation and imagination, uncontrolled or misdirected emotion interferes with the progress of the class, with the normal development of the student, and with the comfort of the instructor.

CHAPTER VII

THE LATER YEARS OF ADOLESCENCE
Moral and Social Attitudes

The present chapter is a continuation of Chapter VI. It will deal with the typical attitudes of undergraduates upon social and moral matters, with their religious beliefs, and with honor among students.

It is quite possible to measure, with a fair degree of accuracy, the attitudes of a group of people to any situation or problem. The type of scale one uses consists essentially of a series of statements which have been graded so as to express many shades of attitude from one extreme to another. A student who takes such a test simply marks the statement or statements that best reflect his opinion. When these tests first appeared there were naturally some doubts as to their validity.[1] To demonstrate this point, one sample study may be quoted.[1] The scale in question was designed to measure the amount of interest a student had in engineering. Groups of prospective engineers and prospective ministers took the test. All but 13 per cent of the engineering students showed more interest than the most interested student from the college of divinity, while all but 10 per cent of the latter scored below the least interested student in engineering. Approximately 88 per cent of the scores in each group were completely exclusive of any scores in the other. Since one may suppose that students pre-

[1] H. H. Remmers, "Further Studies of Attitude, Series II," *Purdue Studies in Higher Education,* XXXI, Vol. 37, No. 4, 1936, 298 pp.

paring for the ministry would hardly have much interest in
the problems of engineering and that the boys in the engineering school were there for the most part because they wanted
to be, the results of the test certainly favor its validity. This
example is only one of the many that could be quoted to show
the accuracy with which scales for measuring attitudes reflect
what they are supposed to reflect.

Investigators have measured various opinions in an effort
to find out what are the typical attitudes, during the later
years of adolescence, to nonacademic problems. These studies
include reports of attitudes toward such social problems as
communism, prohibition, drinking, birth control, sexual morality, war, or racial tolerance; to such beliefs as faith in God
or in the Ten Commandments; to such moral problems as honesty in general, cribbing on examinations, debts, or crime; to
such economic problems as property rights, government ownership, relation of capital and labor, party government, regulation of wages, child labor, relief, or the distribution of wealth;
and to such peculiarly collegiate problems as the value of
fraternities or the comparative merits of the scholar and the
athlete. Although these results are of a somewhat piecemeal
nature, they give, when taken together, some picture of the
ideas in the average college student's mind.

I. TYPICAL ATTITUDES ON SOCIAL AND ECONOMIC PROBLEMS

It is naturally impossible in this summary to present results
from more than a sampling of attitudes on social matters.
I have therefore selected a few that seem especially interesting
and timely. In one recent study [2] the opinions on several matters of over 13,000 young people between the ages of sixteen
and twenty-four were obtained by means of personal interviews. Among other things these adolescents—some of whom
were in college and some of whom were not—expressed their
views about government regulation of wages, child labor, and
relief. The questions used and the different answers obtained
are as follows:

[2] H. M. Bell, *Youth Tell Their Story*, American Council on Education,
1938, 261 pp.

1. Should the government regulate wages?
   Yes, in all types of business.............. 52%
   Yes, in some types of business............ 24%
   No regulation at all..................... 16%
   No opinion............................. 8%
2. Is relief a problem of government?
   Yes 89.5%
   No 8.0%
   No opinion 2.5%
3. Should the government permit child labor?
   Not at all 46.9%
   Under some circumstances............... 47.3%
   Yes 3.5%
   No opinion 2.3%

One especially interesting thing about these opinions is that the youth questioned in this study were so strongly in favor of government participation in the social and economic life of the country. If these attitudes are typical of young people as a whole one must conclude that the days of laissez faire are definitely gone.

The opinions of these adolescents about war and their idea of their probable behavior in the event of war are of considerable significance. Figure 19 tells the story better than words could do. Less than a third stated that they would volunteer for military service. Of the entire group, 9 per cent thought they would refuse to fight and another 4 per cent would take only noncombatant service. The resistance to war increased both with age and, especially, with the amount of education. The attitudes of those who had had a sixth-grade education or less are contrasted in Figure 20 with those who had had four or more years of college work. About half as many of the best-educated group would go to war if drafted, over twice as many would refuse to go, and about the same number would volunteer. The differences between the educated and uneducated were much greater than those between the younger and the older adolescents; there seems therefore no doubt that education had had an effect upon the thinking of youth. Per-

172 THE COLLEGE STUDENT

haps one really educated generation could do a great deal toward stopping the present spread of ruthless warfare.

One other attitude on the part of young people is of some importance. The 13,000 were questioned on their ideas about

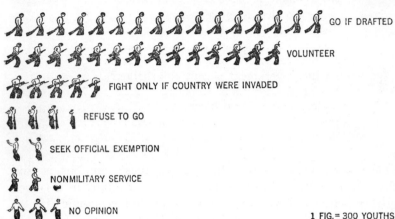

FIG. 19.—Attitudes of Youth toward War.

Bell, *op. cit.,* p. 242. Used by permission of the American Council on Education.

drinking. Of the entire number 52.9 per cent said they drank more or less, 27.8 per cent did not drink but were not opposed to it, and only 19.3 per cent had any real scruples in the matter. The proportions who drank, at least somewhat, increased with

FIG. 20.—Influence of Education upon Attitudes toward War.

Bell, *op. cit.,* p. 244. Used by permission of the American Council on Education.

age, as indicated in Figure 21. In fact, the per cent of men and women of twenty-four who drank is twice that of sixteen-year-old boys and girls. The experiment with prohibition does not appear to have been a success, so far as the children who grew up during it are concerned.

The results below are especially valuable because they were based upon actual interviews. This individual technique pre-

BOYS   GIRLS   DRINK

DO NOT DRINK BUT HAVE NO OBJECTION

OPPOSED

Fig. 21.—Attitudes of Youth toward Drinking.

Bell, *op. cit.,* p. 236. Used by permission of the American Council on Education.

vented, however, the collection of attitudes on a large variety of problems. A few sample results from two other studies in which college students expressed their opinions merely by marking statements are shown on page 174,[3] since they give evidence upon other points. The figures show the per cent of students who either believed or were inclined to believe each statement.

In general, the attitudes expressed in all these investigations are distinctly liberal but not extreme, except perhaps in the matter of the government's responsibility for solving the relief problem. The opinions are about what one would expect to find in the general population. They suggest, therefore, that

[3] G. H. Dudycha, "Social Beliefs of College Freshmen," *School and Society,* 32: 846–49, 1930, and "The Moral and Popular Beliefs of College Freshmen," *ibid.,* pp. 69–72. Used by permission of *School and Society* and the author.

young people are nearer to maturity in their thinking than their elders sometimes give them credit for being.

Per Cent Believing
Each Statement

1. Home is a necessary institution.................... 99
2. Marriage is necessary to society.................... 95
3. Church is necessary to society...................... 93
4. Democratic government is better than monarchy.... 79
5. The United States has the best form of government.. 74
6. The white race is superior to others............... 57
7. All men are free and equal........................ 54
8. Capital punishment is right........................ 46
9. The constitution of the U. S. is a perfect document.. 35
10. Freedom is an absence of restraint................. 33
11. Unjust laws should be obeyed..................... 32
12. There should be class distinctions................. 29
13. Radicalism is a sign of progress................... 26
14. The government is not fair to the working man..... 18
15. Companionate marriage is all right................ 16
16. There should be an equal distribution of wealth..... 11

II. TYPICAL ATTITUDES ON RELIGIOUS PROBLEMS

Two studies of religious attitudes seem worth presenting. One reports the reactions of a small group of students to a series of propositions on religious doctrines.[4] The list of twenty-five items was first submitted, with some of the statements in positive and some in negative form. A few days later the same students marked a second list, in which the same propositions appeared but in a different order and in the opposite form. The correlation between the lists was .93, indicating clearly that the opinions were really reflections of attitude and not mere guesswork. After each proposition the students indicated if they really believed it, were inclined to credit it, did not know whether they believed it or not, were inclined to discredit it, or really did not believe it at all. The results appear in Table 10. Half or more of the students believed implicitly in all but the last seven statements, and half or more were at least inclined to accept all but three of the statements. Some proportion between 25 and 50 per cent were inclined to dis-

[4] G. J. Dudycha, "The Religious Beliefs of College Students," *Journal of Applied Psychology*, 17: 585–603, 1933.

card—or had actually discarded—their belief in the existence of hell, present-day miracles, angels, the devil, and the creation of the world in six solar days. If these results are typical of college students, one need not complain too bitterly about the godlessness of the younger generation.[5]

TABLE 10

Per Cent of Students Having Varying Degrees of Belief or Disbelief in a Number of Propositions [5a]

	A	B	C	D	E
✓ 1. Authority of the Ten Commandments..	93	5	2	—	—
✓ 2. Existence of God...................	87	9	3	1	—
3. Divinity of Jesus Christ..............	79	14	6	1	—
4. Existence of the soul................	80	12	6	2	—
5. Christ died to save sinners...........	81	9	6	1	3
6. Sunday is a holy day................	77	14	4	2	3
✓ 7. Forgiveness of sins..................	74	12	10	2	2
8. Power of prayer.....................	70	17	8	3	2
✓ 9. Genuineness of Christ's miracles......	67	17	10	4	2
✓ 10. Reality of sin........................	65	19	11	2	3
11. Virgin Birth	63	19	11	3	4
12. The Bible is the word of God.........	63	18	6	8	5
✓ 13. Existence of heaven..................	65	12	13	3	7
✓ 14. Existence of the Holy Spirit..........	57	18	19	4	2
15. Sacrament of Baptism...............	61	12	19	2	6
16. Fatherhood of God..................	52	25	15	5	3
17. Man saved by faith, not works........	53	19	13	5	10
18. Resurrection of the body.............	54	10	20	9	7
19. Day of final judgment...............	47	18	23	3	9
✓ 20. Immortality	44	19	24	6	7
✓ 21. Existence of hell...................	45	13	14	8	20
22. Present-day miracles.................	28	19	22	11	20
✓ 23. World created in six solar days.......	27	24	15	14	20
24. Existence of angels.................	30	19	19	8	24
✓ 25. Existence of the devil...............	29	18	16	8	29

A = implicit belief
B = inclined to believe
C = neither belief nor disbelief
D = inclined to disbelieve
E = complete disbelief

[5] See also R. Bain, "The Religious Attitudes of College Students," *American Journal of Sociology*, 32 : 762–70, 1927 ; C. M. Bond, "College Student Attitudes toward Some Basic Christian Values," *Religious Education*, 35 : 109–16, 1940 ; A. R. Gilliland, "The Attitude of College Students toward God and the Church," *Journal of Social Psychology*, 11 : 11–18, 1940.
[5a] Dudycha, "The Religious Beliefs of College Students," *op. cit.* Used by permission of the *Journal of Applied Psychology* and the author.

In the second investigation,[6] undergraduates in college were asked to express their beliefs by checking one of several statements concerning the nature of God. In general, 63 per cent regarded God as a person; 22 per cent regarded Him as an impersonal force; 13 per cent were agnostic, while 2 per cent believed there was no God and the world was a machine. The relationship of these four points of view to earlier religious

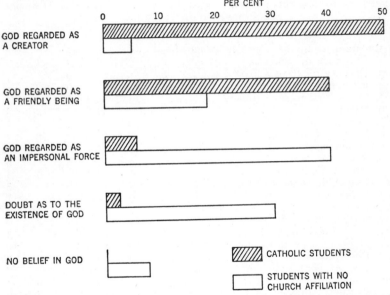

FIG. 22.—Per Cent of Catholic Students and Students with No Church Affiliation Who Expressed Various Attitudes Concerning the Nature of God.

Katz and Allport, *op. cit.,* p. 263. Used by permission of the authors.

training is made quite clear in the chart below. Of the Catholic students, 51 per cent regarded God as a Divine Creator, and another 40 per cent as a friendly and intelligent Being. Only 6 per cent thought of God as an impersonal force, only 3 per cent had any doubts, and no one accepted a naturalistic view of the universe. Of those who had no religious affiliations,

6 D. Katz and F. H. Allport, *Student Attitudes,* Craftsman Press, 1931, 408 pp.

only 22 per cent thought of God as a person, 40 per cent regarded Him as an impersonal force, while 30 per cent were agnostic—leaving 8 per cent who thought the world a machine. The Protestant and Jewish students expressed opinions about halfway between these two extremes, with the largest number believing God to be a friendly and intelligent Being.

From these studies one can hardly conclude that religion is as dead as many writers would have one think. The adolescents that go to college still have faith. Whether or not this is a good thing depends upon one's point of view. Nor does the training in college destroy this faith. The change in attitude from the freshman to the senior year consists mainly in a shift from belief in a personal to a belief in an impersonal God;[7] only a few seniors have doubts about the existence of some kind of righteous force in the world.

Attitudes toward moral problems also leave little to be desired. From 75 to 98 per cent of the students[8] consider it wrong to have debts, to be sexually immoral, to use alcohol to excess, or to be dishonest or unjust. Naturally, one does not suppose that a boy who disapproves of having debts never has any, or that the girl who condemns "blind dates" never goes on one. However, all that a teacher can hope for is to inculcate acceptable moral attitudes. He cannot stand over his fellow man and make him behave morally; he can only help him to see what is right. The expressed attitudes of college students are quite satisfactory.

Indeed, students are too credulous rather than too skeptical. For instance, about 35 per cent of them still believed that they could determine a person's intelligence from his face or that the shape of a person's head was related to his character.[9] Just half of them had no doubts about the reality of telepathy. A recent book lists fifteen hundred unfounded beliefs that are accepted by at least some students as well as numerous adults.[10] Many students will not light three cigarettes on a match or step on the cracks of a

[7] Katz and Allport, *op. cit.*
[8] G. J. Dudycha, "The Moral and Popular Beliefs of College Freshmen," *op. cit.*
[9] *Ibid.*
[10] C. J. S. Thompson, *The Hand of Destiny,* Rider and Company, 1933, 303 pp.

pavement, while many others take fetishes to examinations with them or pick up pins for good luck. It must be admitted that courses in college science do not seem to uproot such ideas nearly as thoroughly as one could wish.[11] On the whole, the average college boy or girl is rather too full of simple beliefs. Like most people they can live in a scientific world and can store up facts about science without ever losing either their faith in God or their dread of black cats. In addition to this very human ability to believe two mutually contradictory theses at the same time, their ideas reveal their essential youthfulness and their inexperience with the world and its ways. Life has not yet disillusioned most of them.

III. TYPICAL ATTITUDES ON PROBLEMS CONCERNING THE SOCIAL LIFE OF THE CAMPUS

Attitudes toward current problems upon the college campus are of interest to teachers because these opinions influence student behavior directly and college work indirectly. The effect of fraternities and that of college athletics upon social development have both been investigated. The data to be presented below are taken from a study of attitudes shown by fraternity and sorority members. These attitudes not only reflect an intensification of normal adolescent prejudice and antagonism, but also show the effect of fraternity life in molding adolescent opinion.

In the course of the investigation,[12] this question was given to over three thousand fraternity members: "Provided members of the groups listed below were otherwise good fraternity material, would you admit the following types of students to your own fraternity?" There then followed a list which included the names of various religious, national, racial, and

[11] See, for instance, O. W. Caldwell and G. E. Lundeen, "An Experimental Study of Superstitions and Other Unfounded Beliefs," *Journal of Educational Research,* 22: 257–73, 1932; F. D. Curtis, "Some Values Derived from Extensive Reading in General Science," *Teachers College Contributions to Education,* No. 163, 1924, 143 pp.; A. R. Gilliland, "A Study of the Superstitions of College Students," *Journal of Abnormal and Social Psychology,* 24: 472–79, 1930; P. O. Johnson, "An Application of Biological Knowledge," in *The Effective College Curriculum,* pp. 373–75; J. H. Sinclair and R. S. Tolman, "An Attempt to Study the Effect of Scientific Training upon Prejudice and Illogicality of Thought," *Journal of Educational Psychology,* 24: 362–70, 1933.

[12] Katz and Allport, *op. cit.* Used by permission of the authors.

social groups. Those who would be excluded from fraternity life include Jews, queer-looking students, atheists, Italians, American Indians, agnostics, Slavs, Armenians, Greeks, students with unconventional morals, Orientals, Turks, Hindus, Bolshevists, anarchists, students of low intelligence, loafers, Negroes. In this list are reflected many racial and national prejudices; there is also the usual adolescent antagonism toward anyone who is "queer"—in appearance, religious beliefs, or moral attitudes.

Another item presented to members of fraternities or sororities was the following:

Check the one of the two following statements which more nearly expresses your general feeling in regard to your fraternity or your sorority: (a) "My fraternity is a group standing for high ideals. The active personnel changes from year to year but the fraternity goes on, always upholding the same standards. A disgrace to my fraternity hurts me and reflcts on all its members. A high standard of conduct should be required of its members so that the fair name of the fraternity should be upheld." (b) "My fraternity is a group of individuals. The fraternity and its standing really exist only in the personnel active at the time. A high standard of conduct should be required of the members because, since they are associated in the fraternity, a disgrace to one might affect the reputation of each of the others."

Approximately 70 per cent of the undergraduate fraternity members checked the first statement; even in the graduate school it was checked by half the students with fraternity connections. The idealizing of a group of individuals is a typically adolescent attitude that is crystallized and perpetuated far beyond its normal limits by the fraternity or sorority. In fact, the attitude expressed is often permanent. I was recently chairman of a committee composed of two forty-year-old women and myself. The other two members had belonged to rival sororities during their student days. At the end of several meetings I had to request a new committee because the two women refused absolutely to agree on any point and alternately visited me secretly for no apparent reason except to arouse prejudice against the other. Each of the two sororities involved had so inculcated loyalty to itself and antagonism to other groups that twenty years later the rivalry was interfering with matters having no relationship whatever to college life.

A further reflection of fraternity influence was shown by answers to a question about the probable effects on the university of continued losses to outstanding rivals by the local athletic teams. Approximately 20 per cent of the fraternity members believed such losses would not affect the merit of the university at all and the reputation only slightly, if any. Another 30 per cent believed the reputation would be considerably lowered but the merit unaffected, while 40 per cent believed the reputation of the university would be utterly lost and the merit considerably reduced. The most extreme 10 per cent believed both reputation and merit would be "completely destroyed." These attitudes are not due to mere youthfulness, because students of the same age but not belonging to fraternities showed a far more balanced attitude. Only one-fourth of them believed the reputation would be seriously affected by athletic losses, while the majority discounted any effect at all of such losses upon merit and more than a moderate effect upon reputation.

The student body in general is not so silly about athletics as one might imagine from their behavior during the football season. In one instance an investigator used a series of statements comparing the value to the college community of the athlete and the scholar. The results are on the whole reassuring. A few excerpts from the scale used are shown below: [13]

	Per Cent Disbelieving	Per Cent Neutral	Per Cent Believing
The athlete is a better sport than the scholar	54	17	29
The athlete is more deserving of a trophy	71	12	17
The athlete is more likely to succeed in life	76	16	8
The athlete has a more desirable personality	54	17	29
The athlete is a better representative of college ideals	71	17	12
The athlete is a better representative of manliness	65	16	19
A college owes the athlete greater recognition than it owes the scholar	81	11	8

[13] G. J. Dudycha, "Student Beliefs concerning the Athlete and the Scholar," *School and Society*, 36: 123–28, 1932. Used by permission of *School and Society* and the author.

These opinions seem as sane as could be expected from those who are still in the later years of adolescence. If students actually succumb no more completely than is here indicated to the hysteria in which they sometimes indulge, one need not be too concerned. They are at an age when excitement is still merely exciting and not exhausting. As long as it remains superficial, it is not likely to have the effect upon scholarship that is often feared.

One minor study bears out this conclusion.[14] At the college in which the investigation was made, the students have the custom—during the football season—of gathering for an hour every evening for a "pep session." They sing and cheer until they are hoarse, and they appear to be worked up into a frenzy of excitement. The investigator examined a group of them with tests in the fundamental operations of arithmetic—as generally monotonous a task as students are often asked to perform. They were tested repeatedly—in the morning, when they were relatively free from excitement, again within ten minutes after the singing, and once more about an hour later. They averaged one more error on the second test than the first, but were just as good on the third as they had been during the morning. About three-fourths of them lost speed on the second test, but only 15 per cent of them continued to be slower on the third test than they had been on the first. In short, most of the students recovered within an hour from any excitement they may have felt, and a fourth of them showed no sign of disturbance at any time. Either their emotion was too superficial to affect their work, or else the recuperative power of youth is quite sufficient to offset any fatigue.

IV. PROBLEMS OF RACIAL PREJUDICE

Theoretically a college education should make one more tolerant toward people who belong to other races or social groups. From available evidence this does not seem to be the case, unless students have taken work in which tolerance is specifically taught—as in the course on "Racial Problems"—and even here there is less effect than one could desire. With-

[14] R. C. White, "The Effect of Emotional Disturbance on Ability to Concentrate," *School and Society*, 22: 343–44, 1925.

out such training the attitudes toward other races continue
without modification from the junior high school level through
the graduate school.[15] In particular is this true of attitudes
toward the Negro; these remain essentially untouched by ordinary college classwork.[16] Sociology students are a little more
friendly toward members of other races than is the average,
and sociology majors who have religious convictions are a
great deal more friendly. This situation suggests that the real
source of the modification is religion rather than education.
The races and nationalities toward which there is the greatest
antipathy are those that are least like American people: Chi-
nese, Negro, Japanese, Mexican, Greek, Turk, Hindu, and
Jew.[17] The national groups receiving favorable ratings are
those with the least difference from Americans: the English,
Germans, French, Swedes, Spaniards, Russians, and Italians.
No college education is necessary for the development of such
attitudes. It would seem as if colleges should make sure that,
at some point in each student's training, he should receive
instruction that would favor the development of a greater
degree of tolerance than is revealed by any of the studies
to date.

V. MODIFICATION OF ATTITUDES BY DIRECT INSTRUCTION

The part generally played by the college in the development
of attitudes seems much too small. When one compares the
opinions of seniors with those of freshmen, there is only a
slight difference.[18] However, what change has occurred is

[15] A. L. Porterfield, "Education and Race Attitudes," *Sociology and
Social Research*, 21 : 538–43, 1937.
[16] V. A. Jones, "Attitudes of College Students and the Changes in Such
Attitudes during Four Years in College," *Journal of Educational Psychology*,
29 : 14–25, 1938.
[17] J. P. Guilford, "Racial Preferences of a Thousand American University
Students," *Journal of Social Psychology*, 2 :179–204, 1931.
[18] W. J. Boldt and J. B. Stroud, "Changes in the Attitudes of College
Students," *Journal of Educational Psychology*, 25 : 611–19, 1934; K. C.
Garrison and M. Means, "A Study of the Opinions of College Students,"
Journal of Social Psychology, 2 : 168–78, 1931; E. S. Jones, "The Opinions
of College Students," *Journal of Applied Psychology*, 10 : 427–36, 1926;
V. Jones, "Attitudes of College Students and the Changes in Such Attitudes
during Four Years of College," *Journal of Educational Psychology*, 29 : 14–
25, 1938; E. Salner, H. H. Remmers, and C. L. Morgan, "The Influence of

always in the direction of greater liberalism. Seniors are slightly less inclined to accept orthodox religious beliefs, slightly more tolerant in their moral judgments, and slightly more appreciative of academic values. They are relatively liberal, however, primarily because they were already so as freshmen.

Although college work in general does not modify attitudes on social problems to any great extent, those students who take courses from which they should derive some change of opinion upon sociological matters do actually show a modification of attitude in a few weeks.[19] Moreover, the majors in social science test significantly more liberal in their attitudes on such matters as property rights, politics, or the relation of capital and labor than the majors in the physical sciences or in languages. The degree of liberalism increases also among students in the same college class in proportion to the number of credit hours they have completed in the social sciences. These differences are at least four times their probable error and are therefore significant.[20]

Students do not modify their attitudes as much as they might, chiefly because they do not receive, in enough classes, the direct type of instruction that would produce this result. Attitudes are relatively easy to alter. If they were not, the amount of propaganda in the world would hardly pay for itself. The ease with which opinions may be changed has been demonstrated experimentally. Two sample studies are given below.

In one case [21] the investigators first measured the attitude of sixty students towards capital punishment. Three weeks later they read them some excerpts from a text in criminology

Certain Factors upon the Liberalism and Conservatism of College Students," *Journal of Applied Psychology,* 17 : 349–54, 1933.

[19] See, for instance, J. R. Gerberlich and C. Jones, "Measurements of Attitude Changes during an Introductory Course in College Sociology," *Journal of Educational Sociology,* 8: 116–24, 1934; and A. W. Kornhauser, "Changes in the Information and Attitude of Students in an Economics Course," *Journal of Educational Research,* 20: 288–98, 1930.

[20] Jones, *op. cit.*

[21] R. M. Bateman and H. H. Remmers, "The Relation of Pupil Attitudes toward Social Topics Before and After Studying the Subject," *Purdue University Studies in Higher Education,* XXXI, Vol. 37, No. 4, 1936, pp. 27–51.

and again measured the attitudes. The change in point of view was in the same direction as the material presented and was a significant change since it was several times its probable error. Before listening to the excerpts only ten out of the sixty students made scores above the median of their own subsequent scores, and after the reading only eight made scores below the first median. On this scale a score of 13 or more

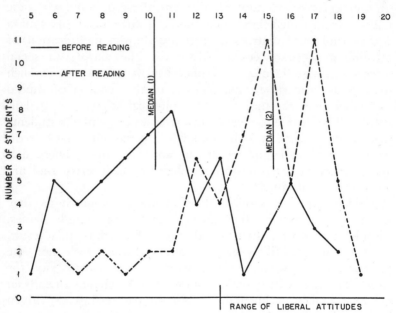

FIG. 23.—Change in Attitude toward Capital Punishment as the Result of a Single Reading.

Bateman and Remmers, *op. cit.* Used by permission of Purdue University.

represents a liberal view. In the beginning only twenty students expressed such attitudes. After a single "dose" of liberalism forty-four students made scores at or above 13.

The second investigator [22] studied the effect of a single dose of propaganda upon attitudes. The subject chosen for investigation was the Japanese occupation of Manchuria. One group

[22] Ke-Ching Chen, "The Influence of Oral Propaganda Material upon Students' Attitudes," *Archives of Psychology*, No. 150, 43 pp. 1933.

of 136 students read a pro-Japanese article; a second group of 145 students listened to a pro-Chinese one; three classes, totaling 243 students, heard nothing on the subject but took the tests at the beginning and end of the experiment. These control classes showed a change of only — .43 from their initial score. The "pro-Japanese" group increased their ratings in favor of the Japanese + 6.78, while the "pro-Chinese" group decreased their ratings of the Japanese — 6.82. The variation in the attitudes of those who had heard nothing is well within the probable error of the measurement; that is, they did not change their opinions. The other two groups showed variations that are more than five times the probable error; the differences are thus true differences and occurred in the expected direction.

If single readings of a short article can produce real changes in attitude it would seem as if four years of college should certainly do so. As in other situations, however, it is direct teaching that gives the clearest results. One cannot rely upon transfer of training or upon the gradual absorption of ideas from a number of sources. If college teachers are to have a hand in the production of sounder attitudes and more tolerant opinions they should follow the lessons implicit in these experiments and teach directly what they want students to believe. This procedure may seem to many professors too much like propaganda for comfort. However, I still have confidence that a college professor's brand of propaganda is greatly superior to the types students will assuredly meet outside the classroom.

This entire chapter thus far has included a sample of attitudes toward many different problems. Except for the lamentably small contribution of classroom work to the formation of opinions, I cannot see that one needs to view the results with any alarm. The students reveal some signs of immaturity, but they also show considerable balance and judgment. The younger generation appears to be quite as sane as previous generations were at the same stage of development. If they translate even a part of their opinions into action they should grow up to be acceptable citizens.

VI. PROBLEMS OF HONOR

1. Development of the honor system: Sufficient time has
now elapsed to provide the honor system with a history. In so
far as its spirit is concerned, it has doubtless always been in
existence in some places and among some teachers. As a system,
however, it made its appearance between 1905 and 1910. Since
that time two investigators [23] have inquired into the extent of
its adoption. By comparing the figures in 1915 with those in
1933 one can note any changes that have taken place in the
official attitude toward this method of securing honesty. A
total of two hundred colleges and universities, both public and
private, from all parts of the country, participated in the first
survey; only eighty-one took part in the second, but the sampling was well distributed as to size and type of institution.
The facts appear below:

	1915: Per Cent of 200 Colleges and Universities Reporting Each Situation	*1933: Per Cent of 81 Colleges and Universities Reporting Each Situation*
Honor system used at all times.....	50	20
Honor system used by some departments	11	13
Honor system now being adopted...	17	0
Honor system used in previous years but now abandoned..............	0	25
Honor system not used............	22	42

Of the twenty colleges that in 1933 reported continued use
of the honor system, only two were satisfied with its effect.
Both of these were Eastern women's colleges with high entrance requirements and a rigid selection of students. In these
two places there is a social solidarity and force of tradition
that do not exist where the student population is more heterogeneous. Under such circumstances the system really works—
and it was for such groups that it was originally intended.
From the figures above only one conclusion is possible: that

[23] B. T. Baldwin, "Present Status of the Honor System in Colleges and
Universities," *Office of Education Bulletin,* No. 8, 1915, and J. T. Wahl-
quist, "The Honor System in American Colleges and Universities," *School
and Society,* 37: 757–60, 1933.

the honor system, as first conceived, is not satisfactory in most places. It is not now being adopted anywhere, it has already been abandoned in more places than are using it at present, and it is not well regarded where it is in use. It may be that sooner or later a different system will be devised, but in its original form the honor system is dying rapidly. Officials and faculty members alike feel that it does not produce honesty.[24] If it does not, the only honest thing for any institution to do is to abandon it and try something else.

It is hard for people to realize how much actual training in dishonesty is given by an honor system that does not work. I once took a course in a state university in which examinations were not proctored. The professor passed out the papers at the first quiz, put the students on their honor, and then left the room. To my surprise the students on either side of me immediately got out their notebooks and began looking up answers. I had left such material at home—a procedure that seemed positively to shock those around me. When the period was half over, I surveyed the room and counted the number of dishonest students. Of the twenty-six people, fourteen were copying answers directly from their notebooks. Three were sitting together and discussing each question before they worked on it. Two roommates had divided the quiz into halves, and each was writing one part and then copying the other from her friend. Six others had their texts open and were referring to them as necessary. In fact, I was the only one who was idiot enough to come unprepared! By dint of application I managed to get a C+. One student failed —a fact I have never understood—and one other got a B—. The remaining twenty-three received A, A—, or B+, depending, I assume, upon how fast and how accurately they could copy. The professor knew perfectly well what was going on but was powerless to stop it. When I told him I had not cheated, he just laughed and said I soon would, because no student could hope to survive such competition without dishonesty. The class in question was

[24] See, for instance, J. R. Geiger, "The Educational Value of the Honor System," *School and Society,* 21 : 516–22, 1925; J. L. Merriam, "Examinations and the Honor System," *Bulletin of the American Association of University Professors,* 17 : 338–41, 1931; University of California, "The Honor System," *Bulletin of the American Association of University Professors,* 16 : 258, 1930; E. H. Wilkins, "Oberlin College and the Honor System," *School and Society,* 32 : 763–64, 1930.

typical of university groups. Aside from the two roommates no
one knew anybody else. Their social backgrounds varied from the
daughter of a day laborer to the son of a college president. Their
ages were anywhere between seventeen and forty-five. The group
had no social cohesion and no common standards of any kind.
Without supervision it simply fell to pieces, and each member
degenerated to the level of the lowest, thus at least producing a
situation from which everyone started the examination at scratch.
I emerged from the course with a clear conscience, a confirmed distrust of honor systems, a good mastery of the subject—necessi-
tated by the intense competition in order to so much as pass—and
a poor grade.

   2. Studies of student honesty: Those interested in this question have used one or more of three different methods of
investigation. Some have given their students opportunities
to score papers that had already been scored but not marked.
Others have used graduate students as "spies" to note who
did and who did not cheat. In most cases these graduates were
supposedly taking an examination of their own and were seated
in the room with the other students for the ostensible reason
that their own room was unexpectedly in use. They were
equipped with examination papers, blue books, and so on, and
they wrote busily—but they merely took notes on the students
near them. Still other investigators have passed back series
of examination papers that had been wrongly scored. Each
student received an equal number of papers with scores that
were correct, too high, or too low. They showed whether or
not they were honest by reporting or not reporting these errors.
Regardless of the method used, the results are about the same,
although naturally some facts are better determined by one
method than by another.

   First, as to the general level of honesty. In six different
studies,[25] made in as many different places, the per cents of

   [25] Anon., "Honesty in College Examinations under the Honor System,"
School and Society, 31 : 577–80, 1930; W. G. Campbell, "Student Honesty
as Revealed by Reporting of Teachers' Errors in Grading," *School and
Society,* 33 : 97–100, 1931; W. G. Campbell and H. L. Koch, "Student Honesty in a University with an Honor System," *School and Society,* 31 : 232–
40, 1930; N. Fenton, "Objective Study of Student Honesty during Examinations," *School and Society,* 26 : 341–44, 1924; G. F. Miller, "An Experi-

dishonesty were respectively 42, 65, 46, 70, 36, and 36. The average of all these figures is 49 per cent. The amount varied, naturally, according to the circumstances of the tests, but in no case were as many as two-thirds of the students honest.

The extent of cheating correlates with a number of other factors. It is related negatively to intelligence. Of students who were below the average intellectually, approximately 50 per cent cheated, while of those above average about 25 per cent were dishonest.[26] In one study the students had three chances to cheat. Those who did so all three times had an average intelligence percentile 20 points below those who did not cheat at all and 10 points below those who cheated once.[27] The difficulty of an examination also has its effect upon the amount of dishonesty. The harder the test, the more cheating occurs.[28] The presence of the instructor very clearly conditions the amount of cheating. Results from two studies [29] agree in general import as to the effect of the teacher's presence. When the teacher was in the room, 16 per cent of one group cheated and 33 per cent of the other. When the teacher was in and out of the room at irregular intervals, 30 per cent of one group were dishonest and 40 per cent of the second. When the instructor left the room for a period of known length, after putting the students on their honor, the amount of cheating rose to 42 and 45 per cent respectively in the two classes. The implications of these facts are too obvious to miss.

The amount of dishonesty is related directly to the standing of students in their classwork. In one of the best studies [30] no A student cheated, 33 per cent of the B students did so, 80 per cent of the C students, 75 per cent of the D students, and 100 per cent of the E students. Another investigator [31] gave students several chances to keep points that they had

mental Test of Intellectual Honesty," *School and Society,* 26 : 852–54, 1927; F. W. Parr, "The Problem of Student Honesty," *Journal of Higher Education,* 7 : 318–26, 1936.

[26] Parr, *op. cit.*
[27] Fenton, *op. cit.*
[28] T. H. Howells, "Factors Influencing Honesty," *Journal of Social Psychology,* 9 : 97–102, 1938.
[29] Campbell and Koch, *op. cit.*
[30] Fenton, *op. cit.*
[31] Campbell, *op. cit.*

earned through a misscoring of test papers. The number of points dishonesty retained varied from none by the A to 15 by the E students. This relationship is to be expected, although it does not settle the question of whether the good student is honest because he wants to be or because he does not need to run the risks of cheating.

The minor form of dishonesty known as "bluffing" showed a clear correlation with the amount of education. In the particular experiment reported [32] the investigator used a set of twenty objective questions, for none of which was the correct answer given. The students were thus asked to select which play an author wrote out of several that he did not write, which meaning a completely artificial term had, and so on. The amount of bluffing increased steadily from the third grade through college. All the college seniors bluffed at least half of the question; their median number of bluffs out of twenty questions was eighteen. This form of dishonesty may not be especially serious, but it is certainly prevalent. Moreover it appears to be a form of behavior learned in school— probably because so many teachers make a pupil feel uncomfortable if he admits he does not know the answer to a question.

Student opinions about honor and honor systems are relevant and of interest. For instance, out of those students who cheated on one examination 20 per cent flatly denied it, even when confronted with the evidence.[33] Of the entire 190 students—regardless of whether or not they cheated on the particular test during which they were watched—approximately 33 per cent admitted cheating on some examination. Not more than 10 per cent of students say they would be willing to report even the most flagrant case of dishonesty.[34] So long as students will not take responsibility for their own and each other's behavior, it is hard to see how any honor system can be made to work. Incidentally, in one of the studies mentioned above, 51 per cent of the students who came from high schools

[32] H. W. James, "Honesty as a Characteristic Trait of Young People," *Journal of Educational Research*, 26: 572–78, 1933.

[33] Campbell and Koch, *op. cit.*

[34] Similar attitudes are reported by T. M. Carter, "Cheating as Seen by College Students," *International Journal of Ethics*, 39: 341–45, 1929, and the University of California, "The Honor System," *Bulletin of the American Association of University Professors*, 16: 258, 1930.

having an honor system cheated, as compared with 31 per cent of those who came from high schools without such a system.

One careful and comprehensive investigation has been made of what 494 undergraduates and 46 faculty members regard as honorable or dishonorable.[35] The method used consisted of a paper-and-pencil test containing thirty-six parts. Each part was a paragraph long and described a typical situation involving honesty. Students and teachers gave their opinions as to whether or not they would condemn each case as wrong. The situations were so well selected as to cover most of the common temptations to cheat. The results appear below:

TABLE II

Per Cents of Students and Faculty Members Regarding Each
Situation as Wrong [35a]

Situations	Students (Per Cents)	Faculty (Per Cents)
1. Two students worked on a theme together and each handed it in as his own	77	96
2. A student was ill and had his theme written for him	94	100
3. A student wrote a review of a movie instead of reading the book on which the movie was based	52	80
4. A student copied from his neighbor because he lacked self-confidence	89	91
5. A student wrote a paper from his roommate's notes because too few books were available in the library	37	54
6. A student did not call attention to an error in the scoring of his test when it was in his favor	62	66
7. A student copied on a surprise quiz because he was unprepared	91	98
8. A student wrote a supposedly original story from another person's plot	60	69
9. A student cheated on a final examination for the sake of his fraternity	94	98
10. A student used suggestions seen accidentally on another person's quiz paper	65	54
11. A student borrowed specimens instead of collecting them himself	62	89
12. When his notebook was to be graded a student copied notes from a friend whose work he knew to be superior	67	87

[35] C. O. Matthews, "The Honor System," *Journal of Higher Education,* 3:411-15, 1932.

[35a] Matthews, *op. cit.* Used by permission of the *Journal of Higher Education.*

TABLE II *continued*

13. A student used a crib on an examination that included only memory questions .... 90 | 96
14. A student profited during an examination by the whispering of two other students to each other .... 20 | 35
15. A student cheated when he had a boasting, egotistical teacher .... 74 | 78
16. A student faked a chemistry experiment to meet a requirement .... 59 | 80
17. A student gave an illegitimate excuse for his cuts .... 50 | 84
18. A student was excited during an examination and copied to calm his nerves .... 81 | 96
19. A student cheated to come up to his parents' expectations .... 88 | 98
20. A student wrote a story for another student and was paid for it .... 40 | 87
21. A student bluffed in a course he thought unpractical .... 40 | 82
22. Two roommates divided the reading for a course and each copied the other's notes.... 51 | 82
23. A student cheated to become eligible for athletics .... 82 | 96
24. A student cheated when he had a sarcastic teacher who ridiculed him .... 64 | 85
25. A student altered the score on an examination before the figures had been recorded .... 57 | 83
26. A student cheated on an obviously unfair examination .... 87 | 89
27. A student cheated in order to keep his standing when others in the class cheated .... 88 | 98
28. A student used a verbal translation after being forbidden to do so .... 67 | 85
29. A student arranged to sit beside a well-prepared classmate so they could help each other 92 | 96
30. A student looked over a copy of an examination illegally secured for him by a fraternity brother .... 38 | 76
31. A student copied another's paper to maintain his eligibility as team manager .... 94 | 98
32. A student used questionable methods in a large class when the teacher did not know the individual students .... 82 | 93
33. A student was willing to do anything to get by in a course in which the teacher had announced that 10 per cent would fail........ 51 | 61
34. A student copied his partner's results in laboratory .... 77 | 86
35. A student cheated on a test but justified himself by saying that he came to college to get an education and not to pass a silly examination .... 74 | 93
36. A student used a crib on an examination because he thought it was no worse than cramming .... 76 | 94

The faculty members expressed 100 per cent condemnation for only one situation; between 95 and 99 per cent of them voted against ten other cases. Some proportion at or above 90 per cent thought fifteen of the thirty-six situations dishonorable. The students condemned, to an extent of 90 per cent or more, only five situations. The per cents that are 90 or above appear on the table in italics. One may not approve of the level of behavior here implied, but in the face of facts, one has to admit that efforts to teach honesty have not been especially successful.[36]

The investigations already quoted indicate the amount of dishonesty in large institutions. I do not want to leave the topic without saying a word about the amount in small colleges. Although I have no objective data on the point I have talked with and written to a number of experienced teachers who have taught for some period between twenty and forty years in one or more small colleges. The testimony is that cases of cheating are few, partly because there is a better chance to instill ideals and partly because the usual classroom situation does not encourage dishonesty. All the students know each other, and the teacher knows all the students. Even though someone could cheat without much prospect of being reported he would find himself more or less ostracized by his age-mates and the object of suspicion from his teacher because his work was too good! The estimates concerning the amount of cheating given me by various professors varied from two known cases in forty years to 1 per cent of the students. Either

[36] There is one study in which the differences between the honesty of students under an honor system appear greater than those under a proctoring system. (W. G. Campbell, "A Comparative Investigation of the Behavior of Students under an Honor System and a Proctor System in the Same University," *University of Southern California Education Monographs*, No. 6, University of Southern California Press, 1935, 74 pp.) Although the differences are statistically reliable, the study is not so valuable in proving the worth of the honor system as might at first appear. The students were compared on the basis of three measurements. In regular examinations 14 per cent of the students cheated under the honor system and 38 per cent under the proctor system; for admitting cheating, the figures were 32 per cent and 43 per cent; for keeping back points on tests that were scored too high, 66 and 77 per cent. The honor system admittedly produced less dishonesty than the proctor system, but who wants an "honor" system under which some proportion between 14 and 66 per cent still cheat? The investigator admits that cheating fell to practically zero when examinations were proctored with sufficient care.

teachers in small colleges are badly fooled, or else there really is far less cheating than in a big university.[37]

Some effort is now being made to determine what kind of person becomes a chronic cribber. The complete case histories needed to settle the matter are still lacking, but a few general results are available. The two studies [38] which have thus far appeared agree in finding the cheater more neurotic than the honest student, more inclined to brag, and less self-sufficient. These same characteristics are even more pronounced among those who cheat but will not admit it. The cribber is usually of lower than average intelligence; he almost always has a low academic standing. One study reports him as introverted and one as extraverted. Some day it may be possible to tell in advance who is likely to cheat. A teacher can then either educate such a student or can watch him to make sure he does not get good marks in return for dishonesty.

3. The conduct of examinations: In the average large college or university, there are relatively few situations in which it is safe to leave a class unproctored. A teacher is probably justified in so doing only if he is teaching a small, selected group of students who are fairly homogeneous as to ability and are well known to each other. In a small college this statement will naturally apply to more classes than in a large one, and in a few places it is true for all classes. When only a little supervision is needed, it is enough for a teacher to sit in the examination room, with his or her back to the class. A teacher's presence almost eliminates whispering; while the students could copy things from their notebooks or from each other, they usually do not. Even the back of a professor's head seems to exert a beneficent influence. In the heterogeneous class in the large institution, however, the teacher should really proctor the group during the period. There is no other way to protect those who are willing to be honest from the aggressions

---

[37] For an excellent summary of the situation in a small institution, see *Report of the Joint Committee on the Honor System*, Oberlin College, 1930, 44 pp.

[38] H. C. Brownell, "Mental Traits of the College Cribber," *School and Society*, 27:764, 1928; and W. G. Campbell, "Measurement in Determining the Personality and Behavior of the College Cribber," *Education*, 53:403–8, 1933.

THE LATER YEARS OF ADOLESCENCE

of those who are not. Cheating is a contagious kind of behavior. Out of a hundred students there may not be more than five who plan in advance to be dishonest, but as soon as one begins to act dishonorably the behavior spreads, until as many as half the class are cheating. The teacher needs to protect not only those who are honest but also the many immature students who so quickly imitate what others are doing.

The college of thirty years ago enrolled mostly students from good homes and good social backgrounds. These students had been trained in honesty by their home environment and by their teachers in the small secondary schools they had attended. They were a select group, not only in intelligence but in character. At the present time, boys and girls from all possible social backgrounds come to college. I have had in class the children of bootleggers, street cleaners, pipe fitters, coal miners, day laborers, and even children of criminals. These students have about the same degree of honesty as is found in the general population; that is, they are more likely than not to be honest in ordinary situations, but they succumb too easily to pressure. For many of them the provocation to cheat on a college examination is greater than one might think, because the curriculum is either too hard for them or quite irrelevant to their needs. A teacher should, of course, do all that is possible to develop each student's sense of responsibility, but—as in all other teaching—it is necessary to start at the student's present stage of development, not above it. Anyone who trusts a class of a hundred ordinary freshmen is beginning his training of character at a point much too high.

It does not pay to become sentimental about student honor. The teacher who says he "trusts his students implicitly" is undoubtedly imposing too great a load of responsibility upon some of them. During the examination period every student should have a fair chance to show what he can do. If an instructor leaves a room of undergraduates completely unsupervised, he is not giving his best students the chance to which they are entitled. *It is the teacher's business to insure honesty.* Blind faith is not enough; nor can one change the fundamental facts by refusing to look at them. There is nothing either kind or educative in permitting students to cheat.

There are a number of things a teacher can do to reduce the amount of dishonesty. Whenever students are to hand in work prepared outside of class, they have a chance to cheat if they wish. They can copy from a paper used in previous years, or they can get help from a friend, or they can have the paper written for them. A professor can avoid being handed the same reports year after year, in different handwriting, by changing his topics. If he does not do so, he will probably find the reports becoming more and more familiar as the years roll by. One can avoid co-operation among students in the actual writing of papers by asking them to bring to class a page of condensed notes and then to write the paper itself in class. To be sure, they may get help from others in their plan, but the composition, at least, is their own production. A term paper cannot be written in this way, because there is not enough time, but book reviews and other short reports can be. An instructor can reduce the amount of copying during an examination by having a special seating plan for all testing. He first spreads out his class, so that there are two or three empty seats between each two people, and puts the poorest students across the front rows where he can watch them easily. Under these circumstances whispering becomes impossible and copying extremely difficult. The students' habit of handing in other people's laboratory work as their own can be largely avoided by the use of individual assignment sheets. In this case, no two students have the same work to do, and the substitution of another person's notes is impossible. Of late years the "Open Book" examination has become popular in some colleges. The students are allowed to use their texts and notebooks as much as they wish during the examination. Naturally the questions given them are such as to require a reorganization of their materials. One result of this method is the great decrease in the amount of cheating.[39]

Some teachers simply encourage dishonesty by their marking system. For instance, if students know that an instructor will give the lowest 3 per cent in the class failing grades, no matter what the level of performance is, the situation becomes one of *sauve qui peut*. If, on the other hand, students know that he will give failing grades only to those who really deserve them and will give none at all if no one does, there is much less temptation to cheat. Marking in terms of a single class distribution, without respect to

[39] For a discussion of this type of test, see J. M. Stalnaker and R. C. Stalnaker, "Open Book Examinations," *Journal of Higher Education,* 5: 117–20, 1934, and 6: 214–16, 1935.

some standard of performance, automatically produces a situation in which a student can increase his standing only by displacing someone else. Like the Red Queen, he has to run as hard as he can in order to stay where he is and twice as hard in order to progress. Under such a system there is naturally a good deal of cheating.

Probably the best plan thus far devised for handling examinations in larger institutions is that used by the University of Chicago. There the teachers assign no grades, although they give tests of various kinds as aids to the students in finding out what they do or do not know. Any student who is fool enough to cheat himself is at liberty to do so. What he does in class, what kind of reports he turns in to his teachers, what he writes on his teachers' examinations are all for his own benefit and have no relation to his grades. His mark depends upon his performance on a rigidly supervised examination, given by a central committee. This solution is not ideal, and many small colleges have found a better one. The complete divorce between teaching and testing does, however, eliminate the type of situation in which most of the dishonesty occurs.

Although most large institutions with a heterogeneous student population have given up the struggle to secure honesty and have come to depend upon strict supervision of examinations as a means for insuring an equal chance to all, the small college has other methods of procedure. There are direct education and training in honesty from both upperclassmen and faculty. The student who is caught cheating is commonly brought before a student court. This group hears the evidence and renders a judgment which is in most cases carried out, although some older persons occasionally have to plead with the student justices for greater leniency! Even though the court may try only one or two offenders a year the realization of possible condemnation by one's equals and subsequent ostracism is enough to prevent cheating. The combined efforts of the faculty members who talk individually with students over minor difficulties, of the student court that considers major offenses, and of the constant pressure of friends and acquaintances, give the undergraduates in a small college little opportunity to be dishonest and even less desire. Such indirect and natural types of control are greatly to be preferred to the impersonal rigidity of the closely proctored examination. However, as soon as a college group grows too large for everyone to know everyone else, the natural social controls break down. Thus far, the big university has found no way to develop sufficient honesty to act as a basis for an honor system. It is in this field of character training that the small college has its greatest advantage.

VII. SUMMARY

College students tend to be liberal in their attitudes on social, economic, and moral questions, although the total range of their opinions is from ultraconservative to ultraradical. The four years in college do not seem to have much effect upon their attitudes, but what little change occurs is in the direction of greater liberalism. There is plenty of experimental evidence to show that attitudes are readily altered by direct teaching.

The facts about honor among students are somewhat discouraging. In large heterogeneous classes there seems no way to protect honest students except by supervision so strict that those who are willing to cheat have no opportunity to do so. In small classes an honor system can still be made to work. It is also possible that more adequate methods of training students in honesty would result in a higher level of performance.

CHAPTER VIII

MENTAL HYGIENE

Mental hygiene represents a fairly new field of human endeavor. It arose from the conviction that much mental disease and suffering could be prevented if one could only reach the prospective sufferer before his maladies had developed too far. By the time most lunatics arrive at an institution they are too deteriorated to make an adequate recovery. Their case histories show, however, that the basic symptoms first made their appearance years earlier, when the individual still had a normal mind. The original purpose was therefore to reach potentially abnormal people before their condition had become too serious for remedial measures. As investigators continued to study mental and emotional problems, however, it became clear that practically everyone had more or less pressing difficulties that were quite needlessly causing distress. As knowledge about human maladjustments increased, the purpose of the mental hygienist broadened. At the present time the worker in this field is more interested in helping normal people to live as normally as possible than he is in preventing insanity. The aims of mental hygiene are therefore twofold. In its more general aspect, instruction in mental hygiene is thought of as being parallel to that in physical hygiene. The main object of the latter subject is to keep well people well; the similar aim of mental hygiene is to keep sane people sane. The treatment of mental abnormality and the prevention of insanity have become somewhat secondary. Indeed the cure—if any—of insanity is outside the field of mental hygiene entirely—just as the cure of physical disease is the business of the doctor, not the hygienist.

The interest in this subject in colleges has developed within the past fifteen or twenty years. In 1920 there were only three institutions of higher learning in which there was even a part-time worker in mental hygiene.[1] In 1937, out of 497 colleges, 41 per cent had a consultant and 93 per cent had some member of the teaching staff who interviewed students.[2] In most instances the hygienist is an adjunct to the medical staff; in others, he or she is connected with either the Dean of Women's office or with the psychology department. The first arrangement is probably best, partly because many of the students who need attention are sick and partly because undergraduates too often associate discipline with the Dean and abnormality with the psychologist. For many of his contacts with students the mental hygienist is usually dependent upon the teaching staff. Instructors who avail themselves of his help in dealing with problem students in their classes find him of great service to them.

The need for mental hygiene has been amply demonstrated. The estimates of how many students per hundred require such treatment vary according to the type and size of the college, the personality of the estimator, the basis for his estimates—whether questionnaire results or interviews—and his conception of what constitutes a "problem." The figures vary from 6 to 86 per cent. The two studies [3] that report the proportion as being over 80 per cent both include as a problem any nonacademic matter about which students are concerned. In this sense these figures are probably too low rather than too high, since practically everyone is concerned or worried or anxious about something. The completely contented person with a perfect adjustment to life is a *rara avis* at any age and almost

[1] W. Richmond, "Mental Hygiene in the Colleges," *Journal of the American Medical Association*, 93: 1,936–39, 1929.
[2] T. Raphael, "Mental Hygiene Services for Colleges and Universities," *Mental Hygiene*, 21: 559–68, 1937.
[3] R. C. Angell, *A Study in Undergraduate Adjustment*, University of Chicago Press, 1930, 173 pp.; and S. L. Pressey, "The College and Adolescent Needs," in *Research Adventures in University Teaching*, Public School Publishing Company, 1927, pp. 81–85.

unknown during the adolescent years. Eight other investigators, who based their opinions upon test results, personnel records, questionnaires, interviews, or some combination of the above, give per cents for serious maladjustment in the general college population as 6, 10, 10, 10, 16, 16, 18, and 20.[4] The proportion of undergraduates who have some degree of maladjustment—enough to prevent them from functioning in an entirely normal manner—is given by six writers [5] at some per cent between 41 and 64; four of these estimates are between 48 and 50.

It would seem, then, upon the basis of such opinions, that the great proportion of college students have minor personal problems, that about half of them have somewhat more serious difficulties, and that about one-tenth show acute conditions. This situation certainly suggests the need for a mental hygienist upon every college campus.

Further evidence of the need for mental hygiene comes from another source that is completely independent of the college situation. This report [6] presents the experiences of one large business firm in dealing with college graduates. At one time the personnel officers of the concern interviewed 344 graduates of Eastern colleges, but could accept only two of this number in important posi-

[4] S. Blanton, "A Mental-Hygiene Program for Colleges," *Mental Hygiene*, 9: 478–88, 1925; S. Cobb, "A Report on the Brief Neuropsychiatric Examination of 1,141 Students," *Journal of Industrial Hygiene*, 3: 309–15, 1922; J. G. Darley, "Tested Maladjustment Related to Clinically Diagnosed Maladjustment," *Journal of Applied Psychology*, 21: 632–42, 1937; A. W. Morrison and H. S. Diehl, "Some Studies of Mental Hygiene Needs of Freshman University Students," *Journal of the American Medical Association*, 83: 1,666–72, 1924; A. W. Morrison, "Further Discussion of College Mental Hygiene," *Mental Hygiene*, 12: 48–54, 1928; H. D. Palmer and E. O. Harper, "College Mental-Hygiene Methods," *Mental Hygiene*, 21: 397–415, 1937; T. Raphael, "Mental Hygiene Survey for Colleges and Universities," *op. cit.*; A. F. Riggs and W. B. Terhune, "The Mental Health of College Women," *Mental Hygiene*, 12: 559–68, 1928.

[5] Blanton, *op cit.*; M. B. Blake, "How Does the Personnel Worker View the Work of a Dean?" *Proceedings of the Fourteenth Regular Meeting of the National Association of Deans of Women*, National Education Association, 1927, pp. 191–95; Darley, *op. cit.*; G. E. Gardner and H. D. Pierce, "The Inferiority Feelings of College Students," *Journal of Abnormal and Social Psychology*, 24: 8–13, 1929; Palmer and Harper, *op. cit.* R. Strang, "Personal Problems of Students," *Sixteenth Yearbook of the National Association of Deans of Women*, 1929, 147–51.

[6] V. V. Anderson and W. M. Kennedy, "Psychiatry in College," *Mental Hygiene*, 16: 353–83, 1932.

tions and only 30 in any job whatever. During several previous years 646 college graduates had taken positions with this firm. Only a small proportion of them were successful; 30 per cent had been dismissed, 20 per cent had never been promoted, and many had left voluntarily. The difficulties were in almost every case of a personal character. These graduates were unable to adjust themselves to the work. In competition with noncollege people they were unsuccessful, although their native ability was undoubtedly greater.

It may appear at first as if the average college instructor had little concern with the mental hygiene program. Actually he has an important role. In the first place, many of the maladjustments come to a head in the classroom, sometimes as mere failures and at other times as disturbing manifestations of personality. The teacher is the one mature person with an adequate opportunity to observe variations of behavior and abnormalities of character among undergraduates. The surest way to get the right students in touch with the mental hygienist is to train the members of a faculty to see what they are looking at. In the second place, teachers can either cause or avoid emotional difficulties according to the methods of instruction they use. In an institution in which young people are presumably being educated, they should certainly not meet with types of teaching that precipitate unnecessary crises. In the third place, teachers themselves need mental hygiene. Their work always involves more or less nervous and emotional strain because of their constant association with human beings. Some teachers have as hard a time keeping on an even emotional keel as any of their students. For their own happiness and well-being they should therefore want to learn what they can about the ways in which a sane person can stay sane.

I. EVERYDAY PROBLEMS OF ADJUSTMENT TO THE COLLEGE ENVIRONMENT

Everyone needs to follow the general principles of mental health. The student has the usual problems of life to meet and, in addition, certain situations that arise in connection with his college work. The problems reported in a large number of articles are remarkably similar from one university or college to another. Apparently the difficulties of adaptation arise, regardless of the size or type of institution, mainly because a student is for the first time trying to live an independent life.

The average college freshman has lived at home during his high school days, has met only a comparatively few people, has attended small classes in which he has received much individual attention, and has been taught subjects that were, in the main, not too hard for him. He has usually never needed before to concern himself with such mundane matters as food, room rent, clothing, or laundry. Both his family and his school have simplified life for him, even though he may not have known it. When he comes to college, he enters a new scene. He has more independence than he sometimes wants, he meets a large number of new people, and his lessons are suddenly much harder. Some of the problems he meets are concerned with classwork, others with adaptation to the social life of the college. Still other difficulties arise from his own personal inadequacies. The following list has been compiled by including those difficulties reported by at least a third of the students examined in the various studies put together;[7] the starred items refer to problems that beset half or more of the students.

[7] Angell, *op cit.;* K. E. Appel and L. H. Smith, "The Approach to College Mental Hygiene," *Proceedings of the 10th Annual Meeting of the American Student Health Association,* 1929, pp. 106–24; E. Bagby, "The Emotional Factors in Human Adjustment," *Proceedings of the 17th Regular Meeting of the National Association of Deans of Women,* 1930, pp. 63–72; J. H. Beard, "Mental Adjustment in College Students," *School and Society,* 32:475–80, 1930; Blake, *op. cit.;* S. Blanton, "A Mental Hygiene Program for Colleges," *Mental Hygiene,* 9:478–88, 1925; D. D. Bromley and F. H. Britten, *Youth and Sex: A Study of 1300 College Students,* Harper & Brothers, 1938, 303 pp.; S. Cobb, "A Report on the Brief Neuropsychiatric Examination of 1,141 Students," *Journal of Industrial Hygiene,* 3:309–15, 1922; E. Conrad, "The Maladjusted Girl," *Proceedings of the 13th Regular Meeting of the National Association of Deans of Women,* 1926, pp. 109–25; H. F. Carson, "Factors in the Development of Psychoses in College Men." *Mental Hygiene,* 11:496–518, 1927; J. G. Darley, *op. cit.;* E. E. Emme, *Adjustment Problems of College Freshmen,* Cokesbury Press, Nashville, Tennessee, 1933, 125 pp.; A. F. Fenlason and H. R. Hertz, "The College Student and Feelings of Inferiority," *Mental Hygiene,* 22:389–99, 1938; G. E. Gardner and H. D. Pierce, "The Inferiority Feelings of College Students," *Journal of Abnormal and Social*

Continued on page 205.

TABLE 12
Problems Commonly Reported by Students

I. Difficulties in connection with classwork
    A. Methods of instruction
        1. Lecturing unfamiliar
        *2. Assignments not clear or too long for the time allowed
        3. Textbooks too hard or too uninteresting
        4. Too little opportunity for reviews in class
        *5. Too little attention to individual needs
    B. Administrative features
        1. Classes too large
        *2. Too little guidance in selection of courses
        3. Registration too complicated
        *4. Library facilities inadequate
    C. Characteristics of teachers
        *1. Inadequate understanding of students as people
        2. Overestimation of the average student's ability
        3. Refusal to talk with individual students outside of class
        4. Indifference to student's welfare
II. Difficulties in connection with social adjustment
    A. Being away from home (including homesickness)
    *B. Newness and strangeness of campus life, with resulting feeling of being insecure and lost in a crowd
    C. Change from being a high school senior to being a college freshman
    *D. Ignorance of how to make social contacts
    E. Too much freedom
    F. Social isolation
    G. Inability to handle money
    H. Too much outside work
    I. Difficulties of adjustment to members of the opposite sex
    J. Friction with parents
III. Difficulties caused by personal inadequacies
    A. Physical difficulties
        1. Constant fatigue
        2. Frequent headaches
    B. Intellectual difficulties
        *1. Inadequate methods of study
        2. Inability to concentrate
        *3. Inability to take notes
        4. Inability to select important facts from reading material
        5. Inability to read fast enough or well enough
        *6. Inadequate budgeting of time
        *7. Inadequate fundamental preparation
    C. Emotional difficulties
        1. General feelings and attitudes
            *a. Feelings of inferiority and insecurity
            b. Depression
            c. Boredom and discontent with college life
            *d. Embarrassment or self-consciousness
        2. Special difficulties
            a. Fear of examinations
            *b. Timidity in class

Some of these difficulties, of course, are unavoidable and are merely incidental to the process of growing up; they would occur wherever the student happened to be. It is, however, desirable that a college should do what it can to solve as many problems as possible, because the fewer such troubles a student has, the more he can concentrate upon his work.

The complaints about classwork suggest mainly that the curriculum is still too hard for the average student, that the red tape is too complicated, and that there are still too many teachers who teach subject matter exclusively instead of subject matter and students together. Gradually colleges are either making the curriculum easier in the first two years or are differentiating their

⁷ *continued*
Psychology, 24: 8–13, 1929; G. E. Gardner, "Causes of Mental Ill-Health among College Students," *Annals of the American Academy of Political and Social Science,* 149: 102–23, 1930; G. Green, "Freshman Problems," *Proceedings of the 16th Regular Meeting of the National Association of Deans of Women,* National Education Association, 1929, 152–54, S. D. House, "Mental Hygiene Inventory," *Archives of Psychology,* No. 88, 1927, 112 pp.; K. W. Jameson and F. C. Lockwood, *The Freshman Girl,* D. C. Heath and Company, 1925, 170 pp.; H. N. Kerns, "The Experiences of a Mental Hygienist in a University," *Mental Hygiene,* 11: 489–95, 1927; F. L. Knapp, "Freshmen Adjustment," *Proceedings of the 17th Regular Meeting of the National Association of Deans of Women,* Nation Education Association, 1930, pp. 101–6; D. A. Laird, "Case-Studies in the Mental Problems of Later Adolescence," *Mental Hygiene,* 7: 715–33, 1923; Z. E. Leatherman and E. A. Doll, "A Study of the Maladjusted College Student," *Ohio State University Studies,* Vol. 2, No. 2, 1925, 56 pp.; E. A. Leonard, *The Problems of Freshman College Girls,* Bureau of Publications, Teachers College, 1932, 140 pp.; K. A. Menninger, "Adaptation Difficulties in College Students," *Mental Hygiene,* 11: 519–35, 1927; A. W. Morrison and H. S. Diehl, "Some Studies of the Mental Hygiene Needs of Freshman University Students," *Journal of the American Medical Association,* 83: 1,666–72, 1924; A. W. Morrison, "Further Discussion of College Mental Hygiene," *Mental Hygiene,* 12: 48–54, 1928; H. D. Palmer, "Mental Hygiene Problems in a University," *Mental Hygiene,* 18: 233–44, 1934; H. D. Palmer and E. O. Harper, "College Mental-Hygiene Methods," *Mental Hygiene,* 21: 397–415, 1937; D. E. Phillips, "Mental Dangers among College Students," *Journal of Abnormal and Social Psychology,* 25: 3–13, 1930; S. L. Pressey, "The College and Adolescent Needs," in *Research Adventures in University Teaching,* Public School Publishing Company, 1927, pp. 81–85; T. Raphael, "Mental Hygiene Service for Colleges and Universities," *Mental Hygiene,* 21: 559–68, 1937; T. Raphael, "Four Years of Student Mental-Hygiene Work at the University of Michigan," *Mental Hygiene,* 20: 218–31, 1936; T. Raphael, M. A. Gordon, and E. M. Dawson, "Mental Hygiene in American Colleges and Universities," *Mental Hygiene,* 22: 221–36, 1938; E. Reinhardt, "Freshmen Difficulties," *Journal of Higher Education,* 4: 307–9, 1933; A. F. Riggs and W. B. Terhune, "The Mental Health of College Women," *Mental Hygiene,* 12: 559–68, 1928; A. H. Ruggles, "College Mental Hygiene

courses of study so that only students of good ability enter the traditional academic courses. In time there should be fewer maladjustments between students and their work. The difficulties with red tape and with inadequate guidance are products chiefly of mere size. Many universities with 5,000 or more students are still using methods of registration, guidance, and general administration that are simply extensions of procedures adapted to the handling of 500 students. Very few institutions manage to get a freshman class of a 1,000 or more registered without wearing down the nerves of all concerned. Finally, the average college teacher is gradually becoming more and more concerned over the students as individuals. On almost any campus there are still a few professors who remain intolerant of the presence in their classes of students who cannot profit from their best teaching efforts. Their attitude is entirely understandable in the light of their own educational history. They are people who, early in life, developed an intense interest in academic work; their potential scholarship received intensive training in a hard school. In the year 1900, for instance, there were about 5,000 graduate students in the entire country in all subjects; now there are over 75,000.[8] Those professors who received their advanced degrees at about this time were therefore the survivors of a terrific elimination;

[7] continued
Problems," Mental Hygiene, 9: 261–72, 1925; G. H. Smeltzer, "A Method for Determining What College Students Consider Their Own Difficulties," School and Society, 32: 709–10, 1930; S. K. Smith, "Practical Modes of Treatment in Handling Mental Hygiene Problems," American Journal of Psychiatry, 13: 56–67, 1933; R. M. Strang, "Problems of Adolescents Which Come to Deans," Junior-Senior High School Clearing-House, 7: 29–34, 1932; R. M. Strang, "Personal Problems of Students," Proceedings of the 16th Regular Meeting of the National Association of Deans of Women, National Education Association, 1929, pp. 147–51; C. M. Thompson, "The Value of Mental Hygiene in the College," Mental Hygiene, 11: 225–40, 1927; C. M. Thompson, "Mental Hygiene and Study," Proceedings of the 17th Regular Meeting of the American Association of Deans of Women, National Education Association, 1930, pp. 97–101; L. T. Thompson, "Mental Hygiene in a University," American Journal of Psychiatry, 8: 1,045–52, 1929; O. H. Werner, Every College Student's Problems, Silver, Burdett and Company, 1929, 370 pp.; G. M. Wiley, et al., "Needs of American Adolescent Youth," Sixth Yearbook of the Department of Supervision of the National Education Association, 1928, pp. 9–37; F. E. Williams, "Mental Hygiene and the College Student," Mental Hygiene, 9: 225–60, 1925; E. G. Williamson, How to Counsel Students, McGraw-Hill Book Company, 1939, 562 pp. (Chapters 7, 9, 22); K. Young, N. Drought, and J. L. Bergstresser, "The Social and Emotional Adjustment of Freshmen at the University of Wisconsin," American Sociological Review, 2: 166–77, 1937.
[8] Biennial Survey of Education, 1930–32, Bureau of Education, 1934.

each was literally "the one in a thousand." These professors have a sincere desire to pass on their learning to those of the next generation who can profit by it, and they are understandably irritated by the flood of students without interest in or ability for scholastic attainments. The younger members of a college faculty have a better comprehension of the changes during the past twenty years because as students they have personally experienced these changes. The present generation of Ph.D. candidates is learning—as an integral part of its training—something about the current trends of higher education. It would therefore seem that many of the bitterest complaints now made by students might become less prominent with the passage of time.

The difficulties of social adjustment arise primarily from the mere fact that students are "on their own" for the first time. Those adolescents who do not go to college have the same troubles, often in a more aggravated form. The change in status from high school seniors to college freshmen is disturbing to those who have been especially active in secondary school. There is really some basis for this feeling. The greater social competition in college operates to subordinate the importance of many a prominent high school graduate. For instance, a typical group of 348 college students, who had received 1,051 recognitions of prominence in secondary school, received only 452 such recognitions in college.[9] This situation is practically unavoidable, and some students find adjustment to it rather hard. With all the social resources of a college campus, however, it would seem as if many social problems could be largely solved by any group of students and teachers which takes the situation seriously. Some methods have already been suggested.

The personal inadequacies are of two kinds—those that arise from unpreparedness for college work and those that are inherent in an individual's personality. The difficulties in the former group are certainly unnecessary. Methods of prevention will be discussed in a later chapter and will not therefore be presented here. Those in the second group require for the most part some elementary mental hygiene.[10]

[9] G. E. Gardner and H. D. Pierce, "The Inferiority Feelings of College Students," *Journal of Abnormal and Social Psychology*, 24: 8–13, 1929.
[10] For a discussion of mental hygiene methods for large groups of young people, see B. B. Robinson, "Mental Hygiene for Youth," *Annals of the American Academy of Political and Social Sciences*, 194: 100–110, 1937.

It is of interest to compare what students say about their difficulties with the diagnoses that a psychiatrist gives to the group he sees. Some of the studies present only general conclusions. Thus, one writer regards one-third of the maladjustments as scholastic, one-third as physical, and one-third as psychological.[11] Another considers half the problems as scholastic, one-fourth as social, and one-fifth as administrative.[12] Other investigators have given more specific classifications. Three of these are shown in Table 13.

Although the classifications vary from one report to another, the three agree fairly well as to the per cent of a student population that is seriously abnormal. The per cent diagnosed as psychotic varied from 2.4 to 7.4. Psychoneuroses accounted for 21.5 to 37.2 per cent of the cases. Of the 2,301 students included in the first study, 21 per cent came to the clinic in an acute emotional condition, and 6 per cent were in such a

TABLE 13

Classification of Diagnoses from Three Studies

First Study: Diagnoses given to 2,301 cases*

	Per Cent
Psychotic: Schizophrenia, manic-depressive, and toxic	2.4
Neurotic:	
1. Nervousness, due to infection of the central nervous system	3.6
2. Depression	10.0
3. Psychoneuroses	37.2
4. Psychopathic personality	2.0
5. Nonclinical—minor personal difficulties	44.8
	100.0

* T. Raphael, "Four Years of Student Mental-Hygiene Work at the University of Michigan," *Mental Hygiene,* 21: 218–31, 1936. Used by permission of *Mental Hygiene.*

[11] A. H. Ruggles, "College Mental-Hygiene Problems," *Mental Hygiene,* 9: 261–72, 1925.
[12] R. Strang, "Personal Problems of Students," *Proceedings of the Sixteenth Regular Meeting of the National Association of Deans of Women,* 1929, pp. 147–51.

TABLE 13 *continued*

Second Study: Diagnoses given to 1,000 cases †

	Per Cent
1. Social maladjustment	31.6
2. Sexual maladjustment	19.8
3. Psychoneuroses	21.5
4. Intellectual inferiority	3.7
5. Psychopathic personality	4.1
6. Psychoses	7.4
7. Glandular disorders	3.1
8. Nervous diseases	7.2
9. Unclassified	1.6
	100.0

Third Study: Diagnoses given to 165 cases ‡

1. Poor work, with no emotional difficulty	16.0
2. Definitely psychoneurotic	27.0
3. Poor physical condition	9.0
4. Cyclothymic personality	13.0
5. Acute emotional condition	5.0
6. Disciplinary cases	6.0
7. Difficult adjustment because of being a foreigner	2.0
8. Sex problems	2.0
9. Feelings of inferiority	2.0
10. Minor problems	18.0
	100.0

† S. K. Smith, "Practical Modes of Treatment in Handling Mental Hygiene Problems in a University," *American Journal of Psychiatry,* 13: 56–67, 1933. Used by permission of the *American Journal of Psychiatry.*
‡ A. F. Riggs and W. B. Terhune, "The Mental Health of College Women," *Mental Hygiene,* 12: 559–68, 1928.

state of depression they had to be kept under observation because of the danger of suicide.

The chief symptoms reported by all investigators are—in order of their frequency—discouragement, anxiety, somatic conditions of emotional origin, depression, dislike of college life or dissatisfaction with it, failing or nearly failing classwork, phobias of various kinds, social isolation, feelings of inferiority,[13] homesickness, lack of purpose, excitement, dislike of or worry about one's family.[14] These symptoms differ from a similar list that could be compiled for the cases admitted to a psychopathic hospital because the symptoms of mental deterioration are strikingly absent. The students were still intact mentally when the psychiatrist saw them. What they needed was a re-education of the emotions, and this help is precisely what the mental hygienist is equipped to give. The degree of success attending his efforts has been commented upon by two writers. One of them,[15] who worked with only 50 students, considers he was successful in 28 cases—of whom 13 showed relatively minor maladjustments—and a complete failure in 4; the other 18 students showed some improvement, but not much. The second worker [16] reports definite improvement in 560 out of 1,000 cases. The real successes came to a little more than 50 per cent of the cases in both instances. In other words, the hygienist does not claim to be God. He can do a great deal of good for about half the students sent him and some good for many others, but he sometimes fails.

The relative importance of poor preparation and emotional condition in causing failure is a matter on which various investigators differ considerably. In some studies practically all the difficulties reported have to do with unpreparedness for classwork.[17] In others, there is a definite statement that inadequate preparation is only a minor problem and that failing work is a result of some personal maladjustment.[18]

[13] Feelings of inferiority seem unusually persistent among those who have them at all. Thus in one study (Fenlason and Hertz, *op. cit.*) 43 per cent of the graduate students who were questioned admitted feelings of inferiority in one way or another.
[14] For further discussions of the effect of families in the production of abnormal conditions among college students see, for instance, H. L. Pritchett, "The Adjustments of College Students' Family Problems," *Social Forces,* 10:84–89, 1931; H. M. MacCracken, "Parents and Daughters," *Harper's Magazine,* 154:454–61, 1927; L. C. Pressey, "Some Serious Family Maladjustments among College Students," *Social Forces,* 10:236–42, 1931; and E. G. Williamson, *How to Counsel Students,* McGraw-Hill Book Company, 1939, 562 pp. (Chap. 9).
[15] A. W. Morrison, "Further Discussion of College Mental Hygiene," *op. cit.*
[16] Smith, *op. cit.*
[17] See, for instance, Smeltzer, *op. cit.*
[18] C. M. Thompson, "Mental Hygiene and Study," *op. cit.*

I have an idea that the point of view depends in large measure upon the student population under consideration. If there has been only what might be called the "natural selection" that occurs as pupils are eliminated in successive grades, the preparation of the average student is hardly sufficient for the strain put upon it, and the failures are due in large measure to this factor. In a small college that has high standards of admission, however, most of the failures come from other sources because those whose preparation is inadequate are not admitted. Of course, in a university there are many students who do poor work because of emotional maladjustments, but these form a much smaller group than those who fail because they simply do not know enough.

From one other source there is some information about maladjustment. Although most college students are well behaved, there are always a few cases of discipline. In 33 institutions there were 275 instances of punishable offense in a month's time—or approximately 8.3 per college.[19] Since some 25,000 students are included, lawbreaking on the average campus is a minor matter, in so far as the number of students affected is concerned. The chief offenses are as follows: driving an auto without permission, staying out late, going to dances without permission, being noisy in either classroom or rooming house, smoking, failure to attend classes, general disregard of rules, cheating, drinking, immorality, and stealing. The offenses listed occurred at the rate of 4 per 1,000 students per month. To the mental hygienist these disciplinary cases suggest immaturity and adolescent revolt against authority.[20] It should be noted that almost all the offenses indicate the presence of overextraverted individuals, whose inhibitions are not adequate under a little excitement. It goes without saying that all offenders should be examined by an expert before they are punished—whether by student courts or by administrative officers. Usually one finds behind the lawbreak-

[19] G. Greene, "A Study of Problems of Discipline Which the Deans of Women in Teacher-Training Institutions Are Handling," *Proceedings of the Sixteenth Regular Meeting of the National Association of Deans of Women,* 1929, pp. 137–42.

[20] See, for instance, K. A. Menninger, "Psychoanalytic Observations on the Mental Hygiene Problems of College Students," *Journal of Nervous and Mental Diseases,* 69: 642–50, 1929.

ing an immature and unhappy child; he may at first appear
sophisticated, but he rarely is.

It is probable that some colleges bring down offenses upon their
own heads by the narrowness of their restrictions. Students are
at a stage of development during which they want to see and experience everything. If the rules are too cramping and existence
on the campus too confining, they will simply "bootleg" life.
Naturally, some of them will get caught at it. For a normal development, however, it is much better to see life illegally than not
to see it at all. I have seen sets of rules for college groups that
ought to arouse resentment in any healthy adolescent; if these
regulations were followed to the letter, a student would be so
sheltered from the world that he certainly ought to find it thoroughly terrifying when his school days are over. In the list of
common offenses given above, smoking is included.[21] On grounds
of health it is undesirable, but it is hardly a crime. I was once
in a university where smoking was completely forbidden; there
were large signs to that effect outside of every building. In between classes, the students used to go out on the steps, smoke
for five minutes, and throw the butts at the sign. Rules that are
too strict do not give protection; they only breed contempt for all
rules.

II. ABERRANT EMOTIONAL TYPES AMONG COLLEGE STUDENTS

As mentioned earlier, the teacher has an important place
in the mental hygiene program because he is the person with
the best opportunity to observe students. He sees them all
against the same background of the class situation and is
therefore in a position to notice which ones are not reacting
in a normal manner. The members of a faculty form, indeed,
the chief connecting link between the mental hygienist and
the students who most need his services. Aside from the obvious value to the student of an early adjustment of his difficulties, the results are of considerable usefulness to the teacher.
One abnormal student in a class of fifty can disrupt the group
and make teaching unduly difficult. If a professor wants his

---

[21] Of course, the offense may refer only to smoking where the fire
hazard is so high that cigarettes are prohibited.

classes to go well, he should do whatever he can, as soon as he can, for those whose behavior is not entirely normal.

It is, of course, impossible to describe all forms of aberrant behavior in so short a presentation as this, but a few types recur so often that a teacher should be able to recognize them. Eight deviations from strictly normal personalities are especially important because they make trouble in the classroom and will—if not modified—continue to make trouble after college days are over. The first five types are well within the range of normality; with them a teacher can often do much. The last three, however, are definitely abnormal and require the services of an expert. The descriptions of these aberrant personalities are necessarily brief, but they may be sufficient to aid teachers in the recognition of such students.[22]

There is, first, the easily excited, effervescent, underinhibited student who laughs and cries at the slightest provocation, gets angry at nothing, and creates scenes. Many people of this type are sick, but that does not make them any easier to get along with. In class they talk too much, volunteer continually, laugh loudly, whisper to their neighbors, interrupt the teacher, and are general nuisances. For these students classwork is more of a strain than their weak powers of inhibition can stand. Either the mental hygienist or the physician can usually help this type of person. There are also some things a teacher can do to make the class situation easier. It is more peaceable for all concerned if such a student sits alone, with at least one empty chair between himself and others. This arrangement reduces the amount of stimulation he receives and allows him to relax better. The volunteering and interrupting can be kept under fair control if the teacher will talk to the student alone and ask for his co-operation in the general

[22] For a good discussion of the underlying theories of personality, see H. A. Murray, *Explorations in Personality*, Oxford University Press, 1938, 761 pp. (Chap. 2). This same reference contains (Chap. 3) a presentation of personality types. Unfortunately the author has seen fit to invent a new language for the expression of his ideas. If one can assimilate such terms as "Harmavoidance, Infavoident, Inviolacy, Succorance, Exocathection, Motones, Verbones, Exterofactive, or Supravertive," and if one can become reconciled to such cryptic lines as "conflict with: n Aba, n Inf, n Suc, n Auto, n Aff, n Nur, n Play, n Def," there is a great deal of value in the presentation. Certainly the types of personality described are so good that the reader is constantly reminded of people he has known who fit the specifications well. The types described in this chapter are with one exception to be found in greater detail in Murray.

conduct of classwork. If the student is bright enough, he may be allowed to remain away from class some of the time and work by himself.

A second type of student who also offends by too much volunteering is the exhibitionist; although his behavior may be somewhat similar to that of the merely uninhibited person, his motives are altogether different. What he wants is attention—at any price; even a reprimand is better than nothing. If the behavior is not too annoying, it is often possible to keep such a student under fair control merely by ignoring him. The situation is greatly complicated if the best student in the class is of this type, because there are some points that only he will see—and these are precisely the ones that give him the best chance to show off. It does not do at all to reprimand the braggart in public, because he is already under more emotional pressure than he can bear or he would not act in this manner. One should, however, have no difficulty in arranging for a private conversation, because the attention-getter is forever lingering after class—a type of behavior that differentiates him from the merely overexcitable person. One does not need to be a psychoanalyst to see that such a student is an unhappy child, who is trying desperately to cover some inferiority. An expert can usually find out what the difficulty is in a short time; there is no person who breaks down and tells all as quickly as the braggart. If a hygienist is not available, a teacher can do a great deal for a student of this type. Honesty, a reasonable amount of sympathy, and a complete absence of emotion are necessary. It is probable that an honest talk will hurt the braggart's feelings, but a teacher can rest assured that these feelings will soon be hurt much worse by someone else if nothing is done to bring about a change of behavior. Incidentally, many of the symptoms disappear quickly as soon as the student himself sees what is causing him to act in a conceited and overbearing manner. One may not like especially to do clinical work with one's slightly aberrant students, but a teacher cannot afford to allow the exhibitionism to continue unchecked because the offending student will annoy others in the class too much and they, in turn, will criticize the instructor for his lack of control.

A third type of general nuisance is the excessively nervous student, who may or may not also be emotional, but often is not. This student is simply restless. He moves about in his seat, he wiggles and twists and squirms, he wraps his legs around the chair

rungs, he sprawls, he drops things, he jerks his head about, he
contorts his face, he twiddles his fingers, he scratches his head,
he writes furiously, he breaks pencils, he shuffles his feet, and by
the end of the hour he is usually tied up like a pretzel. All of this
performance is harmless but very annoying to the teacher who
has to watch it. Since such a student is clearly sick, his behavior
should be reported at once to the college doctor, who can usually
help in reducing the restlessness. In the meantime, there is little
a teacher can do except to possess his soul in patience and to seat
the student off at one side, out of his direct line of vision. If the
teacher is also nervous, this arrangement is almost imperative;
otherwise, he and the student will catch each other's mannerisms,
and both will get worse.

There is one kind of emotional deviate who can hardly escape
the teacher's attention—the rebellious and antagonistic student.
The real trouble with a person of this type lies in the fact that a
teacher represents authority. Such a student has had unfortunate
experiences with someone whose methods of control were extreme; now he revolts at the slightest hint of domination. He objects needlessly to all manner of things. If a teacher wants an
outline of his reading, he protests; if one book is assigned, he
wants to read another. If an instructor tries to assert a little
authority, the student at the very least talks back, often contra-
dicts flatly or refuses point-blank to follow suggestions, and sometimes indulges in profanity or general vituperation. Naturally, the
student should be examined at once by a specialist, but the teacher
is forced into dealing in one way or another with the immediate
situation because the outbursts cannot be ignored. Not one instructor in ten manages to keep his own temper well enough to
handle a student of this type successfully, but if he can only be
patient and unemotional, it is possible to reduce the antagonism
appreciably. Many teachers dread this particular kind of personality because of the tendency to bad manners and violence.
They are, however, overlooking one point that to the hygienist is
most hopeful. Such a student has great vitality and drive. Life
has not beaten him; he is still exchanging blow for blow—even
though some of his returns hit the innocent bystander. Because
there is something to build on, the rebellious student is not as hard
for a relatively inexperienced but intelligent teacher to deal with
as the thoroughly beaten, exhausted down-and-outer, who is willing to sell his soul in return for peace.

Finally, there is the shy, immature, self-effacing youngster who comes to class day after day without ever contributing voluntarily to the discussion, hangs his head in embarrassment if called upon, passes in careful but thoroughly immature work, clearly feels himself inferior to the others, and needs continual reassurance and general bolstering of the spirit if he is to get anything done. Such a student depends upon the teacher, just as at home he has depended upon his parents. He often has ability enough to do college work, but he lacks the capacity to get himself started or—if someone else initiates an activity—to keep himself going. The most extreme students of this type are like millstones around a teacher's neck. They need, of course, to be taught how to stand on their own feet, how to direct their own activities, and how to evaluate their own achievements. With these adolescents the home has obviously failed in its task of educating its children away from their dependency. If teachers and older students do not take a hand the student is likely to grow into an individual with no ability to maintain himself. The re-education of such a student has to be gradual, but with good teaching a freshman who has nothing to say and no courage in the classroom can, in a year's time, develop into a young person with a fair assortment of ideas, the ability to complete short pieces of work independently, and enough selfconfidence to take a small part in group discussions.

The students thus far described are all within the normal range of personalities. They need help in their personal adjustment to the world, but their troubles do not make them anything more than unusual. The difficulties of the next three types are much more serious.

Some students are extremely moody. Their change from excitement to gloom may be so pronounced as to make them seem at different times like two different people. During a period of excitement, such a student shows a type of behavior a good deal like that of the underinhibited student, only in a more extreme form. He laughs at nothing and seems under constant compulsion to chatter. When the mood of depression begins it is just as extreme; nothing seems worth while, there is no interest in anything, and utter despondency is the only possible response to a horrible world. The teacher cannot deal effectively with this type of personality because external situations are likely to be of no importance at all; the moods come in response to some kind of internal pressure and are therefore quite unaffected by environment. A teacher has, indeed, only one function in such a case and that is to recognize it; the treatment is outside his province. He will save himself a great deal of unnecessary trouble if he does not waste time in fruitless adjustments that are at best only palliative and are often worse than useless because they postpone the moment of contact between the student and the specialist.

Another clearly recognizable type of abnormal person is the student with a repressed, overinhibited, introverted personality. Too often these students attract only casual notice and are regarded as being "queer but harmless," even though it should be evident that there is nothing harmless about queerness of any kind. Such a student sits quietly in class, seems to be in a daze much of the time, often answers irrelevantly, occasionally does not realize when class is over, usually has odd mannerisms, often laughs at nothing but fails to laugh when others do, is usually alone, is avoided by his classmates, and is sometimes actually dirty in appearance. All of these symptoms are indicative of disintegration. In most instances, actual mental deterioration does not begin until obvious emotional and social maladjustments have been going on for some time. It is therefore possible to arrest the course of the disease if one can only start early enough. Naturally the treatment of these cases is a highly technical matter. A teacher has done his part when he has reported such a student to the proper authorities. Except for minor adjustments there is nothing a teacher can do that is helpful.

The last type is the suspicious student with ideas of persecution. He complains that he is not treated fairly, that his teachers "pick" on him, that his examinations are not properly graded, and so on. He gives elaborate and patently incorrect explanations of other people's behavior toward him. If a teacher tries to be kind to him, he audibly wonders "where the catch is." His confidence in humanity is approximately nil; he expects to be cheated, imposed upon, and discriminated against. Often his skepticism extends into the intellectual field, and he questions every statement an instructor makes. A student who shows this paranoid disposition is in great need of expert help because he is the kind of person who is the hardest to re-educate and the most dangerous if re-education is not successful. The mental condition here described is rarely accompanied by any deterioration. Therefore a student of this type usually does good work although his conclusions may be affected by his mistaken ideas.

A professor needs to develop a keen eye for certain types of people: the overstimulated, the boastful, the nervous, the rebellious, the childish, the moody, the introverted, and the suspicious. It is to everyone's advantage to get these students under proper treatment as soon as possible. The first and third types need medical attention. A teacher can generally help the braggart, the shy child, and the iconoclast as much as anyone can. This is particularly true if the teacher is one to whom the student is attached. The last three types need to see a psychiatrist. They are not only outside the normal range of personalities, but they are also not influenced by their environment as normal people are. Consequently any special effort a teacher makes in trying to help them is as likely as not to go unnoticed.

III. A COURSE IN MENTAL HYGIENE

From the foregoing discussion it should be clear that all students need information about mental hygiene so that they may conduct their lives upon healthy principles. Most people know too little about the fundamental requirements of a normal emotional, social, and intellectual life. In a state of almost complete ignorance on these matters, the average freshman tries to adapt himself to the demands of a much more complicated life than he has hitherto known. The ordinary college presents the incoming freshman with many problems and too frequently leaves him to his own devices about solving them. If the major objective of the undergraduate years at the present time were to turn out embryo scholars, one might regard this sink-or-swim method as a good means of eliminating the unfit. Since, however, the main objective seems to be the development of each student to his highest capacity and the adjustment of each to his social milieu, a college fails in its duty if it does not help the student to get past the first hurdles of campus life.

The place for a course in mental hygiene is quite clearly

at the very beginning of college, when the problems are thickest and the student least able to cope with them. The work should presumably be required. In the first place, one cannot tell in advance which freshmen will soon be in desperate need of information on how to stay sane; in the second, it is probable that almost every person will need such facts at one time or another during his life. Anyone who is not an idiot has problems of adjustment to the world. Each person has an assortment of faults and shortcomings that may interfere with his progress. Every freshman has some traits of immaturity. It seems reasonable to suppose that students will adjust themselves better, correct their faults more completely, and grow up quicker if all of them receive systematic instruction in these phases of personality development. Students themselves are aware of their needs and express spontaneous interest in such topics. In one study, 33 per cent of all questions asked about personal hygiene by students were concerned with mental health.[23]

The content of such a course should presumably be based upon the range and types of difficulties shown. From all available data the following subjects [24] seem of outstanding importance.

(1) Emancipation from home
(2) New freedom and independence of college life
(3) Social adjustments
(4) Criteria of adulthood
(5) Emotional strain and its effects
(6) Typical worries and conflicts in college
(7) Types of human reaction to emotional situations
(8) Sex attraction—what is healthy and what is not

The first object of such a course is to give insight into everyday life on the campus. Naturally, the emphasis should be upon the normal adjustment of the normal person. The content may be adapted to the needs of any particular group if the

[23] D. Oberteuffer, "Personal Hygiene for College Students," *Teachers College Contributions to Education,* No. 407, 1930, 121 pp.
[24] Topics dealing with study methods have not been included here, in spite of their importance, because they are taken up later in another connection.

THE COLLEGE STUDENT

instructor will ask students to submit questions—preferably by dropping them into a box or by some other technique that preserves anonymity. By this procedure the problems that most worry each successive freshman class can be determined. Aside from any help in general orientation to college work and environment, the course brings freshmen at once into contact with the mental hygienist. Many of those having the worst problems come of their own accord for an interview because they have developed an awareness of their difficulties and a confidence in the teacher.[25] If the instructor asks the students to turn in data about themselves, he or she soon locates the most serious cases. The course acts, therefore, both as general guidance for the healthy and as a first point of contact between the unhealthy and the person who can help them most.[26]

IV. SUMMARY

Most college students are healthy youngsters who have only minor tragedies to contend with. The majority of them, even without other than incidental help, will muddle along somehow and will emerge from their college days with no more than a few superficial emotional scars. I am aware that this point of view is too optimistic to be accepted by some of the people interested in mental hygiene. I must confess I can find little that is alarming in the mental condition of the average present-day undergraduate or in the development of the many middle-aged college graduates I have known. From some of the articles

[25] For further discussion of the content for a course in mental hygiene and for the usefulness of such a course, see F. L. Patry, "Some Suggestions on a Mental-Hygiene Program for Schools and Colleges," *Mental Hygiene,* 18: 621–28, 1934; E. V. N. Emery, "The Content and Method of Instructing College Students in Mental Hygiene," *Mental Hygiene,* 17: 590–97, 1933; and G. H. Estabrooks, "Suggestions as to the Detection and Treatment of Personality Difficulties in College Students," *Mental Hygiene,* 13: 794–99, 1929.

[26] Various measuring devices for investigating the total adjustment of college students have appeared in recent years. Two of these might well be mentioned: the *Bernreuter Inventory* (Stanford University Press, 1935) and the *Washburne Social Adjustment Inventory* (World Book Company). From either, one gets clues as to the nature of a given student's difficulties, provided the student is reasonably co-operative.

in the literature [27] one would conclude that higher education steadily produced more abnormal than normal people. A few college graduates are insane and others are eccentric, but how does anyone know they would not have been madder a good deal sooner if they had not gone to college? After surveying the literature on mental hygiene I am still of the opinion that, for most students, college is a healthy mental and emotional experience.

[27] See, for instance, Anon., "Mental Hygiene and the College Student— Twenty Years After," *Mental Hygiene,* 5 : 736–40, 1921.

CHAPTER IX

INCENTIVES

Every teacher has his or her opinion as to what incentives will produce desirable results. Nor is there any dearth of such opinions in the literature. The difficulty is that these expressions of attitude are not always accompanied by objective proof. Therefore, even though the points of view so often set forth may be entirely correct, one cannot present them as being established facts. In addition to statements of opinion, I have found many articles dealing with well-controlled experiments of a nature that seem to me wholly irrelevant. Some of these investigations are laboratory experiments performed with a small and miscellaneous assortment of subjects under typical laboratory conditions. Others are concerned with the effects of different types of motivation upon such activities as the learning of nonsense syllables, or upon the ability to cross out the "a's" on a page of pied type, or upon the development of color discrimination. None of this—interesting though it may be—explains a student's incentives to master the content of any course. There is also a host of experiments on the strength of different stimuli in causing white rats to run through a maze more or less quickly. These experiments, while both sound and valuable, seem to me to shed even less light upon problems of motivation in college. Students are not white rats and they are not learning to run through a maze; nor can a teacher provide them with either food or electric shocks of any intensity whatever. Finally, there are a number of investigations that are relevant in their examination of possible stimuli, but the results are unfortunately negative. Since I do not trust unsupported opinions and since laboratory experiments with human beings or with rats seem to me quite irrelevant, I have had the greatest difficulty in getting information of value about what motivates John Smith, human and aged twenty, to learn chemistry well and French poorly. As a result, this chapter will be much shorter than the importance of the topic warrants.

The question of motivation has, unfortunately for the average teacher who wants practical suggestions, been treated mainly from a theoretical point of view. People have wanted to know what effect pleasure or pain had upon learning. They have consequently selected any kind of learning that was easily measured, have tried this or that pleasant or disagreeable stimulus, and have noted the results. Such experimentation has shown, for instance, what effect punishments of varying intensity have upon the speed with which one can tap a pencil against a desk. They have shown also what effect knowledge of one's progress has upon the ability to estimate the comparative length of lines. Other investigations indicate the effects of a successful response upon the learning of isolated words and the extent to which this pleasant result tends to spread to the learning of other words.[1] Indeed, the main objective of much of the research seems to have been the proving or disproving of the law of effect. Because of the largely theoretical approach the investigators have not bothered much about the possible relevancy of the learning situation to the reality of the schoolroom. One does not, therefore, know to what extent conclusions based upon the effect of an electric shock in learning a series of responses with a telegraphic key are true of the effects of sarcasm upon a freshman's ability to see through a problem in physics.

I. EXPERIMENTAL EVIDENCE

There have been some good experiments on motivation in elementary school. It has actually been proved that praise of a child's efforts will cause him to learn addition combinations faster than these same combinations will be learned by another

[1] E. L. Thorndike, *An Experimental Study of Rewards,* Bureau of Publications, Teachers College, 1933, 72 pp.

child of the same initial standing and ability who is blamed for his errors.[2] It is probable that this same situation holds true after the children become college students. It is even probable that the oftener a college student feels the warm glow of success, the faster he will progress—but this is only an assumption. Moreover, it is known that children will react to immaterial just as well as to material rewards.[3] Whether the college student is more or less practical is not known. School children are stimulated to greater effort than usual by the prospect of gaining some free time if they finish a task satisfactorily in less time than is needed by others.[4] From observation of college students it seems likely that they also find this situation an incentive to learning, but how effective a stimulus such free time may be has not yet been proved.

There are, to be sure, a few reports on the value of this or that form of motivation upon learning in college, but most of the results are negative. Knowledge of what kind of work a student is doing does not seem to encourage him to appreciably greater efforts than he makes without such information.[5] The exemption from examinations in return for good work has an effect upon those who are just below the exemption point, but it does not influence the progress of the group.[6] That is, if one excuses all those who have an A standing, there will be more B's than usual, but no more A's. The hope of getting into a fraternity motivated freshmen into obtaining better marks than those received by equally capable freshmen without

[2] E. B. Hurlock, "Evaluation of Certain Incentives Used in School Work," *Journal of Educational Psychology*, 16 : 145–49, 1925.

[3] C. L. Leuba, "Preliminary Experiment to Qualify an Incentive and Its Effects," *Journal of Abnormal and Social Psychology*, 25 : 275–88, 1930.

[4] G. Forlano, "School Learning with Various Methods of Practice and Rewards," *Teachers College Contributions to Education*, No. 688, 1936, 114 pp.

[5] C. C. Ross, "The Influence upon Achievement of a Knowledge of Progress," *Journal of Educational Psychology*, 24 : 609–19, 1933; and E. C. Deputy, "Knowledge of Success as a Motivating Influence in College Work," *Journal of Educational Research*, 20 : 327–34, 1929.

[6] C. W. White, "Effect of Exemption from Semester Examinations on the Distribution of School Marks," *School Review*, 39 : 293–99, 1931. See also H. H. Remmers, "Exemption from College Semester Examinations as a Condition of Learning," *Purdue Studies in Higher Education*, XXIII, Vol. 34, No. 3, 1933, 52 pp.

this stimulus, but from the time they were actually admitted
to the fraternity the marks made by these same men became
poorer than those in the control group of nonfraternity men.[7]
The holders of scholarships did somewhat better work, until
their last year, than was typical of nonscholarship students
having the same ability and the same initial standing. Of course,
this motive affects relatively few individuals and apparently
does not stimulate them for long.[8] None of the above-mentioned
types of motivation—so far as investigations to date have
shown—furnish much driving power for the average student.[9]

An interesting experiment [10] showed clearly that students usually work at a lower level than is necessary. A group of freshmen
who had been hazed steadily, day and night, for an entire "Hell
Week" were required—as their final task—to add columns of
figures of ten addends, from which all zeros and ones were
omitted. The freshmen began a new sheet of exercises each five
minutes for an hour; then after a ten minutes' rest, they worked
in similar fashion for another hour. The number of addition problems solved per five-minute period decreased only from 22 to 21
during the two hours, and the accuracy only from 85 to 83 per
cent. In spite of fatigue and the monotony of the task these freshmen did more work and were more accurate than a group of
juniors who performed the same experiment for a single hour
under no pressure.

Two types of stimulus have received careful consideration—
the choice of a vocation and the amount of interest in the subject. It would seem as if students should do good work in
courses they elect because of relation to vocational objectives.
Such has not, however, been the case. Two investigators [11]

[7] H. C. Lehman, "Motivation," *Journal of Applied Psychology,* 19: 9–28,
1935. See also A. C. Eurich, "Relation of Achievement between College
Fraternity and Non-Fraternity Groups," *School and Society,* 26: 624–30,
1937.
[8] A. B. Crawford, "The Effect of Scholarships," *Journal of Personnel
Research,* 4: 391–404, 1926.
[9] The best single reference for this whole subject of motivation in
college is probably A. B. Crawford, *Incentives to Study,* Yale University
Press, 1929, 94 pp.
[10] F. B. Knight and H. H. Remmers, "Fluctuations in Mental Productivity
When Motivation Is the Main Variable," *Journal of Applied Psychology,*
7: 209–23, 1923.
[11] N. B. Cunningham, "Student Grades in Required and Elective Courses,"

found no increase in the level of work done in courses taken for vocational reasons over that done by the same students in other classes. Indeed, there was in one instance [12] a negative relationship. The men students showed no change in performance after they began taking courses that led to their vocational objective, whereas the women did appreciably poorer work thereafter. It may be, of course, that many students select occupations for which they are unfitted and that they consequently are not able—in spite of presumably greater interest —to excel their own earlier averages. If the counselors finally succeed in their tremendous task of getting the majority of students headed for occupations for which they have both interest and ability the vocational motive may prove more powerful than it at present appears.

II. INTEREST

The matter of interest remains, and on this point there is quite an accumulation of evidence. Most people feel that interest is the chief motive in college work. Perhaps this general assumption is correct, but the results of investigation have thus far failed to prove it so. The usual method of procedure has been to obtain at the beginning of a course some statement from students concerning their degree of interest in the work and then to correlate this measure with the marks received. In five such investigations [13] the relationship was definitely low, the coefficient being no higher than .25. There are two obvious sources of error in these studies, however: the absence of any really good measure of interest and the tendency of interest

Pedagogical Seminary, 30: 389–92, 1923 and G. S. M. Zorbaugh and G. J. Kuder, "College Grades and the Vocational Motive," *School and Society,* 46: 62–64, 1937.

[12] E. G. Williamson, "Scholastic Motivation and the Choice of a Vocation," *School and Society,* 46: 353–57, 1937.

[13] J. M. Bridges and V. M. Dollinger, "The Correlation between Interest and Ability in College Courses," *Psychological Review,* 27: 308–14, 1920; D. Fryer, "Predicting Abilities from Interests," *Journal of Applied Psychology.* 11: 212–25, 1927; D. Fryer, "The Significance of Interest for Vocational Prognosis," *Mental Hygiene,* 8: 466–505, 1924; M. Meenes, "Comparison of Measures of Interests," *Journal of Applied Psychology,* 19: 85–92, 1935; R. S. Uhrbrock, "Interest as an Indication of Ability," *Journal of Applied Psychology,* 10: 487–501, 1926.

to change during a semester as a student continues with his classwork. Indeed, the measures of interest and those of achievement are both decidedly unreliable. The low relationship may therefore be only a result of correlating two inaccurate estimates. In one further investigation of this matter,[14] the relation of interest to achievement was high, but was clearly influenced by other factors than attitude. The students were asked to state which of all their courses in high school or college they had liked best and which they had liked least. The difference between the grades received in the two courses was large, but one has no way of knowing to what extent the retrospective estimate of interest was affected by the students' knowledge of their marks. They may have failed a course because they disliked it, or disliked it in retrospect more than they had in reality because they failed it.

One further study [15] provides a little more information about motives. In this case the students stated their reasons for electing certain courses. Those who took the work because they thought the content would help them in solving professional problems, or because they wanted to add to their store of knowledge in the subject, or because the course bore directly upon their main field of interest, did better—but not conspicuously better—work than those who elected the course because it came at a convenient hour, because some friend had suggested it, or because it gave three points' credit. There is again, however, one obvious source of error. At the low end of the interest measurement are only those who admit the casualness of their motives. No one knows how many of those who said they wanted to add to their knowledge really took the course for that purpose and how many thought this reason sounded well. Until some more accurate measure of interest than a student's own incidental statement is used, the real relation between interest and ability will not be known.

There is some evidence that the amount of interest necessary for success in a type of work is not so great as one might think. In recent years inquiries have been made into the

[14] B. O. Nemoitin, "Relation between Interest and Achievement," *Journal of Applied Psychology*, 16 : 59–69, 1932.
[15] D. H. Kulp, "The Role of Purpose in Achievement," *Journal of Applied Psychology*, 19 : 479–89, 1935.

attitude of successful adults toward their work.[16] An A rating on these scales reflects a great deal of enthusiasm, a B rating a moderate amount, and a C rating so little as to be almost indifference. Among the engineers tested 11 per cent received C ratings; among the teachers, 23 per cent; among insurance salesmen, 14 per cent; among accountants, 32 per cent; among office clerks 11 per cent. From these figures it would seem as if an absence of dislike were as much as was absolutely necessary for success, although one's subjective pleasure in one's work must be greater if the interest is on a higher level. One reason for the low relationship between interest and marks may be that once a student is over the "threshold" of enthusiasm he is sufficiently stimulated to pass his work; the grade he receives is, then, primarily a function of his ability and his previous preparation for the course.

It appears generally true that ability and interest do not have a high relationship. That is, people can do well things they do not enjoy and can do only poorly things that give them pleasure. Mathematically stated, the chances that ability can be predicted from interest are only 49 out of 100.[17] It may therefore be that students who elect a course because of real enthusiasm are just as likely to lack the ability as to have it. This situation seems to be one of the many contradictions in human nature. Anyone can think of friends or acquaintances who have genuine talents which they never bother to develop because they have no urge to do so, and of others with great interest in some field but no talent.

There are other types of motive that could be investigated but have not been. Perhaps there is a relationship between the marks obtained in a course and the degree to which the subject matter explains everyday problems, for instance. Or the attitude of a student toward his teacher may affect his work.

[16] E. K. Strong, *Manual of Vocational Interest Blank for Men,* Stanford University Press, 1936, and I. R. Berman, J. G. Darley, and D. G. Paterson, "Vocational Interest Scales" *Bulletin of the Employment Stabilization Research Institute,* University of Minnesota Press, 1934, Vol. 3, No. 5, 35 pp.
[17] D. Fryer, "Predicting Ability from Interest," *op. cit.;* see also K. Van Tuyl and A. C. Eurich, "Measuring the Interest of College Students with Different Major Subjects," *Journal of Applied Psychology,* 18 : 27–44, 1934.

Certainly, dislike of a teacher often seems to overshadow attitude toward subject matter in the production of poor work, although there is no actual data on this point. There is, however, a little evidence on the relation between liking a course and liking the teacher. In a total of 470 courses both teacher and subject were liked in 62 per cent of the cases and both disliked in 17 per cent—giving an agreement between attitude to the course and the teacher of 79 per cent.[18] It would thus seem that a favorable attitude toward the instructor increased the appeal of subject matter. Presumably the students did better work as a result, but there is no evidence to show whether or not this assumption is true. The prospect of being allowed to do special types of work after one has reached a given degree of excellence has not been adequately investigated as a motive. The gradual increase in the number of students who voluntarily read for honors suggests that this type of incentive is effective.[19] The relation between the preparation for a course and the interest in it is probably high, but no one knows how high. In short, most of the information teachers want is lacking. One is left essentially with one's own convictions as to what motivates students.

Other investigations of interest contain information that a college teacher might like to have. For instance, how much interest does a student need in order to obtain at least a minimum motivation? And what range of interests can one expect to find in college classes? Evidence on these points comes from extensive use of rating scales.[20] A total of 2,101 beginning students in chemistry rated their degree of interest in their work by marking from a long series the statement that best reflected their attitude. The opinions range from complete absorption in the subject to a violent distaste for it, as shown in

[18] S. M. Corey and G. S. Beery, "Effect of Teacher Popularity upon Attitude toward School Subjects," *Journal of Educational Psychology,* 29: 665–70, 1938.

[19] E. S. Jones, *Comprehensive Examinations in American Colleges,* The Macmillan Company, 1933, 436 pp.

[20] H. H. Remmers, A. D. Taylor, and K. E. Kintner, "Student Attitudes toward Basic College Courses," *Purdue Studies in Higher Education,* XXXI, Vol. 37, No. 4, 1936, pp. 145–76. This reference contains ratings on other courses as well as the data in chemistry.

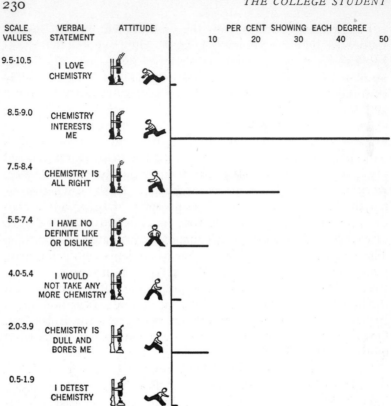

FIG. 24.—Degrees of Interest in Chemistry.

Based upon figures from Remmers, Taylor, and Kintner, *op. cit.* Used by permission of Purdue University.

Figure 24. It should be noted, however, that the majority of the students showed some degree of liking for this course and that only 12 per cent expressed a dislike. The amount of interest revealed by this group was clearly adequate for purposes of motivation—as far as merely passing college work is concerned—because very few of them failed. Since the ratings were anonymous one cannot tell what relation there may have been between interest and success.

Most of the evidence on human development shows that only a few desires and motives come from within. The majority are either derived entirely from the environment or are greatly influenced by environmental factors. Any experienced teacher has known students who were utterly purposeless at the beginning of a course but were subsequently stimulated by the material into great activity. Because attitudes are modifiable [21] and because adequate motivation is important, many of the experiments in college education have been essentially modifications of the environment in such a way that any native interests will be encouraged and new enthusiasms awakened. The entire programs of such colleges as Sarah Lawrence, Bennington, Bard, Stephens, or Black Mountain are applications of what is known and surmised about motivation. The idea is that, if one arranges an environment that is favorable to learning and stimulating to interest, any normal student will develop in a desirable way. These colleges are usually not trying to arouse one particular interest or even one particular type. A quotation from a college catalogue expresses the basic idea.

During registration the student guided by her registration adviser chooses the field (art, dance, drama, music, literature, social studies, science) in which she wishes to try out her interest and have her ability tested. This choice will automatically enroll her in what is called a trial major. It consists of individual work under guidance of the counselor in the field of her tentative choice, plus one or more introductory groups in that field. The two will approximate one-half of the student's working time. This is only an approximation. Schedules will vary and working time will change under the control of the counselor. When a student at entrance has a serious specialized interest and a desire to concentrate immediately, the trial major work may be enlarged in scope and character so as to include more of her time and effort. No student should divide her time between more than three different fields in any semester.

For both first-year and second-year students the trial major work, as the title implies, is a trial rather than a settled choice. If, during either of the first two years, a student's interest seriously turns to another field, she may apply to the Committee on Student Personnel for transfer to the appropriate trial major.

[21] See, for instance, D. Fryer, *Measurement of Interest,* Henry Holt and Company, 1931, 488 pp.

Such changes are frequently made, in accordance with the exploratory purpose of Junior Division work.[22]

Whether or not students learn more about subject matter under such conditions as those just described has not yet been proved, but at all events they should be able to find stimulation of interest in their environment.

As a further means of arousing enthusiasm and of appealing to those with a primarily practical mind, modern colleges are utilizing community resources more and more. For instance, students who have only a perfunctory interest in a course called "The Causes of Delinquency" may become quite entranced by visits to a juvenile court and subsequent talks with the children and social workers. Once this attitude is established, the desire to learn more about delinquents in order to understand particular children better soon urges a student into covering with interest the same material he would otherwise have covered without any real motivation.

The advisors in the modern college make special efforts to find out what students like to do and to think about outside the classroom and then to arrange a plan of work that will develop these already existing enthusiasms. To the best of their ability they break down any previous barriers between what goes on inside of class and out so that every spark of interest a student has can be brought to bear upon the business in hand. This idea has become so generally accepted that there are not many teachers left who would give a student a failing grade because he wrote poems for the school yearbook instead of the formal compositions that had been assigned.[23] Teachers of today, especially those in the experimental colleges, are supposed to look for interests and to use everything they can find.

In these various ways colleges are trying to develop greater motivation. Presumably a higher level of accomplishment will result, but even if it does not, the students should derive greater satisfaction from their college years and should develop

---

[22] *Bennington College Bulletin,* Vol. 8, No. 1, 1939, p. 12. Used by permission of the College.
[23] An actual instance.

an attitude toward their work that will allow them to go as far as their abilities permit.

III. SUMMARY

From the actual evidence that exists a few suggestions emerge. It is probable, although by no means proved, that praise for a student's small successes from day to day, adaptation of work to his interests, provision for use of the material outside of class, and the prospect of being allowed to do independent work upon the completion of the regular assignments will motivate the average undergraduate into doing his best. These motives are all directly connected with classwork and are perhaps effective because they are not appeals to anything extraneous to the learning situation. There is nothing new about any of these suggestions. Good teachers have always stimulated students in these ways. Perhaps all that is needed is a more conscious use of methods already sensed as effective.

One further point about interest as a motive might be kept in mind. Some of the articles on this subject have rather implied that a teacher should vary the content of his courses according to the interests of his students. With this implication I cannot agree. Interest is a powerful incentive and, as such, should be used for all it is worth, but not with a disregard of other possible factors in the situation. The inclusion of facts and principles in a course should depend upon what value they have—not upon their momentary appeal. In short, teachers *should teach worth-while material in a way that will interest students, but they should not try to teach only what is interesting.*

CHAPTER X

ARTICULATION AND PREPARATION

At the beginning of his college career a freshman's progress is affected by the extent to which his work articulates with what he has taken in high school and the degree to which he has in readiness the particular skills and understandings that his teachers will assume him to have. These problems are, of course, related, but they are sufficiently distinct for separate consideration. Both are important because they determine in large measure the start a student is able to make in his new environment.

I. PROBLEMS OF ARTICULATION

The relationship of high school and college was originally close because the former was thought of as being a preparation for the latter. The course of study was therefore so planned as to lay a good foundation for college subjects. By 1900, however, high schools began to have objectives of their own, and the courses that led toward college entrance were put into a curriculum by themselves for the benefit of such students as wished to pursue them. For a while this arrangement was satisfactory. As the pressure of numbers in the high schools became greater and as more and more pupils from the elementary levels continued into secondary education, the high school modified its program to fit the needs of its new pupil material. For about twenty years the articulation between high school and college was very poor because the colleges remained essentially conservative while the lower schools had been forced into a more progressive curriculum that was better adjusted to the needs of a boy or girl who did not go to college than to the needs of those who did.[1] Eventually the pressure of increased enrollments reached the colleges also and forced them into the same kind of curricular revision that had earlier been necessary in secondary school. At the present time secondary schools and colleges realize that their problems are much the same—the development of a type of higher education that will be adapted to the needs of boys and girls throughout their entire period of adolescence. Consequently they are beginning to work together again, and the articulation is in many places becoming distinctly better.

One can easily find evidences of poor articulation between the two levels of education. For instance, out of 517 colleges and universities [2] only a few reported any modification whatsoever of the work in various fields for those who had taken a largely duplicating course in high school. In chemistry 2 per cent of the institutions treated a student differently if he had had high school chemistry; for the languages and physics, 3 per cent made modifications; in mathematics, biology, and history, only 1 per cent did so. This wholesale disregard of high school work—regardless of its quality—forces thousands of students every year to repeat courses unnecessarily. The arrangement represents practically zero articulation. The same 517 institutions reported a number of ways in which they were trying to improve the situation. Unfortunately, the direct methods, such as providing the secondary schools with information

[1] For a good summary of high school developments see, "The Development of the Curriculum," *Sixth Yearbook of the Department of Superintendence*, National Education Association, 1928, 584 pp.

[2] P. R. Brammell, "Articulation of High School and College," *Office of Education Bulletin*, No. 17, 1933, 96 pp. See also H. R. Douglass, "The Relation of High School Preparation and Certain other Factors to Academic Success at the University of Oregon," *Oregon Studies in Education*, Vol. 3, No. 1, 1931, 61 pp. and D. Segel and M. M. Proffitt, "Some Factors in the Adjustment of College Students," *Office of Education Bulletin*, 1938, No. 12, 49 pp.; W. C. Eells, "Collegiate Success of Secondary School Graduates: a Report on One Phase of the Cooperative Study of Secondary School Standards," *Journal of the American Association of Collegiate Registrars*, 13: 285–302, 1938.

about college courses as guidance for the pupils, made up
only 21 per cent of all the suggestions.

Colleges and universities use the high school record primarily
as a form of educational currency, by means of which a freshman buys his way into higher education. There the matter
generally ends. The record is filed, and the main use thereafter
made of it is to determine which "group requirements" a
student has not yet met. The personnel officers, to be sure,
have learned to make good use of the record and of any comments made about a student by the high school principal or
teachers. Presumably a good deal more value could be derived
from the record than usually is.

A second kind of evidence comes from the analysis of the
textbooks most widely used in high school and college.[3] The
topics taken up are for the most part much the same, although
the treatment of them is somewhat fuller in the college books.
For instance, high school texts in chemistry contain an average
of 261 topics and 61 lines of print to a topic, while college
texts contain 306 and 90 lines.[4] It is a question, however, if
it is a valuable use of time for a student to take a largely
repetitive course in which matters are discussed in more detail
and on a slightly higher level instead of taking an entirely
new course. The evidence of just how much and just what
overlapping there is between a given college text and the books

[3] See, for instance, R. H. Bush, "Integrated Secondary Curriculum,"
Junior College Journal, 1 : 299–304, 1931 ; A. Cassell and E. Wolf, "Over-
lapping in Literature and Mathematics," *California Quarterly of Secondary
Education,* 6 : 322–26, 1931 ; T. Hunt, "Overlapping in High School and
College Again," *Journal of Educational Research,* 13 : 197–207, 1926 ; A. W.
Hurd, "High School Physics Makes Small Contribution to College Physics,"
School and Society, 31 : 468–70, 1930; L. V. Koos, "Overlapping in High
School and College," *Journal of Educational Research,* 11 : 322–36, 1925 ;
H. C. Mills, "Analysis of High School and College Courses in Elementary
Economics," *University of Buffalo Study,* 9 : 263–79, 1934, and his "Analysis
of High School and College Courses in Elementary History," *ibid.,* pp.
280–86; M. E. Sarbaugh, "Anticipating College Credit in English," *School
Review,* 44 : 100–18, 1936; W. J. Osburn, *Overlapping and Omissions in
Our Course of Study,* Public School Publishing Company, 1928, 167 pp. ;
W. E. Vaughan "Articulation in English between the High School and
College" : A Study of Freshman English in 21 State-Supported Southern
Higher Educational Institutions and of Senior English in Their Accredited
High-Schools, *Teachers College Contributions to Education,* No. 370, 1929,
76 pp.
[4] Koos, *op. cit.*

used in the secondary schools from which the students come can be collected by any intelligent person who wants to take the trouble. In fact, many more such studies should be made as a necessary basis for proper articulation of work.

Further evidence comes from an examination of the work done in college classes by those who have had similar courses in high school. In general, the work done in the first semester of a duplicating college course is somewhat better for those who have as compared to those who have not had previous contact with the field.[5] But even this advantage—usually small —disappears during the second semester. The most recent figures on this point show rather more influence of one course upon the other than is often the case. The per cent of students receiving each letter grade for the two semesters is given in Table 14.[6]

TABLE 14

Grades for Freshmen Who Had Had or Had Not Had Chemistry in High School

	First Semester						Second Semester					
	A	B	C	D	E	F		A	B	C	D	E	F
No chemistry in high school.......	2	16	28	23	9	38	} Per Cents {	2	10	12	19	8	12
Chemistry in high school...........	2	34	32	20	7	6		3	11	28	22	6	14

[5] See, for instance, W. J. Bray, "Achievement in General Chemistry as It Is Related to Certain Learning Abilities," *School Science and Mathematics,* 32: 19–29, 1932; C. A. Buehler, "The One College Chemistry Course for Freshmen," *Journal of Chemical Education,* 6: 510–12, 1929; I. D. Garard and T. B. Gates, "High School Chemistry and the Student's Record in College Chemistry," *Journal of Chemical Education,* 6: 514–16, 1929; G. A. Herrmann, "An Analysis of Freshman College Chemistry Grades with Reference to Previous Study of Chemistry," *Journal of Chemical Education,* 8: 1,376–85, 1931; *N. E. A. Research Bulletin,* "From High School to College," Vol. 16, No. 2, 1938, 122 pp.; M. E. Sarbaugh, "Articulation in English," *University of Buffalo Studies,* 11: 57–78, 1936; C. A. Smith, "High School Training and College Freshman Grades," *Journal of Educational Research,* 32: 401–9, 1939; L. E. Steiner, "Contribution of High School Chemistry toward Success in the College Chemistry Course," *Journal of Chemical Education,* 9: 530–37, 1932.

[6] From H. C. Mills, "Contribution of High School Chemistry to Elementary College Chemistry," *University of Buffalo Studies,* 9: 250–62, 1934. Used by permission of the University of Buffalo.

The greatest difference between the two groups appears in the failing grades for the first semester. Six times as large a proportion failed completely among those to whom chemistry was altogether new. There were also twice as many B's among students having previous contact with the subject. It seems probable, however, that the boredom from repetition frequently offsets the advantage of familiarity. In a number of the studies there is no difference in grade level between freshmen with and without a duplicating high school course.

This situation becomes more clearly inefficient when one tests the achievement of high school students with examinations that are used in the corresponding college courses. In one such investigation [7] high school students took a total of 726 final college tests in 27 courses and passed 60 per cent of them. Under ordinary circumstances if these students took any work in college along these lines they would have been obliged to repeat classes, the final examinations for which they could already pass. In all investigations of intelligence or reading ability unselected groups of college freshmen and of high school juniors or seniors show almost exactly the same range and nearly the same median.[8] If one were to compare the scores made by those who actually went on to college with the scores of freshmen already in college the difference would be extremely small.

One of the more pressing problems of the modern college is this one of adequate articulation. Until it is solved freshmen will continue to begin their college careers on either too high or too low a level. There is a necessary break in the life and habits of the high school senior when he becomes a college freshman because his environment alters in the direction of greater self-direction and responsibility. It would seem, however, as if his course of study might proceed with fewer malco-ordinations than the usual number.

Various state universities have initiated a more or less ade-

[7] H. C. Mills, "Contribution of Articulatory Examinations in Articulation of High School and College," *University of Buffalo Studies,* 11 : 5–36, 1936.

[8] M. E. Wagner and E. Strabel, "Comparison of the Ability of High School and College Students," *University of Buffalo Studies,* 9 : 51–57, 1934.

quate plan of co-operation with the high schools of the state. Generally these programs are directed toward the development between the two levels of a greater understanding of each other's problems and points of view. The steps thus far taken are for the most part only paving the way for some actual adjustments of a practical nature. Just what these will be is difficult to foretell, but most probably they will consist of (a) an agreement between high school and college teachers as to who will teach what, (b) a better adjustment of beginning college courses to the work done in high school, and (c) a placement of freshmen in college work on the basis of actual knowledge rather than of credits. The movement toward a better articulation has been especially strong in departments of English, probably because English composition comes close to being a universal requirement in colleges and therefore affects more students than any other class does. During the last ten years Ohio State, the University of Denver, and the University of Buffalo have taken the lead in the practice of excusing from the course freshmen who were already proficient and giving them full college credit.[9] Several institutions maintain a non-credit English course for those who are not yet ready to begin freshman college work.[10] If similar arrangements can be made in other departments, the number of maladjustments should be considerably reduced. An adequate program will take time and can hardly be initiated in a given institution until after both college and high school teachers have developed a more sympathetic grasp of each other's difficulties than most of them have at present.

II. THE PREPARATION OF COLLEGE FRESHMEN

The fundamental tools by means of which a freshman pursues the first stages of his college education are his skills in

[9] H. C. Mills, "Contribution of Articulatory Examinations in Articulation of High School and College," *op. cit.;* J. F. Fullerton, "A Proficiency Test in English Composition," *Journal of Higher Education,* 4: 33–34, 1933; E. K. Schuman, "A Letter," *Journal of Higher Education,* 4: 203, 1933.

[10] According to M. E. Sarbaugh ("Articulation in English," *University of Buffalo Studies,* 11 : 57–65, 1936) about 45 per cent of colleges have these subcollege courses and 60 per cent have sectioned their classes in freshman English on the basis of writing ability.

reading, in written English, in arithmetic and algebra, and his knowledge of several hundred elementary concepts in the fields of science, mathematics, social studies, and English grammar. Naturally, the needed assortment of skills and ideas differs from one course to another, but it is safe to guess that, at some time during his first two years, a student will need all these items of preparation. It is, of course, obvious that he does not need every fact and skill to which he has ever been exposed during his previous twelve years in school, but there is a certain nucleus that is of the utmost importance. The main problem of preparation is concerned with this essential core of skills and ideas, without which a freshman cannot prepare his assignments.

1. Determination of minimum essentials: The essentials that a student needs as preparation for his first year's work have been determined by a thoroughly objective technique. The method consists of four steps. The first (1) is an analysis of the most commonly used college texts in those subjects most frequently taken by freshmen. The subjects included in the results to be presented shortly are based upon a detailed analysis of elementary texts of the following subjects: English composition, foreign language grammars (German, French, Spanish, and Latin), mathematics (college algebra, solid geometry, and trigonometry), sciences (physics, chemistry, zoology, botany, geology, geography), and the social sciences (American and European history). In the course of this work every problem in the science and mathematics books was solved, and a count was kept to determine just how often a student in these subjects would need to divide a decimal, extract a square root, solve an algebraic equation, multiply common fractions, and so on. For all the language texts, frequency counts were made of every technical word—such as "preposition," "case," "perfect tense," and the like. In fact, the analysis included frequency counts of the special terms in every book in every subject. In addition, the history texts were studied to find out what geographical place names occurred with such frequency that ignorance of them would handicap a student's understanding of history. Every diagram, chart, map, table, and formula

was also listed, since these items present unusual reading difficulties. Finally, the textual material was all read consecutively
and classified, by half pages, as to its general type. In short,
the analysis determined in detail exactly what mathematical
operations a freshman would need, what background facts—
including technical words—he should know, and what types of
reading matter he should be able to understand. The results
of this investigation took the form of a long list of over ten
thousand items, for each of which the frequency of occurrence
was known. Many of these items appeared only once in all the
texts put together, and many more were used on an average
of only once per book in a given subject. On the other hand,
there were some that occurred as often as eight hundred times
per book. This list is an expression of the total possible preparation, plus much of the actual content of the courses. It does
not show the minimum essentials because these are snowed
under by a welter of other details.

It was obviously important to differentiate between the
preparation for and the actual content of college work. Many
items included on the lists in their original form were not
regarded by the textbook writers as matters of preparation.
It was therefore necessary (2) to check each item against the
texts to find out if it were adequately explained. Thus in a
physics text such words as "ampere," "velocity," "convection,"
and so on, are defined and discussed. If an item were thus
shown to be a part of the content of any course, it was simply
crossed off the list; if it were assumed as known, it was retained. This procedure reduced the length of the lists by
about 50 per cent.

The third step (3) was to boil down the list still further.
The total assortment of items was first grouped by putting
together those concerning the work of each department for
which the texts had been analyzed. The investigator then submitted the appropriate list to the members of each department
involved and asked them to mark each item as being essential
for the work of his freshman classes, as of secondary importance, or as unnecessary. Thus the professors of freshman
chemistry, physics, and mathematics gave their judgment as

to the need for each mathematical skill and each technical word; the language professors marked the list of grammatical terms; the history professors went over both the geographical background and the vocabulary; and so on. The lists given the professors did not contain the results of the frequency counts but did contain every relevant item, regardless of its frequency. The ratings from each department were then tabulated. For the most part the teachers agreed in their estimates as to what was or was not important, but there were in all cases a few items that showed a great divergence of opinion. These were further considered at departmental staff meetings until, eventually, the approximate value of each word or skill in the class-work of each freshman course had been determined. Indeed, there was the most painstaking attempt to obtain from college teachers their best judgment as to what points were of greatest value for the teaching they did in their classrooms. These opinions operated to reduce the length of the lists, because any items marked as unnecessary or even of only moderate value were eliminated.

Finally (4) the greatly shortened lists were considered in the light of what is known about the difficulties of freshmen in preparing their work. Some of this evidence came from the results of tests, some from daily observation of large numbers of failing freshmen who studied under supervision, and some from analyses of papers and compositions written by students. For instance, the original analysis showed that freshmen needed to know how to add a short column of three-place numbers. On the tests, nearly 100 per cent added such columns correctly. While this skill is necessary, it is so sure to have been mastered that there seemed little use in keeping it on the list, because its presence there would only obscure those items that were equally needed but known by smaller proportions of the student population. In the results to be presented shortly, only those facts or skills are included that were *proved by the original analysis to be necessary, are not usually explained in texts, are considered by college professors as essential, and are not known to more than 85 per cent of the average entering class.*

These items make up the minimal, essential, critical preparation for college.

The final list of items is not long. It includes approximately 325 technical words, over 100 place names, 25 skills in mathematics, and about 20 skills in written English, plus the ability to read the material in college texts at a rate and with a comprehension of at least tenth-grade level, a fair skill in reading such special materials as diagrams or maps, and a capacity to "see through" simple verbal problems. All of the items have been taught at some level of elementary or high school.

2. Mastery of the essentials: The results presented in this section are based upon tests given to entire freshman classes during "Freshman Week" at different colleges and universities. In all cases the number of students tested is adequate to be representative of the average situation. By using results from several places in different parts of the country it has been possible to obtain evidence of typical mastery in each of the fields previously studied.

The lists themselves appear in the Appendix. They are intended primarily for reference and not for consecutive reading, but there would be no sense in presenting them at all unless they were given in detail. Anyone who tries to "read" them, however, is almost certain to be bored, and any teacher of a single subject will find some of the data of no value to him. The precise information within his field will, however, be of use when he is preparing work for a class of freshmen.

(1) *Mathematics:* [11] The fundamental skills in arithmetic— aside from operations with whole numbers, addition and subtraction of decimals, and the finding of simple per cents when there is no remainder—are inadequately learned. The remaining skills can be demonstrated during "Freshman Week" by some per cent between 30 and 85. None of the necessary skills in either algebra or geometry were in a good enough state of repair to be shown by as many as 80 per cent of the freshmen. The situation in essential vocabulary was somewhat better. The entire original list of essential terms in arithmetic totals 116; in algreba, 58; and in

---

[11] See pages 597–601 for the lists of skills and concepts. The references on which these conclusions are based also appear there.

geometry, 96. The terms listed in the Appendix are those that were identified [12] by less than 85 per cent of the entering freshmen. There are 33 in arithmetic, 44 in algebra, and 54 in geometry.

The degree of mastery shown in either skills or vocabulary is distinctly below that needed for work in college sciences or mathematics. Part of the poor showing comes, of course, from too little recent use of mathematics, but even after this factor is discounted, the mastery is too low to be a safe foundation upon which to put college work of a nature that requires any mathematics at all. The moral is fairly clear. If students need more proficiency than is here revealed, the professor of the course in question should make provisions for developing it. How this is to be accomplished is the business of the department involved, but it has to be done if college work is to be kept on an appropriately high level.

(2) *Written English:* These results are based partly upon objective tests given during "Freshman Week" and partly upon error analyses of themes written by freshmen. The objective tests call, of course, only for recognition of a given usage; these results were therefore quoted only for those items that could not be derived from the papers. The students either intentionally or accidentally avoided writing sentences that required certain usages. Consequently it was impossible to tell what they might have done if they had attempted to employ them. The tests covered every needed skill systematically; when students did not volunteer a given usage, the test results were substituted for the error analysis. The list of skills will seem incomplete [13] because those on which the students made relatively few errors were eliminated from the original list of essentials.[14]

The total list contains 21 types of error, the majority of which are in sentence structure and punctuation—many of the latter probably being due to the existence of the former.

Since students are still making errors such as those listed, they will need a minimum technical vocabulary in order to understand

[12] The results quoted for all the vocabulary items in this section are based on objective tests that required only recognition of each term.

[13] The errors listed account, however, for over 85 per cent of all the mistakes on freshman themes. See, for instance, J. T. Seaton, "The Errors of College Freshmen in the Mechanics of English Composition," in *Research Adventures in University Teaching,* Public School Publishing Company, 1927, pp. 96–99.

[14] See pages 602–3 for the lists and references.

the nature of their mistakes and to correct them. The total vocabulary [15] necessary for this purpose contains 112 words. Of this number 37 were still unfamiliar to at least 85 per cent of the freshmen.

Clearly, many freshmen have not learned the elements of grammar. In recent years the trend of teaching written English in elementary and high school has been away from such formal items. Undoubtedly, in the past, grammar was overemphasized, largely on account of its supposed value in training the mind. In their efforts to offset earlier excesses, however, the public schools have perhaps swung too far in the direction of complete informality, with the result that students do not know how a sentence is constructed and therefore have understandable difficulties in either writing or revising sentences of their own. While one cannot recommend a return to formal discipline, it does seem absurd that children should practice writing from the fourth through the twelfth grades without finding out, for instance, that verbs have subjects and objects.

(3) *Foreign language:* The main type of preparation in this field consists of understanding grammatical concepts in English. The list of necessary words includes, of course, all those that have just been cited for English, plus some additional ones. In the interests of brevity the background for all languages is treated as a unit; actually, most of the words peculiar to a single language are items of content rather than of preparation.

The degree of mastery shown by freshmen in public institutions varied from 6 per cent who could recognize which of four English words was "inflected" to 93, 91, and 90 per cent who could identify which words were respectively in the masculine, feminine, and neuter gender. None of the other necessary words except these three were known by more than 77 per cent of those tested. This mastery is obviously insufficient to serve as a basis for a foreign language, unless the teacher intends to use a grammarless approach. In any case, one should not make the mistake of assuming as known the many special words that are emphatically not known, but should rather teach these words as an essential part of the course. The figures given in the Appendix include results from entire freshmen classes. Most students have already

---

[15] Any reader who is interested in this problem of technical vocabulary can find a report of the researches and the resulting lists for thirteen school subjects in L. Cole, *The Teacher's Word Book of Technical Vocabulary,* Public School Publishing Company, Bloomington, Illinois, 1940,

had at least two years of some foreign language; obviously, one cannot depend on the teaching in high school for the mastery of essential vocabulary.

(4) *History:* As far as available evidence shows, the preparation for reading a textbook in history consists of an adequate special vocabulary, a knowledge of geographical background, an ability to read maps and diagrams, and a speed and comprehension of historical matter not lower than that of the tenth grade.[16] Whatever information about history a freshman brings with him from his previous work in the subject is, of course, so much to the good, but if he is equipped to read his text intelligently he can, if necessary, obtain enough facts and ideas as he goes along to compete with other students.

The competition is not nearly so severe as one might expect, because the general level of preparation in both geography and history is low. A single sample of the general level is shown by results obtained from an entering class of 800 freshmen in one university.[17] The test used had norms for the various grades, by means of which the scores of the freshmen could be interpreted. In history, 59 per cent of the students scored below the average for the eighth grade, 33 per cent below that for the seventh, 12 per cent below that for the sixth, and 5 per cent below that for the fifth. In geography the showing was worse. Five per cent scored below the third grade average, 10 per cent below the fourth, 21 per cent below the fifth, 35 per cent below the sixth, 55 per cent below the seventh, and 76 per cent below the eighth grade norms.[18] With the preparation in the way of factual material so meager, it is no wonder that a student's readiness for history consists mainly of reading skills.

The original list of special terms in history contains 346 words. Learning in the grades and high school has reduced this total to 121 which are still unknown to 15 per cent or more of the freshmen. The geographical background is fairly adequate for American history but quite poor for European. In addition to a special vocabulary and geographical background a student needs a fair speed and comprehension in reading. Since, however, reading is

[16] For the lists and references see pp. 605–8.

[17] M. J. Van Wagenen, "The College Freshman's Range of Information in the Social Sciences," *School Review*, 35: 32–44, 1927.

[18] All percentages given in this paragraph are cumulative; they are not supposed to add up to 100.

an element in the preparation for many subjects it will be treated later on as a unit.

(5) *Sciences:* The section on previous preparation for the sciences is soon over, for the very simple reason that writers of college textbooks assume hardly anything to be known. Neither apparently do college teachers, as may be inferred from their almost universal habit of putting into the same class freshmen who have and have not had work in high school science. On the basis of the original analysis, the preparation for reading the science texts consisted of four parts. There was, first, the technical vocabulary. These words were, in almost every instance, explained in the texts; they are therefore part of the content and, as such, were eliminated. Second come the mathematical skills and concepts; these have already been presented. Third is the ability to read diagrams and schematic drawings; and finally the ability to read the text. These last two types of skill will be discussed in the section on reading. There remains, therefore, essentially nothing! To be sure, it helps a freshman if he brings with him the beginnings of a special vocabulary and an initial experience with the subject,[19] but the knowledge of technical words is generally so low that a good reader can compete on practically equal terms with those who have already had work in science before reaching college.[20]

(6) *Reading:* The average college text makes heavy demands upon reading skill. A freshman has to read not only textual material but also a variety of maps, graphs, drawings, tables, formulas, and problems. The material itself is harder than anything he has probably read before, and the assignments are longer. It is therefore not surprising to find students unable to read their books either well enough or fast enough. Adequate reading skill is so essential to progress in college that many places have established classes in remedial reading at the college level.[21] To some people the presence of such a class in an institution of higher learning is an insult—perhaps justifiably so, although that is not the point here. Experience in these classes has shown that im-

[19] See page 237.
[20] A few samples should illustrate this point sufficiently. The figure after each of the words in the following list indicates the per cent of freshmen who were able to recognize a correct definition of these terms: alloy, 57; adulteration, 57; combustion, 46; decomposition, 40; filter, 79; humidity, 81; inertia, 51; immunity, 76; molecule, 62; nutrition, 69; organic, 72; osmosis, 38; radiate, 64; vacuum, 85; velocity, 60.
[21] See the references on page 379.

provement in reading ability is almost always accompanied by
better grades in those courses for which reading is the chief type
of preparation.

The average degree of skill in reading [22] shown by unselected
freshmen is clearly not sufficient for the needs of college students.
While 82 per cent of them could get adequate meaning from a
narrative, less than 70 per cent understood typical samples of
other types of material—directions for experiments, descriptions
of processes or organisms, presentation of theories or laws, and
discussions of causal relationships. The ability to get new ideas
from diagrams or graphs was also inadequate. About 70 per cent
could "read" diagrammatic drawings, linear graphs, or maps, but
less than half understood a cross-section drawing. Those teachers
who use books full of diagrams should obviously give freshmen
some help in reading them. Only a few of the texts analyzed
contained any formulas or problems, but when these did occur
they presented great difficulty. Less than 45 per cent of the freshmen could match the correct verbal statement to even the simplest
formula and not even the easiest problem could be read by as
many as 85 per cent.[23]

As may be inferred from these results, freshmen are by no
means ready to read their textbooks,[24] no matter how much time
they are willing to invest in their work. They need to develop a
greater capacity for understanding the printed word than they
have at matriculation. In a later chapter there are some suggestions
for teaching students to read their texts; this matter is therefore
omitted here.

In addition to inadequate comprehension, freshmen show great
variability in rate. According to all investigators, those freshmen
who read most rapidly cover ground at three and one-half to five
times the speed of those who are slowest. An assignment that some
can prepare in an hour will therefore take others from three and
one-half to five hours.[25] The slowest readers progress at a rate
of two words per second and the fastest at a rate of 7 per second;
this difference permits the latter to read 18,000 more words an

[22] See pages 609–10 for both skills and references.
[23] "Read"—not solved.
[24] About one-tenth of an ordinary entering class scores below the average
for eighth-grade pupils. See page 259.
[25] See, for instance, E. M. Anderson, "Individual Differences in the Reading Abilities of College Students," *Journal of Educational Research,*
19: 309–10, 1929.

hour than the former.[26] Such wide variations emphasize again the need for the individualization of instruction.

III. ADJUSTMENTS TO FRESHMAN ABILITIES

It seems a particularly stupid waste of time to bemoan the low academic preparation of the average freshman class. The students are the product of their native ability, as modified by the amount and type of education they have received to date. As more and more people continue their education beyond high school, the average ability per class becomes less and the retention of previous schoolwork poorer. Until the last twenty or twenty-five years, colleges were able to influence to a considerable extent the curriculum of the high school and to a lesser degree that of the lower grades. It was tacitly assumed that the main objective of secondary education was to prepare for college those pupils who were capable of going on with their education. Any boy or girl who did not continue his study after graduation simply took the work intended primarily for those who did. This arrangement was pleasant for the colleges, and one can sympathize with them in their resentment at having it disturbed. The work of the high school was so hard and so relatively unrelated to an adolescent's daily life that it automatically eliminated those who were not well above average in both ability and scholarly interests. Within the last twenty years, however, the high school has changed both its objectives and its methods. It is now trying to educate as many adolescent boys and girls as possible, along whatever lines are most suitable for them, without respect to what colleges think or want. Most educators conceive of the first twelve years of school as being the period during which the members of the next generation are learning whatever facts, principles, skills, or habits will best fit them to live normal lives in an average American community. The curriculum is therefore based essentially upon the daily needs of ordinary people.

[26] I. A. Booker, "Measuring the Improvement of Silent Reading among College Freshmen," Doctor's Thesis, University of Chicago.

Although a high school may still have in its curriculum some classes whose names remain unchanged, the content of these courses has usually been greatly altered. Thus, there may be a class in "First-Year Latin," but when one investigates it one finds that it is concerned chiefly with showing children the relationship in word meanings and forms between Latin and English. At the end of an entire year the pupils may be unable to read a sentence in Latin or to recite a single declension. As a basis for college work in any language such a course is inadequate. As a means of enlarging the average pupil's vocabulary in his own language, it gives as good results as the traditional type of Latin class. The course is, then, doing what it is supposed to do; it is quite unfair to criticize it for not doing something else. Out of one hundred children entering the fifth grade, only seven will—according to available statistics—ever go to college,[27] but seventy-five of them will enter high school.[28] The curriculum is planned for the sixty-eight who will not go to college—not for the seven who will.

This arrangement, while in the interests of society, is by no means in the interest of scholarship. The situation can, however, be remedied—but not by an exchange of recriminations. There are at least four procedures that are productive of results. One (1) is for each department to determine for itself, on the basis of objective and unprejudiced research, exactly what essentials are necessary for beginning its work. It can then test its entering freshmen and exclude temporarily from membership in its classes those who are not yet ready. Many departments, notably English, have already done this, although the essentials are sometimes not so rigidly determined as they could be. By this method the college can make sure that students have the needed preparation, even if some freshmen have to lose a semester's credit in order to get it. Because most of those who go to college come from the upper third of the high school population, they usually have sufficient ability to remedy their inadequate preparation in a short time if the remedial work is centered upon essentials.

[27] J. H. Beard, "Mental Adjustment in College Students," *School and Society*, 32: 475–80, 1930.
[28] E. M. Foster, "School Survival Rates," *School Life*, 22: 13–14, 1936.

I happen to know one language department that has succeeded unusually well in solving the problem of inadequate preparation. On the first day of school the students in all beginning classes take a test, which calls for recognition, in English sentences, of the various necessary grammatical concepts.[29] On the next day each student receives a list of all the terms on which he was tested; those that he did not know are marked. The teacher hands out also some mimeographed pages, on which the entire number of terms is explained and illustrated. Item No. 10 on these pages corresponds to Item No. 10 on the student's list of terms, so that he need only look at the marked items to know what he should study and where he can find the explanation he needs. The instructor next tells the class that they will have three weeks in which to remedy any faults revealed by the test. Incidentally, the same test is used for selecting special groups of students for "fast" sections.

During the following three weeks the class time is spent upon pronunciation, vocabulary work, and the reading of simple sentences involving little or no grammar. On the appointed day, the students take a duplicate form of the test, each student filling in only those items he missed on the first form. Anyone who misses more than five items on his scond trial either drops the course or is put into a noncredit section. The first time the department tried this procedure a good many students had to be eliminated, but in subsequent years the number has become very small—never more than 1 per cent of the enrollment and usually less. Once the freshmen realized the department meant business there was no real trouble in remedying preparation in the three weeks allowed. This method pays excellent dividends in the more rapid progress of all classes and in the absence of the dragging weight teachers feel when their students are inadequately prepared.

In some places,[30] a second type of adjustment (2) has been made. Some proportion of the freshman class is asked to report three weeks early. During this time, before college opens, these students are helped both to remedy their defects and to learn good methods of study. The trouble with this plan is that the time is too short for remedial work along in more than one

[29] These concepts are approximately those listed on page 604.
[30] See, for instance, E. S. Jones, "A Preliminary Course on 'How to Study' for Freshmen Entering College," *School and Society*, 29: 702–5, 1929.

field, and the number of freshmen affected is too small. It would probably work very well if all pupils below the highest third of the high school graduating class were to be in residence for six weeks at least before the opening of the term. In colleges that have called in even a small number for a short time, the freshman mortality has decreased considerably [31] and the level of scholastic work has risen.

As a further method, to be used in conjunction with either of the above two, a college could (3) put out a brief bulletin that contained a precise list of all the basic skills, facts, and principles that a freshman needs for his first year's work at college. Every high school could be supplied with a sufficient number of copies, not only for the teachers but also for every pupil who has any idea of going to college. The better students will make intelligent use of such a manual [32] in getting themselves ready for their work. If the bulletin contained suggestions of where and how a pupil could find the books necessary for remedying any defects he found, many students would spend time during the summer before their entrance to college in making sure they were ready. Such a list of items, published with the approval and on the authority of colleges and universities, would also have a salutary effect upon those prospective freshmen who are unable or unwilling to prepare themselves. There are few things more discouraging than a long list of things one does not know but will shortly be expected to. Many potential failures would never come to college at all if they knew in advance what would be expected of them.

One somewhat less obvious type of adjustment (4) is being made by a few institutions that are introducing a formal stopping place at the end of the first two years of college.

[31] In the above instance, from 40 to 15 per cent.
[32] An individual attempt to formulate such a manual has already appeared. See, S. L. and L. C. Pressey, *Essential Preparation for College,* Farrar & Rinehart, Inc., 1932, 59 pp. The University of Buffalo already publishes outlines and syllabi for the guidance of high school students. (See H. C. Mills, "Anticipating College Work," *University of Buffalo Studies,* 9: 287–97, 1934.) A suggestion for similar guidance in English has appeared, M. Shackelford, "Shall We Change Entrance English?" *English Journal,* 14: 98–107, 1925.

The courses leading up to this level, for those that are not expecting to go further, are of the same type as those the pupils have been studying in high school. For much work, which is admittedly intended to produce an informed public rather than a group of scholars, the current level of preparation is not far from adequate. In short, a college can adjust its procedures to what the high school sends it, instead of trying to adjust adolescents to a type of training for which many of them were never intended by either nature or inclination.

IV. SUMMARY

If an institution really wants to do something constructive about these matters of articulation and preparation, it can, as soon as it learns to accept the inevitable. No one really likes to have the mental and emotional habits of a lifetime altered by circumstances. Those who are now professors received their own education in a period during which the college students were a far more highly selected group than they are at present. These teachers understandably are distressed by the presence of so many poorly prepared freshmen. However, time marches on, and no one thus far has had much luck in turning back the clock. In the course of time, college faculties will get over the shocks they have experienced during the recent period of increased enrollments and will bend their undoubted talents to the tasks of articulating beginning courses with the work done in high schools, of estimating freshmen as they are, of retraining those who are worth the trouble, of selecting the brilliant for special attention, and of devising some form of higher—if not highest—education for those who never will be anything more than average men or women. No one ever solved a problem either by pretending it was not there or by getting into an emotional state about it. The problems of articulation and preparation are already on the way to solution. The next ten years should see a much better relationship between secondary and higher education.

CHAPTER XI

STUDY METHODS

A student is by definition a person who studies. Most undergraduates are willing enough to go through the motions of studying, but the results are often not commensurate with the effort. One of the objectives mentioned in educational literature is the development of good habits of work during the college years. To some extent students will acquire reasonably good habits through mere experience and by their own efforts. That is, they learn to work by working. This sink-or-swim method has advantages in developing the moral fiber of those who swim, but it is obviously fatal to those who sink. Moreover, it is a wasteful and painful method of learning anything. With all that is known about good and poor techniques of study, it seems inexcusable for a college to let freshmen flounder about for weeks before they learn to study with whatever efficiency they may possess. Since good methods of work are an important outcome of a college education, it is only sensible to make sure that students acquire them as quickly as possible. If each instructor would conscientiously teach study methods along with his subject matter, the level of efficiency, especially during the first year, would rise appreciably, and the teacher would be better satisfied with the work of his classes.

I. STUDY HABITS OF COLLEGE STUDENTS

The first point to consider about the study methods of college students is the amount of time they spend in studying.

There have been many investigations. In some cases the results are based upon mere estimates, but in others they rest upon actual diaries kept from day to day by large numbers of students who recorded their time in fifteen-minute or half-hour intervals. The figures to be quoted presently have been compiled by combining results from several studies.[1] The facts are so consistent from one investigation to another as to suggest that the amounts indicated are close approximations to the actual time spent in most colleges. The average amount turns out to be 2.7 hours per week per credit hour. Since one of these hours is spent in class, the preparation must come to 1.7 hours. For a three-hour course, the total would be 5.1 study hours per week. The variation shown by different students and by different small groups is from 4.0 to 1.7 hours. Of the twenty-seven investigations [2] from which results

[1] A. Comstock, "Time and the College Girl," *School and Society,* 21: 326–27, 1925; H. L. Donovan and W. C. Jones, "Study Habits of College Students," *High School Quarterly,* 21: 61–62; P. D. Converse, "Time-Studies in the University," *Journal of Higher Education,* 2: 258–62, 1931; A. C. Eurich, "The Amount of Reading and Study among College Students," *School and Society,* 37: 102–4, 1933; J. R. Gerberich and C. Jones, "The Optional and Required Reading of College Students," *School and Society,* 38: 93–6, 1933; A. G. Goldsmith and C. C. Crawford, "How College Students Spend Their Time," *School and Society,* 27: 399–402, 1928; R. G. Hutchinson and M. H. Connard, "What's in a College Week?" *School and Society,* 24: 768–72, 1926; H. C. Martin, "How Students Spend Their Time," in *Research Adventures in University Teaching,* Public School Publishing Company, 1927, pp. 86–91; H. Moore and L. Graham, "Study of Freshman Distribution of Time," *School and Society,* 45: 336–38, 1927; K. H. Pollak, *et. al.,* "The Vassar College Time Survey," *Vassar Journal of Undergraduate Studies,* 1: 3–56, 1926; F. W. Reeves and J. D. Russell, "The Student's Working Load," *Journal of Higher Education,* 1: 85–90, 1930; E. H. Wilkins, *Report of Faculty-Student Committee on the Distribution of the Student's Time,* University of Chicago Press, 1925, 101 pp.; A. W. Shaw, and O. Parsons, *Methods of Study Used by College Students,* Western State Teachers College, Gunnison, Colorado, 1936; R. S. Uhrbrock, "The Freshman's Use of Time," *Journal of Higher Education,* 2: 137–43, 1931; N. A. Wade, "Comparison of the Time Spent by First-Year Students and Expected by Teachers in a State Normal School," *Journal of Educational Research,* 19: 183–87, 1929; J. D. Weinland, "How Successful College Students Study," *Journal of Educational Psychology,* 21: 521–26, 1930; F. L. Whitney and W. D. Armentrout, "The Total Load of Students," *Journal of Higher Education,* 3: 427–30, 1932; L. Jones and G. M. Ruch, "Achievements as Affected by the Amount of Time Spent in Study," *Twenty-seventh Yearbook of the National Society for the Study of Education,* Part II, 130–34, 1928.

[2] Many of the studies above listed included reports from more than one college or university.

were included, seventeen gave averages between 2.5 and 3.0 hours. Instructors commonly expect students to spend two hours in preparation for each class. The average time is thus a little short of this expectation. It is, however, not likely that longer assignments would bring about more study. The remaining hours of the day are already taken up with other activities that students would be loath to abandon. It is therefore probable that longer lessons would merely be less well prepared. One further point mentioned in some of the studies is the relation between the time spent on a course and the mark received. There seems to be no connection whatever. In fact, students in general do not fail work because they do not put enough time into their preparation, even though in individual cases this may of course be true. Nor do extra hours of work necessarily bring high grades.

A great deal is known about methods of study. In considering what is or what is not a "good" method of work, one has to forget one's own prejudices and individual methods of procedure. Nor is it enough to sit comfortably in an armchair and apply the "laws of learning" to absentee students. This procedure is neither sufficiently impersonal nor sufficiently related to reality. Perhaps the most objective definition of a good method of work is as follows: a method is good if a student who uses it gets appreciably better marks than those obtained by another student of the same ability who does not use it. An adequate experimental procedure for determining objectively which techniques are good and which are poor is neither difficult nor abstruse, although it is admittedly time-consuming and wearisome. An investigator first locates, by searching among the records, several pairs of students. The two members of each pair should both have the same level of intelligence, but one of them should be an A student while the other is failing in his academic work. Because of the relatively low relation between intelligence and grades, and the numerous individual exceptions to what trend there is, an investigator can find many such pairs. He then arranges for these students to do all their studying in groups of five or six in some room where they can be observed. Thereafter the investigator settles down to long weeks of observation with first one group and then another. He not only questions students about what they do and how they do it, but he watches them, day after day, until they have become so immune to his presence that they go about their work without embarrassment. With enough time and patience such an investigator can study the methods of a sufficiently large number of students to get reliable results.

The methods used almost automatically classify themselves into the following types: first come those that are used by everyone; second are those that are used by no one—even though some of these latter are recommended in books on study. The methods in these two classes are neither good nor bad. They are merely irrelevant—and they will become neither better nor worse by being commended or disparaged by teachers. In the third class are those methods used by appreciably more A than E students; these are good. Finally come those used by an excess of E over A students; these are bad.

The results to be presented below are based upon three such studies as that just described, plus some additions from other and less rigidly objective investigations.[3] By combining results from all sources one can arrive at a fair idea of what methods are of real value to a college student.

The specific habits used by good and not by poor students are listed in Table 15.

[3] J. A. Charters, "Methods of Study Used by College Women," *Journal of Educational Research,* 10: 344–55, 1924, and "How 258 Junior College Women Study," *Journal of Educational Research,* 11: 41–48, 1925; H. R. Douglass and H. C. Bauer, "The Study Practices of 395 High School Pupils," *Journal of Educational Psychology,* 29: 36–43, 1938; A. C. Eurich, "Analysis of Self-Ratings on Studiousness Traits," *Journal of Applied Psychology,* 14: 577–91, 1930; L. C. Pressey, "Problems of Study," in *Research Adventures in University Teaching,* Public School Publishing Company, 1927, pp. 4–21, and an unpublished study of the author's; C. C. Ross and N. M. Klise, "Effective Study Procedures," *University of Southern California Education Series,* No. 8, 1927, 117 pp.; J. D. Weinland, "How Successful College Students Study," *Journal of Educational Psychology,* 21: 521–26, 1930.

TABLE 15
Habits Typical of Good Students

A. Items concerning the study environment
  1. Usually studies in the same place
  2. Has a daily plan of work
  3. Keeps regular hours of study
  4. Keeps desk clear of things not concerned with study
  5. Does not smoke while studying
  6. Avoids distraction, especially people who talk
  7. Studies alone
B. Behavior in class
  1. Observes methods and personality of instructor
  2. Asks about what is not clear
  3. Takes notes only when necessary
  4. Listens carefully
C. Note taking
  1. Takes fairly full notes
  2. Keeps notes on each subject together
  3. Takes notes in roughly outline form
  4. Rarely rewrites notes
D. Reading
  1. Skims new chapter and looks at summary before reading chapter in detail
  2. Looks up new words in the dictionary
  3. Stops from time to time to think over what has been read
  4. Recites each section to himself and then rereads any forgotten parts
  5. Distributes memorizing over several short practice periods
E. Reviews and examinations
  1. Reviews mainly those items not already known
  2. Organizes the entire course in outline or other condensed form
  3. Gets plenty of sleep during examination week
  4. At time of examination reads over all questions before answering any of them
F. General attitudes
  1. Keeps preparation up to date by studying each day
  2. Tries to analyze weaknesses and correct them
  3. Uses what is learned in class as often as possible outside of class
  4. Spreads out work on term reports over the whole term
  5. Uses material from one class to help in another

Since most of these habits can be learned by a person of average intelligence, one can reasonably expect a poor student to become as good as his ability will allow if he learns to use techniques known to be good. A teacher can help in this process by giving assignments that will call for the use of desirable habits.

II. HELPING STUDENTS TO STUDY MORE EFFECTIVELY

A college teacher may feel that teaching students to study is not part of his job because they should know how before they enter college. They certainly should, but the fact is that many of them do not. Until they achieve at least a moderate degree of efficiency they will waste not only their own time but that of their teacher and their classmates. It is therefore desirable that an instructor should do what he can to improve the study methods of his students. Naturally he cannot stand over them and make them use one technique rather than another—even if this were profitable—and there are some items of procedure to which he cannot contribute much if anything. On the other hand there are certain matters that are more or less under his control. As he proceeds with his regular work from day to day he can contribute a good deal to the development of good study habits by introducing a word of advice here and there or by modifying his own presentation. The following discussion covers only such points as frequently need emphasis and normally come under the control of the teacher. It is not my purpose to write a systematic manual of study methods [4] but merely to indicate some of the ways in which the average teacher of any subject can contribute to the efficiency of his students without any great inconvenience to himself.

1. Reading the textbook. It is not safe to assume that college freshmen can "read." Indeed, about a tenth of them cannot read with more efficiency than the average eighth-grade child.[5]

[4] See footnote, page 269.
[5] Thus, one typical group of fifty-one students, who scored in the lowest decile of the Iowa Qualifying Examination (A. C. Lemon, "An Experimental Study of Guidance and Placement in the Lowest Decile of the Iowa Qualifying Examination, 1925," *University of Iowa Studies in Education,* 1927), showed the following degrees of mastery along these lines:

Average Scores

Reading comprehension ....11th grade
Reading speed .... 6th grade
Reading vocabulary .... 9th grade
English composition .... 7th grade

The materials assigned—whether limited to a single text or scattered through a number of references—make heavy demands upon both speed and comprehension. Moreover, technical books in any field have their characteristic difficulties, most of which are ascribable to the nature of the material rather than to the idiosyncrasies of the author. These peculiarities mean trouble for the student.

Texts in the social sciences, for instance, are usually long, and some of them are extremely discursive. They contain a large assortment of ideas drawn from various areas of human activity and not always too well co-ordinated. Too often these books are decidedly hybrid in style. It is still a tradition that such texts should have a semiliterary flavor; in some cases an author has succeeded in being both a social scientist and a man of letters, but in others the basic material is obscured by literary flourishes which provide reading difficulties for students by saying in polysyllables what could be better said in simple Anglo-Saxon. Textbooks in the natural sciences are generally so loaded down with facts and more facts that a coherent view of the subject is difficult. From the first page, the student is lost in a welter of detail that is too confusing for him to synthesize alone. Moreover, some of them are dry beyond the point of human tolerance, having in fact all the disjointed effect of a Sears, Roebuck catalogue without the human interest. Books in both the social and the natural sciences contain diagrams, charts, maps, and schematic drawings. All of these present such special problems in reading that many students skip them altogether. In the languages there are other difficulties, wholly aside from any actual training in the language. One cannot "read" a list of vocabulary words by any technique useful for cursive material. The explanations of grammatical points are often too short and not adequately illustrated. The special terms used in the explanations are not numerous but they are essential—and, as already pointed out, not more than half the freshmen will know them. The situation in mathematics is even worse. What reading there is appears in the most condensed form. The explanations are sometimes brief to the point of obscurity; the main effect upon the student is the conviction that most of the connecting links have somehow been omitted. Nor is the situation improved any by the insertion of formulas, and other expressions involving symbols, or numbers, or both. The eye movements needed to read problems, numbers, or formulas are totally different in rhythm, pattern, length, and number from those required by print. In fact, such types of reading material call for special skills that many students simply do not possess. In certain of the less well-established subjects, of which education is unfortunately an example, the ratio between words and ideas is altogether too high. The resulting repetition is confusing and merely obscures the ideas that are undeniably lurking behind the verbosity.

In addition to the special characteristics of various textbooks in each subject there is one problem common to all. In any subject there is a technical vocabulary, the essential terms of which must be mastered before a student can read the book with any likelihood of success.[6]

An instructor should, then, assume that beginning students in any field will be unprepared to read the text. Teachers in the elementary and high schools are concerned with preparing children for everyday living, not with getting them ready for college. A textbook in college botany, for instance, is a highly specialized type of reading matter. It would be a waste of time for the majority of high school pupils if teachers were to try to teach the reading of such materials. The public schools are busy teaching those skills and facts that no citizen in a democracy can get along without. The reading of cross-section diagrams of tree trunks, of formulas showing the interrelation of volume, pressure, and density, or of such phases as "terminal moraine," "inversely proportional," or "imperfect subjunctive" are not among these essentials. Since they are, however, necessary for college work, they have to be learned there—and they will be better learned if they are specifically taught.

2. Note taking: just what notes should be taken and in just what form depends upon the nature of the subject matter and upon the type of assignments used. The notes a student gets into his notebook, whether from classwork or reading, are of great importance in conditioning his work. Some years ago a certain professor[7] compared the ideas in his students'

---

[6] For material concerning the mastery of technical vocabulary in various fields, see pages 599–601 and 603–6.

[7] C. C. Crawford, "The Correlation between College Lecture Notes and

notes with those upon their quiz papers. The agreement was
not only high in general but extended even to specific facts.
To be sure, not all the ideas in the notebooks got into the
quiz papers, but almost nothing found its way into the quiz
that had not been in the notes first. The same investigator
found that the taking of notes improved the recall of lectures
after a week's time, although it did not increase the immediate
recall appreciably.[8] Further evidence of the value of good notes
has been given in the report of the study habits of successful
students.

Such instruction as a college teacher can give is usually
incidental, but from time to time he can develop certain general
principles of note taking, especially in interviews with those
students who have a tendency to write frantically from the
beginning of an hour to the end or to reproduce in written
work practically whole sections of material from the books
they read without the alteration of even the examples. In many
classes the students sooner or later have occasion to hand in
their notes on a reading assignment. A teacher almost automatically discovers what deficiencies his students have and can,
with a little extra effort, help them to improve. Some teachers
of freshman groups post on a class bulletin board or make
otherwise available two or three good sets of notes that show
desirable types and amounts of organization and condensation.
Students are so dependent upon what goes into their notebooks that an instructor cannot afford to let them take notes
badly, especially when the great majority of them can learn,
with a little help, how to do this particular academic chore
reasonably well.

3. *Reviewing:* One of the outstanding faults of students is
their failure to review either often enough or well enough. As a
result they forget far too great a proportion of what they have
learned. A teacher can do much to stimulate regular reviewing
by using a few unannounced quizzes for which only systematic
reviewing will keep one ready. The student mind seems to be

Quiz Papers," and "Some Experimental Studies of the Results of College
Note Taking," *Journal of Educational Research,* 12 : 282–91, 379–86, 1925.
    [8] C. C. Crawford, "Some Experimental Studies of the Results of College
Note Taking," *Journal of Educational Research,* 12 : 379–86, 1925.

constructed on the principle that it will not attend to that which the instructor neglects. Students will review regularly if a teacher gives them any good reason for doing so; otherwise most of them will not. A second weakness of the unsuccessful student is his method of procedure when he does review his work. If he spends ten hours he usually spreads it evenly over all the material of the course, without respect to his mastery of the various parts. Selective reviewing seems obvious enough to most teachers, but many freshmen have evidently never been shown how to do it and consequently do not use their time as effectively as they could.

Most teachers make some provision for a review of an entire course before the final examination. An instructor's best contribution at this point is, I think, the assignment of some type of work that will require a synthesis of the main facts and ideas which have been discussed. The exact nature of such a summary depends, of course, upon the material. The real essential is that it should call for a thorough review of the entire course in such a way as to make the students organize the details, find the main ideas, and isolate their own weaknesses. This matter is so important that it seems worth while to insert an example (Table 16, page 264). This particular one shows a section of work in elementary chemistry; the student has underlined the facts he did not know and has thus isolated the points he needs especially to study.

4. Memorizing: The amount of memorizing varies greatly from one course to another. When verbatim learning is necessary, however, a teacher should expect to help students by showing them the most efficient ways of going about this work. Poor methods produce such inferior mastery that the work of a course is seriously handicapped. In self-defense, therefore, a teacher should be willing to give what aid he can.

The first point on which students need assistance, especially at the beginning, is in deciding what to memorize. Many of them spend hours in learning word-for-word many things that are much better learned by association. In his early assignments an instructor can indicate what, if anything, should be memorized. In almost any course there are some things that

TABLE 16
A Review Chart
CHEMISTRY

	Oxygen	Hydrogen	Nitrogen
Discoverer	Priestley 1774	Cavendish 1778	Rutherford 1772
Occurrence	21 of oxygen to 100 of dry air.	Small amount in air, in water, and in all living organisms. 10 per cent of human body in combination with carbon.	Dry air is 78 parts nitrogen. It occurs in all living organisms.
Preparation	1. From mercuric oxide. 2. From potassium chlorate 400°. 3. Commercial preparation decomposition of water by electricity. Both O and H obtained.	1. By action of metals on water. $2Na + H_2O = H + 2NaOH$ at ordinary temperature $2Fe + 3H_2O = 6H + Fe_2O$ with steam. 2. Action on metals, on acids. $Zn + H_2SO_4 = ZnSO_4 + 2H$ 3. Commercial preparation electrolysis.	1. From air decompose air by combining O with Cu. 2. From compounds $NH_4\ NO_2 = 2H_2O + N$
Properties	Gas Colorless, tasteless, odorless. 1 liter weighs 1.4290 grams at O° and 1 atmosphere of pressure slightly soluble in water liquid oxygen boils at −182.7° and freezes at −235°.	Gas Colorless, tasteless, odorless. Lightest substance, 1 liter weighing 0.08987 grams. Liquid hydrogen boils at −252.7° melts at −259°	Gas Colorless, tasteless, odorless. 1 liter weighs 1.25079 Insoluble in H_2O Liquid boiling point −194° freezes at −210.5°
Chemical conduct	Not very active at low temperature. Very active at high temperature. Oxidation — union of substance with oxygen. Oxides — any compound of oxygen and another element. Combustion — oxidation accompanied by light. Heat of oxidation — very slow but equal to combustion. Spontaneous combustion.	Not active at ordinary temperature. At high temperature hydrogen explodes. Does not support combustion. Reduction — process of withdrawing oxygen from a compound. Opposite of oxidation. $CuO + 2H = H_2O + Cu$	Very inactive at ordinary temperature. At high temperature it combines partly. Assimilated by plants. Legumes: clover, alfalfa, beans get nitrogen from air and deposit it in soil.

are most efficiently acquired verbatim. The various periods of geology, the table of valences in chemistry, a series of significant dates in history, or the names of authors and their chief writings in any period of literature are all things that one can learn either by remembering them on purpose or by waiting for them to dawn gradually as the year rolls on. Because teachers—being adults—often shy away from memorizing, and because they do not like parrotlike repetition, they often discourage verbatim learning in the places in which it is efficient.

The second point about memorizing is to learn material in the way in which it will be used. Textbooks, because they are summaries, are prone to present items in the form of a list. The only items one should ever learn in this form are those that will subsequently be used as lists. Since almost nothing is actually used in this way, the form of presentation is definitely bad and encourages students to learn facts in a setting from which they must be torn before they are of service to him.

The elementary schools found out a long time ago that the child who had memorized the multiplication table for "6's," and then wanted to multiply 46 by 8, had to recite the table to himself until he reached 8 times 6 before he could even get started on his problem. Since the number facts are used in isolation, not in a series, children no longer learn these items in any relation at all to each other. In grammars, however, one still finds paradigms (which are, of course, useful in showing the relationship between forms) and long vocabulary lists. Of the two, the second is the more objectionable. For instance, in learning the list below by the usual method of reading it through from top to bottom, one makes just as many associations between "the day" and "le cheval" as between "le jour" and "the day," although the wrong associations are not as strong as the right because the learner's attention is not upon them.

le jour—the day	*la chaise*—the chair
le cheval—the horse	*la chambre*—the room
la fille—the daughter	*la plume*—the pen
le papier—the paper	*le ciel*—the sky

All incorrect associations, even though relatively faint, are not merely unnecessary; they are definitely bad. Moreover, words are often associated with their position in a list, especially by a person who visualizes readily. Thus *la chaise* is associated not only with both "the chair" and "the paper," but also with its position in the middle of the list. As a result of all of these harmful associations most people learn such a list both slowly and poorly. Language teachers know this fact well enough and some of them try to substitute the learning of words in context for the memorizing of lists. The great difficulty with this technique is that, except for a few constantly recurring words, the students do not get enough drill; the great majority of the words are underlearned and then promptly forgotten. Moreover, there are numerous irrelevant associations to handicap the person who tries to acquire a vocabulary by this means. Many beginners in a language are in the same condition as the small child who complained to me that she always knew the word "porridge" in the story of Goldilocks but never knew it anywhere else! The only object in learning a word is to know it the next time one sees it, regardless of its context. For this purpose it is more efficient to learn words in isolation than with any irrelevant associations whatever.[9]

Although language books are perhaps the worst offenders when it comes to presenting material so that students are encouraged to learn it with as many unnecessary associations as possible, other texts fall into the same error from time to time. For instance most texts in physiology list the cranial nerves, their points of origin, their course, their termination, and their function in a series, although no one is likely to use them that way. In fact, almost every textbook presents more or less often a list of disparate items, thus giving a student a chance to learn them in as useless a way as he can.[10]

It remains to say a word about the effective spacing of repetitions when one is memorizing. The main point rests upon ordinary common sense—namely, that such work should be

[9] For experimental results on this topic, see L. C. Seibert, "An Experiment on the Relative Efficiency of Studying French Vocabulary in Associated Pairs Versus Studying French Vocabulary in Context," *Journal of Educational Psychology,* 21 : 297–314, 1930.

[10] The student's main problem in memorizing material from textbooks consists of breaking into units items that should not have been joined together. The simplest way is to make a card catalogue. If, for instance, a student is to learn the valence of each element, he can do so with the least number of interfering habits if he will first write each symbol with its valence on a small card. Then he should read the cards through, shuffle

done a little at a time over several days. A teacher cannot, of course, stand over students and make sure that they spread out their repetitions, but he can contribute the information that such spacing is desirable, and he can make assignments involving memory far enough ahead of time to permit spacing.

5. *Analysis of error:* Sometimes a student is fortunate enough to make a faultless first reaction to a new situation, but usually he learns by making and correcting errors. Almost any mistake is worth making if by so doing one learns not to repeat it. The trouble arises when a student makes an error and does not recognize it as one. Under such circumstances the error will perpetuate itself, becoming more and more firmly established as time goes on. It is therefore necessary that a teacher analyze work constantly, so as to correct errors before they have had time to be ground in by repetition. An error is not a mere absence of correctness. It is a reaction that is just as positive and persistent as a right answer. Nor does a correct response have any native advantage over a mistake. Unless the consequences are unpleasant, the human nervous system is quite as well satisfied with one as with the other. If an error is not detected by either student or teacher, it will continue to function.

Errors are not all equally important. In most cases there are a few "key" difficulties upon which the other mistakes are heaped in a somewhat disorderly confusion. To the student one error looks like another, but a teacher should not be so naïve. The following story is a case in point.

One day a girl brought me a composition that had been corrected and returned. On the two pages that it occupied there was a total of 127 corrections. I could not get any coherent picture from such

them to break up chance connections between any two successive cards, read them again and shuffle them again, until he feels that he knows some of them. At this point he should test himself, sorting the cards into two piles —those he knows in one and those he does not know in another. The latter he continues to study, stopping from time to time for an attempt at recall and adding any new acquisitions to the pile of cards already learned. By this method a student puts all his time on the things he does not yet know, and if he constantly shuffles his cards he never makes unnecessary associations. Since he will want to use the facts about valence as independent units, it is most uneconomical for him ever to let them get connected in an alphabetical or other series.

a complete mess, so I tabulated the errors according to type. Out of the 127 mistakes, 92 came from wrong punctuation. There were no errors of capitalization or grammar. Two sentences were incomplete, 19 were far too long and involved, 8 contained wrong references, and 6 lacked parallelism. This girl had another composition to write at once. I told her to go to work on it, but to concentrate on the avoidance of a single error—the long, loose-jointed sentences. In fact, I was so sure from the analysis that her key mistake was mere length that I instructed her to use not over fifteen words per sentence. She promised to keep within this limit and went into an adjoining laboratory. I did not see the finished product, but I know she went directly to class where she handed in her work, and I know she got no help from anyone. The total length of this second composition was about twenty words more than the first, but when it came back there were only eight errors— one incomplete sentence, three errors in spelling, and four unnecessary commas. All of the mistakes the girl had made earlier had been pyramided upon the single error of trying to write sentences that were too long. Naturally, this girl still needed to learn how to write sentences that were of greater length than fifteen words, but the situation was much clarified for all concerned by this isolation of the key difficulty.

As students get older, they should of course take over the analysis of their own errors in so far as they can. The habit of analysis is—like any other habit—contagious. If a teacher looks for mistakes and makes diagnoses, the students are not long in making what analyses they can. Although not too much transfer of training can be expected, a teacher can hope to build up a general habit of objective self-analysis that may, and often will, carry over into other subjects and into activities outside the classroom.

III. SUMMARY

A student's native ability is not alterable in any real measure, but his habits of work are subject to change without notice. It is unreasonable to expect that students will discover efficient methods for themselves or that they will arrive at college with such methods already developed. Since it takes a trained investigator a minimum of six months of research to find out what is and what is not a good study habit, one can hardly expect freshmen to evolve these habits out of their own inner consciousness.[11] Even though some students will eventually discover by themselves how to study effectively, they will almost certainly waste a great deal of their own and their instructors' time during the process. The really essential habits are not numerous or particularly difficult. If these few are adequately established, other and less vital methods will soon be added, usually on a student's own initiative. A college teacher is not supposed to "spoon-feed" his students, but he is supposed to help them provide themselves with the tools they need for getting an education.[12]

[11] If students ask about manuals on methods of study an instructor can conscientiously recommend any one of the six given here: A. W. Kornhauser, *How to Study,* University of Chicago Press, 1924, 43 pp.; L. Cole and J. M. Ferguson, *Students' Guide to Efficient Study,* Farrar & Rinehart, Inc., 1935, 38 pp.; N. Fenton, *Self-Direction and Adjustment,* World Book Company, 1926, 122 pp.; R. A. Brotemarkle, *How to Study,* University of Pennsylvania Press, 1928, 15 pp.; C. G. Wrenn, *Practical Study Aids,* Stanford University Press, 1931, 16 pp.; and M. G. Rigg, *Making Good in College,* Thomas Nelson & Sons, 1939, 55 pp.

[12] Sometimes a teacher wants to investigate the study habits of a group of freshmen. In this situation he can make use of a simple questionnaire such as that given below. The questions cover those habits of work that are most crucial and most likely to be neglected by freshmen. The answers to the questions are so arranged that the further a mark is to the right the less established is the method of work.

Directions: Answer the questions below by drawing a line under the word that gives the correct answer.

1. How regularly do you have a plan of work for each day?
   always   often   sometimes   seldom   never

2. If so, how closely do you stick to it?
   always   seldom   sometimes   often   never

3. How often are your study hours interrupted?
   never   seldom   sometimes   often   very often

4. How often, when you are reading an assignment and come to a word you do not know, do you look it up in the dictionary?
   always   seldom   sometimes   often   never

5. How often do you make a preliminary survey of a chapter before reading it in detail?
   always   often   sometimes   seldom   never

6. How often do you skip the tables and graphs that you find in your books?
   never   seldom   sometimes   often   always

7. How often do you have trouble in understanding graphs or tables?
   never   seldom   sometimes   often   very often

8. How often do you make original graphs or tables to summarize your own work?
   very often   often   sometimes   seldom   never

9. After reading your lesson through once, how often do you recite to yourself to see how much you remember?
   always   often   sometimes   seldom   never

10. How often do you read the summary of a chapter before reading the chapter itself?
    always   often   sometimes   seldom   never

11. How often do you read through the paragraph headings of a chapter before starting to read the main text of the chapter?
    always   often   sometimes   seldom   **never**

12. How often do you take your reading notes in outline form?
    always   often   sometimes   seldom   **never**

13. How often do you take your lecture notes in outline form?
    always   often   sometimes   seldom   never

14. How often do you take notes on the backs of envelopes, or on loose sheets of paper that you happen to have with you, instead of in your notebook?
    never   seldom   sometimes   often   very often

15. How often do you get to class without your notebook, or other equipment that is needed during the hour?
    never   seldom   sometimes   often   very often

16. How often do you have difficulty in expressing yourself in writing?
    never   seldom   sometimes   often   always

17. About how much time do you spend each week reviewing each subject?
    3 hours   2 hours   1 hour   ½ hour   none

18. How often do you try to analyze your difficulties to find out your own weak points?
    always   often   sometimes   seldom   never

19. How often do you get excited over examinations?
    never   seldom   sometimes   often   very often

20. If an examination is given without announcement, how often do you fail?
    never   seldom   sometimes   often   very often

21. If you do not fail an unannounced examination, how often do you get a poor mark?
    never   seldom   sometimes   often   very often

22. How late do you usually sit up preparing for an examination?
    11 o'clock   12 o'clock   1 o'clock   2 o'clock   almost
                                                           all night

23. How often do you do most of your reviewing for a course the night before the final?
    never   seldom   sometimes   often   always

24. How often do you try consciously to associate the ideas of a chapter with those you already know?
    always   often   sometimes   seldom   never

25. How often does what you learn in one class help you in some other class?
    very often   often   sometimes   seldom   never

26. How often do you try to memorize the exact words of a text in preparing for an examination?
    never   seldom   sometimes   often   always

27. How often do you try to memorize the exact words of a text in preparing for your daily assignments?

    never   seldom   sometimes   often   always

28. How often in class do you take notes just about as fast as you can write during most of the hour?

    never   seldom   sometimes   often   always

29. How often when you are reading, do you take down the exact words of the author in your notes?

    never   seldom   sometimes   often   always

30. How often do you review the work of a 3-hour course?

    once a   once every   once a   twice a   once a
    week   two weeks   month   semester   semester

CHAPTER XII

LEARNING AND FORGETTING

College teachers are certainly interested in how much students learn and by what methods. Unfortunately, only a small proportion of the many experiments reported are of real value because so few of them deal with either human beings or college material. It may be that a freshman learns geology according to the same principles shown by a chimpanzee in putting two sticks together, or that he refrains from errors in written English by the same methods observed in the backward conditioning of the eyelid response—but I am too dubious of such assumptions to accept them. Nor does it seem to me at all certain that the learning curve for twenty-year-old juniors in economics is the same curve as that shown by seven-year-old children in learning multiplication combinations. In short, there is only a scattering of information about learning in the college subjects. Somewhat more work has been done on the topic of forgetting, although many additional studies are needed to determine how the amount of forgetting can best be reduced. Because I intend to exclude all material that does not bear directly upon the work of college students, this chapter will be considerably shorter than it should be, in view of the great importance of the subject for the teacher.

I. LEARNING

As far as I can find out, there is no experiment reporting the learning of even one student in a single college subject. No one knows at what rate or by what methods students master any field of knowledge. Such results as there are relate mostly to the acquisition of specific skills or to the development of

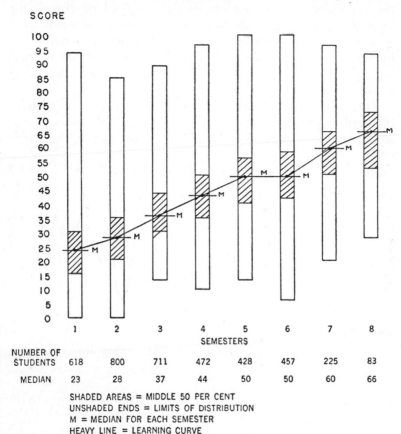

SHADED AREAS = MIDDLE 50 PER CENT
UNSHADED ENDS = LIMITS OF DISTRIBUTION
M = MEDIAN FOR EACH SEMESTER
HEAVY LINE = LEARNING CURVE

FIG. 25.—Learning Curve for Acquisition of Vocabulary in Spanish.

specific abilities that form only a small part of an entire course. A few typical examples of such reports as there are will appear below.

In the field of foreign languages the development of vocabulary, either in general or in detail, has been traced. The growth of vocabulary during four years of work in Spanish is shown in Figure 25.[1] The amount of learning here indicated is far from satisfactory. In fact, since there were 618 students in the beginning classes and only 83 at the end of the eighth semester, it is probable that even less progress was made than appears. Most of the increase in score could be accounted for by the mere elimination of poor students. In terms of total vocabulary this improvement would amount to about 270 words per semester.

The above report shows only mass learning. A more interesting study from the teacher's point of view is the record of a single person's acquisition of skill in translation.[2] The curve

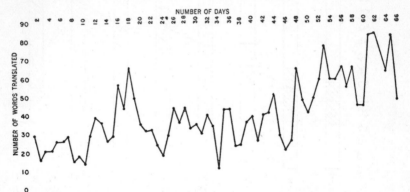

FIG. 26.—Learning Curve for Translating Russian.

Swift, *op. cit.*, p. 198. Used by permission of Charles Scribner's Sons.

is given here because it illustrates what probably happens in the day-to-day course of learning. This person recorded the number of words he could translate in a given amount of time each day. Naturally the passages he attempted were not of equal difficulty, but this fact does not influence the value of the results for a language teacher, because the passages he assigns from day to day are not equal in difficulty. The many

[1] V. A. C. Henmon, *Achievement Tests in the Modern Foreign Languages,* The Macmillan Company, 1929, p. 141. Used by permission of The Macmillan Company.

[2] E. J. Swift, *Mind in the Making: A Study in Mental Development,* Charles Scribner's Sons, 1908, 329 pp.

and extreme variations in performance were probably produced by several factors—the interest and vitality of the learner, and the difficulty and complexity of the work. It is likely that such peaks and valleys are typical of all human learning.

One other individual curve seems worth presenting, even though it deals with the learning of an elementary school phase of English composition.[3] This record shows the re-education

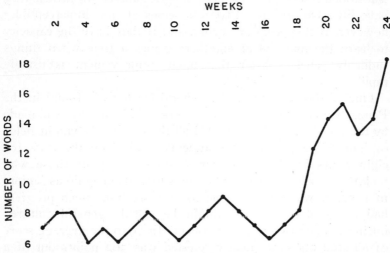

FIG. 27.—Learning Curve for the Re-education in Spelling of a Partially Deaf Girl.

Pressey, *Psychology and the New Education, op. cit.,* p. 321. Used by permission of Harper & Brothers.

in spelling of a partially deaf girl. Certain sounds she could not hear at all, while her hearing of all sounds was blurred. Before the period of training she misspelled as many as thirty words per page. Her English teacher was unwilling to accept otherwise acceptable compositions because the spelling was so illiterate. The girl therefore began learning to read lips in order to see the sounds she had never heard. She was also trained to stare hard at each word and try to remember its

[3] From S. L. Pressey, *Psychology and the New Education,* Harper & Brothers, 1933, 594 pp.

appearance. Each week during the twenty weeks of the treatment she took a test. All tests used were of approximately equal difficulty. Her scores on these tests show her rate of learning. For eighteen weeks, while she was mastering the elements of lip reading, she made essentially no progress at all. Then, all at once, she began to make great gains, which were apparently permanent. Learning often takes place in this way, especially for students who are just beginning a subject for which they have little background. Progress seems at first imperceptible; however, if they keep on trying, and if they have the capacity to learn the material at all, there comes a time when things suddenly "click." After this point, improvement is usually rapid.

One of the few studies of general learning is found in the Pennsylvania survey of college work.[4] This survey was made by the use of tests that sampled all the commonly taught fields of human knowledge. The students worked on the tests for eight hours in four two-hour sessions. Many of those who took the tests in 1930 as sophomores took them again as seniors in 1932. It was thus possible to measure how much progress had taken place in what might be called "general culture" during the last two years of college. In 1930 the average score of all students subsequently retested was 562 points out of a possible 1,882; in 1932, it was 641—a gain of only 79 points in two years. The senior class in the college making the greatest improvement over its sophomore scores made a gain equal to approximately one-fifth of the difference between the best and poorest sophomore classes at the beginning.

The learning of individual students is more interesting. Figure 28 shows the record of 69 seniors in one small college. all of whom had been tested during their sophomore year. The average gain is less than one-seventh of the difference between the highest and lowest scores for this same group in 1930. Of the 69 students, 16 made lower scores as seniors than they had made as sophomores, 49 made higher scores, and 4

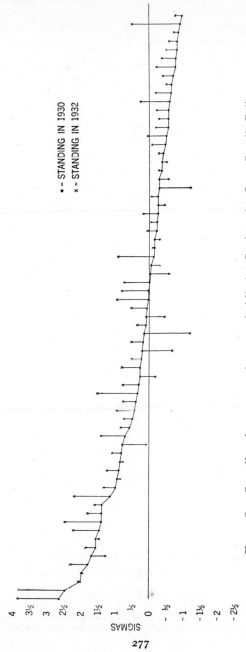

FIG. 28.—Standing in 1930 and 1932 of All the Seniors in One Small College.

Learned and Wood, *op. cit.*, p. 262. Used by permission of the Carnegie Foundation for the Advancement of Teaching.

made essentially the same score. The amount of learning does not seem to have been excessive.

A recent experiment has shown that even in such general matters as background and culture real progress can be made if a college wants to work hard enough at the problem.[5] At the beginning of the experiment the freshmen in the college studied averaged 249 points on a general culture test and the seniors 287, with the other two classes in between. This small increase suggested that the students were not getting some of the desired values from their college work. A number of survey courses were therefore instituted, and advisors tried to influence the lower classmen to elect more purely cultural courses. Six years later the tests were repeated. The general average for the entire sophomore class was 336 points; those who had taken all the survey courses offered had an average of 352. This change was not due to differences in general intelligence, because the comparable groups showed the same distribution and average on the mental tests. Whether or not the objectives or the methods of this particular experiment are desirable is not the point at issue here. The investigation shows that students can learn a great deal more than they usually do.

One important outcome of experimental work in the lower grades has been the discovery that pupils can learn much faster than they usually do. When the method of teaching is made as diagnostic as possible, when the learning situation is adequately adjusted to the nature of the pupil, and when the motivation is made as strong as possible, the results are phenomenal. A single instance of such results appears in Figure 29. This learning curve comes from an experiment in teaching fifth-grade children to read more rapidly.[6] This child's original rate was 160 words a minute— exactly the average for the fourth grade. In twenty-one school days or about four weeks, his rate just equaled that of the average eighth-grade pupil. At the end of six weeks this child had increased his speed to 425 words per minute with the same degree of comprehension he had had at the beginning of the work. This speed, which is good for a graduate student, is two and a half times the original rate. Both the materials and methods of the experiment were adapted for the one purpose of increasing the speed

[5] T. E. Newland, "Some Objective Evaluations," *Journal of Higher Education*, 7 : 415–21, 1936.
[6] J. A. O'Brien, *Silent Reading, with Special Reference to the Development of Speed*, The Macmillan Company, 1921, 289 pp.

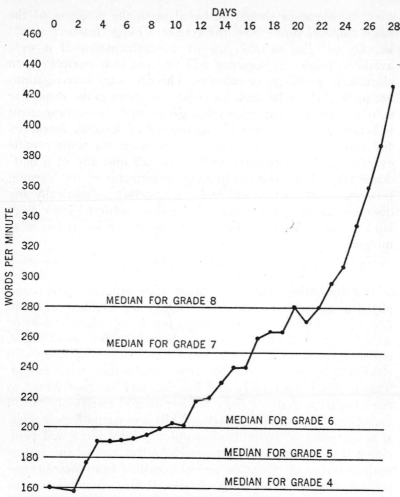

FIG. 29.—Increases in the Rate of Reading of One Pupil as a
Result of Special Training.

O'Brien, *op. cit.*, p. 221. Used by permission of The Macmillan Company.

of reading. The results show what can be done in the way of
producing greater learning than usually takes place.

This section on learning is lamentably short. There should
be curves showing the mastery of each college subject. More-

over, these curves should be based upon the progress of the same students throughout the course. College teachers would be only too glad to make use of this information if it were available. Some day someone will find out how students learn chemistry, sociology, or calculus. The necessary investigations are most likely to be made by college teachers in the respective subjects, rather than by psychologists—and this arrangement is better for all concerned. The teacher of English literature, for instance, may not know how to keep his testing units exactly equal in difficulty, or he may fall into any of a half-dozen traps that await the unwary investigator of the learning process, but at least he will find out *something*. Practically any discovery about the learning of a college subject by a college student will be of value because the present information is so meager.

II. FORGETTING

The forgetting that takes place after students have completed a course has been called rightly the greatest waste in education.[7] The more pessimistic of professors often wonder of what value all their efforts are when, in a few years' time, not more than 20 to 40 per cent of the ideas they discuss in class will be remembered by those whom they have taught. This notion is admittedly discouraging and has contributed to the conviction that a college teacher should teach only "main ideas," leaving out all the facts. While one would hardly question the value of concentration upon general ideas and principles, it does seem as if some teachers had applied the system without too much discretion and had omitted from their presentations altogether too many details. People cannot learn the general ideas a teacher would like to have them learn without facts upon which to rest them. Certainly no professor should be willing to teach nothing but minutiae, but it is only through the mastery of detail that students can arrive at principles. A teacher can shorten this rather laborious process of wading through facts if he himself never loses sight of the conclusions

[7] B. R. Buckingham, "The Greatest Waste in Education," *School and Society*, 24: 653–58, 1926.

and if he encourages his students to make deductions and inferences just as soon and as often as possible; but it is not safe to omit the details—even though these will subsequently be forgotten—because they are necessary to the development of thought at the time. One cannot think in a vacuum. If one tries to do so he gets into the state of the freshman who asked about the Spanish word for "swamp." According to his notion, if the word for "gulf" was *el golfo* and that for "ocean" was *el oceano,* then the one for "swamp" should be *el swampo;* this boy had got hold of a principle, but he lacked facts. It is because of this same condition that students defend earnestly a theory exploded fifty years ago. Their mental processes are often unexceptionable, but their minds do not contain enough concrete data. It is therefore necessary for students to be taught facts, even though a few years later only general principles remain.

1. Experiments in retention: The early experiments in learning and forgetting produced results that were far from reassuring. The method of investigation was roughly the same in all cases. The instructor used an objective test at the end of his course and then re-examined the members of the class with the same test at some subsequent time, the length of the intervening period varying from three months to three years. Typical results show that by the end of a few months students forgot about half their information in zoology, psychology, Latin syntax, chemistry, algebra, physiology, and botany.[8] If

---

[8] J. A. Cederstrom, "The Retention of Information Gained in Class in College Zoology," *Pedagogical Seminary and Journal of Genetic Psychology,* 38: 516–20, 1930; E. B. Greene, "The Retention of Information Learned in College Courses," *Journal of Educational Research,* 24: 262–73, 1931; P. O. Johnson, "The Permanence of Learning in Elementary Botany," *Journal of Educational Psychology,* 21: 37–47, 1930; L. R. Kennedy, "The Retention of Certain Latin Syntactical Principles by First and Second Year Latin Students after Various Time Intervals," *Journal of Educational Psychology,* 23: 132–46, 1932; E. T. Layton, "The Persistence of Learning in Elementary Algebra," *Journal of Educational Psychology,* 23: 46–55, 1932; R. I. Watson, "An Experimental Study of the Permanence of Course Material in Introductory Psychology," *Archives of Psychology,* No. 225, 1938, 64 pp.; L. H. Ziegler, "Learning and Forgetting," *Journal of Higher Education,* 2: 144–46, 1931. See also E. Ellis, "The Permanence of Learning in World History," *Social Studies,* 25: 133–36, 1934; M. E. Haggerty, "The Improvement of Medical Instruction," *Bulletin of American Medical Colleges,* 1929; P. O. Johnston, *Curricular Problems in Science at the College Level,* University of Minnesota Press, 1930, 188 pp.

one waited a year, the scores decreased to approximately a third of the standing on the final examination. In these studies, however, there is one conspicuous source of error. Although objective tests are not necessarily restricted to the measurement of mere facts, they often fail to measure anything else, because questions calling for details—and often rather unessential ones —are so much easier to construct than those that require reasoning. It is more than probable that the final examinations used in these investigations were incapable of measuring the extent to which general principles had become a part of the students' permanent intellectual equipment.[9]

The investigators whose results have just been reported have usually constructed curves of forgetting on the basis of their materials. These match closely the curve of forgetting for nonsense syllables, except that the initial loss is not so great. This similarity is no compliment. Nonsense syllables drop out of one's mind for two reasons: the learner does not intend to remember them permanently, and he has no use for them. If the human mind did not forget what was useless, it would become so cluttered up that it could not think at all. Since students forget the facts about botany in the same way that they forget nonsense, it is either because they do not intend to learn the material in the first place or because they have never had any occasion to use it. In either case, these details were worth teaching *only if they contributed at the time to a better understanding of the principles.* That some forgetting will occur after a student stops actively reading, studying, and thinking about a topic is inevitable, but if as much as 80 per cent of the final achievement in a course disappears in a few months, he has obviously been taught something for which he has no possible use. Not even dull human minds forget at that rate the things they use with moderate frequency. It is also likely that many students have no intention of recalling at any future date what they have learned in a subject. I have certainly taken courses that I was only too glad to forget;

[9] It is of interest that, in the case of Latin syntax for which the test used covered only principles, the forgetting was appreciably less than that for other types of material.

they were of no interest to me at the time, and what tag ends of knowledge I may have acquired from them have long since been pushed into the limbo of forgetfulness by other things that are for me more important. This type of purposeful forgetting should be expected from anyone who does not have a mind like a piece of flypaper.

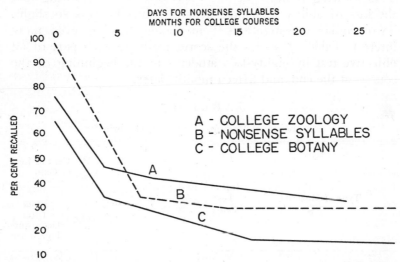

FIG. 30.—(a) The Curve of Forgetting for Nonsense Syllables, and (b) Similar Curves for Two College Courses.

Curve for nonsense syllables from H. Ebbinghaus, *Memory: A Contribution to Experimental Psychology,* Leipzig, 1885; curves for college courses based on results given by Greene, *op. cit.* and P. O. Johnson, *op. cit.* Used by permission of the publishers and authors.

Some of the recent experiments have been more reassuring, largely because the investigators have made consistent efforts to measure something besides mere detail. In one study [10] the students, after an interval of one and one-half years, recalled the following proportions of information of different types concerning their courses in chemistry.

[10] F. P. Frutchey, "Retention in High School Chemistry," *Educational Research Bulletin,* 16: 34–37. 1937. Used by permission of the *Educational Research Bulletin.*

Type of Information	Per Cent Recalled
1. Technical words	66
2. Balancing equations	72
3. Symbols, formulas, and valence	70
4. Main facts of the course	84
5. Application of general principles	92

This showing is much better. Especially is it reassuring that the loss of ability to handle general principles was so slight. Two similar investigations [11] in zoology are of even more interest. Table 17 shows the scores made on each part of an objective test by eighty-two students at the beginning of the course, at the end, and fifteen months later.

TABLE 17

Retention of Various Types of Material[11a]

Type of Material	Initial Test Score	End Test Score	Gain during Score	15 Months Later, Score	Per Cent of Loss or Gain	
					From Final Score	From Total Gain during Course
1. Names of organs identified from pictures.............	22	62	40	31	50	22
2. Recognition of technical terms	20	83	63	67	80	72
3. Recall of facts..............	34	102	68	88	86	80
4. Application of principles.....	35	65	30	65	0	0
5. Interpretation of new experiments..................	30	57	27	64	112	126

The first column of per cents was obtained merely by dividing the retention score by the final examination score. This figure does not, however, tell the whole story. The actual gain during the course is reflected by the difference between the initial and end tests—being 40 points for the first type of material. The retention score contains presumably not only the amount of new material retained but also the 22 points with which the

[11] R. W. Tyler, "Permanence of Learning," *Journal of Higher Education,* 4 : 203–4, 1933.
[11a] Tyler, *op. cit.* Used by permission of the *Journal of Higher Education.*

students began their work. Assuming that they still knew fifteen months later what they knew to start with, the retention is only 9 points. That is, they kept only 22 per cent of the 40 points they acquired during the course. The new words they learned and the main facts have been retained much better. The students kept everything they knew earlier about principles and—probably because of greater maturity and because of the other college work they had taken in the meantime—they had improved their ability to see through new experiments.

The second experiment [12] is largely a repetition of the first but was carried on for a longer period of time. The students took the final course examination at intervals of one, two, and three years after completing their work. The results (in Figure 31) are based on the final examination score and show the per cent that each successive score was of the standing at the end of the course.

These results are even more encouraging. Growth in those abilities that teachers most want to develop apparently continues throughout at least three years, although the details have been largely forgotten. Half of the terminology and half of the main facts are also permanent acquisitions. These students showed clear evidence of being able to think better in terms of zoology because of their course—and that is all any teacher should ask of those who do not become zoologists. Does anyone really care whether or not after three years students can identify the duodenum, the jejunum, and the ileum, provided they can still think intelligently about the subject of zoology?

Even in the matter of verbatim learning the general ideas are recalled after the words are forgotten. There is a report of a long series of experiments,[13] of which I will quote only two. For both of these, students memorized a short prose selection. Immediately afterward they took a test that included some verbatim sentences from what they had learned and some summary statements concerning the general import of the pas-

[12] J. E. Wert, "Twin Examination Assumptions," *Journal of Higher Education*, 8 : 136–40, 1937.

[13] H. B. English, E. L. Welborn, and C. D. Killian, "Studies of Substance Memorization," *Journal of General Psychology*, 11 : 233–60, 1934.

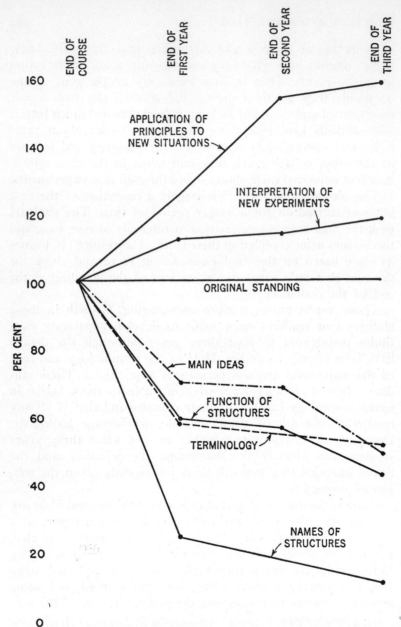

FIG. 31.—Recent Results as Regards Retention.
Wert, *op. cit.* Used by permission of the *Journal of Higher Education.*
286

sage. After an interval of time the students took the tests again. Their recollection of the verbatim statements decreased an average of 4 points in one experiment and 6 in the other, but their recall of the summaries increased 8 and 5 points respectively. Again there is evidence that students forget details —even though these are actually memorized—but remember more about the main ideas after a period of time than they did immediately after they finished learning.

These experiments indicate that investigators are at last on the right track. Students do not forget the principles of a subject, and they become better able to apply these principles as their subsequent work in college gives them more knowledge and better judgment. The relation of detail to this retention of main ideas is still not clear, however. If the same type of experiment were repeated with different groups, some of which studied details of structure and function while the others did not, one could find out to what extent the minutiae were essential during the process of acquiring general ideas. If the improvement of ability to think in terms of a subject is just as good whether or not details have been temporarily mastered, it seems a waste of time and energy to include them, since they will most assuredly be forgotten. In this case, the time saved by omitting minor points could be used for further development of "thinking." If, on the other hand, those students who did not study details did not learn to think, it would be clear that minor facts—even though soon forgotten—serve a necessary purpose at the time the students learn them. It is merely my own impression that the latter case is the truth. No one knows definitely at present, but the question can be answered. By carrying on the necessary experiments, a teacher could determine just which facts and how many are needed by students if they are to achieve a reasonable grasp of principles. Until such proof is forthcoming any further discussion is as futile as the famous dispute about the number of angels that could dance on the point of a pin.

2. *The prevention of forgetting:* In the earlier part of the chapter three main reasons were given for the loss that appears with the passage of time. A student may forget because he

does not intend to learn, because he does not use the facts, or because he has too much competition from other ideas. The problem of bringing about less loss from the first cause is one of more adequate motivation, while loss from the last is inevitable. The teacher can, however, reduce the amount that is lost through disuse by restricting his work primarily to such elements as are of use or by relating his material to everyday life. There is, of course, no knowledge in the world that is not useful to someone, any more than there is any knowledge that is not interesting to someone, but there are portions of subject matter in any field that are of value chiefly to the specialist. If the average person concentrates his learning efforts upon these portions he soon forgets them because he has no use for them. It seems more sensible to teach students by the usual methods something they will not forget because of frequent use than to expend effort in teaching them by more elaborate techniques things that are completely removed from their daily life and will therefore be forgotten anyway. There are "social" values in any subject that undergraduates are likely to elect. If a teacher will concentrate upon these, his teaching will be more profitable.

A few examples may make this point clearer. I remember one course in English composition in which each week we wrote one letter home and passed it in as an assignment. The instructor returned the letters the next day. We were at liberty to send them or not, to add further items or not, or to copy them or not, as we saw fit. Most of us simply sent them, corrections and all. Naturally we had other assignments, but this one continued throughout the year. We developed a socially useful skill for meeting a situation that would recur so often throughout our lives that we were not likely to forget it. In one chemistry course the instructor asked us—after we had had about a semester of introductory work—to bring to class an object made from inorganic substances and analyze it. Our "unknowns" were of our own choosing. Since we chose something about which we were already curious, we were stimulated to learn more chemistry than we otherwise would have done and, hence, to remember more. In one history course we spent the major part of most class hours in discussing the implications of the morning newspaper. As we proceeded, we found various points that were not clear. Our assignments consisted chiefly in assembling data to make them clearer. We learned as much history as any teacher could wish, but we did not go through any period chronologically. In later years we probably forget many of the facts, but we did not forget how to read a newspaper. In a course on the psychology of adolescence the teacher required each student to read six modern novels from a list of about fifty. The students were not quizzed on the story content of these books but on their ability to see wherein the facts they had learned in the course illuminated the stories. The students also wrote case histories of their own adolescent years in the light of what they had just learned about the period. In a course in French literature my professor made unusual efforts to build up our vocabularies. Each day he discussed two or three new words. He told us all he could about them, including their derivation, their relation to other words containing the same stem, their cognates—if any—in English or other languages, their common idiomatic uses, and any other details about them. I have no way of knowing whether or not we learned more words, or even if we learned them better, but I do know that I cannot now—after a lapse of nearly thirty years—go by an unknown French word because it is too likely to prove interesting.

By such means as the above, or by any others that suggest themselves, a teacher can attach the main ideas of a course to everyday life or can present his material in such a way as to guarantee its frequent use. The college graduate who becomes a scholar recalls the details of what he has learned because he uses them every day, but the graduate who becomes a businessman does not use them and soon forgets them. Since one cannot tell in advance what any student will become, the elementary courses might well be limited to those phases of a subject that will be of the greatest use to the greatest number, no matter what type of work they subsequently enter. Since advanced work in a field presupposes at the very least an interest and often an intention of continuance, the teacher is reasonably safe in presenting details for their own sake, because most of the students will actually use them throughout their lives and will therefore not forget them. Training the future specialist is easy compared to training the general public.[14]

III. SUMMARY

Almost nothing is known about the progress of learning in any college subject—and what is known is not especially encouraging. The matter of forgetting has been investigated many times for different subjects. Although the earlier experiments gave rather depressing results, the better types of measurement more recently developed indicate that students do not forget the particular kind of thing that teachers most want them to remember. Since general principles and ability to interpret data within a given field of study seem to be permanent acquisitions, a teacher should presumably concentrate upon them, using details to bring about understanding of the main issues. The exact number and type of detail necessary could be worked out experimentally, but thus far has not been.

[14] It has been suggested that students should take during their junior year review examinations in some of their freshman subjects. (See H. T. Moore, "The Skidmore Plan of Review Examinations," *Journal of Higher Education*, 7: 173–75, 1936.) This suggestion might prove valuable provided the material of the freshmen courses was such as to be worth the work involved. Otherwise it might as well be forgotten.

CHAPTER XIII

PREDICTION OF SUCCESS OR FAILURE

The sooner a college can find out about its students' prospects, the sooner it can adjust its procedures to their needs. Some sort of prediction is the first step for the elimination of the unfit from the academic courses and for the selection of the unusually fit for advanced work. It is to everyone's advantage that the prediction be made as early and as reliably as possible. The larger an institution is and the more motley its student body, the more acutely it needs some means of accurate prediction.

There are at least six bases that can be used for making a forecast: scores on intelligence tests, scores on achievement tests, high school grades, first-semester college marks, scores on tests of personality, and some summary of the personnel records. In many instances an investigator has combined two or more of these measures. From a scientific point of view it is desirable to include in the basis for prediction as many measures as possible, but one has to be careful lest the prediction formula become so complicated that no ordinary person can use it. I have purposely omitted from this summary the reports of experiments in which the methodology was too complicated for the average person who does not have a battery of statisticians awaiting his command.

I. PREDICTION OF THE GENERAL LEVEL OF WORK [1]

The earlier efforts in this direction were distinctly discouraging, largely because only tests of intelligence were available as measuring instruments. The intelligence test is valuable, particularly at the lower end, but it measures at best only one element that goes into the production of college marks. Usually the correlation between it and college grades comes out at some figure between .40 and .50, although it sometimes rises as high as .65.[2] If one looks at the scattergram from which such a coefficient is calculated, one finds a clear relation between low scores and failure. There are, however, many failing students who score in the higher levels of intelligence and many students with good grades who have compensated by extra industry for less than average ability and achievement; in both cases the amount of interest and effort has introduced a new factor. The test of intelligence gives a reasonably accurate statement of what it is intended to measure; it should not be condemned for its failure to measure some-

[1] For the benefit of those who have not had work in statistics it might be said that a "coefficient of correlation" below .50 is of practically no use for general prediction. Only those above .60 are at all valuable. Any that are above .70 will show a good prediction that can be used in practical ways. I do not attempt to define coefficients but merely to give some basis for interpreting them.

[2] See, for instance, H. R. Douglass, "The Relation of High School Preparation and Certain Other Factors to Academic Success at the University of Oregon," *University of Oregon Publications, Education Series,* Vol. 3, No. 1, 1931, 61 pp.; J. R. Gerberich and G. D. Stoddard, "Personnel Survey of 100,000 Iowa High School Seniors," *School and Society,* 30: 515–20, 1929; L. L. Thurstone, "Psychology Tests for College Freshmen," *Educational Record,* 6: 69–83, 282–94, 1925; J. V. Waits, "The Differential Predictive Value of the Psychological Examination of the American Council of Education," *Journal of Experimental Education,* 1: 264–71, 1933; D. W. LeFever, "The Prognostic Value of Certain Groupings of the Test Elements of the Thorndike Intelligence Examination for High School Graduates," *University of Southern California Studies, Education Series,* No. 9, 1930, 116 pp.; H. E. Garret, "A Study of the CAVD Intelligence Examination," *Journal of Educational Research,* 21: 103–8, 1930; A. H. MacPhail, *Intelligence of College Students,* Warwick and York, 1924, 124 pp.; R. A. Kent and E. Schreurs, "Specific Factors for Freshmen English and Mathematics," *School and Society,* 27: 242–46, 1928; L. M. Terman, *A Report of the Stanford University Committee upon the Uses of Psychological Tests as Admission Tests,* Stanford University Press, 1923; L. L. Thurstone and T. G. Thurstone, "The 1930 Psychological Examinations," *Educational Record,* 12: 160–78, 1931.

thing else. It has its values, but for purposes of prediction it cannot stand alone.

In recent years colleges and universities have been using "aptitude" or "scholarship" tests. Some of them are naturally better made than others, but the essential idea behind all of them is the same. They are supposed to sample all types of previous work; the scores are therefore functions of preparation. If such a test is well constructed, it samples systematically the various possible fields and it is both long enough and hard enough to give the superior student a chance to show his ability. Typical scholarship tests have been developed at Iowa and Wisconsin. Results with these tests have sometimes been relatively good and sometimes not. Average coefficients of correlation between test scores and grades vary from .45 to .65 with a median of .55,[3] as compared to an average of .44 for tests of intelligence.

Prediction at the lower end of the distribution has been better than at the upper. Thus, at one university, 208 or the 211 entering freshmen who scored below the thirty-fifth percentile on the aptitude test made failing records.[4] The prediction at the upper end is far more difficult, because the situation is more complex. While a student who does not know the facts he needs for college classes will rarely pass a course with more than a D, a student who is well equipped may spend his time loafing around a fraternity house, in working his way

[3] D. Segel, "Prediction of Success in College," *Office of Education Bulletin*, 1934, No. 15, 98 pp. See also L. B. Kinney, *The Use of Aptitude Tests for Subjects Taught at the College Level* (Mimeographed Report), University of Minnesota, 129 pp.

[4] J. B. Johnston, "Student Aptitude and the Prediction of Student Scholarship," *Report of the Survey Committee*, No. 10, University of Minnesota, 1927. See also G. D. Stoddard, "The Iowa Placement Examination," *School and Society*, 24: 212–16, 1926; C. E. Kellog, "Relative Values of Intelligence Tests and Matriculation Examinations as Means of Estimating Probable Success in College," *School and Society*, 30: 893–96, 1929. In many instances the prediction is too low to be of much practical value. It is not clear why there is so much variation. Some of the tests used are probably better than others and sometimes the content of the tests is more closely related to the content of the courses than in other instances. It may be difficult to select students as to number of type or the situation may be complex. In spite of the general mediocre results, there is enough encouragement in the few highly successful experiments to suggest that predictions can be made much more accurate than they usually are.

THE COLLEGE STUDENT

through school, or in having a desperate love affair, with sad results to the predictive value of his aptitude rating. A lower relationship at the upper end than one could wish does not, however, diminish the value of the scores. Their chief use should, in fact, be to call the attention of instructors to the presence of superior students in their classes. College teachers often complain bitterly about the lack of "pupil material" in the modern college. When one of them gets a student with an aptitude rating at the ninety-fifth percentile or higher, he ought to be more than willing to furnish help and guidance. These students are the ones who are already well started on the road to learning. Presumably if a bright freshman's first teachers would make a real effort to interest him and would invest time and effort in his development these students would do work more nearly commensurate with their high standing. At present, these able freshmen are too likely to get lost among their many less capable classmates.

Table 18 presents results from one of the more successful attempts at prediction.[5] The proportion of students in each decile who made C grades or better decreased steadily from 97 per cent in the highest decile to 0 per cent in the lowest. In fact, no one whose score was below the fifteenth percentile made a passing record.

One further investigation merits attention.[6] In this case the results used as a basis for prediction came from tests in essential preparation for work in English composition, modern languages, mathematics, history, and general reading, plus scores in intelligence. The aim of the investigation was to predict both failure and unusual success, rather than to foretell the level of work over the entire range of scores. About a week after the beginning of college the investigator went over the list of scores made by the entire entering class. Any incomplete records were ignored. From 2,000 or more freshmen, 168 were selected as being excellent "educational risks" and

[5] J. B. Johnston, *The Liberal College in a Changing Society,* The Century Company, 1930, p. 126. Used by permission of D. Appleton-Century Company.
[6] L. C. Pressey, "Report on an Attempt at the Prognosis of Unusually Good and Unusually Poor Scholastic Work," *Journal of Educational Psychology,* 23: 387–99, 1932.

169 as being poor "educational risks." A list of these names was deposited with the head of the Bureau of Educational Research, who had agreed to act as a sort of referee. Before the end of the first semester, 3 students had withdrawn from the upper group and 13 from the lower. The remaining freshmen made first-semester grades as shown in Figure 32.

TABLE 18

Relation of College Success to College Aptitude Ratings

College Aptitude Percentile	Number	"C" or Better	Per Cent	Prospects
96–100	88	85	96.6	Very
91–95	125	116	92.8	Unusual
86–90	156	121	76.3	Superior
81–85	135	98	69.5	
76–80	137	89	65.0	
71–75	123	69	56.1	Good
66–70	131	57	43.5	
61–65	144	66	45.2	
56–60	144	57	39.6	
51–55	150	45	30.0	Fair
46–50	141	34	24.1	
41–45	129	20	15.5	Poor
36–40	137	19	13.7	
31–35	116	13	11.2	
26–30	90	6	6.4	Very Poor*
21–25	76	1	1.3	
16–20	85	2	2.3	
11–15	47	—	—	
6–10	44	—	—	
1–5	14	—	—	

* In the years under consideration not less than 5 per cent of those whose entrance scores were below the twenty-fifth percentile graduated. See J. B. Johnston and E. G. Williamson, "Follow-up Study of Early Scholastic Prediction at the University of Minnesota," *School and Society,* 40:730–38, 1934.

The prediction of decidedly poor work was good for 84 per cent of the unpromising freshmen. Since most of those who withdrew left because of low standing, the per cent of accuracy is actually a bit higher. The prediction of superior work was not as good, although 67 per cent of those selected actually did make A or B records; all but 2.5 per cent of the total made at least C records, however. If the teachers of these well-

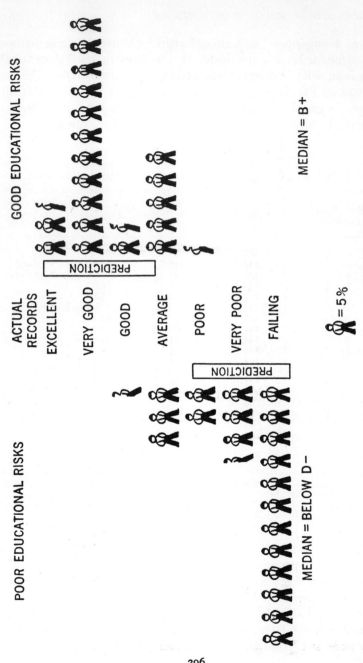

POOR EDUCATIONAL RISKS

GOOD EDUCATIONAL RISKS

ACTUAL RECORDS
EXCELLENT
VERY GOOD
GOOD
AVERAGE
POOR
VERY POOR
FAILING

PREDICTION

PREDICTION

MEDIAN = B+

MEDIAN = BELOW D−

= 5%

FIG. 32.—Prediction of Unusually Good and Unusually Poor Work.

296

prepared freshmen had made definite efforts to interest and stimulate them, the prediction might easily have been much better, and the students would have begun their college career on a higher level.[7]

Recently the prediction of general level has become in the same universities less successful than it was ten years ago.[8] The reasons given for this decline are interesting. First the work of advising students in the high schools has resulted in a narrowing of the distribution of abilities because the poorest students do not go to college but are diverted by guidance into other types of education. The second is that colleges are working much more efficiently with their poorer students who now succeed better in their academic courses. The third is that many special courses have been established for below-average freshmen—courses in which they can receive good grades. As a result of all this adaptation to native capacities the accuracy of prediction has been lowered. The statistician may regret the decline in accuracy, but teachers should feel greatly encouraged that their efforts at individualization have produced measurable results.

Many efforts have been made to predict success in college from marks in high school. In the early experiments the relationship was low, probably because of the great variability in the performance of students coming from different schools. It is not a question of the reliability of marks within each school system. The real trouble is that each teacher tends to assign grades within whatever range of abilities her particular group of pupils may show. A glance at Figure 33 should convince one of the statistical difficulties involved in

[7] For other articles on the use of aptitude or placement tests, see H. P. Hammond and G. D. Stoddard, "A Study of Placement Examination," *University of Iowa Studies in Education,* Vol. IV, No. 7, 1928, 59 pp.; T. A. Langlie, "Iowa Placement Examinations at the University of Minnesota," *Journal of the Society for the Promotion of Engineering Education,* 17: 842–60, 1927; C. V. Mann, "An Evolution of Placement Examinations," *Journal of the Society for the Promotion of Engineering Education,* 19: 288–300, 1928; J. B. Johnston, "Predicting Success in College at the Time of Entrance," *School and Society,* 23: 82–88, 1926; Segel, *op. cit.;* C. C. Upshall and H. V. Masters, "Differences between Good and Poor Students Chosen on the Basis of College Entrance Test Scores," *Educational Administration and Supervision,* 19: 507–10, 1933.

[8] E. G. Williamson, "The Decreasing Accuracy of Scholastic Prediction," *Journal of Educational Psychology,* 28: 1–16, 1937.

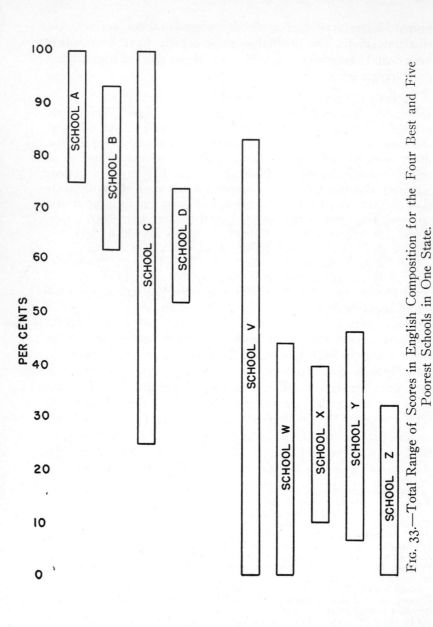

FIG. 33.—Total Range of Scores in English Composition for the Four Best and Five Poorest Schools in One State.

Remmers, "Achievement in Our High Schools," *op. cit.* Used by permission of Purdue University.

using high school marks in their original form as the basis for prediction. The chart shows the complete range of scores on a test of English composition for the four best high schools in a single state and the five poorest.[9] The marks assigned within each school may have a direct relationship to achievement, but the schools show no common standard. If the teacher of School D assigns grades from A to E within the distribution shown, the A's will represent a degree of mastery lower than the average in School B, below the lowest score in School A, and about average for School C. The E's in this same school will, however, represent a higher level of achievement than that of the A pupils in the four lowest schools and above average for School V. Naturally if one were to put together in a college group any selection of students from these schools and were then to correlate high school grades with marks in college English, one would find practically no relationship. The actual correlations in different studies have varied from .15 to .65, but most of them are nearer to the former figure than to the latter.[10] The exact amount of agreement in any given case depends presumably upon the extent to which contributing high schools have had a common standard of marking.

The same high school marks can, however, be used quite

[9] H. H. Remmers, "The Achievement of Our High Schools," *Purdue Studies in Higher Education,* XVIII, Vol. 32, No. 2, 1931, 30 pp.

[10] See, for instance, A. B. Crawford, "Forecasting Freshman Achievement," *School and Society,* 31 : 125–32, 1930 ; H. R. Douglass, "Selecting Good College Risks," *School and Society,* 35 : 140–47, 1932 ; E. T. Ellefson, "Predicting College Freshman Scholarship," *California Quarterly Journal of Secondary Education,* 3 : 179–85, 1928 ; R. Gilkey, "Relation of Success in Certain Subjects in High School to Success in the Same Subjects in College," *School Review,* 37 : 576–88, 1929 ; J. B. Johnston, "Prediction of Student Scholarship," in *Problems of College Education,* E. Hudelson (Ed.), University of Minnesota Press, 1928, pp. 232–38 ; H. H. Mills, "Predicting Scholastic Success at the Time of Entrance," *University of Colorado Studies,* Vol. 23, No. 4, 1936, pp. 305–14 ; C. W. Odell, "Predicting the Scholastic Success of College Freshmen," *Bureau of Educational Research Bulletin,* No. 52, 1927, 54 pp. ; C. B. Read, "The Prediction of Scholastic Success in a Municipal University," *School and Society,* 48 : 187–88, 1938 ; E. G. Williamson, "An Analysis of Scholastic Aptitude of Freshmen in Some Private Colleges in Minnesota," *School and Society,* 34 : 674–80, 1931 ; M. E. Wagner, *The Relation of General and Specific College Achievement to Previous Academic Performance, Intelligence Scores, and Subject Content Tests,* University of Buffalo, 1934, 78 pp.

effectively if they are expressed in terms of rank order instead of letter grade or per cents. If teachers simply list their pupils in order, from the best to the worst, and if a statistician then converts those judgments into the properly equated values, one can obtain a correlation as high as .63.[11] In one study [12] the rank order, plus rating on themes written at entrance to college, gave a correlation of .70. Marks that have been corrected for the variation from school to school still furnish the best single criterion of success in college—that is, the correlations show less variation than those between scholarship tests and college work, and the average coefficient is higher.

Various combinations of tests have been found especially valuable. The coefficients often run between .60 and .75 and occasionally as high as .81.[13] These combinations usually include a measure of intelligence and one of preparation, plus— in a few instances—measures of study habits or other personal traits.

The grades that students receive during the first semester are usually indicative of those they will continue to get. In individual cases, this statement is not, of course, always true; any teacher knows some students who reform after a bad start and some who begin well but backslide. In general, however, the preparation and ability that produce first-semester grades determine the level of later work. In one study all the students who had poor averages for the first semester's work, but who nevertheless went on in college, were ineligible for entrance to the junior year.[14] Of those who made D, D+, or

[11] J. B. Johnston, "Predicting Success or Failure at the Time of Entrance to College," *op. cit.*

[12] J. B. Johnston, "Tests for Ability before College Entrance," *School and Society,* 15 : 345–53, 1922.

[13] C. C. Crawford, "Some Criticisms of Current Practice in Educational Methods," *Harvard Teachers Record,* 3 : 67–81, 1933; J. H. Edds and W. M. McCall, "Predicting the Scholastic Success of College Freshmen,". *Journal of Educational Research,* 27 : 127–30, 1933; E. G. Fleming, "College Achievement, Intelligence, Personality, and Emotion," *Journal of Applied Psychology,* 16 : 668–74, 1932; L. D. Hartson, "The Most Valid Combination of 23 Tests for Predicting Freshman Scholarship at Oberlin College," *Ohio College Association Bulletin,* No. 58, 1928.

[14] E. F. Potthoff, "Predicting the Ultimate Failure of College Students on the Basis of Their First Quarter's Records," *School and Society,* 33 : 203–4, 1931; and Read, *op. cit.*

C records the first semester, 7 per cent, 28 per cent, and 57 per cent, respectively, were eligible for junior work. The initial efforts of students, especially those at the lower end of the distribution, are highly prognostic of their subsequent academic achievements.

Another basis for prediction is the college board examination. It has sometimes been found to be relatively unsatisfactory,[15] and sometimes quite good.[16] These examinations are usually of the essay type. It is therefore probable that they do not have a wide enough selection of topics to give an adequate sampling of the students' achievement. The tests themselves vary a good deal from one year to another, with a resulting variation in their value for prediction.

Finally, there are various tests and ratings of personality. These measures are still relatively new, but some of them seem to correlate with success in college. Even though the coefficients are not high, use of them represents an effort to introduce into the problem of prediction some measure of nonintellectual and nonacademic traits. In one case [17] the correlation between tests and marks rose to .74 with the addition of the data of this character. In the course of time it is probable that temperament and interest can be measured well enough to yield a fair estimate of the characterological elements that influence college classwork.

It is, then, possible for a college or university to predict with some accuracy, by a combination of previous marks and tests given at entrance, the probable failure of incapable or ignorant students and with fair accuracy the success of its best "pupil material." Such knowledge is of great value. The college can at once set about remedying the defects of such poorly prepared students as seem to be worth the effort—

[15] See as an example, A. B. Crawford and P. S. Burnham, "Entrance Examinations and College Achievement," *School and Society,* 36 : 344–52, 378–84, 1932.

[16] M. E. Wagner, "Prediction of College Performance," *University of Buffalo Studies,* 9 : 125–44, 1934.

[17] C. M. Scott, "Background and Personal Data as Factors in the Prediction of Scholastic Success in College," *Journal of Applied Psychology,* 22 : 42–49, 1938. See also N. E. Drought, "Analysis of Eight Measures of Personality and Adjustment in Relation to Relative Scholastic Achievement," *Journal of Applied Psychology,* 22 : 597–606, 1938.

before they fail too much work and the machinery eliminates them. It can also begin immediately to direct the attention of its least promising freshmen away from academic pursuits into some more appropriate type of work. Most important of all, it can locate its best talent early. There is still plenty of good academic material in every freshman class, but it may be overlooked. Such youngsters are already so much ahead of their fellows that the work of the first year or two may bore them unutterably and may even cause them to leave college.

One of my own friends was a good example of this situation. During her freshman year she took English, French, Chemistry, American history, and mathematics. In neither English nor French did she read anything she had not already read. Her chemistry and history courses were almost exact repetitions of what she had had in high school. On the four courses together she spent about half an hour a day. She was normally industrious, but she simply had nothing to do. With this slight expenditure of time she was able to get A's. She was saved from complete boredom by her teacher of mathematics—the only instructor who sensed the girl's capacity and scholarly interests. After the first two weeks of school this teacher dismissed the girl from further class attendance for the rest of the year. During this time the student completed an entire course in solid geometry, a second in trigonometry, a third in non-Euclidian geometry, and a fourth in analytics. Her other four classes were a sheer waste of time. In fact, they were worse than that, because they could easily have bored her into leaving college.

Brilliant students are rarely docile. If they do not find something to think about in their classes, they will not put up with being bored. They may disrupt the class by misbehavior, they may plunge into campus activities, they may leave school to take a job, or they may do almost anything else that is wasteful of a promising scholar's time. Their independence is one of their most valuable traits, but it easily leads them away from an education instead of toward it, unless it can be attached from the first to the work in which they would be vitally interested, if only given a chance.

II. PROGNOSIS OF SUCCESS OR FAILURE WITHIN A SUBJECT

There has been more or less experimentation with the forecasting of grades in the fields of study commonly open to freshmen. The results vary considerably from one subject and one institution to another.

The best prognosis within a single subject has been in the field of modern language. The lowest coefficients are about .50 [18] and the highest .81.[19] Indeed, in the best of these investigations the prognosis on the two ends of the distribution was nearly perfect. In this case both the test and the teaching stressed a grammatical approach. The teaching of a subject often does not agree with the type of aptitude test used, and the relationship of scores to marks is naturally low. In another instance [20] the designers of a prognosis test established a "threshold" score—that is, a score below which the preparation in language was inadequate for the work. Out of 300 beginning students 74 per cent of those scoring below this threshold actually did fail while 80 per cent of those scoring above actually did succeed.

Prediction of grades in mathematics should be easier than in other subjects because the tests are almost sure to be objective and reasonably reliable. The relationship between test results and marks is not, however, as high as one would expect. The coefficients are usually about .40 and .50, occasionally, .60.[21] One

[18] M. E. Wagner and E. Strabel, "Predicting Success and Failure in College Ancient and Modern Foreign Languages," *Modern Language Journal*, 19: 285–93, 1935; C. D. Stoddard, "Iowa Placement Examinations," *School and Society*, 24: 212–16, 1926; L. C. Seibert and E. R. Goddard, "The Use of Achievement Tests in Sectioning Students," *Modern Language Journal*, 18: 289–98, 1934; M. E. Wagner, "Prediction of Specific College Field and Course Performance," *University of Buffalo Studies*, 9: 145–74, 1934.

[19] B. E. Tomlinson, "General and Specific Prognoses of Academic Success, Based upon Tests of Intelligence and Preparation," Doctor's Thesis, Ohio State University, 1930, 165 pp.

[20] R. Blakely, "Use of Prognosis Tests in Modern Languages," *School Review*, 35: 692–698, 1927.

[21] See, for example, G. H. Ayers, "Predicting Success in Algebra," *School and Society*, 39: 17–18, 1934; M. R. Dickter, "The Relationship between Scores on the Scholastic Aptitude Tests and College Marks in Mathematics and Science," *Journal of Educational Psychology*, 29: 363–73, 1938; R. Gilkey, "The Relation of Success in Certain Subjects in High School to Success in the Same Subjects in College," *School Review*, 37: 576–88, 1929; J. W. Gowen and M. Gooch, "The Mental Attainments of College Students in Relation to Previous Training," *Journal of Educational Psychology*, 16: 547–68, 1925.

of the studies [22] throws some light upon a possible reason for
these relatively low correlations. In most universities the students
in the elementary mathematics courses are mainly freshmen in
engineering. The instructors are supposed to do a good deal in
the way of elimination, because there are always more freshmen
than could conceivably be used by society as engineers. The marking is therefore very strict. On the other hand, most of the boys
who enter engineering have a relatively high standing in mathematics; if their interest in mathematics were low they would have
entered some other college. As a result of these two factors, a
curious situation develops. The two sets of figures in Table 19
show the relation of the placement scores made by 287 freshmen
engineers to the normal distribution for the whole university and
the similar relation for the grades received by these same boys in
their first course in mathematics.

TABLE 19

Relation of Marks in Mathematics to Other Criteria

Test Scores, in Percentiles

	1-5	6-25	26-75	76-95	96-100
Per cent of 287 engineering freshmen	1	1	25	52	21
Entire freshman class	5	20	50	20	5

Marks in Mathematics

	E	D	C	B	A
Per cent of 287 engineering freshmen	19	21	31	18	11
Normal distribution	3	14	66	14	3

All but 2 per cent of these boys scored above the twenty-fifth
percentile on the placement tests, 73 per cent scored above the
seventy-fifth percentile, and 21 per cent above the ninety-fifth.
Yet 40 per cent received either E or D. Although 73 per cent were

[22] Tomlinson, *op. cit.*

in the highest fourth of the entering class in their preparation for mathematics,[23] only 29 per cent received either A or B. This is an example of thoroughly ruthless elimination. It is not surprising that the correlation was only .47. If this same factor of an artificially high elimination enters into the situation in other universities the prognosis of success in mathematics is likely to remain low.

Reports of prediction in history are not numerous. Two efforts were quite successful, one coefficient being .70[24] and the other .75.[25] In the former case, the aptitude test used measured knowledge of geographical background, mastery of technical vocabulary, and ability to read typical selections from textbooks in history. For the four hundred students involved, the relation between marks and intelligence scores was only .51; the prognosis by use of the more specific test was therefore much better. Other efforts at prediction in this field have produced coefficients anywhere between .20 and .60.

Prediction of marks in English composition has not been especially satisfactory, largely because it is so hard to construct a test that is both reliable and relevant. The usual grading of themes or other written work is distinctly unreliable. This point has been thoroughly proved by the efforts of the examiners at the University of Chicago to devise an adequate test which would predict success in this subject. Even when the written selections are only a paragraph long and are read by two people, the resulting scores are still too uncertain to give a good prognosis.[26] On the other hand, an objective test is rather irrelevant. It does measure some of the elements of composition, but by its nature it can test only recognition—not spontaneous composition. While there is, of course, a relationship between ability to recognize errors and ability to compose, the connection is not high enough to give a good prediction.[27] The coefficients range in general from .20 to .55.

[23] Incidentally, the reading and intelligence scores of these students were equally high.

[24] Tomlinson, *op. cit.*

[25] F. A. C. Perrin, "The Freshman Psychological Examination in the College of Arts and Sciences at the University of Texas," *University of Texas Bulletin,* 1924.

[26] F. W. Reeves, N. E. Peik, and J. D. Russell, "Instructional Problems in a University," *University of Chicago Survey,* Vol. 4, 1933, 245 pp.

[27] In one case the investigator (L. C. Pressey, "The Needs of Freshmen in Written English," *English Journal,* 19: 705–10, 1930) used a test which has the advantages of objective measurement and also calls for some ele-

In only one or two instances has the relation between tests and grades been high enough to afford much hope of a reliable forecast.[28] Although many tests will pick out a few students who are unusually good and a few who are outstandingly bad, they fail to catch all the extreme cases and they do not give a reliable relationship throughout the middle levels of performance.

At the lower end of the distribution, prediction within a subject is not too difficult. In one instance [29] all but one of the students thus selected for the precollege, noncredit course in English really needed the work, according to the opinions of their teachers. It is something to be able to foretell the level of work over even a narrow range.

There have been a few scattered efforts to work out a prognosis in both chemistry and physics,[30] but the results have not been satisfactory except in one investigation.[31] The other coefficients of correlation varied from .20 to .60; of the twenty reported in the above references, eleven were less than .50.

The various investigations here reported suggest that prediction within a subject is feasible and will probably be worked

mentary skill in sentence structure. A few sample items from this test appear below:

5. Rewrite the following sentence, inserting the words "If he tries" after "the boy" and making any other necessary changes.
   This boy can do good work.
9. Rewrite the following sentence, beginning with the words "If he does not stop and plan" and making any other necessary changes.
   His work is likely to become hurried and superficial.
22. Rewrite the following sentence, omitting the word "and" and making any other necessary changes.
   The speaker arrived promptly at six o'clock, and then he went to his room.

Although this test does not measure more than a single skill, this one is important. Its relation to marks was .58.

[28] McCall, *op. cit.;* Garrett, *op. cit.;* Gilkey, *op. cit.;* and Wagner, *op. cit.*
[29] L. K. Shumaker, "The Prediction of Success in English Composition," *Office of Education Bulletin,* No. 12, 1930, pp. 72–79.
[30] R. M. Bear, "Predictive Value of the Iowa Physics Aptitude Placement Test," *Journal of Applied Psychology,* 11: 381–84, 1927; M. E. Dickter, "Relationship between Scores on the Scholastic Aptitude Test and College Grades in Physics," *American Physics Teacher,* 5: 263–67, 1937, and "Relationship between Scores on the Scholastic Aptitude Test and College Grades in Chemistry," *Journal of Experimental Education,* 6: 40–45, 1937; F. Palmer, "A College Physics Testing Program and its Significance for Guidance in Secondary Schools," *Educational Record,* 16: 82–96, 1935; G. D. Stoddard, "Iowa Placement Examination," *op. cit.;* Tomlinson, *op. cit.;* Edds and McCall, *op. cit.;* Gowen and Gooch, *op. cit.*
[31] Perrin, *op. cit.*

out in a satisfactory manner in the course of time.[32] The measurement of preparation for the work is—except in the case of composition—relatively simple. Once the members of a department can settle upon what essentials contribute to success, these elements can be measured accurately and reliably. In addition, however, one must have some measure of industry, studiousness, ambition, interest in the subject, and attachment to the teacher. Thus far these nonacademic traits have not been adequately considered, and until they are the prognosis is likely to remain lower than it should be. Even with these added elements the relationship between test scores and marks will not be high unless the grades are distributed in a more normal manner than was the case in one of the above illustrations. In fact, every deviation in the marking system immediately affects the prognosis. If, for instance, a professor keeps students at work until they either drop out of his course or finish an entire series of problems with a score of 95 per cent or better, he will obviously have a distribution composed exclusively of A's, and there will be no relation whatever to any prediction, except in so far as one might foretell the amount of time needed to get an A. At present a good beginning has been made upon the problems of prediction, but much remains to be done before the scores are of more than suggestive value to the average college teacher.

There is, however, one use that can even now be made of prediction test scores. While there are any number of reasons why a student may make a low score on such a test, there is only one reason why he makes a high one—namely, that he is well prepared to do the work. If teachers would locate and encourage those who score in the highest 10 per cent on a prognosis test, they could make contact at once with most of the promising students. To be sure, there are a few freshmen who should score equally high and for some reason do

---

[32] For good summaries see A. B. Crawford, "Individual Differences in Educational Guidance," *Psychological Monographs,* Vol. 47, No. 212, 1936, pp. 148–72; Segel, *op. cit.;* R. R. Wolf, "Differential Forecasts of Achievement and Their Use in Educational Counseling," *Psychological Monographs,* Vol. 51, No. 1, 1939, pp. 1–53.

not do so. However, it is better to locate 60 or 70 per cent of the good educational risks than not to locate any of them. The prognosis tests, even as they stand, can point out many an embryo scholar. A college teacher should be glad of this help because he can concentrate at once upon those students who can most profit by his instruction.

III. SUMMARY

Prediction at the time of entrance of the general level of college work is reasonably good at the lower end of the distribution and fair at all levels. Within a single subject it is somewhat better—presumably because the tests can be made more precise. Any information that a teacher can glean from prediction is of value because he has a better idea of the level at which to begin his work and upon whom to concentrate. To date in many colleges the results of predictive tests have not been put into the hands of the faculty because of the feeling that the scores were not sufficiently reliable for use with individuals. Although these test results should not be regarded as infallible, they are—when used cautiously and sensibly and when backed by other data—of considerable value to the average teacher.

III.

THE PROBLEMS OF CLASSWORK

CHAPTER XIV

ADMINISTRATIVE PROCEDURES AFFECTING CLASSWORK

———

The assignment of students to classes and sections is largely an administrative matter, even though certain decisions are sometimes left to departmental control. The three main administrative procedures affecting teaching are the determination of class size, the division of large classes into homogeneous sections, and the use of quiz sections to supplement lectures. There has been fairly adequate experimentation on the first of these points, though some of the issues involved remain unsettled. Naturally teaching is affected by both the size and character of the group with which one is dealing. A college teacher needs therefore to have a basis of fact upon which to rest his conclusions about class size, homogeneous grouping, and the value of quiz sections. He will almost surely be forced into having some kind of opinion, and it is obviously to his advantage that his conclusions should rest upon something more than personal prejudice.

I. CLASS SIZE

Most experienced teachers want small classes, not merely because the "paper work" is less but because they are sure they can teach students more effectively in groups of not more than twenty than in groups that are larger. Almost the only exceptions to this opinion are those voiced by the few professors who enjoy lecturing and feel they can do better work when stimulated by an audience. Until about twenty-five years ago such large classes as existed were conducted by lecture chiefly because the person in charge preferred this method. It cannot be denied that there are people who teach a large class extremely well and make the material they present both interesting and worth while. One of my own best teachers always lectured—regardless of the size of his group; the difference in his work between a large and a small class was only that before the former he lectured much better. For the great majority of teachers, however, a large class is, subjectively at least, unsatisfactory.

With the increases in enrollment since 1900, and especially since 1915, colleges and universities have been faced with the necessity of giving mass instruction. The reasons are primarily financial. In one careful investigation the cost per student for classes of 125 to 150 was $4.12; for groups between 8 and 15 it was $33.41.[1] The typical tuition fee in a state university is about $20.00 each semester—outside of laboratory and other special charges. If a student takes five courses he pays about $4.00 a course. In a college in which the classes are purposely kept below ten students the tuition is about $250.00 a semester—or $50.00 for each of five courses. Although the influx of students in the first few years might have precipitated a few large classes until enough qualified teachers could be found, the situation would not have continued if the cost of instructing thousands of students in small groups had not been prohibitive. For most public institutions the tuition fees are too low to provide for anything but mass instruction during the first year or two at any rate. No sensible person quarrels with expediency. The practical circumstances are what they are, and many administrators are so well satisfied with such results as those to be quoted shortly that they are making

[1] E. Hudelson, *Problems of College Education,* University of Minnesota Press, 1928, 449 pp. See also F. W. Reeves, N. B. Henry, J. D. Russell, "Class Size and University Costs," *University of Chicago Survey,* Vol. 11, 1933, 229 pp.; and F. Von Borgersrode, *Relation of Class Size to the Effectiveness of College Instruction,* University of Minnesota Library, 1929, 238 pp.

little effort to change the situation. Large classes will therefore continue to exist—but the nature and interests of superior teachers will have to change considerably before most of them become reconciled to this reality. They will undoubtedly keep on exerting what pressure they can for the reduction of class size and eventually they may succeed. In the meantime, however, any teacher who does not work in an institution that insists upon small classes needs to know to what extent instruction is efficient when given to large groups.

The actual facts from the most outstanding of the investigations can be summarized in a brief space. At Minnesota [2] the students in classes with enrollments between 115 and 150 averaged 72.7 points on their final tests, while the students in classes with enrollments between 8 and 15 averaged 71.4. At the University of Oregon [3] the differences in achievement between classes averaging 29, 37, or 104 students were all very small and in all cases favored the biggest group. At Purdue University,[4] where the work was done in trigonometry classes, the investigators took great care to match students as to intelligence and previous preparation in mathematics. In three successive semesters the experiment was repeated—with identical results. The difference in percentage standing between classes was not over 2 per cent and was always in favor of the large groups. At the close of each semester the students rated their teachers on a rating scale that covered such points as attitude toward students, ability to stimulate intellectual curiosity, presentation of subject matter, and so on. The experiment had been arranged in such a way that every teacher had an equal number of large and small sections during the

[2] Hudelson, *Problems of College Education, op. cit.,* pp. 403–420. See also H. A. Erickson, "An Experiment on Class Size in the Department of Physics," *ibid.,* pp. 421–25.
[3] H. R. Douglass, "Controlled Experimentation in the Study of Methods of College Teaching," *University of Oregon Publications, Education Series,* Vol. I, No. 7, 1929.
[4] H. H. Remmers, L. Hadley, and J. K. Long, "Learning Effort and Attitude as Affected by Class Size in Beginning College Engineering Mathematics," *Purdue Studies in Higher Education,* XIX, Vol. 32, No. 9, 1932, 31 pp. See also B. F. Holland, "The Effects of Class Size on Scholastic Acquirements in Educational Psychology," *School and Society,* 27 : 668–70, 1928.

year. He was therefore rated an equal number of times by the two types of class. In 53 per cent of the instances an instructor was rated higher on a given trait by a small than by a large group. As far as the students were concerned, then, the teaching was about as satisfactory in one as in the other.

There are at least four reasons why large classes should have proved superior for the learning of facts. I have worded this statement in this way because the tests used in the various investigations have measured very little except factual achievement. In the first place, the teacher is almost inevitably an expert; he has to be. No one who is not can keep a class of several hundred under control long enough to teach it anything. In the second place, a professor can never neglect his preparation and trust to his skill in improvising. The moment he wavers, the class falls to pieces. Consequently the teacher is always ready. Third, the material is presented in logical units without the interruptions or diversions that are sure to occur when the group is small enough to permit discussion. Many students have great difficulty in synthesizing a discussion, but they can learn material that is set before them with the conclusions already drawn. Finally, the presentation is usually geared to the abilities of those at the lower end of the distribution. As a result the teacher pounds away at the fundamental points and succeeds in getting them well understood. Small classes rarely get drill that is so intensive.

In a few of the experiments the same instructors have taught both a very large and a very small class in the same course. They have used the same readings and, within reasonable limits, the same methods of presentation. This arrangement eliminates the inevitable differences that are introduced into an experiment by variations in personality among teachers. The results, however, remain unchanged; the large classes are still superior. Such outcomes suggest that many teachers are definitely stimulated to better work in direct proportion to the number of people who will listen. In fact, some of the instructors involved have said as much.

For all of the experiments thus far mentioned the teaching was, in general, the same for both small and large groups. Investigators at the University of Chicago [5] tried the effect of changes in method upon the situation. When the teaching was the same in classes of eighty and twenty students, six out of the seven bases of comparison in regard to the value of the work favored the large class. When the work in the small group was partially individualized, six out of seven comparisons—although slight—were in favor of the small class. When the work was still further individualized, all comparisons favored the small class by a considerable margin.[6] The students rated their courses as to the time required for study, the intellectual challenge of the work, the interest they developed, and the benefits they derived. On the first two points the large and small classes received equal commendation, but on the last two the small group was considered superior. From these results one can conclude (1) that the mere placing of students into groups of fifteen or twenty will—in and of itself—do no particular good, (2) that small classes will yield results in direct ratio to the appropriateness of the methods for the handling of such groups, and (3) that the students derive more profit from a small than a large class if it is properly taught.

All educational issues in regard to class size are not, however, settled because one can prove that students master as many facts in a large as in a small class. While one gets rather tired of the statement that a school consists of Mark Hopkins on one end of a log and a student on the other, one cannot deny the value or the importance of student-teacher relationships. Thus far the examinations used in investigations of class size have been primarily factual, although they probably contained some general questions. When other types of measurement can be used it may appear that the large class is not as satisfactory as it now seems to be. Indeed, most teachers regard other results of teaching as far more important than

[5] F. W. Reeves, W. E. Peik, and J. D. Russell, "Instructional Problems in the University," *University of Chicago Survey*, Vol. 4, 1933, 245 pp.

[6] See also F. A. Moss, "Impersonal Measurement of Teaching," *Educational Record*, 10: 40–50, 1929 and *Proceedings of the Forty-first Annual Convention of the Association of Land-Grant Colleges and Universities*, 1927, 73 pp.

the acquisition of information. The matter then is not settled because adequate information in certain important phases of the subject is still lacking.

It may turn out eventually that students in the introductory classes in some subjects, because of the factual content of the courses, are about as well off in a group of three hundred as in a section of fifteen. At least if a college cannot afford to have small classes under all circumstances, it should probably save money at the lowest level in some of its departments and thus conserve its funds for the teaching of those students who continue beyond the first course. At present in the large universities the introductory course in many departments enrolls eight hundred freshmen; two dozen or so sequent courses have about one hundred students each, and the numerous advanced classes about forty apiece. If the freshmen are placed in twenty sections the expense will be so high that the intermediate and advanced courses will also have to remain too large for the development of personal contacts between students and teachers. With the money a department can save by teaching all its freshmen in a single group it can divide its more advanced courses and can give some degree of individual attention to its major students. Such an arrangement is by no means ideal, but it may be the best that can be made under the existing circumstances. This whole matter is related to the efficiency of the lecture method and will be discussed further in the next chapter.

II. SECTIONING UPON THE BASIS OF ABILITY

Some years ago, when mental tests first appeared, both their originators and teachers in general thought the results could be used for grouping students into sections on the basis of innate ability, with a consequent reduction of difficulties in teaching. This assumption led to various plans for segregation at all educational levels. Testimony as to the results has been somewhat contradictory. The most tenable conclusion at present seems to be that segregation in the lower schools makes the teaching situation only slightly easier, does not produce any great educational advantages for the pupils, and often contributes to the development of undesirable traits of personality. These conclusions do not, however, necessarily hold for work in college. During the elementary school years a child may become intolerably conceited because he is a member of a "fast" section or develop marked feelings of inferiority because he is assigned to a "slow" one. These reactions are partly the products of his immaturity. He does not yet know that his ability at any one point in time is the result of his inheritance plus his training; consequently, he regards any unusual capacity as something he has invented and any defect as something he should be ashamed of. College students are old enough to grasp the idea that membership in a fast section means merely greater opportunity and greater responsibility, while membership in a slow section offers a chance to remedy defects or to adjust to them. Even if freshmen do not have these ideas at entrance to college they are mature enough to understand them. The teacher of brilliant students can guard against conceit and can nip it in the bud when it appears; the teacher of dull students can guard against discouragement. In any case the possible effects of segregation are not so serious because the personalities of freshmen are already well formed. Hence some of the objections raised against sectioning in the lower grades do not apply to work in college. The matter can therefore be decided wholly by the instructional situation for the teacher and the learning situation for the student.

There are many reports upon the effects of sectioning in various college classes. Of these, three are especially interesting. The first experiment [7] had three subdivisions. During the first term the students were segregated at three levels according to ability and preparation, but all sections were taught in the same way. There were no differences on any given level of ability in the achievement of students who attended a homogeneous section over those on the same level in heterogeneous classes. During the second term the curriculum was enriched somewhat for the fast groups and re-

[7] O. A. Ullrich, "An Experimental Study of the Effect on Learning of Sectioning College Classes," Doctor's Thesis, University of Texas, 1926, 56 pp.

duced somewhat for the slow. The students in the former made
10 per cent more gain than those in the middle group and 22 per
cent more than those in the slow section; the middle section showed
an achievement of 11 per cent over the lowest. During the third
term the curriculum was enriched still more. The highest class
then made 33 per cent more gain than the middle and 48 per cent
more than the lowest, while the middle group exceeded the slow by
the same amount as before.

Similar results are reported by two other investigators. One [8] of
them used the relation between intelligence and achievement as the
criterion of effective teaching; on this assumption teaching is good
if every student is working up to his capacity and poor if the
relationship is low. The correlations remained unchanged after
the sectioning was first made. That is, the mere placing of students
in special groups did not affect the relationship. In subsequent
semesters the teachers tried to push every student into doing all
the work of which he was capable. The correlations between ability
and marks rose appreciably.

The third investigator [9] based his sectioning upon the general
average of students in their work before they took his course in
descriptive geometry. For the best sections he selected those with a
previous average of B and for the poorest those with an average
of slightly more than D, or less. The work done, as reflected by
marks, is indicated below:

Students	Grades				
	A	B	C	D	E
77 students with excellent records	35%	44%	21%	—	—
80 students with poor records....	—	—	42%	30%	28%

Although there is some overlapping in the middle of the distribution, the segregation seems in the main to have been adequate.
Grades are not, however, the best possible criterion. If the teacher

[8] H. E. Burtt et al., "Proficiency of Instruction in Selected Sections of
Elementary Psychology," *Journal of Educational Psychology,* 14: 154–61,
1923.
[9] H. W. Miller, "Segregation on the Basis of Ability," *School and
Society,* 26: 84–88 and 114–20, 1927. Used by permission of *School and
Society* and the author.

of a low section has a flair for diagnostic and remedial teaching, some of his students will do work far in excess of expectation—thus upsetting the statistics but augmenting the human values of education.

One other variation in treatment should be mentioned. In the above experiments the time allowed for the course was the same for all sections, but in many cases the content was different. It is possible to keep the content uniform and alter the time. Two such experiments have been reported.[10] In the first case, the best groups met three times a week, the middle ones four times, and the poorest five times. The achievement was supposed to be roughly the same for all classes, thus making the problem of articulation with the next course somewhat easier. Because of the saving of time the students in the highest sections were able to elect one more course than they would normally have carried. In some situations this arrangement may prove more practicable than the alternative plan of enriching or reducing the content of a course.[11]

Sectioning at the college level would appear to be worth while if the teaching, or the content of the course, or both, are changed to suit the needs of the learner. As to any possible bad effects upon personality the literature is silent. It has

[10] J. B. Tharp, "Sectioning Classes in Romance Languages," *Modern Language Journal,* 12 : 95–114, 1927; C. M. Brown, "An Experiment in Sectioning," *Journal of Higher Education,* 1 : 269–73, 1930.

[11] There have been, of course, a large number of other experiments, many of them interesting and valuable, but a presentation of them would be repetitious. A few references may, however, be listed. F. D. Cheydleur, "Placement and Attainment Examinations in Foreign Languages," *Educational Record,* 15 : 176–91, 1934; H. S. Colton, "Segregation of Zoology Students on the Basis of Ability," *School and Society,* 23 : 471–72, 1926; H. W. Miller, "Profits Derived from Segregating College Students on the Basis of Ability," *Science,* 65 : 427–29, 1927; R. E. Monroe, "Adapting Instruction to the Ability of the Student in the Romance Languages," *Bureau of Educational Research Monograph,* Ohio State University, No. 15, 1932, pp. 123–34; G. W. Munroe, "Selected Sections at Double Pace," *Purdue University, Studies in Higher Education,* VII, Vol. 27, No. 4, 1926, 20 pp.; J. W. Price and J. A. Miller, "An Experiment in Sectioning Students in the Second Course in Zoology," *Bureau of Educational Research Monograph, No. 15,* Ohio State University, 1932, pp. 79–92; H. E. Schoonmaker, "The Value of the Hotz Algebra Scales in Sectioning College Classes in Freshman Mathematics," *School Science and Mathematics,* 28 : 880–84, 1928; L. C. Seibert and E. R. Goddard, "The Use of Achievement Tests in Sectioning Students," *Modern Language Journal,* 18 : 289–98, 1934; M. B. Scofield, "Further Studies on Sectioning in General Chemistry," *Journal of Chemistry Education,* 7 : 117–26, 1930; J. B. Tharp, "How Shall We Section Beginning Foreign Language Classes?" *Modern Language Journal,* 13 : 433–49, 1929.

always seemed to me as if the grouping of students into sections were only a halfway station between class and individual instruction, and—like most compromises—not especially valuable. It may be desirable, however, on grounds of either expediency or socialization. Sometime there will presumably be enough evidence to justify a conclusion rather than an opinion.

III. QUIZ SECTIONS

In most colleges and universities the students in the large lecture classes attend small quiz sections once or twice a week. The ratio of section meetings to lectures is apparently a function of tradition rather than of research. I have found variations all the way from one quiz for five lectures, to three quizzes for one lecture. Thus far I can find only one article [12] that bears in the least upon the value of quiz sections. In this case students who were in a lecture course with no quiz made as good progress as others who had one quiz each week. This single contribution is too slight to prove anything. The subject is discussed here at all only to call attention to the need for investigation. It should be possible to find out what ratio between quizzes and lectures will produce the best results, and whether or not quiz sections actually add to the mastery students achieve on the basis of lectures alone.

IV. SUMMARY

The one outstanding lesson of this chapter is that no administrative procedure by which students are placed in classes of different sizes or types is automatically and inevitably of value. Indeed, unless a rearrangement is accompanied by adequate changes in teaching and content, it is more likely than not to be quite futile. The administrative task is merely to produce a situation in which a teacher can most easily teach; it is then the instructor's job to adapt his presentation so as to get the greatest possible value out of the new arrangement.

[12] H. R. Douglass and D. G. Barnes, "The Value of an Extra Quiz Section in the Teaching of English History," *University of Oregon Publications, Education Series*, Vol. 1, No. 7, 1929, pp. 276–84.

All the problems need further investigation—although it is already clear enough that changing the size or character of a class without altering anything else does not have as much effect upon learning as might be supposed. Especially is there need to measure student growth under different plans along other lines than mere learning of facts. There is nothing inherently impossible about giving instruction to groups of any type or any size, but unless teachers have flexible methods they are not likely to get the best educational results from whatever arrangement they have.

CHAPTER XV

PROCEDURES IN CLASS

In recent years there have been literally hundreds of experiments on methods of teaching in college. Their scope has ranged all the way from simple investigations of the comparative value of two techniques for teaching vocabulary in first-year French to complete reorganizations of undergraduate work.[1] From the mass of available data I have tried to pick out representative samples of various types of investigation. It is naturally not possible in one short chapter to describe all variations and methods, so I have included only those that were either recurrent in the literature or of some special interest.

There are three typical and traditional methods of procedure in college classes—the lecture, the discussion (or recitation), and the laboratory experiment. In recent years various forms of individualization have made their appearance. These four general methods are all used by most teachers at one time or another and in one situation or another. The lecture is the customary method of mass instruction; in some universities one finds classes with enrollments as large as 1,500 meeting in an auditorium, where the lecturer's words are amplified by

---

[1] For summaries of this work see F. V. Speek, "One Hundred Twenty-Eight Outstanding Changes and Experiments," *Thirty-first Yearbook of the National Society for the Study of Education,* Part II, 1932, pp. 43–155, and H. M. Wriston, "A Critical Appraisal of Experiments in General Education," *Thirty-eighth Yearbook of the National Society for the Study of Education,* Part II, 1939, pp. 297–321.

loud speakers. For classes that contain 60 or more students, the lecture is almost the only possible technique. In smaller classes the discussion method is more in vogue; it may take various forms, but the essential feature is that students participate in the development of ideas and points of view. Until recently the laboratory method was regarded as an essential element for all work in any science. Indeed, its advocates have imputed to it many Christian virtues in addition to various intellectual advantages. There is no space in a book of this type to describe in any detail the different plans for individualization. The main element in them all is that each student is treated as a person and is allowed to proceed at his own rate and in his own way.

In the past decade many people have become agitated about (1) the lecture method of teaching—especially as compared to the discussion or individual methods, (2) the use of laboratory work as an introduction to science, and (3) the value of applying to higher education the same principles of individualized work, educational analysis, and remedial teaching that have been found so effective in the lower schools. The experimental results to date seem far from conclusive, but they should serve at least to indicate the problems involved.

I. LECTURES VERSUS DISCUSSION

The growth in college enrollments has precipitated the establishment of many large courses that can be taught only by a lecture method. There is little else one can do with a class of 100 or more students. This number could, of course, be distributed into several sections, if the expense involved were not so great. Suppose, for instance, that a course has enrolled 760 students and that a single professor gives all the lectures. If he has four assistants—usually graduate students—to help him in scoring papers, the total cost of the course would add up about as follows:

Professor's salary $5,500
Four assistants @ $600 each 2,400
$7,900

Suppose, however, that these 760 students are put in classes of 20 to 25. There would be about thirty-three such sections. If they are to be even fairly well taught, the institution will have to employ teachers who already have their degrees. One teacher could handle not more than four small sections effectively, so there would have to be eight of them. If each received what is about the minimum salary of $2,000, the cost of the course becomes $16,000—or approximately twice the expense involved if a single professor lectures. In order to keep the cost the same, the work would need to be done by only four young instructors each of whom would then have three sections with an average enrollment of 63 students. Such classes are too big for the students to obtain the benefits that may accrue from personal contacts between student and teachers and too big for more than an occasional discussion, especially in the hands of a young teacher. Consequently, the 760 students would get lectures in groups of 65 from inexperienced instructors, instead of getting much better lectures in a single class from an experienced person. Unless one is prepared to double the expense, the entire group might therefore better be left together. This solution is so far from ideal that one hopes it is only temporary; colleges and universities should eventually make a better adjustment to their increased enrollments than they have made thus far.

Naturally the administrative officers in colleges and universities are interested, not only in keeping the budget within reasonable limits, but also in supporting teaching efficiency. From the first appearance of large classes there have been doubts as to the possibility of effective work in them. What people wanted was some demonstration of the efficacy of lectures as compared with class discussions. Because of the relation of this matter to the budget there have been a number of carefully controlled experiments to determine the educational value of the lecture method.

The outstanding conclusion of all the experiments is inescapable: that in so far as mere mastery of elementary subject matter is concerned the lecture method is as good as any other. The results are sometimes almost identical for the lectures and discussion groups, sometimes slightly in favor of the discussion classes, and often appreciably in favor of the lecture classes.[2] One sample experiment should suffice to show the nature of the results.[3]

In the fall of 1930, the students who would normally have formed four sections of an elementary subject were put together in one large lecture group two days a week; for the third hour they met in small groups. At the same time there were six other sections in the same subject. All of these were small and were taught by a discussion method. The students were assigned to one type of section or another in such a way that the level of intelligence and of achievement upon placement tests was the same for all groups. Those students who had two lectures and one discussion a week were superior on the various short tests given throughout the semester, on the objective final examination, on the nonobjective final, and in the distribution of marks. The wholly discussion classes showed a slight superiority in their daily lesson sheets—a set of exercises that could be handed in or not according to the students' wishes. The investigators thought the failure of the small sections and the discussion method to show superiority might be due to a difference in the teachers who worked with the various groups. During the following year (1931) therefore the staff was rotated so that each person used each method with

[2] C. L. Bane, "The Lecture Versus the Class-Discussion Method of College Teaching," *School and Society,* 21 : 300–2, 1925; S. M. Corey, "Learning from Lectures Versus Learning from Readings," *Journal of Educational Psychology,* 25 : 459–70, 1934; D. R. Davis and H. R. Douglass, "Relative Effectiveness of Lecture-Recitation and Supervised-individual Methods in the Teaching of Unified Mathematics in College," *University of Oregon Publications, Education Series,* Vol. I, No. 7, 1929, pp. 313–16; V. P. Morris and H. R. Douglass, "The Relative Effectiveness of the Problem and Lecture Methods of Instruction in Principles of Economics," *ibid.,* pp. 285–92; J. R. Gerberich and K. O. Warner, "Relative Efficiency of the Lecture and Discussion Methods in a University Course in American Government," *Journal of Educational Research,* 29 : 574-79, 1936; E. B. Greene, "The Relative Effectiveness of Lecture and Individual Reading as Methods of College Teaching," *Genetic Psychology Monographs,* 4 : 463–563, 1928; C. W. Gwinn, "An Experimental Study of College Classroom Teaching," *Contributions to Education,* George Peabody College, No. 76, 1930, 135 pp.; S. H. McGuire, "Two Procedures in Teaching Modern European History," in *A College Looks at Its Program,* 1937, pp. 65–74; H. H. Remmers, "Learning Effort and Attitudes as Affected by Three Methods of Instruction in Elementary Psychology," *Purdue Studies in Higher Education,* XXI, Vol. 33, No. 6, 1933, 48 pp.; R. B. Spence, "Lecture and Class Discussion in Teaching Educational Psychology," *Journal of Educational Psychology,* 19 : 454–62, 1928.

[3] Remmers, *op. cit.*

equal frequency. The results remained essentially unchanged, except that the lecture section was better on all counts. To make the matter still clearer the experiment was repeated in 1932, but this time the four sections that had been combined were given three lectures a week and no discussion at all, while the other six continued with all discussion and no lectures. All differences were in favor of the lecture group, and most of them were large enough to be significant.

Other investigations [4] have been concerned with student reactions to discussions or lectures. In most cases the students seem about equally divided as to their preferences. Those who favor lectures state that they learn more, that they dislike the time wasted in aimless discussion when their age-mates do much of the talking, that they feel more mature and responsible under the lecture system, and that the teacher is both more interesting and better prepared when lecturing than when guiding discussion. Those who prefer discussions state that lectures give them no chance to ask questions or to talk, that the lectures are too formal, that they are not interesting, and that they cannot be adapted to a student's personal problems as a discussion can be. From these comments it seems to me that two types of individual are involved. An emotionally mature student who wants to learn as much as he can about a subject appreciates the preparation and keenness the professor brings to a large audience and resents the constant interruptions that are inevitable in small groups. When he is in class he wants to hear what the teacher has to say; he can listen to his confreres anywhere. The other type of student is not happy unless he can talk; he wants special help, which he cannot get in a large group; he wants attention paid to his individual peculiarities and interests. The one type wants to get something from the class hour; the other wants to put something into it. Since it is hard to imagine a student world in which both types do not exist, the argument among undergraduates as to lectures versus discussions is not likely to be settled.

It will of course be noted that the experimental results thus far have been concerned almost entirely with the mastery of

---

[4] See, for instance, W. D. Armentrout, "College Students' Preferences for Certain Mechanics of the Class Period," *School and Society*, 24: 739–40, 1926; E. L. Holton, "A Study of Methods of Presenting Subject Matter to Undergraduates in Colleges," *School and Society*, 11: 58–59, 1920; H. H. Horne, "University Students on the Discussion Method," *School and Society*, 16: 218–21, 1922.

facts. For this purpose lecturing is probably an effective method of procedure. This conclusion runs counter to the pet convictions of many people, especially those who define lecturing by the well-known phrase, "The method by which the facts in the professor's notebook get into the student's notebook without passing through the mind of either." This is a definition of a poor lecturer and a poor student. If the same student and professor changed to the discussion method, I see no reason to think that matters would be improved any. It is naturally true that some people lecture badly, and that some types of material do not lend themselves to this method of presentation, but these facts do not prove the method to be useless; some teachers lecture with excellent results.

Since lecturing seems to be a quick and direct way of supplying students with a survey of the basic facts in a given field it would seem a method adapted for introductory courses, especially in the sciences since these subjects require the mastery of so much factual material. At the beginning of a science the students have relatively little to contribute; nor are they yet ready for intelligent discussion. The lecture has its chief value, perhaps, in the elementary course and becomes less and less useful as students advance in their work.

Too many people judge the lecture method by its poorer exponents, of whom there are unfortunately some on every campus. In the hands of an expert, lecturing is an educative way of teaching some courses, in some departments, at some levels. There are so many kinds of lecturers—good and bad—that it seems worth while to give specific examples of the extremes.

Mr. C has remained in my mind as my one first-class lecturer. In a small class of a dozen students he was always ill at ease and often actually dull. He did not, however, often have small classes because he was too popular. His interest in students as individuals was not far from nil, and he apparently found the task of talking to them two or three at a time unbearably wearing. His manner—except when he was teaching—was detached, impersonal, and distant, but when he began to lecture he became a different person. His lectures were marvels of close organization, keen thinking, crystal-clear exposition, gay humor, and forceful presentation. Every day's lecture was meticulously joined on to that of the previous day; the work of the whole semester flowed on in an even stream from the first hour to the last. Even if one were a poor student, one could still construct a coherent outline of the entire course merely by taking down Mr. C's main points and matching the degree of subordination of each item to the amount of emphasis apparent at the moment in Mr. C's flexible voice. But supreme clarity was not the whole story. Mr. C sprinkled clever illustrations throughout his lectures. Indeed, he was an excellent raconteur—but only during working hours. The only intimate details the students ever knew of his life were those he described at length to illustrate general principles during his lectures. From a large class he obviously derived great stimulation, and the bigger it was the better he talked. On the lecture platform he was alive, interesting, intimate, and exciting. As he talked, the students sat on the edge of their seats, eyes wide, and attention riveted on the speaker. There was nothing passive about those who listened to Mr. C. He was so entertaining that one did not want to miss a word. The elements of humor and ingenuity were, however, strictly subordinated to the business of teaching the essential facts and theories of an introductory course. They merely provided such good butter that students ate a great deal of bread without finding it dry. The doubting Thomas in the matter of lectures does not need to take the verbal testimony of Mr. C's former students that the method he used was satisfactory. Cold statistics prove the same point. During the period from five years after Mr. C began teaching to five years before he resigned, almost 75 per cent of all the undergraduates in the institution elected his introductory course. It was not required in any student's curriculum unless he wanted to take advanced work in the same department. Moreover, there is evidence that the work was not merely amusing and interesting. In the national organization of teachers and research workers in Mr. C's field, the largest single contingent comes from this one college. In the face of these facts even the person who is most prejudiced against the lecture method can hardly say that this procedure is always and inevitably ineffective.

Unfortunately there are relatively few exponents of lecturing as an art. I am quite convinced that a successful use of the method requires a certain combination of traits that most teachers do not possess—and those that do sometimes do not have the necessary scholarship to use their skill in the most productive and educative way. The objections to the lecture method are perhaps based fundamentally upon observation of such performances as that described below:

Mr. W was the lecturer in charge of a large required course. His assistant came to class at the beginning of the hour and kept the students from leaving until Mr. W chose to arrive. In the meantime, there was a great deal of talking, some moving about, occasional bursts of laughter, and sometimes whistling, stamping, or singing. When Mr. W put in an appearance, some fifteen or twenty minutes late, the students were in no mood for working. By the time he got the class under control, about half the period had elapsed. It then became evident that he was totally unprepared. He hemmed and hawed, told jokes that were not funny, related personal anecdotes, fussed with papers on the desk, and broke the chalk into bits, until finally some topic in which he had an interest occurred to him. Unfortunately, it rarely had much relevance to the course. We heard his views upon such divergent topics as woman suffrage, slavery, the sanctity of marriage, the sad state of politics, the broadening influence of foreign travel, the duties of citizens in a democracy, the need for freedom of speech, the values of a college education, the morals of modern youth, and the nature of the federal government. Once he got under way, he became an impassioned orator. He shouted, waved his arms, shook his fists, and got red in the face. About once a week he actually talked about some matter relevant to the course. When he did, another defect became evident; he was completely out of date. The experiments he quoted were twenty to thirty years old, and the general theories he defended had usually been exploded. Mr. W had probably once been an average teacher, but he had been doing administrative work for many years. He kept control of this large class because he could get a bigger salary by so doing. It is my impression that Mr. W was a good administrator and that he could have been a good teacher if he had not preferred to spend his time and energy playing campus politics. He neglected his teaching, he was "rusty" and out of date, he substituted bombast and shouting for knowledge, he insisted upon clinging to a job for which he was no longer equipped, and he bored his students almost unbearably. I have no doubt that he lectured primarily because he thought this method took less effort than a class discussion. On almost any campus one or two such lecturers exist and do much toward arousing wholesale condemnation of the method.

There are other results of teaching, however, beside the learning of facts. Whatever value may lie in personal relationships between a teacher and his students is certainly better obtained in a small class in which an informal discussion is carried on largely by student initiative. These as yet unmeasured results of instruction should have their influence in determining teaching method. Everyone admits the value of personal relationships,[5] but remarkably little seems to be objectively known about them. There is a general conviction that they cannot or do not develop in large classes—although in isolated instances they undoubtedly do.

One might reach a conclusion about the value of student-teacher relationships, if one knew how many teachers were of real influence as persons in the lives of, say, 1,000 students, for what reasons, and whether or not the methods used by these teachers were responsible for their influence. At the risk of becoming tiresome, I intend to quote my own experiences with college teachers in an effort to estimate what and how much effect they had upon me. I have tried to disregard what they taught and to center attention entirely upon their influence as individuals. For instance, one professor from whom I learned many useful facts and theories had no personal influence upon me; if his work had been given through a dictaphone the degree of personal contact could have hardly been less. Merely as people, then, I would estimate the value of personal contacts between myself and twenty-four college teachers as follows:

No influence 18
Some influence 4
Great influence 2

By "no influence" I mean that, although I remember the teacher, she or he might just as well have been someone else; if another

[5] See, for instance, C. Gauss and K. Blunt, "Student-Faculty Relationships," *Association of American Colleges Bulletin*, 18: 196–204, 1932; C. C. Little, "The Relation between Faculty and Students," *Bulletin of the American Association of University Professors*, 13: 219–29, 1927.

person had said and done the same things, I cannot see that I would have cared. By "some influence" I mean that my relation to these teachers was close enough that substitution of another individual would have made a difference in the value I derived from their courses. By "great influence" I mean that these two teachers influenced me as much as anyone I have known. Out of twenty-four instructors, then, only six had any more influence than any other equally well-prepared person would probably have had. Nor was it because of either large classes or lecturing, since I was in almost no class of more than twenty students and rarely heard any lectures. The point seems to be that, even under the best of circumstances, only a few teachers will attract any one student—but those few may have a tremendous effect. Although the above instance is only one isolated record, the general conclusion seems to be in accord with the experiences of many college graduates with whom I have discussed the matter.

Until the measures of teaching efficiency are modified so that they take account not only of factual mastery but also of general intellectual and personal development the questions about teaching method will not be settled. If teaching consists primarily of pouring knowledge into students, the lecture technique is as good as any other and certainly less expensive; if it consists in guiding individual development, there would seem to be some a priori doubts as to its value. One cannot, however, actually prove the value of discussion in small groups over lectures in large ones until one has some objective measure of all the types of progress that one wants students to make. While the experiments to date are of their kind excellent, they side-step some of the main issues.

II. LABORATORY WORK

For a good many years after the sciences became established college subjects no one doubted the absolute necessity of the laboratory work in the introductory courses. Aside from any value it might have in the learning of a science, it was considered indispensable in training the mind, in teaching students to observe, and in showing them how to reason inductively—apparently from any premise to any conclusion. Gradually it has become clear that a student learns to think about a given type of material primarily by thinking about it—not by transferring patterns of thought from some other subject. Thus the social scientist learns to reason well in social science, the Latin scholar learns to reason about Latin, and the chemist learns to reason about chemistry. The idea—once vigorously defended—that training in a chemistry laboratory would make one think better about anything whatsoever, including present-day politics, has been completely exploded. The question remains, however, as to the value of the laboratory in the learning of elementary science. Until the last few years this value was unchallenged and might still be so had not the expense for both the necessary equipment and the teachers, if a college is to give laboratory work to enormous freshman classes, brought the matter forcibly to the attention of all concerned. Out of a total group of some 2,000 freshmen who are taking chemistry in a large university there are likely to be not more than 30 embryo chemists—all subdivisions of the subject included—and not more than 200 others who will go into lines of work—such as medicine, dentistry, dietetics, or pharmacy—for which a considerable amount of laboratory work in chemistry is of obvious practical use. The experimental results to be quoted shortly are concerned with the value of the laboratory for the 1,770 other entering freshmen for whom the chemistry course represents merely a sampling of one field of knowledge. These students use chemistry every day of their lives, but it does not necessarily follow that those who have laboratory work will understand the phenomena any better than those who have had the same material presented in some other way. If it should turn out that the students are about as well prepared for daily living and for a nontechnical understanding of chemistry without laboratory work as with it, the saving of time, money, and nerve strain will be considerable for all concerned.

To date the results are only partially conclusive. The measurement has been concerned almost wholly to the mastery of facts—a restriction that in elementary science is not as objectionable as in some other fields—and the comparisons have often involved only immediate rather than delayed recall. Of fifteen experiments in which the lecture-demonstration-by-the-teacher was compared with individual laboratory work, seven deal with immediate recall, only three with recall over a longer period than two months, and none with a longer period than five months.[6] The differences in immediate recall were almost uniformly in favor of the lecture-demonstration method, but they are all small and many of them are within the probable error of the measurement. Of the nine investigations that measured retention after some lapse of time between two weeks and five months, six favored the laboratory method and three the lecture-demonstration; the latter differences were however larger than the former. The whole matter of effectiveness, even for the learning of facts, is therefore still open to question and needs more and better experimentation before the truth can be known.

Four special investigations seem of sufficient value to merit reporting in some detail. The first [7] dealt with dissection work in anatomy. It had been the custom to provide one cadaver for each two students; during the year of the experiment, one was provided for each four. There was no discernible difference in the knowledge gained from the dissection, although each student watched someone else do many of the things that in former years he would have done himself. The second experiment [8] was designed to determine to what extent laboratory work could be reduced without deleterious effects upon achievement. Some of the classes had the usual five lectures, two quizzes, and seven and one-half hours of laboratory each week; others had the lectures and quizzes, but only five hours of laboratory—the remaining two hours being spent in the library. The results show the slight superiority of those having the greater amount of laboratory work, but the difference was not large enough to warrant the extra time and expense. In another experiment of similar nature [9] the amount of laboratory was reduced from five to three hours.

[6] E. R. Downing, "Methods in Science Teaching," *Journal of Higher Education,* 2: 316–20, 1931. This article contains reference to fifteen experiments.

[7] A. W. Hurd, *Problems of Science Teaching at the College Level,* University of Minnesota Press, 1929, 195 pp. Also C. M. Jackson, "Experiment in Methods of Teaching Gross Human Anatomy," in E. Hudelson, *Problems of College Education, op. cit.,* pp. 444–49.

[8] V. H. Noll, *Laboratory Instruction in the Field of Inorganic Chemistry,* University of Minnesota Press, 1930, 164 pp.

[9] V. H. Noll, "The Optimum Laboratory Emphasis in College Chemistry," *School and Society,* 32: 300–3, 1930.

Again, the students with less work in laboratory made slightly lower scores than the others, but the differences are too small to be reliable.

The last of the four experiments [10] reports a comparison of progress in botany by 282 students who made their own drawings and 286 students who used printed drawings prepared for them. The former group scored lower on the tests throughout the year than the latter. In fact the differences were large enough to leave little doubt that students were better off with a set of correctly made drawings and no laboratory work of this character than they were with their own, often badly drawn sketches.

The moral of these last few experiments is that, for the ordinary elementary student who does not intend to make technical use of his laboratory technique, there can be a considerable reduction of time, effort, and expense without any significant reduction of achievement. Just how many hours of laboratory work constitute the optimum amount is not known. Indeed, I do not see any prospect of solving this particular problem by the procedures thus far used because the measurements have simply compared mastery of traditional material by two different methods; they have ignored the much more important question of whether or not this traditional material is appropriate for the average educated adult to learn by any method. For most students, to whom a year's work in a science is an introduction to some phase of the physical universe, a different course altogether is presumably needed. Once the content of such a course is established, it will be time enough to find out by what method of instruction it can best be taught. It now seems as if laboratory work would eventually be restricted, for the most part, to those intending to become chemists, physicists, zoologists, botanists, psychologists, and so on, but probably omitted altogether for those who want only a survey of main facts and general conclusions. The trend at the present time is certainly in this direction.[11]

[10] L. E. Taylor, "The Ready-made Drawing with Relation to Student Achievement," *School and Society,* 32: 371–74, 1930.

[11] See, for instance, H. C. Sampson and L. H. Tiffany, "Methods Followed in the Teaching of General Botany," *Bureau of Educational Research Monograph,* No. 15, Ohio State University Press, 1932, pp. 3–42.

III. VARIOUS "MODERN" METHODS OF PROCEDURE

Within the last twenty-five years there have been numerous suggestions for the improvement of college teaching. Most of the "new" procedures have already been used in the elementary schools with considerable success. For that matter, they are methods that good college teachers have been using from the beginning but—like so many other things—they are discovered all over again by every other generation and become for a time the latest thing in the educational world. They are definitely good procedures, but they are hardly the unique products of modern educational research, although recent studies have done much to prove their value objectively and to extend their use.

The investigations to be considered in this section group themselves quite naturally under four heads—the use of projects, the integration of tests with teaching, the socializing of classwork, and the complete individualization of instruction. These four topics will be taken up in order. There will also be a short section giving some suggestions that have appeared in the literature for the improvement of lectures.

1. The project method: In its essentials this method has three fundamental features. In the first place, the material of a course is divided into "units" or topics, each of which is large enough to cover several days' work, to require some degree of reorganization, and to constitute a fairly independent section of subject matter. Below are a few samples of teaching "units."

SAMPLES OF TEACHING UNITS

Physics:
1. Molecular nature of matter
2. Induced currents
3. Magnetism

Chemistry:
1. Oxidation
2. Equivalent weights
3. Chemical equilibrium

Sociology:
1. Emergence of wage-earning class
2. Personal management in business

History:
1. The feudal regime
2. Islam and the Crusades
3. Imperialism [12]

There is, of course, nothing unique about breaking subject matter up into such subdivisions, but a project is more than merely a logical section of an outline. To be effective it should have the following characteristics:

(1) It should serve some useful purpose in the lives of the students.

(2) It should reproduce actual life conditions by utilizing material as it occurs in life.

(3) It should involve a considerable amount of student activity and of free informal association among students.

(4) Within the limits of their capacity, it should provide students with a chance to judge, choose, and evaluate.

Whenever possible, the students themselves should take part in the conception of the project, although this feature is not essential.

In addition there are certain highly practical but necessary elements that are too often neglected. The directions for the work must be clear and accurate. The amount of work must not be so great that a student cannot finish it in the allotted time. All reference books and necessary equipment should be available when they are needed. It may seem absurd to mention such elementary matters in a book intended for college teachers, but many an otherwise excellent project has gone on the rocks because of a teacher's lack of attention to exactly these details.[13] If the students cannot find the books, or if the work takes time from their other subjects, the teacher

---

[12] From C. V. Good, *Teaching in College and University*, Warwick and York, 1929, pp. 122–23. Used by permission of the publisher.

[13] This point is well brought out by H. H. Whetzel, "An Experiment in Teaching," *Journal of Higher Education*, 1: 125–35, 1930.

who initiates a project will find himself in the exact center of a storm of protests—and the project method will probably get the blame, since most teachers are too human to admit their own mistakes.

Teachers in various departments have reported use of this method. In one case, the work in elementary French was divided into projects.[14] By the end of the year 10 per cent of the students had completed so much extra work that they could go at once into third-year French, and no student did so poorly as to deserve either a D or an E. In some instances teachers have used a variation of the method, usually called the "unit-contract plan." The only essential difference is that the students make a contract to complete a given unit of work at a given level. Thus for example, a "D" contract may require only mastery of basic facts from a restricted amount of reading matter, while a "C" contract calls for this work plus reports on added references; the "B" level may include everything on the first two and a number of short papers on relatively specific topics, while the "A" level includes all the first three, plus a long and somewhat comprehensive term paper. The student picks out the mark he wants—or compromises between the mark he would like and the amount and type of work he can do.[15]

In general, the results gained by the project method, in so far as mastery of facts is concerned, are only a little better than those obtained by day-to-day assignments or by lectures.[16] The interest of the students seems, however, to be greater.

[14] See F. Payne and E. W. Spieth, *An Open Letter to College Teachers,*. Principia Press, Bloomington, Indiana, 1935, 380 pp.

[15] For a more detailed explanation see S. S. Stockwell, "A Normal School Experiment with the Dalton Plan," *Education,* 46: 12–17, 1925.

[16] See, for instance, V. E. Esson and R. D. Cole, "The Effectiveness of the Contract Method as Compared with the Ordinary Method of Teaching," *School Review,* 37: 272–81, 1929; N. M. Funk, "Comparative Study of the Results Obtained by the Method of Mastery Technique and the Method of Daily Recitation," *School Review,* 36: 338–45, 1928; C. E. Persinger, "An Experiment in Quantity-Quality Assignments in College Classes," *Historical Outlook,* 17: 293–95, 1926; N. V. Scheidemann, "An Experiment in Teaching Psychology," *Journal of Applied Psychology,* 13: 188–91, 1929; M. Shirley and K. Hevner, "An Experiment in Teaching Laboratory Psychology by the Project Method," *Journal of Applied Psychology,* 14: 309–54, 1930; H. S. Tuttle and H. R. Douglass, "Project Teaching in a College Course in Educational Psychology," *University of Oregon Publications,*. *Education Series,* Vol. 1, No. 7, 1929, pp. 293–99; L. Weber, "The Use of the Unit-Contract Method in Teaching Biology," *School Science and* *Mathematics,* 28: 399–413, 1928.

The experiments referred to here were carried out in subjects as divergent as biology, history, and psychology. Although no greater knowledge was usually gained, it may well be that the project method is still superior because it calls for a reorganization of data. It is not likely that the tests upon the results of which comparisons have been based, gave students in the project classes a chance to show any superiority they may have possessed in organizing ability, in initiative, or in self-direction. Some of the main values claimed for this method have had, therefore, no chance to show themselves. Until these outcomes of teaching are also measured no one will know whether or not the project method is better than others.

One further variation in the project technique is of interest. Sometimes, instead of contracting for work of a given level or type, a student is allowed to repeat units as often as he wants, until he has earned whatever grade satisfies him or whatever grade is demanded by the teacher. In one instance [17] a teacher divided the work of the course into fifteen major problems, on each of which the students were to write a short paper. If their first draft of a paper received a mark of C or better, the teacher was satisfied, although a student could rewrite his work for a still better grade if he wished. All D or E papers were rejected. Table 20 shows the effect of this procedure upon the number of papers actually written.

Since each student was required to turn in 15 papers and there were 136 students in the class, the total—if all contributions had been accepted in their first form—would have been 2,040 reports. Actually, 787 papers—or, 39 per cent of the work—were revised. As a result of this technique no one in the class who finished the course received a grade of less than C.[18]

A good adaptation of the project method to work in plant pathology has been reported.[19] The professor in charge made out a list of problems of which the students were required to do three and from which they were to select at least another twelve. He left

[17] E. W. Dolch, "Mastery in College," *Journal of Higher Education,* 5 : 121–24, 1934.
[18] A somewhat similar experiment is reported by S. L. Pressey and L. W. Pressey, "Experimenting with the Examination," *Journal of Higher Education,* 1 : 396–98, 1930.
[19] Whetzel, *op. cit.*

the laboratory open all day long. Students might come whenever they wanted to. If a student needed help he could ask someone for it. When he thought he had completed a given unit of work, a student presented himself in the professor's office where he was examined orally. At the end of this quiz the professor told him what mark he would get. If a student were not satisfied he could repeat the work and try again. This method was proving very satisfactory both in the achievement and in the interest of the students.

TABLE 20

Number of Times Papers Were Rewritten* [19a]

Rewritten Papers	Number of Students	Extra Papers
0	1	0
1	4	4
2	11	22
3	18	54
4	18	72
5	12	60
6	17	102
7	21	147
8	11	88
9	8	72
10	7	70
11	3	33
12	3	36
13	1	13
14	1	14
TOTAL......	136	787

* This table is to be read as follows: One student did not rewrite any paper; four students rewrote one paper; eleven students rewrote two papers; one student rewrote fourteen papers.

Naturally some kinds of subject matter are more easily broken up into units than are other types, and undoubtedly some teachers find this method more sympathetic than do others. It is certainly not the educational panacea that its more ardent advocates believe it to be. It is, however, a sufficiently useful technique in some situations that no instructor can afford to neglect it. The teachers I have happened to know who condemned it most bitterly were of three types—those

[19a] Dolch, *op. cit.* Used by permission of the *Journal of Higher Education.*

who had never tried it, those who had tried it and had got
themselves tied up in the red tape, and those who depended
for teaching effectiveness upon the inspiration of the class
rather than upon systematic preparation. This method is, however, valuable to some people in some situations and should
receive a fair trial before it is condemned.

2. Integration of tests with teaching: There is nothing new
about the giving of tests. The new elements in the situation
are the extreme frequency with which some teachers use them
and their careful integration of the tests with their teaching.
Both features resulted from the development of objective
measurement. Few teachers have sufficient courage to use essay
questions at the end of every class hour, for instance, even
if there were time, because the papers pile up so relentlessly.
The short objective test is different. In five minutes students
can answer seven or eight questions, and in ten minutes a
teacher can score these answers from a class of thirty students.
Objective tests may be integrated with teaching in a more
complete manner than essay tests, because their nature permits
a teacher to cover *all* the essential ideas that have been developed during one or two class periods. Suppose, for instance,
that on Monday and Tuesday a group has discussed five main
ideas and nine important but less significant points besides
the usual assortment of details. On Wednesday the teacher
can give fourteen objective questions covering the fourteen
important ideas. Every student thus has a chance to give
evidence of his understanding of the entire number. The scoring almost automatically tells the teacher which ideas are not
clear to the class as a whole, while the marks on each student's
paper tell him which ones he individually did not understand.
The essay test does not produce results of this type because
the points on each student's paper represent his voluntary
contribution; of the fourteen ideas the teacher wishes to in-
quire about, a single student may mention only six; whether
or not he is well informed on the other eight remains a complete mystery. The objective test results can, therefore, be
integrated in teaching—especially with review—in a more
immediate way than can the results of essay tests. It is these

two features of frequency and relevancy that are probably responsible for the relative efficiency of the methods about to be described.

Two experiments [20] of quite similar nature illustrate the value of frequent tests. In both cases, the tests were given during the last part of a class hour once a week. In one case the control groups had two and in the other three essay examinations during the semester, but both were taught by the same teachers and used the same reading materials. In the first experiment the class in which the frequent tests were given made 43 per cent more gain than that shown by the students in the control classes; in the other, the students gained 18 per cent more. In both experiments the students expressed a preference for the short frequent tests over the longer and less frequent ones.

A thorough integration of tests with the teaching procedures brings results. In one unusually good experiment [21] the teacher used the following method. He first divided the work of the quarter into eleven units—one for each week. On Tuesdays, Wednesdays, and the first half of the hour Thursdays he lectured. During the last twenty minutes of the Thursday period the class took an objective test covering the essentials. On Friday the teacher handed back the scored papers and discussed the various misunderstandings, ending with a general summary of the unit. Those students who had received either A or B on the weekly test were excused from class on Monday. With this reduction in class size it was possible to have a discussion of the points raised during the work of the previous week. The best students got a reward in the form of a free day while the poorer ones got the extra help they needed. The results of this procedure in terms of achievement were excellent, as shown in Table 21. The outstanding ad-

[20] A. H. Turney, "The Effect of Frequent Short Objective Tests upon the Achievement of College Students in Educational Psychology,'" *School and Society*, 33: 760–62, 1931; S. L. Pressey and L. W. Pressey, "Practical 'Educational Engineering' in a Teacher-Training Course," *School and Society*, 35: 67–70, 1932. See also N. Keys, "The Influence on Learning and Retention of Weekly as Opposed to Monthly Tests," *Journal of Educational Psychology*, 25: 427–35, 1934; D. H. Kulp, "Weekly Tests for Graduate Students," *School and Society*, 38: 157–59, 1933; A. C. Eurich, H. P. Longstaff, and M. Wilder, "The Effect of Weekly Tests upon the Achievement in Psychology," in A. C. Eurich, *The Effective College Curriculum*, University of Minnesota Press, 1937, pp. 333–47.
[21] C. H. Smeltzer, "Improving and Evaluating the Efficiency of College Instruction," *Journal of Educational Psychology*, 24: 283–302, 1933.

TABLE 21

Results of a Teaching Experiment [21a]

Scores in Points	Experimental Groups		Control Groups	
	Pretest*	End Test	Pretest	End Test
280–89		2		
270–79		2		2
260–69		5		5
250–59		6		6
240–49		8		10
230–39		16 Med.		13
220–29		13		10 Med.
210–19		11	1	7
200–09		7		9
190–99	1	5		8
180–89	1			6
170–79	2	1	2	4
160–69	3 90th		2 90th	3
150–59	3		10	1
140–49	2		4	2
130–39	6		10	1
120–29	17		15 Med.	1
110–19	11 Med.		9	
100–09	9		8	
90–99	3		8	
80–89	7		9	
70–79	6		4	
60–69	3		4	
50–59				
40–49	1			
30–39	1		2	
Number of Students......	76	76	88	88
Medians.........	117	231	120	222

* The same examination was given on the first and last day of the course.

vantage of the experimental method does not appear in the gain of the group as a whole but in the narrowness of the range on the final test and in the elimination of the low scores that appear in the distribution for the control group. This method was especially valuable in raising the performance of the low end of the class. All the experimental students scored, at the end of the quarter,

[21a] Smeltzer, *op. cit.* Used by permission of the *Journal of Educational Psychology* and the author.

above the ninetieth percentile of their own distribution at the beginning. In the control groups, the two distributions overlap down to the median. The total gain from pretest to end test was appreciably greater for the students taught by the more modern method.

As already indicated, with reference to the project method, there is no technique that is applicable to all situations, or students, or teaching temperaments. The test-teach-test method has its values, especially in elementary courses; it becomes less useful in small advanced classes. It should certainly never be used as a substitute for all other techniques. The method provides, however, an opportunity for the systematic learning of a body of facts and almost automatically produces remedial teaching, because it diagnoses—for both student and teacher— what has not yet been mastered.

3. Socialized classes: During the last two decades there have been two fundamentally antagonistic points of view about the manner in which the work of a classroom should be carried on. According to some people, all work should be individualized; according to others, all work should be socialized. Many elementary schools try to retain the values of both methods by having socialized classes in the afternoon and individual work in the morning. At the college level the socialization of classwork—beyond what students do of their own accord— has not in general developed as far as it has in the lower schools.

In the literature I have come across only two reports of actual experiments that dealt with a socializing technique in classes of ordinary size. In both instances the students in several sections of a large course were divided into committees of about five members each.[22] These small groups met and discussed what they had read. There was some guidance from the teacher, but the majority of the instruction was given by the students to each other. The results in one case were not compared objectively with the achievement of similar students under other methods of instruction. In the second experiment those who did the major part of the work

[22] F. G. Davis, "Methods in College Teaching," *Educational Administration and Supervision,* 14: 476–84, 1928; Pressey and Pressey, "Practical 'Educational Engineering' in a Teacher-Training Course," *op. cit.*

through committees scored 12 per cent lower than the students
in the lecture sections. In neither case did as many as half the
students like the method. There were constant complaints that a
few of the members did practically all the talking, with the result
that each committee became a very small class, badly taught by a
young and totally inexperienced student-teacher. While there are
values to be gained from committee work, the method does not
seem to yield good results if it is made the sole type of instruction.
When used as an auxiliary procedure once in a while it may prove
of greater usefulness.

In addition to these two minor experiments there were many
descriptions of college classes carried out on the "workshop"
principle. To some extent these undertakings are individual
and should therefore be discussed in the next section of this
chapter, but rather more often they are group efforts. The
workshop in dramatics, in other types of writing and in art,
and the community surveys are the commonest forms of socialized classwork at the college level. Most teachers are familiar
with such activities, but a few samples may illustrate the matter for those who are not.

Thus, in one college the members of the sociology classes surveyed a small town, making house-to-house visits and gathering the
basic information. The statistics class took the raw data and
tabulated and summarized it. Then advanced students in political
science, sociology, economics, and history met in a special seminar
and worked out a set of recommendations to the town council
for the improvement of the situation. In another instance the
students of a class in child psychology wrote their own textbook,
since at that time no good book in the field was available. At many
colleges one finds groups of students writing, costuming, and producing their own plays. Occasionally they correlate their work in
history and dramatics by producing a pageant or play dealing with
some period in history. More and more undergraduates are being
encouraged to carry on a project away from the campus. Students
in archaeology go to some near-by site of an Indian encampment
and dig up arrowheads; embryo teachers go out into the community for their classes; prospective social workers handle actual
cases in juvenile court; a major in physical education supervises
children on a playground; geology students collect a complete set

of specimens for the county in which the college is located; students in anthropology work as volunteers in a museum—cleaning, labelling, and arranging specimens; language majors spend a year abroad; undergraduates in engineering install the electrical and plumbing fixtures in a new building; members of a class in landscape gardening take over some neglected area in the community and beautify it, and so on.

All of these undertakings require more or less time away from the campus, give a student a sense of accomplishing something real, and provide him with a chance to make an adjustment to the conditions of adult life and work. They also force him into independence because in minor matters at least he must make his own decisions. Such activities are especially valuable in the development of the whole individual because they provide training in personal traits as well as training of the intellect. Although there seems to be no actual measurement on this point it is the unanimous testimony of college teachers that students who carry on work of this type avoid the bookishness and separation from reality that sometimes characterized the successful scholars of previous generations.

4. Individualization of instruction: In recent years one clearly discernible trend in college work has been the introduction of individual adjustments to the needs of students at all levels of ability. As already pointed out in the chapter on objectives, the characteristic aim of the modern college is to develop the individual, to the extent of his capacities, whatever these turn out to be. It is therefore quite understandable that methods for treating students as persons rather than classes as groups should have become popular.

There have been, in general, three different techniques that come under the heading of individualization or "personalization" of teaching. The first consists essentially in establishing a greater degree of personal contact between a teacher and his students. For instance, an instructor may interview each member of a class within the first two or three weeks of a semester in order to get acquainted with each; the information and impressions thus gained he makes use of in his daily teaching and in his assignments. Toward the end of the semester he again talks individually to each student. In fact, he may have interviews with certain students from time to time throughout the semester. This particular kind of personalization has been tried on a rather large scale. In zoology and botany classes [23] the "interview" sections showed some degree of improvement in learning over ordinary groups; for educational psychology classes the superiority of such sections was 18 per cent.[24] In both cases the only appreciable difference in the treatment of the classes thus compared lay in the amount of personal contact between students and teachers. The only criterion of effectiveness used was the standing of classes on objective tests. If improvement showed even here, it is a fairly safe guess that the students in the interview sections profited even more in non-academic ways as a result of the interest taken in them by their instructors. If there had been no gain at all in mastery of subject matter, the work might still have been eminently worth while.

A second technique consists in the actual individualizing of the material taught in the course. In this case the students use tests and exercises that are self-instructional and work on them alone unless they need help from the teacher. Because the instructor is free from the burden of lecturing or holding discussions, he can give individual aid or guidance when a need is indicated. He can also analyze the work of students who are having difficulties. In general, the idea of those who have experimented with individualization seems to have been to cover the usual material of a course in this way, rather than to enrich it for the gifted or reduce it for the dull student, although some adjustment of content may have been introduced in a few instances.

Three fairly adequate experiments have reported [25] that the students who did individual work had a slightly higher standing in the course than those who were taught in classes. The difference was not so great as is the case with most such experiments in

----

[23] R. W. Tyler, "Certain Administrative Procedures in Botany and Zoology," *Service Studies in Higher Education,* No. 15, Ohio State University Press, 1932, pp. 109–22.

[24] Pressey and Pressey, "Practical 'Educational Engineering' in a Teacher-Training Course," *op. cit.*

[25] Tuttle and Douglas, *op. cit.;* W. E. Lessenger, "An Experiment in Individualized Instruction at the College Level," *Sixteenth Yearbook of the National Society of College Teachers of Education,* 1928, pp. 36–41; N. V. Scheidemann, "A Comparison of Two Methods of College Instruction," *School and Society,* 25 : 672–74, 1927; see also D. D. Feder and C. Cochran, "A Study of Individualized Instruction at the College Level," *Modern Language Journal,* 21 : 23–35, 1936; E. O. Miller, "An Experiment in Individualized Instruction," *Progressive Education,* 7 : 221–24, 1930.

grades below college. Whether this result was due to inappropriateness of the technique or to inexperience of the classroom teachers who carried on the work is not clear, but I suspect the latter explanation is the true one—especially since individualized work has been proved of great value in dealing with both bright and dull students.[26]

Finally, there is a more extensive technique that consists of an individualization and adaption of both classwork and reading assignments to the needs of each student. Most of the independent study and guided-reading plans come in this category. There is often some degree of ordinary classwork, but the essentials of these procedures lie in adjusting the content of a course more or less for each person—with the result that no two students have exactly the same work although they get the same credit—and in enriching the usual amount of reading for anyone who can profit by the change. Many of the "experiments" with individualized plans are unfortunately not experiments at all, because they were not adequately controlled. In fact, no one knows whether or not most of the best-known plans of this type are successful. From a scientific point of view there are numerous sources of error. Sometimes those in charge of the work (1) did not know what was achieved under the traditional methods of teaching in their college and hence had no basis for comparison with the new method; sometimes they (2) did not measure objectively the progress made by the experimental groups and had therefore only opinions to go by; or sometimes they (3) did not control such factors as intelligence, previous training, college level, or economic background in their comparison of the results obtained by the newer and older methods and could not therefore know to what extent observed changes were due to such extraneous influences. Consequently, even though these large-scale individualized plans may be extremely successful, there is no actual proof that they are. In the few sample studies with small groups of students the differences in actual achievement between group and individualized work have been small, but they are usually in favor of the latter.[27]

Probably the most talked-of method of individualization in college is the "tutorial" system. The details vary somewhat from one

[26] See especially the references on pages 378–84 and 407–9.
[27] See, for instance, E. B. Greene, "Certain Aspects of Lecture, Reading, and Guided Reading," *School and Society,* 36: 478–80, 1932, or J. G. Umstattd, "The Independent Study Plan," *Journal of Higher Education,* 6: 143–48, 1936.

place to another, but the basic idea is the same. Each student is
assigned as a "tutee" to some faculty member. He and his tutor
plan his work, talk it over every week, and discuss any problems
that arise. Although the conversations generally begin with consideration of academic matters they may roam as far afield as the
student's interests demand. If the personal relationship is as close
as it should be, the student feels free to consult his tutor about
anything and the tutor contributes to the student's emotional and
social growth quite as much as to his intellectual development.
The tutor is, in fact, the guide, philosopher, and friend of his
tutees. Where the system is in full force the tutors live in dormi-
tories with their charges and keep a big brother's eye upon each
student's total development. The system does not, in and of itself,
involve individualized work in the classroom, although it sometimes results in greater personal attention there also. More often,
however, the instructional methods continue as usual, with the
tutorial relationship acting as a counterbalance to group instruction. Is is extremely difficult to obtain an objective and unprejudiced opinion as to the merits of the tutorial system. I have heard
many tutors at Harvard express themselves; their estimates vary
from complete confidence to complete distrust.[28] In general, however, there is an acceptance of the work as being worth while in
contributing to the healthy growth of undergraduates.

In the lower schools teachers are often provided with diagnostic and remedial materials by use of which they automatically give individual instruction, whether they intend to
or not. For an occasional introductory course in college such
materials—in the form of special texts and exercises—do exist,
but for the most part a college teacher has to do his own
individualizing. Good teachers have always adjusted work to
individual capacity—ever since the days of Socrates. A good
illustration of the common methods by which such adapta-
tions are carried out appears below:

Miss A taught geometry to a class of twenty girls, of whom not
more than two had the slightest real interest in the subject; several
of them at the beginning of the course disliked it violently. Miss

[28] For an official statement see, "General Examinations and Tutors in
Harvard College: Prepared in Answer to Numerous Inquiries," *Official
Register of Harvard University,* 1929, 32 pp.

A showed, however, three elements of marked superiority by means of which she changed antagonism or indifference into real enthusiasm. First, she could explain a difficult point in geometry with such lucidity that the most stupid member of the class could understand. The girls made progress, not because she fascinated them with the charm of her personality, but because she could make clear a difficult and—to most girls—uninteresting subject. In addition to utter clarity she had a positive genius for diagnosis. She always knew exactly what was the matter, even when a student could not herself give a coherent account of her troubles. After listening to some poor girl's garbled efforts at proof, Miss A would unerringly put her finger upon the exact "key" difficulty. In the third place, Miss A was careful to adjust the load of work to individual capacity; although this class was held thirty years ago, she individualized the work as thoroughly as if she had been brought up in the most modern educational doctrines. No two girls had exactly the same assignment, and from no two did Miss A expect the same amount or type of work. The best students in the class had no text. She gave each, from time to time, a typewritten sheet containing several theorems; so far as I could see, no two sheets were ever alike. These students worked by themselves, made their own figures, wrote out their own proof, and often remained away from class for days, coming to Miss A only when in difficulty. From them she exacted the most meticulous work; every proof had to be perfect. At the other end of the distribution there was a small group of girls to whom Miss A gave only a few theorems, for which the proofs were already complete; with these girls she worked unremittingly to make clear a small body of facts. Between the two extremes she graded her assignments according to capacity. When Miss A gave examinations she used different forms for different groups of girls within the class. The best two or three students were required to solve a number of original theorems; the poorest two or three had only to reproduce proofs already studied and to apply them to slightly different figures. On each girl's examination paper Miss A wrote just how many and what types of problems she would be held responsible for. I rate Miss A as among my best teachers because of her clarity, her ability to diagnose errors, and her careful adaptation of work to the ability of each girl. She had no modern gadgets for individualization, but she did not let their absence prevent her from regarding each girl as an unique human being, or from adjusting the material of the course to her capacity.

One outcome of a thoroughly satisfactory method of supervising and teaching students should be a great achievement on their part, but this is by no means the only outcome. There is the well-known but poorly defined "ability to think" about the problems presented by a course and the even-less-well-defined "development of personality." I have no doubt that the ability to think, the development of initiative, and the growth of normal personalities are more important as end results of teaching than the mere mastery of subject matter. It is also my opinion that individualization is superior to group methods for achieving these objectives, but I cannot prove any of these assumptions.[29]

5. *The improvement of lectures:* There is a little evidence on minor techniques by means of which a teacher can improve his lectures. This small amount of data concerns (1) the use of short review summaries at the beginning of each lecture, (2) the value of short daily tests for the purpose of preventing forgetting, and (3) the student reactions to lecturing with or without notes.

At the beginning of a class period lecturers often make a summary of the previous day's work. Such a review, although it may take not more than three to five minutes, does help students to understand the material slightly better.[30] It does not, however, make any appreciable difference whether this brief review is given to the class ready-made by the teacher, or if it is developed by the students themselves. Before accepting this result as definitive I should want to repeat the investigation, but if this conclusion proves to be correct a lecturer can save time by using his own summary.

[29] For further references on this subject see O. F. Bond, "Adapting Instruction in the Modern Languages to Individual Needs," *Proceedings of the Institute for Administrative Officers of Higher Institutions,* University of Chicago Press, Vol. 4, 1932, pp. 132–43; W. Blair, "Individualization of Instruction in English Composition," *ibid.,* pp. 125–31; A. D. Henderson, "Curricular Provision for the Individual at Antioch College," *ibid.,* pp. 79–97; C. S. Boucher, "Curricular Provision for the Individual at the University of Chicago," *ibid.,* pp. 98–108; J. B. Johnston, "The Junior College of the University of Minnesota," *ibid.,* pp. 109–24; G. A. Works, "Survey of Curricular Provisions for Individual Instruction," *ibid.,* pp. 71–78.

[30] O. A. Ulbrich, "An Experimental Study of the Method of Reviewing the Lesson of the Previous Day," *Journal of Educational Research,* 17: 211–14, 1928.

It has already been shown that short tests at frequent intervals have an effect upon learning. In the present investigation the teacher gave a five-minute test at the end of each class hour.[31] The test items dealt exclusively with the main ideas of the lecture just concluded; it thus offered an immediate review of what the lecturer had said. Without this aid to memory the 872 students involved in the experiment forgot half the ideas of a lecture at the end of three days, 60 per cent by the end of one week, and 70 per cent by the end of two. With the help of immediate review by the tests these same students forgot, after corresponding intervals of time, 39, 40, and 47 per cent of the ideas. Since most forgetting takes place within the first few days, it would appear that the test reinforced the teaching enough to save approximately a fifth of what would otherwise have been lost.

One very careful report [32] concerns the value of lecturing with and without notes. The professor first wrote out entire lectures. He then selected certain passages and memorized them. Next he practiced speaking these passages until he could say them with the same intonations he used in reading them from his notes. For some of the classes he then read the lectures, but for others he looked up when he came to the memorized passages and spoke them directly to the students—carefully avoiding, however, any variations in inflection from his previous rendition. The difference lay then merely in the fact that he was looking at his class. The absence of notes had an effect upon retention. The students to whom the passages were spoken recalled 18 per cent more of the ideas contained in the selections than those to whom the same passages were read in the same tone of voice against the background of an otherwise identical lecture.

IV. SUMMARY

Naturally no reader is likely to experiment with all the technique just described: some will be already familiar and

[31] H. E. Jones, "Experimental Studies of College Teaching," *Archives of Psychology*, No. 68, 1923.
[32] H. T. Moore, "The Attention Value of Lecturing without Notes," *Journal of Educational Psychology*, 10:467–69, 1919.

some will be of a character unsympathetic to his temperament. It is reasonable to suppose, however, that every method is of more or less use to someone. In any event, college teachers should know the facts about such experimentation as has been done with different methods of teaching so they may have an opinion based upon information rather than upon prejudice.

CHAPTER XVI

PREPARATION AND ASSIGNMENTS

This chapter will be short because there is no research to present. If adequate preparation and stimulating assignments were not such important elements in successful teaching I should, in view of the absence of data, omit discussion of them. Since, however, they are vital and since no definite experiments along these lines have been carried out on the college level, I shall have to summarize the opinions of various experienced college professors. In some cases the opinions are expressed in the literature; in others they were given to me orally.

I. PREPARATION FOR CLASS

This matter of preparation is not so simple and obvious as it may at first seem. There are at least four different kinds that a college teacher may find desirable. The first is the preparation for the entire semester or year—depending upon the length of the course. This long-time planning is one of the numerous activities that prevent a teacher from ever getting his work done. By the middle of one school year he should be reading books and articles in preparation for the next. During the summer it is not safe for him to put his work entirely out of his mind or he may find himself in a sad state of unreadiness when the fall term opens. Once classes start, a teacher is so busy with day-to-day tasks, red tape, and contact with students that he does not have a sufficient number of consecutive, uninterrupted hours for working out a complete and systematic plan for an entire course.

At the beginning of the year an instructor should know what he intends to cover, how long he expects to spend on each major topic, and what books he will use. If he wants to have a syllabus or outline of any kind, it should be in readiness on the first day of class. Indeed, a really good teacher goes to class on the opening day so loaded with ideas that he can hardly wait for class to start. The value of a semester's plan is illustrated by the following incidents:

I once took a course in "World History" which ran through an entire year. The instructor in the first semester was supposed to begin with the dawn of time, proceed from one mountain peak to another, and finish with the fall of Rome in 476 A.D. He set off at top speed the first day and did not remove his seven-league boots during the semester, with the result that we arrived—somewhat breathless—on the last day of class just in time to view the smoking ruins. From the first it was clear (1) that he had decided exactly how many days could safely be spent on each period, and (2) that he had mastered the materials himself. Whenever the students showed a tendency to get off the main track he herded them back on to it. He drove the class, quietly but relentlessly; if an unexpected event deprived us of an hour's time, he merely gave the screw another twist. I know he had a schedule—not only from his occasional comments about where the class should be at a given point in the semester but because he one day dropped it on the floor! Although he did push us a good deal, there was no confusion and no cramming of facts into an inadequate amount of time. He had such good mastery of the data that he could concentrate upon what was vital for our understanding. By having a schedule and sticking to it he gave his students precisely the overview of "World History" that was advertised in the catalogue.

The second semester was a distinct contrast. We dawdled along, got completely lost in one cul-de-sac after another, loitered to admire Charlemagne, spent a whole week with the popes at Avignon, worked out an interesting but time-consuming project on social organization under feudal conditions, and suddenly found ourselves—a week before the final examinations—centuries away from the announced objective. The teacher tried to crowd all the remaining events of history up to the present into a week, but she was so unprepared herself that she did not know what to omit and what to include. The result was a hodgepodge, delivered under conditions of considerable mental and emotional stress. This second teacher had obviously no large plan whatever, although—with the exception of the last few days—her daily preparation was excellent. The classwork was not only good but stimulating; the difficulty was that she had no scheme for the semester as a unit.

It is valuable for a teacher to sit down with a calendar, in the peace of a summer's day and to work out the main structure of a course. It gives him a most comfortable feeling of firm ground under the feet.

A second type of preparation is needed when a teacher is about to introduce special work of some kind—a project or some other such unit. As an observer watches a class it often seems as if a project just grew spontaneously out of the discussion. Sometimes it does, but if the teacher at once knows what to do and how to do it, he has probably been egging the students on to propound some plan much like that which they have actually suggested.

I recall one class in which the students decided, supposedly by themselves, that they wanted to write a pageant depicting the main events of a certain period in history. The enthusiasm was clearly real and apparently spontaneous. At first I thought the teacher was remarkably quick in capitalizing on the students' interest, in organizing them into groups for the purpose of preparing different episodes, and in working the assignment into his schedule of class hours. By the end of the hour I decided that the whole pageant had been carefully thought out and time left for it. The red tape took so little class time because he was all prepared, down to the last detail.

Good projects sometimes come wholly from the students, but more commonly they are the result of careful and detailed planning on the part of the teacher. Even though the students can and do add elements and make suggestions here and there, the basic organization is usually the instructor's. So also is the collecting of the necessary books and materials. Since the whole matter of teaching by means of projects has been discussed at some length in the previous chapter, further remarks here seem unnecessary.

Third, there is the matter of daily preparation, which goes on endlessly. Unless it is made, the students will not profit as much as they should from the teaching; and unless it is well made, the teacher will not profit much from it either. There is nothing more utterly boring than to make the same preparation year after year for the same section of subject matter. Even though a particular approach works, an instructor has to have all the qualities of a machine to use it for every repetition of a course. An important part of mental hygiene for a teacher consists in preventing him from boring himself into a coma. A series of dull preparations, without ingenuity or newness, will produce this effect as soon as anything.

Too well do I remember one professor who came to class totally unprepared. In his case I am sure of my facts, because he told me so himself—even if I had been unable to deduce as much from his behavior. He explained to me that it was no use for him to make a preparation because he derived all his inspiration from the "alert and interested" faces of his students! His customary technique was to come into class and start talking about anything that occurred to him, whether or not it was relevant to the course. During the first fifteen minutes or so he rambled on by free association, gradually getting closer and closer to some topic that was pertinent. By the middle of the period he was really under way, and during the last ten minutes he was often interesting and stimulating. At the end of the hour he was generally annoyed because the class walked out—just about the time he was ready to become expansive. On certain days the students' bright young faces were apparently blank, since he sometimes did not get started at all but rambled on for an hour about all conceivable matters. Although he said many worth-while and interesting things in the course of the semester, there was almost never any relation between the points discussed at any two consecutive periods.

Another one of my teachers made a somewhat different kind of mistake. He had extensive and detailed notes from which he lectured. The notebooks were obviously far from new; indeed, I suspect their age exactly equaled the length of time he had been teaching. He had the notes marked off into lectures for each successive day; if anything interfered with his finishing the exact amount of material at a given period, he was visibly disturbed. Almost ten years after I took the course I visited his class—only to see the same notebook and to hear one of the lectures, almost verbatim, that I had heard before. This man's lectures were clear but hopelessly dull, and they quite evidently bored him about as much as they did his students. In a sense he was prepared for his work. At some time before I knew him he had evidently made a preparation that was to last him for a lifetime. Since he locked up his notebooks in the desk drawer before leaving the classroom, I can only infer that he made no daily preparation whatsoever. On several occasions I debated robbing that drawer of its contents, because I felt he could be a good teacher if he had no notes to lean upon and was forced to work from day to day.

In sharp contrast to these two instructors were two others. One of them used to close and lock her door every evening from seven to ten in order to make her preparation for her next classes. Since she rarely had more than two classes a day, she had an hour and a half for each—in addition to any other moments she might have used before seven o'clock. Twenty years after my first acquaintance with her, I wanted her to go with me to an evening meeting. Because of this appointment she worked from four to five upon a course that she had been giving for nearly forty years, while I read a book and covertly watched. I would have thought she was giving the subject for the first time. Even after her preparation was completed, she spent a half hour in planning her assignment for the next week.

Another teacher who was once a colleague of mine in the same department, was similarly industrious. We were both teaching sections of a required course. Hardly a week went by that she did not have some new and clever assignment. In several years' time I never knew her to repeat an assignment in exactly the form in which she had first thought of it. She was continually constructing models, borrowing exhibits, arranging slides, making charts, and so on. Her examinations were ingenious and interesting, but no matter how successful a test was, she never repeated it; she produced another that was equally good, only quite different. Even such a simple thing as a book report would receive a new twist from her fertile brain. On one occasion the students had read a certain book on behaviorism. Instead of asking for a mere summary, she first wrote out the names of twenty psychologists upon slips of paper, had the students draw lots, and then required each to review the book from the point of view of the person whose name he had drawn. This woman spent hours in her daily preparation—and her results were phenomenal in terms of student achievement. She is still hard at work. I visited not long ago a section of the course we had once both taught. Although not more than ten years had elapsed, the material was almost all new, the reading list contained only one familiar reference, the syllabus was a remote cousin of the earlier one, and the flow of clever assignments continued unabated. This teacher has developed and thrown away more good lesson plans than any three ordinary people.

A fourth type of "preparation" has no direct connection with classwork but is intended to aid in the development of the teacher as a person. It has been suggested to me by experienced teachers that every day one should read something not in the least connected with what one is teaching. The reading of something outside his immediate field helps a teacher in four distinct ways. It keeps him from becoming too specialized; the man who knows "more and more about less and less" is useful within the narrow limits of his field, but his general value is low and his personal development often retarded. Second, the reading gives a teacher something to think and talk about beyond the inevitable "shop talk" of the profession; in every college there are a few faculty members who are generally avoided because they have no topics for conversation outside of campus events and activities. They may be efficient and useful people, but they do bore their colleagues. In the third place, the reading allows a teacher to escape for a while from the constant adjustment of ideas to adolescent minds. The college population never grows up; the social and mental life of a college campus has all the effect of a defective phonograph record that plays the same groove over and over, endlessly. If a teacher wants to grow up he has to escape from eternal youth into the world of adult opinions and ideas. Finally, the reading is a form of mental and emotional old-age insurance. There will inevitably come a time when a professor has to stop his work; if he has spent all his reading time in concentration upon classwork he is likely to feel unbearably lonely when this need no longer exists.

The successful college teacher—as will appear in a later chapter—is an interesting and exciting person. A stimulating personality does not develop without adequate nourishment. If a young instructor wants to grow into an interesting adult he can find no better means of doing so than the daily reading of something outside his narrow professional and academic interests.

Almost every book on methods of procedure in the class-room recommends to a teacher that he or she should have a definite lesson plan before going to class. On the college level this suggestion is perhaps superfluous, but various people who read the manuscript of this book asked that a brief section about lesson plans be added. The need for some kind of system is obvious enough. The main difficulty seems to be to strike just the right balance between definiteness of purpose and adaptation to the passing interests of students. At one extreme is the teacher with a rigid and logical plan who pursues his system no matter what other possibilities are indicated by the questions or comments of his students. At the other extreme is the teacher who depends for guidance largely upon the day-to-day interests of his class and develops whatever points the members want to talk about. Somewhere between these two extremes is a middle way that good teachers try to follow: to have a definite goal for each class hour and a definite approach to that goal, but to utilize momentary interests when they appear and—as the class hour continues—to adapt the general plan to the needs of the group. In short, they use a lesson plan that is flexible without being weak and definite without being rigid.

Young instructors learn to make such plans largely by making whatever kind they can and then altering these plans in one direction or another until the necessary balance has been reached. No one can tell anyone else how to proceed. Each teacher has to use trial and error—not only at first but throughout much of his teaching career.

As a sample of an adequate groundwork for an experienced

teacher I can present the following set of questions which were
used by an acquaintance. A younger person would perhaps
need more guidance than is here indicated.

1. What kind of man was Martin Luther?
2. What elements in his environment would be especially irritating to a man of his temperament?
3. What were the chief reforms for which he worked?
4. What relationships are there between (a) his character and
his reforms and (b) the influences acting upon him and his character?

This teacher clearly knows what he wants to do with the
time, but he has left room for a great deal of discussion by
his students.

According to the evidence of students in their ratings of
instructors,[1] the teacher who is too rigid appears far less frequently than the one who has no ostensible plan of procedure.
The case history below gives a description of a rather typical
rambler.

Mr. Z was in some respects a good teacher. His interest in and
knowledge of his subject were excellent. In fact, his mind was a
little too encyclopedic for his powers of organization. At the beginning of an hour he would often announce the general topic for
discussion during the period. He would say, for instance, "Today
we shall consider the main characteristics of economic life among
primitive peoples." From such a statement he always started off
well enough, but soon he wandered from the matter in hand.
There seemed to be two sources of trouble. First, he knew far too
many interesting and alluring details. Within ten minutes—even
when he was not interrupted—he had got lost up some cul-de-sac,
where he would sometimes remain for the entire hour, telling the
class things that were interesting but did not advance the discussion one iota toward the announced goal. The students all knew
this failing and introduced a second source of difficulty by often
deliberately leading him away from his objective. Thus, on a day
when he had intended to talk about economic life some student
would raise his hand and say, "I was reading in a magazine yesterday that the Brahmans would not kill anything and that when

[1] See pages 568–69.

a plague of locusts descended on them they would stay indoors for days rather than risk stepping on one. Is that true?" In answer to such a question Mr. Z would spend twenty minutes. As soon as he threatened to run down, another student would raise his hand and contribute, "In that reference you assigned yesterday there is a statement that geography often has a negative effect on culture but frequently fails to have a positive effect. I don't understand what that means." There would follow an exposition of the point involved—usually a good exposition, but it took up another twenty minutes. The net result of the spontaneous wandering and the specious questioning was that we regularly spent four or five class periods in getting through with a topic that should have taken one or two. The entertaining ramble would go on for days; then Mr. Z would suddenly realize that he was not so far along with his work as he should be, and he would lecture in a fast and furious manner for about a week—rushing through points without waiting for the students to grasp them, touching only lightly upon matters that needed discussion, and refusing point-blank to be interrupted by questions. After a week of this technique he would again slow down, begin to meander among his delightful details and quaint reminiscences, and welcome the queries of students. As a result of this methodology I emerged from the course with a fund of entertaining anecdotes, a good grasp of a few points, and a blurred comprehension of all the intervening parts. Although Mr. Z did rate high in his ability to interest and stimulate students, the results of his instruction were meager, scattered, and un-co-ordinated. The students learned little of permanent value; they merely enjoyed a pleasurable semester of diverting stories. Often the teacher who rambles is much worse than Mr. Z, who really did have something to say, but had no systematic way of developing his ideas.

Summary: The daily preparation is the part of a teacher's work that puts verve and freshness into his teaching. It supplies the details that make the next day's work exciting. It removes the slight fog that always gathers around ideas about which one has not thought specifically for a few months. It permits a teacher to relax in class, because he is so completely ready that he can watch his students and adapt his work to their needs. It prevents disciplinary difficulties and general restlessness because the teacher is always ahead of the class.

In short, no matter how long a person has taught, he cannot safely neglect the reviewing and refreshing of his memory through his daily preparation. Successful teachers know this. They know also that making the same kind of preparation day after day is extremely monotonous. In self-defense they vary their plans all they can, they introduce new points and whole new sections, they change their reading requirements, they try out something new whenever possible, they polish illustrations already used and think up new ones, they devise different kinds of tests from time to time. They are not only willing but eager to try anything once—but rarely more than once. Most of the little additions that make the difference between a class that is monotonous and one that is exciting are due to the teacher's daily review. The planning of an entire semester's work contributes a great deal to clarity and efficiency; the daily preparation contributes an equal amount to interest and stimulation.

II. THE ASSIGNMENT

A second important element in class management is the assignment. The value that students derive from a course is usually in direct ratio to the kind of work they are asked to do. On the college level there has been almost no research in this matter, probably because supervisors do not walk into college classes and listen. Consequently, no one knows what per cent of the assignments consist simply of directions to read a given number of pages in a single text, without any reorganization of the subject matter. This type of lesson is undoubtedly the poorest, although the instruction to "just go on with what you have been doing" is not much better.[2] Because investigations are lacking, I have to depend for the data of this section upon such information as I have been able to gather from college teachers and students. Most of the material is therefore mere opinion; but for what it is worth, I

[2] For a good report of assignments in high school see J. O. Powers, "Analysis of the Use Made of the Recitation Period," *Second Yearbook of the National Conference of Supervisors and Directors of Instruction,* 1929, pp. 145–63.

would make the following suggestions to a young person just entering college teaching.

(1) An assignment should always be perfectly clear and definite. This point may seem obvious enough, but I have heard many that had neither of these characteristics. An assignment is not definite unless students know not only what they are supposed to do but also why they are supposed to do it. One way of increasing clearness and, incidentally, of producing a greater degree of learning is to provide the class with a set of questions for their guidance in reading.[3]

(2) Assignments should be given in as large units as practicable. Aside from the nuisance of spoon-feeding small daily doses, the practice is undesirable because students are encouraged to learn the material in little pieces that are often never joined together. Moreover, the responsibility for organization remains the teacher's instead of being passed along to the students. The subject matter of any course breaks up naturally into a number of small units, each of which will require from two to six weeks for completion. If assignments are made at the beginning of each such unit, the results are likely to be better than if they are made day by day. For one thing, a teacher gives out such a major assignment with far more care and system than he is likely to devote to any lesson for a single class period.

(3) The assignment should be flexible and adapted to the needs of different students. One of the common practices in elementary school is quite valuable in this connection. Most grade teachers make a minimum assignment that is to be completed by all the pupils and then add materials for those who are unusually capable. Sometimes teachers divide a class into three or four subgroups and hold each successive section responsible for the work of those below, plus a bit more. Some such arrangement is desirable in college classes as well. Otherwise the more capable students learn chiefly how to get good

[3] For the advantages of this procedure see E. Holmes, "Reading Guided by Questions Versus Careful Reading and Re-Reading without Questions," *School Review*, 39:361–71, 1931, and L. B. Wright, "The Value of a Motivated Assignment," *University of Pittsburgh School of Education Journal*, 5:64–67, 1929.

marks in return for very little effort. Anyone who makes a uniform assignment is tacitly assuming that all students are alike, no matter how well he knows that they are all different.

(4) The assignment should be ingenious and should call for more or less reorganization of subject material. Too many lessons are frightfully dull. A student reads his text, learns what is in it—in precisely the form and order in which it appears—and then goes to class and recites it like a parrot. Of course, there are some things like the conjugation of verbs that have to be learned verbatim, but for any other kind of material this procedure is extremely uninteresting and wholly unnecessary. If students do not think about their work, it is to some extent the fault of their teachers, who have not asked them to do any thinking. Ingenuity is the best prevention for boredom.

(5) The assignment should be, if possible, of some practical use, in and of itself, especially when one is dealing with a group of undifferentiated freshmen. For advanced classes this matter is not so important. For many freshmen, however, a lesson is of value in proportion to its usefulness in their daily lives. While any teacher uses some textbook assignments, he can supplement these with applications of various kinds so that the students may feel they are learning something of immediate value to them. Naturally, some subjects and some parts of subjects can be treated in this way more easily than others, but the practicability of a lesson is always one point to keep in mind.

An assignment should, then, be clear, flexible, ingenious, and as practical as possible. A few illustrations may serve to give greater reality to these general statements. Every example is not perfect on every possible count, but each illustrates one or more points about the making of assignments.

A teacher of statistics had her students collect data of all kinds about their friends in the college community—amount of time spent in studying, number of dates per week, number of week ends absent from college, number of dances attended, membership in organizations, marks in different classes, number of hours spent in nonacademic activities, incidence of illness, size of families, and many other such details. The students first secured complete data from one hundred classmates and then spent the rest of the semester on such interesting questions as "Does frequent absence over week ends interfere with academic progress?" "Do the students from the cities have more social life than those from the country?" "What is the relation between participation in extra curricular activities and marks?" "Who has the most dates and why?" The practice in manipulating machines and applying techniques was just as good as it would have been for more abstruse problems, but the work was far more entertaining and the students could check directly upon the accuracy of their results.

In a history course the teacher wanted his students to look over some of the newspapers published during a certain period in order to find out what points of view were prevalent at that time. His assignment was, however, to look at the papers as much as seemed necessary and then to write an editorial for one of them. Each student was free to select whichever paper he or she wished, but each had to read enough in at least one paper to make the editorial fit the policy of the paper, and each had to think up some topic that might have been written about but actually was not— in the issues examined, at any rate. This assignment has clarity, flexibility, and ingenuity.

In a class on mental hygiene the instructor wished to have the students consider the long-time effects of maladjustments in childhood and adolescence. He therefore assigned the reading of any three of a long list of novels, all of which gave a personification of the problems involved. The students were not to write a summary of the plot; they were to trace the effects of maladjustment throughout the life of some one character.

In an English composition class the teacher was working on the imitation of literary styles. She realized that the task of imitating a classical author would be too discouraging for the students; she therefore used another plan of procedure. She asked each student to write a letter purporting to come from her and addressed to some other teacher with whom the student was studying; the letter was to be concerned with some matter of local campus interest. As an aid in this work she passed out several samples of letters she had written so that the students would have something to imitate. Then she said, "Now, all of you know me, all of you know the teacher to whom you will address the letter, and all of you know at least one topic on which we might converse. You have the pieces of the puzzle, now put them together." The students learned a great deal about imitating the style of one individual and adapting it to the personality of another—and the resulting letters were worth the price of admission.

In a chemistry class the professor wanted to convince his students that his subject was of universal interest and importance. He asked each student to keep a diary for a single day, putting into it everything he did and noting what chemical phenomena were involved. The student did not have to explain any of them— merely to note their existence. A little later in the course this same professor handed out in the laboratory some pieces of white cloth, each with a stain on it. The students were to find out what the stain was—which could be done in most cases by mere inspection —and then record their efforts to get it out, telling why they chose the reagents they did. The practical usefulness of these assignments is especially striking.

In a course in anthropology the professor asked the students to write an account of a hypothetical visit of either a Navajo or Crow Indian to a church service in any church with the customs of which the students were familiar. This assignment required, first, a great deal of reading about the religious customs of the selected tribe and then a comparison of them with some modern church service.

The teacher of a physics class borrowed from the local gas and electric company the record of complaints that had come in to the "trouble department" over a period of about six weeks. He then passed out a copy for a different day to each student in the class and asked him to tell what he thought was probably wrong in each case, why he thought so, and how he thought the defect could be remedied.

The students in Latin composition were getting bored with the usual set of exercises to be rendered from English to Latin, so the teacher proposed that the class choose something of their own to translate. The students selected "Bluebeard," translated it, costumed it, and enacted it.

In a mathematics class there were three failing students and four others whose work was barely passing. At the top of the class were two excellent students and three more whose work was very good. When it came time to review for an examination in the middle of the semester, the teacher gave a unique review assignment. The five superior students were to tutor the seven poor ones—the two best having two inferior classmates apiece. The good students were excused from the examination, but they were to receive a mark, which would depend upon how much their pupils improved on the examination over their standing up to that time. Both groups of students were excused from class for ten days before the test and left entirely to their own devices. No student thus tutored got a lower mark than a C and two of them received B's—increases of two or three letter grades over their previous standing. The teacher quite rightly reasoned that by the time a superior student had worked for a while with someone for whose progress he was responsible, he would know the material so thoroughly that examining him would be a waste of time.

A history professor asked her students to imagine they were citizens of some Italian city during the Renaissance and to imagine further that they visited some other Italian city. Each was to write what impressions he or she would have gained from the visit. By this assignment the students became acquainted with the development of two cities. In another history class the teacher asked each student to write a series of letters supposedly exchanged between a Northerner and a Southerner in about the year 1850. The object was to make the students realize the antagonism that existed between the two sectional points of view.

In a class on the Old Testament the professor asked each student to write a denunciation of modern society after the general style of any one of the Old Testament prophets he preferred.

In a course on the history of art each student was asked to select some theme around which many pictures had been painted, then to examine what pictures he could find, and to report on the developments in style and technique he had noticed in the treatment of this one theme.

All of these assignments are interesting and ingenious; all are definite without the sacrifice of flexibility. They demand both the collecting and the organizing of facts. They are adapted to various levels of ability, since one student can always produce more of the same type than another; they therefore permit the best students to demonstrate their superiority. Most of them are, of course, assignments for a period of time from one to six weeks. They were presumably preceded, accompanied, and followed by assignments that were less unusual. Even a small admixture of such tasks as those just described does a good deal to lift the student's preparation of his lessons from the dead level of monotony that is produced by too lavish a use of "Take the next twenty pages for tomorrow."

Summary: Assignments are the student's sailing directions. If they are confused or boresome, he either will not know where he is supposed to go or will not care whether or not he ever gets there. Although not every assignment needs to be original—after all a teacher is only human and cannot be expected to have inspirations daily—a dash of ingenuity and novelty in assignments adds greatly to their value. It is the consensus of opinion that the progress of students in a course bears a direct relation to the degree of challenge in the work required of them. One of my friends once expressed a characteristic student attitude toward a really stimulating assignment when she said, "I am willing to walk to the Library to work on any lesson, but when Miss F gives me one of her assignments I want to run."

CHAPTER XVII

THE INFERIOR STUDENT

College teachers vary in their attitudes toward the presence in their classes of numerous students who are unable, at the time of entrance, at any rate, to profit by work at the college level. Some professors resent the situation and believe that such freshmen should be eliminated as soon as possible. At the other extreme are those who are inclined to be sentimental; more than one teacher has passed inefficient students because the latter "tried so hard." Between these two extremes are various shadings of opinion. What any individual professor thinks depends partly upon his beliefs as to the objectives of a college education, partly upon the amount of experience he has had, partly upon his own personality, and partly upon how many inferior students have recently been annoying him. If one is quite convinced that college work should be reserved for the intellectually elite or for the training of leaders in the next generation, one is naturally impatient with those who obviously belong to neither of these groups. On the other hand, if one believes in spreading out educational advantages over as many people as possible—even if the layer is sometimes a bit thin—then one becomes automatically more tolerant toward the less capable individuals in the student population.

It is always necessary to make some kind of adjustment to the lower end of the distribution of ability. Even if one cuts off the distribution arbitrarily at any point by the use of admission standards, there is still a low end that cannot quite keep up with the middle and upper divisions. The problem cannot, therefore, be solved by elimination alone.

In any program of adjustment the first step consists, obviously, in a careful study of the students involved in order to determine why they are unsuccessful. Any treatment of failing students that is not based upon adequate investigation is largely an expression of prejudice.

I. CAUSES OF FAILURE

There have been numerous investigations into this matter of why students fail. From these studies two kinds of cause have emerged. These may be classified roughly as academic or nonacademic. The former type of difficulty has already been discussed in the chapter on the preparation of college students. Deficiencies exist in every field, but those which especially influence work in college are inability to read the textbooks, inability to write simple sentences, and inability to solve problems in elementary school arithmetic.[1] The importance of defects in preparation is too obvious to need further comment.

In nonacademic matters the difference between good and poor students is neither so clear nor so easy to determine. The most adequate study on this point is an analysis of the personal handicaps of 204 probation students who were studied over a period of at least one semester by means of interviews, physical examinations, and careful observation during their daily attendance in small sections of a class in study methods. Various assistants compiled adequate case histories of all students. The statements to follow are based upon these his-

[1] A. C. Lemon, "An Experimental Study of Guidance and Placement in the Lowest Decile of the Iowa Qualifying Examination, 1925," *University of Iowa Studies in Education,* Vol. 3, No. 8, 1927, 136 pp.; O. F. Bond, "Causes of Failure in Elementary Freshman and Sophmore Courses at the College Level," *School Review,* 32: 276–87, 1924; J. A. Highsmith and M. S. Bean, "Why College Freshmen Fail," *North Carolina College for Women, Studies in Education,* No. 2, Greensboro, North Carolina, 1928, 22 pp.; K. L. Heaton and V. Weedon, "The Failing Student," University of Chicago Press, 1939, 286 pp.

TABLE 22[2]

The Most Common Symptoms of the Inferior Student

	Per Cent		Per Cent
A. Physical condition		f. Wrote as fast as possible during lecture	32
1. Infections		3. Reviewing	
a. Ear infection	21	a. Reviewed 5-hour course only once a quarter	37
b. Dead teeth	62		
c. Infected tonsils	17		
d. Rheumatism	17	b. Reviewed only night before examination	56
2. Enlarged thyroid	29		
3. Hay fever	15	c. Got excited over examination	52
4. Colds			
a. Chronic cold	27	d. Did not read examination questions over before writing	57
b. Chronic cough	14		
c. Four or more colds per year	22		
5. Headaches		C. Social difficulties	
a. Severe	24	1. Home conditions	
b. Frequent	37	a. Constant criticism	19
6. Digestion		b. Uncongenial home	19
a. Frequent indigestion	21	c. Broken home	22
b. Frequent intestinal cramps	38	2. Outside work	
		a. Working for all expenses	14
7. Insomnia	16		
8. Recent loss of weight	14	b. Working for part of expenses	28
9. Fatigue		3. Social relations	
a. Chronic	18	a. Isolation	24
b. Always tired upon waking	45	b. Excitement over sorority or fraternity	40
10. Some eye defect	57	c. Social life restricted because of being a Jew or Negro	24
11. Nervousness	31		
B. Methods of work			
1. Reading		d. Adjustment to college life hard	43
a. Inability to skim	76		
b. Failure to read paragraph headings	43	D. Vocational difficulties	
		1. No choice made	24
c. Failure to read summary	51	2. Obviously wrong choice	27
d. Failure to read graphs	87	E. Emotional difficulties	
e. Skipping unfamiliar words	73	1. Worry over	
		a. Previous failure	71
2. Note taking		b. Money	11
a. Notes from all classes mixed together	40	c. Personal defects	14
		d. Health	12
b. Notes taken on loose sheets of paper because notebook forgotten	16	e. Failure to get into sorority or fraternity	19
		2. Difficulties of personality	
c. Reading notes not in an outline form	52	a. "Shut-in" type	11
		b. Moody type	10
d. Lecture notes not in an outline form	59	c. Rebellious, un-co-operative type	16
		d. Immature type	18
e. Copied words of author from book	32	e. Feelings of inferiority	25

[2] Pressey, *op. cit.* Used by permission of the *Journal of Higher Education.*

tories.[2a] This list includes all symptoms of any kind shown by 10 per cent or more of the entire group.

From the foregoing description it seems clear that these students were in somewhat poorer physical condition than the average, that their study habits were ineffective, and that their social and emotional problems were rather more numerous than is customary. There is, however, nothing unusual about any of their handicaps; there are merely more of them. Over half of the students showed difficulties in four of the five fields recorded, and all but about a dozen had handicaps in more than one field. It is a reasonable conclusion that students do failing work because they have too large an assortment of simple troubles. A student can get along with relatively low ability, or with some physical handicap, or with inefficient methods of work, or with poor preparation, or with common emotional and social problems, but he cannot do passing work if he has three or four of them in combination.

The probationer is, then, a person with an inadequate academic preparation and more personal handicaps than the student whose work is satisfactory. Sometimes this condition is doubtless the freshman's own fault, but quite as often the blame, if any, lies with the schools he has attended earlier, with the lack of proper articulation between high school and college, with his family, or with a personality that is an outgrowth of his entire previous life. Since the situation differs from one case to another, it is dangerous to make generalizations, but it is only fair to remember that many students are in trouble through no fault of their own.

II. DESIRABLE TREATMENT OF FAILING STUDENTS

Some twenty or more years ago, as authorities came to realize that an unreasonable proportion of each entering class failed to make acceptable progress, a number of people tried various methods of dealing with the situation. Probably the most common of these was the establishment of a "how-to-

[2a] L. C. Pressey, "A Class of Probation Students," *Journal of Higher Education,* 2: 506–10, 1931.

study" class for those who were in academic difficulties. In other places a clinical psychologist was asked to interview failing students and determine what maladjustments were causing the failure. The approach in any one school depended usually upon what talent was available among the faculty. The resulting treatments ran all the way from an occasional personal interview with inferior students to a re-education of their ocular-motor responses or a fairly complete psychoanalysis. In some instances the experimenters obtained excellent results; in others they had no success at all. One finds therefore the most divergent opinions in the literature. Much of this difference is due, however, to the differences in treatment. Those who merely told students how to study without giving them a chance to do so under supervision or those who merely talked with students about their difficulties but did little or nothing to remove them got understandably poor results. The students reacted favorably to the individual attention they received, and that was about all. The better efforts at remedial work consist of actual studying under supervision, actual analysis of error in subjects with subsequent remedial drill, actual alleviation of physical ailments, and actual adjustment of emotional difficulties. The values of such work are related directly to the practical action taken and inversely to the amount of sheer talk.

Since remedial work of the type to be described is relatively recent and since its nature is often misunderstood, I want to discuss the various problems involved a little more fully than I should were the work of a generally accepted character. There is on almost any faculty some amount of opposition to courses designed explicitly for inferior students. The objections voiced are sometimes valid and are sometimes mere rationalizations of some emotional attitude. Because the question of what to do with the students who have neither interest nor ability to pursue an academic course successfully is so important, a prospective college teacher needs to have an informed opinion as to the value of the various methods already in vogue for handling the situation. The remedial class is only one, but its use is widespread.

1. Planning a remedial program: In planning for remedial work the first matters for attention are frankly administrative. Although something can be done by even a single earnest person and although in particular instances much has been accomplished in spite of unfavorable circumstances, I feel sure that the best work is not possible unless four definite arrangements have been made in advance of any actual meeting with students.

Most of those who need help are freshmen. It is therefore necessary to fit the remedial work into the existing pattern of instruction and treatment accorded to the beginner in college. The first step should be to obtain approval for the work from all departments that enroll any considerable number of freshmen. If this precaution is not taken, the remedial work and the regular classwork are almost certain to fall afoul of one another because the former is new and its nature not well understood by the average instructor. Most of the prejudice that exists in some colleges against remedial treatment rests upon ignorance and the garbled accounts of students. Work can, of course, be done in the face of faculty disapproval and misunderstanding, but it cannot be well done.

Unless some plan as to who does what is agreed upon, such situations as the following may develop. In one college a member of the education department was asked by the administration to look into the problems of failing students and to take whatever steps seemed indicated. The professor soon found that the freshmen he interviewed needed help in study methods. Among other things he gave his charges some instruction about outlining. In a week's time there was a protest from the freshmen English teachers that they taught outlining. Further difficulty arose because the particular method of note taking he recommended did not meet with the approval of the history department which issued to all beginning classes some instructions of its own on note taking. Presently the method of memorizing came in for criticism by the language teachers. Even the registrar was perturbed when certain students—entirely on their own initiative and certainly without any suggestion from the teacher of remedial work—began to raise objections to the assignment of classes because the hours given them did not accord with the study schedule they had been advised to follow! All these misunderstandings, although eventually adjusted, weakened and discredited the remedial work.

The only safe procedure is to make a definite arrangement with each department as to what articulation can be made between remedial training and classwork. Several adjustments are possible, but three are especially valuable. Presumably if freshmen have average preparation the regular teachers are more capable of teaching them the content of subjects than any remedial teacher is likely to be. On the other hand the regular teachers have to assume a minimum preparation. If the special work is restricted to reviewing grammar school and high school subjects in order to provide an adequate basis for college work, there is not only no friction but the faculty members are glad to have the remedial work done. As such work develops, the person in charge soon needs assistants. Some of these obviously should be clinicians in order that the difficulties of personality may be properly handled, but some of them should be subject-matter experts. I have found it very useful to recruit assistants from among the graduate students of the content departments—especially English, mathematics, modern language, history, and chemistry. These graduates can not only give more help in their own field than an education-alist can, but they also almost automatically act as liaison officers between their departments and the remedial class. A third method is to arrange for frequent visits to the study class by all ranking members of all departments that enroll many freshmen. One should be especially careful to invite any people who are opposed to the work. I usually show the visitors the materials, tell them where the case studies are kept, familiar-ize them with the general procedure of the group, and then leave the room while they talk with any students they like and ask any questions they see fit. They generally stay for an entire afternoon, converse with one student after another, and find out what is really being done. To be sure, they are not always convinced that the outlay of time, effort, and money is justified by the results, but at least their criticisms are based upon knowledge.

A second matter of administrative nature concerns the assignment of the remedial work. Commonly the class is given in the education or psychology department, unless it is under the supervision of the personnel office. It is far better if the work—like that of many of the survey courses—remains entirely independent of departmental lines. If this arrangement is not made the work sometimes falls heir to any interdepartmental jealousies or misunderstandings that exist between the one to which it is assigned and any other on the campus. Since remedial training is relatively new, it cannot afford to handicap itself with old quarrels.

A third administrative problem concerns the actual arrangement of the work so that the students who most need it can get it with the least difficulty for all concerned. In some cases, especially in small colleges, the whole matter has been handled by means of voluntary individual interviews. For some elements in the total procedure this method is highly desirable, but it is too time consuming for use in large universities, and for certain common problems it is not especially valuable. In many institutions the remedial work has been given as a regularly scheduled class in which the students enroll either upon recommendation of their deans or upon their own initiative. The class serves as a nucleus around which various individual treatments can cluster, it is useful in the development of good study methods, it is attended more regularly than most individual appointments, and it serves as an efficient medium through which information on certain matters of mental hygiene can most easily be conveyed. For its numerous practical values a "class" —but by no means of a traditional type—is strongly recommended.[3]

A final administrative problem relates to the students' schedules. Unless a freshman has adequate time for the remedial treatment he needs, the work will not get done, and at the end of the semester he will hardly be better off than at the beginning. It should

[3] It is also desirable that the course should carry one hour or more of college credit. Objections are sure to be raised against this procedure on the grounds that students should not receive credit for repeating work they should already have mastered before entrance. For a further discussion of this point see pages 235–38.

be clear enough that a student who is having difficulty in passing
fifteen hours of classwork will not progress as well with this load
plus a "how-to-study" class, but it is surprising how often the
work is merely added to whatever other courses a freshman is
carrying. I have always made it a condition of doing remedial
work at all that I should have control of each student's schedule
during the semester he was in the class. After a conference with
each one, I reduced the load to an amount that would give the
student enough time to concentrate upon correcting his weaknesses.
If a normal schedule calls for fifteen hours, the probationer's
should call for some number between three and ten. Both the
amount and type of work must be considered. Thus, if a student
who has just failed the first semester of Spanish has put the course
on his schedule again, it should be removed. Whatever handicap
caused him to fail in the first place is still present, and he should
not repeat the course until he has remedied his original weaknesses. The amount of time a student spends in the class should
depend upon how much he has to do. I always required a student
who was carrying only one five-hour course to spend fifteen hours
a week; if he were carrying two five-hour courses he spent ten
hours a week. In addition, he could come in and study any time
he wished. It is essential for the success of such a program that
the students have adequate time for concentration upon their
remedial work. Otherwise everyone's energy is wasted.

It may seem that I have spent too much time and space in
dealing with administrative phases of the problem. The reason
is that in at least a dozen colleges with whose work I am familiar the development of the work has suffered severely because
the person in charge had rushed into action without first clear-
ing his administrative lines. As a result he aroused the antagonism of his colleagues mainly because he was misunderstood, he
accomplished less than he should have because he had to rely
upon purely voluntary contacts with his students, and he had to
make the best of whatever odds and ends of time remained
after they had finished their other work. These matters, though
of course secondary in importance to the actual conduct of the
course, are so vital to its continuance and so often neglected
that I have presented them in more detail than some may
think justified.

2. Nature of the remedial class: The visitor to the class on methods of work generally finds a small group of students meeting in a laboratory room. At the beginning of the hour there are often some announcements for the entire group, but soon the class breaks up and each student goes about whatever business he has on hand. One or two leave the room for interviews, some get out their regular assignments and start to study, others practice various types of drill exercises, one over in a corner is memorizing Spanish vocabulary, another is making an outline of a paper, while a third is engaged in constructing a review chart. The teacher moves about the room, noting the progress of each student and making sure that each is following the type of assignment that will best remedy his shortcomings. If the teacher observes some common mistake or if some point of general interest is suggested to him, he may stop the class and have a few minutes of classwork. The procedure is quite informal and develops each day according to the needs of the group at the moment.[4]

Against this background the work of the course should proceed along three lines. Some time is given to methods of study, some to a review of essential preparation, and some to the adjustment of such personal difficulties as are not automatically relieved by the improvement of classwork. For an adequate program one cannot neglect any of these three. Naturally, in some colleges there are local reasons why the program has to be restricted to a single approach. In such cases, since less is done, less should be expected.

First (1) come the methods of study. Most people have found it best to develop desirable habits through the use of each student's own daily assignments, rather than by means of special exercises, because of the greater motivation. This arrangement is not as difficult as might at first appear. The number of courses open to freshmen is not large, and in a short time one becomes familiar with the texts. In no case is it desirable to make any effort at teaching students the

---

[4] If a large laboratory can be secured for the purpose, and if each student can be given a place in which he can keep his belongings, many students will do practically all their studying under supervision during the whole semester.

content of the books; one should merely use the texts for working out assignments in study methods. Most investigators have concentrated their efforts upon the development of five techniques of study—taking notes from reading material, taking notes from lectures, combining materials from several sources into a coherent plan and then writing from the plan, reviewing, and reading to find the structure of a chapter and its main ideas.

In my class I usually begin with reading.[5] The first assignment required the students to read their next day's work in any text that contained consecutive reading material and to write out a statement of the main idea of each paragraph. Naturally, some paragraphs have no main idea, but it is just as valuable for students to discover that a paragraph does not have one as to find that it does. This work continued until each freshman could read his book with reasonable comprehension of the paragraphs as units. Then I made an assignment on outlining sections or whole chapters. These two types of work usually extended over the first six weeks of the semester. As soon as the students could take notes

[5] Some very good experiments have dealt with reading exclusively. In some cases a considerable improvement in scholastic work has followed an adequate training course in the reading of college texts. Some of the better investigations are listed below:
M. B. Blake and W. F. Dearborn, "The Improvement of Reading Habits," *Journal of Higher Education*, 6 : 83–88, 1935 ; W. F. Book, "How Well College Students Can Read," *School and Society*, 26 : 242–48, 1927 ; R. F. Carroll and C. C. Jacobs, "Drill in Silent Reading for College Freshmen," *School and Society*, 30 : 656–58, 1929 ; J. D. Davis and H. S. Tuttle, "Remedial Measures for College Freshmen," *Regional Conference on Higher Education*, 1931, pp. 80–104 ; R. W. Deal, "The Development of Reading and Study Habits in College Students," *Journal of Educational Psychology*, 25 : 258–73, 1934 ; J. R. Gerberich, "Five Years of Experience with a Remedial Reading Course for College Students," *Journal of Experimental Education*, 3 : 36–41, 1934 ; L. W. Pressey, "College Remedial Reading Classes," *English Journal*, 19 : 566–69, 1930 ; F. P. Robinson, "Can College Freshmen in the Lowest Tenth in Reading Be Aided Scholastically?" *School and Society*, 34 : 843–46, 1931 ; C. W. Howe, "Improving the Reading Abilities of College Students," *Journal of Educational Method*, 2 : 8–23, 1922 ; G. E. Nelson, "Correction of Visual Defects and Improvement in College Studies," *School and Society*, 27 : 107–8, 1928 ; G. B. Watson and T. M. Newcomb, "Improving Reading Ability among Teachers College Students," *Teachers College Record*, 31 : 535–39, 1930 ; H. H. Remmers and J. M. Stalnaker, "An Experiment in Remedial Reading at the College Level," *School and Society*, 28 : 797–800, 1928 ; R. M. Strang, "Improving Students' Reading," *Journal of Higher Education*, 5 : 426–32, 1934, and "Improvement of Reading in College," *English Journal* (College Edition), 26 : 548–59, 1937.

fairly well from their books, I lectured for the major part of one hour each week while they took notes. Then we discussed what had been said and compared the notes of various students. During the rest of the semester I required them to show me their lecture notes from one of their regular classes once a week. About a week before the mid-term examinations I made an assignment on selective reviewing. The freshmen brought all the materials from any one class to the laboratory and organized the work to date; this assignment was repeated at the close of the semester. Most students have at least one paper to prepare at some time during the term. As soon as the paper had been assigned, they began collecting their notes, arranging them into an outline form, and then writing from the outline. My own contribution to this procedure consisted (1) in being sure they took down each item on a separate card so that their units of thought could be arranged and rearranged in any desirable order, (2) in making certain that they had a coherent plan before they began to write, and (3) in seeing to it that they followed their outline. What they put into the paper was strictly their business. These five types of assignment seemed adequate for developing in the students whatever skill in studying they were capable of developing.

The second part of the course (2) should be concerned with the remediation of inadequate preparation in one or more fields. It is usually possible to tell from a freshman's high school record which subjects need attention. If not, one can always give an objective test and find out. Suppose, for instance, that a freshman had always had trouble with languages and needed further work in this field. I started his remedial training by giving him an old-fashioned English grammar and some exercises in sentence structure. He kept on working at this material until he could analyze an English sentence into its parts and tell me what modified or agreed with what. If a freshman had failed chemistry, I gave him first a series of remedial exercises in reading—including the reading of graphs and tables—then a series in arithmetic and algebra, and finally a series of vocabulary drills covering basic scientific terms. In brief, I required each student to remedy whatever elements in his preparation had been neglected. Moreover, I did not excuse him from further work until his performance was between 95 and 100 per cent perfect—no matter how long it took. One trouble with these freshmen was that too many of their previous teachers had let them pass with a 70 per cent mastery—which through normal forgetting soon became not more than 40 or 50 per cent. This part of the course was hard work for all concerned, but I have never found any substitute for a mastery of elementary facts.[6]

The third section of the program (3) should be devoted to the elimination—in so far as practicable—of personal difficulties. Since most problems will yield to adequate information, one can approach the matter through short lectures interspersed with other phases of the work. Common problems of mental hygiene, of vocational choice, and of social adjustment can be presented and discussed. In addition, one needs a complete case study of each student, including a physical examination by the college physician. Naturally, those in charge of such work try to carry out such adjustments along personal lines as may seem desirable and possible. The reading that students do in the course may be so assigned as to give them information and help with their personal maladjustments. If this part of the work is omitted, some students profit little from the class because they already study reasonably well

[6] Various people have worked on this phase of remedial teaching. Almost without exception the progress of an originally low group of students has been phenomenal. For instance, 80 freshmen made scores in punctuation between 60 and 91 on a test for which a score of 85 was just average for the ninth grade. At the end of a few weeks in a remedial class their scores ranged from 98 to 119 with a median at 110—the average for college sophomores. (These figures are from the first article by Guiler, below.) This result is typical of the improvement brought about by diagnostic work. The references below report similar experiments in various fields. W. A. Coit, "A Preliminary Study of Mathematical Difficulties," *School Review,* 36: 504–9, 1928; F. R. Conkling, "Student Self-Help in Composition Drill," *English Journal* (College Edition), 20: 50–53, 1931; W. S. Guiler, "Remediation of Teachers College Freshmen," *School and Society,* 30: 242–44, 1929; W. S. Guiler, "Improvement and Permanency of Learning Resulting from Remedial Instruction," *School Review,* 41: 450–58, 1933, and "Remediation of College Freshmen," in Capitalization, *Educational Method,* 11: 540–44, 1932; in Punctuation, *Peabody Journal of Education,* 9: 152–58, 1931; in Grammatical Usage, *Journal of Educational Research,* 26: 110–15, 1932; R. G. Simpson, "Effect of Specific Training on Ability to Read Historical Materials," *Journal of Educational Research,* 20: 343–51, 1929.

and their preparation is already adequate. The study below summarizes such a situation.

John was a boy from the backwoods of Kentucky. He had come to college only because he wanted to become a minister and he had been advised to get at least two years of college before entering divinity school. At home John belonged to a violently fundamentalist family and to a fundamentalist church. Such young people as he had been allowed to know were a good deal like himself. In the simple environment from which John came he had had no great difficulty in leading a chaste life. What he did not realize was that he had never been really tempted. John's entrance to college precipitated him onto a large campus in the middle of a big city. The local mores struck him as infamous, and the students seemed to his inexperienced eyes to be headed straight for perdition. The coeds were especially distressing because, while being doubtless wicked, they were strangely exciting. Not even in class was John safe. Both his biology and his history teachers told him things that were at variance with the Bible. And his English teacher regarded the Bible merely as an excellent sourcebook of phrases. Before the end of the first semester John was in academic difficulty. He had failed zoology because he had not attended class during the last month or taken the examination. When asked for an explanation of this conduct he said shortly that he would not go to such a godless class. His marks in both English and history were low, chiefly because he insisted upon arguing about religion instead of answering examination questions in a manner that could be scored. In addition to the religious conflict John had many personal troubles. He felt inferior and unsure of himself. He doubted that a person to whom no one would pay attention had any business becoming a minister. He fell in love with a popular coed, who only laughed at him. The infatuation was so intense that he spent much time in daydreaming, which more often than not ended in masturbation, followed by intense shame and regret. At the beginning of the second semester when John reported for remedial work he was in a state of great excitement, anxiety, bewilderment, and despair. Most of the work done with him consisted of personal interviews, plus reading of selected references for the purpose of broadening his outlook on life. There was no need to teach the boy how to study because he already knew how when his fantasies would let him concentrate. Nor was his preparation below average in anything but written English. Nothing could have been sillier than to subject John to the usual routine of remedial work. He did, to be sure, study in the laboratory, but this arrangement was merely for purposes of keeping him under supervision three or four hours a day until his acute fears and anxieties could be checked. John remained in the remedial class for a year and a half. During this time he gradually learned to accept the modern world as it is, to adjust himself to it, and to get along with his age-mates. If he lost some of his crusader's ardor in the process, he acquired a poise and tolerance that promised greater success in his chosen calling. Perhaps the best single element in this boy's re-education was the requirement that every day he should tell his counselor something funny that he had noted. This incident had to be an actual experience—not a joke out of a newspaper. It was nearly three weeks before this sober lad saw anything even faintly amusing. It was not until John began poking gentle fun at himself that he was regarded as really "cured."

Although not many students have as severe difficulties as this boy, who had to adapt reactions built up in one environment to a completely different situation, there are always some freshmen in any group of probationers whose problems are primarily personal. No one who deals with probation students can afford to neglect clinical work. On the other hand, neither can he afford to neglect educational diagnosis or training in good methods of study.

Such a program as that just outlined should not be regarded as a nebulous ideal. It has been carried out in its entirety in a number of places. Moreover, it gives results.[7] Whether or

[7] The various experiments listed below are all good. In some cases the training was more extensive than in others and the results correspondingly better. H. D. Behrens, "Effects of a How to Study Course," *Journal of Higher Education*, 6: 195–202, 1935; W. P. Book, "Results Obtained in a Special How to Study Course Given to College Students," *School and Society*, 26: 529–34, 1927; C. C. Crawford, "Some Results of Teaching College Students How to Study," *School and Society*, 23: 471–72, 1926; A. C. Eurich, "Improvement in Scholarship During the Probationary Period," *School and Society*, 35: 129–34, 1932; J. M. Ferguson, "Saving the Probationer" and "Probation Students under Guidance," *Educational Review*, 75: 142–45 and 224–28, 1928; P. L. Harriman, "Orientation of College Freshmen," *Peabody Journal of Education*, 3: 159–61, 1925; P. W. Holaday, "The Long Time Effects of Freshmen Counseling," *School and Society*, 29: 234–36, 1929; E. S. Jones, "The Preliminary Course on 'How to Study' for Freshmen Entering College," *School and Society*, 29: 702–15, 1929; E. S. Jones, "Testing and Training the Inferior Freshman," *Personnel Journal*, 6: 182–91, 1927; E. S. Jones, "How Freshmen Needs are

not the results are worth as much as other outcomes that could be achieved by a different use of the same time and money is another matter.

III. RESULTS OF REMEDIAL WORK

The first result of remedial work cannot be expressed in terms of academic progress. It refers to the number of students who were persuaded, during their probation semester, to leave college and go into some type of work that promised greater success. Many teachers do not seem to realize that there is no graceful way for a failing student to get out of college. Either he is put out or he leaves just before the machinery catches up with him. Many academic delinquents are acutely miserable and want to quit, but like other human beings, they do not want to admit they are failures. One of the most valuable features of the remedial program is the opportunity it offers for removing the academic failure without distress to anyone. Some freshmen do not have the native ability to do college work, and many of them do not have one spark of interest in anything taught in school. They are not, however— as many of their professors suppose—mentally empty. They have interests that, if developed, will make them valuable citizens. It is an important phase of remedial work to find these interests and to persuade the freshmen having them to leave college and go where they can get the training they need.

Met at the University of Buffalo," *Ninth Yearbook of the National Education Association, Department of Superintendence,* 1931, pp. 158–61; G. F. Kay and D. D. Feder, "Some Effects of Curriculum Adjustment at the College Level for Students Low in Scholastic Aptitude," *School and Society,* 47:772–76, 1938; A. C. Lemon, "An Experimental Study of Guidance and Placement of Freshmen in the Lowest Decile of the Iowa Qualifying Examination," *University of Iowa Studies in Education,* Vol. 3, No. 8, 1927, 136 pp.; F. W. Parr, "Teaching College Students How to Read," *Journal of Higher Education,* 2:324–30, 1931; L. C. Pressey, "The Permanent Effects of Training in Methods of Study on College Success," *School and Society,* 28:403–4, 1928; H. H. Remmers, "A Diagnostic and Remedial Study of Potentially and Actually Failing Students at Purdue University," *Purdue Studies in Higher Education,* IX, Vol. 28, No. 12, 1928, 164 pp.; R. Strang, "Another Attempt to Teach How to Study," *School and Society,* 28:461–66, 1928; P. A. Witty and H. C. Lehman, "Teaching College Students How to Study," *Education,* 48:47–56, 1927.

A few cases may make this point clearer. There was, for instance, the girl whose one real interest in life was marcelling hair. Moreover she was, even without special training, so expert that her friends used all her spare time in having her curl their hair for them. I explained to her that an expert marcellist was much too valuable a member of the community to waste a college education on and persuaded her to leave college and go to a school of beauty culture. There she was a great success.

One amiable young man from the college of engineering had such a serious deficiency in his mathematical preparation that I doubted if he could remedy his defects in any reasonable amount of time—if at all. After a few minutes' conversation with him, it became perfectly evident that he did not want to be an engineer; he wanted to be a mechanic. I advised him to make a trip to his home town and see what he could do about arranging for a job in some garage. In a few days he was back with a glowing account of a position that he could get in a new garage that was to be opened in about two months. He stayed at the college for another six weeks, during which time he finished the equivalent of eighth-grade work in arithmetic and written English. It is not likely that he will ever need much more formal training. He now owns the garage.

One of the colored girls in the class was very evidently unable to do college work because of her inferior mental ability. No amount of remedial training would raise her average of preparation above that of the seventh or eighth grade. Her ambition was to become a dietitian. Since she would almost certainly never reach it, it seemed best to develop her interest in some related field. In the first interview she accounted for her interest in dietetics on the grounds that she liked to cook. I began talking to her about the advantages in being a cook and succeeded in getting her to withdraw from college and enter cooking school. She was an immediate success. After her course she obtained a good position where she has been ever since.

One of the boys wanted to be a doctor and had registered for premedical work. The first semester he failed both chemistry and zoology. During his probation semester he was allowed to take only English, in which he did good work. He had average intelligence, but his whole training had been in the humanities rather than in science. It seemed likely that he would need at least two years of remedial training before he could prepare himself for the scientific courses required by his curriculum. This boy had a real interest in doing something to alleviate pain and to take care of people who were sick. It was therefore suggested to him that he leave college and take up training as a male nurse. In this work he was both happy and successful.

The main thing to notice about these cases is the psychological effect of the treatment. The students were not eliminated by failure. They did not leave the university with a sense of discouragement and without any idea of what they would or could do next. There was no period of painful readjustment at home. They left of their own accord, with a definite objective about which they are enthusiastic. In their new work they had every hope of success. Usually it is possible to get rid of about one-third of the probationers in this manner. They do not belong in higher education, but this fact is no excuse for allowing their college experiences to leave permanent emotional scars. The first although intangible value, of the remedial work is, then, the relatively painless elimination of the most unfit.

As regards academic progress the results are of interest, although one may subscribe to either of two possible interpretations of them. In one early study [8] that reported the permanent result of training for fifty cases, there is evidence that the work was by no means wasted. The progress of the students who had been trained was compared with that of untrained students who entered college at the same time, had the same score of intelligence, failed the same courses, were in the same college, had the same number of academic credits at the end of the first semester, carried the same number of hours throughout the year, and took the same courses in the second semester. The main variable was, therefore, the training given to one member of each pair. Figure 34 indicates the level of work done by these two groups of students in the three years following the semester, during which half of them took a course on methods of study. Nearly 60 per cent of the trained group showed normal progress as compared with 18 per cent of the untrained. In the university where this work was done,

[8] Pressey, "The Permanent Effects of Training in Methods of Study on College Success," *op. cit.*

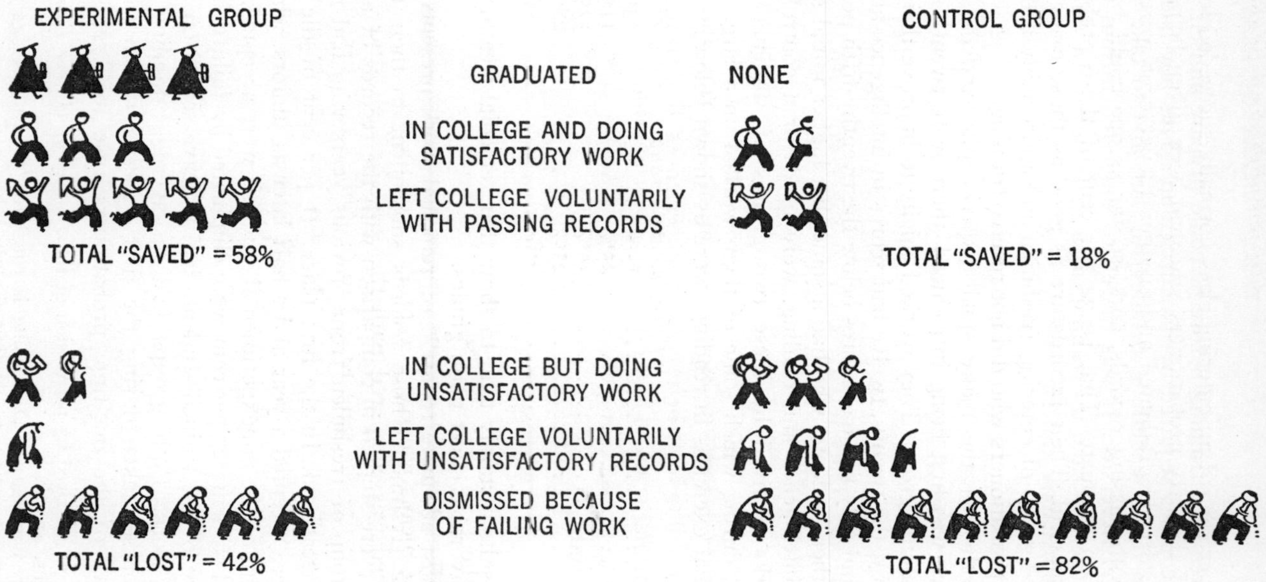

EXPERIMENTAL GROUP

GRADUATED

IN COLLEGE AND DOING
SATISFACTORY WORK

LEFT COLLEGE VOLUNTARILY
WITH PASSING RECORDS

TOTAL "SAVED" = 58%

IN COLLEGE BUT DOING
UNSATISFACTORY WORK

LEFT COLLEGE VOLUNTARILY
WITH UNSATISFACTORY RECORDS

DISMISSED BECAUSE
OF FAILING WORK

TOTAL "LOST" = 42%

NONE

CONTROL GROUP

TOTAL "SAVED" = 18%

TOTAL "LOST" = 82%

Fig. 34.—The Long-Time Effects of Training in Methods of Study.

387

only 35 per cent of an entering class normally succeeded in graduating. Of the fifty probationers who had been given help, 20 per cent had already graduated and another 14 per cent were still in college with passing records, and—so far as one could foresee— would soon graduate. That is, 34 per cent of these probationers were successful. Their records are as good as those made by any unselected group of entering freshmen and appreciably better than those of probationers who did not receive training.

In another of the many small experiments carried on when such work was first being introduced, there were twenty students in the training group. They worked chiefly to improve their ability to read. Of the twenty, twelve had scores in intelligence above the median and only five had scores below the twenthy-fifth percentile. Thirty other students, who had a somewhat higher initial standing in both intelligence and reading, were used for a control group. The marks received by these two groups of students for the semester, during which some of them worked on a large number of remedial exercises in reading, were as shown below: [9]

	Experimental Group	Control Group
A	15%	3%
B	25%	11%
C	35%	53%
D	25%	28%
E	0%	5%

These results certainly tend to show that remedial treatment does have a favorable effect upon grades.

The most adequate report [10] of remedial work presents results from 282 freshmen whose records subsequent to their training semester were studied in comparison with the records of a closely paired group of freshmen from previous years who had received no such treatment. In the first place, 41 per cent of the trained group were accepted a year and a half later as juniors, while only 23 per cent of the nonexperimental students were accepted. Of the untrained students 27 per cent were eliminated by failure, but only 3 per cent of the trained students had to leave school on account of poor work. Both groups had an average standing of .86 in the courses taken during the first semester. From this level the grades of the one-time probationers rose to 1.72 [11] in the

[9] Parr, *op. cit.* Used by permission of the *Journal of Higher Education.*
[10] Behrens, *op. cit.*
[11] In this university a D standing is equal to "1." An average of 1.7 is required for graduation, a standing slightly below a C.

course of the subsequent three semesters, while the average of the control group rose only to 1.39—still much below the level needed for admission to junior standing. In other words, those who had a chance to remedy their preparation and to learn efficient methods of work made measurably better records than equally poor students who did not have such an opportunity.

It should be noted that no investigator claims anything like a 100 per cent success. It is not far from the truth to say that of all the students who get on probation about one-third can be academically rehabilitated and can make average or slightly better than average records from that time on. Another third lingers on in college and eventually leaves after one or two years of mediocre or barely passing work. The last third is eliminated by the rules, or leaves with records too low to enter the junior year, or drops out of school while not actually failing but very close to it. One's attitude toward the whole remedial program depends in large measure upon how one views these outcomes. No one can object greatly to the salvation of those probationers who profit by the work. Whether or not it is worth anyone's while to improve the second third enough to permit them to pass two years of college, but not enough to continue further, is a question. If there were always a stopping place at the end of the first two years, one could view this group with more equanimity. In some colleges the curriculum is so arranged that these students can complete two years of training and get a junior certificate; in this case it seems to me that the work justifies itself for this group also. If, however, these students are merely postponing the day of failure from their first to their third year, there is no kindness in the arrangement. To be sure, some of them get a great deal of emotional satisfaction out of the two years of college life and do profit by some of the nonacademic activities, in spite of their final elimination, but perhaps this value is not sufficient. For the lowest third, it is my own opinion that the work can be justified only if the most strenuous efforts are made to get these freshmen out of college at once under their own power and headed into an occupation in which they have some prospect of success. As a convenient escape from the burden of maladjustment such a course is of value, regardless of academic achievement. The whole problem is, of course, open to argument. The only stipulation is that one should argue in the light of facts and not on the basis of preconceived prejudice.

IV. CURRICULAR ADJUSTMENTS

There seems little question that the traditional academic curriculum furnishes an inappropriate diet for the inferior student. This statement does not imply that there is anything wrong with either student or curriculum; they simply do not belong together. Even if these students could get passing grades, they still should not be taking work of this character. There are plenty of useful things a dull freshman can learn. Whether or not these things are of college caliber is to me unimportant because no one assumes that such students are mentally and emotionally capable of profiting by any more purely academic training than they have already received. On the other hand, every citizen in a democracy needs all the education he can get. The elimination of such a large proportion of students from college as was demonstrated in Chapter IV represents a great waste of human material.

The best type of adjustment to the needs of inferior students is preventive rather than remedial in character. In several places—the Universities of Texas, Minnesota, Florida, and Chicago—there is a special curriculum which does not lead to a degree and which has as its objective the development of whatever native capacities average and below-average students may show. On a smaller scale one finds the same kind of arrangement at Mills College and other small institutions; students who do not want to graduate or do not have the ability to complete the regular work have a considerable choice of curricular offerings designed especially for them. While the "special" student has always existed, he has often wasted much of his time because the courses offered were arranged for those who were going on with their education, not for those who wanted to stop soon. The resulting smattering of work was often far from educational. Wherever a school has evolved a constructive plan for dealing with the situation, the inferior student finds an array of nontechnical, general courses of the survey type. These are geared to his interests and ability. Usually this curriculum runs for two years and leads to a certificate. If, during these two years, a student shows enough ability, he may transfer to the academic courses at the end of any semester. In the meantime no one tries to make a scholar out of him, and his presence does not in the least prevent other students in college from doing superior work. This preventive approach is far better than even the best remedial work, although it does not entirely supersede the latter. It does, however, permit the remedial instruction to be given to those who will profit most by it, and it prevents the expenditure of time and money in an effort to fit students for a curriculum ill adapted to their needs. Educational diagnosis and individual guidance pay better dividends if applied to the otherwise brilliant freshman who cannot spell, who gets confused when confronted by a formula, who is afraid of his teachers, who is bombastic, or who suffers from social handicaps. An adequate program of prevention also operates to reduce to a total that can be handled efficiently the number of students who require detailed individual treatment.

The first step in adjusting work to the needs of the inferior student lies in accepting reality; the second step consists in doing something intelligent—not emotional—about it. Naturally, not all college teachers are able, either by disposition or education, to teach students of this type, or to find interest and stimulation for themselves in the task of helping common people to become better common people. If a professor's own emotional life is tied up with the development of geniuses and leaders, he will be of little use in dealing with mediocre freshmen, and it would be a waste of human capabilities to let him try. There is both room and need for the enthusiastic specialist to teach small advanced classes of brilliant students. On the other hand, there are many college teachers who are interested in the development of their students, no matter who these may be or at what level they start. These teachers like to teach and guide youth; they do not want to be research workers or specialists. With their aid a college can develop the capacities of its poorer students and can serve society by meeting the needs of the common people, of whom Lincoln so wisely said the Lord had made a very great many.

V. SUMMARY

Every distribution has a lower end. In the case of college students the lower fourth or fifth of the group in either ability or preparation is not ready—and perhaps never would be ready —to take work of an academic character. At least two attitudes toward them are possible. Teachers can continue to give nothing but academic work with true college standards and let the failures fail, or they can alter the work in either quantity or quality so that the potential failure will pass. Presumably the courses thus established should not lead to the same degree as those for which the normal standard is upheld. In any event the student who does unsatisfactory work should at least be studied before he is eliminated. The problem of just what to do with the potential failure is far from being settled, although some institutions have made better and more fundamental adjustments than others. In the course of time it seems probable that teachers and administrators will find some solution that is humane without being sentimental and appropriate without being detrimental to college standards.

CHAPTER XVIII

THE SUPERIOR STUDENT

Any college teacher is interested in brilliant students. They are the people for whom a college education was originally intended, and they are the ones who can profit most from it. In former years the bright youngster was not hard to find, because classes were small and teachers knew their students. By the end of the first year most outstanding freshmen were already known to the entire faculty. Those who complain about the lack of brilliant students today do not realize that there are, in actual numbers, more of them in the colleges now than there ever have been. They do not attract the attention that they once did because their proportional number is smaller and the classes are too large. Indeed, too often they are completely unnoticed during their entire college career.

In studying the problems presented by the upper range of ability there are three main questions that require answers: (1) What are the traits shown by brilliant students? (2) How can they be located in the shortest time? (3) What treatment should they receive? These three questions will be considered in order.

I. CHARACTERISTICS OF BRILLIANT STUDENTS

Perhaps the first thing should be a definition of what is meant by "brilliancy." It is sometimes used as a synonym for "brightness" and sometimes in place of the phrase "mental maturity," even though these two concepts are by no means identical. Throughout the public school years a differentiation is made between a bright and a mature pupil. The former is merely a child who learns faster than most but shows no other sign of unusual development. The latter is a child who seems in size, judgment, poise, social ability, and adjustment to the world—as well as learning capacity—to be older than he is. This difference between a quick memory and real maturity continues into the college years, although many of the merely bright pupils from the grades become only average as freshmen. A common complaint from freshmen is: "In high school everyone thought I was bright, but here I'm just like the others." This feeling that one's superiority is slipping away is frequent among the merely bright. Every college teacher knows some students with alert minds to which facts stick like flies on fly paper—and with about as much system. These youngsters can and should take a heavier schedule than the average, but they do not belong to the most superior group of students.

TABLE 23
Traits of the Intellectually Mature Person

Trait	Number of Times Mentioned
1. Forms rational judgments uncolored by emotional tones	32
2. Can perceive relationships and correlate materials	19
3. Has a critical, evaluating attitude toward problems	19
4. Is independent	16
5. Has a wide background of information	15
6. Shows intellectual initiative	12
7. Is able to apply knowledge	11
8. Keeps an open mind	10
9. Assimilates new facts with the old	9
10. Has a good sense of values	7
11. Can separate the important from the unimportant	7
12. Shows tolerance toward those who differ in their opinions	6

The intellectually mature person has a number of characteristic traits. The particular list shown in Table 23 was compiled by a comparison of students picked out as being mature with those selected as merely bright.[1] The figures refer to the num-

[1] R. E. Eckert, "Intellectual Maturity," *Journal of Higher Education,* 5: 478–84, 1934. Used by permission of the *Journal of Higher Education.*

ber of times each trait was mentioned by the fifty-six teachers who gave their judgments as to the difference between the two groups of students. It should be noted that the speed with which a person learns is not included in Table 23—presumably because it has nothing much to do with maturity. Some mature students are "quick studies"—as the theater jargon describes an actor who memorizes his part rapidly—but some of them are not.

This list indicates four outstanding differences between the mature and the bright student. The former thinks with his mind instead of his emotions, he is nobody's disciple, he sees through facts to their implications, and he uses his mind continually. It is this type of student about whom this chapter is written.

There have been a few studies that measured more or less adequately the personal and nonintellectual differences between brilliant and average students. The basis of selection for the highest group was sometimes an intelligence test score, sometimes the academic record, and sometimes both. The results are similar from one investigation to another. The traits to be listed are those found by the study—with various tests, by interviews, and through personnel records—of approximately 1,250 outstandingly capable students, who comprised about the highest 5 per cent of their respective college groups.[2] The differences found are shown in Table 24.

One gets a clear picture from this list of traits. The brilliant student is an efficient person about his work, he comes from a superior home, and he finds his classmates a little too adolescent for his taste. He is willing to participate in anything that gives him a chance to use his mind, and he is not antisocial by any

[2] M. E. Herriot, "Honor Engineering Students: Their Characteristics and Reasons for Success," *Society for the Promotion of Engineering Education Journal*, 19:871–83, 1929; R. E. Eckert, "Who Is the Superior Student?" *Studies in Articulation of High School and College*, Vol. 9, Series 1, University of Buffalo, 1934, pp. 11–51; M. O. Neel and C. O. Matthews, "Needs of Superior Students," *Journal of Higher Education*, 6: 29–34, 1935; M. Newcomer, "The Phi Beta Kappa Student," *School and Society*, 25: 24, 1927; H. H. Remmers, "Distinguished Students—What They Are and Why," *Purdue University Studies in Higher Education*, XV, Vol. 31, No. 2, 1930, 36 pp.; C. G. Wrenn, "Aiding the Fit," *Journal of Higher Education*, 6: 357–64, 1935.

TABLE 24

Characteristic Differences between Superior and Average Students

I. Differences in academic achievement
   A. Study habits
      1. They make a rapid survey before reading a chapter
      2. They notice the headings in the textbooks
      3. They recite to themselves
      4. They associate what they learn in one course with work in another
      5. They clear up any point they do not understand before going on to another
      6. They spend a little more time than the average in study
      7. They study alone
   B. They take a slightly lighter schedule
   C. They are happy in college
   D. They usually have the abilities necessary for success in their chosen profession

II. Differences in nonacademic activities
    A. They tend to be nonsocial
    B. They are more introverted
    C. They are more self-conscious
    D. They are relatively indifferent to the opposite sex
    E. They are persistent
    F. They are less assertive but more independent
    G. They participate in more extracurricular activities, but mostly in clubs in which the interest is intellectual rather than social

III. Home background
     A. They come from small families
     B. They come, three times as often as the ordinary student, from families in which the father is a professional man
     C. They are younger than most students

means; he is merely so mature that he gets bored with adolescent chatter, puppy love, and social functions. An illustration of the usual situation appears below:

Frank entered college at the age of sixteen. He was as big as the average boy of eighteen but did not have as good muscular co-ordination. In the gymnasium classes and intramural games he was always the boy who dropped the ball at critical moments or fell over his own feet. As soon as his required athletic participation was completed, he took no further part, although he would have liked to do so. By the time he had reached a normal muscular development he had lost contact with others who were interested in the athletic activities he liked. In his classes he was an outstanding scholar from the start. Ideas fascinated him. He exercised his mind in the same way that an athlete exercises his muscles. Frank went to summer school each year, took a heavy schedule at all times, and graduated before he was nineteen. At once he entered the graduate school, where he majored in Egyptian archaeology. He had already—to the mystification of his acquaintances—studied Latin and Greek. When he began Hebrew and Egyptian, he became simply incomprehensible to others of his age. He is now in his second year of graduate work and will presumably get his Ph.D. before his twenty-second birthday. He is a fine scholar, with a burning enthusiasm for his subject, and a thoroughly charming boy. He finds himself, however, greatly isolated. His age-mates are all so immature that their conversation bores him. Their thinking is not nearly as clear and concise as his own, and their efforts at discussion strike him as puerile. Many of his former friends he likes as personalities, but he wishes they would stop talking. Their interest in girls, social events, and "bull sessions" merely irritate him. The people with whom he can most easily and naturally make friends are all about forty years old. They are as much too mature for him socially as he is for his classmates intellectually. His professors are almost the only people to whom he can really talk with any satisfaction. For the next few years life will be relatively hard for this boy. He has the mental and scholarly development of a man and the social skills of a college sophomore. There is nothing abnormal about his personality, and he will probably settle down comfortably to academic life just as soon as he has had time to grow up socially. Because he is at present something of a misfit he seems seclusive and self-conscious, although he is not actually either.

One reason that the brilliant student tends to become a nuisance to his teachers is merely that they are the only people he knows who talk about ideas. When he lingers after class and pesters the instructor he is getting a glimpse into what constitutes for him an intellectual paradise. For a few minutes he can escape from the mental immaturity of his friends and have a bit of adult conversation. It is his misfortune that he is too old for his classmates and too young for his teachers. It is not surprising that many superior students become a little odd; they are cut off from everyone for one reason or another. Many who have been through the experience give eloquent testimony of how a mature mind that is forced to associate for the most part with juvenile intellects longs for an exchange of ideas with another mind of equal or greater maturity.

The practice of encouraging brilliant children to make rapid progress through school precipitates some of the problems faced by the superior student. No one doubts that a clever child should have enough work to keep him as busy as other children are kept by ordinary assignments. Some people believe in accelerating such children until they are in a group with whom they belong intellectually, while others favor keeping them in the group to which they belong socially. In the one case they study only the usual academic offerings, completing the work in less time than most children require, while in the other they study enough additional material to keep them thoroughly occupied but progress through the grades no more rapidly than any one else. As long as one is dealing with the merely bright child, the second treatment is probably satisfactory. Such a pupil has the capacity to learn quickly and he is better off if he uses it, but he is not in most respects any more mature than his age-mates. He has the same interests and enthusiasms. For the really mature child, however, the solution is not so easy. If the curriculum is enriched he will certainly profit by it in his mental growth, but he will not be any less bored by his companions. One of the tasks of a brilliant mind is to learn somehow to get along in a world that is full of mediocrity.[3] Holding a child back in school will not necessarily help him to make a better social adjustment. The problem of what to do with the adolescent boy or girl with a mature mind has not yet been solved. There is no question that young students can do just as good college work as students of average age at entrance. In fact the youngest freshmen are usually superior academically.[4] What is not clear is the effect of early entrance upon the development of personality.

[3] See E. D. Bond, "To a Graduating Class of Geniuses," *Mental Hygiene,* 13: 520–28, 1929.
[4] See, for instance, M. W. Moore, "A Study of Young High School Graduates," *Teachers College Contributions to Education,* No. 583, 1933, 78 pp.; C. W. Odell, "The Effect of Early Entrance upon College Success," *Journal of Educational Research,* 26: 510–12, 1933; M. E. Sarbaugh, "The Young College Student," *School and Society,* 40: 823–24, 1934.

II. THE DISCOVERY OF THE BRILLIANT STUDENT

As colleges are usually organized, the discovery of out-standing ability is left mainly to the teaching staff. Naturally, faculty members are the right people for the job, but they often do not have the right opportunities to make their discoveries early enough. During a student's first year he often comes in contact only with assistants and young instructors— most of whom are too busy keeping ahead of the class to have much time for anything else. Because the first year is often a repetition of what a brilliant student already knows, he does not always make as good an impression as he could because he is bored to death, and what new tasks he is given are much too easy to bring out his superiority. Many such students are not discovered through the ordinary processes of classwork until their junior or senior year. Then there is not enough time left to give them the training they need, and they have in the meantime developed the habit of working far below their capacity. This arrangement is undesirable. The sooner a brilliant student can be located and stimulated the better.

In the chapter on prediction of college work it was pointed out that one main purpose in giving tests of scholastic aptitude should be to locate as many of the superior students as possible at their entrance to college. Such a program could, without much extra work, become a valuable method of guidance. One essential thing is often not done, but could be. Those who give the tests could make sure (1) that every promising freshman is put into classes with experienced teachers, (2) that these teachers are informed of the situation, and (3) that these students do not repeat work they have already mastered. In large courses it is worth while to form a section of the most brilliant freshmen. In smaller classes special attention from the instructor should be adequate. In any case, the mere recognition of excellent promise is not enough. It is only a first though necessary step.[5] College teachers should all be vitally interested

[5] See, for instance, C. E. Seashore, "The Placement Test as a Means for the Early Discrimination and Motivation of the Future Scholar," *Journal of the Proceedings and Addresses of the Twenty-Seventh Annual*

in such a program as that outlined above because it would help them to get in touch with the best prepared and most intelligent students at the earliest possible moment—before these brilliant minds have had any period of monotony and boredom to dull the enthusiasm which most of them originally bring to college work.

III. TREATMENT OF BRILLIANT STUDENTS

From a number of sources comes evidence that college work is not at present very well adapted to the needs of the brilliant mind. Four studies are worth quoting on this point.

The first[6] reports an investigation of the extent to which superior students live up to their promise. It is not necessary to go in detail into the statistical treatment of the data. The 118 students in the study varied between surpassing their expectations by an index of +21 to falling below them with an index of —70. The median was —7. In other words, these students on the average fell below what could reasonably be expected of them—some of them far below.

Another investigator[7] tried giving the final examination on the first day of his course. Out of the 185 students, 8 stood higher than the average student after taking the course and two scored above the eighty-fifth percentile for the end of the semester. All of them had high ratings in intelligence. From some source these students had already learned the main facts and principles, with which they were obviously bored during the subsequent semester, because some of them made either the same or lower scores some months later. This study indicates one reason why the superior student does not always make high marks.

The third investigation[8] compared the progress of freshmen with an A rating in scholastic preparation—about the highest 7 per cent—and those with a B rating—about the next 15 per cent.

Conference of the Association of American Universities, University of Chicago Press, 1925, pp. 50–56.

[6] M. O. Neel and C. O. Matthews, "Needs of Superior Students," *Journal of Higher Education,* 6: 29–34, 1935.

[7] D. A. Worcester, "Twice-told Tales," in *Research Adventures in University Teaching,* Public School Publishing Company, 1927, pp. 45–54.

[8] F. C. Touton and B. T. Berry, "Superior Scholastic Aptitude and Success in College," *Education,* 53: 387–92, 1933.

There were 49 in the first group. Of this number 63 per cent made first-semester records of C or better; of the 41 who returned for the second semester, 61 per cent made similar records. Of the 161 freshmen with the B rating, however, 82 per cent made a C average or better; 141 of them continued into the second semester, and 81 per cent had the same standing. The B students not only surpassed those who knew more at entrance but more of them continued in college. During the same year 21 freshmen were admitted by special permission; among them were 5 A and 16 B aptitude ratings. Only one of the first group made a good enough record to remain in college while 13 of the second group succeeded. The same investigator studied the ratings of those who were elected to honor societies or received honors at graduation. Out of 183 such students 73 per cent had had B aptitude ratings and 4 per cent C ratings; only 23 per cent of them had entered with an A standing in scholarship. Even though the particular tests used were not perfect, they gave some measure of previous preparation. To make a high score on such a test a freshman had to be well prepared for college work. Yet from every point of view those with the best start were inferior to their classmates with somewhat less knowledge at entrance.

The fourth report bears out the implications of the other three.[9] Those students with the highest scores in both intelligence and scholastic aptitude worked far below their capacity and accomplished less in proportion to their ability than inferior students. Indeed, the accomplishment ratio—between ability and work—decreased steadily as the aptitude increased. The more promise a student showed at entrance, the less, in proportion to his ability, he accomplished.

Other writers report such facts as the following.[10] Out of 502 freshmen with abilities above the median, 100 made an average of less than C in their work. On the New York Regents' Examination, 195 out of 750 freshmen showed a negative deviation of one probable error in their subsequent college work and 99 showed a negative deviation of two or more probable errors.[10] Taken out of statistical language this statement means that 39 per cent of

[9] P. H. DuBois, "Achievement Ratios of College Students," *Journal of Educational Psychology*, 30:699–702, 1939.

[10] J. G. Darley, "Report on the Study of 502 Freshmen Entering in the Fall Quarter of 1937," Unpublished Report, 1938; and M. E. Wagner, "Studies in Academic Motivation," *University of Buffalo Studies*, Vol. 13, Series 2, No. 5, 1936, 188 pp.

these freshmen did poorer work in college than could reasonably be expected from their high standing on the examinations and that 13 per cent did much poorer work. In neither of these cases did the superior student live up to his promise.

From these and similar studies one can only infer that ordinary college work is not appropriate for the stimulation of the superior student. This situation represents a great loss in educational values and a loss to the next generation of scholars. If these results are typical—and they seem to be—it is time that colleges developed some special technique for harnessing the abilities of its best material to the task of getting an adequate education. The remaining parts of this chapter will deal with methods that have already been tried and with various suggestions for dealing with the total situation.

The brilliant student needs in general two things.[11] He requires comradeship with mature minds, and he needs enough to think about. The amount and type of work that is appropriate for others leave him in the ranks of the mentally unemployed.[12] Since a brilliant mind requires something to chew on, it will find stimulation outside the classroom if it does not find enough inside. The essential task in educating an intellectual leader is to attach his brilliancy to something that is worth his and society's while. From that point on, the alert mentality may need guidance, but it will for the most part run itself.

Many teachers have no clear idea how quickly and thoroughly a superior student can learn. A few examples may illustrate this point. I have selected these from my own friends because I can vouch for their accuracy. One of my friends arrived at college five days before classes began. Not wanting to waste her time she looked up her teachers to see if there were not some subject on which she could start work. The one professor she found in residence loaned her a copy of an Old English grammar and reader. The girl memorized the various word forms and read the stories in the back of the book in exactly five days, returned the book at

---

[11] See also E. S. Jones, "A Charter for the Superior Student," *University of Buffalo Studies,* 10: 51–87, 1936.

[12] For a good discussion of the problems and results of inadequate scholastic motivation see E. G. Williamson, *How to Counsel Students.* McGraw-Hill Book Company, 1939, 562 pp. (Chaps. 16, 18, 19).

the first class meeting, and made no preparation whatever during the following semester. In fact, she did not even buy a book—but she got an A. Another friend remained at college over the Thanksgiving holidays. Between Wednesday noon and the next Sunday night she did the necessary reading, planning, and writing for term papers in two courses. Each occupied about twenty typewritten pages, and both were retained by the professors as excellent examples to show subsequent classes. Another friend loafed along through the semester, doing practically no work and living on her wits. About two weeks before the end of the year she decided to review her courses; she read every assignment, actually absorbed as much as most students who had studied regularly, got excellent grades on examinations that required judgment and organization—and enjoyed the two weeks' review plus the examination period enormously because she had enough to think about to keep herself from complete boredom. Another friend who was a brilliant freshman in chemistry—and has since become an outstanding research chemist—left twenty "unknowns" that she was supposed to solve one at a time during a whole semester until one spring afternoon, when she ran the entire lot through the analysis at once. The work took her about seven hours—and she was the only student in the class who found every element in every unknown. Another friend was given two weeks in which to look up such materials as she needed to write a one-act play based upon some dramatic incident during a given period in history. She went home from class about three o'clock in the afternoon, wrote the play at once, typed it before dinner, put it away in her desk for two weeks, and did no work on the course during that time. Still another friend returned to boarding school after the Christmas holidays after having been absent until that time. She was registered for five courses. Between the first and last week in January she made up all her work, took her semester examinations with her classmates, and stood at the top of the honor roll with an average of 98 per cent.

Brilliant minds such as have just been described are simply wasting their time in the ordinary college class. What they need is something to think about. Unfortunately, they do not often get it before their last year, and by then many of them have learned to loaf or have become so involved in extracurricular activities that their interest in scholarly pursuits has evaporated.

The second thing a superior student needs is comradeship [13] with mature minds. This requirement can be met to some extent if brilliant freshmen have some way of getting acquainted with each other, but the best help can come only from the faculty. It is especially important that the contact between an experienced teacher and a brilliant student should be made at the earliest possible date. The more or less prevalent system of letting the least mature members of the faculty teach the freshmen is positively vicious as far as the best human material is concerned.[14] These students ought to be stimulated by the best minds there are. Because of the almost inevitable isolation that appears before college days are over—even if it is not in evidence during the first year or two—the typical superior student has no one to whom he can really talk. His mentality annoys his age-mates, and his youth annoys his teachers. It is not necessary for a teacher to make bosom friends out of his brilliant students, but an investment of time spent in threshing out ideas pays excellent dividends in growth. Incidentally many such students outgrow the irritating traits of youth in a short time if they are treated as adults.

Various practical plans have been worked out for meeting the needs of the superior student. Perhaps the logical starting point in treatment is to determine where each student should begin his college work. Such an arrangement is already in practice at Columbia.[15] There the students are allowed to get credit for courses by examination and to enter a department at whatever level they are best fitted for. The need for this practice is shown by the fact that 48.6 per cent of the freshmen in the first year of its use entered higher classes than they would have done had they been assigned on the basis of high

[13] For a good discussion of this point see B. D. Wood, "The Sifting Out of the Exceptional Student and His Relationship to the University Curriculum," *Journal of the Proceedings and Addresses of the Twenty-fourth Annual Conference of American Universities,* University of Chicago Press, 1922, pp. 32–39.

[14] See F. S. Breed, "A Guide for College Teaching," *School and Society,* 24: 82–87, 1926. In this instance, 70 per cent of the beginning courses were given by teachers on one-year appointments, of whom nearly a half changed from year to year.

[15] H. E. Hawkes, "Report of the Dean of Columbia," *Columbia University, Bulletin of Information Series* 30, No. 2, 1929.

school credits. In one year, a total of 1,115 semester hours of work was anticipated in this way—or 37 student years. Of all those who took advanced work as a result of this procedure only one student failed and only one other received a D in any course.

In another case [16] 466 superior high school seniors passed 60 per cent of a series of college examinations. Some students passed as many as 9 hours of college work in this way. At Princeton it has been found possible to place over 50 entering freshmen cach year in sophomore English classes.[17] When so much work is anticipated by the brighter students in high school it is no wonder that college classes are not sufficiently stimulating to call forth their best efforts. If capable freshmen can start their work where it is sufficiently hard to be interesting and if they can avoid the fatal repetition that so often falls to their lot during the first year in college, they should make better progress than is now the case.

In other places brilliant students get credit by examination for as much elementary work as possible and are then allowed to take a heavy schedule, so that they can graduate in three years. Students at the University of Buffalo who have received this treatment are in favor of it.[18]

In some colleges there is a personnel officer or member of the faculty who is supposed to interview all promising freshmen soon after entrance. This arrangement is merely a modification of the "faculty advisor" system that was in vogue for many years in many colleges. The objections to this system as originally conceived were three. The student did not always like the particular instructor to whom he was assigned; some members of the faculty were not equipped by either temperament or training to do work of this kind well; and usually there was no reduction of instructional duties to make adequate time in the teacher's day for this increased load. As a result of these factors

[16] H. C. Mills, "Anticipating College Work," *University of Buffalo Bulletin,* 9: 291–97, 1934.
[17] C. C. Brigham, "Admission Units and Freshmen Placement," *Educational Record,* 15: 56–67, 1934.
[18] H. C. Mills, "Evaluation of the Three-Year Program Leading to the Baccalaureate Degree," *University of Buffalo Studies,* 9: 75–86, 1934; *ibid.,* "Plan for Articulation with Reference to the Superior Student," *English Journal* (College Edition), 25: 557–61, 1936.

the guidance was often given in a perfunctory way or not at all. There is an obvious advantage in having one or two persons who are supposed to devote a considerable portion of their time to this work. No one unfitted for the work is likely to hold such a job for long, and the person who does keep it has time enough to do it well.[19] Usually the advisor helps materially in making contact between promising freshmen and those members of the teaching staff from whom the students can get the greatest assistance and to whom they would be of the greatest interest.

An obvious and relatively old method of treatment is the establishment of special classes or sections for the best students in a department, especially in the elementary courses. Typical reports of the progress of students thus selected have appeared.[20] In the elementary German course no student in the special section failed, and after the first quarter none received a grade lower than a C. At the end of the second quarter the amount of reading done was equal to that usually finished in three quarters; by the end of the year the group had read enough to get credit for five quarters' work. In zoology and French all the selected students scored above the middle of the distribution for the entire class. In European history twenty-five of the thirty-seven best-prepared students received either A or B in their work. These results are to be expected. There is nothing new about such sections; there should merely be more of them.

One variation upon the general theme of the special section is worth noting. In some cases [21] the amount of time devoted to a course is reduced. In this way the students can get one more course

[19] For a good account of such an arrangement see H. Dupré, "Encouraging the Superior Freshman Student in the College of Arts and Sciences," in R. Tyler, *Service Studies in Higher Education,* No. 15, Ohio State University, 1932, pp. 221–30.
[20] D. F. Miller, "A Special Treatment for Superior Students in General Zoology," pp. 72–78; W. S. Monroe, "Adapting Instruction to the Abilities of the Student in the Modern Languages," pp. 123–34; A. H. Noyes, "Some Recent Developments in History Instruction," pp. 151–56; W. Gausewitz, "German for the Gifted Student," pp. 135–40. All these articles appear in Tyler, *op. cit.*
[21] See, for instance, C. M. Brown, "An Experiment in Sectioning," *Journal of Higher Education,* 1 : 269–73, 1930.

on their schedules, and can thus progress into upper division classes more quickly. In one basic course in home economics the section of brilliant students met only three times a week instead of five. In spite of the reduced instruction no student in it received less than a C, and 69 per cent of them had either A or B. The marks were determined on the basis of a common examination for all sections.

From some points of view the best answer to the problem of instruction for these students is a partial individualization of work from the beginning. This plan is relatively easy to administer because there are not many brilliant minds and those that exist have enough independence to work alone. Some classwork is at first desirable, in order that the freshmen should not become too isolated, but part of their work can be individualized at once. If each member of the faculty were willing to be the guide, philosopher, and friend of one brilliant student a proper amount of individualization could be brought about. This method is expensive, but for the highest 3 per cent of the student body it is worth the money. No other students repay a teacher so well for his efforts.[22]

A few colleges have instituted a whole special course of work for their best students, sometimes from the beginning of their college careers. These independent study plans [23] have not yet been in operation long enough for a thorough evaluation of their merits, but the testimony to date seems in their

[22] For further discussion see R. H. Frazier, "An Experiment in the Honors Treatment of Students in Electrical Engineering," *School and Society*, 39: 271–72, 1934; J. R. Gerberich and W. M. Roberds, "Individualized Instruction for Superior Students in Introductory College Physics," *Scientific Education*, 18: 28–33, 1934; E. Hassold, "The Honor Seminar in Louisville," *Journal of Higher Education*, 7: 137–40, 1936; G. W. Stewart, "A Problem in the Education of College Students of Superior Ability," *School and Society*, 14: 439–47, 1921; S. L. Pressey, "A New Program for the Degree with Distinction in Education at the Ohio State University," *School and Society*, 36: 280–82, 1932; L. M. Terman, "The Gifted Student and His Academic Environment," *Journal of the Proceedings and Addresses of the Fortieth Annual Conference of the Association of American Universities*, University of Chicago Press, 1938, pp. 67–76. (Also in *School and Society*, 49: 65–73, 1939.)

[23] See, for instance, E. G. Robinson, "The Independent Study Plan at Stanford University," *Association of American Colleges Bulletin*, 14: 431–36, 1938, and J. G. Umstattd, "An Independent Study Plan," *Journal of Higher Education*, 6: 143–48, 1935.

favor. In their essence these plans consist of releasing a student from class attendance except on his own volition, of letting him work by himself under fairly close guidance of an interesting professor, of organizing his procedures on an adult level, and making him responsible for his own educational fate. The teaching is sometimes carried on wholly by individual interviews and sometimes by discussion of problems with a small group of these special students. In short, the plans are intended to train the brilliant student in becoming a well-adjusted adult who has a good mastery of the tools of learning, a good sense of problems, and a good foundation in scholarship.

Probably the most widespread type of adjustment in the two last years of college is the "reading for honors" system. The main idea of this plan is that superior upperclassmen should spend a large part of their time in supervised reading that covers a whole field and includes material they would ordinarily read only if they took a large number of courses. It is also the intention of its founders that this reading should co-ordinate ideas in several fields and should break down any barriers that may exist between departments. The work is wholly individual. The student's progress is usually measured by a comprehensive examination, either written or oral, or both. In some colleges the honors work is done in addition to the regular courses; in others it is substituted for part or almost all the classwork a student would otherwise take. Almost everywhere an honor's candidate writes a paper on some more or less original topic.[24] For the upper years of

[24] For discussions of the history and methods of the honors plan see F. Aydelotte, "Honors Courses in American Universities and Colleges," *Bulletin of the National Research Council,* Vol. 10, No. 52, 1925, 80 pp.; A. L. Barrows, "Studying for Honors in American Colleges and Universities," *School and Society,* 13: 432–34, 1921; R. C. Brooks, *Reading for Honors at Swarthmore,* Oxford University Press, New York, 1927, 196 pp.; E. S. Jones, *The Comprehensive Examination in American Colleges,* The Macmillan Company, 1933, 436 pp.; J. Park, "Tutorial Instruction at the University of Buffalo," *Bulletin of the Association of American Colleges,* 22: 624–26, 1936; J. H. McNeely, "Changes in Traditional Methods of Collegiate Instruction," *School and Society,* 41: 213–17, 1935; W. F. Sanders, "Honors Work in a Small Middle-Western College," *School and Society,* 28: 455–56, 1928; J. H. Sinclair and M. B. Taylor, "Honors Work in Institutions Accredited by the Association of American Universities," *School and Society,* 33: 247–50, 1931; R. Walters, *et al.,* "Honors Work, the Tutorial System, and General Examinations," *Thirty-first Yearbook of*

college these courses have been found quite satisfactory. Naturally they are better taught in some colleges than in others, but the defects—where they exist—seem to be in the handling of the work rather than in its conception. They provide exactly the flexibility in study, the independence for the student, and the personal contact with some faculty member that are so needed by superior students.

Although comprehensive examinations are now used in some colleges for all upperclassmen, in at least their major subject, the growth of this type of test gives some indication of the increasing interest in adapting work to the abilities of superior students. The following table shows the development of the comprehensive examination from 1900 until 1935. Of the total number of colleges reporting use of such a test, 71 use it exclusively for their honor students. The examinations, properly constructed,[25] give a student a chance to show what he can do in the way of independent thinking. They are therefore especially well adapted for giving the unusual mind a chance to demonstrate its superiority.

One further plan has been used for developing the interests of good students.[26] They can sometimes participate in the work or research being done by various members of the faculty. Of course students should not be exploited, as they occasionally are, but their work can often be integrated with research in such a way that they receive great stimulation from the arrangement. The thrill of doing "real" as compared to "practice" work is not to be underestimated. If the tasks are well arranged the participation of superior students is highly educational for them and brings them into close and spontaneously natural contact with the people they like best. The brilliant student ceases at once to be a pest and becomes an enthusiastic young colleague.

the *National Society for the Study of Education,* Part II, 1932, pp. 165–80; R. Walters, "Teaching Honor Students at Swarthmore," *Bulletin of the Association of American Colleges,* 14:419–24, 1928.

[25] For a collection of sample comprehensive examinations see P. O. Johnson, *Comprehensive Examinations in Biological Science,* 1935, 30 pp.; *in Economics,* 1935, 20 pp.; *in Physical Science,* 1935, 35 pp.; University of Minnesota Press.

[26] S. L. Pressey, "A University Activity Program," *Journal of Higher Education,* 8:211–14, 1937.

TABLE 25

Number of Colleges Reporting Use of Comprehensive
Examinations[2]

	For Honors Only	For Degrees in Two or More Departments	For Degrees in at Least One Department
1900	2	2	3
1905	2	2	3
1910	3	2	3
1911	3	3	3
1912	3	3	3
1913	3	4	4
1914	3	4	6
1915	3	6	7
1916	3	6	8
1917	3	7	9
1918	5	6	8
1919	8	6	8
1920	9	7	9
1921	10	9	12
1922	18	10	12
1923	22	10	15
1924	36	11	17
1925		12	24
1926	43	17	23
1927	51	18	25
1928	58	21	30
1929	64	27	36
1930	67	32	44
1931	72	42	55
1932	75	54	73
1933	74	66	85
1934	72	74	92
1935	71	77	94

By means of admission to advanced courses, by personal attention, by special sections, by individual instruction, by honors
courses, and by participation in the research of faculty members, colleges are attempting to meet the needs of their best and
most promising students. The basic idea is to catch such stu-

[27] From E. S. Jones, *Comprehensive Examinations in American Colleges,*
The Macmillan Company, 1935, 436 pp. Used by permission of The Macmillan Company.

dents at an early age, work them hard, and give them kindly sympathy. Any investigation of the progress made by a freshman class shows that the ordinary college loses from 10 to 25 per cent of its most capable freshmen during the first year. This loss to society is, in the aggregate, serious. There are not many superior minds in the world; educators cannot afford to waste any of them.

IV. SUMMARY

A brilliant mind enjoys thinking. In fact, it thinks all the time—if not about one thing then about another. The main problem in educating it is to give it something worthy of its superiority. It is senseless to let a student in the highest 1 per cent of his class expend the major part of his mental effort upon fraternity life, intramural handball, or dance committees. All these things are acceptable diversions, but they should not occupy the focus of attention. A superior mentality also needs contacts with mature minds against which it can strike sparks. College professors are the best-equipped people in the world to stimulate the brilliant student into doing the work for which he is by nature intended. It is through their influence on brilliant students that college teachers can be most useful to their colleges and to society.

CHAPTER XIX

EXAMINATIONS

―――――

Many teachers regard examinations as the bane of their lives. This attitude arises largely because they are concerned primarily with the police functions of an examination rather than with its educational values. Examinations can be interesting and profitable to students, but they are not likely to be if the teacher looks upon them with irritation, boredom, and a general feeling that "there's constabulary duty to be done." This attitude soon transfers itself to the students, and the educational values disappear. From time to time one reads an article that contains a vehement attack upon the use of any examinations whatever. Some writers object to the final examination on the ground that it is a totally unnecessary academic chore, that it encourages cheating, that it does not give a fair indication of a student's knowledge, and that it is generally an anachronism. The reasons given for these expressions vary—but I doubt that they are more than a rationalization of the basic boredom which soon arises if a teacher uses examinations merely for the assignment of grades. This attitude creates a sort of game between a teacher and his students in which the former propounds difficult questions and the latter bluffs the answers if he can. The whole business is just as uneducational as its critics feel it to be. The point is that an uneducational test is the teacher's own fault.[1] An examination is not futile unless some teacher has made it so.

――――――

[1] For a good discussion on the use of tests for guidance, see C. M. McConn, "Examinations Old and New: Their Uses and Abuses," *Educa-*

The value of a final examination at least can be and has been proved.[2] Thus one investigator who had equivalent classes excused one group from the final examination, but told the students to read over the work and remember the main facts for their own sake; he told the other group to remember the main points because they would be needed for the test. Actually he gave both groups the examination. Those who had read merely for their own development scored 17 per cent lower than those who had had a purpose in their review.

The students do not enjoy uneducational examinations any more than the teacher does. In fact, they would much rather get some benefit from their work. One investigator asked a number of students for suggestions about the improvement of teaching. The comment made most frequently[3] was that teachers should pass back examinations and discuss them with the class. Any instructor who does not give back papers or who returns them without comment is losing one of the chief values of examinations. Nor do students object to frequent tests. A total of 213 students were asked to state how often they preferred to have examinations. The replies are shown below:[4]

	Per Cent
One examination a semester	3.3
Two examinations a semester	20.7
One examination a month	23.0
Two examinations a month	25.8
One examination a week	22.5
An examination every day	4.7
	100.0

In this group at least there were more students who preferred one test a day than voted for one a semester.

One interesting study[5] shows clearly the value of discussing

tional Record, 16:375–411, 1935; P. O. Johnson, "The Differential Functions of Examinations," *Journal of Educational Research,* 30:93–103, 1936.

[2] T. H. Schutte, "Is There Value in the Final Examination?" *Journal of Educational Research,* 12:204–13, 1925.

[3] C. R. Wiseman, "Methods of College Teaching," *School and Society,* 28:433–34, 1928.

[4] J. R. Gerberich, "Attitudes of College Students toward the Use of Examinations for Determining Course Marks," *School and Society,* 44:284–88, 1936. Used by permission of *School and Society* and the author.

[5] R. E. Breeze, "Correcting Examination Papers," *School Review,* 33:57–61, 1925.

papers after they are handed back. On the first examination the
instructor returned the papers and discussed the errors; two weeks
later without warning he repeated the test. A second set of examination papers he returned at the end of a class period when
there was no time for discussion and did not subsequently mention the matter; again at the end of two weeks he repeated the test.
The results appear below:

TABLE 26
Results of Discussing Examination Papers[5]

	Total Number of Errors on Test, First Trial	Total Number on Test, Second Trial	Number of Errors Common to Both Trials	Number of Errors on First but Not on Second	New Errors on Second Trial	Per Cent of Errors Cor-rected
Examination that was discussed in class..	447	302	233	214	69	47.9
Examination that was not discussed in class.	409	432	290	119	142	29.1

In spite of the fact that the students may have suspected a repetition of the retesting technique and therefore may have done some
surreptitious reviewing, they corrected a far smaller number of
errors between tests when they had not had a chance to discuss
the matter in class. Although the second examination was slightly
easier, they added more new mistakes on the second trial than
they did after a class discussion. Similar results appeared in another study.[6] When the instructor handed back scored examination papers and discussed them, the students improved on subsequent tests a great deal more than did those to whom papers were
returned with the errors marked but without class discussion. It
appears, then, that students will derive educational value from examinations in proportion as they have opportunities for doing so.

At the present time four different types of examination are
in vogue: the essay, the partially objective, the objective, and

[5a] Breeze, *op. cit.* Used by permission of the *School Review.*
[6] H. Y. McCluskey, "An Experimental Comparison of Two Methods of
Correcting the Outcomes of Examinations," *School and Society,* 40: 566–
68, 1934.

the oral. Each has its values and its weaknesses. The first thing to know about any of them is when to use it, and the second thing is how to evaluate the results. Some people have found the essay examination too general and too inaccurate for their taste, while others have become equally disgusted with the frequent trivialities of the objective examination. The oral test is too time-consuming for wide use, but it has both its protagonists and its critics. The remaining sections of this chapter will be devoted to a discussion of the nature and values of these types of test.

I. THE ESSAY EXAMINATION

Teachers are familiar enough with the essay examination. To it belong all the questions that ask students to outline, describe, explain, discuss, evaluate, summarize, compare, or contrast. For purposes of showing the nature of good essay examinations I have included a number of samples. Most college teachers still use essay tests some of the time, and those in small colleges use them a great deal. If one prefers this type of test he should so formulate his questions as to bring out the values inherent in them. This precaution is not always taken, with the result that the questions asked are little if any different from those found on other kinds of tests. For instance, if a teacher has brought out in class three commercial uses of glycerin and then asks on a test, "How is glycerin used commercially?" the question looks like an essay question but calls for nothing but regurgitation of a student's notes. It should be noted in the sample examinations given below that the questions call for a selection of relevant materials from the sum total of ideas presented in the course and their independent organization into a coherent whole.[7]

No one can say that these examinations do not require concentrated thought and constructive planning. They may also measure abilities that should not enter into the measurement of the subject matter, but at least no student taking such a

[7] I am indebted to members of the Vassar College faculty for all but one of these specimens.

test is likely to find it dull. All of these tests demand thinking, organization, and personal reaction. They therefore stress exactly the values that are claimed for the essay test.

THE FRENCH REVOLUTION

How far do the following statements seem to you to be true? Give the facts on which you base your opinion:

I. The Revolution of Violence
1. "The Terror was the most important period of the Revolution."
2. "The Girondin party was the party of moderation."
II. The Reaction
1. "Personal rivalries took the place of ideas."
2. "Napoleon Bonaparte did not receive the chieftaincy of France at the age of thirty because of his proven capacities but because the nation had need of him."
III. The Napoleonic Era
1. "Bonaparte, who in his own words, was the son and testamentary executor of the Revolution, had received his bequest. How much of it he was to squander, how much he was to save, how much he was to add, the next fifteen years were to tell."
2. "Napoleon was never to be depended on for taste, truth, or charity."

PSYCHOLOGY

Professor A is an extreme behaviorist; Professor B is strongly in favor of Gestalt psychology; Professor C is an introspectionist. All three are submitting papers for a symposium on Human Learning. Select any one of these three points of view and write the professor's paper for him. Be sure (a) that you make clear what the fundamental concepts are, (b) that you defend yourself against possible objections from the other two points of view, and (c) that you base any theoretical discussion upon experimental evidence. (Remember the advice from Stevenson: To add irrelevant material is not to lengthen but to bury.)

RELIGION

1. Explain the Mass to a non-Catholic who knows nothing about it in such a way that he will be able to understand it and appreciate it.

2. In what ways are Christianity and Judaism alike and in what do they differ?

3. People often say that all the evils of our civilization would disappear if we would go back to the simple gospel of Jesus, follow his teachings, and pattern our lives after his. Is this possible? Why? What parts of the course can help you in answering this question?

N.B. You will be graded on your knowledge and your understanding—not on the number of words you write or on the careful way in which you reproduce your notes. Take time to think before you write, and think as you write.

PRINCIPLES OF EDUCATION

During the semester we have considered some general principles. Describe either the elementary or secondary school that you attended and show to what extent each of the important principles was followed in ordinary classroom procedures.

HISTORY[7a]

DIRECTIONS: *It is generally admitted that the study of history enables one to read more critically and with greater understanding. The little news-sheet inside the folder will help you to test the truth of this statement in an important field, the press. It is made up of excerpts from newspapers that are in campus houses and the college library daily throughout the year.*

I. *The excerpts are numbered. Identify or explain briefly as many as you can of the historical allusions in 12 and 14.*

II. *Show how your knowledge of its historical background enables you to understand better the chief thesis or point of view expressed in any one of each of the following groups. Use concrete evidence to show why you agree or disagree with the thesis set forth.*

    1. Item 2 or 6 or 8.
    2. Item 3 or 4 or 10 or 13.
    3. Item 1 or 5 or 7 or 9 or 11.

Do not read the entire paper through at first, but read carefully *all items in each group before answering the question pertaining to that group. Spend approximately one hour on I and two hours on II.*

[7a] Used by permission of the History Department of Vassar College. The cartoon is from *Le Rire*, Paris.

| Vol. I. No. 1 | HISTORY BEHIND THE HEADLINES | The Weather—
Fair if not cloudy |

MAY 31, 1939

REICH HAILS HITLER AS EMPIRE BUILDER

MINISTER OF EDUCATION SPEAKS TO YOUTH

(1)
Berlin, Mch. 19.—

The official German viewpoint on the incorporation of Czecho-Slovakia was expounded to-day by Bernhard Rust, minister of education, in a broadcast speech to the nation's youth. . . . Claiming that Prague was a product of old German culture, he said, "This Prague of a hundred spiries is sacred to us as an old German city, which in the great years of our history was the capitol of the Holy Roman Empire of German nationality. By taking Bohemia and Moravia under its care once more the Reich is reawakening forces that for many centuries enabled Czechs and Germans to live together and help one another. . . . We express our deepest thanks to the Fuehrer, who alone succeeded in building a bridge from the great German past to the present and beyond, that to the new German future."

EDITORIALS

NATIONAL ASSOCIATION OF MANUFACTURERS

(2)
Dec. 10.

The real issue today is not whether there is to be government interference and supervision, or whether labor is to have a larger share in shaping the conditions under which it works; it is rather the question of what form such interference and such influence are to take. Any uncompromising affirmation of past rights and privileges on the part of our industrial leadership could only furnish ammunition to those who like to assert that industry fails to adjust itself to the changing needs of changing times. . . . For this reason the willingness of the National Association of Manufacturers to abandon time-honored ground is a propitious sign.

THE GREAT CHARTER

(3)
April 28.

There are three outstanding documents in American history. The first two, the Declaration of Independence and the Constitution of the United States, were

A FRENCH IDEA OF THE FUEHRER'S DREAMS

Hitler "Who shall I be? Bismarck? A duffer? Charles the Fifth? Hand me over Spain? Le Rire, Paris
Otto the Great? Hand me over Italy? Charlemagne? Yes, Charlemagne, and hand me over France!"

drafted in the final quarter of the eighteenth century. The third was drawn up in what is now an English park long before there was any American history. It is, of course, the Magna Carta, which is the foundation of all our liberties.

Magna Carta was signed and sealed in 1215 by "John, by the grace of God, King of England, Lord of Ireland, Duke of Normandy and Aquitaine." The grim barons at Runnymede who waited for the royal signature with their hands grippings the pommels of their swords may, indeed, have accepted John as King by the grace of God. But they knew him for a double-dealing despot and were determined that he should rule only by the grace of the nation. The long list of royal rascalities they required him to renounce included this famous clause: "To no one will we sell, to no one will we refuse or delay right or justice." From that day the principle of equal rights and equal justice has inspired the Anglo-Saxon world wherever it extended on the earth. Again and again it was denied, but never for long, and when it was kings and governments fell. Charles I lost his head and George III his colonies because of Magna Carta.

This precious parchment, its monkish script the fairest of the four copies still extant, is now in New York City. It will be the central treasure of the British Pavilion at the World's Fair.

BISHOPS' COLLEGE MEETS AT FULDA

CONDEMNS NEW CREED OF HITLER

(4)
October 3.—

Assembled beside the tomb of St. Boni-

face, the German Catholic Bishops today addressed a joint pastoral letter to all people of the dioceses and archdioceses. . . . They ask whether it is not an irrefutable fact that Christianity and Germanism in spiritual union created the German culture of the Middle Ages. Whether it is not true that the present German culture springs from Christian as well as German racial roots.

NOBEL PRIZE WINNER ADDRESSES SCIENTISTS

(6)
March 15.—

The everchanging panorama of history shows man's technique advancing at an ever increasing rate. This was the theme of Dr. Arthur Compton's address this afternoon. "The growth of technology," said the Nobel Prize winner, "has changed our social life and customs, and has supplied the tools with which we can shape our world to our needs. . . . A century and a half ago one sees every member of the family hard at work, closely dependent upon nature, but largely independent of his neighbors. Today's family lives in relative comfort and leisure protected from the rigors of nature, but very dependent on organized society and the products of science. . . ."

PATRIOTISM SWINGS BACK TO PAGAN TRIBALISM

(7)
January 24.—

The age in which we live is an age of intense national patriotism. . . . This triumphant nationalism of our day is a novel union of two very old phenomena, the fact of nationality and the sentiment of patriotism. . . . We must remember that while nationality is a fact of long standing in the world, it has not always been a fact of prime importance . . . for centuries of recorded history men have been wont to attach as much or more significance to some other grouping of which they were members—a church, an empire, a town, a guild. . . .

Patriotism itself is a sentiment of ancient and ancient vigor . . . yet throughout past ages there has been no constant uniformity about the object of that impulse. . . . St. Paul displayed as much patriotic pride in the Roman Empire n the Jewish nationality, and a famous medieval hymn celebrated the empire of heaven as the "patria," the fatherland of good Christians. Marcus Aurelius was patriotic about the "world," and so too were the cosmopolitan rationalists of the 18th century. "The world is my country," said Thomas Paine, "Mankind are my brothers." . . . In the modern world, patriotism signifies only loyalty to the national state. In its methods it is reverting to a primitive pagan tribalism: to a supposedly blood relationship reviving the legendary pre-Christian demigods of virility and valor, nd professing a sublime faith in being the hosen people in a world of inferior people.

LETTER TO THE EDITOR—
)
ept. 25.—
". . . You see I've always believed that he way to succeed was to work hard. I m one of these dumb people that believe their government is on such a solid oundation that it can never be shaken r undermined. I like to feel that we not nly have an economic and social system that has brought us to our present reatness, but a system which will continue to enable every man with ambition nd industry to make a decent living for imself and his family, free from governmental interference. . . . As long as I ave good health and am able to work or my own living I want no help from he government or anybody else. . . . I ill cast my vote for any person or any arty I believe will not knuckle under to rganized groups. . . ."

RANCE TURNS
            TO HER EMPIRE
)
aris, October 29.—
Into his speech on Thursday, Premier douard Daladier suddenly thrust a significant reference to France's colonial empire. . . . That he should do so at this me is curiously in accord with tradition. or it has always been the habit of the rench to turn their attention to colonial evelopment when they have suffered ome reverses at home. The Bourbon kings d it in the sixteenth and seventeenth enturies. When France had been stripped f her overseas possessions at the end of e Napoleonic wars she turned to Africa recover both territory and prestige. lgiers was captured by Charles X and at conquest was extended by Louis hilippe.
As time went on Napoleon III for internal political reasons, continued this ork of colonial expansion. Later, within few years of the defeat of 1870, the Republic began to add Tunisia, the Algerian Sahara, Madagascar, the upper Congo nd much else in Africa with Tonkin and nnam in Asia. It has been said that hile the British always added to their verseas possessions so as to consolidate

their position after a victory, the French did so after defeat and revolution. . . .
In the French empire there is plenty of room for enterprise. . . . The colonies are France's best customers. They are also the best source of supply for many raw materials. Finally they provide a reservoir of men who are for the most part loyal to the Republic.

TOPICS OF THE TIMES
(10)
Sept. 20.—
British commitments and responsibilities in Czecho-Slovakia are now presumably an academic question. But if Henlein is right and the Czechs are a lot of Hussite-Bolshevik criminals, then it might be argued that England is morally involved in the conspiracy. For it is pretty generally acknowledged that John Huss's ideas were borrowed from the English reformer, John Wycliffe. It is not however a point to be pressed. By now it is commonplace that the most explicit treaty obligations and the strongest moral commitments fade with time and John Wycliffe has been dead more than five hundred and fifty years.

FOR THIS TOO WAS GERMAN
(11)
February 1.—
The union of the German states was part of the program of the eighteen-forties, a union which it seemed useless to expect from the selfish and jealous princes, and when the program failed many of its adherents thought of migration. Some did migrate, others remained in the fatherland. . . . When later Bismarck unified most of the German race a good many of these emigrants forgave him and the Hohenzollerns, even though the government they established was very far from what the exiles of Forty-eight would have wished. . . . Now these descendants of the democrats of Forty-eight claim that theirs too is a German tradition . . .; Roman writers, they point out, noted that liberty was an early German trait.

CONCLAVE TO BEGIN
            SESSION TODAY
(12)
Rome, March 1.—
The mass of the Holy Spirit in the Pauline Chapel this morning was a prelude to the conclave of the Cardinals who today began their session to elect a successor to Pope Pius XI. . . . All were in agreement that the new pope must carry out a policy based on the church's unchangeable principles in dealing with its chief problem—its struggle with state absolutism. . . . The fact that the conclave is occurring in Lent has given rise to comparisons by those versed in the church's mystical law as well as in its more objective history and organization. . . . One thinks that the conclave could

be linked up as to its hidden meaning with the first conclave to elect a pope ever held in the Vatican. This was in 1377, the year of the return of the pope from "exile in Babylon," in Avignon, France. "The church in those evil days," said the commentator, "had been the tool of the secular state of France. Saints like Catherine of Sienna, and poets like Dante, prayed and made propaganda against the state's tyranny over the church." . . . Is not the church today returning from the exile into which it was drawn by modern materialism . . . and are not there modern states whose rulers would emulate France's ancient monarchs and reduce the universal church to a national tool. . . . And so I pray may the present conclave give the world a pope as strong as Hildebrand, and as powerful as Leo XIII.

MEDIEVAL LORE EXTOLLED
(13)
June 2.—
In his address before the Institute of Post-Biblical Literature, Dr. Alexander Marx discussed the work of a famous Jewish physician, Jacob Ben Makir who lived in Montpelier, France, in the thirteenth century. His Almanach which was translated into Latin, was used by Dante in his Divine Comedy. . . . In enumerating the scientific contributions of medieval scholars in fields of medicine, astronomy, and mathematics, Dr. Marx pointed out that "the Jews have played an important part as mediators in the movement which brought Greek and Arabic learning into western civilization, and thus served as a connecting link between our modern culture and Greek culture."

BOOK REVIEW
Catherine D'Medici and the Lost
    Revolution by Ralph Roeder.
(14)
There are many reasons why Catherine de Medici is a fit subject for a biography. . . . She shared history with astounding events. . . . She was a toddling infant, and as such could not have been aware of it, when her future father-in-law surrendered Pavia. . . . She was eight, and in a way a minor victim of the catastrophic sack of Rome. . . . Lepanto took place in her lifetime and the loss of Calais "open my heart and you will see," and the destruction of the Armada; and so also did the judicial murder of her former daughter-in-law, Mary Queen of Scots, and the savageries of the Duke of Alba in the Low Countries, and the calculated holocaust of Saint Bartholomew which caused even Ivan the Terrible to protest in horror. She saw further the ending of the Renaissance which had been symbolized in France by the wholesale importation of Italian artists . . . and the beginning of the Reformation. She was a contemporary and closely shared the stage with John Calvin, Coligny, and Philip II.

The salient points to consider about any test are four in number. (1) How good is the selection of questions, and what per cent of the important ideas of the course is included? On this point the essay examination is relatively weak—although some teachers manage to make it include considerably more than others do. Unless one takes great care, there are likely to be large sections of the material that do not figure in the examination at all and that cannot be dragged in by even the most ingenious student.

(2) What does the student do when he takes the test? What mental operations are involved? It is on this point that the essay test is undoubtedly strongest. A student must first remember whatever relevant facts he can, must then organize his ideas, and must write out an answer that has sufficient clarity to convey to the teacher's mind the essential points he has to offer. This entire procedure takes real thinking. Unfortunately, the mental efforts are all mixed up with many other elements—chiefly skills in written English. However, there can hardly be any question that a really good essay examination calls for more constructive thinking and concentrated organizing on the student's part than any other type.

(3) How accurately can the examination be scored? And, incidentally, how much time must be used for the purpose?

Clearly an examination is not valuable if the same paper gets an A from Miss Jones and an E from Miss Smith, or if Miss Jones gives it an A on Monday and an E on Friday. In the first investigations of this matter the results were disheartening. Thus [8] 142 high school teachers varied in their scoring of an English examination from 50 to 98 per cent and 115 teachers gave scores from 28 to 88 per cent to the same paper in geometry. At intervals other people repeated this type of experiment with roughly similar results.[9] Gradually the conviction grew that the teacher could score essay examinations as accurately by dropping a batch of them down a stair well—giving grades in accordance with the number of flights each paper fell—as by any other technique, and inci-

[8] D. Starch and E. C. Elliott, "The Reliability of Grading High School Work in English," *School Review,* 20: 442–57, 1912, and "The Reliability of Grading High School Work in Mathematics," *School Review,* 21: 254–59, 1913, and "The Reliability of Grading High School Work in History," *School Review,* 21: 676–81, 1913.

[9] See, for instance, W. C. Eells, "Reliability of Repeated Grading of Essay Type Examinations," *Journal of Educational Psychology,* 21: 48–52, 1930, and C. L. Whitner, "Just How Much Do Teachers' Marks Vary?" *Education,* 52: 97–99, 1931.

dentally save a good deal of time and nerve strain. Once this conviction had gained general acceptance, there was a rush to objectify all examinations, regardless of the subject matter involved. For about a decade, in fact, a teacher was regarded as hopelessly old-fashioned if he did not use objective tests.

In the last few years further investigations have appeared. The development now seems to be in the direction of finding ways by which the scoring can be made more accurate. No one supposes that an essay test hastily or carelessly read will yield accurate results. It now appears that the grading can be made quite reliable if it is properly done. Coefficients of .85 to .95 have been reported between readings of the same tests by different people.[10] In one of the instances the improved reading resulted in an increase in reliability from .42 to .92. For the most part the methods used consist in having some kind of "key" on which the essential ideas are listed. With this objective aid the agreement between scores becomes much higher. It is therefore not necessary for an essay test to be utterly unreliable.

The influence of handwriting upon the mark assigned to a paper is quite definitely known. In the best study on this point [11] the investigator first selected four compositions that had already been rated by a large number of teachers; the average grade was thus already known. These four pieces of writing were rated twice, at intervals of about six months, by 43 teachers, on a scale from 0 to 100. One composition appeared both times in bad script, one both times in good script; the other two were written once well and once illegibly. The results appear in Table 27.

[10] A. C. Eurich, "Four Types of Examination Compared and Evaluated," *Journal of Educational Psychology,* 22: 268–78, 1931; F. P. Frutchey, "Close Agreement Found in Marking Essay Examinations," *Journal of Higher Education,* 4: 376, 1933; R. W. Leighton, "Improvement of the Essay-Type Examination," *Office of Education Bulletin,* No. 12, 1932; J. M. Stalnaker and R. C. Stalnaker, "Reliable Reading of Essay Tests," *School Review,* 42: 599–605, 1934; and J. M. Stalnaker, "Attempts to Measure the Ability to Write with Clarity and Accuracy," *School and Society,* 37: 69–72, 1933; and "Weighting Questions in the Essay-Type Examination," *Journal of Educational Psychology,* 29: 481–90, 1938; J. M. Stalnaker, "Essay Examinations Reliably Read," *School and Society,* 46: 671–72, 1937; V. M. Sims, "Reducing the Variability of Essay Examination Marks through Eliminating Variations in Standard of Grading," *Journal of Educational Research,* 26: 637–47, 1933, and "The Objectivity, Reliability, and Validity of an Essay Examination Graded by Rating," *Journal of Educational Research,* 24: 216–23, 1931.
[11] H. W. James, "The Effect of Handwriting upon Grading," *English Journal,* 16: 180–85, 1927.

TABLE 27
Effect of Handwriting upon Grading[11a]

	Composition A		Composition B		Composition C		Composition D	
Quality of handwriting.....	Good	Good	Good	Bad	Bad	Good	Bad	Bad
First rating...............	65		71		66		55	
Second rating.............		65		60		73		57
Difference between ratings..		0		−11		+ 7		+ 2

Since the successive ratings on Compositions A and D varied so little from each other it is evident that the ratings were carefully made. Good handwriting made an average difference of 8 points for Compositions B and C. This variation may not seem large, but it is significant when taken in relation to the normal marking system.

In many schools the passing marks (A, B, C, and D) represent the distance from 70 to 100 per cent; each mark is, then, the equivalent of 7.5 points. Good writing therefore raised these compositions an amount equal to one letter grade over the rating received when the script was poor. This effect is produced presumably because a teacher is too human not to be annoyed when he has to put forth extra energy in order to read a paper. If a teacher uses essay examinations, he should take two precautions that will minimize this particular error in grading. First, he should tell the students of the effect bad handwriting has; they can either type their papers or write them with care. Second, he can guard against his natural irritation and make every effort to dissociate the content of the paper from the accidental element of script.

The essay test is not necessarily impossible to grade with reasonable accuracy, but it is often poorly graded because teachers do not restrict their scoring to the ideas presented, but are distracted by a number of incidental and subjective elements. If these latter can be brought under better control, it would seem that this type of examination might yield about as accurate results as any other.

(4) What relation exists between the examination score and a

11a James, *op. cit.* Used by permission of the *English Journal.*

student's actual mastery of the subject matter? This question remains unanswered, although it is obviously the most basic of the lot, because the criterion of mastery is usually the grade assigned on a series of examinations. Actually almost nothing is known about the validity of any test. I shall, therefore, omit further discussion of this question when considering other types of test—not because it is not important but because I cannot answer it.

In general, then, one may say fairly that an essay examination has the virtue of making students select, organize, and present their ideas on the topics offered. Unless great care is taken in the formulation of the examination, the questions are likely to sample the subject matter in a hit-or-miss fashion. But it is in the scoring of an essay test that the real difficulty arises. Like any other complex phenomenon, it is hard to evaluate, and people differ in their judgments because they attach different degrees of importance to different elements. The same person differs somewhat from day to day, because first one feature and then another gets the focus of his attention. A teacher can correct an objective examination with only enough of his mind on what he is doing to count accurately, and he can go on correcting papers after he is bored; but he cannot score an essay examination with anything less than his full attention and concentration. An essay test properly constructed and properly graded gives a teacher information about a student that cannot be gained by any other type of test, but such an examination can easily be so poorly made and scored that it is not worth the time of either teacher or student.[12]

II. THE PARTIALLY OBJECTIVE EXAMINATION

This type of test, which includes the short-answer and completion forms, represents a sort of halfway station between the essay and the objective examination. It is not applicable to all types of material but it has its uses. It can be constructed

[12] For a fruitful suggestion about the construction and use of essay questions see H. Cason, "An Intelligent-Question Method of Teaching and Testing," *Pedagogical Seminary and Journal of Genetic Psychology,* 54: 359–90, 1939.

in such a way as to preserve some of the values of both test forms.

1. The short-answer test: The first example below demands for the most part facts or previously learned conclusions, and it does not specify the form of the answer. That is, as far as one can tell from the questions, a student may use a phrase, clause, or single word for his answer, if he wishes; in some items he is obviously not supposed to write more.

SAMPLE 1[13]

1. State three differences between Athenian and American democracy.

    1. ....

    2. ....

    3. ....

2. What are three basic ideas of mercantilism?

    1. ....

    2. ....

    3. ....

3. Name six new states formed in Europe during the 19th century as a result of nationalistic movements.

    1. .... 2. .... 3. ....

    4. .... 5. .... 6. ....

4. Give three instances in the history of Europe since 1648 in which the balance of power was threatened and state by whom.

    1. ....

    2. ....

    3. ....

5. What are two causes which may be assigned for the rise of the middle class during the later Middle Ages?

    1. ....

    2. ....

6. Give a specific instance in which the French Revolution tried to give effect to the principle of liberty, and one in which it tried to give effect to equality.

    1. ....

    2. ....

[13] M. W. Richardson, J. T. Russell, J. M. Stalnaker, and L. L. Thurstone, *Manual of Examination Methods,* University of Chicago Bookstore, 1933, 177 pp., p. 118. Copyrighted 1933 and 1937. Used by permission of the University of Chicago Bookstore. This permission covers all excerpts from this reference.

The second example requires somewhat greater powers of expression, because whole sentences are necessary. It also demands careful thinking and the condensation of one's thoughts into a small space. It is a little harder to score than the first sample, but it measures more.

SAMPLE 2

DIRECTIONS: Answer each question below in not more than three sentences. If you use more than three, the answers will be counted as wrong, regardless of their content.

1. What are the chief physical symptoms by which one can tell that a girl is approaching puberty?
2. What historical evidence is there that puberty has always been regarded as an important period of life?
3. When one speaks of secondary sexual characteristics what developments are meant?
4. What is the range of ages and average age of puberty for boys and girls?

The same questions that were asked about the essay examination need to be answered for this type also. The selection of questions for the short-answer test can be made to cover all the essential points of a course more easily than the essay test because there are more of them. There is, however, the danger that the questions will call only for minor details. The form lends itself to this fault, but a teacher can avoid the temptation—unless, of course, details are exactly what he wants to test at the moment.

What the student does is somewhat the same as for the essay type, but the processes of recall are simpler and the organization element is lacking. He must, however, condense.

The score is for the most part objective. Some questions can be scored as unquestionably right or wrong. The amount of disagreement among scorers on a single answer to a single question may be considerable, but when the scores for all the questions are totaled the sum is almost the same for different graders; the individual variations average themselves out in the total. The short-answer test is, then, fairly accurate and can be made more so by assigning values to the questions. Thus if a teacher counts each good answer as 3 points, each average answer as 2, each poor but possible answer as 1, and any unsatisfactory response as zero, he will get a more accurate score than if he depends entirely upon his general impressions.

2. The completion test: Examinations of this kind consist of items after the nature of those shown below:

1. Dogs are used by the .... for herding reindeer and by the .... for pulling sledges.
2. Some Tungus are not classed as pastoral but as .... because they ....
3. Incorporeal property includes our .... and primitive man's .... It refutes early communism because ....
4. Belief in the survival of the soul is not belief in immortality because the latter ...., the former .... For example, the Jagga believe ....
5. Because it is oral, primitive prose is characterized by .... and .... Prose tales are myths if they explain .... or treat of .... Two types of character found in many mythologies are the .... and the .... The Crow figure of .... combines both characteristics; this is possible because .... The Polynesian equivalent is called .... This character assumes a different personality in one island group because ....

The first item lacks only two words. Even though a student might not know these words, he would surely know that the names of two tribes were missing. He has the context and needs only details for the completion. The last item, however, needs so many additions that there is almost no context. While a student might guess the answer to the first, he can do nothing with the last unless he can supply a whole complex of ideas.

Like the short-answer test, the completion form occupies a place part way between the essay and objective tests, but it is somewhat nearer the latter. In making up items of this type a teacher usually writes out a series of sentences containing important facts or conclusions about a course. He then omits certain of the "key" words.

In a two-hour period a student can answer enough such questions to cover all the basic ideas of a semester's work and many of the details.

In taking the test, a student has to write in whatever is missing. For such an item as the last one shown above, he must have what used to be called an "apperceptive mass." To the ordinary person the question means nothing at all; if a student can fill in the space correctly he must know a good deal about the subject. The wording of an item may suggest what type of thing is missing, but the student must actually recall whatever he writes into any space; unlike most objective forms, he cannot merely recognize his answer.

The scoring presents some difficulties because it is not wholly objective. From time to time a student writes in an answer that is correct, although it is not the one which was expected; sometimes answers are partially right. Although one cannot score papers by mechanically counting up correct responses, there is no real difficulty in obtaining a reliable score.

If a teacher wishes to cover a number of facts and ideas in a short time this type of test is useful. It demands actual recall rather than recognition. It is relatively easy to grade. Although it does not call for any organizing, it is a satisfactory form from other points of view.

III. THE OBJECTIVE EXAMINATION

The objective test is a relatively new thing under the sun. It has revolutionized education, often in ways that are considered not too desirable. It has made possible new types of educational research. Like most innovations, it has aroused a good deal of emotional heat. There are those who regard objective tests as not only the last word in modernity but as a panacea for any and all educational ills. At the other end are those who think them mechanical and stupid. In fact, the objective test has been accused of squeezing the life and interest out of both teaching and learning and of reducing education to the addition of plus and minus signs by a forty-cent-an-hour clerk. Undoubtedly both extreme views are in error. The objective test is a useful instrument in some situations and of no value in others. It will do what it can do at all in a more efficient way than any other examination, but there are plenty of things it cannot do.

A college teacher needs to have a sound point of view about objective examinations because he is sure to find them in use by some of his colleagues wherever he goes, and he is almost certain to be asked for his opinion on the matter. In a recent survey of three hundred colleges [14] 85 per cent reported use of objective tests. In some cases the use was limited to standard measures of intelligence or scholastic aptitude, but in many other instances faculty members used them for diagnostic work and for classroom examinations. Since the time of this survey the use has increased rather than decreased. As long as colleges and universities are crowded with students, the ease with which an objective test can be scored will guarantee its appeal to the instructor who has so many students that he could not possibly grade well the essay examinations that would otherwise accumulate. When a teacher has four sections with about eighty students in each, the timesaving charm of the objective test is well-nigh irresistible—no matter what he may think of its other values.

Perhaps the first point to consider is the essential nature of an objective test. The fundamental thing about them is not their form; indeed, they may assume any of several forms. A test is objective if any number of people who score it always get the same answer. The characteristic forms have been devised merely to help produce this result. The objectivity of a test does not, in and of itself, make a test either valid or reliable; it merely insures the obtaining of the same score by any number of people who care to correct it.

A second point about objective examinations is their comprehensiveness. In the time needed to write the answers to five essay questions a student can mark a hundred objective ones. It is therefore possible for a teacher to cover all the basic ideas of a course in the usual period allowed for a final

[14] A. S. Raubenheimer and F. C. Touton, "Present Status of the Use of Objective Tests in Institutions of Higher Learning," *Eighteenth Yearbook of the National Society of College Teachers of Education,* University of Chicago Press, 1930, pp. 73–87.

examination. The test almost automatically becomes an instrument for diagnosis and remedial teaching because the mere marking of the wrong answers on a paper indicates which of the important ideas a given student has failed to understand. A well-made objective examination of 250 questions is far more reliable than an essay examination of any reasonable length can be, simply because it includes so much more.[15]

Several characteristic forms have been developed. Of these at least five types are well known and widely used. Even though a teacher does not want to use tests of this kind often, he would do well to become familiar with the various types because from time to time he may want to give an examination covering material that is much better tested objectively than in any other way.

1. Forms of objective tests: The first type is (1) the true-false examination. Most people who have done research in test construction have little use for this form,[16] but it is so widely used by teachers that I feel something should be said about it. The customary test of this type contains items such as the following:

DIRECTIONS: If you think a statement is true, mark it with a T; if you think it is false, mark it with an F.

1. The percentage of delinquency in Chicago is highest in the "Loop" district.
2. The juvenile delinquency rate in Chicago declined from 1920 to 1930.
3. Delinquency "runs in" families.

Unfortunately the true-false test has become more widely disseminated than any other form of objective examination, presumably because the items are so easy to construct. The results of these tests have not been altogether satisfactory to either the college teacher or the college student. Many people have become so much annoyed by the general futility of the true-false

[15] E. P. Wood, "Improving the Validity of College Achievement Tests," *Journal of Educational Psychology*, 18: 18–25, 1927.
[16] See, for instance, G. E. Buckingham and R. E. Lee, "A Technique for Testing Unified Concepts in Science," *Journal of Educational Research*, 30: 20–27, 1936.

examination that they have condemned all objective forms as mechanical, untrustworthy, and contrary to the whole spirit of higher education.

The most usual method of selecting items for a true-false test is perhaps the fundamental reason for its unsoundness. Unfortunately many of the statements are taken verbatim from the textbook; others come from the same source but have been changed from positive to negative, or vice versa. The items are numerous enough and often well enough selected to cover the essentials of a course, but they usually do not succeed in covering the main ideas because they are concerned with details. Perhaps they could be formulated so as to test comprehension of general principles, but they usually are not.

When students take such a test, they read, guess mark, hope, and pray for the best. The mental effort involved makes one slightly groggy because the series of items is such a hodgepodge, with no evident rhyme or reason. The test rests, of course, wholly upon recognition and affords no opportunity for initiative and very little for any kind of constructive thinking.

Provided a teacher can count, the scoring can hardly help being fairly easy and reliable. Most true-false tests are at least fifty items long, and many of them are nearer one hundred. Like all other objective measurement, the more there is of it the more reliable is each individual score—but I shall not attempt to explain why.

There are at least four objections to the true-false test. The first is that it almost inevitably measures knowledge of minutiae. An occasional expert can measure conclusions and opinions by it, but most people do not succeed in doing so. If one tries to introduce nuances, one usually produces items that are neither right nor wrong. A second objection is not so fundamental, but it is important because of its indirect results. Many teachers tend to take sentences from the textbook, sometimes using them as they stand and sometimes altering them slightly. The result of this method is to encourage students to memorize the text. In fact, the testimony of students on this point is clear.[17] If they know there is to be a true-false examination they prepare for it by learning minutiae and by scanning the wording of the book with great care so that they can recognize deviations. In the third place the test does not give a sufficiently wide variation in scores to be ade-

[17] This point will be discussed at greater length in a later section.

quate as a basis for marks. There are several different systems of scoring, but none gives more than a narrow range. Finally, it is extremely difficult to construct test items without producing some that are ambiguous, absurd, or impossible. Even experienced workers have these troubles, and the average teacher is practically certain to prepare quite an assortment of "boners." A few samples of items actually used appear below:

—One should never permit a child to conduct a losing battle every day.
—Feeble-mindedness is the sole cause of delinquency.
—The yolk of an egg is not nonliving matter.
—The flesh of only some of the known animals is probably unsuitable for food.
—As symbolism has been badly overworked, few writers now use it.
—The electroscope is a very delicate electrical instrument and measures current in amperes.
—Shakespeare thought of Othello as a Negro.
—Perfumed soaps help to make a girl attractive.
—Recognized independence for women will bring about mutual responsibility of man and wife in the home.
—Pauperism is a relative term but as generally employed it means that economic and social state in which persons have not sufficient income to maintain health and physical efficiency.
—The stimulus for smell is olfactory.[18]

Some of the items are partly right and partly wrong; some contain tricky double negatives; some refer to points that cannot possibly be proved one way or another; some are so involved that no simple positive or negative word answers them; and some are either ridiculous or inaccurate. Unless a teacher wishes to produce such items from time to time, he had better avoid the true-false form.[19]

The one advantage that unquestionably lies in this form is the speed with which students can answer a number of ques-

[18] Richardson, Russell, Stalnaker, and Thurstone, *op. cit.*, pp. 18–21.
[19] For further discussion see J. C. Chapman, "The Individual Injustice of Guessing on a True-False Examination," *Journal of Applied Psychology*, 6: 342–48, 1922; H. E. Jones, "A Comparison of Objective Examination Methods," *Educational Method*, 8: 273–76, 1929; N. Keys, "The Influence of True-False Items on Specific Learning," *Journal of Educational Psychology*, 25: 511–20, 1934.

tions. Thus a series of questions that required thirty-five minutes for writing out single-phrase responses could be answered in eighteen minutes when the series was presented in the form of true-false items.[20] It is also possible to use a modification of this form by asking not only for a response as to the correctness of each item but also for comments of various kinds. An example of this type appears below.[20a]

Read These Instructions Carefully before Beginning to Write

Consider carefully each of the following statements. If it is precise and accurate, enter its number and write the word "Satisfactory." If it is not, enter its number and write what you believe to be a precise, reasonably complete and accurate statement of the matter discussed. If it is an argument or conclusion based on quoted facts, do not attempt to restate the facts, but if the proposition as a whole is not satisfactory, revise only as respects the other statements about the data or the conclusion drawn from the data.

(All questions equally weighted.)

1. The author of your text is mistaken in the emphasis he places on the need of equity in insurance. In fire insurance, for example, it is impossible to get rates which are precisely equitable between individual risks. Yet the business exists and serves the community well.
2. Insurance companies make considerable pretense about being interested in removing the causes of loss. But really they are not, because if the causes of loss are removed, there will be no more risk and no need for insurance companies.
3. Insurance brokers are agents of insurance companies who represent them in the metropolitan centers where it is not profitable to have many local agents.
4. Your textbook says the cost of competitive selling is chiefly due to the attitude of the buyers of insurance. That is not true. It is chiefly due to the hunger of companies for premiums.

[20] G. M. Ruch and J. W. Charles, "Comparison of Five Types of Objective Test in Elementary Psychology," *Journal of Applied Psychology,* 12: 398–403, 1928.
[20a] Loaned me by a colleague at the University of California.

5. Since the law of large numbers is an expression of natural phenomena, insurance companies do not need the elaborate underwriting organizations they have built up. All that is necessary is to get a large enough volume of risks and the business will take care of itself.

6. One of the great difficulties in adjusting fire insurance losses is the fact that the insured feels his contract entitles him to be put back in at least as good a position as he was before, which is usually only possible by putting him back in better position. Doing the latter is questionable public policy since it tends to increase the cost of insurance and may well lead to indifference to protection of property.

7. The investment earnings of well-established fire and casualty companies usually furnish an adequate return to stockholders, without the necessity of underwriting profit.

Naturally this test cannot be scored as easily or objectively as the usual true-false one. Indeed, the fundamental function of the questions is to concentrate the thinking of the students within relatively narrow limits by giving them a number of clues and suggesting to them the desirable form for presenting whatever ideas they care to add.

The next most widely used type of objective test is (2) the multiple-choice form. It consists merely in presenting questions that have been supplied with a number of more or less possible answers and letting the student mark the one he thinks is best. A few items from various subjects appear below: [21]

1. The measurable parallax of the stars is due to the:
—rotation of the earth on its axis.
—revolution of the earth about the sun.
—procession of the equinoxes.
—inclination of the equator to the ecliptic.

2. Of the following factors, the most important cause of the seasonal variation in the solar energy received on the earth is the:
—rotation of the earth on its axis.
—procession of the equinoxes.
—inclination of the equator to the ecliptic.
—earth's atmosphere.

[21] Richardson, Russell, Stalnaker, and Thurstone, *op. cit.* (for Items 1–5), pp. 31–43.

3. If one gram of sugar is burned to carbon dioxide in a calorimeter, a certain amount of heat is evolved. If an equal quantity of sugar is converted to carbon dioxide by body metabolism:
—a greater amount of heat will be supplied to the body.
—an equal amount of heat will be supplied to the body.
—a small amount of heat will be supplied to the body.
—the amount of heat supplied to the body will depend upon the individual.

4. A man breathing air which is 20 per cent oxygen and 5 per cent carbon dioxide enters an atmosphere which is 40 per cent oxygen and 10 per cent carbon dioxide.

RESULT:
—Respiratory rate decreases.
—Respiratory rate increases.
—Respiratory rate remains the same.

EXPLANATION:
—The primary stimulus to respiration is carbon dioxide.
—The primary stimulus to respiration is oxygen.
—The increase in quantity of the two constituents did not alter their productions.

5. The average depth of the ocean is (greater than, equal to, less than) the average height of the land; the greatest known depth of the ocean is (greater than, equal to, less than) the height of the highest mountain.

6. In Grade 4 there is a boy with an I.Q. of 87 who has not yet learned how to read. His eyes seem to be normal. Number the explanations below in the order of probability as reasons.
—He tried to read at too early an age and became discouraged.
—He is too dull to learn.
—His eye movements are inaccurate.
—He is of an auditory type and will have to be taught by some nonvisual method.
—He did not like his first-grade teacher.

7. Which adjectives would you use to characterize Martin Luther? (Choose three.)
gentle, thoughtless, considerate, opinionated, stupid, deceitful, courageous, ambiguous, fanciful, noble, illogical, cruel, determined.

Sometimes it is desirable to use a reverse form in which the student is to cross out the item that does not contribute to the answer. For instance, he may be asked to eliminate the one incorrect or irrelevant response as in the sample below:

8. The reasons why the Napoleonic Empire finally broke up are
   A. Its too close connection with the destinies of but one single person.
   B. The failure of the continental system.
   C. The growth of nationalism in France.
   D. Its dependence upon continued military success.
   E. The growth of nationalism in Europe.[22]

This reverse type can often be used for the testing of several interrelations.

The main advantage of this form is its great flexibility. Almost any kind of subject matter can be tested in this way. As answers, one can use single words, numbers, phrases, whole sentences, or paragraphs. If desired, the teacher can request the students to rank all the answers in the order of their probability, as in the sixth item on page 434. There is a second advantage. Items of this type may deal with complexities, theories, inferences, or appreciations—as well as with facts.

The selection of questions can be, and often is, excellent. In a two-hour examination period a teacher can cover most, if not all, the main ideas and facts of a semester's work. An instructor cannot providentially take the items directly from the textbook, as he can for the true-false examinations; he has to make them up. This process necessitates a rather thorough review of the whole course on his part and a careful consideration of what he will include.

When students take a test of this type, they have to balance a number of answers, one against the other, in order to select the correct one. If the questions have been properly constructed, some of the decisions will call for concentrated and careful thinking. There is, of course, no chance for a student to show originality or organizing ability, and the questions do not require independent recall.

As with all objective tests, the grading of this form is easy though monotonous, and the scores are reliable. The usual score is merely the number of correct answers. If the questions have

[22] From M. E. Haggerty, *Studies in College Examinations,* University of Minnesota, 1934, 204 pp. (p. 69).

been selected so as to cover the main points of the course and if a teacher marks each student's errors, he almost automatically makes a diagnosis of weaknesses and sources of misunderstanding.

In the actual construction of the items—as distinct from the selection of ideas to be put into them—there are a few common difficulties to be avoided. In the first place there must be a right answer. This point seems too obvious to mention but I have seen too many items without any true answer to ignore the possibility that it could happen again. The question below is a case in point.[23]

> A rattlesnake is harmful because of its (a) rattles (b) fangs (c) forked tongue (d) spotted skin (e) strength.

The right answer, "venom," does not appear. Another error in the selection of the right answer arises when *a* correct but not *the* correct answer is used. The item below illustrates this situation:

> Eskimos eat fatty foods because such foods (a) are cheaper (b) produce more calories (c) are easy to preserve (d) need no cooking.

Presumably the true answer is that fatty foods are what the Eskimos can get.

It is necessary also that the right answer should not have any artificial or incidental advantages over any other. It should not be the longest, or the only one with proper names, or the only one with formal wording. The question below appears in two forms to illustrate this point:

With what do you associate the name of Pasteur?

1. diphtheria
2. smallpox inoculations
3. treatment of a formerly incurable disease called either hydrophobia or rabies
4. insulin for diabetes

With what do you associate the name of Pasteur?

1. prevention of diphtheria
2. prevention of smallpox
3. prevention of rabies
4. prevention of diabetes

In the second form the correct answer has no advantage over any of the others. It is quite all right to have one extremely long answer in an item, providing it is not the right one.

The position of the correct response is another matter to be

[23] This and the next illustration are taken from Richardson, Russell, Stalnaker, and Thurstone, *op. cit.,* pp. 87–88.

considered. If each of the questions is followed by four answers, the correct one should occupy all four possible positions an equal number of times. I have seen examinations so arranged that the right response never came first. It does not take long for students to find out that they can safely ignore the first answer and concentrate on the others. This performance reduces the number of choices and makes the items easier.

After the correct answer has been decided upon there have to be three or four "confusion" answers. As their name implies, they must really confuse. Consider the item below:

A governor is elected by (a) the senate (b) the empire (c) the voters (d) the League of Nations.

The supposed distractions simply do not distract. Even a child could throw out two answers, leaving the choice between the other two. Unless a confusion answer is plausible, it is just so much deadwood and is operating to make the question unduly easy.[24]

As can be inferred from these numerous cautions, it is no easy task to construct items of this type. The form is, however, one of the best, if only a teacher has the patience and the ingenuity to use it.

(3) The outlining test is a form of objective examination that is not as widely used as it should be, in view of its capacity to make students think. Anyone who believes that no objective test can require reasoning should try the following exercise.[25]

BONDS AND DEPRECIATION

1. The first requirement for a good bond is that it must be seasoned.
2. Some weak raw-material countries in Latin America undertook doubtful public improvements in order to provide bond issues for New York banks.
3. The resultant oversupply of building space in the U.S. in depression times lowered rents radically.
4. High-grade corporation bonds that were good in 1929 were still good in 1932.

[24] See also J. N. Stalnaker and R. C. Stalnaker, "Chance Versus Selected Distractors in a Vocabulary Test," *Journal of Educational Psychology*, 26: 161–68, 1935.
[25] Richardson, Russell, Stalnaker, and Thurstone, *op. cit.*, p. 109.

5. All U.S. Government bonds were still sound in 1932.
6. The American public has almost stopped buying bonds.
7. The various bonds eligible for savings bank investment in New York have shown little depreciation in value.
8. More than 80 per cent of all foreign defaults since 1929 were Latin American.
9. The Brazilian Importing Company has not defaulted on its bonds.
10. Municipal bonds have shown very few defaults—only 11 out of 309 major cities in the U.S. were in default in 1932.
11. Brazil and Chile (who furnished the greatest total of defaults) fell into political disorder.
12. Construction of buildings in the U.S. (construction based on optimistic expectations) ran ahead of requirements.
13. The market price of U.S. real estate fell.
14. Great as the loss in foreign bonds was, there was a much greater loss in U.S. building bonds.
15. Some Latin-American countries with bad financial records marketed bonds on the theory that the future was going to be different from the past.
16. Holders of building bonds lost many billions of dollars as a result of the fall in U.S. real-estate values.

From these statements (and these alone) construct two outlines which adequately develop each of the purposes given. Write the number of a statement in its proper place in the outline. Not all the statements listed are required, but all of the blanks in the outline are necessary.

Purpose I: To enumerate the types of bonds that have depreciated the least during the depression.

I. ....—
II. ....—
III. ....—

Purpose II: To show why Latin-American bonds and U.S. building (or real estate) bonds have done badly since 1929.

I. ....—
   A. ....—
   B. ....—
   C. ....—
II. ....—
   A. ....—
   B. ....—
   C. ....—
   D. ....—

To construct a test of this kind a teacher merely mixes up the order of headings in some well-made outline and then adds a few extra items that might be relevant but are not. The student must first sense the topic of the outline and then arrange the points in some logical fashion. This form is one of the few objective types that require organizing ability from the students.

Among the oldest forms of objective examinations are (4) the matching tests. In its simplest form this method gives students such materials as a list of words numbered from one to ten and a list of definitions; they are to put the number of each word in front of the correct definition. This technique is too well known to require illustration and too simple for frequent use in college. In some of its refinements, however, the matching method is excellent. Two samples appear below: [26]

SAMPLE 1

In the blank space before the description of each member of a circus, write the number of the disorder which you suspect.

1. Hypofunction of the pituitary (hypophysis).
2. Hyperfunction of the pituitary (hypophysis).
3. Hypofunction of the adrenal cortex.
4. Hyperfunction of the adrenal cortex.
5. Hypofunction of the thyroid.
6. Hyperfunction of the thyroid.
7. Cleft palate.
8. Injured semicircular canals.
9. Pierced eardrums.
10. Middle ear infection.
11. Vitamine A deficiency.
12. Vitamine B deficiency.
13. Vitamine C deficiency.
14. Vitamine D deficiency.
15. Hypofunction of the parathyroids.
16. Hyperfunction of the parathyroids.
17. Malfunction of the liver.
18. Malfunction of the pancreas.

—The Tall Man: 7 feet, 8 inches tall; 30 years old; measurement indicates great abnormal growth in the long bones, arms, legs, and lower jaw.
—An Englishman posing as a "wild man": age 30; height 4 feet; heavy featured; body hair sparse; sexually immature.

[26] Both samples come from Richardson, Russell, Stalnaker, Thurstone, *op. cit.,* pp. 52 and 61.

—The Living Skeleton: height 7 feet; weight 110 pounds; nervous and irritable; basal metabolic rate much above normal; low intelligence; first appearance of the condition in the family.

—The "Bronze Man": age 30; pigmentation began at age 29; blood pressure very low; kidney and digestive functions deranged; history of tuberculosis.

—José X: an acrobat; out of the show because of a succession of broken bones following a series of trivial falls; teeth brittle.

—Proprietor: underweight; tires quickly; susceptible to infection; sugar present in urine.

—"Goofus": American; city bred; age 30; legs bowed almost to semicircles; arms and ribs malformed; teeth abnormal, subject to cavities; due to condition present in childhood.

—A tribe of African natives: have refused to eat American food, and subsist upon dried meat and other foodstuffs brought with them from Africa; teeth loose; gums sore and bleeding; swollen and very painful joints.

—John R: by holding mouth and nose shut is able to expel cigarette smoke from left ear.

—A former tightrope walker: fell and struck the side of his head; now cannot keep his balance, even on the ground, with eyes shut; no symptoms of brain injury.

SAMPLE 2

Consider the following statements as describing isolated acts and policies of governments. Mark each statement with the number of the economic theory which it best illustrates.

> 1. Mercantilism
> 2. Laissez faire
> 3. Socialism

—Steps were taken by the government of Edward II to protect the home industry by discouraging the export of wool and taxing the import of cloth.

—The improvement of the roads was left almost entirely to groups of individuals, who formed themselves into Turnpike Trusts.

—As a result of the policy of the government, the Elizabethan Statute of Artificers, which required a seven years' apprenticeship, was replaced.

—Roads, bridges, tunnels, and water-supply systems, once in

greater or less degree operated privately and for profit, were taken over by the state.

—The inheritance tax which Congress passed provided for a variation in the rate according to the size of the estate left by deceased persons.

—All goods coming into England from Europe were to be imported in English ships, or in those of the country exporting the goods.

—The ownership of the machinery of production passed from the hands of private individuals to the State.

—The government encouraged the immigration of alien craftsmen into England.

—It was conceded that individuals who were actually engaged in industry or trade were the best judges of what was likely to promote the development of the country's economic resources.

—The regulations of the Tudors, although they remained on the Statute Books, were gradually allowed to fall into abeyance, and their very existence was frequently forgotten.

—Several states have enacted statutes which include the requirement that all employers coming within its scope must insure their employees against accident.

—The government enacted an income tax law which differentiated between "earned" and "unearned" incomes, as well as between incomes of various sizes.

—The government offered bounties to encourage the production of shipping stores, masts, spars, and pig iron.

—Congress passed a tariff which was more protective than any previous one had been.

—By means of loans from the Federal government at low rates of interest, municipalities were enabled to provide housing accommodations to workers' families at far less than the usual rentals.

In constructing a test of the kind shown by the first example, one should be careful to include a number of extra items. In this case there were only 10 "freaks" but 18 "causes." The "confusion" elements make the test somewhat harder, and they also prevent a statistical difficulty that otherwise arises. If the number of examples just equals the number of principles to be illustrated, for instance, the errors are always made in pairs; that is, if a student uses as an answer to item 5 the correct answer to item 7, he will obviously get item 7 also wrong. Even with many extra answers it is still possible for students to make two errors at once, but they are not forced to do so.

Taking a test of this sort requires a considerable amount of thought and reasoning. It is also likely to involve altogether too much eyestrain, because of the need to look constantly back and forth from the key at the top of the page to the items, especially when the key is too long to be memorized. This form does not produce wide variations in score, and it occupies a good deal of space. For instance, the possible scores of the first sample would run from 0 to 10, although the test occupies an entire page. The scoring is objective, but an accurate translation of the number into any system of grades is difficult.

The last of the commonly used types is (5) the classification form. A few items of this type are illustrated below: [27]

DIRECTIONS: In each of the following groups place an X before the one name which does not belong with the others in the group, and indicate the category in which the remaining five belong by writing it in the space provided.

CATEGORY——	CATEGORY——	CATEGORY——
—Caesar	—Caesar	—Corneille
—Catullus	—Gibbon	—Goethe
—Ovid	—Plutarch	—Molière
—Petrarch	—Socrates	—Racine
—Tacitus	—Tacitus	—Seneca
—Virgil	—Thucydides	—Sophocles

CATEGORY——	CATEGORY——	CATEGORY——
—Aristophanes	—Chaucer	—Helmholtz
—Beaumarchais	—Descartes	—Galileo
—Molière	—Kant	—Newton
—Plautus	—Plato	—Archimedes
—Spinoza	—Rousseau	—Priestley
—Terence	—Schopenhauer	—Pasteur

This form is excellent for material with which it can be used at all, but it is rather limited in applicability. It gives more score per square inch of paper than any other form. The

[27] Richardson, Russell, Stalnaker, and Thurstone, *op. cit.,* pp. 87–88.

student who takes the test must have sufficient background to recognize the nature of the various classifications. The test therefore measures somewhat more than might at first seem to be the case.

2. Effect of objective tests upon college work: Those college instructors who have appreciated the insidious effects of objective tests upon the thinking of both students and teachers are usually antagonistic to their use. They attack these types of measurement on three grounds: that they do not make students think, that they do not measure the same abilities as those tested by essay examinations, and that they put the emphasis upon nonessentials instead of upon main ideas. If these critics are talking about the hastily constructed true-false tests that Mr. Smith has made by copying—with a few alterations—fifty sentences out of textbook, they are quite right. They are wrong, however, if they condemn the objective form instead of Mr. Smith's laziness; any other examination he made might be just as bad. Before leaving the topic of objective test form it seems desirable to consider the nature and justification of the commonest criticisms against their use.

Unfortunately many objective examinations call for nothing but a good memory for unimportant details. This situation is not necessary, but it will remain true until teachers learn to make better tests than most of them do at present. When a test is poor it is not usually the form that is at fault but the content, which might be just as inacceptable in any other form. The fact is that a teacher has to work hard to make a good test of any kind. Contrary to general opinion, the time needed to construct a good objective test is so much more than that required by a good essay test that—unless a class is enormous—a teacher does not actually save any time in using the objective form; he simply uses it in construction instead of in scoring.

An objective examination can be so devised as to call for plenty of thinking; if it does not require anything but memory for minutiae, it is merely a bad test. Just to illustrate the degree of thinking which can be demanded by an objective test, I am including the following two samples.

SAMPLE 1[28]

DIRECTIONS: In each of the following exercises a problem is given. Below each problem are two lists of statements. The first list contains statements which can be used to answer the problem. The second list contains statements which can be used to explain the right answers. In doing these exercises, then, you are to place plus signs (+) in the parentheses after the statements which answer the problem and which give the results for the RIGHT answers.

1. Coal gas which has not been previously mixed with air is burning in a gas jet. At another similar gas jet the coal gas is mixed with air before it is burned. Will there be any differences in the amounts of light given off by flames of the two given jets? Why? If a cool aluminum pan is placed over each flame will there be any difference in the amounts of soot deposited on the pans in the two cases? Why?

The flame at the first gas jet will give off:
   (a)   more light than the flame in the second gas jet.   ( ) a.
   (b)   the same amount of light as the flame at the second gas jet.   ( ) b.
   (c)   less light than the flame at the second jet.   ( ) c.
   (d)   more soot than that deposited by the second gas jet.   ( ) d.
   (e)   less soot than that deposited by the second gas jet.   ( ) e.

Check the following statements which give the reason for the answer or answers you checked above.

   (f)   Incomplete combustion leaves some uncombined carbon in the flame.   ( ) f.
   (g)   The presence of nitrogen retards combustion.   ( ) g.
   (h)   Particles of uncombined carbon glow when heated.   ( ) h.
   (i)   Combustion is more complete in the first flame.   ( ) i.

[28] B. C. Hendricks, R. W. Tyler, and F. P. Frutchey, "The Ability to Apply Chemical Principles," *Journal of Chemical Education*, 11:611–13, 1934. Used by permission of the *Journal of Chemical Education*.

(j) The amount of air mixed with the gas does
     not affect the amount of light produced by
     the burning gas.   (   ) j.

(k) Some uncombined carbon in the flame is de-
     posited on a cool surface placed in a flame.   (   ) k.

2. The equation for the reaction by which methanol (methyl
alcohol) is prepared from carbon monoxide gas and hydrogen
gas is:

$$CO + 2H_2 \leftrightharpoons CH_3OH + heat.$$

In one experiment carbon monoxide and hydrogen gas are mixed
under pressure in the presence of a catalyst and heated to 350° C.
In a second experiment the same quantities of carbon monoxide
and hydrogen gases are mixed under the same pressure and in the
presence of the same catalyst and heated to 1500° C. Will there be
any difference in the reaction? Why?

(a) The reaction in the second experiment will
     proceed less rapidly than the reaction in the
     first experiment.   (   ) a.

(b) A smaller amount of methonal will be ob-
     tained in the first experiment than in the
     second experiment.   (   ) b.

(c) The reaction in the second experiment will
     proceed more rapidly than the reaction in
     the first experiment.   (   ) c.

(d) The amount of methanol will be the same in
     both experiments.   (   ) d.

(e) A larger amount of methanol will be ob-
     tained in the first experiment than in the
     second experiment.   (   ) e.

Check the following statements which give the reasons for the answer or answers you checked above.

(f) Temperature has no effect upon the rates of
     the reaction in these experiments.   (   ) f.

(g) In the chemical reaction, an increase in tem-
     perature favors the rate of the reaction of
     decomposing the product.   (   ) g.

(h) Some catalysts retard the rates of chemical
     changes.   (   ) h.

(i)   Raising the temperature increases the rate of
      chemical reaction.   (   )   i.
(j)   Some catalysts increase the rates of chemical
      changes.   (   )   j.
(k)   Catalysts do not undergo chemical changes
      in reactions.   (   )   k.
(l)   The temperature of a reaction which evolves
      heat depends on the rate of the reaction.   (   )   l.
(m)   If more heat is applied to reacting sub-
      stances in equilibrium, the equilibrium point
      of the reaction is changed so that reactants
      are produced which absorb heat or increase
      in amount.   (   )   m.
(n)   Increasing the speed of the molecules in-
      creases the number of collisions of molecules
      in a unit of time.   (   )   n.
(o)   The rate of chemical reaction is increased
      by increasing the speed of the molecules of
      the reacting substances.   (   )   o.
(p)   Methyl alcohol burns readily in air.   (   )   p.
(q)   Increase in the concentration of interacting
      substances increases the speed of the chemi-
      cal reactions.   (   )   q.

SAMPLE 2[29]

DIRECTIONS: Read the quotation from "What Is a Poet?" and place a letter before each statement following the passage. If a statement is a correct interpretation of the author's viewpoint, place the letter "A" on the blank line before the statement; if a statement is a wrong interpretation of the author's viewpoint, place the letter "B" on the blank line before the statement; if a statement is an exaggeration or an overstatement of the author's viewpoint, place the letter "C" on the blank line before the statement; if a statement is an unjust criticism of the author's viewpoint, place the letter "D" on the blank line before the statement; if you think the criticism just, put an "E."

[29] M. E. Haggerty *et al.*, *Studies in College Examinations*, University of Minnesota Press, 1934, 204 pp., pp. 175-77. This reference contains many good samples of tests in all subjects. Used by permission of the University of Minnesota Press.

Read the quotation and the statements carefully; base your interpretations upon the specific passage quoted; remember that

      A = correct interpretation.
      B = wrong interpretation.
      C = overstatement.
      D = unjust criticism.
      E = just criticism.

What Is a Poet? [30]

Poetry speaks for itself. But poets, curiously enough, do not; and so it is time that someone spoke for them and said what they would say if they spoke in prose. It is time that they be defended against the silent charge—all the more damning because it is so silent—that they are a special race of men and women, different from all other creatures of their kind and possessed of faculties which make them, if we knew them, only too wonderful to live with, not to say too embarrassing. I should like to relieve them from the burden of being queer. Poets are supposed to be a suffering race, but the only thing they suffer from is the misapprehension that they are endowed with a peculiar set of thoughts and feelings—particularly feelings—and that these endowments are of the romantic sort. It consists, to speak for the moment historically, in the notion that the poet has always and must always cut the same figure he has cut during the past hundred years or so. It consists in expecting him to be a Shelley, a Keats, a Byron, a Poe, a Verlaine, a Swinburne, a Dowson. He may be another one of those to be sure; but he also may be any kind of person under the sun. My only conception of the poet is that he is a person who writes poetry. That may sound absurdly simple, but it is arrived at after reflection upon the innumerable kinds of poetry which poets have written, and upon the baffling variety of temperaments which these poets have revealed.

— 1. Poets are more romantic than people in general.
— 2. There is a tendency for people in general to assume falsely that poets have peculiar feelings and thoughts.
— 3. Poets regard themselves as though they had thoughts and feelings different from those of people in general.

[30] Mark Van Doren, "What Is a Poet?" *The Nation,* 134: June 1, 1932, 624. Reprinted with permission.

— 4. The position taken by the author is open to serious attack, because he generalizes from his own personal observations and experiences that poets in general have the same type of thoughts and feelings as other people.

— 5. No poets have peculiar feelings and thoughts.

— 6. Poets are characterized by specific types of emotions.

— 7. Poets suffer from the misunderstanding, on the part of other people, that they are peculiar in temperament.

— 8. A study of the innumerable kinds of poetry which poets have written indicates that no poets are peculiar in temperament.

— 9. In general, poets tend to be nervous.

—10. It seems that the opinions of people in general are more valuable than the single opinion of the author in determining what a poet is.

—11. All people have certain misconceptions concerning the traits of poets.

—12. The author's point of view would be more convincing if he had some facts to show that poets have the same traits as other people.

—13. The author contends that poets have peculiar endowments or abilities which qualify them for their work.

—14. The fact that some poets have peculiar habits, ideas, and personal traits indicates that the author has taken a prejudiced viewpoint in his conception of the poet.

—15. The fact in itself that the author is in a sense a poet makes his conception of the poet prejudiced.

—16. The only thing that differentiates the poet from any other person is that the poet writes poetry.

—17. The viewpoint of the author is supported by scientific investigations which disprove the existence of psychological types.

—18. The only thing that poets suffer from is their own misunderstanding that they are peculiar.

—19. Shelley, Keats, Byron, Poe, Verlaine, Dowson, and Swinburne are typical examples of the poetical personality type.

—20. All poets are misunderstood because they refrain from speaking for themselves.

—21. The many kinds of poetry which have been written reveal that poets differ widely in personality and temperamental traits.

—22. All poets would be understood if they wrote prose instead of poetry.

—23. The poet is generally a timid, bashful person who rarely speaks up for himself.

—24. The purpose of the author is to point out that many people have false conceptions concerning poets.

—25. Because the biographies of some poets show that they have peculiar personality traits, one is justified in concluding that the author has generalized from too few facts.

—26. Conclusions such as those of the author which are based upon personal observation and opinion are always open to serious criticism.

Critics cannot say that a student taking either of these tests does not need to think; this objection applies only to badly constructed measures.

A second criticism is that new-type tests do not measure the same mental functions as those involved in an essay examination. On two counts this is obviously true. A student has no chance for either spontaneous recall or reorganization of ideas. It should not, however, be supposed that all essay examinations are automatically better in these respects than any objective test. For instance, out of 428 essay questions one investigator [31] found that 34.5 per cent required nothing beyond simple recall of isolated facts, while another 35 per cent demanded only a short answer without any reorganization. Only 30.5 per cent of the questions called for what is usually referred to as "thinking." In other words, a bad test is a bad test regardless of form.

There is some evidence [32] to show that objective and essay tests do measure some of the same mental functions. Scores on the

[31] V. M. Sims, "Essay Examination Questions Classified on the Basis of Objectivity," *School and Society*, 35: 100–2, 1932.

[32] A. R. Gilliland and L. E. Misbach, "Relative Values of Objective and Essay Type Examinations in General Psychology," *Journal of Educational Psychology*, 24: 349–61, 1933; A. W. Hurd, "Comparisons of Short-Answer and Multiple-Choice Tests Covering Identical Subject Content," *Journal of Educational Research*, 26: 28–30, 1932; J. B. Tharp, "The New Examination Versus the Old in Foreign Languages," *School and Society*, 26: 691–94, 1927; C. C. Weidemann and G. F. Newens, "Does the Compare-and-Contrast Essay Test Measure the Same Mental Functions as the True-False Test?" *Journal of General Psychology*, 9: 430–49, 1933.

two types usually correlate between .60 and .70; if some of the same mental operations were not involved, the relationship would be lower. In one rather elaborate study [33] a statistical analysis indicated an overlapping of about 60 per cent between the mental functions required by essay and true-false examinations. In general, the objective tests correlate higher with intelligence scores than do the marks based on essay examinations, but the differences are not large; those that exist may be due to the greater similarity of the intelligence test form to one type of test than to the other. In any case, there are so many other factors than intelligence that operate to produce the level of work done by students that the relationship of intelligence scores to achievement is not a valid criterion in this connection.

The third criticism—that objective tests may have a bad effect upon the thinking and the study habits of students—is all too true. But again I am certain that the fault lies with the careless construction of the tests, not with their essential nature. An opinion does not, however, affect the facts about how students prepare for an objective examination. Indeed the evidence on this point forms what to my mind is the most serious criticism of these tests as they are usually constructed. Three studies [34] are of interest, but since all of them show precisely the same conclusions, I will present them together in Table 28. The methods students use in studying for an examination they know will be objective appear in one column of the following list; those they use when they expect an essay examination appear in the other. These results are based upon the testimony of hundreds of students.

A worse indictment of the objective test could hardly be imagined.[35] The students have done exactly what students have always done—adjusted their methods to the demands of their

[33] Weidemann, *op. cit.*

[34] C. C. Crawford, "How to Study for Objective Tests," *Education,* 53:143–16, 1933; H. R. Douglass and M. Tallmadge, "How University Students Prepare for New Types of Examinations," *School and Society,* 39:318–20, 1934; P. W. Terry, "How Students Review for Objective and Essay Tests," *Elementary School Journal,* 33:592–603, 1933. See also P. W. Terry, "How Students Study for Three Types of Objective Examination," *Journal of Educational Research,* 27:333–43, 1934.

[35] For a similar discussion see G. Meyer, "The Essay Type of Examination," *American School Board Journal,* 89:17–18, 1934.

TABLE 28

Methods of Study

Methods Valuable in Preparing for Objective But Not for Essay Tests	*Methods Valuable in Preparing for Essay But Not for Objective Tests*
1. Hunt for details.	1. Try to find the main ideas of the course.
2. Underline all epigrammatic, startling, strongly positive or negative sentences.	2. Consider the general trends.
3. Look up meanings of all unfamiliar words.	3. Draw the important conclusions from tables or diagrams.
4. Write out and memorize a list of authors and experiments.	4. Reread the text and lecture notes, without memorizing them.
5. Associate the examples given with the rules they illustrate.	5. Understand underlying relationships between ideas.
6. Memorize any series of related items.	6. Form one's own opinion on important points.
7. Reread two or three times all the sentences that have been underlined.	7. Read the summaries and table of contents.
8. Consider which sentences the teacher is likely to select and memorize them.	8. Make and learn a short outline of the whole course.
9. Study any diagrams or tables and memorize details [36]	9. Recite the main points.
10. Hunt for debatable issues and learn the textbook writer's opinion.	10. Make an outline of each chapter.
11. Note all the exceptions to any rules.	11. Think up new examples of all general principles.
12. Learn as many isolated facts as possible.	12. Organize related chapters into groups.
	13. Recite to oneself from the main headings in the text.

teachers. In two of the four investigations, the students mentioned the habit of looking in the text for sentences that they thought the teacher might select, and in all four they voted for underlining and learning any sentence that stood out in

[36] The comparison of techniques in studying diagrams was well brought out in one of the investigations (Douglass and Tallmadge, *op. cit.*). Ninety one per cent of the students testified that they studied tables and charts for minute details when preparing for an objective test, but 86 per cent of the same students said they looked for the main conclusions to be drawn from such material when they studied for an essay test.

452 THE PROBLEMS OF CLASSWORK

any way. This result is clear evidence that the atrocious habit of taking examination items direct from some book is extremely prevalent. If any instructor is fool enough to do this, his students will checkmate him neatly by finding the sentences and memorizing them. What the inside of a student's mind is like after making such a preparation as that described above, I hate to think, but certainly his mental state cannot lead to lasting educational values. I should imagine such students would suffer considerably from mental indigestion. Their methods of work reveal better than anything else the dangers inherent in the use of objective tests. The form lends itself to such abuses. If students always were given such examinations as those shown on pages 444–49 they would abandon their hunting for minutiae because this procedure would do them no good. Students are not fools, and their fundamental maxim is to give the professor what he wants. If his examinations call for details, no student in his right mind is going to concentrate on anything else. If it calls for conclusions, opinions, and reasoning, students will produce them.

A student's "mental set" when he is reviewing his work is important. If he is "set" for recalling main ideas and evaluating conclusions, he is also ready for any type of recognition test, but if he is "set" only for recognition he is unable to recall his work on his own initiative.[37] Even though a teacher intends to use an objective test, it is better not to let the students know it, because if they are ready for recall the process of recognition is easy—provided the test does not demand minutiae.

The retroactive effect of tests upon teaching should also be considered. It has been said with considerable truth that the makers of tests—especially of standardized tests—have become the real curriculum makers and the real determiners of teaching method.[38] Teachers will prepare their students for the type of examinations that will be used, and students will study in whatever way will bring them the best grades. It is therefore

[37] G. Meyer, "An Experimental Study of the Old and New Type Examination," *Journal of Educational Psychology*, 25: 641–61, 1934, and 26: 30–40, 1935.
[38] W. S. Monroe, "Effects of Measurement on Instruction," *Journal of Educational Research*, 28: 496–97, 1935.

vital that teachers should produce not only the best tests they can, but the kind of tests that will have the most desirable retroactive effect upon all concerned. This statement does not mean that objective tests should be abandoned but that they should be constructed with greater care as to their content. In some instances measurement has undeniably had a bad effect upon teaching, but this situation is the fault of the material included in the tests—not the fault of their form.

This retroactive effect is nothing new. I recall one course in my own student days, during which the class had been working along on an interesting project, when suddenly it was interrupted by the introduction of a totally new and—to me, at least—quite irrelevant topic. We proceeded to spend about two weeks in endless drill on this new material. In a burst of probably undeserved confidence, the teacher one day told me she had not intended to include this topic at all; she had, however, learned that the head of the department was going to devise the final examination and she did not want her students to make a poor showing! No teacher is immune to this sort of stimulus. He or she will prepare students for what they are likely to meet on a test, regardless of personal convictions as to the worth of materials.

Naturally some degree of supervision over teaching is a good thing. Otherwise an instructor with a series of pet ideas can spend the entire time in airing them. In an advanced class this procedure does no great harm, but for elementary work it is undesirable because the students do not get the foundation they need. Modern measurement is, however, so thorough and exact that the retroactive influence upon teaching is far greater than it has ever been before.[39] If an instructor wants to use an

[39] For further discussion of new-type examinations see A. C. Eurich, *The Effective General College Curriculum as Revealed by Examinations,* University of Minnesota Press, 1937, 427 pp.; M. E. Haggerty, *et al., Study in College Examinations,* University of Minnesota Press, 1934, 204 pp.; E. S. Jones, "Comprehensive Examination Questions in History, Economics, Government, Sociology, and Psychology," *Supplement to the Bulletin of the Association of American Colleges,* 1933, 128 pp.; R. W. Leighton, "Studies to Determine the Relative Achievement of Students at Different Potentiality Levels," *Studies in College Teaching,* No. 1, University of Oregon Press, 1934; C. C. Weidemann and B. D. Wood, *Survey of College Examinations,* Bureau of Publications, Teachers College, Columbia University, 1927, 30 pp.; P. O. Johnson, *Comprehensive Examinations in Biological Science,* University of Minnesota, 1935, 30 pp.; *in Economics,* 20

objective form for some of his examinations, he should make very certain that he is emphasizing elements which are of permanent educational value.[40]

IV. THE ORAL EXAMINATION

The oral examination is presumably the oldest type. It comes down from a time when there were so few students that each one could be questioned at length, not only once but repeatedly. In most universities the oral examination is now given only to candidates for the Ph.D. degree, but here and there one finds a college in which the comprehensive examinations are either entirely or partly oral. The average teacher therefore needs to have some opinion about the worth of an oral test.

There have been two reasonably good studies on this question. For the first [41] a graduate student presented herself for four oral examinations with different committees, each composed of two professors. The eight faculty members rated her independently on a scale of 100 points at the close of their examination, then talked over the situation, and finally made out a committee report. The individual ratings varied from 40 to 88 per cent, and the committee averages from 55 to 90. Two committees passed the candidate, and two flunked her. During the examinations—unbeknown to the professors—two stenographers took down every question and answer. The num-

pp.; *in Physical Science*, 35 pp.; P. Hartog and E. C. Rhodes, *Marks and Examiners*, The Macmillan Company, 1936, 344 pp.

[40] There is one technique that cuts down materially the amount of time needed in preparing objective examinations. This procedure is highly recommended. Whenever a teacher gives an objective test he should keep one blank copy, cut up the questions, and mount each upon a separate card. Library cards, eight by five, cut in half lengthwise, are excellent for this purpose. He then files the cards by subject and under whatever additional subheadings may seem useful. In a course of a year's teaching he may thus accumulate a library containing several hundred objective questions. When he repeats the material during subsequent years he can use some of the questions already constructed and add more that have since occurred to him. If this process is continued over a period of time he will have a collection of several thousand objective questions. There is no sense whatever in throwing away good items which have been made with much labor and thought.

[41] S. L. Pressey, L. C. Pressey, and E. J. Barnes, "The Final Ordeal." *Journal of Higher Education*, 3: 261–64, 1932.

ber of questions was twice as large on one examination as it was on another, no question was asked on all four tests, and only five of the twenty-three different topics came up on more than two examinations. In short, nothing much in one oral examination agreed with anything in another.

The second study [42] reports ratings by fifty-nine faculty members of twenty-six examinees on the following specific traits: (1) importance of thesis topic, (2) intelligibility of thesis, (3) methods used in special research, (4) accuracy of conclusions, (5) candidate's insight into implications of his thesis, (6) candidate's ability to develop his methods and conclusions, (7) candidate's background of knowledge, (8) quality of candidate's general vocabulary, (9) general estimate of candidate. The ratings assigned on each point varied as follows:

TABLE 29
Ratings on Nine Traits of Twenty-six Candidates [42a]

Percentage Rating	Number of Traits*								
	1	2	3	4	5	6	7	8	9
96–100	2	1	3		4	1			2
91–95	1	4	1	3	1	4	2	2	2
86–90	8	7	6	8	3	3	1	2	2
81–85	2	6	3	6	6	3	1	2	2
76–80	4	11	7	11	3	8	4	2	2
71–75	12	5	9	7	7	7	4	10	8
66–70	6	7	5	2	9	6	8	11	8
61–65	2	3	6	9	5	4	7	7	7
56–60	3	8	6	1	5	4	9	4	10
51–55	7	2	6	4	8	3	7	9	5
46–50	4	3	1	2	1	6	4	5	5
41–45	2	2	3	1	3	1	4		4
36–40	2			3	1	3	2	2	
31–35	2		2	1	1	1	2	3	
26–30			1				1		1
21–25					1	1	2		
16–20	1								
MEDIAN......	65.7	72.4	61.8	70.8	66.4	66.7	58.9	63.1	64.4

* These columns do not all add up to 59 because some of the professors submitted incomplete ratings.

[42] P. C. Trimble, "The Final Oral Examination: Its Limitations and Its Possible Improvement as a Major Academic Hurdle in the Graduate School," *Purdue Studies in Higher Education*, XXV, Vol. 35, No. 3, 1934, 38 pp.

[42a] Trimble, *op. cit.* Used by permission of Purdue University.

In spite of the wide variation in all these ratings, only three of the twenty-six candidates failed to pass! The ratings of the different examiners for two of the candidates were intercorrelated. The relationship varied from —77 to .73. Out of forty such correlations, twelve were negative and only seven were above .50. In short, these examiners did not agree with each other at all.

It would seem as if the oral examination were somewhat more unreliable than any written examination. It has some of the same faults as regards the selection of questions; indeed, the questions are quite often the result of only casual interest on the part of the examiners. No two orals are even approximately equal in difficulty. The one element added by the oral examination is some estimate of personality. Most people do not succeed in conveying much about themselves in writing. The oral answers give teachers a chance to become better acquainted with a student. It would seem, however, quite unfair to use these examinations as a basis for important grades of any kind, because of the great unreliability of the marks assigned.

The oral examination introduces one source of error that is of no importance in an objective test and of little influence in written work. I mean the error of overrating sheer verbal facility. Perhaps an illustration will make the point clearer. I was once a member on a doctoral committee of five professors. The candidate had done her major work with me and had written a thesis on a matter so detailed that probably only she and I knew what it was about. By a series of chance happenings and substitutions, the committee that heard her final examination contained only one other person besides myself from her major department; one professor came from an allied subject, and two were complete strangers. Only I could ask her intelligible questions about her thesis, so the other four members proceeded to wander over the entire field of clinical psychology. The candidate answered glibly, impressively, and for the most part incorrectly. The notion that a person with such complete aplomb could be utterly wrong apparently did not enter the heads of the three professors who had no adequate background for evaluating her answers. They were, in fact, enchanted by the candidate's brilliance. Whenever the other psychologist or I tried to pin her down, so as to demonstrate her ignorance, she either told a joke or launched into an interesting but irrelevant case study. After the candidate had been dismissed, I found myself in the unenviable position of voting against my own candidate, while one colleague hesitated and the other three voiced the heartiest commendation. The candidate passed her oral examination chiefly on the fluency and charm with which she imparted misinformation. This personal element does not enter in any important way into written work, but it does have an undeniable influence upon the outcome of an oral test.

V. PURPOSES IN TESTING AND THE SELECTION
OF AN APPROPRIATE FORM

It is important to realize the shortcomings of any examination and the particular deficiencies of each type. Various people have expressed the opinion that examinations should be abolished. There is something to be said for this point of view. Without doubt an examination of any kind favors the student who reacts quickly and is emotionally stable. An essay test gives a further advantage to a student with these two characteristics who does not know too much and is fluent in his written work. If examinations had no time limit, some of these advantages would disappear. Speed would become no factor at all, and the student who knew a great deal would have time to organize it properly.

I remember once studying for a final examination with a friend who simply appalled me by the amount she knew—not merely details but many important ideas that had escaped me altogether. On the examination we were given six essay questions of a type neither of us had anticipated. She got a poor grade and I got a good one, for reasons having nothing to do with the course. In the first place, she was a person who becomes disorganized by surprise and recovers slowly, while I tighten up and work better under pressure than otherwise. In the second place she knew so much that she had no time to organize it all; I had only a few ideas, which I could rearrange quickly. In the third place she wrote slowly and carefully, whereas I can always express an idea if I have one. None of these traits had anything to do with our respective understanding of the material, with the profit we derived from the course, or with the amount of work we had done. She finished only one question, and even it was not well organized because she had too many relevant ideas to weave into a logical pattern in the time at her disposal. Moreover, her sentence structure was often awkward. I finished all the questions, arranging the half-dozen ideas in each in an orderly sequence—no great intellectual achievement—and wrote better sentences. When we compared our papers, it appeared she had more substance in her one answer than I had in all six. She was penalized for being hesitant, too well informed, and a bit clumsy in expression, whereas I reaped undeserved benefits from being adaptable, ignorant, and fluent.

Any experienced teacher could quote similar instances. Indeed, such situations have arisen so often that many people have an active prejudice against formal tests. Because of these factors, test results should always be considered with care and interpreted sensibly.

No examination is more than a sampling. The theory is that a given sample will correlate highly with any other equally well-selected sample, also that a single examination will correlate highly with total mastery of the entire course. Neither assumption is wholly true, and in specific instances both are false.[43] The more inclusive and the longer a test, the greater is the chance that the results will correlate with the criteria. A teacher would do well to keep these assumptions in mind when dealing with students' papers.

Most teachers feel that the advantages of examinations outweigh the disadvantages. The imminence of a test causes students to review and organize. The results give at least some insight into their achievements. When tests are used often and are only one means of judging a student's work, when time is given for all to finish, and when the tests are constructed

---

[43] For example, I once took an examination on which there were two questions—one about Roman law and one about the growth of towns during the Middle Ages. The professor added that if neither question suited us we might write on a topic of our own choosing. I wrote three bluebooks on Abelard—who had up to that time not been mentioned—and got a high mark. The idea that this performance correlated with anything else I might have done or with my general information about the course is absurd.

with care, the results are likely to be satisfactory. The difficulty arises in large classes in which a student is judged entirely upon his work on one mid-term and one final examination. Such a sampling, administered under ordinary time limits, is inadequate for assigning a mark that is supposed to reflect what a student has gotten from a course.

Assuming, however, that a test of some kind is to be used, the next step is to make up one's mind as to exactly what is to be tested. If a teacher wants to find out how well his students can, for instance, recognize and classify a set of specimens, he does not want a paper-and-pencil examination at all. If he wants to obtain individual reactions or expressions of opinions, he needs a different type of test from that by means of which he can measure comprehension of main ideas. Test forms should be flexible enough to permit a teacher to stress the values in which he is interested.

One excellent example of clearness in the planning of tests has come to my attention. A professor who gives a course on Shakespeare uses several types of measurement. She first assigns two or three plays, asking that the students read them before a certain day. At that time she gives a detailed objective examination covering the essential facts in the plays. No marks are assigned on the basis of this test. It is used merely to tell her which students know enough about the assignment to be ready for discussion. Those who make perfect or nearly perfect scores constitute the group that takes part in the ensuing classwork. Any student who did not pass the examination may come to class and listen but may not participate—on the principle that he is not yet ready to talk, because he does not know enough. At intervals during the year she gives essay tests, the results of which she uses in deciding upon her final grades. In addition, she calls for a long paper or other project suggested by some phase of the classwork. Finally, she maintains a workshop in which the students carry out such group activities as costuming and producing one of Shakespeare's plays each semester, dramatizing his life, devising modern stage settings, and so on. Her final examination has three sections. The first is objective and requires judgment on a number of more or less correct statements. The second consists of several essay questions, from which a student may select any two she likes. For the third section the students draw slips of paper out of a box and each goes either to the library or the workshop to complete a small but individual project. Her grades for the course are based partly upon written work, partly upon class discussion, and partly upon initiative and ability in the workshop. She thus has the various kinds of measures and uses each in accordance with what she wants at the moment to find out.

In general, the multiple-choice, completion, short-answer, and matching forms are suitable for measuring the mastery of facts and the ability to draw simple conclusions from them. Questions of all these types can be so formulated as to require real thinking. Since a teacher can cover the main points of a course with any of these forms it is possible to obtain a diagnosis of each student's shortcomings merely by marking his errors. This technique is valuable in proportion as the test is inclusive.

The outlining and classifying forms are useful as summaries or cross sections. They are, however, so special that only a few types of material will fit them. There can be no objection to them, however, on the grounds that they require too little thinking. The outlining test even calls for some degree of organizing ability but not for written expression.

The essay examination has virtues that the other forms do not have. For some purposes it is desirable to find out how well students can recall relevant ideas, organize them, and express their opinions in writing.[44] The one thing this kind of test does badly is to measure the mastery of facts. One cannot obtain from it a systematic diagnosis, partly because it does not often cover all the important points of a course and partly because no two students produce the same assortment of ideas.

An essay test can, however, be made to yield a good deal of diagnostic information, even though it is not always of a system-

[44] One other virtue has recently been brought to my attention by an acquaintance who divides his examinations into several parts and lets his students select whichever series of questions appeals to them. The parts are so arranged as to be appropriate for students of different personalities and interests. While equivalent in difficulty they are totally different in type. This refinement might well be used more widely.

atic character. I well remember one professor who called each student to her office after every test and went over almost every sentence. She asked why we said this or did not say that, what unexpressed ideas were behind one statement and what errors in thinking behind another, what the basis was for this deduction, the authority for that comment, or the logical conclusion from facts we had given. At the end of such an interview a student felt that she had a perfectly transparent mind, about the workings—and especially the shortcomings—of which the teacher knew more than she did. This diagnosis of a student's thought processes is better done from an essay test than from any other type, but it requires time, penetration, and concentrated effort on the part of the professor.

The selection of a particular form thus depends upon what the immediate objective is in testing and the use to be made of the results. A teacher who is willing to experiment soon learns what kind of test is most useful at what times. The common error to be avoided is the use of a test form for a purpose for which it is not intended. There is no objection to a test that measures only facts, because there are parts of any course that are factual; there have to be facts or there would not be any content. There are also some things that do not need to be learned beyond the level of recognition. If teachers adapt the test form to the aims they have in mind they should find all forms valuable—but not at the same time or for the same purpose.[45]

Finally it must be remembered that tests have retroactive effects upon both the attitudes and the study habits of students. A good examination tells students what their weak and strong points are, develops a desire for more tests rather than fewer, and emphasizes such values as can be gained only through desirable methods of work. Tests that are so general and so subjective in nature that students cannot see why they received the estimate they did are not satisfactory, partly because they engender misunderstandings and partly because they give the student so little help. Examinations that cause

[45] See also P. O. Johnson, "The Differential Function of Examinations," *Journal of Educational Research*, 30: 93–103, 1936.

students to memorize sentences or to cram their minds with isolated and unassimilated facts are worse, because they produce methods of work that will decrease a student's efficiency along all lines. These indirect results are relatively permanent and are therefore of great importance, since they may persist long after 90 per cent of the details and half of the main ideas have been forgotten.

VI. SUMMARY

Examinations should be helpful to both teacher and student. When they are not, the teacher is to blame. If tests are not consonant with the aims of higher education, that is also the teacher's fault. If students dread examinations it is because their instructors have overemphasized the measuring and policing phase of tests to the exclusion of their educational values. Once students learn how to use their examination papers as guides to individual study and remedial work, they want frequent tests for their own use. No form of test will protect a careless teacher against the results of his own carelessness, and no form will guarantee an acceptable content. The really important thing about any test is what goes into it, not its external form. Therefore any kind of test can be either as bad or as good as any other kind. The selection of one type or another depends upon an instructor's objective and the nature of the material he wishes to include. Examination forms are neither right nor wrong; they are merely appropriate or inappropriate to a given situation.[46]

[46] See C. S. Boucher and F. S. Beers, "Improved Examinations," *Bulletin of the Association of American Colleges,* 21 : 94–114, 1936.

CHAPTER XX

MARKS

As higher education is at present organized a teacher has to assign marks whether or not he believes in them. Many teachers do not. A priori there is something to be said both for and against the practice of giving grades to students. The arguments against are briefly as follows: (1) If students receive grades they become interested in their marks rather than in the material they are learning. (2) Grades are based only upon mastery of subject matter and do not take into consideration the student's total development during the course. (3) Marks are—even as reflections of knowledge—too inaccurate to be useful. Finally, (4) the assigning of grades permits the vicious practice of reducing education to arithmetical units. The main arguments in favor of grades are: (1) that they are necessary in order to keep an objective record of a student's progress—a record used for many purposes by many people and of great service to the student himself, (2) that students earnestly desire grades, and (3) that only by the use of objective records can students know where they stand and when they are improving. All of these points need discussion.

The "work-for-work's-sake" school of thought is always more or less vociferous and perhaps more so than usual at the present time. This attitude, as far as I can tell from reading about it and from talking with teachers who espouse it, seems to have a number of bases. Some instructors think they can develop greater interest if students do not have their minds divided between the subject matter and their probable mark. Others feel that every student should do his best all the time without thought of possible results. A few believe that marks are juvenile and should not be of interest to mature people.

For myself, the most convincing argument on this point has been mere personal experience; while this is admittedly only hearsay evidence to anyone else, I shall present it. The college I attended gave marks, but these were entered on a record not available to a student until her graduation. At that time she could find out how many grades of each level she had received during the previous four years if she wanted to take the trouble to ask for them, but she had no prospect whatever of discovering what mark she got in what course. This arrangement was intended to prevent students from thinking about their grades, but it did not produce this result. The one steady topic of undergraduate conversation was the matter of who was probably getting what mark in what course, and why. The comparison of actual grades can go on for only a short time, but for conjectures and arguments there is no terminus. Far from reducing interest, the secrecy of the whole procedure greatly heightened it. In this particular instance, at least, the suppression of marks had no appreciable effect upon the preoccupation of the students with them—it only altered the nature of the interest.

Thus far no one has presented any experimental results to show that students do better work or are any happier without grades than with—or vice versa. Until such evidence appears each person is equally entitled to his own opinion, inconvenienced by any embarrassing facts. One element in a teacher's thinking should be, however, that students are normal human beings who like to know what they are doing and rarely become so wrapped up in ideas as to overlook the possible approval or disapproval of other people.

The second objection to the usual mark—that it overemphasizes subject matter—is well taken. The more modern attitude is that a student's report in a given course should cover all phases of growth. Naturally the mastery of ideas would be one basis for judgment, but it should not be the only one. In individual cases it never has been the sole basis. Teachers raise or lower marks in view of a student's original standing, his effort and industry, or his improvement in attitude. Those who oppose the ordinary mark because it is too narrow want mainly to have a report that will tell what a student's total development has been and will present in some detail the bases upon which the various judgments were made. Some such modification of the marking system will probably come, but just what form it will take is not yet clear. In the lower schools teachers commonly grade children for various traits of which knowledge is only one. This form may be used, but it seems more likely that colleges will devise their own type of report. That it should cover more than mastery of facts would seem obvious.

The argument against grades on the grounds that they are inaccurate is unfortunately all too valid. At best a mark is only an estimate, and, like any other estimate, it is subject to error. It seems to me that this error can be reduced by carefulness and even corrected for those teachers who have a consistent bias, but that it can never be eliminated. As far as a student's entire record is concerned, however, these inaccuracies are not so important as one might think, because the too-high estimate of one instructor is soon offset by the too-low guess of another. Very few teachers assign either an A or an E without much careful consideration and much real evidence. There may be, and probably are, errors in the intervening grades, but in a student's total record these are not of great importance. In any case, since instructors are human, they will remain as full of frailty as anyone else.

The fourth argument is often heard. At the present moment American education is still suffering from an effort to reduce achievement to credits. Undoubtedly the ready availability of grades has helped in this movement, but marks cannot be regarded as the sole or even the main cause, since they existed for generations before the current arithmetical computations came into vogue. The real cause is the great increase in enrollment, with its resulting terrific pressure upon the teaching staff. Instead of having only 20 students in a class, as they had had in former years, teachers suddenly had 120. Instead of an acquaintance with each student, with a resulting consideration of personal factors, they had only a record of examination grades. A system of complicated and formal credits is one outgrowth of this situation. The impersonality and the rigidity of the system is not, however, caused by the assigning of marks but by the hordes of students who figure in a teacher's consciousness only as names in a class book.

A good summary of the present situation in many colleges and universities is given in the following excerpt.

The usual transcript is a really significant document, in part because of its value as educational currency but more particularly because it reflects all too clearly certain basic educational concepts. It usually solemnly affirms that the bearer has on deposit in the office of the registrar credits for a specific number of hours in German, French, Latin, History, Economics, Government, Mathematics, Chemistry, Physics, or other such subjects. It testifies that he has marks of 75, 80, or 85 per cent, but whether this means 75 per cent of what he is capable of learning, 75 per cent of the content of the course, or 75 per cent of what the instructor knows is never quite clear. . . . When the guesses of different instructors are combined to derive an average (hour-point-ratio, grade-point-ratio, etc.), we have much the same result as though we added apples and pears, multiplied by doorknobs, and divided by peanuts.[1]

This statement may be something of a *reductio ad absurdum,* but it is a fairly accurate exposition of the situation. Something should be done to produce a better kind of record and to get away from the senseless complexity here indicated. It is as bad as its critics think it is. I am not sure, however, that the wholesale elimination of all grades is the best solution.

On the other side of the argument is the undeniable fact that marks are useful. A student's record is important in a number of wholly practical ways. During his college career he gains or loses special privileges on the basis of it. In getting

[1] A. J. Brumbaugh, "Achieving Greater Unity in General Education," *Report of the Fifteenth Annual Meeting of the American College Personnel Association,* 1938, pp. 23–26. Used by permission of the American College Personnel Association and the author.

a job he has a record to present as proof of his competence. If he goes on into the graduate school, his record follows him and helps him to get—or prevents him from getting—scholarships or teaching assistantships. Whatever one's feelings about the keeping of records, it is hard to see how these practical affairs could be carried on without some indication of academic standing. Of course, a student's record should include other factors besides his marks, but without these the various personal recommendations would be difficult to estimate. The red tape of education is sometimes ridiculously involved, but it has such practical values that one can hardly dispense with it altogether.

There have recently been scattered efforts to develop some kind of permanent record other than marks.[2] At Bennington College, for instance, the teachers make a series of comments about each student's work and personal development during the period of contact. No grades are given. If a student's work is not up to standard this fact appears in the report, together with the bases for this opinion. To quote the catalogue:

Each counselor receives from other members of the faculty confidential descriptions and estimates of his counselee's work from time to time. Through conferences with counselor and faculty the student may obtain frequent assessment of her accomplishment. At the end of each year she is sent a summary of her record indicating her success or failure in the work of the period with an assessment of her abilities. Since the College has no final examination period, competitive grades or numerical accumulation of course credits, the student's record is a cumulation of specific judgments on specific achievements: reports, papers, investigations, projects, discussions, pieces of creative work and written tests when desired. So far as possible a single, critical, terminal test is avoided as the main basis for decision as to promotion.[3]

[2] See, for instance, C. S. Boucher, "Achievement Tests and Substitutes for Course Credits," *31st Yearbook of the National Society for the Study of Education,* Part II, 1932, pp. 193–96.

[3] *Bennington College Bulletin,* 1939–40, Vol. 8, No. 1, p. 14. Used by permission of the College.

Progress in the field of knowledge is naturally one basis for judgment, but it is not the only one. This type of record may eventually come to be accepted in higher education. It has, of course, the advantage of being flexible and of giving a complete picture of a student. Whether or not it can be made sufficiently objective for general use remains to be seen. In any case the development of such records in even a few places is almost certain to effect modifications and improvements throughout the country.

The second argument in favor of grades is that students undeniably want them. They are just as naturally and spontaneously interested in their marks as a businessman is in his salary; in fact, classes and marks occupy the same place in a student's life as are occupied by work and wages in the life of an adult. Students invest hours of time and effort, and they want some objective return on their investment. It is my opinion that a student has a right to know, in as exact terms as possible, what kind of work he is doing in each course. Even though he has no undue preoccupation with his academic record he may very well be sufficiently interested to desire precise information. Students want also to experience the thrill of success as often as possible, and presumably they should be allowed to do so, since success leads to greater learning.

It may be argued that students ought to become independent of the teacher's judgment of their work and ought to think only of the value of the work to themselves. This argument is very nearly a psychological absurdity; no normal human being is independent of the attitude of others toward what he is doing. In the student's case the person best equipped to render a judgment is the teacher.

It might also be argued that comments written by teachers are adequate substitutes for marks. On the basis of a practically uninterrupted observation of students from my entrance to college thirty years ago to the present time, I can only say that students do not seem to regard anything—no matter how complimentary—as a substitute for an objective grade. This attitude is perhaps unfortunate, but it is so characteristic of late adolescence that a college faculty might as well give in to it at one time as another. Allowing students to know their marks saves time and much nervous wear and tear. One may not always approve of human nature, but there is very little one can do about it.

A student's mark is important also because it tells him the extent to which he has succeeded in doing what he was supposed to do. Without grades an inefficient student will work happily and busily for months and never know that he is not improving. A person of any age has a right to know what those best equipped to judge think of his competency. Failure to receive such estimates is sometimes unfortunate.

In a certain college the authorities refused to give students their marks on the principle that each person should follow his interests and should not be concerned with the academic returns on his investment of time and effort. At the end of his sophomore year, Allen was in doubt whether to major in chemistry or history. He assembled all the information he could, but none of his teachers in either department would tell him what kind of work he had done. Everyone advised him to follow whatever subject most appealed to him. After some debate Allen continued in chemistry, largely because it seemed a field that would be more likely than history to lead to a job not too long after his graduation from college. In due course of time Allen graduated and set about finding a position. To his consternation the firms to which he applied all received reports from his college that his work in chemistry had never been above average and was in some cases almost failing. Allen returned to the college and demanded to see his academic record, which was finally given to him to look at. He then discovered that during his freshman and sophomore years he had received A's in three semesters of history and D's in two semesters of chemistry. As far as he could recall, his interest in both fields had been about the same. He decided upon chemistry on practical grounds, although it was certainly a subject in which he had a keen interest. He would never have made such a decision, however, if he had had any idea of his relative competence in the two fields. By concealing his standing from him his college sent him out into the world with such a poor academic record in his main subject that he could not get a job in his expected field, although he had an excellent record in another subject in which he had taken so few courses that his record was of no practical value to him.

A student's teachers—past and present—the college officials, his parents, and his future employers will all demand to know how well he did in various subjects, and they will lay considerable stress upon his academic record. The student is the person whose life will be affected more or less by the marks he gets in college. He is in no position to improve that record unless he at least knows what it is.

There are, then, arguments both for and against the use of marks. They can easily become too important to everyone, but if they are assigned with discretion, treated with respect, and kept associated in everyone's mind with the person to whom they belong, they are both of great practical use and of real emotional value to students.

I. METHODS OF ASSIGNING MARKS

The assignment of marks is always a problem—no matter upon what kind of evidence they are based. Every teacher has his own standard; so does every department. The distribution of grades is influenced by many other considerations than the achievement of the students. Much of the data in this chapter will deal with the situation as it exists rather than with solutions for it—the latter being decidedly scarce and still in the experimental stage.

One method of assigning marks is to use the "normal curve" as a basis. According to this criterion a teacher should distribute his grades so that 5 per cent of his students get A, 12.5 per cent B, 65 per cent C, 12.5 per cent D, and 5 per cent E.[4] This arrangement reflects the normal distribution of human abilities. For most classes, however, its use is questionable. In the first place, at least the lowest third of the total distribution of abilities—if not the lowest half—never comes to college. One is always dealing with a group from which the lower end is missing. In the second place,

[4] The exact per cents vary from one plan to another, depending on just where one puts the dividing lines in the normal curve. The important thing is not the exact per cents but the fact that they are rigidly determined in advance.

even the most ardent defenders of this technique admit there must be a large number of students in a class or the selective factors will make application of the principle impossible. Thus, a class of twenty students in Chaucer is so small and so selected that the marks may turn out to have any distribution from all A's to all C's and D's. Groups of upperclassmen—even though large— rarely arrange themselves "normally," because all of them are survivors of many previous eliminations; all are therefore at the top of the normal curve, and any effort to redistribute them in accordance with it is an injustice. This principle is, then, of little use except in large freshman courses and is of questionable service there. Although the marks from such a class may sometimes fall into a normal distribution, any attempt to force them into it on principle is likely to produce a distortion of the facts.[5]

The other system in vogue at present is to assign marks in terms of the class distribution, whatever it may turn out to be and without any reference to outside standards. Suppose, for instance, that a group of students had made the following scores on a test:

TABLE 30

Three Possible Values of the Same Test Scores in Terms of Grades

Scores of Tests	First Plan	Second Plan	Third Plan
80–84	1 ⎫	1 ⎫	1 ⎫
75–79	2 ⎬ A	2 ⎬ A	2 ⎬ A
70–74	1 ⎭	1 ⎭	1 ⎭
65–69	3 ⎫ B	3 ⎫ B	3 ⎫
60–64	2 ⎭	2 ⎭	2 ⎪
55–59	2 ⎫ C	2 ⎫	2 ⎪
50–54	3 ⎬	3 ⎭	3 ⎬ B
45–49	1 ⎭	1 ⎫ C	1 ⎪
40–44	2 ⎫ D	2 ⎪	2 ⎭
35–39	1 ⎭	1 ⎭	1 ⎫
30–34			⎬ C
25–29	1 ⎫ E	1 ⎫ D	1 ⎪
20–24	1 ⎭	1 ⎭	1 ⎭

The teacher might distribute the grades in either of the three ways indicated. In one case the instructor located the two ends of the distribution at A and E, in the second case at A and D, and in

---

[5] As shown by S. M. Corey, "Use of the Normal Curve as a Basis for Assigning Grades in Small Classes," *School and Society*, 31 : 514–16, 1930.

the third at A and C. In each instance the distribution is divided evenly into whatever number of parts is indicated by the marks assigned at the two extremes. The number of grades at each level differs accordingly. The decision as to where the limits are always rests with the particular teacher involved; her only guide—if it is one—is to turn the scores into per cents and then decide what range of per cents equals what letter grade.

When this same system is applied to classes in successive years one is likely to discover such variations as are shown in Table 31.

TABLE 31

Scores from Four Classes in the Same Subject during Four Different Years

Score	1926–27	1927–28	1928–29	1929–30
400			1 } A	
390			(A)	
380			2	
370	1 } A		2	
360	2	(A)		4 } B	
350	3	2 } A	6	
340		5	9	
330	1 } B	2	4 } C	
320	6	7 } B	7	
310	8	4	2	
300	4	8	6	
290	7 } C	9	1 } D	
280	7	3		4 } A
270	1	1 } C		6
260	4	1		10
250	} D		1 } E	8 } B
240	3			10
230		1 } D		3
220				
210	1 } E			1 } C
200	1			
190		} E		2
180		1		
170				1 } D
160				
150				1
140				} E
130				1
TOTAL.....	49	44	45	47
MEDIAN....	301	309	342	266
RANGE....	208–371	185–352	255–401	132–296

Over the entire four years here presented the total range of scores was from 408 to 136 points—or 272—but in any one year it was not more than 167—or slightly more than half the actual variation among students. If a teacher assigns grades in terms of

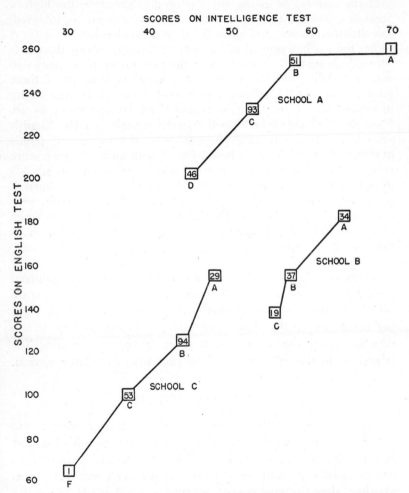

Fig. 35.—The Relationship between Marks and Both Intelligence and English Scores in Three Schools in the Same State.

Learned and Wood, *op. cit.*, p. 170. Used by permission of the Carnegie Foundation for the Advancement of Teaching.

a single distribution only, he will certainly vary his standards greatly from year to year. The mark any given student receives is quite as much influenced by the competition he happens to meet as by his actual achievement.

If the method of giving the top of a distribution the highest possible grade and the bottom the lowest possible one is followed, the situation shown in Figure 35 is sure to develop. This chart shows the marks assigned in English by the teachers of three different high schools. It shows also the relation of these marks to both the ability and the achievement scores in English of these same pupils. The "A" students in School A had an average rating in intelligence of 70; those in School C an average rating of 48. Even the "D" pupils in School A were superior on the English achievement test, with an average score of 205, to the "A" pupils in either of the other two schools. Pupils with an intelligence score between 50 and 60 and an English test score of about 150 got A's in School C and B's in School B. The same level of intelligence, associated with a considerably higher level of achievement, produced only C's in School A. The habit of marking within the limits of a particular class distribution inevitably results in such situations as those shown above.

There is no good system for assigning grades. The standard is artificial if one uses the normal curve; it is not sufficiently related to the abilities of modern students if one uses rigid per cents; and it fluctuates violently from year to year if one depends upon the class distribution. Some suggestions for adjusting to this situation will be presented in a later section.

II. THE PRESENT SITUATION

Investigations of the actual results of marking systems are numerous and varied, but all of them give roughly similar results. A few typical studies will be summarized. From them one can easily see that an A from one teacher equals a C from another, that the chances of getting a good mark are twice as good in some courses as in others of the same level, and that the grades from some departments represent better work than identical grades from others.

One relatively simple statement of the facts is shown by the per cent of A's given by various instructors.[6] The table below tells what per cent of teachers in one institution gave what per cent of A's. No conceivable difference in the groups of students taking

Per Cent of Teachers	Per Cent of A's
7	Less than 10
30	10–19
24	20–29
17	30–39
7	40–49
12	50–59
3	60–86

different courses could explain the variations here revealed. Nor is all this variation due to differences of standards between departments, since within the same department one teacher gave 77 per cent A's and another none at all.

A second investigator [7] presents similar but somewhat more detailed data. He found the per cent of passing grades and the average grade for twelve departments enrolling freshmen. The three most lenient departments passed 95, 92, and 86 per cent of their freshmen with average grades of 81, 76, and 75 respectively; the three strictest departments showed corresponding figures of 78, 68, and 63 per cent passing and grade averages of 71, 70, and 68. Since the same students were involved, it is evident that some teachers required more than others in order to assign the same grade.

A third investigator [8] studied the consistency of marks from one semester to another within the same departments. All the entering freshmen who remained for six semesters were included in the study. The marks they received in the first, third, and fifth semesters were correlated by departments with those received in the second, fourth, and sixth. If teachers tend to assign similar grades in successive years, these correlations should be fairly

---

[6] E. Hudelson, *Problems of College Education,* University of Minnesota Press, 1928, 449 pp. Used by permission of the University of Minnesota Press.

[7] A. B. Crawford, "Rubber Micrometers," *School and Society,* 32: 233–40, 1930.

[8] H. R. Taylor and C. L. Constance, "How Reliable Are College Marks?" in *Research in Higher Education,* Department of the Interior, *Bulletin,* No. 12, 1932, pp. 5–14. For a recent dissenting report, see J. B. Shouse, "Teachers' Grades Mean Something," *Journal of Educational Psychology,* 30: 510–18, 1939.

high. Actually they varied from .56 to .90. In some departments, at least, the marking was not consistent from year to year.

Finally, there are various studies in which the investigators [9] used the average performance of students upon tests, or in their freshman courses, or both, as a criterion of what should be expected of them, and then compared various courses and teachers with this criterion to see what differences there were. A few of these comparisons from the first study appear below: [9a]

Name of Course	Median Grade	Average of Intelligence and English Placement Tests	Amount of Error
Latin X............	81.5	73.4	9.1
Mathematics X......	80.5	74.6	5.9
German Y..........	74.1	73.1	1.0
French Y..........	71.4	74.3	−2.9
Latin Y............	66.0	76.9	−10.9
Latin Z............	65.0	77.2	−12.2

In the first three cases the average grade in per cents exceeded the average expectation expressed in percentile standing; in the last three the average mark was less than the expectation. Regardless of what one may think of the bases here used for determining the probable success of students, there seems no good reason why in one course (Latin Z) well-prepared and intelligent students should get an average grade 16.5 points lower (81.5 minus 65.0) than less intelligent and less well-prepared students got in another course (Latin X).

In the last study to be presented there is a comparison of individual teachers. The grades given by each instructor were first compared with the average marks received by the same students in all their other courses combined. Then the excess or deficiency of points assigned by each teacher above or below this average

[9] R. S. Ellis, "The Correction of Constant Errors in College Marks," *School and Society,* 24: 432–36, 1926; and F. W. Reeves and J. D. Russell, *Instructional Problems in the University,* University of Chicago Press, 1933, 245 pp. See also J. E. Bohan, *Students' Marks in College Courses,* University of Minnesota Press, 1931, 133 pp., and I. J. Lubbers, "College Organization and Administration," *Northwestern University Contributions to Education, School of Education Series,* No. 7, 1932, 155 pp.
[9a] Ellis, *op. cit.* Used by permission of *School and Society* and the author.

was calculated and expressed as an index number. A few of these are quoted below: [10]

Instructor	Number of Students	Index of Grading
Lower Division Courses		
A	9	1.79
B	21	1.58
I	37	1.12
P	21	.96
X	6	.80
Y	105	.79
Z	25	.78
Upper Division Courses		
H	30	1.25
AC	17	1.03
U	18	.88
AF	69	.80
AG	34	.70

Thus, Teacher A gave marks that averaged 79 points higher than the average mark received by his students in all their other courses. In short, he was an easy grader. Teacher Z, who gave marks that averaged 22 points below the average of his students in their other work, was a hard marker. In this case also it is clear that the grade a student receives depends quite as much upon who marks him as upon what kind of work he does.

One might think that the situation would be better in a small college in which the faculty members have a more favorable opportunity for knowing and understanding each other's points of view. In some cases this is probably true, but a small number of teachers and students will not, in and of itself, produce uniform marks. In one careful investigation in a college [11] with an enrollment of 660 and a faculty of 65 members the marking was just as lacking in uniformity as in the large universities. Thus of two teachers, both of whom had students whose previous marks and intelligence scores were the same, one gave grades averaging B+ and the other C–. It seems, however, quite possible that the teachers in a small college could by an informal exchange of ideas come closer to each other than they ordinarily do when they are

[10] Reeves and Russell, *op. cit.* Used by permission of the University of Chicago Press.
[11] R. W. Ogan, "The Appraisal of Grading Practices," in *A College Looks at Its Program,* pp. 255–66.

not aware of the problem in more than a general way. The environment should permit a *rapprochement,* even though it will not function automatically.

From all of this evidence the conclusion is inescapable that the same mark does not mean the same level of accomplishment from one teacher to another or from one department to another. Presumably, if grades are supposed to mean anything at all, they should represent roughly the same degree of excellence in all cases. Everyone is familiar with the "cinch" course, in which no one gets less than a C and with the "tough" course in which no student has had an A for the last ten years. Sometimes two such courses are in the same department and are taken by the same students. It is simply not possible that so much variation could be a true reflection of any real difference in achievement. Although some of the variation can be explained on the basis of differences in the selection of students for different courses, not all of it can. The fact of glaring inequalities in the marking system—or lack of it— remains.

III. SUGGESTED SOLUTIONS

Thus far there appear to be only two solutions for the situation. Both are based on the assumption that nothing can be done to bring about any real unanimity among professors as to what constitutes work of a given level. In large colleges and universities this conclusion is probably well grounded, although in smaller places the permanent members of the staff often develop a fairly uniform standard. Both solutions therefore leave the actual assignment of grades to a central office. In one case [12] the teacher merely lists his students in order from the best to the poorest. An administrative officer then performs some statistical feats and assigns the grades upon the basis of each student's intellectual level, his previous record, and his work in other courses. That is, the teacher gives his judgment as to relative excellence, but he does not decide

---

[12] R. B. Spence, "The Improvement of College Marking Systems," *School and Society,* 28: 224–27, 1928; C. C. Nicol, "The Ranking System," *Journal of Higher Education,* 3: 21–25, 1932.

where the A's stop and the B's begin. A single person who has all available information about the students, the teachers, and the courses, is responsible for keeping the marking uniform.

The other system is in essence of a somewhat similar character,[13] but more extensive. The administration first determines to what extent and in what direction each individual teacher varies from the average of those who assign grades to the same students. Each teacher then turns in his grades as he sees fit, but the central office corrects them in terms of the known deviation. Since the actual marks are assigned each semester by the teacher, the person in charge of equalizing the grading can—and presumably would—determine each semester what the deviation was at the moment. Naturally, teachers are sure to alter their procedures when they find that their marks are either too high or too low. This method necessitates constant research and checking, but with care it could be made to work. Thus a teacher might turn in a list of forty names with A's after twenty-nine of them, but twenty-nine students would not receive A's because the exact amount of leniency on the part of this particular instructor would be known and the equalizer would reduce the number by putting the dividing line closer to the top of the list—the position depending upon the data assembled about both students and teacher.

In the small college already referred to [14] the procedure was much the same except that it was less formal and the final step of actually correcting grades was not taken. Each professor was informed of his variations from the marks given by other teachers to the same students and to other students of the same intelligence and previous academic record. Other elements, such as the amount of time students said they spent upon their assignments and their degree of interest in the course, were also presented. Everyone had a chance to talk over his results with others and with the director of the research. The results soon showed that with adequate informa-

[13] Reeves and Russell, *op. cit.*
[14] See Ogan, *op. cit.*

tion and understanding the teachers voluntarily compiled their marks with more care and tried to approximate the standard for the faculty as a whole. This informal method is naturally desirable wherever the group is not too large for a free interchange of ideas and attitudes.

It goes without saying that many teachers are sure to resent such an interference with what they regard as a prerogative. I am not at all certain, however, but what such an arrangement as that just described would be a good thing. If a professor gives up his right to mark his students as he wants, he at least gets in return protection from the competition of those teachers who build up enrollment by permitting low standards. The snap course would at once disappear, with a resulting lessening of tension among faculty members. In the course of time such a system of grading would probably result in a much more uniform standard of marking than is now possible. Each teacher would want to know to what extent his grades had to be corrected and would presumably raise or lower his standards accordingly. The variations should therefore become less than they are on any campus at present. Those who were willing to conform to the level of their colleagues would suffer no unpleasant results because their grades would need little if any correction. Those who were totally unwilling to conform would have their marks corrected for them. The rugged individualist could still assign grades to suit himself, but he could not actually give an A student a C or an E student a B, because the equalizer would not let him.

One other worth-while suggestion of an entirely different type has been made.[15] The usual principle in planning classwork is to keep constant the amount of time students are to spend in a course and to let their performance vary. It would be possible to demand a single level of achievement from all and to let the time vary. A preliminary study to test the feasibility of this change has already been made. In this case students were allowed to repeat

[15] S. L. Pressey and L. W. Pressey, "Experimenting with the Examination," *Journal of Higher Education,* 1 : 396–98, 1930. Still another suggestion is made by W. D. Ellis, "Grade Versus Credit," *School and Society,* 51 : 59–61, 1940.

work as often as they wanted until they received whatever grade satisfied them. Although the experiment was not carried to its logical conclusion, it did show that such an arrangement would produce a bimodal distribution of grades. At one end there would be a great majority of A's—some of them achieved in one semester and some in several—and at the other end a small number of E's obtained by those who were unwilling to complete the work at the required level. In other words, the "ideal" distribution [16] under this system would consist of practically all A's, no differentiation being made as to how long a given student needed to reach this level of attainment. In passing it may be said that anyone contemplating such a method would do well to start by proselyting the registrar; otherwise the red tape ties itself into knots that defy unraveling.

IV. SUMMARY

Marks are valuable on two grounds : college students want to know what kind of work they are doing, and they need an objective record for various practical purposes. The marks given to students have a high degree of unreliability, which comes partly from a lack of any uniform standard and partly from the tendency of teachers to assign grades within the limits of whatever distribution a single class happens to show. The outstanding suggestion to date for remedying this situation is to correct each teacher's constant error before issuing grades to students.

[16] For further discussion of this idea see S. L. Pressey, "Fundamental Misconceptions Involved in Current Marking Systems," *School and Society*, 24: 736–38, 1925.

IV.

THE SOCIAL AND ECONOMIC ASPECTS

CHAPTER XXI

COLLEGE OR UNIVERSITY ORGANIZATION

There is more to the job of being a college professor than merely going to class and teaching. In fact the average teacher in a university spends only 44.4 per cent of his total working time in activities directly connected with teaching.[1] This proportion is probably greater in small colleges, but in no place is a teacher's work restricted exclusively to instructional activities. Nor are his social or professional contacts restricted to his relations with students. Although a college teacher's first loyalties are to his subject and his students, he has more or less direct concern with his department, his colleagues on the faculty, and the administration. As long as a college remains small, these contacts are informal and easy to maintain because everyone knows everyone else, but in a large institution the single problem of getting merely acquainted with all one's colleagues presents almost insuperable difficulties. In general, the larger an institution, the more complex is its machinery, but any college has some degree of organization to which teachers must adjust themselves.

I. DEPARTMENTAL DIVISIONS

The division of a faculty into departments is almost universal. Indeed, there is undoubtedly more such division than is

[1] F. W. Reeves, *et al., The University Faculty,* University of Chicago Press, 1933, 326 pp.

485

either necessary or desirable. I knew, for instance, one university in which there were three departments of English in three different colleges upon the same campus. Another university had a department of psychology, one of educational psychology, and one of education. Another had a department of geography in the Arts College, one of commercial geography in the College of Commerce, and a third of agricultural geography in the College of Agriculture. The sub-divisions within the science of chemistry are numerous; I know a university in which there are eight. Even though there is often more complete and rigid departmentalization than is essential, some degree is evidently useful or the practice would not be so universal.

There are numerous matters of departmental interest that engage the time and attention of teachers—the schedule of classes, the adoption of new courses, the consideration of any fundamental course that is prerequisite to those taught by several different people, the interchange of ideas about both subject matter and students, the standards of marking, the approval of schedules for major students, the yearly budget, the recommendations for promotion, the selection of new members, the assignment of assistants, and so on. Naturally, no one person has to manage these details, but all of them have to be considered if a department is to develop. A division of labor in terms of personal abilities and preferences is commonly made. Thus some teachers are more successful than others in advising students and therefore do most of this work; others are objective and unprejudiced about the distribution of available funds and are consequently given charge of such details. In any department which consists of a half-dozen or more people there are some departmental chores for all to do; if the work can be distributed so that each person does what he is best fitted for, so much the better. The actual amount of work is often not large if each person does his share, but it becomes a heavy burden when it must be carried by one or two people.

In most departments there is an appointed or elected head. In some places the headship is automatically handed around among the permanent staff; in others, the position is elective; in still others, the administration appoints someone each year, sometimes keeping the same person from year to year and sometimes making changes. All of these arrangements have their drawbacks and their advantages. If a different person becomes chairman each year there is little continuity, either in details or in policy; no one is responsible for a long enough time to devote himself in earnest to the development of the department. A permanent chairman, however, is always potentially a menace to peace, even though at a given moment everything is harmonious. Sooner or later most permanent chairmen become possessive about their position and resentful about turning it over to another person. If the head is appointed by the administration, another type of difficulty arises. Wholly aside from the opportunity given by this arrangement for an administrator to further the career of some favorite, any official is almost sure to appoint a person who will keep the red tape unrolling smoothly, regardless of other qualities. Under this system the natural leader within a group rarely becomes chairman. He is so busy doing other things he regards as more important than managing the mechanics of administration that he does not attend to business. Probably the best method is the election of a head by the members of the department. They all know each other and are in a better position than anyone else to select the right person for chairman; they know also when it is time to change leaders.

The emotional atmosphere within a department may vary all the way from open hostility to brotherly love. I have known departments in which there were two or three cliques so antagonistic to each other that an outsider had to be brought in as head; and I have known others in which all members of the group were completely congenial. On every campus there is at least one department that is dominated by a single outstanding person who keeps himself surrounded by satellites and will not permit the appointment of anyone who might detract from his own brilliance. I knew one such department that was composed of one full professor, one instructor who had been in residence for years without advancement, and eleven assistants! The problems of adjustment within any given department vary with the size, the personalities involved, the extent of domination by a single person, and the position of the group in the minds of other similar groups. In any case, there is always the problem of fitting oneself into this social and professional milieu with as little friction as possible.

Relations within one's department are sometimes tranquil enough while those with other departments are not. The typical organization of a college easily leads to jealousy and rivalry between departments because in the last analysis teachers are dependent upon enrollments for keeping their positions. This situation is especially likely to develop when two or more departments of widely different standards are included within a single "group" of subjects, one of which must be taken by every student regardless of interest. Under these circumstances the department with the lowest standard may get the enrollment and grow apace—to the great discomfiture of the others. Antagonisms and rivalries between departments develop partly as a result of such external factors and partly because of personal animosities. This condition is all the more undesirable when it involves two departments that should be allied because of their common interests. Correlative fields are, however, often fatal to cooperation. Thus, for instance, the psychologist may be violently opposed to the educationalist, or the botanist to the zoologist, or the chemist to the physicist, or the professor of European to the professor of American history. In all these cases the people involved use some of the same data and have therefore more to argue about than if their subject matter were wholly discrete. For the student such antagonisms are a constant source of trouble in a practical way and a threat to the growth of his own tolerance. Departments as groups pass on their characteristic attitudes and points of view to their major students at least, thus breeding in the next generation either more intolerance and misunderstanding or greater friendship and alliance, as the case may be.

In recent years there has been some effort to lessen the sharpness of cleavage between departments. The college student is understandably bewildered when he is faced with a catalogue containing some four hundred courses listed under thirty-five to fifty departments with innumerable cross-referencing, plus a complex system of "group electives" and requirements. He cannot possibly get adequate information about the nature of so many courses; as a result he often fails to take the work he would like best. It is no wonder that students cannot read a catalogue to good effect. I have known several institutions in which the faculty members could not grasp the essential facts in the catalogue with much more success. In one university, where an unusually large enrollment was expected for summer school, several professors were asked to help the regular staff in approving schedules. At the end of the first day all of them were asked not to "help" any more; they had made so many mistakes that the permanent advisory staff had more rather than less work to do. Since the mechanics of getting an education have become overcomplicated there has arisen a movement to simplify the course offerings [2] until they are intelligible to someone except the secretary of each college. One result of this movement has been the breaking down of the watertight divisions between departments.

Wholly aside from practical inconveniences, rigid departmentalization tends to break up knowledge into little pieces, thus preventing a student from ever getting exactly the main ideas and insights that he is supposed to derive from a general education. The piecemeal effect is enhanced if courses within a department are multiplied unduly—as is sometimes the case. I know one catalogue that lists the following courses: "The Infant," "The Preschool Child," "The Nursery School Child," "The Elementary School Child," "The Adolescent," "The Junior High School Pupil," "The High School Pupil," "The Defective Child," "The Brilliant Child," "The Handicapped Child," "The Normal Child," and "The Unstable Child." Just how any student could get a clear idea of normal growth from birth to maturity from such an array of courses I do not know.

[2] In one instance a university catalogue was so revised by a faculty committeee that 377 courses were permanently dropped, 69 given only in alternate years, and 30 offered fewer times per year. See G. W. Eckelberry, "Faculty Control of Courses," *Journal of Higher Education,* 7 : 141–46, 1937.

He would have to take and synthesize at least five in order to obtain an overview—and most students take only one or two courses in a department. Such extreme specialization has probably done more to create the recent interest in generalized courses than the mere inconvenience of the situation.

For the first two years many colleges now require "survey" courses, the object of which is to provide students with a general background of information and general points of view in a number of fields before they begin to specialize. Four such courses are becoming increasingly common: one each in the social sciences, the physical sciences, the biological sciences, and literature. It is the purpose of these classes to give an overview of the field in question. An incidental result is the breaking down of departmental lines.[3] In some colleges it is possible for students to continue such a synthesis by majoring in a combination of departments. Perhaps the movement will go to extremes before it becomes an accepted thing, but eventually there should develop a better relationship between general and special education than has existed in the past two decades, during which the tendency has all been in favor of extreme specialization without adequate general background. A natural correlation to this development has been an over-emphasis upon departmental importance.

Another influence that is operating to reduce the sharp delineation between departments is the present tendency to make a definite stopping place after the first two years of college. This movement is reflected in the number of junior colleges; there were only 46 in 1917, but there were 428 in

[3] A few sample courses that are joint undertakings of two or more departments are listed below:

Name of Course	Institution
Consumers' Education	Stephens College
Nature of the Living World	Pennsylvania State College
Biological Survey	Oberlin College
Contemporary Society	Reed College
Books	Ripon College
Energy and Life	Mills College
College Aims	Antioch College
Introduction to Social Science	Albion College
Survey of the Humanities	Judson College
Introduction to Natural Science	University of Omaha
Christian Service	Whittier College

1938.[4] Even four-year colleges often give a junior certificate at the end of the first two years and require a reasonably good scholastic record for entrance to the senior college. This change, like so many others, is due primarily to the changes in the nature of the student population. The freshman and sophomore years are thought of as forming a unit with the four years of high school; real college and university work starts beyond that point. Specialization is therefore postponed until the students have had time to mature and to be selected more carefully than they are at entrance. This horizontal division is superimposed upon the vertical division by departments and has had its influence in obliterating sharp departmental lines.[5]

A young instructor has to adjust himself to the demands made by his department and to the relationship between his group and others upon the campus. The exact nature of the adjustment depends upon the local situation, but in all cases he should do his best to promote both the development of his own field and a cordial relationship with those to which it is most naturally allied.

II. COLLEGE AND UNIVERSITY ADMINISTRATION

The number of administrative officials necessary for running an institution of higher education is at least three—the president, the dean, and the business manager.[6] In large colleges and universities there are several other persons—vice-

---

[4] *Biennial Survey of Education,* 1938–39, Part III, United States Department of the Interior, *Office of Education Bulletin,* No. 1, 1939.

[5] See R. L. Kelly and R. E. Anderson, "The Extent of the Divisional Development of the Curriculum," *Association of American Colleges Bulletin,* 19: 418–24, 1933.

[6] For good discussions of typical administrative organizations in higher education see I. J. Lubbers, "College Organization and Administration," *Northwestern University Contributions to Education,* No. 7, 1932, 155 pp.; J. S. Kinder, "The Internal Administration of the Liberal Arts College," *Teachers College Contributions to Education,* No. 597, 1934, 160 pp.; E. J. McGrath, "The Control of Higher Education in America," *Educational Record,* 17: 259–72, 1936; E. E. Lindsay and E. O. Holland, *College and University Administration,* The Macmillan Company, 1930, 666 pp.; J. D. Russell and F. W. Reeves, "Administration," *Evaluation of Higher Education,* Vol. VI, University of Chicago Press, 1936, 285 pp.

presidents, college secretaries, the registrar, the bursar, deans of women or of men, deans for the separate colleges, an admissions officer, health officials, a director of publicity, an alumni secretary, the head of a placement bureau, plus numerous advisors.[7] The total amount of administrative machinery is often appalling to the uninitiated. The details of organization vary from place to place because, within any given college, they are the result quite as much of historical accident as of intention. Both the names and the duties of the officials vary, and the relation of teachers to the existing officials is often not well defined.

The nature of administrative machinery is clearer when viewed from a diagram than when expressed in words. I am therefore presenting a comprehensive scheme of university organization.[8] In any one institution some of the officials mentioned in Figure 36 are almost certain to be missing, but most of the functions here indicated are performed by someone.

At the head of the college or university administration is the board of trustees. The members are often elected by the board itself, sometimes by the alumni, and sometimes by people who have a vested interest in the institution. In some cases the boards are wholly self-perpetuating. For the most part the activities of the trustees are centered upon financial matters and care of the physical plant. Trustees do not usually interfere with the work of the college teacher or concern themselves in any detailed way with what goes on in the classroom. In fact, most teachers carry on their business year after year without more than a general awareness that the trustees exist. In most instances the board acts favorably upon recommendations of the faculty, in so far as new appointments or salary increases are concerned, unless the suggestions made are beyond the possibilities of the existing budget.

The main interests of the board of trustees may be inferred from the nature of its standing committees. Of these, three are

[7] The number of such officials has increased greatly as colleges have grown. Thus Harvard, which originally had three administrators, now has more than two hundred.
[8] From Lubbers, *op. cit.*

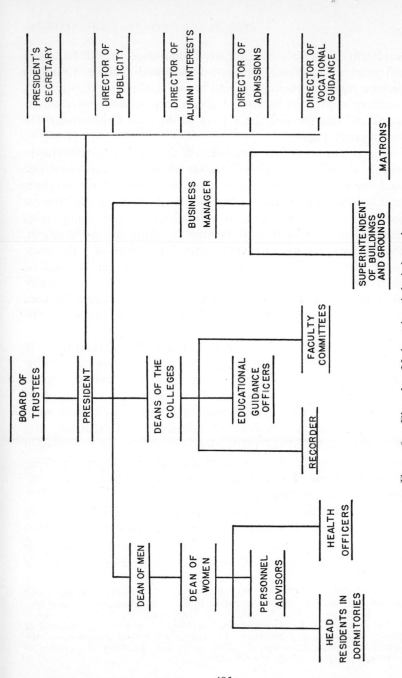

FIG. 36.—Plan for University Administration.

Lubbers, *op. cit.* Used by permission of Northwestern University Press and the author.

practically universal—an executive committee, one on buildings and grounds, and one on investments and finance. Common also are committees on gifts and bequests, the budget, auditing, honorary degrees, educational policy, and nominations to the board. All but the last three have to do with either money or the physical plant.

The extent to which members of the faculty participate in college or university administration differs greatly from one place to another. There are practically certain to be some faculty committees that are concerned with administrative matters. In a few colleges, of which Oberlin is a conspicuous example, the teaching staff is also in effect the government. Even in large institutions, such as the University of California, the faculty may have the main control of the budget and of educational policy.[9] In general, however, while the faculty takes the initiative in such matters as are of direct concern to teachers or students, the final decisions are made by the board of trustees.

Sooner or later almost all college teachers are asked to serve upon a committee, the work of which will contribute in some way to administrative procedures. It is therefore advisable for any teacher to know how his institution is organized. It is also essential that when a teacher is put upon such a committee he should do his work so objectively and faithfully that the best interests of the institution may be served. One should forget departmental loyalties and abstain from campus politics during his term of office; otherwise he is likely to defeat the purpose of the committee.

In the majority of colleges the relationship between teachers and administrators is amicable, although often somewhat distant. Each group has its own work to do, and each accords the other both respect and support. When friction arises, it

[9] See also E. Y. Blewett, "A New Type of Faculty Organization," *Journal of Higher Education,* 9: 201–6, 1938; A. G. Ruthven, "Administration at Michigan: A Plan by Which the Members of the Faculty Receive a Larger Measure of Self-Government, but More Responsibility," *Journal of Higher Education,* 2: 7–10, 1931; O. Tead, "Place and Functions of the Faculty in College Government," *Bulletin of the American Association of University Professors,* 25: 163–68, 1939.

is usually because teachers and administrators have different points of view.

For instance, I have taught in two institutions in which no teacher of any rank whatever could get his last pay check for a given semester until he had a "clearance slip" from the registrar's office that his grades were turned in. Many members of the faculty resented this arrangement as an insult to their dignity. The point was that some teachers, during previous years, had been altogether too free with their prerogatives and had left for parts unknown without first handing in their marks. As a result, certain seniors had either been unable to graduate or had done so only after complicated adjustments. In a college in which such a rule was not in force a certain professor left for a year's leave of absence; after his departure the maid who cleaned his room found his grade book in the wastebasket. She gave it to another teacher in the same building who eventually handed it along to the head of the missing professor's department. The chairman, however, could make nothing whatever out of such entries as the book contained. For a week the department kept the telegraph wires humming, but to no avail. In the end it was decided to give each student a mark that corresponded with the average for all his other courses. Such episodes as this give rise to friction between teachers and administrators. The registrar wants a grade for each student within three days of the final examination simply because he has so many marks to record that he cannot afford to waste time. On almost every college faculty there is at least one person who persistently hands in grades from a week to a month after the end of the course. These people do a good deal to damage cordial relations between administrators and the instructional staff.

III. THE BUSINESS OF THE COLLEGE FACULTY

In any college certain matters are of immediate concern to faculty members. Especially important are problems of instruction and of student welfare. Most of the business of a faculty has to do with one or the other of these points. The casual observer attending a faculty meeting for the first time would not get more than a glimpse into the large volume of business that is done each year or into the vast amount of work involved. The usual technique for carrying on affairs is the appointment of standing committees. If membership on these groups has been passed around with a fair degree of evenness practically every member is on at least one such committee.

The best and quickest way to get an overview of the business done by a college faculty is to consider the nature of these standing committees. The number naturally varies with the size of the institution. In a small college a single committee is responsible for several matters, while in a larger place each topic is referred to a separate group. All the points get attention sooner or later, however. The standing committees fall naturally into five main classifications—those dealing with teaching, student welfare, general college service, teaching personnel, and administration.

In the first group come the committees responsible for the following matters: the curriculum, catalogue, schedule of classes, calendar, and teaching methods; admissions, entrance examinations, relations with high schools, registration, transfers, and advanced standing; individual work, scholarships, honors, and prizes; requirements for degrees; and the library. All of these are directly or indirectly connected with instruction. The three commonest and most important are the curriculum, admission, and library committees. These are practically universal.

In the second group come the even more numerous committees that deal with some phase of student welfare. The following matters are all included although there is not always a separate committee for each: student affairs, student housing, student publications, student health, student discipline, supervision of student clubs and organizations, student religious life, athletics, debating, fraternities and sororities, student employment, student loans, and auditing of student accounts. In almost every college one finds at least four of the above committees—those concerned with student affairs, athletics, publications, and student aid. Generally the faculty group works with undergraduate representatives, who are elected through the student government. Whatever the details of the arrangement, these various phases of welfare are the business of the faculty.

In the third group come the committees on college publications, public lectures, convocation or chapel, commencement, alumni, community relations, and educational conferences. These matters concern the welfare and development of the college as a whole and its service to and relations with people off the campus.

The fourth group of committees is concerned with teaching personnel. Usually there are four topics to be considered—the appointment of new teachers, the promotion of teachers, leaves of absence, and faculty research. The last two committees are less frequent than the first two, which exist in almost any college and are extremely important.

Finally, there is a small group of committees having administrative or advisory functions. The faculty's own executive committee, for putting through routine business and keeping the red tape in order, and the budget committee—if there is one—are both administrative. The advisory committee and the committee on committees [10] are extremely important groups. One or the other or both can dominate college developments more completely than any other subdivision of the faculty. In a large university the real power is often vested in the committee on committees, because its members select the personnel of all the other groups. If it wishes to it can assign the adherents of a single small clique to so many offices that the faculty in general has little opportunity to control its own destiny. In addition to the above groups there is sometimes a committee on rules and another on educational policy. In both cases the work is primarily advisory.

From this account it is clear that a college faculty has many things on its collective mind and many duties for the adequate performance of which it is responsible. It may seem to the uninitiated as if there could be no need for so many committees. Actually, however, if a single group neglects its work, something goes wrong and complaints arise. The outsider does not see all this machinery and sometimes thinks college teachers have no burdens except their classes. At least a fifth of a college professor's time and often nearer a third [11] of it is spent upon committee work of some kind.

The instructional staff meets at stated intervals to consider its problems. The usual arrangement in colleges is a biweekly meet-

[10] These two are sometimes synonymous, but in a few institutions both exist.
[11] See pages 501-3.

ing [12] of the entire faculty; in universities the college faculties meet not oftener than once a month, while the university faculty—composed of the permanent staff—meets only at irregular intervals. The college faculty has typically two officers—the president and a secretary who keeps the minutes. In small colleges there is no senate; anyone belonging to the staff may vote. In universities a senate to which only those of professional rank belong commonly decides many matters without the vote of the whole group. This smaller legislative body becomes in effect an oligarchy. In general, the larger an institution is, the less does the faculty have to say about its management.

One other function of the college faculty should be noted. Somewhat irregularly most groups of teachers meet to discuss new methods of instruction or to exchange ideas on other matters related to classwork. Once in a while the staff makes a self-survey of some kind. These meetings are eminently worth while, not only because of their actual content but also because they furnish the best opportunity for a young person to find out how successful college professors work. In most institutions there is relatively little chance for teachers to visit each other's classes. Informal conversations between teachers naturally take place constantly but are often not very illuminating as to teaching procedures because the occasion is too incidental and the opinions expressed are too offhand. When a professor is asked to tell the entire group of his colleagues how he deals with certain recurrent classroom problems, he prepares a careful and balanced answer. Such meetings of the faculty are consequently of great value and help materially in disseminating every teacher's bright ideas as widely as possible.

The faculty's main business has to do with teaching, in all its ramifications, and with the welfare of students. Most teachers have enough of the missionary in them to put their own welfare in third place. Although there are sundry other duties that devolve upon somebody, these three matters constitute the vital business of a college faculty.[13]

[12] Most of the facts in this paragraph come from Lubbers, *op. cit.*
[13] For a good discussion of the contribution of faculties, see, W. M. Hepburn, "The Reconstruction of Higher Education: The Faculty's Part," *Bulletin of the American Association of University Professors,* 25: 169–81, 1939.

IV. SUMMARY

A college or university has to be run along business lines, and there has to be a division of labor among the various people and groups concerned. The trustees and the president usually control all matters pertaining to finance and development of the physical plant; they also contribute more or less to educational policy. The faculty initiates and to a considerable extent controls all matters concerned with teaching. Through its numerous standing committees it keeps contact with student groups, with administrators, and with its own subdivisions. It also contributes largely to educational policy. Between the faculty and the trustees, between the faculty and the students, and between the faculties of separate colleges within a university there are liaison officers—the president, the deans of men or of women, the personnel officers, and the college deans. Trustees, the administration, and the faculty participate to various degrees in anything that concerns the institution as a whole. Many matters, however are of interest only to those teachers who are within a single department. For convenience and greater speed of adjustment each department usually has almost complete autonomy in its own affairs.

There are, of course, innumerable minor variations on this general plan of government. Any college has some peculiarities that are mere historical accident and owe their existence to some dominating individual in an earlier period. The broad outlines can, however, be found behind any idiosyncrasies of this kind. A college teacher should develop a working knowledge of the machinery by which his institution is managed as soon as he can and should do his part in keeping the business of the college moving forward.

CHAPTER XXII

TEACHING LOAD, PROFESSIONAL ACTIVITIES, AND PROMOTION

As pointed out in the previous chapter, teachers do more than merely instruct students. The teacher's day includes, indeed, a considerable diversity of activities. In addition to whatever work there may be to do on the campus, a teacher is usually engaged upon some kind of research or publication. Aside from any practical values—such as faster promotion— to be gained from this additional work, he usually wants to do it because it offers him an escape from adolescent personalities and minds into the world of ideas. He is constantly intrigued by this or that problem that he wants to study further. If college teachers did not have this spontaneous interest in scholarship they would not enter the profession. There have been enough studies of how much time teachers spend and how they spend it to provide a good picture of probable developments in the life of the young person who intends to become a college professor.

I. THE TEACHER'S LOAD

Most of the larger universities and some of the colleges require each semester a report of work done by each faculty member. These "time sheets," as they are often called, are only estimates, but if one averages enough of them, the accidental errors disappear, and a reasonably accurate view of faculty activity emerges. That is, for everyone who over-estimates his time there is almost certain to be someone who makes an underestimate. In any case, the present question concerns merely the proportioning of time—not the amounts. The relative accuracy of these estimates when combined for a large group of teachers is shown by the fact that the figures change little from year to year. One summary of the time sheets for an entire faculty appears in Table 32.

Although teaching is the largest single item, it accounts—with home study—for only 44.4 per cent of the average teacher's time. The next largest item is research and writing. These two, plus departmental service and research, make up a total of 81.7 per cent of the teacher's working hours. General service, administration, and extramural activities nibble away an hour here and another there until the aggregate is nearly one-fifth of the total.

These figures are only averages. For individual faculty members the results may take almost any form. A few samples of the reported variations appear in the second set of figures in Table 32. The first person in the list did nothing but research and teaching, while the fifth one put in practically all his time in administration. One teacher was working under a subsidy during most of his hours at the university and was receiving compensation for extramural work. The last person listed reported 83 per cent of his time in either teaching or home study. In a small college a somewhat larger proportion of time is usually spent in activities connected with teaching, but almost everyone, except a brand-new instructor, can expect to have from 10 to 25 per cent of his working hours diverted from teaching into other activities.

There are a few reports on the actual number of hours in a college teacher's working day. One study [1] gives the average hours per day for activities directly connected with teaching as 5.8, with a range for individual teachers from 2 to 14. The total working time per day averaged 8.5 hours, with a range from 4 to 15. In short, college teaching is a full-time job. There is constant complaint on the part of professors that either the day is not long

[1] L. V. Koos, "The Adjustment of the Teaching Load in a University," *Office of Education Bulletin,* No. 15, 1919, 63 pp. See also C. S. Yoakum, "Functions of the Faculty: The Work Load," *University of Michigan Administration Studies,* Vol. 1, No. 2, 1932, 64 pp.

TABLE 32

How a College Faculty Spends Its Time[2]

Per Cent of Time Spent in Different Types of Service

Field of Study	Research without Compensation	Research under Subsidy	Teaching	Home Study	Departmental Service	General University Service	Administration	Extramural, with Compensation	Extramural, without Compensation
Humanities..........	23.1	2.3	48.2	4.6	6.3	4.2	2.7	3.7	4.9
Social Science......	19.1	1.2	40.3	5.0	7.2	4.7	9.1	5.4	8.0
Physical Science....	35.3	—	42.9	1.5	7.1	2.6	6.3	1.5	2.8
Biology............	28.7	1.1	32.3	0.8	25.6	2.2	4.3	3.2	1.8
Professional Schools	13.3	0.2	49.4	1.8	12.4	4.7	6.6	5.2	6.4
TOTAL.........	24.6	1.1	41.6	2.8	12.7	3.6	5.4	3.7	4.5

Individual Working Load, in Per Cents

Teacher	Research without Compensation	Research under Subsidy	Teaching	Home Study	Departmental Service	General University Service	Administration	Extramural, with Compensation	Extramural, without Compensation
A	60	—	40	—	—	—	—	—	—
E	15	—	60	12	10	3	—	—	—
F	5	—	60	—	10	3	22	—	—
N	—	60	27	—	1	—	—	—	13
P	1	—	—	—	5	3	90	—	5
Q	—	—	55	28	5	5	—	7	—

[2] F. W. Reeves et al., The University Faculty, University of Chicago Press, 1933, 326 pp., pp. 163 and 177. Used by permission of the University of Chicago Press.

enough or the tasks to be done are too numerous.[3] Especially do teachers find committee work and administrative duties burdensome. I have known faculty committees that met for as many as fifteen hours a week over a long period of time. During one year of particularly violent curricular changes, I was on exactly six university, three college, and two departmental committees, the aggregate of which came to something like twenty hours a week, and I knew at least three other people who were on fifteen or more such committees—all important and all time-consuming. Often the work of these groups is extremely interesting and valuable, but unfortunately there is rarely any reduction in teaching schedule to compensate for the hours demanded. One's teaching always suffers more or less as a result. Although these committees make inroads upon the time of faculty members, much of the work is of a type that only they can do. There is, for instance, the ever-present problem of the curriculum. If anyone outside a given department tries to alter the offerings by a hair's breadth there is a riot of protest. Even if a college calls in an expert who studies the situation in detail and makes recommendations concerning his results, the faculty must have its say before anything will be done—and professors take a lot of time to reach a conclusion. The faculty-committee method of procedure is admittedly wasteful—in fact, it sometimes seems as if it were democracy at its worst—but it is apparently the only procedure for getting done many of the things that need to be done if a college is to develop. The point is that those who are especially useful upon such committees should have a reduced teaching load during their terms of service.

The figures thus far presented have been rather general. One detailed report, based on an actual record of the hours spent by one teacher, seems well worth presenting. This teacher worked a total of 84.1 hours per week. Omitting Sunday—which she probably did not—this number works out to 14 hours a day. This investigator was a really conscientious teacher who spent enough time on her work outside of class hours to have something worth while to say during class. Moreover, she made a reasonable effort to maintain with her students the personal relationship that a

[3] See, for instance, C. F. McIntyre, "The Professor and the Side-Shows," *School and Society*, 32: 444–47, 1930; E. M. Michell, "The Need for Time Analysis of Instruction," *Journal of Higher Education*, 8: 311–14, 1937; and C. H. Titus, "The University Professor at Work," *School and Society*, 37: 672–75, 1933; W. H. Cowley, "The Professor's Numerous Functions," *School and Society*, 38: 88–89, 1933.

TABLE 33
Working Hours for One Teacher

	Hours	*Totals*
A. Work per week for each nonduplicating course		
1. Review material for presentation..........	1.0	
2. Plan presentation—illustrations, problems...	3.0	
3. Plan assignments and select readings........	2.0	
4. Devise brief biweekly tests (four hours per test twice each month).................	2.0	
5. Score tests................................	1.0	
6. Correct reports (30 in class, and about 500 words per paper).......................	1.5	
7. Hours spent in class......................	3.0	
SUBTOTAL—		13.5
B. Work for each duplicate course (includes items 4, 5, 6, and 7 above)........................		7.5
C. Office conferences		
1. With students (8 students 15 minutes each, and 6 students 30 minutes each)..........	5.0	
2. With advisees (30 students, one hour per semester)	2.0	
3. With colleagues..........................	1.0	
4. With officers of student clubs..............	1.0	
SUBTOTAL—		9.0
D. Clerical duties (Inspecting class rolls, filing papers, tabulating marks, recording marks, reading and answering official bulletins, making reports)...		5.0
E. Meetings		
1. With student club........................	1.0	
2. Staff (2 hours once a month; subcommittee, the same).............................	1.0	
SUBTOTAL—		2.0
F. Examinations		
1. Mid-term and final examinations for five courses (10 hours for construction and 10 for scoring)		
2. Selecting books for library purchase (15 hours per semester)		
3. Writing recommendations (5 hours per semester)		
SUBTOTAL—		6.6
G. Summary		
1. Time for four nonduplicating courses (4 times 13.5 in Item A)............ 54 hrs. per week		
2. Time for one duplicating course .... 7.5 hrs. per week		
3. Additional responsibilities. 22.6 hrs. per week		
GRAND TOTAL—		84.1

teacher is supposed to have. The results of this conscientiousness in terms of hours are appalling.[4]

No teacher can continue year after year to do effective work with such a load. Frequent but unsatisfactory solutions to this common situation are (1) to use last year's preparation instead of making a new one, (2) to see students as little as possible outside of class, (3) to use examinations from previous years without revision, (4) to read very little, and (5) to reduce as many procedures as possible to routine in order to save time. These adjustments keep a teacher from suicide, insanity, or an early grave, but they do not produce good teaching. If a college really wants superior instruction for its students it has to give its teachers time to think.

A college instructor has many different things to do and not enough time or energy to do all of them. In large universities a typical teacher spends about half his working hours in activities directly associated with teaching; in a small college he may spend as large a proportion as 80 per cent. In any case, he always has some other duties and interests that he cannot afford to neglect.

II. PUBLICATIONS AND RESEARCH

One of a college teacher's numerous functions is to be a scholar and intellectual leader. Of course, not all teachers are equally well equipped by nature for original study and research; indeed, there are some excellent teachers who would like to put their entire time into their instructional activities and the development of their students. Since there are only twenty-four hours in a day, it becomes almost necessary to limit one's major efforts to either teaching or research. A few people succeed in doing both well, but most human beings are not so gifted. The typical research man has neither the interest nor the personality for the instruction of any but advanced students in his own field, and the typically successful undergraduate teacher has neither the interest nor the personality to do outstanding research. Both types of person

[4] Michell, *op. cit.* Used by permission of the *Journal of Higher Education.*

are needed in the present-day college or university. As will be
discussed in more detail in a later chapter the brilliant teacher
often does not rise in rank as fast as the research worker.
However, most people have to make a choice between research
and teaching, in so far as their major efforts are concerned.[5]

The first objective point to consider about publication is perhaps
the amount of writing done by a typical faculty. Table 34 shows
the per cent of teachers on one university faculty who, in a five-
year period, had published something. About four-fifths of the
professors, three-fourths of the associates, and half the assistant

TABLE 34
Faculty Publications [6]

Rank	Number of Persons	Number Who Had Published	Per Cent
Professors..............	155	135	87.1
Associate professors.....	70	54	77.1
Assistant professors.....	68	37	54.4
Instructors.............	34	5	14.7
	327	231	70.6

professors had added to their record at least one publication during
the previous five years.

The next point is the number of publications by these same
teachers. Table 35 gives this information.

TABLE 35
Number of Publications of All Kinds in Five Years [7]

Number of Publications	Number of Teachers	Per Cent
21 or more	14	4.3
13–20	19	5.8
10–12	19	5.8
7–9	34	10.4
4–6	57	17.4
1–3	88	26.9
0	96	29.4
	327	100.0

[5] For a good discussion see H. F. Davidson, "The Puzzled Professor,"
School and Society, 15: 559–61, 1922.
[6] Reeves, *op. cit.* The material contained in Tables 34–36 is used by permission of the University of Chicago Press.
[7] *Ibid.*

Over one-fourth of these faculty members had not published anything, while 15.9 per cent of them had produced more than ten articles or books. In a college the proportion of those without publication is generally higher.

The third point concerns the nature of the materials published. For these same 327 teachers the results appear in Table 36.

TABLE 36

Nature of Publications [8]

Type	Average Number Per Faculty Member
Books, monographs............................	0.7
Articles in technical journals....................	3.9
Articles in proceedings of associations...........	0.4
Articles in local journals.......................	0.3
Articles in collaboration.......................	1.4
Reviews.......................................	3.8
Other types...................................	0.3

During the five-year period covered by this report, these faculty members produced an average of less than 1.0 book, 4.6 independent articles, 1.4 joint articles, and 3.8 reviews. The rate of publication would be roughly one book in seven years, one article each year and occasionally two, and one review almost every year. This amount of writing may seem somewhat high, but one has to remember that the most fluent 16 per cent of the faculty produced about 60 per cent of the books and articles. Nearly three-fourths of the teachers published an article or a review no oftener than once a year.

A college teacher should do some kind of independent intellectual work for the sake of his own development. Whether or not he publishes his results is, for this purpose, unimportant. If a teacher neglects this type of work he is likely to become rusty and out of date. In a recent study of the teaching staffs in 225 colleges, 10 per cent of the faculty were reported as rusty.[9] Of these, nearly half had once been considered good

[8] *Ibid.*
[9] A. V. Reed, *The Effective and the Ineffective College Teacher*, American Book Company, 1935, 335 pp.

teachers. Although failure to continue with independent study and research is not the only cause of the condition described as "rusty," it is an important one. Sometimes this situation is not the teacher's fault; he may have neglected his own scholarship because he had to. Too heavy a teaching load, too much time spent with students, or too many administrative duties can all operate to lower a teacher's productivity and scholarship.[10]

The amount of time spent in research by faculty members varies from none to 100 per cent. Research within one's own subject is usually a highly specialized job, the nature of which does not fit one for undergraduate instruction. It is my candid opinion that a college would do well to underwrite a few research workers, relieve them of all teaching except perhaps one seminar, and let them do what they are best fitted for— at the same time removing all pressure for research from everyone else.[11] Those who wanted to make investigations in their own field would still be free to do so, but no one would feel forced to publish, as altogether too many teachers now do.

Naturally a graduate student who intends to become a college professor cannot foresee what the future will bring him in the way of a position, but he can be fairly sure that he is more likely to need a higher degree of teaching than of research skill. If, however, he does research at all he should be prepared to concentrate upon it. A recent study of the preparation and actual work done by a group of graduate students in previous years is of interest in this connection.[12] Thus, 85 of these students prepared for research jobs only, but 105 of the group were later engaged exclusively in research. On the other hand, only 186 prepared for teaching only, but 309 were doing nothing else. The remaining graduate students had had more or less preparation along both lines and were engaged in both, although the proportions were not stated. From these results

[10] H. M. Wriston, "Report of the Commission on Faculty and Student Scholarship," *Association of American Colleges Bulletin,* 17 : 37–40, 1931.
[11] Further comment on the nature of promotion for excellence in teaching alone will be made in a later chapter.
[12] F. W. Reeves and J. D. Russell, *Instructional Problems of the University,* University of Chicago Press, 1933, 245 pp.

it would appear that rather too few people had been trained intensively for research and that far too few had prepared intensively for teaching.

One excellent suggestion has been made concerning the division of labor among the members of a faculty group.[13] This writer believes, in common with most other people, that all college professors should be teachers and scholars in their respective fields. In addition, each person should select one other field of interest from the following four: research, professional or civic service, student leadership, or administration. Each should follow his natural interests and abilities, but no one should be expected to carry on these four types of activity, in addition to a teaching schedule and the reading necessary for maintaining scholarship. Actually many engage in all these activities simultaneously, but the resulting dispersal of their energies prevents them from doing anything as well as they could. On a faculty there are people of many types. If each could be allowed to concentrate—in addition to his teaching and scholarship—upon one other kind of activity, all the necessary work would get done—and with far less friction than is the case at present.

Before leaving this topic of research there is a further point I would like to make. One type of research—whether or not it leads to publication is unimportant—can and should be carried on by every teacher. I mean research in effective methods of teaching. Any good instructor is continually trying new procedures. With very little more time and effort he could find out objectively if the changes he makes are effective. As it is, he usually has only his own impressions to go by in estimating the worth of any technique. This kind of investigation is especially vital to the teaching profession, and only teachers can carry it on. The trouble is not that college teachers fail to experiment but that they fail to measure or control the results. There are literally hundreds of general questions concerning college teaching that need to be answered, and every teacher finds innumerable questions of his own as he proceeds with his work from day to day. If each college teacher would carry on one sound experiment in one course once every five

[13] P. D. Converse, "The Work of the College Professor," *Journal of Higher Education,* 5: 299–304, 1934.

years there would soon be a large body of accurate knowledge about effective methods and desirable subject matter. A few of the possible questions that need answers are listed below:

But does anyone know that a year of freshman English really changes a student's capacities sufficiently to justify the time it requires? In what way and to what degree, if at all, is an introductory orientation course for college freshmen superior to some other curricular offering? What changes are wrought in a student through a four-year, five-year, or six-year requirement in English that may not be achieved through some simpler and less coercive program? What does a two-hour, four-hour, six-hour, or eight-hour per week requirement in laboratory practice add to the simpler lecture or demonstration program in introductory chemistry or zoology? To what degree does the recently extended program and highly lauded curriculum in history and the social sciences actually accomplish the results its champions so vigorously claim for it? Is an introductory course in science for college students defensible in terms of the changes it works in student intellect and attitudes? Is anyone prepared to defend with objective data the wilderness of prerequisite courses into which the young student plunges upon college entrance? Certainly no one is, and before these and scores of similar questions we shall stand helpless until, through long-extended investigation, the processes of scientific study shall have created for us a body of educational knowledge as yet nonexistent.

What are the changes wrought in a college student when he "takes," as we say, a certain curricular dosage? The naïve assumption underlying college work, that every unit of the curriculum will produce some desirable or useful alteration in character or intellect if the student will only master the course, is certainly to be called in question. Widespread among students is the contrary view, and alumni generally discredit the usefulness of portions of their college work. It is the business of the faculty, through research and objective evidence, to determine the degree of validity in their own assumptions and the measure in which student and alumni criticism is justified.[14]

Such questions as those mentioned above are likely to remain unanswered until college teachers themselves do the

[14] M. E. Haggerty: "Improvement of University Instruction through Educational Research." From Kent's *Higher Education in America.* Boston, 1930. Used by permission of the publishers, Ginn and Company.

needed research upon both the content of college courses and the methods of presentation. I do not mean to imply that everyone should engage in research whether or not he has the inclination for it but only to emphasize the need for educational work as well as work in one's own field of knowledge. There are plenty of problems for all tastes.

III. PROMOTIONS

The data about the frequency of promotions and the length of time required to pass from one academic rank to another are included in a later chapter.[15] Here I want only to present briefly the bases upon which promotions are made, since this topic is closely related to the matters discussed in this chapter. The most objective statement of why an individual is promoted has been published by an investigator who asked thirty-one prominent administrators to give their reasons for advancing teachers.[16] The reasons were—in order of their frequency—as follows: publications, new degrees, completion of some particular research, recent honors or other form of public recognition, efficiency in administrative work, high ratings by members of the administrative staff, new membership in learned societies, service on important committees, election to some office in a learned society. Conspicuous for their absence are both excellence in teaching and ability to guide students into better ways of living and thinking. In short, the college teacher is promoted for almost any reason except that he can teach. If I had no professional conscience I would advise a young person just entering the profession (1) to publish as many papers as he can, (2) to serve on as many committees as possible, and (3) to make himself very useful to every administrator. By these procedures he will almost certainly gain promotion more quickly than if he spends his time in preparing ingenious ways of presenting ideas to his classes or in laboring faithfully with Susie Smith about the use of commas. While I would certainly prefer that teachers should

---

[15] See pages 537–38.
[16] J. L. Ward, "Promotional Factors in College Teaching," *Journal of Higher Education*, 8 : 475–79, 1937.

be promoted mainly for teaching, the fact is that they are not—although they could be.[17]

The reasons above given are doubtless more operative in large than in small institutions.[18] In the latter the students talk so continually about what this or that teacher does in class that every member of the faculty knows a great deal about every other member. When those in a given department meet to consider recommendations for promotion, they have plenty of information about each individual. Teaching skill is therefore taken seriously into consideration, with the result that expert teachers with no publication record may be promoted as regularly as those who publish or are superior in research. This situation is unfortunately not true in larger institutions, where the individual faculty members do not know each other and the students do not know either each other or their teachers well enough to disseminate the necessary data about what goes on in class. As a result, advancements are made on the basis of objective data—usually publications, research, or election to learned societies. Probably the person who moves fastest from rank to rank is the one who becomes a useful errand boy for the administration. This is not as it should be, and most colleges and universities are making earnest efforts to alter the situation. In the course of time a teacher may actually be advanced in proportion to his ability to bring about desirable changes in the students whom he instructs.

IV. SUMMARY

Many points in this chapter will make a somewhat melancholy impression upon the reader. College teachers have too much work and too many different things to do. About half the load typically consists of activities directly connected with teaching. The remaining hours go into departmental business, administration, research, or extramural service. Faculty committees make heavy demands upon a teacher's time. There is

[17] See pages 589–93 for a further discussion of this point.
[18] See, for instance, *Report from the Committee on Progress and Promotion,* Oberlin College, 1930, 4 pp.

more pressure for publication than there would be if expert teaching brought results commensurate with research, and promotions are much too dependent upon publication records. In the large university the situation is not perhaps as serious as in a small college, where the facilities for research are often inadequate. Perhaps the most fruitful suggestion in this whole matter is one already mentioned—that each teacher should, rather early in his career, settle upon research, administration, student leadership, or community service as his field of activity in addition to his teaching. Such action cannot, however, be taken by faculty members until the chances for advancement are equalized. The arrangement now prevalent in most colleges and universities does not allow for the individual differences in talent among its teachers and thus flouts one of the most basic doctrines of education.

CHAPTER XXIII

ETHICAL BEHAVIOR

College teaching is one of the oldest and most honored professions. Like medicine and law, it has its own code of ethics. College teachers guard jealously their right to teach what they believe to be the truth, but they have among themselves definite standards of behavior to prevent any possible misuse of their position.

The consideration of proper behavior for a college teacher subdivides itself rather naturally into three topics. There is, first, the accepted code of ethics. This statement of principles covers some matters that enter into a teacher's daily activities, but it is more concerned with major issues, attitudes, and decisions. A teacher's behavior is influenced also by his conception of academic freedom. There has been so much discussion of this point in recent years that definite and authoritative formulations of a desirable point of view have appeared. Finally, the teacher is guided from day to day in his personal relations with students and colleagues by certain minor but important considerations. The three sections of this chapter will correspond to these three general topics.

I. THE TEACHER'S CODE OF ETHICS

Various codes have been published, but none is any better than that which appears below. I have selected this one largely because it is a little more specific than some and because it seems to me to include more topics.

A Code of Ethics for Teachers in Colleges and Universities

I. Relations of the Teacher to His Profession

A. A profession is delimited in part by the necessary training. The minimum training and performance for different levels of teaching are prescribed by law and by the regulations of responsible bodies. Moreover, it is the duty of the teacher to secure the best training possible in the mastery of his field of study, in knowledge and understanding of the behavior of his students, and in teaching technique.

B. The teacher should expect to be governed in accordance with a clear formulation of the conditions for appointment and promotion by the authorities of his institution and, in the absence of such formulation, he should press for it.

C. The first duty of the teacher in all circumstances is the discovery and exposition of the truth in his own field of study to the best of his ability. This necessarily involves a clear orientation within the general field of knowledge. Discovery as here used means the thorough, critical, and independent canvass, so far as possible, of available sources of knowledge and the carrying on of original investigation in so far as time, circumstances, and ability permit. Exposition means the conscientious and thought-provoking presentation first of all to his students and secondarily to others with whom he has occasion to deal. So far as this aim is development of skills rather than knowledge and understanding, discovery and exposition have to do with methods of training rather than with content.

D. Every teacher should be ready to assist to a reasonable extent in the administrative work of his department and in the more general administrative work of the institution, when called upon to do so.

E. Reasonable participation in professional societies, including not only those having to do with subject matter, but also those concerned with the interests and normal affiliations of classroom teachers, is a duty resting upon all teachers.

II. Relations of the Teacher to His Students

A. The ethical obligation to give due time and attention to effective teaching requires of the teacher the prompt and regular meeting of his classes, faithfulness to student consultations, and constant refreshment in the daily work of his classroom programs.

B. The teacher should strive for a timely, just, and unprejudiced appraisal of all student work in terms of whatever grading system may be commonly accepted throughout his institution. He owes students the right of review of their work and grades given and, in cases of serious grievance or dispute, the right of appeal to a faculty committee, or similar agency, regularly provided for this purpose. The individual teacher, staffs, and whole faculties should, from time to time, make comparative studies of grades given and of the effectiveness of their appraisal systems in general.

C. The teacher should be actively concerned for the general welfare of his students so far as this has a clearly discernible bearing upon the success of the educational process.

D. The teacher should secure permission and give credit for the use of original student contributions in his lectures or publications, in the same manner and degree as for borrowed materials from other sources. He should not, in any case, use students to their detriment in fostering his own research, publications, or other ventures.

E. The teacher, who rightfully asks academic freedom for himself, should be extremely careful to accord his students a like freedom.

F. The teacher should not tutor students from his own classes for pay, or those from the classes of colleagues in the same department or elsewhere except under conditions known and approved by responsible authorities.

G. The teacher should be alert and co-operative in the detection and reporting to appropriate disciplinary agencies of all cases of student dishonesty and of other misconduct that is seriously harmful to the objectives and ideals of the department or institution in which he serves. It is his duty, however, to take care that students charged with offenses of this sort have opportunity for a hearing such as to ensure the submission of all relevant facts and a just disposition of their cases.

H. The teacher should treat the ideas, needs, weaknesses, and failures of students in confidence, whether he has gathered his knowledge in the course of routine activities or from personal consultation, and he should not reveal such facts to others except in the line of duty.

III. Relations of the Teacher to His Colleagues

A. The teacher should give his colleagues active co-operation and encouragement in their individual development as teachers and in measures in behalf of the objectives of his department and institution.

B. The teacher should in no case indulge in unfair competition with his colleagues for position, rank, salary, students, or other advantages of any sort.

C. The teacher should avoid indiscriminate disparagement of his colleagues. He owes to his institution and to the profession a reasonable tact, both as to content and place, in the utterance of disparaging facts. This should not restrain him, however, from an honest and timely appraisal of a colleague that is for the betterment of educational service, or from his duty to submit to appropriate authorities any substantial evidence in his possession concerning the unfitness of a colleague.

D. A teacher should always secure permission and give credit for the use of materials borrowed from colleagues or elsewhere in his own lectures, publications, or other public presentations.

E. A teacher should not sponsor or promote the rendering of services to students for pay by individuals who would not meet the approval of the department most closely concerned with such services.

F. A teacher should not fail to recommend a colleague for a better position through desire to retain him in his present position, or for any cause other than that of unfitness for the place.

IV. Relations of the Teacher to His Institution and Its Administrators

A. The teacher should at all times insist upon and exercise his right of untrammeled investigation and exposition of any matter within his own field or specifically germane to it, but he is also morally bound not to take advantage of his position for introducing into his classroom the discussion of subjects not pertinent to his special field.

B. The teacher should maintain his right as a citizen to speak outside his institution on matters of public interest, so far as this does not interfere with proper attention to his educational duties; but he should make clear always that the institution is in no way responsible for his extra-mural utterances, except where he is specifically acting as its agent.

C. It is the duty of the teacher loyally to support the principles of tenure, promotion, demotion, and dismissal adopted by the profession and to press for the formulation and use of such principles where none have been adopted.

D. The teacher should not intrigue with administrative officials to enhance his own position or to injure that of a colleague.

E. The teacher should always recognize his responsibility to administrative officials, unless their acts conflict with a higher loyalty with reference to which he makes his position clear.

V. Relations of the Teacher to the Nonacademic World

A. The teacher should maintain and exercise his right as a citizen to take part in community and public affairs, except for such restrictions as are necessary to prevent the neglect of his professional duties.

B. The teacher should make his abilities and influences available for the service of the public relations of his institution. He should not, however, attempt on his own account to initiate or promote any policy relating to his institution, or seek advancement in rank or salary for himself or a colleague, through connivance with or influence upon governing boards or public officials. In case such officials initiate discussions with him concerning matters of this sort he should report the substance of the discussions to the president or appropriate officers of his institution.

C. The teacher should not, during the academic year, undertake for pay extensive activities outside his institution, such as would consume his time and energy, except with the approval of the proper institutional authorities; and he should not, in any case, exploit his teaching position to secure outside income or favors in competition with non-academic colleagues.

D. The teacher should avoid occasioning sensational publicity by unbecoming speech or conduct.

E. A teacher should not accept pay, directly or indirectly, from outside individuals, groups, or agencies of any sort, for the teaching of partisan views or the promotion of partisan projects, either within or outside his institution.

F. The teacher should maintain a non-committal policy in public on all controversial issues arising within the school. He should maintain in strict confidence all departmental or school matters not intended for dissemination. If any issue or matter is of such public concern that he must, for his own integrity, speak out, he should make this clear to all concerned.

G. A teacher should defend any member of the profession who is unjustly attacked.[1]

This code requires little comment. Any young person who is planning to enter the teaching profession should not only read it but should think about it and practically memorize it until it becomes so much a part of himself that forgetting is impossible.

II. ACADEMIC FREEDOM

One hears a good deal at present about academic freedom, especially since the rise of totalitarian states in which the teacher is not allowed to discuss certain topics at all and is permitted to present only one side of any controversial question. Thus, for instance, in Germany a professor of anthropology must support the idea of "Nordic supremacy," although he knows that Nordics present the same distribution of abilities as other groups; and he must condemn the "Jewish race," even though there is no such thing, because Jews always resemble physically whatever national group they happen to live with. There have been of late certain indications that some degree of regimentation may develop in America also. Against this possibility scholars have sought to defend themselves by official protest.[2] At any time a college teacher should have a clear conception of what is meant by "academic freedom," but never is he likely to need it more than at the present.

[1] From "A Code of Ethics for Teachers in Colleges and Universities," *Bulletin of the American Association of University Professors,* 23: 143–48, 1937. See also B. Y. Landis, "Profesisonal Codes: A Sociological Analysis to Determine Applicability to the Educational Profession," *Teachers College Contributions to Education,* No. 267, 1927, 108 pp. For the official N.E.A. code see the *Research Bulletin of the National Education Association,* 9: 88–89, 1931. The above code is quoted by permission of the *Bulletin of the American Association of University Professors.*

[2] See, for instance, the publications of the Committee for Cultural Freedom under the leadership of John Dewey or those of the American Committee for Democracy and Intellectual Freedom under the leadership of Franz Boas.

Rather than attempt to explain the matter in my own words, I shall quote from official sources. Below are two excerpts that summarize the situation.[3]

The primary object of a formulation by this Association is, as far as it may be attained by this means, two-fold: first, to secure for competent, judicious teachers in the colleges of the Association the sense of security and the peace of mind which are indispensable to the efficiency of their work; second, to insure protection of the colleges against wanton, persistent injury from utterances of the incompetent and injudicious.

Academic freedom is not a myth, neither is it license unrestrained and irresponsible. What it should be may be stated best in terms of liberty and responsibility. The ideal college atmosphere is one in which, on the one hand, competent, judicious scholars exercise their freedom with fitting regard for the welfare and reputation of the institution they serve. Such an atmosphere should be the ultimate aim of every institution of learning; in it every trace of the problem of academic freedom would disappear.

Impediments to immediate and general realization of ideal conditions inhere in the very nature of the parties to the relation. Colleges are hampered in their approach to it by two facts. One is that many, perhaps most, of them owe their origin and present support to constituencies whose convictions on certain controversial topics do not allow complete freedom in the teaching of those topics, even in the privacy of the classroom. The other is the immaturity and consequent extreme impressionability of the student body. Topics and doctrines that are in themselves entirely suitable material for thought and study are in some cases wholly inappropriate for consideration in college, and in others call for the most careful and considerate handling. Exclusion of restriction in such cases results from the necessary exercise of "pedagogic common sense."

Since there are no rights without corresponding duties, the considerations heretofore set down with respect to the freedom of the academic teacher entail certain correlative obligations. The

[3] The first is from the Report of the Commission on Academic Freedom and Tenure of the Association of American Colleges in the *Bulletin of the American Association of University Professors,* 18: 376, 1932; the second is from Appendix B of the same volume, pages 386–87, 1932. See also *ibid.,* 26: 49–51, 1940. Used by permission of the *Bulletin of the American Association of University Professors.*

claim to freedom of teaching is made in the interest of the integrity and of the progress of scientific inquiry; it is, therefore, only those who carry on their work in the temper of the scientific inquirer who may justly assert this claim. The liberty of the scholar within the university to set forth his conclusions, be they what they may, is conditioned by their being conclusions gained by a scholar's method and held in a scholar's spirit. The university teacher, in giving instruction upon controversial matters, should, if he is fit for his position, be a person of a fair and judicial mind; he should, in dealing with the divergent opinions of other investigators, cause his students to become familiar with the best published expressions and he should, above all, remember that his business is not to provide his students with ready-made conclusions, but to train them to think for themselves, and to provide them access to those materials which they need if they are to think intelligently.

The American Association of University Professors has also published an official statement in regard to academic freedom. The following excerpt was agreed upon by the Association, together with representatives of the American Association of University Women, the Association of Land-Grant Colleges, the Association of Urban Universities, the National Association of State Universities, and the American Council on Education. It appeared originally in 1925, was reaffirmed in 1935, and again in 1940. It is, then, an approved expression of those groups of people most interested in college and university work.

(a) A university or college may not place any restraint upon the teacher's freedom in investigation, unless restriction upon the amount of time devoted to it becomes necessary in order to prevent undue interference with teaching duties.

(b) A university or college may not impose any limitation upon the teacher's freedom in the exposition of his own subject in the classroom or in addresses and publications outside the college, except in so far as the necessity of adapting instruction to the needs of immature students, or in the case of institutions of a denominate or partisan character, specific stipulations in advance, fully understood and accepted by both parties, limit the scope and character of instruction.

(c) No teacher may claim as his right the privilege of discussing in his classroom controversial topics outside of his own field of study. The teacher is morally bound not to take advantage of his position by introducing into the classroom provocative discussion of irrelevant subjects not within the field of his study.

(d) A university or college should recognize that the teacher in speaking and writing outside the institution upon subjects beyond the scope of his own field of study is entitled to precisely the same freedom and is subject to the same responsibility as attaches to all other citizens. If the extra-mural utterances of a teacher should be such as to raise grave doubts concerning his fitness for his position, the question should in all cases be submitted to an appropriate committee of the faculty of which he is a member. It should be clearly understood that an institution assumes no responsibility for views expressed by members of its staff; and teachers should when necessary take pains to make it clear that they are expressing only their personal opinions.[4]

Most colleges have their own statement concerning academic freedom. One sample from a private college is given below:

Within the limits of national and state law all teachers in the service of .... College shall enjoy liberty of research, instruction, and utterance upon matters of opinion. The teacher's exercise of the rights and obligations of a citizen and of a member of the community shall in no way be affected by academic tenure.

In enjoying these rights based upon the principle of academic freedom the teachers in the service of .... College recognize certain correlative obligations. The teacher will bear in mind that the good name of the college rests upon its faculty. The teacher's conclusions should be the fruits of competent and sincere inquiry, set forth with dignity, courtesy, and temperateness of language. The teacher should accept full responsibility for all utterances. His essential function as a teacher is not to dogmatize but to train students to think for themselves and to provide them access to the necessary materials.

Three points about these various excerpts seem worth stressing further. The first is that a college teacher must not abuse

---

[4] From the *Bulletin of the American Association of University Professors*, 26: 52, 1940. Used by permission of the *Bulletin of the American Association of University Professors*.

his right to speak the truth. The second point to note is the restriction upon speech that a teacher must accept if he agrees to hold classes in a college supported by particular interests. Once he has signed a contract to instruct in such a school, he has temporarily given up his freedom of expression on certain topics. If he is a gentleman he will simply avoid these topics in his classwork; anyone who cannot control himself under such circumstances should not sign a contract of this type. Finally, a teacher must always remember that he is dealing with students who, because of their immaturity, will be unduly influenced by what he says. No one is easier to proselyte than an eager college student with an emotional attachment to a teacher. In fact, the average student's best protection against proselyting and indoctrination is his bland indifference toward most of his professors. At all times a teacher would do well to follow the precept of one of my professors who told me she never made extreme statements of any kind in class because she was afraid there might be one student present who would believe her!

The general principles underlying academic freedom and proper relationships with students are easy enough to understand. The actual situations that arise are not always so simple. For the protection of students against undesirable influences it is necessary to avoid the development of "disciples" among one's best students and to treat certain topics in class from an objective, judicial point of view. One extreme example of each of these situations has come to my attention.

In a certain college there was a professor who had at his disposal a few assistantships in his department. Generally he used them to support some of his best students immediately after their graduation from college, while they were getting their degrees. One year he had in his beginning course two young men who showed unusual promise. He made friends with them, complimented them on their work, and encouraged both to major in his department—holding out as an inducement a chance for a job as his assistant after their graduation. In return he wanted them to let him guide their work during their next two years. Both were delighted at the attention they received and at the prospect of security at a time when their classmates would be looking for work. The professor took the two boys under his wing, gave them a good deal of extra reading, asked them to help him in various small matters, and generally adopted them. Among other things he wanted to approve their schedules. One of the boys greatly admired the professor, but the other disliked him. The former followed his teacher's advice to the last item, but the latter soon became tired of being dominated by someone he did not care for. Eventually friction developed between the second boy and the professor over the student's schedule, and they came to a parting of the ways. One student of this pair remained at his alma mater after graduation, became an assistant and later an assistant professor. The other left, took his advanced degree elsewhere, and is now a full professor in the same subject. Both are at present about fifty years old. The one who was successfully proselyted has, within the past fifteen years, found himself increasingly out of date. The only material he really knows is that which he learned under the tutelage of the professor he admired. He realizes now that he learned only one side of every topic in a highly controversial subject. While he would very much like to modify his views he finds he cannot because he was too thoroughly indoctrinated in his youth. Since he is an honest person he has recently resigned his teaching position and has gone into administrative work. He does not especially enjoy it, but he likes it better than being an out-of-date teacher. The second student is a success largely because he had the good luck to dislike the professor. This history shows some of the long-time results of an unwise use of "academic freedom."

The other incident is entirely different in character. At one time I gave a course on the psychology of adolescence in a summer school. To my surprise I received a note from my administrative superior telling me that there had been some objection to the course as given by my predecessor on the grounds that there was too much discussion of sex problems. He therefore requested that I give the course without any mention whatever of sex. On theoretical grounds I thought the content of the course was my business rather than his, and on practical grounds I did not see how I could follow instructions and give the course at all. I therefore asked him to attend my first few class hours, in which I intended to discuss physical changes at puberty and the effect of these changes upon the behavior of boys and girls in their early adolescent years. He came to several classes, listened to the discussions, and went away satisfied that I was not corrupting the young. I told him that for some sections of the course there was only casual reference, if any, to matters of sex, but that whenever I expected to go in any detail into such topics I would let him know in advance so that he might attend if he wished. Actually he did come to class fully a dozen times. At no point did he raise the slightest objection. In class the students discussed such topics as mother-fixations, homosexuality, promiscuity, masturbation, and prostitution. They were intelligently interested but clearly not excited or disturbed. At the end of the course the administrator gave me carte blanche to repeat the work in subsequent summers without interference or supervision. In one sense he was trespassing upon my freedom to present the truth as I saw it, but in another he was merely protecting students from what might have been—and evidently had been—a possible source of undesirable stimulation. I considered him quite within his rights, but I thought I also had a right to speak the truth—as did the students to learn it. Many cases of "interference" with academic freedom are of this general type and are the result of some abuse of liberty at a previous time. In all such instances one has to use the "pedagogic common sense" already mentioned. If teachers use it, they should be able to retain their freedom; if they do not, they are likely to lose it.

One further point about academic freedom should certainly be mentioned, since there has been so much agitation about it. In some states college teachers have been required to take an oath of allegiance to the government. In and of itself there is nothing objectionable in such an oath, inasmuch as any citizen expects to support his government. It is in the implications that serious objections arise. In the first place there is no justification for making a teacher sign an oath when other people do not have to. Such a requirement singles out members of the profession as being so unreliable that an oath is necessary. In the second place the promise could be used to throttle academic freedom completely. Whether or not it ever would be is beside the point. Teachers do not resent an oath of allegiance because they are plotting against the government but because they see in it a powerful weapon for oppression.

There is nothing new in this idea so often expressed by the layman that colleges and universities are hotbeds of radical opinion. They have been thus regarded ever since they were founded, and they are almost certain to remain so because truth has nothing to do with expediency or vested interests. The present agitation is largely along political and economic lines. At an earlier period it was in the field of religion. No present-day excitement over communism or nazism is any more extreme than the furor about evolution during the last decades of the nineteenth century. Crises in the intellectual life of the world come and go. During them a college teacher can only continue to guard his right to seek and teach the truth, confident that when the shouting dies down the "radical" ideas around which the battle has surged will have become the commonplaces of succeeding generations. In the meantime the scholar's position is clear. He should be as judicial, careful, and objective [5] in political or social matters as he is in academic affairs. His knowledge should make him a leader in any search for truth, and he should be the last person in the world to succumb to hysteria.[6]

III. SPECIFIC SUGGESTIONS CONCERNING DAILY BEHAVIOR

Every year a number of young assistants and instructors are dismissed from their positions because of undesirable attitudes or activities. Many more have difficulties of adjustment to their students or to their colleagues. Even the best-intentioned and most capable young instructors get into trouble once in a while. There are a few articles in the literature giving data on the reasons why college teachers are dismissed.[7]

[5] See C. A. Beard, "The Scholar in an Age of Conflict," *Bulletin of the American Association of University Professors,* 22 : 324–29, 1936.
[6] For an excellent discussion of this whole question see H. Kohn, "Academic Freedom in Our Time," *Bulletin of the American Association of University Professors,* 25 : 183–87, 1937. See also E. P. Cheyney, "Intellectual Freedom in a Democracy," *ibid.,* 23 : 383–95, 1937.
[7] See, for instance, G. C. Brandenburg, "Why College Teachers Fail," *Bulletin of the School of Education,* Indiana University, Vol. 9, No. 1, 1932, pp. 49–60; C. C. Crawford, "Defects and Difficulties of College Teaching," *School and Society,* 28 : 497–502, 1928; J. A. Starrak, "Student Rating of Instruction," *Journal of Higher Education,* 6 : 88–90, 1934; F. H.

The following suggestions are based upon these reports, plus the testimony of nearly thirty experienced college professors of whom the majority were or had been heads of departments. The reasons for dismissal are largely personal or social. Two points struck me as being especially important. The first was that most of the habits and attitudes were so commonplace and obvious that the usual code of ethics took them for granted, and the second was that practically all of them were easily avoidable. The only logical conclusion seems to be that many young instructors go to their first position ignorant of certain simple conventions of academic life. As a result, they do things that offend and antagonize the older members of the teaching staff or they belittle themselves in the eyes of their students. It seems a waste of human material when a person who has spent years to prepare for teaching—often doing so at great personal sacrifice—diminishes his usefulness to society by getting into difficulties through sheer ignorance of their existence. The habits and attitudes to be discussed account for a large proportion of the maladjustment and for the majority of dismissals among members in the lower academic ranks. Some of the points will seem completely obvious to any experienced teacher but these matters are not obvious to the beginner; if they were, fewer beginners would have trouble during their first years of teaching.

One source of difficulty lies in the development of a too familiar relation with students. In an effort to be friendly, young teachers sometimes let students call them by their first names, or they throw an arm casually across a student's shoulders, or they do similar things that are quite appropriate between members of the same generation but not between members of different generations. Even though at first the instructor is only a little older than his students, he is unwise to let them address him informally. The good-natured young man of twenty-eight who is glad to be hailed as "Tubby" by his freshmen will be considerably less happy about it when he is fifty and they are still eighteen.

Another and frequent cause of friction is the habit some young

Kirkpatrick, "What about the Problem Professors," *School and Society,* 38: 406–7, 1933; H. R. Douglass, "Rating the Teaching Effectiveness of College Instructors," *School and Society,* 28: 192–97, 1928.

teachers have of chatting with students about departmental and college affairs that are of concern only to the faculty and administration. Such a "leak" is usually not intentional; the assistant or instructor gets a little excited and says more than he means to say. One professor I consulted had just been dealing with a case of this sort. The latest addition to his staff had told a major student that the members of the department did not get along well together and were going to divide into two groups, each with its own organization. Although it seems incredible, I heard a young instructor this last year tell a senior, "Your academic record is not really good enough for Phi Beta Kappa but I think I can get you in if I do a little lobbying." Unprofessional comments of this sort are practically certain to make trouble.

For young men on the faculty there is one special caution that was mentioned by many of the people I consulted. Rarely does a year go by that some young man is not accused of improper conduct toward some girl with whom he has had an interview behind a closed door. In all probability the teacher against whom such a complaint is made had done nothing wrong or even unwise, but his usefulness to a college may terminate abruptly. Only one hysterical girl needs to accuse a man of making advances in order to cast suspicion upon him. Sooner or later the emotionally unstable girl who is doing poor work and feeling sorry for herself arrives for an interview. Such a girl will, perhaps unintentionally and quite unconsciously, use every means at her command to enlist her teacher's sympathies; this is normal feminine behavior. She may even make some advances herself; if they are refused she is likely to accuse the teacher of having made them. The latter is without protection—unless people in the corridor have had a chance to see what he was or was not doing. The only safe procedure is to keep the door open and to put the desk in the direct line of vision through it.

There are a few cautions concerning one's conduct in class. Many a young teacher gets into difficulty because he either wisecracks or expresses extreme ideas in which he does not really believe. In both cases, he is talking just to be smart. One has to remember that students will repeat to other faculty members any remark that is even faintly clever; they will, in point of fact, tell it in season and out, with an infinitude of variations and additions.

For instance, in one department there was a young man who gave a course on the contemporary developments in his field. One year about thirty majors in the department took this course as a means of reviewing material for their comprehensive examinations. At the end of the year these students were asked on their comprehensive to identify certain prominent men. Imagine the consternation of the examining committee when about twenty of the thirty seniors wrote that a certain famous professor in another institution was too old for his job and ought to get out and give a younger man a chance! In another case, a youthful instructor made an excellent pun on the president's name; he was not reappointed. Radical opinions are almost as certain to backfire as wisecracks. I know one man, now about thirty-five, who cannot get a promotion from the rank of instructor very largely because he has repeatedly exhorted his students to have trial marriages, to support strikers—regardless of the issues involved—and to vote for various radical measures. If he really believed in any of these ideas, he would be within his rights to express his views—although it is a little hard to see how he works them into a course on Spanish literature—but he does not believe in them at all. He talks about such matters merely to amuse and excite the students. In private life he is an inoffensive person with one wife, and he votes the Republican ticket. By talking loudly in class he has succeeded only in arousing distrust through the many garbled quotations that his students have removed from what may have been a sensible context and have repeated anywhere.

One other classroom habit of young teachers sometimes causes friction. An instructor usually has at least one section of an elementary course. He is given an outline or syllabus, which he is supposed to follow. There is almost nothing that so immediately reveals the inadequacy of one's preparation as the need to cover systematically the basic ideas in one's field. The average young teacher finds portions of the syllabus about which he knows very little, and he may be tempted to substitute something else—such as the details of his doctor's thesis. Sooner or later he is found out because the older members of his department discover in their classes former students of his who have never had certain sections of the elementary work. The only safe thing to do is to follow the outline. Naturally one does not need to accept without protest a syllabus that is inadequate or out of date but the changes should be made by the common consent of everyone teaching the elementary course and not introduced independently by an instructor, either because he thinks his ideas are better or because he does not want to remedy his own weaknesses of preparation.

In addition to getting along with students in a properly dignified manner both in class and out a young teacher has to adjust himself to the personalities of his colleagues and to the conventions of college administration. Three situations were mentioned with considerable frequency by those I consulted. Some beginners make the mistake of criticizing their colleagues before their students. This habit leads at once to open friction because such criticisms almost invariably get back to the individual criticized. This type of behavior is particularly likely to occur when a young person enters a department in which the others are from twenty to forty years older. It is always possible that some or all of them are out of date, or at least are not thoroughly conversant with the latest developments, but if the new arrival wants to make this comment, he should make it to them—not to the students.

It does not take the average person long to discover that there are antagonisms between certain members of the permanent staff. The problem of staying out of a feud does not arise frequently, but when it does, it is extremely important. The only safe course for a young person is to ignore its existence for as long as he can, and to remain aloof from it when he can no longer pretend that it is not there. The roots of any feud are many and complex. Whoever—if anyone—may have been "right" in the beginning, it is a safe conclusion that both people are at the moment about equally in the wrong. Joining one side or the other is almost certain to be disastrous, regardless of the merits of the case.

Sometimes a young person finds himself becoming a great favorite with some prominent member of the faculty, and he may think that he is helping his own career by fostering this attitude. Many a young teacher in a large university has been greatly pleased because some more or less prominent campus politician singled him out for personal interest and patronage. In a few instances this interest is real, but more often the politician merely wants a chestnut pulled off the fire and prefers not to burn his own fingers; the charm of his manner is usually in direct ratio to the heat in the chestnut. Even though being some older person's favorite does not involve a young teacher in any open breaks with his other colleagues he usually finds sooner or later that he has automatically inherited the animosities aroused by his sponsor, with the result that academic progress is slower than it might otherwise have been.

Heads of departments frequently complain that some instructor has approached the administration directly upon some matter. Going over the head of one's department without first trying to work through him is sheer idiocy, if for no other reason than that he has the last word. Naturally the head is not always right or even always reasonable. An instructor's first efforts should, however, be to proceed in the usual manner by consulting his immediate superior. He is not supposed to draft letters to the president or other administrative officers, or to interview them on matters that are the primary concern of his department. Sometimes a departmental head is not willing to support a member of his staff in some project but is willing that he should write the administration directly about it. As long as he or she knows what is going on, there is no objection to such a procedure, but approaching the administration first is practically certain to be interpreted by all concerned as an operation carried out behind the back of one's superiors.

In some colleges and universities the instructors have no vote. They are, however, allowed to talk during faculty meetings if they want to do so. It is safer not to want to. Young teachers have little to say that their more experienced elders either wish to hear or will attend to. Those who talk too much and too soon merely bring upon themselves the antagonism of others, even when the points they make are entirely acceptable. There is no place where silence is more golden than in a faculty meeting.

It remains to say one or two things about general relationships between the college and the world outside its gates, since beginners sometimes bring down unfavorable comment upon themselves by behavior or remarks that give an erroneous impression to the general public of what goes on in the college. Two situations are especially important. Since a college is always dependent to some extent upon the good will of the place in which it is situated, anyone who makes slighting remarks about the community or the people in it is disturbing what should be a harmonious relationship. The old "town-and-gown" rivalry, which is a relic from earlier times, is becoming distinctly unpopular. The more modern attitude is a desire to use the community as a laboratory for various campus and classroom activities and to co-operate with it in any of its own worth-while undertakings. On various counts this relation is healthier and better than rivalry, but it does not thrive upon disparaging comments, no matter how witty.

Most teachers participate more or less in off-campus activities and often play a rather important part in various organizations. A teacher has, of course, a perfect right to belong to any group he enjoys or to work for any movement in which he is interested. He has, in short, the same rights as any other citizen. Indeed, college teachers should be leaders in the intellectual life of the world, because they are better equipped for it than other people. As leaders they may have shortcomings, but rarely do they have as many as those who otherwise take their places. People from off the campus tend to identify a teacher with his college and to regard his utterances as official. A teacher has to be especially careful when he expresses personal convictions that are in sharp contrast to the generally accepted views either of the community or of the college. He is free to commit himself, but never free to commit his institution, unless he has been authorized to do so.

Most young teachers get into one or more of these difficulties at one time or another, either from sheer ignorance of their existence or from too casual an estimate of their importance. In the first years of teaching one has trouble enough with subject matter and teaching methods without having difficulties of the types indicated. Such situations are extremely destructive to either good work or normal progress.

IV. SUMMARY

Academic life has its code of ethics and its principles of behavior with which every young teacher should become acquainted as soon as possible in order that he may avoid accidental offense and may mold his activities into the accepted pattern. As the installation service of an honorary educational organization puts the matter in its address to initiates: "Take your place in the long procession of light-bearers, nor ever bring shame on those with whom you march." In large matters and in small, correct behavior is essential.

CHAPTER XXIV

ECONOMIC ASPECTS

A college professor has invested a great deal of time and money in his preparation for his work. He therefore has a right to expect a reasonable return on his investment and a reasonable wage for his highly trained services. Although college teaching has certain emotional compensations and satisfactions, most teachers have found that "atmosphere" alone does not compensate one for an inadequate salary. The whole question of what salary is adequate is highly complicated because there are so many factors to be considered. There is, first, the matter of how much training is needed—that is, how much the original investment comes to. After a person has completed his training, he has to find a position; at this point, the law of supply and demand enters the picture. During some periods not all those who are adequately prepared can be absorbed into the profession. Consequently, their entire specific training may be wasted. Once a teacher has a position, his salary has to be considered in the light of the security of tenure offered, the amount of work he has to do, the extent to which he has opportunities for self-development while he is working, his opportunities to add to his salary by other activities, and his chances of getting a pension when he is too old for active service. Finally, there is the question of what protection is given a person by his legal status as a college teacher. All these matters have to be taken into account when one is discussing the financial returns of teaching.

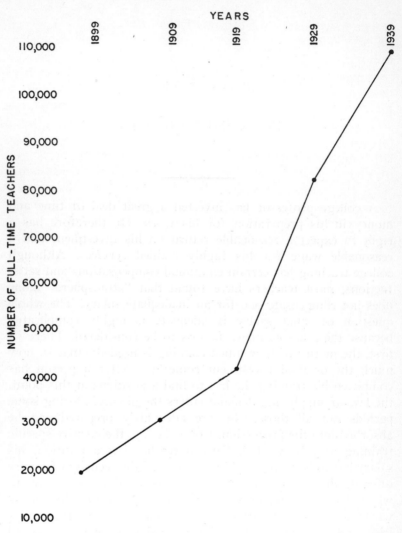

FIG. 37.—Increase in Number of College Teachers during the
Last Forty Years.

I. FACULTY PERSONNEL

The first points to consider relate to the number of college teachers now working in the United States, their academic rank, the growth trends in the numbers employed, and the training these teachers have had. The total number of college teachers of all ranks, as given in the last Biennial Survey of Education, is 110,000. Similar figures at ten-year intervals since 1889 produce the curve shown in Figure 37. The growth in actual number of teachers is from 19,496 to 110,000; the latter figure is 564 per cent of the former. In the same length of time the enrollments increased nearly 900 per cent; naturally, the number of students per teacher became greater. In twelve selected institutions—four universities, four colleges, and four technical schools—the increase in size of faculties between 1900 and 1933 was 359 per cent.[1] The demand for adequately trained workers in higher education is therefore increasing—and the end is not yet. Although the number of teachers decreased during the depression, the present figure is larger than ever before.[2] College enrollments continue to climb, and there is every indication that they will climb further. There are, then, still opportunities for adequately trained teachers.

The best single study of faculty personnel comes from the University of Chicago.[3] Although the number of teachers included is far larger than that for the average college, the distribution by ranks does not seem to differ much from the situation elsewhere. For all members of this faculty the number and per cent in each academic rank are shown below.[3a] For the 337 members in 27 academic departments, the per cents are slightly different in that the proportions for the two highest ranks are larger. Any faculty

[1] W. A. Lunden, "Economic Changes and Faculty Changes," *Journal of Higher Education*, 8: 253–56, 1937.

[2] Malcolm M. Willey, *Depression, Recovery, and Higher Education*, McGraw-Hill Book Company, 1937, 543 pp.

[3] F. W. Reeves, *et al.*, *The University Faculty*, University of Chicago Press, 1933, 326 pp.

[3a] Reeves, *op. cit.* The material contained in the next three short tables is used by permission of the University of Chicago Press.

Rank	Total Faculty		Teachers in 27 Academic Departments	
	Number	Per Cent	Number	Per Cent
Full professor..................	265	34	146	43
Associate professor............	139	18	65	19
Assistant professor.............	177	22	50	15
Instructor.....................	203	26	76	23
	784	100	337	100

is always "top-heavy" because competent people usually reach the highest rank by the time they are fifty and then continue to teach another fifteen or twenty years. As a result there are more full professors than members of any other rank.[4]

The amount of training needed for college teaching is not fixed. Out of 8,743 teachers whose records were studied in 1928, 2.5 per cent had no A.B., and 33.9 per cent had no Ph.D.[5] Even among the 5,686 professors included in this study, 13.1 per cent did not have the doctorate. At the University of Chicago the figures for the whole faculty and for the members of the 27 academic departments appear below:[6]

Members of the Faculty	For the Entire University		For 27 Academic Departments	
	Number	Per Cent	Number	Per Cent
No college degree..............	13	1	4	1
A.B. only......................	65	8	38	10
A.B. and A.M..................	78	10	54	16
A.B., A.M., and Ph.D..........	301	40 ⎱ 81	230	70 ⎱ 73
Professorial degree equal to the Ph.D.......................	327	41 ⎰	11	3 ⎰
	784	100	337	100

[4] Many differences in this respect appear, however, from one institution to another. For further data on this point, see W. A. Lunden, *The Dynamics of Higher Education,* Pittsburgh Printing Company, 1939, 402 pp.

[5] F. Payne and E. W. Spieth, *An Open Letter to College Teachers,* Principia Press, Bloomington, Indiana, 1935, 380 pp.

[6] Reeves, *op. cit.*

Although it is possible for a person of unusual ability to enter college teaching and even become a full professor without having a Ph.D. degree, the prospects of success without the doctorate are low. In a single small college, however, the per cent of teachers lacking a Ph.D. may be as high as 50, but those without it are usually in the upper age groups. It is becoming increasingly difficult to so much as enter college teaching unless one has an advanced degree.

In the Chicago group the amount of training in education varied from none at all to several courses. Slightly less than half the members had had no formal training, a fourth had had one or two courses in education, and the remaining fourth three or more courses. In the past, then, college teachers have not considered it necessary to study methods of teaching as an integral part of their preparation. Whether or not they benefit by such courses remains an open question. There is, however, considerable agitation for a more adequate training in all fields, including work in education.[7]

Progress from one rank to the next takes an average of four years, but the range is from one to sixteen years. That is, an instructor who gets his first position at the age of thirty cannot expect to become a full professor before he is forty-five; it is more likely that he will not reach this rank until he is fifty. The amount of time spent by the Chicago faculty in each position and the average age of those classified in each group reflect the situation. The majority of these faculty members spent from one to five years as instructors, two to nine years as assistant professors, and two to seven years as associate professors.

Rank	Average Age for Members of Each Rank		
	1908	1918	1928
Professors	48.5	53.1	51.4
Associate professors	44.1	45.7	44.0
Assistant professors	39.8	39.9	36.2
Instructor	36.2	35.4	32.2

[7] H. M. Byram, "Some Problems in the Provision for Professional Training of College Teachers," *Teachers College Record,* 35: 724–26, 1934; L. B. Richardson, "Desirable Types of Graduate Training for Prospective College Teachers," *Proceedings of the Institute for Administrative Officers of Higher Institutions,* University of Chicago Press, 2: 27–41, 1930; H. Suzzallo, "Reorganization of Postgraduate Work for Prospective College Teachers," *ibid.,* pp. 61–69; W. S. Gray, *The Training of College Teachers,* University of Chicago Press, 1930, 242 pp.

The table showing the average ages contains data over a period of twenty years. In this university the teachers are beginning their work at an earlier age than formerly, but their progress is slower. In 1908 the difference in age between professors and instructors

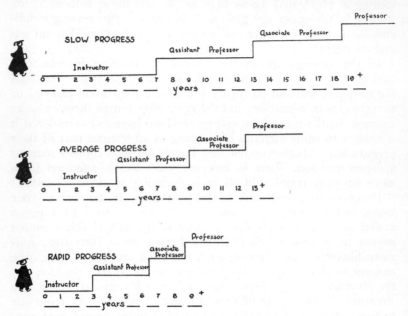

FIG. 38.—Different Rates of Progress from One Academic Rank to Another.

was 12.3 years; in 1928 it was 19.2 years. In a small college promotion is sometimes faster than this and sometimes slower, the rate depending upon the amount of local competition and the policy of the administration.

The upper end of the distribution—the full and associate professors—constitutes a relatively stable group upon the college campus. In 4 Eastern colleges, the annual turnover was only 3 per cent for professors and 8 per cent for associates;[8] in 117 institutions the corresponding figures were 6 and 5

[8] A. C. C. Hill, "The Appointment of College Professors," *Bulletin of the Association of American Colleges,* 14: 522–40, 1928.

per cent.[9] These figures include new appointments made necessary by retirement, illness, and death, as well as those due to changes of position. For the full professors at least there is little change beyond replacement as the ranks are depleted by normal causes. The per cents of new appointments for assistant professors were 22 and 15 in the two studies, and for instructors 50 and 44. The turnover for the lowest rank is high. Every year some instructors are discharged, some are promoted, and some leave the profession voluntarily. There is, then, constant change at one end of the academic distribution and only slight change at the other.

One further point about the personnel of college faculties is of interest and importance to the young person who intends to enter the profession. Institutions sometimes hire their own graduates, thus producing what is known as "inbreeding." The extent of such inbreeding varies considerably from place to place. There are two excellent studies on this matter. In one case [10] the investigators considered results from all the accredited institutions on the list of the American Council on Education that could supply adequate information. A total of 219 colleges and universities, both public and private, in 42 states contributed data about 16,837 faculty members. Of this number 5,707, or 34 per cent, taught in the institution from which they received at least one degree. The amount of inbreeding in the different colleges is shown below: [10a]

Per Cent	Number of Institutions
0	6
1–9	31
10–19	48
20–29	51
30–39	37
40–49	28
50–59	11
60 or more	7
	219

[9] Report of Committee B, "Methods of Appointment and Promotions," *Bulletin of the American Association of University Professors,* 14: 95–102, 1928, and 15: 175–217, 1929.

[10] W. C. Eells and A. C. Cleveland, "Faculty Inbreeding," *Journal of Higher Education,* 6: 261–69, 1935 and "The Effects of Inbreeding," *Journal of Higher Education,* 6: 323–28, 1935.

[10a] Eels and Cleveland, *op. cit.* Used by permission of the *Journal of Higher Education.*

In general the per cent was higher in the East than in the West, in private than in public schools, and in denominational than in nondenominational institutions. In men's colleges the average per cent was 41, in coeducational schools 35, and in women's colleges only 17. The large universities with the best-developed graduate schools had unusually high percentages. It was clear also that the practice is on the increase. Among instructors the amount was 45 per cent; with each rank the percentage decreased until it was only 25 for the full professors. In 34 colleges that had adequate records since 1902 the amount had increased from 31 to 41 per cent during this period. The total number of teachers involved in these 34 colleges rose from 718 to 4,569. In numbers, then, the difference in inbreeding is between 222 faculty members and 1,873. Inbreeding may come from the employment of those who have an A.B. from an institution, an M.A., a Ph.D., or some combination of the three degrees. In the colleges studied, 5 per cent of the teachers showed all three types of inbreeding—that is, they had never been at any other institution since they left high school.[11]

The effects of inbreeding are as interesting as the amount. In the second article already referred to the investigators paired each of the 5,707 "inbred" teachers with another person in the same department of the same college, of the same length of service, sex, and academic rank. The two groups were then studied in detail. The members of the inbred group made somewhat slower progress than the others; fewer of them were listed in *Who's Who, American Men of Science,* and *Leaders in Education;* fewer of them had publications of any kind to their credit, and the number of their publications was far smaller. In short, they were not so successful—as far as one can tell from objective evidence—as those who had had wider experience. This result may be due to several factors. Perhaps the more capable graduates of an institution get jobs in other colleges, and the less capable are eventually employed in the place where they got their last degree; or perhaps the graduates of a college feel more secure in their positions and have less urge to work; or perhaps the relative narrowness of

[11] At the University of Chicago, 52 per cent of the faculty members have their highest degree from the University and 31 per cent have their A.B. also. See Reeves, *op. cit.*

their training makes them less able to make adjustments as time goes on. In any case, inbreeding does not seem desirable.

The situation as regards college personnel may be summarized as follows: The total number of college teachers is still increasing. On the average faculty about half the members are either full or associate professors. At least half the teachers have a Ph.D. and the percentage for a single college may run as high as 85. Progress from instructor to full professor is almost certain to take fifteen years and may take longer. The annual turnover is high for instructors, much lower for assistant professors, and very small for the two highest ranks. Almost all colleges show some degree of inbreeding, although the people who stay at their alma mater, as a group, are not so successful as those who do not.

II. SUPPLY AND DEMAND

It is not enough that a young person wants to teach in college or even that he is prepared to do so. His services are required in accordance with the number of positions open and the number of other equally well-prepared applicants. The best single study [12] of supply and demand covers the situation in 184 colleges between the years 1920 and 1931. It is particularly unfortunate that the study was terminated in the middle of the depression. During this period the number of new appointments per college decreased from 10.7 in 1920 to 6.9 in 1931. At the same time the proportion of Ph.D.'s among the new appointees increased from 9 to 22 per cent.

A later study [13] by the same investigator revealed the fate of 1,939 young people—649 men and 290 women—who received their doctorate in 1932. At the end of 1933, 400 of them, or 22 per cent, were still unemployed. The proportion of those who found work varied from one department to another. In psychology only 14 per cent of the new Ph.D.'s

[12] J. G. Umstattd, *Supply and Demand of College Teachers,* University of Minnesota Press, 1934, 41 pp.
[13] J. G. Umstattd, "Supply and Demand of College Teachers," *The Nation's Schools,* 14: 44, August, 1934.

were placed; in Latin, 33 per cent; in forestry, 50 per cent; in mathematics and the social sciences, over 70 per cent. Because of the depression there were too many prospective teachers for the amount of work to be done. Moreover, the training in different fields was by no means proportionate to what demand there was. During the period from 1930 to 1935— that is, during the worst of the depression—the number of Ph.D.'s granted rose 27 per cent.[14] At the same time the number of instructorships—into which rank the new candidates would presumably go—declined by some amount between 8 to 13 per cent, according to the size of the institution. By the end of the period the number of positions as instructors was still below that of 1931. In other words, the demand declined while the supply rose.

At the present time the market continues to be overcrowded, partly because of the "leftover" Ph.D.'s from earlier years and partly because many previous instructors are still out of work. The result is a steadily falling market in which the young teacher cannot get a good price for his services. It is likely that this condition will continue for a few more years, until the graduate schools reduce the number of degrees granted and the colleges have had time to overcome the financial effects of the depression. Since undergraduate enrollments are still rising, it is reasonable to suppose that a larger proportion of each year's graduate students will succeed in getting placed, but this result is by no means certain. Indeed, the worst effects of the depression, both immediate and continued, among college teachers were felt by those in the rank of instructor. The number of professorships declined a little, mainly because colleges did not make new appointments when someone died or resigned, but the loss in the number of instructorships came mostly through actual dismissals. Many of the positions have within the last two or three years again been established, but the number of instructors is still nearly 4 per cent below the total for 1931. Any young person who is planning to go into college teaching should look carefully into this matter of supply and demand for teachers of his

[14] Willey, *op. cit.*

subject, especially within his own state, before investing time and money in an advanced degree.

III. SALARIES

The earnings of college teachers are relatively low and are not likely to become much higher for some time, partly because the supply is greater than the demand and partly because the teacher has a greater degree of security than most workers in other fields. The figures as to salary cannot, therefore, be taken on their face value but must be interpreted in the light of other considerations. A typical salary scale for college teachers runs as follows:

```
Instructors  ...........................  $1,500–$2,200
Assistant professors  ..................  $2,200–$2,800
Associate professors  ..................  $2,800–$3,250
Full professors  .......................  $3,500–$5,500
```

The average salary of all members of fifty-one land-grant institutions was $3,277 in 1928, $3,307 in 1929, and $3,343 in 1930; because of reductions during the depression, the average fell to $2,906 in 1934.[15] The salaries vary a good deal from place to place and from one type of school to another. Some pertinent figures appear below.[16]

Institutions	Median Salaries							
	Professors		Associate Professors		Assistant Professors		Instructors	
	No.	Median	No.	Median	No.	Median	No.	Median
55 state and land-grant colleges and universities.	365	$4,078	211	$3,198	311	$2,680	280	$2,076
194 denominational colleges and universities...	294	$3,000	51	$2,550	99	$2,279	95	$2,032

[15] Willey, *op. cit.*
[16] E. S. Evenden, G. C. Gamble, and H. G. Blue, "National Survey of the Education of Teachers," *Office of Education Bulletin,* 1933, Vol. 2, No. 10, 258 pp., p. 179. Used by permission of the U. S. Office of Education.

Two interesting facts emerge from these data. In the denominational schools there were three times as many full professors as there were either instructors or assistant professors, while in the state schools there were only 1.3 times as many full professors as instructors and only 1.1 times as many of the former as there were assistant professors. In short, the denominational schools have faculties that are extremely "top-heavy." It is therefore not surprising that, while the youngest members of the two groups have about the same salaries, the denominational schools make an increasingly poorer showing at each successive level. One reason they cannot pay the members of the upper ranks more is that there are too many of them. The median amount in favor of the state schools rises from $44 for instructors to $401 for assistant professors, to $648 for associates, and to $1,078 for full professors.

The average life earnings of a college teacher have been computed at $74,000; [17] the corresponding figure for doctors and lawyers is $117,000; for engineers, architects, and dentists $108,000. In any comparison with other learned professions the teacher always comes out at the lower end.

The actual salaries, however, do not mean much until one considers other elements in the situation. One of the obvious points is the relation of the teacher's income to the cost of living. This relationship from 1913 through 1935 has been traced.[18] Using 1913 as a base, this author produced a chart (Figure 39), which shows the increases in salary level, the increases in the cost of living, and the relation between the two. Salaries rose slowly through 1919, when there was a large increase, followed by slightly smaller ones in 1920 and 1921. The level then continued to rise, but more slowly, until 1930. The cost of living rose slowly until 1917 and then began to climb rapidly; in 1919 it was nearly twice what it had been in 1913. From then on until 1930 it declined gradually, but between 1930 and 1933 it dropped about 35 per cent.

[17] Harold E. Clark, "Medicine, the Most Lucrative Profession," *Columbia Alumni News,* 1932.
[18] Viva Boothe, *Salaries and the Cost of Living in 27 State Universities and Colleges from 1913 to 1932,* Ohio State University Press, 1932, 157 pp. (Summary in the *Journal of Higher Education,* 3 : 504–6, 1932.)

The purchasing power of the average faculty salary was lowest between 1917 and 1921. It did not catch up with the increases in the cost of living until 1926. From then on, the

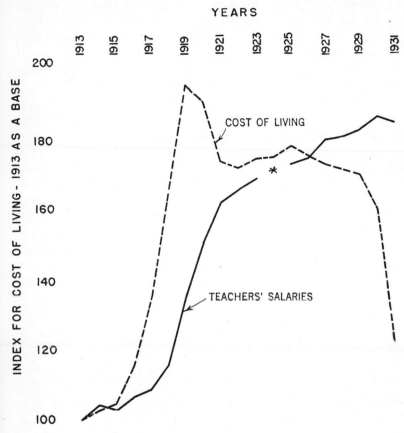

Fig. 39.—Relation between Faculty Salaries and the Cost of Living from 1913 to 1931.

* Data for this year not given.

Boothe, *op. cit.* Used by permission of the Ohio State University Press.

salary increases have been actual raises; until then the additions to salaries did not represent real increases at all, because the cost of living was rising so much faster. In spite of the depression the average faculty salary will still buy more than it would in 1913.[19]

A second matter for consideration in estimating the salary of college teachers is the degree of security they can expect. In general, the greater the security the less the financial return per year needs to be. The principle is the same as that which governs investments. Stocks pay more than bonds in good years, but their value fluctuates so much that they often pay less; bonds are sufficiently more secure that the public will invest in them, even though the yearly return is lower. A savings bank can pay an interest rate below that of bonds because it provides even greater security. An intelligent person can be content with a low salary if he is sure of getting it year after year, once he has proved his ability. The security is, however, essential. It will be quite impossible to attract capable young men and women into the teaching profession unless there is a reasonable guarantee of safety. In fact, from such evidence as has appeared, it would seem that the best minds are not being attracted. From some 125 accredited colleges, with a total number of 129,194 graduates in 1930, 6,022 or 4.6 per cent were expecting to enter teaching.[20] Barely more than half of these students, however, stood in the upper fourth of their respective graduating classes.[21] With adequate security enough superior graduates may be attracted by teaching to meet the demand without lowering the quality.

[19] For further references see T. Arnett, "Teachers' Salaries in Certain Endowed and State-supported Colleges and Universities, 1926–27," *General Education Board, Occasional Papers,* No. 8, 1928, 84 pp.; and "Teachers' Salaries," *Bulletin of the Association of American Colleges,* 15: 9–19, 1929; Y. Henderson and M. R. Davie, *Incomes and Living Cost of University Faculty,* Yale University Press, 1928, 170 pp.; J. B. Peixotto, "Family Budgets of Faculty Members," *Bulletin of the American Association of University Professors,* 15: 144–49, 1929; S. H. Slichter, "Economic Condition of the Profession," *Bulletin of the American Association of University Professors,* 19: 97–105, 1933; 20: 105–11, 1934; 21: 154–60, 1935; and Willey, *op. cit.*

[20] J. L. McConaughy, "Report of the Commission on the Enlistment and Training of College Teachers," *Bulletin of the Association of American Colleges,* 18: 82–90, 1932.

[21] See also the Reports of the Commission on Enlistment and Training of College Teachers, *Bulletin of the Association of American Colleges,* 13: 126–44, 1927; 14: 95–107, 1928; 15: 40–45, 1929; 17: 24–36, 1931; 19: 72–79, 1933; and E. H. Wilkins, "Enlistment of Prospective College Teachers," *Proceedings of the Institute for Administrative Officers of Higher Institutions,* 2: 70–79, 1930.

Tenure is by no means so secure as it should be, and there is rather more moving about from one college to another than is consistent with the most satisfactory professional development. One study [22] of 106 liberal arts colleges showed the following results concerning the number of years the faculty members had been connected with their present institution.

Years of Service	Per Cent
1–5	56
6–10	22
11–15	9
16–20	5
21–25	2
30	2

These figures suggest that the members of the profession are decidedly on the move. It takes about five years before a teacher gets really adjusted to a new college and is able to do his best work. College classes would receive better instruction if there were greater stability in the faculty.

The American Association of University Professors has for years been active in trying to bring about greater permanence of tenure. It is certainly not the object of this organization to encourage mediocrity, although such a charge has been made, but to protect the capable college teacher so that he can give his full attention to his duties. The unsatisfactory person should be eliminated during his first few years, while he is still an instructor. After a person has proved his ability he should have security of tenure to compensate him for his low financial return. Even though, as in many colleges and universities, a professor can have by law only a yearly contract, the institutions should feel a moral responsibility to renew these contracts unless there is a most adequate reason for dismissal. The general principles in regard to tenure are embodied in the quotation below:

(a) The precise terms and expectations of every appointment should be stated in writing and be in the possession of both college and teacher.

[22] N. M. Grier, "Teaching Tenure," *Journal of Higher Education,* 4: 483–84, 1933. Used by permission of the *Journal of Higher Education.*

(b) Termination of a temporary or a short-term appointment should always be possible at the expiration of the term by the mere act of giving timely notice of the desire to terminate. The decision to terminate should always be taken, however, in conference with the department concerned, and might well be subject to approval by a faculty committee or by the faculty council. It is desirable that the question of appointments for the ensuing year be taken up as early as possible.

Notice of the decision to terminate should be given in ample time to allow the teacher an opportunity to secure a new position. The extreme limit for such notice should not be less than three months before the expiration of the academic year. The teacher who proposes to withdraw should also give notice in ample time to enable the institution to make a new appointment.

(c) It is desirable that termination of a permanent or long-term appointment for cause should regularly require action by both a faculty committee and the governing board of the college. Exceptions to this rule may be necessary in cases of gross immorality or treason, when the facts are admitted. In such cases summary dismissal would naturally ensue. In cases where other offenses are charged, and in all cases where the facts are in dispute, the accused teacher should always have the opportunity to face his accusers and to be heard in his own defense. In cases of professional incompetence the testimony of scholars in the same field, either from his own or from other institutions, should always be taken. Dismissal for other reasons than immorality or treason should not ordinarily take effect in less than a year from the time the decision is reached.

(d) Termination of permanent or long-term appointments because of financial exigencies should be sought only as a last resort, after every effort has been made to meet the need in other ways and to find for the teacher other employment in the institution. Situations which make drastic retrenchment of this sort necessary should preclude expansions of the staff at other points at the same time, except in extraordinary circumstances.[23]

These provisions appear sane, yet during every year there are a few dismissals of professors for either no reason or no adequate reason.

[23] From a Report in the *Bulletin of the American Association of University Professors,* 26: 53–54, 1940.

While the security of the college teacher is not so high as it needs to be, it is higher than in other types of work. For instance, during the depression the median reduction in the

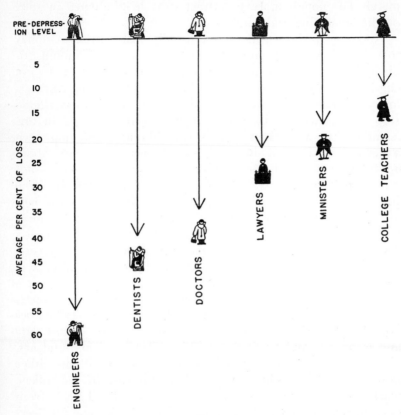

FIG. 40.—Relative Security of Income as Revealed by Average Losses during the Depression.

size of faculties was only 4 per cent and in salaries only 15 per cent.[24] The amount of unemployment was therefore much less than that in other fields. While comparisons of incomes of different types are always a little dangerous, there seems no doubt that college faculties weathered the depression better

[24] Willey, *op. cit.*

than did members of any other profession. Figure 40 gives an indication of relative security.[25] There is, then, already a fair degree of compensation for low salaries. There should merely be enough more to attract capable graduates in spite of the small financial returns.

A college professor does not usually make enough money to bring up a family and still save a reasonable amount for his old age. If he teaches in a state university, he is not eligible for any old-age security.[26] As a result of this situation many professors continue working long after they should stop and would like to stop. About half the colleges in this country have no retirement system, although there has been a revival of interest in all kinds of pensions since about 1936.[27] In the most common pension plan the college holds 5 per cent of each teacher's salary, adds an equal amount from its own funds, and—when the teacher retires—buys the best annuity it can with the joint savings. Where this arrangement is in force a teacher has much more security than otherwise. More and more colleges are adapting some sort of pension system, and it is probable that eventually every teacher will have this type of protection.

In addition to financial security a teacher needs more opportunity to study than he can get while he is working. If he does not have time to read and study he soon becomes out of date and is of less and less value to his college and his students. No professional man or woman can ever stand still; he either moves forward or slides backward. In the case of the college teacher there is the further need for an occasional leave from duty because he needs to get away from adolescent intellects and eternal youth. Many a professor has failed to realize his full possibilities because he has spent too large a part of his adult life among his intellectual and scholastic inferiors. A sabbatical or other type of leave is not as common as it ought

[25] *Ibid.* Figure 40 is based upon a table on p. 41. Used by permission of the McGraw-Hill Book Company.
[26] At present he is not eligible even in a private college, but the laws may be altered in this respect. See C. Wilcox, "The College Professor and the Social Security Act," *Bulletin of the American Association of University Professors,* 25: 284-94, 1939.
[27] Willey, *op. cit.*

to be. One investigation of 268 colleges [28] reports 43 per cent as having leaves for its faculty members, while another study [29] of practices in 419 colleges and universities reports 44 per cent. It appears, then, that in less than half of the institutions can a teacher expect this chance to refresh his soul. Where such leaves exist, under the usual arrangement the college provides full pay for a semester or half pay for a year.

In this connection one point should be made concerning the "four-quarter-plan" about which one hears conflicting reports. It originated as an administrative device for keeping a university plant continually busy—thus producing more income. Many faculty members regard it as a system designed to prevent any teacher from living long enough to claim his pension. After it has been in force in an institution for a few years, however, most teachers come to like it because of the system of automatic leaves that it includes. The usual procedure is as follows: a professor teaches for six consecutive quarters—for instance the fall of 1930, the winter, spring, summer, fall of 1931, and the winter of 1932 [30] and then gets seven months' continuous vacation on full pay. He not only does not have to ask for these leaves—he has to take them whether he wants to or not, because he is not allowed to teach at his own institution during his free quarters. He can go elsewhere and teach if he wishes to augment his salary. If a person is a language teacher he can usually arrange to teach nine consecutive quarters and then have a whole year to spend abroad; thus, by teaching from the fall of 1930 through the fall of 1932 he could be away all of 1933. Under no other plan of work does a teacher get such regularly recurring, automatic leaves on full pay. This feature compensates in large measure for the feeling of being hurried which results from the shorter time between classes. The actual number of class periods per credit hour is the same as for the semester plan, but the classes meet oftener—usually every day.

From an economic point of view, then, a college teacher can expect a lower salary but greater stability than he would

[28] H. G. Bennett and S. Scroggs, "Sabbatical Leave," *Journal of Higher Education,* 3: 196–99, 1932.
[29] O. J. Campbell, "Systems of Sabbatical Leaves," *Bulletin of the American Association of University Professors,* 17: 219–34, 1931.
[30] Actually there are two week vacations between quarters and the whole month of September as rest periods, so the six consecutive quarters are not as strenuous as they may sound.

receive in other types of professional work. He has a reasonable expectation of receiving a pension and some chance of being allowed an occasional leave of absence for purposes of his own development.

IV. LEGAL STATUS

Most college professors, like most citizens, go through life without ever bothering over their legal status. In an emergency, however, it is well to know where one stands before the law. A college teacher, regardless of rank, is an employee, not a public official.[31] The latter cannot be discharged except by legal removal, and he draws his pay whether he works or not, while the former can be discharged—though not wrongly— and gets his pay only upon fulfillment of his duties. As long as a teacher is employed under contract he has a remedy against arbitrary dismissal before the end of the stipulated term— just as any other employee has—unless the contract in question reads that the governing board has the right to discharge him at their pleasure, with or without cause. In many contracts there is a clause to the effect that the trustees of an institution can remove a professor at any time without notice, if in their opinion the best interests of the college require the discharge. Just what the "best interests" are and in what ways a teacher can work against them is not stated. However, most professors have the best interests of their college at heart and are therefore in no danger of discharge under this clause.

What the teacher is not protected from is the failure of his institution to renew his contract. The maximum term of employment in public institutions is usually fixed by statute, and there is no law covering the moral responsibility of a college or university to rehire a satisfactory employee. College authorities have thus a legal though not a moral right to discharge a professor at the end of any year by the simple expedient of withholding his contract for the next year. Although this is not often done, it can be, and therefore constitutes one of the

---

[31] M. M. Chambers, "The Legal Status of Professors," *Journal of Higher Education*, 2: 481–86, 1931.

hazards of the profession. It would seem, then, that the law
is on a teacher's side during the term of service for which
he has a contract, but that there is a decided loophole between
contracts.[32]

V. SUMMARY

It does not take a graduate student of today long to find
out that the supply of college teachers is greater than the
demand. The first step is to get a job at all. Once an instructor
has a position he soon discovers for himself that progress is
moderate and the financial returns low. There are, however,
some compensations in the matter of security. The teacher's
tenure—except for gross violations of conventional standards—is already more secure and his income steadier than is
the case with other professional workers. The main difference
between him and them is perhaps that he never has "boom"
years, during which he can get far enough ahead financially
to weather a depression. All his years are lean ones. Consequently he needs security of tenure during his active service
and security of pension when he retires. If the profession can
offer safety, its attractiveness is sufficient to interest a fair
proportion of the best minds in each generation. Higher education cannot afford to depend upon the services of those few
gifted souls who are destined to teach, no matter what the
disadvantages to themselves may be, plus those who are content with a low salary and partial security because in any other
position they would get an equally low income with no secruity
at all.

[32] For a good history of the specific cases on which opinions have
been based, see E. C. Elliott and M. M. Chambers, *The Colleges and the
Courts,* Carnegie Foundation for the Advancement of Teaching, 1936,
564 pp.

V.

THE MEASUREMENT OF TEACIIING

CHAPTER XXV

THE RATING OF COLLEGE TEACHERS

In recent years the rating scale as a means of estimating a teacher's success has appeared upon the scene. Any young person who is now preparing to become a college professor will probably at one time or another be rated. It is therefore desirable that teachers should understand the nature of these scales and should form their opinions upon the basis of actual facts about what measurement of this type will and will not do.

Whatever one may think about the scales themselves, one cannot but approve of one by-product that has emerged from the research upon which the scales rest. In order to rate a teacher it was obviously necessary first to know what were the traits of good teaching and wherein lay the difference between excellent and unsatisfactory instruction. Investigators have therefore studied this question in its numerous ramifications until it is now possible to list the outstanding and basic characteristics of both good and poor teachers. The first section of this chapter will deal with results of such research. Once the rating scales were prepared, they were, of course, used. The discussion about their value has centered mainly around two points—the reliability of the measures themselves and the reliability of such ratings when made by students. There is a great deal of quite conclusive evidence on both these points. Finally, there is the question of what value, if any, teachers derive from being rated. If no benefit accrues to teachers, the scales have only a police function and cannot be regarded as educational. What data there is on these matters will be presented in the following sections.

I. CHARACTERISTICS OF GOOD AND POOR TEACHERS

It is obviously for the good of a college community if faculty members know what characteristics good teaching has. In most colleges the average instructor has little or no chance to observe his colleagues at work. Even if he knows that Professor X is an expert, he cannot usually visit classes and see what makes Professor X so unusual. Students will undoubtedly tell him something about this expert's methods, but a teacher cannot solicit such information without discussing his colleagues with his students—a most undesirable practice. A college teacher is therefore thrown rather completely upon his own resources in the development of his methods, and he rarely has any objective yardstick by which he can measure himself. The numerous investigations to be reported should therefore contain worth-while information.

The usual procedure in studying teaching methods has been to select two groups of teachers, the outstandingly poor and conspicuously good, and then to study both extremes in as great detail as possible. The opinions of students, faculty members, administrative officers, alumni, and departmental heads are commonly taken into consideration in selecting the teachers. The traits shown by each group have been determined partly by actual observation and partly by student testimony, either spontaneous or in answer to specific questions. The results from the numerous studies agree; there seems little doubt that the essential elements in good and poor teaching are definitely known. The list of traits that will be presented shortly is the outcome of many separate pieces of research. I have combined the results partly to condense them and partly to give a more complete picture of the good and poor teacher.[1]

[1] The studies from which the results have been taken appear below. Not every trait is mentioned in every study, but all characteristics included in the lists appear in the majority of these investigations.

A. G. Barr, "Scientific Analysis of Teaching Procedure." *Journal of*

The traits of the oustandingly good teacher as revealed by research are summarized in the list below:

TABLE 37
Traits of the Good Teacher

I. Scholarship
    A. He knows his subject matter thoroughly
    B. He is interested in his profession
    C. He never stops studying and learning
    D. He shows mental growth from year to year

II. Handling of class
    A. He is orderly, systematic, and careful to have details properly arranged
    B. He organizes his courses; uses syllabi, summaries, and outlines
    C. He is always prepared for class
    D. He uses various methods of teaching, adapting them to the subject matter under consideration
    E. He has definite standards of work and holds his students responsible for meeting them
    F. His assignments are clear and varied; he emphasizes the purpose of the work and leaves enough time to make his assignments properly
    G. He uses many illustrations; whenever possible he shows the relation of his work to daily life; he has a bulletin board, charts, etc.
    H. His tests are fair; he grades papers accurately and carefully; he gives examinations frequently and keeps students informed of their standing; he returns papers promptly and discusses them; he gives adequate time for review
    I. His conduct of the class is informal; he lets students participate in the classwork and express their opinions freely; he

Educational Method, 4: 369–71, 1925; G. C. Brandenburg, "Why College Teachers Fail," *Indiana University, School of Education Bulletin,* Indiana University, Vol. 9, No. 1, 1932, pp. 49–60; F. S. Breed, "Factors Contributing to Success for College Teaching," *Journal of Educational Research,* 16: 247–53, 1927; C. D. Champlin, "The Preferred College Professor," *School and Society,* 27: 175–77, 1928; R. J. Clinton, "Qualities College Students Desire in College Instructors," *School and Society,* 32: 702, 1930; C. C. Crawford, "Defects and Difficulties in College Teaching," *School and Society,* 28: 497–502, 1928; C. O. Davis, "Our Best Teachers," *School Review,* 34: 754–59, 1926; E. M. Dexter, "Determining What Constitutes Campus Popularity," *School and Society,* 23: 758–60, 1926; H. L. Donovan, "Faculty Effort in the Improvement of College Teaching," *Peabody Journal of Education,* 7: 259–63, 1930; C. C. Eckhart, "Faculty Self-Survey and the Improvement of College Teaching," *School and Society,* 27: 336–38, 1928; E. S. Evenden, "The Improvement of College Teaching," *Teachers College Record,* 29: 587–96, 1928; F. C. Hockema, "Earmarks and Question Marks," *Journal of Higher Education,* 8: 471–74, 1937; H. F.

gives them a chance to think; he knows his students
individually
J. He keeps work adjusted to the learning capacities and compre-
hension of his students
K. He constantly analyzes errors, does remedial teaching, and
individualizes his instruction
L. He speaks clearly and has no annoying mannerisms
III. Personality
A. He is kind, human, friendly, sociable, willing to see students
outside of class
B. He is polite, tolerant, mature, objective
C. He is enthusiastic, interesting, and vital
D. He is intellectually honest and willing to admit his own short-
comings and errors
E. He has a sense of humor
F. He is neat in appearance and orderly in his habits

From this list, the picture of the excellent teacher emerges
clearly. He is a true scholar, he is efficient, he works at his
job, he always considers the nature of the youthful mind, he
is resourceful, he is objective, he is human, and he is a gentleman. Of course, few teachers are superior in every possible
trait, but the best college professors stand well above the
average on all and are outstanding in some. Because of their
scholarly attainments they have something to teach, because
of their attention to business they present their knowledge

Martin, "Methods of Teaching in College Classes," *Pedagogical Seminary,*
31 : 285–92, 1924; J. E. Moore, "Annoying Habits of College Professors,"
Journal of Abnormal and Social Psychology, 30 : 43–46, 1935, and "A
Further Study of the Annoying Habits of College Professors," *ibid.,* 32 :368–
75, 1937; F. P. O'Brien, "The College Student's Viewpoint," *Sixteenth
Yearbook of the National Society of College Teachers of Education,* University of Chicago Press, 1928, pp. 8–15; L. B. Richardson, "Deficiencies
in Current College Teaching," *Proceedings of the Institute for Administrative Officers of Higher Institutions,* 2 : 5–18, 1930; Q. A. W. Rohrbach,
"How College Teaching Could Be Made More Interesting as Viewed
by the Student," *Sixteenth Yearbook of the National Society of College
Teachers of Education,* University of Chicago Press, 1928, pp. 16–23; A. R.
Root, "Student Ratings of Teachers," *Journal of Higher Education,* 2 : 311–
15, 1931; L. P. Sieg, "Who Are the Good Teachers?" *School and Society,*
36 : 481–85, 1932; G. E. Snavely, "Who Is a Great Teacher?" *Bulletin of
the Association of American Colleges,* 15 : 68–72, 1929; J. A. Starrak, "Student Rating of Instruction," *Journal of Higher Education,* 5 : 88–90, 1934;
H. M. Wriston, "Requisites of Successful College Teachers from the
Administrator's Point of View," *Proceedings of the Institute for Administrative Officers of Higher Institutions,* 1938, pp. 76–92; W. A. Bous-
field, "Student Ratings of Qualities Considered Desirable in College Professors," *School and Society,* 51 : 253–56, 1940.

well, and because of their personality they are always considerate of students.

The traits of the unsuccessful teacher are to some extent simply the reverse of those already listed, but in addition he has some peculiarities of his own. The characteristics attributed to the unpopular college instructor are shown below :

TABLE 38

Traits of the Poor Teacher

I. Scholarship
   A. He does not know his subject matter and is often quite out of date
   B. He does not continue to work and study in his own field
   C. He is often interested primarily in either research or writing and not in teaching

II. Handling of class
   A. He does not control his class; he assigns readings in books that are not in the library; he does not allow time enough for the work
   B. He does not use an outline or syllabus; he jumps from one thing to another in an illogical fashion
   C. He is vague and indecisive [2] in class; he rambles; he has no discernible objective; he bluffs and "stalls"
   D. He uses the same methods day after day; he depends almost wholly upon the textbook, practically paralleling it in class; he is so dependent upon his notes that he cannot look at the students while he talks; he sometimes reads his lectures
   E. He has no clear standard of work
   F. He often makes no assignment; when he does, he assigns only pages in the text
   G. He makes no effort to connect what goes on in class with anything outside; he repeats the examples given in the text and rarely has supplementary materials of his own
   H. His tests are poorly made and unfair; he sometimes does not pass back papers; when he does return them, he delays for several days; he gives no help in reviewing; his grading is inaccurate and careless
   I. He does not allow his students to talk much and does not permit them to disagree with him
   J. He talks over the students' heads; he is technical
   K. He makes no evident effort to individualize his work
   L. He uses poor English; he has numerous annoying mannerisms [3]

[2] As the freshmen are warned in the "Cheater's Bible," published by students at Stanford University: Don't select a professor who says, "It is probably true to some extent but only to a certain degree."

[3] A list of such habits has been compiled and reads as follows: twisting

III. Personality
   A. He is lazy, conceited, impatient, and indifferent
   B. He is sarcastic,[4] prejudiced, dogmatic, intolerant; he shows marked favoritism
   C. He is dull
   D. He will not admit his own errors or shortcomings
   E. He has either no humor or an unkind humor
   F. He is untidy in appearance and unsystematic in his habits

This list is most revealing. The poor teacher is a slovenly scholar, he has many forms of personal inefficiency, he is too lazy to apply himself properly to his job, he shows a minimum of ingenuity, he pays no real attention to his students, he takes everything personally, he is immature, and he has no manners. I strongly suspect that he hates teaching and wishes his students were all in Jericho. Between the lines of this list one can see a profoundly unhappy, tired, maladjusted person who is under more social and emotional strain than he can bear. His students suffer, but so does he. Although no teacher is likely to have all the traits mentioned, a person with only a few of them is unsatisfactory in the classroom.

II. RATING SCALES

1. Nature of the scales: Once the main characteristics of good and poor teaching had been determined objectively, it was a natural further step to devise a scale by which an observer could estimate the methods and personality of any given teacher. These scales have taken one of three forms. In some cases they consist merely of a list of questions that the observer is to answer, either positively or negatively; in other cases it is a series of traits, and the rater is to indicate to what degree the teacher shows each of them. For rating

mouth into odd shapes, frowning, playing with objects, cocking the head, pulling ears or nose, sticking hands into pockets, standing in awkward positions, allowing long pauses, using pet expressions, scratching the head, looking off at the corners of the room, talking too low to be heard, pacing the floor, sitting on the desk, talking too fast, moving nervously all the time. For further details, see Moore, *op. cit.*

[4] For a list of supposed witticisms that were actually heard, see T. H. Briggs, "Sarcasm," *School Review,* 36: 685–95, 1928. According to student testimony sarcasm caused them to do poorer rather than better work on at least two-thirds of the occasions when they received such treatment.

teachers in elementary and high school the observer sometimes tabulates on a list of activities the things a teacher actually does and how often he does each. This last type is the most objective, but as far as I know it does not exist for use with college teachers.[5] The series of questions generally covers many points in some detail, while the rating scale is restricted to only a few characteristics about which the user expresses his general opinion. One sample of each type is reproduced below:

TABLE 39
A Sample List of Questions [6]

1. Does he treat you in a democratic spirit?
2. Does his general scholarship seem to be of a high order?
3. Is his scholarship in his specialty adequate for the job?
4. Does he know what he is talking about?
5. Are the statements he makes accurate and reliable?
6. Does he seem fair in his presentation of debatable points?
7. Is he master of the class situation?
8. Does he admit his lack of information on points of weakness?
9. Does he deal honorably with you?
10. Does he give you a wholesome opportunity to learn?
11. Does he invite and welcome critical questions upon the subject matter of the course?
12. Are his examinations comprehensive enough to be a good sampling of your educational experience in his course?
13. Is he a mere rubber stamp of the textbook?
14. Do you leave the class feeling that you have made profitable use of the hour?
15. Is he willing to make inquiries about points on which his preparation was inadequate?
16. Does he have definite prejudices that make him partial?
17. Does he create a cheerful spirit in the room?
18. Does he give you an adequate chance to prepare for examinations?
19. Is his classwork prepared thoroughly?
20. Does he play "aboveboard" in preparing examinations?
21. Does he play "aboveboard" in giving examinations?
22. Does he play "aboveboard" in grading examinations?
23. Is he sympathetic to your interests and points of view?
24. Do you consider him a constructive influence in your life?
25. Does he stimulate interest in the subject matter of the course?

[5] For a good example of such a scale for use in the public schools, see A. S. Barr, "Scientific Analysis of Teaching Procedures," *Journal of Educational Method,* 4: 360–71, 1925.

[6] A. R. Root, "Student Rating of Teachers," *Journal of Higher Education,* 2: 311–15, 1931. Used by permission of the *Journal of Higher Education.*

26. Does he wander from point to point?
27. Does he hurt your feelings in the classroom?
28. Does he understand your needs in the field?
29. Does he show any degree of nervousness and tension in class?
30. Does he bluff in class by evasive answers?
31. Does he make examinations unwarranted ordeals for you?
32. Does he have any distracting or annoying peculiarities of dress?
33. Does he tolerate well-meant but poorly worded questions in class?
34. Does he relate the parts of the course and synthesize the whole into a meaningful progression?
35. Does he have any annoying peculiarities of speech?
36. Does he have any annoying peculiarities of action?
37. Does he stimulate and maintain interest in the subject matter of the course?
38. Does he hold your interest during the class hour?
39. Are his examinations fair?
40. Is his vocabulary beyond your comprehension?
41. Is he accessible and approachable outside of class, so that you may talk over difficulties or problems with him?
42. Does he create in you a gross inferiority by his classroom treatment of you?

This series of questions has a high reliability. A group of two hundred students who used it for rating a teacher agreed with themselves so well that the coefficient of reliability was .95.

Probably the best-known and most widely used scale for judging the work of college teachers is that developed at Purdue.[7] It covers only ten traits, all of which are quite general. A copy of this scale appears in Figure 41. The phrases inserted under the lines are for the guidance of the student in making up his mind.[8]

This list of qualities, when taken together, tend to make any instructor the sort of instructor that he is. Of course, no one is ideal in all of these qualities, but some approach this ideal to a much greater extent than do others. In order to obtain information which may lead to the improvement of instruction, you

[7] H. H. Remmers, "The College Professor as the Student Sees Him," *Purdue University Studies in Higher Education,* XI, Vol. 29, No. 6, 1929, 63 pp.
[8] Other scales may be found in F. S. Breed, "A Guide for College Teaching," *School and Society,* 24: 82–87, 1926; G. W. Hartman, "Measuring Teaching Efficiency among College Instructors," *Archives of Psychology,* Vol. 23, No. 154, 1933, 45 pp.; H. Patterson, "An Experiment in Supervising College Teaching," *School and Society,* 21: 146–47, 1925. There is a good collection of scales for use in college in the "Report of the Committee on College and University Teaching," *Bulletin of the American Association of University Professors,* Vol. 19, No. 5, Sec. 2, 1933, 122 pp.

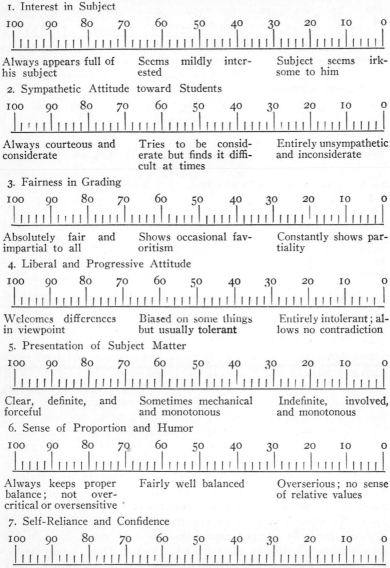

FIG. 41.—The Purdue Rating Scale.
Used by permission of Purdue University.

FIG. 41.—(*Continued*).

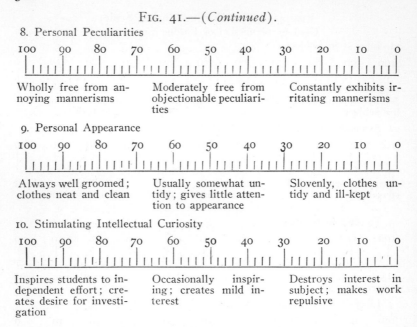

8. Personal Peculiarities

100   90   80   70   60   50   40   30   20   10   0

Wholly free from an-   Moderately free from   Constantly exhibits ir-
noying mannerisms   objectionable peculiari-   ritating mannerisms
                             ties

9. Personal Appearance

100   90   80   70   60   50   40   30   20   10   0

Always well groomed;   Usually somewhat un-   Slovenly, clothes un-
clothes neat and clean   tidy; gives little atten-   tidy and ill-kept
                             tion to appearance

10. Stimulating Intellectual Curiosity

100   90   80   70   60   50   40   30   20   10   0

Inspires students to in-   Occasionally   inspir-   Destroys interest in
dependent effort; cre-   ing; creates mild in-   subject; makes work
ates desire for investi-   terest   repulsive
gation

are asked to rate your instructor on the indicated qualities by
making a check on the line at the point which most nearly describes him with reference to the quality you are considering.

One is naturally interested in the sort of results obtained from
such a device. A few illustrations should make clear the facts of
the case. First, there are some "profiles" for several professors;
these are made by joining together the average on each trait for
the same person. Professor A rated above 90 in his interest in
his subject, his presentation, his sense of proportion, his absence
of mannerisms, and his ability to stimulate students; his ratings
in sympathy toward students, fairness, progressiveness, and selfconfidence were slightly lower but are still good; his students
apparently did not think much of his clothes, however, since they
rated them decidedly below the usual level for this trait. Professor C was so bad as to require no comment. Professor J
showed decidedly uneven capacities. He was rated high in his
presentation of subject matter and freedom from mannerisms;
his students thought him rather uninterested in his subject, only
moderately self-confident, careless about his appearance, and be-

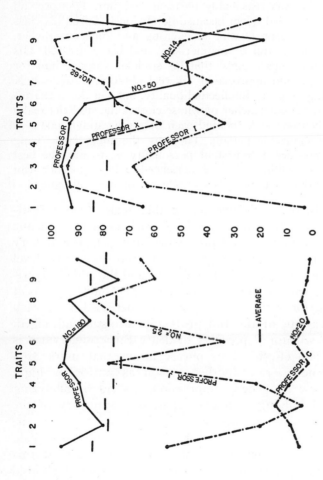

FIG. 42.—Profiles of Several College Teachers.

Remmers, "The College Professor as the Student Sees Him," *op. cit.* Used by permission of Purdue University.

The short, straight lines on this figure indicate the average rating, based upon much use of the scale. All the averages are high, but students do not hesitate to give an individual teacher a rating at the bottom of the scale, as will appear shortly. It may surprise people that teachers dress so well.

low average in ability to stimulate intellectual curiosity; they were apparently annoyed by his lack of sympathy, his unfairness, and his rigidity. Professor I impressed his students as being uninterested in his subject, quite unstimulating, and poor in his presentation, but he was reasonably pleasant and fair. I suspect all his ratings were pulled down because he obviously bored his class unspeakably. Professor D was an exciting and superior teacher, but he was hesitant, full of mannerisms, and badly dressed. His extremely high ratings suggest that his students forgave him for his shortcomings and appreciated his real abilities. Professor X got a low rating on every intellectual quality, but she was a charming person and the one teacher of whose clothes the students really approved. When one looks behind each of these ratings, one sees a real and recognizable person. The way the judgments "hang together" to produce a consistent personality is, to me, the best proof of their validity. Any experienced college teacher can identify every one of these types among his or her colleagues.

There is further evidence about this scale. One investigator [9] collected ratings on 213 college teachers of all academic levels from assistants to full professors. The per cent of very superior teachers should be greater at each successive level because of the elimination of the least fit and the added experience of those who remain. Of the assistants, only 5 per cent received superior ratings; the per cent increased with each grade, 48 per cent of the full professors being so adjudged. Another investigator [10] presents evidence concerning what is called the "halo effect." This phrase means that users of a scale may tend to rate another person as uniformly high, average, or low on general impression, instead of analyzing his traits and judging each one separately. Summary of the statistical treatment on this point is not necessary, but the conclusion seems to be that there is remarkably little halo effect observable in the judgments obtained by use of this scale. Certainly the students who rated Professor J showed discrimination.

2. Ratings by students: From the first appearance of the scales there has been constant discussion about allowing stu-

[9] Brandenburg, *op. cit.*
[10] Starrak, *op. cit.*

dents to make out the ratings. Naturally, everyone knows that students have always passed judgment upon their teachers, but these opinions have remained until recently merely matters of campus gossip. Presumably even the most bitter critics of rating scales would have no objection if a teacher wished to use them with his own classes for his own information; academic freedom certainly allows a teacher to ask his students what they think of him. The opposition arises when the opinions of students are used as a basis for supervisory or administrative action. On this point various people have expressed themselves with more or less emotional fervor.[11] The fundamental objection is that these ratings are not reliable. The reasons advanced are numerous: the students are too young to have any worthwhile opinion, they do not know good teaching when they see it, they are not able to analyze teaching into its elements, they make out their ratings carelessly, their opinions depend upon their marks in the course, they use the scale as a means of expressing their prejudices or of "getting even" with the instructor, and they develop an undesirable attitude toward their teachers. If any of these objections should prove true, the use of scales would become questionable.

On some of these points there is already objective and conclusive evidence. The scales are undoubtedly reliable in the sense that the same students rate the same teacher the same way on different occasions.[12] The coefficient of reliability for the Purdue Scale is .95. If teachers are not told what their students said about them and consequently do not have this impetus to alter their methods, student opinion remains stable from one year to the next in the same classes.[13] For more than one hundred college instructors there was, under such

---

[11] See Anon., "Rating the Professor," *School and Society,* 28: 311–14, 1928; H. G. Hullfish, "Student Rates the Teacher—Officially," *Educational Administration and Supervision,* 17: 314–16, 1931; M. I. Pretzman, "Student Rating of College Teachers," *School and Society,* 29: 513–15, 1929; L. Detchen, "Shall the Student Rate the Teacher?" *Journal of Higher Education,* 11: 146–53, 1940.

[12] See, for instance, Remmers, *op. cit.;* H. R. Douglass, "Rating the Teaching Effectiveness of College Instructors," *School and Society,* 28: 192–97, 1928.

[13] E. R. Guthrie, "Measuring Student Opinion of Teachers," *School and Society,* 25: 175–76, 1927.

circumstances, extremely little fluctuation. In short, the students are not guessing. They are rating something that to them is real and about which they have definite opinions.

Although the scales are demonstrably reliable they may still not be valid. That is, students' evaluation, while the same from day to day, may always be wrong, because it rests upon the wrong premises. What evidence there is supports the view that students know whereof they speak. In one instance an investigator [14] obtained the best possible information he could about teachers by visiting their classes, collecting opinions from colleagues and departmental heads, looking over their assignments and tests, finding out how many of their students went on into advanced work in their department, reading their publications, and so on. This composite evaluation of teaching effectiveness was correlated with student ratings. The coefficients varied from .72 to .89. Another investigator [15] of this same point concluded that the students gave valid ratings in at least 75 per cent of the cases. In short, if anyone is right about teaching skill, the students are equally right.

Undoubtedly there have been occasions on which students made out their ratings carelessly, but this fault is not inherent in the nature of the scales. Any experienced teacher knows that students are careless if they are allowed to be and careful if they are asked to be. The problem of obtaining thoughtful opinions is not different from that of getting any work well done. If some administrative officer takes over a class during the teacher's absence and tells the students that their ratings will be used for serious purposes, the students will produce their best judgment.

There has been no study so far as I can find out of the relationship between an individual student's rating and his emotional attitude toward an instructor. I have, however, seen a good many scales that had been filled out by students. Thus far, I think, I have never been over a large set of ratings in

[14] Douglass, "Rating the Teaching Effectiveness of College Instructors," *op. cit.*
[15] Starrak, *op. cit.*

which I did not find at least one that ranked the teacher as a complete paragon and one that ranked him a little short of a fiend in human form. These extremes are just projections of "grouches" or "crushes." No teacher should be in the least disturbed by an occasional outburst of either type; they are infrequent and they have no influence upon the general results. In fact, the person who bases protests upon them has fallen into the familiar error of arguing from the single instance. If, out of fifty students, one gives an extremely low rating, the matter is of no importance; if three or four produce such opinions, the situation becomes worth looking into; if a dozen have this idea, something is undoubtedly wrong. The same discretion should be used in considering abnormally high ratings. One in a class means nothing; a sprinkling of them suggests superior teaching; enough of them prove it. These occasional extreme fluctuations do not affect the statistical results if one uses the median instead of the arithmetical average; even one low rating in a small class can pull an average down, but it does not alter the position of the median.

The criticism that students express opinions in direct relation to their standing in a course is entirely without foundation. There is no relation whatsoever.[16] Although ratings are not signed, it is easy enough to introduce faint markings that differentiate one paper from another and then to pass out the papers in accordance with a prearranged seating plan. The students think their judgments are anonymous, but actually they are identifiable. The correlation between marks and ratings is usually about .15.

The criticism that students do not know good teachers when they see them does not seem to be borne out by the agreement of their ratings with those of departmental heads and faculty members. Moreover the point is debatable from other angles. Students probably do not know what elements constitute expert teaching, but they do know when they find a course of interest

---

[16] H. H. Remmers, "The Relationship between Student Marks and Student Attitude toward Instructors," *School and Society*, 28: 759–60, 1928; Starrak, *op. cit.*

and value to them. They are in the same position as the person who views an art exhibit; he does not know how the various artists produced their effects, but he is quite certain what his reactions are. An artist may express his soul in totally unintelligible ways, bore the public, and die in a garret. A teacher may similarly express himself, infuriate his students, and lose his job. This sort of thing may not be either art or education, but it is undeniably life. The students are the consumers of teaching, and they know what they can and cannot consume, even if they are foggy about the reasons. Students admittedly cannot analyze teaching ability into its elements nor do they often have a clear standard of what constitutes good teaching, but they do not need to have either. They can answer specific questions about their own reactions, and that is all any scale asks them to do. The interpretation of the results is not their business.

Before leaving this topic I should like to stress the point that students are the only people who can or should rate a teacher, as far as his work in the classroom is concerned. They are poor judges of a teacher's scholarship or his general worth to a college, but they are the only individuals who know what goes on in class. No supervisor or departmental head ever finds out what a teacher's daily performance is like, because no class is normal when there is a visitor in it. I well remember one instructor who was intolerably prejudiced and sarcastic. Apparently some rumors of the situation had reached the head of his department because one day the head visited class. The subsequent hour was the only one in the entire year during which the instructor showed neither sarcasm nor prejudice. He was kind, gentle, and sympathetic. The visitor found out exactly nothing about this teacher's usual classroom procedures and, I fear, never suspected how the students paid in subsequent days for that one hour of amiability. The ability to impress students favorably day after day is important; the ability to impress a supervisor once in a while is not. The students are the only people who see a teacher in all his moods and can sample all his methods. They are therefore in a position to give a rating that is based on enough observations to mean something. They give their judgments anyway; the rating scale merely makes these opinions systematic and official.

Naturally there has been opposition by professors to the idea of being rated by their students.[17] The whole business is sometimes regarded as an insult to academic dignity and freedom. Some of the resistance comes from teachers who fear low ratings, some from those who cannot face the prospect of being rated at all, and some from those who think students totally unfit to judge their work. Members of the first group are justifiably agitated, and one can only feel sorry for those in the second, many of whom are superior teachers and know it. The idea that college students, especially upperclassmen, cannot give reliable opinions about a teacher with whom they have spent from thirty to sixty hours is rather ridiculous. It is much easier to fool one's colleague than one's students.

One of my students brought this point home to me with considerable force. I had not realized that I had developed the habit of holding on to the back of a chair and generally playing with it while I lectured. In the course of time the janitor, in a fit of industry, removed the chair from the platform. My next two lectures went badly. I consulted no less than three colleagues, all of whom made suggestions, which I followed. The work continued to be below par. After about a week of indifferent lectures one of the boys in the front row got up in the middle of the period, brought his chair up onto the platform, and said, "Here, hang on to this, and everything will be all right." I got a firm grip on the chair back, and my ideas began to flow easily for the first time in several days. Within five minutes I was completely out of the woods. Neither my colleagues nor I could make a diagnosis, but a student knew the answer.

Rating scales, if properly used and sensibly interpreted, give information that cannot be obtained in any other way. They have their place in any plan for the evaluation or improvement of college teaching. Although a single student may be prejudiced in one way or another, the testimony of an entire group is both reliable and valid.

[17] A good summary of arguments for and against student ratings appears in R. C. Bryan, "A Study of Student Ratings of College Teachers," *Educational Administration and Supervision,* 19: 290–306, 1933.

III. USES OF RATING SCALES

The most valuable use of a scale is to inform a teacher of the effect his own performance has had upon his audience. Any instructor who does not use them for this purpose is overlooking an excellent source of information. There is some evidence that teachers realize this fact.[18] Repeated ratings provide a teacher with objective evidence of his development. In one case [19] an instructor's first rating totalled 789 points on a scale, for which the average in his institution was 818 points. This teacher studied the opinions recorded about him by his students and tried to remedy his weaknesses. On five subsequent ratings by different classes he scored 801, 863, 873, 887, and 982 points. At the end he was among those with the highest ratings. In another case [20] two teachers attempted during four successive semesters to improve their relationships with their students. At the end of each term they obtained ratings from their classes. Their scale consisted of a series of forty-two definite questions. The per cent of students answering unfavorably on each rating to a few sample questions is shown in the table on the next page.[20a]

The differences in these opinions were not due to differences in the type of student, since in the successive years the intelligence, general aptitude, and specific aptitude scores were all similar in average and range. It was the instructors who changed—not the students. One important outcome of this work was the increase in achievement during the course. The average score on the same final examination rose by an amount three times the probable error of the measurement.[21]

A second use of ratings is for purposes of supervision, the

---

[18] See, for instance, Anon., "Student Help in the Growth of a Teacher," *Journal of Educational Method,* 10: 30–33, 1930; O. M. Clem, "What Do My Students Think about My Teaching?" *School and Society,* 31: 96–100, 1930.

[19] W. D. Armentrout, "Improving College Teaching by Consulting the Consumers," *School Executives Magazine,* 51: 476–77, 1932.

[20] A. R. Root, "Student-Teacher Rapport," *Journal of Higher Education,* 5: 133–35, 1934.

[20a] Root, *op. cit.* Used by permission of the *Journal of Higher Education.*

[21] In the report by Starrak, *op. cit.,* there is also evidence of a general rise in the level of teaching efficiency as a result of the scales.

Item Number	Per Cent Answered Unfavorably of Successive Ratings			
	First	Second	Third	Fourth
6. Does he seem fair in his presentation of debatable points?.............	14	10	11	1
12. Are his examinations comprehensive enough to be a good sampling of your educational experiences in the course?........................	18	15	8	1
8. Does he admit his lack of information on points of weakness?...........	12	8	6	2
36. Does he have annoying peculiarities of action?.......................	32	28	16	4
40. Is his vocabulary beyond your comprehension?........................	58	40	25	10
26. Does he wander from point to point?..	32	20	12	6

ultimate objective of which is the improvement of instruction. Although supervision on the college level is not common, it does exist. Sometimes it is limited to the junior members of the teaching staff, and sometimes it includes the entire faculty. In one extremely interesting investigation [22] every teacher in a college was rated by his students. A total of 960 classes submitted evidence. Each person received his own ratings. One member of the faculty who had worked on the ratings and was familiar with the entire situation was available for consultation by any teacher who wanted to talk over his results. Many of them did. The outcomes of this investigation were an awakened interest in teaching and a general increase in the level of instructional efficiency.

A third and thus far almost unused value of student ratings is the location of the "problem professor."[23] These individuals exist upon every college campus. They are not to blame for being what they are, since each is a product of his own experi-

[22] W. R. Wilson, "Students Rating Teachers," *Journal of Higher Education,* 3 : 75–82, 1932. See also F. J. Kelley, "Improving Instruction at the University of Idaho," *Proceedings of the Institute for Administrative Officers of Higher Institutions,* University of Chicago Press, 2 : 165–77, 1930.

[23] See, for instance, F. H. Kirkpatrick, "What about the Problem Professors?" *School and Society,* 38 : 406–7, 1933.

ences and inherited abilities, but their presence is a constant source of trouble. The customary attitude is thoroughly fatalistic, and the only solution proposed is to wait patiently until Father Time removes them. In the meanwhile they remain unhappy, and they have an undesirable effect upon many generations of students. Any good rating scale will give objective evidence as to which teachers are "problems." Often the students, faculty, and administrative officials already know—but they have no proof. With the evidence supplied by a scale, much can frequently be done to make life happier for the maladjusted teacher and indirectly for his students. On many campuses there is now a mental hygienist. The problem professor offers him an excellent opportunity for an exercise of his talents.

Some years ago I observed such a use of rating scale results. The professor in charge of a large elementary course wanted to get information about the work of his nine or ten instructors. When the students came to the final examination they were asked to answer a number of questions about their teachers. Among others was the query: How often was your teacher sarcastic? (Never, seldom, sometimes, often, continually.) The students in one instructor's sections reported him as being either often or continually sarcastic. The young man was given his ratings and asked to the professor's office for a conference. It then appeared that this evidence had come as a complete surprise. The instructor was a "smart-aleck" sophisticate, and it had simply never occurred to him that his acid comments and mordant humor might be offensive to those whom he taught. He had merely been trying to enliven the proceedings a bit. The same characteristics had earned for him the dislike of his colleagues and the suspicion of his superiors. In fact, he was already well started on the way to becoming a problem. After a few interviews he began to see that his biting wit was making him a bore rather than the man of the world he liked to think he was. He took himself firmly in hand, learned to appreciate his students' point of view, lost his objectionable traits, and is now a well-liked associate professor. He readily admits that he was caught just in time, before the habit of sarcasm became too much a part of him to break and before he had alienated those whose respect and liking he most needed.

Finally there are the administrative uses of ratings. One of these is quite frankly the dismissal of unsatisfactory teachers. Naturally they are not dismissed on the basis of student opinions alone, but these attitudes as expressed through a scale are often the starting point of an investigation that ends in the termination of a teacher's contract. If administrators evaluate the results in the light of other evidence and if they give a teacher a chance to improve before eliminating him, I can see no objection to this use of the results. In some cases an official may misuse the ratings, but such instances do not prove that the scales are to blame. The other administrative use of ratings is to discover unusual teaching talent, with the specific intention of giving these teachers an increase in salary.[24] I know of one instance in which student opinion was used in precisely this way. If officials are willing to investigate an unusually low rating in order to protect students from bad teaching, they should be equally willing to reward an unusually high one. By taking such evidence into consideration they can promote teachers on the basis of classroom success, instead of depending upon publications or seniority alone.

There are many uses for student ratings, provided these are handled with common sense. Students are not fools. They see, hear, discuss, and think about every little thing that goes on in the classroom. The information they can give is worth having. It does not tell all there is to know about a teacher, but it is good evidence concerning those points upon which only students are in a position to testify.

IV. TEACHING PERSONALITIES

After the average teacher or administrator has finished reading such an account of rating scales as that given in this chapter he is likely to look up in preplexity and want to know

[24] Actually, the campus reputation of a teacher enters into any deliberations about dismissals or promotions, but usually it is not official. Administrators in some thirty colleges admit that student opinion is influential in such matters. (See H. R. Douglass, "Rating the Teaching Effectiveness of Instructors," *op. cit.*) If this is true, then the ratings should be collected as objectively, officially, and carefully as possible.

why there has been no judgment of personality. There has, of course, been a good deal said about individual traits, but the term "personality" has hardly been used at all and certainly not discussed as an entity. Because of this omission, one may feel that the ratings are incomplete and that they do not get to the heart of the problem. Moreover, there are some people who hold—perhaps rightly—that even the best rating scale used in the most careful way necessarily omits certain imponderables that are of great importance for teaching. Indeed, the charge has been made that the use of scales has depersonalized and devitalized the art of teaching. Even the most ardent enthusiast for objective measurement cannot defend the thesis that at the present time all elements in teaching skill can be analyzed and measured. In fact, there may always be some artistic intangibles left over after the scientist has done his best.

The material in the present chapter up to this point should give a general picture of good and poor teaching. It is, however, rather depersonalized and concerns traits rather than people. Analysis of a complex skill like teaching is most useful, but at the end one should employ a little synthesis. A teacher is a human being—not a collection of traits. In this section about personality I would like, therefore, to put Humpty Dumpty back together again and to describe a number of college teachers as they function in their daily work.

The matter of personality is often uppermost in the minds of those who have a hand in hiring or judging teachers. It is also of great importance in the thinking of students when they talk among themselves about their instructors. There is, indeed, almost complete unanimity as to the value of personality, but remarkably little concrete information about its nature. Since the matter is so important, some comment upon it seems required, although in the absence of adequate objective evidence I shall have to present case histories or other forms of opinion.

In the first place, it appears practically axiomatic that there is no such thing as a single, coherent, "teaching" personality. One need only think over one's own good teachers to see a whole array of different types of individual. It is true that certain traits do correlate with success in teaching, but the constellation of these characteristics into personalities does not seem to have a relationship. Suppose, for instance, that there were no more than five traits that lead to teaching success and that each teacher in a group had some four out of five, and that these traits varied somewhat in amount. There are no less than 120 orders in which these four out of five characteristics might be grouped. Moreover, a personality is an entire constellation that inevitably contains some traits having nothing at all to do with teaching skill. Since these will also vary from one person to another, the number of different personalities is almost infinite. The best one can do at the moment at least is to consider specific characteristics that are linked positively or negatively with teaching skill and then to judge how many of them a given person shows.

To some extent personality is measured indirectly by any rating scale. For the particular scale described above it is certain that a student who judges his teacher as to "sympathetic attitude," "fairness," "humor," or "self-reliance" is reacting more or less to the total personality. Certainly his inclination to rate a teacher generally high, generally low, or generally average rests quite as much upon personality as upon any changes the course may have brought about in him.

The whole matter is further complicated because the effect of a teacher upon a student depends upon the interaction of two personalities—the teacher's and the student's. This factor emerges from any discussion of the topic among undergraduates. Thus John Jones goes to great lengths to have his younger brother Fred enrolled in the class of his favorite teacher, whereat Fred develops an intense dislike for the professor and fails the course. Or Susie Smith warns her roommate Mary away from a certain professor's class, but Mary decides to take it anyway and is entranced by the personality of her new instructor. There is simply no accounting for tastes. Nor is it possible to foretell with any accuracy who will like whom. It would be nice if enough were known about personality—either in general or in the case of teachers—for a coherent presentation of the problem. In the absence of such data I shall have to rely upon experience and observation. Since the personality of the student enters so much into any rating of the teacher's personality—I cannot use case histories reported by another person. I am therefore forced to describe my own professors, who, while they seemed to me to be possessed of excellent teaching personalities, might have aroused totally different reactions in others. In fact, I am reasonably sure they sometimes did! I have picked out from a total of some sixty different teachers to whose personalities I have at one time or another been exposed the two best and the two poorest teachers of each sex and have given as good a picture of each as I can. Even though these brief sketches are all based on the experiences of a single person, they do reveal something about personality.

1. *Good teachers:*

If there is such a thing as an "ideal" personality for teaching, Miss B had it. Her geniality and wit flowed out to the class in an unending stream and completely entranced each student. She fascinated both boys and girls by the same kind of charm as that which comes across the footlights from an especially bewitching actress in the years of her full maturity. Her alert and mobile face mirrored each passing thought and feeling; her shrewd eyes twinkled at the world with kindly humor. Miss B was by no means pretty, but she had a sensitive loveliness that stirred the adolescent imagination and was no small element in her success. Her manner with students outside of class was delightful, and she had too great a sense of responsibility to turn aside from anyone who needed her help. To those who came to her for comfort and advice—and almost everyone did—she gave equal doses of mature judgment and irresistible humor. The student who came to cry stayed to laugh—usually at himself. Miss B taught literature, but it would not have mattered if she had taught Hindustani; her courses would still have been full. In class she often aroused the emotions of her students, perhaps not deliberately but because she was so alive and felt everything so keenly that she transferred her own feelings to others. Her teaching was quietly skillful and effortless; there was probably some machinery behind the scenes, but no one ever heard it clank. As she talked, the world outside the four walls of the classroom faded away, and Miss B's ready flow of ideas seemed the only important reality. Actually her method of procedure in class consisted chiefly of being herself. She sat at the desk and talked about whatever points in the day's lesson happened to interest her. A person with less clarity of mind and less mastery of subject matter would simply have rambled, but Miss B always brought out her ideas with complete lucidity—aided by a quick insight and a brilliant wit. She was more successful than any other teacher I have known in combining scientific precision and clear thinking with literary appreciation and aesthetic values. Unlike many "inspirational" teachers, she never sacrificed accuracy or content; rather, she emphasized both as the necessary basis upon which appreciations could be developed. She accomplished the difficult feat of being simultaneously a scientist in dealing with facts and an artist in dealing with implications. Miss B's classroom methodology was only one contributing item to her success. What she did—in spite of its excellence—paled into insignificance beside the fascination of what she was.

Miss D was undoubtedly my strictest teacher. Some of her students found her unduly distant, and a few even disliked her, but everyone gave her a spontaneous and genuine respect. As a person, her outstanding characteristic was a fearless intellectual honesty. She never compromised with the truth, and she could reach a conclusion distasteful to her with the same unfaltering logic that led her to one of which she approved. In class she frankly admitted her ignorance on some points and her mistakes about others. Because of her honesty she had no favorites, and because of her high standards of scholarship she was severe with everyone—including herself. Behind the severity there lay, however, a real kindness, a sincere desire to help students grow in wisdom, an excellent understanding of their needs, and a magnificent sense of humor. In class Miss D was a dynamic, skillful, exciting teacher. Her sheer determination that every student should profit by the work and her frequent flashes of amusement effectively banished the boredom that so often creeps into the college classroom. As a teacher she showed three outstanding characteristics. First, she always came to class completely prepared; even to my immature mind it was clear that Miss D had worked for hours to master and assimilate her material. Any teacher is sometimes full of her subject, but Miss D was always loaded with ideas and sparkling with eagerness to discuss them. The second trait was her ingenuity. Every class hour produced something new, stimulating, and unexpected; the assignments were clever, they demanded real thinking, they were never twice alike, and they were so arranged that students of varying capacities could all derive profit from them; the examinations intrigued even those who failed them. The third characteristic was her objectivity. Matters were presented, discussed, and judged upon their merits. Miss D definitely encouraged independent thinking based upon evidence, but she effectually banned the airing of personal prejudices or unsubstantiated notions. I rate Miss D as a superior teacher because of her personal integrity, her immense driving power, her maturity, and her resourcefulness. She certainly did not suffer fools gladly, and she was admittedly the nemesis of the slacker, but she never committed the unforgivable sin of boring her students.

Mr. E was a genial scholar. The amount and range of his information were both unbelievable. His mind was an orderly storehouse of precise information on an enormous number of subjects. His position as a professor of astronomy did not in the least prevent him from developing a profound knowledge of such diverse topics as Ming pottery, German classical literature, primitive music, Latin coins, modern philosophy, and phonetics. Nor was he a mere dabbler. When he became interested in some topic he read and worked until he had satisfied himself—and the level of information necessary to this state of mind more than satisfied others. In spite of his learning he was, however, no pedant. Everything in the world and almost every person in the world interested him. His social capacities were as surprising as his intellectual attainments. His students told him their troubles, borrowed his books, and smoked his cigarettes. He had, theoretically, two office hours a week, but actually he kept open house all day long. Almost every afternoon he could be found drinking coffee in the student cafeteria, surrounded by boys and girls, and chatting as gaily as any of them. He had never married, and he seemed to adopt the youngsters in his classes as substitutes for the children he never had. In spite of his friendliness and interest, however, no student ever called him by a nickname or tried to establish any personal intimacy; he had a natural reserve which prevented emotional attachments of an undesirable type. His social life never seemed to interfere in the least with his productivity as a scholar, for his list of publications occupies seven typewritten pages of single spacing. Even after knowing him for several years one comes upon new capabilities. Little by little it dawned upon me that he spoke four languages and read six or seven others, but it was a long time before I identified him as a national champion in both handball and chess. In class, he was a simple, kindly person, with a vast store of knowledge that he was only too willing to share with others. Sometimes he lectured—with great lucidity and verve— sometimes he reminisced, and sometimes he discussed points with his students—changing from one method to another as the spirit moved him. Occasionally he crammed so many facts into an hour that one's head was bursting, but at other times he proceeded in a leisurely way with philosophical reflections. I rate him as a good teacher because of his profound scholarship, his geniality, his unfailing kindness, his simplicity of spirit, and his natural ability to lead students both intellectually and morally into better ways of thinking and living.

Mr. F was a teacher of advanced composition. He was a gentle, patient man with an absent-minded air. One would have said that he did not notice what went on around him, but one would have been completely mistaken. In class Mr. F usually spent the time listening to our productions and discussing them. He gave every- one a fair chance, listened with apparently equal interest to the best and the worst, and gave his criticisms so kindly that no one could feel offended. The student who was reading sat at the desk; Mr. F sat with the class and was so unobtrusive that the students soon forgot he was not one of them. The boys and girls might, with adolescent intolerance, condemn each other's work, but he could find something commendatory to say about stories that limped badly, plays that lacked an adequate plot, or poems that seemed to us devoid of either form or content. Moreover, he could really teach another person to write. When he finished discussing a piece of work the student knew exactly what needed to be done to im- prove matters. At the end of the first six weeks of the course, during which time we had handed in one or two samples of each type of writing, he called each student to his office for an interview and worked out a plan of procedure for the rest of the year. I do not know what he said to other students, but his interview with me still lives in my memory. He told me that I needed chiefly to live another twenty years in order to write an acceptable story or play, that I could produce a clear exposition if I were careful—and carelessness was my problem, not his—that my poems were too hopelessly bad to bother with, and that I did not have much idea how to write a description. He then left to me the decision as to what I should do during the rest of the year. To my surprise I found myself voting for descriptions, which I thoroughly detested. For the remainder of that course and during the following year I wrote nothing else. Mr. F gave all kinds of interesting assignments to other members of the class, but these did not apply to me. I had to rewrite the first description I attempted exactly twenty-two times before he would accept it. He was uniformly gentle and patient, but incredibly persistent. I imagine he was as sick of the thing as I was, but he seemed just as interested in every rendition as in all the previous ones. Through weeks of discouragement he kept me plodding along. When I complained, he was understanding and charming—although the assignment remained unchanged. The pressure was always kindly, but I could never squirm away from it. It was a year and a half before I was able to produce a description that he could accept in its first form, and he was far more elated than I. Mr. F was a good teacher because of his quick sympathy, his serene detachment, his patient but steady persistence, his genuine pleasure in another person's moments of success, his willingness to work unremittingly for a student's development, and his ability to make others think objectively about their own work.

The good teachers in these descriptions show some traits in common. They knew their students—although their techniques for getting acquainted were certainly different—they knew their subject matter, they were exciting people, they were intensely human, and they were thoroughly mature. Each had his or her own methods of procedure. As teachers they had assessed themselves accurately and had learned to do superlatively well the kind of teaching they did at all. As people they were simply and naturally themselves—and very charming selves. It should be noted, however, that in personality the differences between them were greater than the similarities.

2. Poor teachers:

Miss S was without doubt the worst teacher I ever had the misfortune to meet. Indeed, I can think of almost nothing to say in her favor. First, there was her personality. Two traits were especially outstanding—her biting sarcasm and her favoritism. She settled upon one boy as her main victim, about five minutes after the beginning of the first class. I have no idea what caused the antagonism. The unfortunate boy sat next to me and neither spoke nor in any way called attention to himself during the first few minutes. Throughout the year Miss S hounded him with unrelenting demands, from which she seemed to derive a sadistic pleasure. She also had two marked favorites, upon whom she fawned. Both were embarrassed at being held up to the class as paragons, but their attitude did not seem to penetrate Miss S's consciousness. All members of the class, except these two and myself, were targets for her sarcasm; students were frequently reduced to tears by her outbursts. For reasons I never bothered to investigate she did not speak to me once during the entire year, either in class or out—and I was perfectly willing to be ignored. On one occasion I went back to the classroom after a test to get a book I had forgotten and found her tearing the examination papers into shreds without reading them. After that I checked on her by slipping back into the room after each test; the papers were always in the wastebasket. I can imagine no sensible process by which she decided upon what mark to give me. I rate Miss S as a poor teacher because she was an utterly impossible human being.

Mr. T was a limp, unhealthy-looking man with a low voice and a monotonous manner of speaking. He taught English composition. The work of his class was of a uniform dullness and drab monotony. Literally nothing ever happened. For an hour a day he droned on about something—I do not know what, because after the first week I rarely listened. Each day he read and discussed somebody's paper. Each punctuation mark, each phrase, each detail was considered. I remember one day when he spent fifteen minutes in teaching the whole class to spell the word "daguerreotype" because one student had used and misspelled it. From time to time he gave us drill exercises in punctuation. These were undoubtedly the most interesting part of the course! They would have been more valuable if he had not been so careless in preparing them that they contained many errors. Mr. T gave his assignments each day with meticulous care and long-winded precision. No detail was too small for him to waste time over. We were told how wide a margin we should have on our papers, at what slant we should write, and how many words long each theme was to be. Most of the topics he assigned for writing were of little interest to me at least, and he permitted no deviations. Early in the course he asked

us to read an English translation of either the Iliad or the Odyssey
and write a summary of the story. I already knew the story of
both; so I asked him for permission to read the Nibelungenlied in
German and write a résumé of it instead. As I explained to him,
I could get practice in two subjects at once if he would allow this
substitution. He refused. I read the German epic anyway and
handed in a summary of the story, but I was given a failing grade
on this assignment because I had not followed instructions. After
this experience, when he wanted a thousand words, I gave him a
thousand; when he wanted five hundred, I gave him five hundred.
Mr. T was a poor teacher because he was utterly rigid in his thinking and hopelessly dull, both in class and out.

Mr. Y was a brilliant young man who taught German. In a
somewhat gloomy Byronic way he was handsome, but the petulant,
sulky expression of a thoroughly unhappy person rather marred
the effect. One felt almost at once that Mr. Y "smoldered" and
might explode at any moment. He began his remarks on the first
day by telling us that he was wasting his time teaching a beginning class. He assured us we would never learn German and
went on to explain how insular Americans were in regard to
foreign languages. After about fifteen minutes in this vein he
brought up what proved to be his favorite subject—the failure of
the institution to segregate its students, with the result that the few
able ones were lost in a crowd of nincompoops. He gave us illustrations of how he—in his rather recent undergraduate days at
the same institution—had been overlooked by his teachers because
he was surrounded by so much mediocrity. Throughout the
semester Mr. Y complained steadily. He told us about sundry
departmental wranglings and went in detail into what attitude he
had taken, why he was right, and what insidious influences were
almost certain to overcome the righteousness of his side in the
dispute. In the actual presentation of classwork Mr. Y was quite
good, except that he was always argumentative and—in an impersonal sort of way—entirely pessimistic as to our probable work
in German. About the middle of the semester Mr. Y began to
dictate a few sentences in German at the beginning of each hour.
It happened that we had in the group one boy whose parents spoke
the language at home. One day this lad challenged Mr. Y's pronunciation of some word on the grounds that Mr. Y had spoken
it with a slightly Yiddish accent. This comment may or may not
have been justified, but the results were magnificent. Mr. Y ex-

pelled the boy from class then and there and proceeded to spend
the remaining part of the hour in telling us how the Jews had
been persecuted for centuries and how his superiors had discriminated against him because he was Jewish. It occurred to me
that Mr. Y was precisely the type of Jew for whom the Wailing
Wall was devised; if he could have wailed there instead of in
class he might have been more successful. In disposition he was
melancholy, sensitive, suspicious, and insecure; these traits he
could perhaps not help having, but he did not have to pass his own
difficulties and disappointments on to his students. As it was,
students and colleagues alike were annoyed with his emotional
attitudes, bored by his complaints, and hesitant about trusting him
because no one knew where his prejudices might lead him. Mr. Y
lasted as a teacher for three years at his alma mater, where he
had been a phenomenally good student, but he could not obtain a
permanent position. He is now doing translations for a museum—
a sad, oldish man with a permanent grouch.

Miss X was a most amiable young woman who taught history.
She was well prepared for her work and had come to her college
with the best of recommendations. I had the misfortune to be in
the first class she ever taught. Even at the time I realized she was
painfully embarrassed and upset. She was afraid of her students
and did not have the least idea how to catch their interest. At the
first meeting her voice was barely audible, she looked steadily at
her own feet, and she was either so underprepared or so rattled
that she ran completely out of material before the middle of the
hour. It was her bad luck that she had in the class three girls of
the immature, silly type who like nothing better than to make
trouble for the teacher; this particular trio would have discouraged
even an experienced professor. Before the class had been in session
for ten minutes the three had begun to whisper and giggle; soon
the disturbance spread to other parts of the room. Miss X was
totally unprepared for anything of the kind. She blushed and
stammered for a while and then let the class go. The next day
was no better. During the hour several girls began to hum softly;
by keeping their heads bent over their notebooks, they could prevent Miss X from seeing who was singing at any given moment.
This obligato threw her completely off what little balance she still
had, and again she was forced to dismiss the class early. The
disturbances continued during the whole first week, getting somewhat worse every day. By the end of the second week Miss X

began to cry in class. The first outburst took everyone by surprise and produced a quiet room, but the effects soon wore off, and subsequent tears were barely noticed. The students learned nothing, and the room was usually in a state of noisy confusion. Once in a while some of the girls got tired of the situation and "cracked down" on the others for a day or so. During these periods of respite Miss X's work was interesting and worth while. She had clever ideas and ingenious methods of presenting them, but her voice remained weak and her manner diffident. During the rare quiet periods Miss X showed real promise of teaching ability, if she could learn to keep a group under control. Unfortunately, she did not learn in time to hold her first job. Although she was later more successful, she has never been the really good teacher she should have become in view of her undoubted capacity. Her most satisfactory work has been done as a tutor rather than as a teacher. In such individual relationships she is excellent. I rate Miss X as a poor teacher because she was so afraid of her students and so unsure of herself that she could not maintain order in her classroom.

These unsatisfactory teachers all had definite defects of personality. One was devastatingly sarcastic; another was so fixed in his thinking that he had not had a new idea in ten years and was not willing to have one for another ten; the third was morbidly sensitive, and the fourth was pathologically shy. In addition to these characterological difficulties they had certain traits in common. These traits are the same ones that characterize inadequate parents or an inadequate home. Parents are inadequate if they do not give security to their children, if they do not provide an atmosphere in which normal childish development can take place, if they show favoritism toward one child or antagonism toward another, or if they pass on their own maladjustments to their children. The teachers just described gave little or no security to their students, often suppressed normal growth, failed to treat their students uniformly, made little effort to become acquainted with their charges, and constantly presented their classes with situations arising from their own embarrassments and difficulties. They regarded their students either as ever-present victims or as ever-present nuisances. As I look back upon these teachers I can now see that they were immature, unhappy, bored, unsocial, and generally out of sympathy with teaching. Every one of them would have been eliminated from his position—and thus prevented from cramping and twisting the development of any more students—by the poorest rating scale ever made.[25]

In addition to the preceding general summary of traits one general point about personality emerges from these histories; namely, there is no single "teaching personality." Not even the same specific characteristics appear in all four good teachers or in all four bad ones. There are no two constellations of traits that are even roughly alike. Indeed, these eight people were highly individualistic. On the basis of the above studies and of numerous other observations I venture the conclusion that a wide range of personalities is acceptable in higher education, presumably because there is an even wider range of personalities among the students, so that—with the possible exception of definitely abnormal people—almost any teacher is sure to be liked by someone. It may be that eventually the scientist will measure personality in its many phases, but until he can tell why Miss M's appearance, manners, and techniques thrill one student, merely interest another, and put a third to sleep, the essential problem of what is a good teaching personality will remain.

V. A PROPOSED PLAN

It is a commonplace in academic circles that a teacher is more likely to be promoted for mediocre research than for excellent teaching. This discrimination is perhaps not intentional; it may, in fact, be due in large measure to the mere objectivity of publication and the practical difficulties of obtaining any similarly objective evidence about teaching skill. If this is the case, the rating scale should meet a real need.

In recent years there has been great concern over the improvement and vitalizing of college teaching. Many methods,

[25] For another informal evaluation of teachers see D. McCaslin, "Specifications for an Ideal Teacher," *Journal of Higher Education,* 10: 314–19, 1939.

ranging all the way from classroom supervision [26] to the intensive study of great teachers of the past, have been tried.[27] At the University of Chicago, at least, the authorities have specifically recognized teaching excellence.[28] This procedure is a step in the right direction.

I should like to submit a definite plan for a further development that integrates student ratings with recognition for superior teaching effort. If a member of a faculty becomes a scientist of moderate or higher merit, he is commonly admitted to scientific societies. If he is a scholar in any field, his name is proposed for some organization, membership in which is an honor. Teachers have their professional groups, but they do not have any organization based upon superiority in teaching. I think there should exist what, for want of a better name, I will call a "guild of master teachers." To belong to this group, a teacher would have to obtain high ratings from several groups of students. I see no reason for a lot of machinery in the development of such an organization. All a college needs to do is to have its teachers rated regularly every year and to select for membership those exceeding some specified level of excellence. Each college could give whatever form of award seemed most desirable.[29] The matter of salary increases could

[26] I. J. Lubbers, "College Organization and Administration," *Northwestern University Contributions to Education Series,* No. 7, 1932, 155 pp.; A. Y. Reed, *Personal Characteristics of Effective and Ineffective College Teachers,* American Book Company, 1935, 344 pp. Both references contain tables showing the frequency of actual supervision.

[27] See, for instance, F. W. Reeves, "Critical Survey and Analysis of Current Efforts to Improve Teaching," *Phi Delta Kappan,* 11:65–71, 1928; or "Constructive Activities in Improving Instruction in 87 Institutions," *North Central Association Quarterly,* 4:371–76, 1929; J. M. Hughes, "An Analysis of Instructional Handicaps within a University," *Educational Method,* 8:310–13, 1929; R. L. Kelly, "Great Teachers and Methods of Developing Them," *Bulletin of the Association of American Colleges,* 15:49–67, 1929; E. S. Evenden, "The Improvement of College Teaching," *Teachers College Record,* 29:587–96, 1928.

[28] C. S. Boucher, "Honored for Excellence in Teaching," *University of Chicago Magazine,* 24:291–92, 1932. See also "The Evaluation of Faculty Services," *University of Michigan Administrative Studies,* Vol. 1, No. 3, 23 pp., and *School and Society,* "Citations for Distinguished Teaching at the University of Chicago," 35:758, 1932, and "Awarding of Prizes to Teachers of Undergraduate Students at the University of Chicago," 50:12–13, 1939.

[29] Personally I favor a medal with the college seal and the words "Master Teacher of —————— College" on one side and the person's name, the date, and the words "Honored For Excellence in Teaching," on the other.

be left to look after itself; when administrators discuss promotions they take into consideration the election to any honorary group.

On a small scale this plan has already been tried,[30] with thus
far excellent results. The seniors of a small college decided to
give their alma mater a bronze tablet that was to be hung in the
entrance to the recitation hall. On the tablet they wished to have
engraved the names of the institution's most outstanding teachers.
Since the college had been in existence less than twenty-five years,
not many teachers were eligible for such an honor from the mere
point of service, but when the students came to discuss those who
had been at the college for ten years or more they could not agree
upon what constituted excellence. In their difficulty they consulted
the president who—perhaps for reasons of his own—recommended
the use of rating scales. Eventually a joint student-faculty investigation was planned and carried out. Some of the results are summarized in Figure 43. These ratings indicated the presence of two
really superior teachers, both of whom had been at the college for
ten years or more. These two names were all the seniors wanted,
but various faculty committees used the complete results. The
bronze tablet with its two names and plenty of blank space for
additions was duly installed and promptly forgotten by the students. The local "kudos" within the faculty was more than anyone
had anticipated. The two teachers were asked to allow visits by
the other members of the staff. Everyone talked over his or her
rating with everyone else. There was a great flurry of experiments,
projects, and revisions. The impetus given by the survey was still
strong enough two years later to bring about a second rating, with
the addition of three more names to the tablet. Instead of two
master teachers from a faculty of eighteen members the college
now had five out of nineteen. The surveys, with the presumptive
addition of names to the rostrum, are rapidly becoming a biennial
tradition. It is, the faculty members explain, not the sight of their
names on the tablet that gives them pleasure but the knowledge
that they are successes in their chosen work. To the sophisticate
the whole thing may sound childish and silly, with a strong flavor
of the gold star for a perfect spelling lesson. In the college here
described, however, the matter is taken not only seriously but
almost reverently by both teachers and students. Whatever one

[30] The institution involved prefers to remain unidentified.

may think of the technique, there is no doubt that the level of teaching has greatly improved. It is my own opinion that—human nature being as it is—the public citation gives much pleasure.

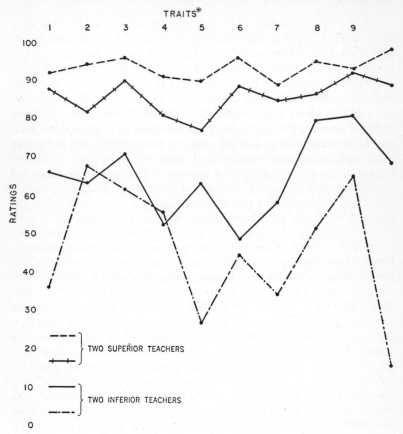

FIG. 43.—Sample Results from One Survey.

Even if this simple satisfaction is lacking, the instructors are certainly pleased by the additions to their salaries, which followed upon their recognition as superior teachers.

Such an arrangement as that already described puts a great deal of responsibility upon the students, but, like other people, they respond to whatever burden one gives them. Some faculty members would probably have a fear that the teachers of "snap" courses would be honored, when a more worth-while but less popular teacher was not. It has been my experience that students will elect snap courses, will take a childlike pleasure in getting a good mark for no effort, will be more or less flattered by any attention from an instructor, and will be amused at the "popular" professor's antics—but they will not give him a high rating. They see through his toadying, they recognize the superficiality of his work, and they are aware of his low standards. While they accept an unearned good grade with pleasure, they have only contempt for the teacher who gave it to them. In the surveys already made, the "easy" teacher has fared badly; he has obviously fooled no one but himself. I have confidence that students—especially upperclass-men—recognize and appreciate good teaching. Awards based upon their evidence, carefully collected and sensibly interpreted, would go to the people who deserved them.

VI. SUMMARY

From the tone of the reports in the literature it would appear that the rating scale has come to stay. Before long it is likely to be as much of a fixture in American colleges as the objective test already is. Wherever it has been properly administered and intelligently interpreted, it has given teachers results that were of value to them in their daily work. Once a faculty has overcome its initial opposition to being judged at all, it usually wants the ratings repeated at frequent intervals because the results are useful and enlightening. Although the scales have administrative uses, these are not so important as the educational values. It is therefore better for a faculty to survey itself than for it to be surveyed by some-one else—unless the members prefer to call in an outsider who will not be subject to domestic pressure and antagonisms.

Such an organization as that suggested in the last section of this chapter might help considerably in making a great teacher the respected person he should be in his college community. People who have some natural talent for teaching often do not develop their ability to its highest possible level because there is so little "future" in it. They may live in the hearts of their students, but they certainly make little impression upon administrators. College teaching is a full-time job. The person who uses part of his time and energy upon research or publication is practically certain to lower the level of his instruction. As many colleges are organized, the only sure way a young man can progress is to neglect his teaching—for which he is presumably paid, but through which he cannot win public recognition—and do something else, for which he is not paid but through which he accumulates objective evidence of his competency to teach. This state of affairs is absurd. A promising instructor should be encouraged to develop into a superb teacher, but he usually will not if he feels that the doors of advancement are closed against him. The rating scale should open them and should permit potentially good teachers to realize their possibilities. It is with this idea in mind that I have proposed, for what it is worth, this suggestion that colleges give public recognition to their master teachers. *The only way in which a college can get superior teaching is to recognize it, emphasize it, respect it, honor it, and reward it.*

APPENDIX

APPENDIX

The material in this section is too detailed and special for inclusion in the main text. Since, however, the data are available and might be of value to some teachers, it seems best to present them somewhere.

The various lists are all based on research as to what is (a) necessary for reading college books and (b) often unknown to entering freshmen. A total list of all the essentials would be extremely long. Those below include only the specific items known by 85 per cent or less of the students. These items are, then, the ones that are most crucial.

1. MATHEMATICS

The essential skills that are not yet mastered are listed at the left in the following table. The figures in the column show the per cent of freshmen in public colleges and universities who were able to demonstrate each skill during "Freshman Week." [1]

[1] These results are based upon the following publications: W. A. Coit, "A Preliminary Study of Mathematical Difficulties," *School Review*, 36: 504–9, 1928; W. S. Guiler, "Background Deficiencies," *Journal of Higher Education*, 3: 369–72, 1932; L. C. Pressey, "The Preparation of Freshmen," *Journal of Higher Education*, 1: 149–53, 1930; H. J. Arnold, "Defects of College Students in Arithmetic," in *Research Adventures in University Teaching*, Public School Publishing Company, 1927, pp. 107–12; L. C. Pressey, "The Needs of Freshmen in the Field of Mathematics," *School Science and Mathematics*, 30: 238–43, 1930. See also M. L. Elveback, "Progress of General College Students in Mathematics," in A. C. Eurich, *The Effective General College Curriculum as Revealed by Examinations*, Committee on Education Research of the University of Minnesota, pp. 316–24. The preparation in mathematics as shown below may seem low. Actually, preparation in this field is much better than it used to be. See H. H. Remmers, "The Quality of Freshman Preparation, Then and Now," *Bulletin of Purdue University*, Studies in Higher Education, XIII, Vol. 30, No. 2, 1929, 35 pp.

[2] This proportion was able to solve three out of the five cases of factoring above given.

B. Simple equations with fractions, such as
$$\frac{2x-4}{3} = \frac{6x}{2}.$$ 39

VII. Formulas
    A. Substituting values in such formulas as
        $x = \frac{1}{2} mn^2,$
        $m = 3,$
        $n = 2,$
        Solve for x. 32
    B. Rewriting an equation so as to solve it for any terms:
       rewrite for y
       $x = \frac{1}{2} a^2 y$ 35

GEOMETRY

  I. Finding the length of the hypotenuse of a right triangle, given the lengths of the sides 48
  II. Bisecting an angle 67
 III. Finding the circumference of a circle 47
 IV. Finding the area of a circle 32

MATHEMATICAL VOCABULARY

  I. Arithmetic [3]

	Per Cent of Freshmen Recognizing Term		*Per Cent of Freshmen Recognizing Term*
unit	60	bushel	76
cancel	66	peck	68
common fraction	83	quart	68
denominator	81	square mile	71
factor	81	cubic inch	84
improper fraction	50	cubic foot	84
invert	78	perimeter	72
mixed number	80	area	66
numerator	79	dimensions	79
prime factor	8	base	78
terms	43	hypotenuse	70
reduce	67	diagonal	76
solid	80	radius	48
avoirdupois	69	pi	84
acre	74	volume	78
rod	61	graph	72

[3] See M. K. Elam and L. C. Pressey, "The Fundamental Vocabulary of Elementary School Arithmetic," *Elementary School Journal*, 33: 46–50, 1932; S. S. Brooks, "A Study of the Technical and Semitechnical Vocabulary of Arithmetic," *Educational Research Bulletin*, 5: 219–22, 1926.

II. Algebra: [4] This list does not include terms that have already appeared on the arithmetic list.

Per Cent of Freshmen Recognizing Term [5]		*Per Cent of Freshmen Recognizing Term*	
symbol [6]	79	degree	31
coefficient	18	simple equation	21
positive	28	simultaneous equation	16
negative	36	quadratic equation	14
monomial	11	independent	23
binomial	41	clear of fractions	58
polynomial	18	transpose	36
algebraic	32	eliminate	74
consecutive	57	formula	43
parentheses	63	evaluate	61
brackets	51	unknown	22
ratio	16	substitute	53
proportion	7	collect	62
descending	56	variable	32
factor	54	power	69
factorable	48	exponent	68
expand	23	root	35
x-axis	43	radical	45
y-axis	43	extract	60
graph	32	ascending	57
plot	50	descending	56
linear	24	$\pm$	38
		$\sqrt{}$	40

[4] S. L. Pressey, L. C. Pressey, and F. R. Narragon, "Essential Vocabulary in Algebra," *School Science and Mathematics*, 32:672–74, 1932.

[5] Figures for both algebra and geometry are from W. S. Moore, "The Growth of Mathematical Vocabulary from the Third Grade through High School," Master's Thesis, Ohio State University, 1931; this material is summarized in *School Review*, 40:449–54, 1932.

[6] There are naturally many courses for which no mathematical terms are needed, but when any are necessary these represent the minimum.

III. Geometry.[7] This list does not include terms that have already
appeared on the arithmetic or algebra lists.

Per Cent of Freshmen
Recognizing Term [8]

angle	45
acute angle	57
obtuse angle	48
straight angle	40
bisect	52
supplementary angle	36
complementary angle	32
degree	33
right angle	52
corresponding angle	16
bisector	22
common angle	37
adjacent side	34
included angle	44
tangent	44
secant	46
inscribe	33
radii	43
right triangle	60
equiangular triangle	37
isosceles triangle	36
congruent	11
vertex	37
vertices	25
similar triangles	47
external angle	29
perpendicular	28

Per Cent of Freshmen
Recognizing Term

transversal	16
intersect	47
opposite side	33
equilateral triangle	38
corollary	14
chord	41
axiom	49
theorem	47
equidistant	18
coincide	50
segment	42
locus	27
parallelogram	66
rhombus	36
hexagon	33
trapezoid	45
quadrilateral	27
polygon	64
equivalent polygons	12
symmetry	31
triangle	67
arc	56
circumscribe	31
plane surface	47
geometric	56
respectively	53
parallel	49

[7] S. L. Pressey, L. C. Pressey, and R. C. Zook, "The Essential Technical Vocabulary of Plane Geometry," *School Science and Mathematics,*
32: 487–89, 1932.

[8] In addition, there are some twenty symbols whose meaning is known by
approximately 45 per cent of the students.

2. ENGLISH [9]

SKILLS   *Per Cent of*
                                                  Freshmen with
                                                  Correct Usage

1. Errors in capitals in titles of books or themes.......... 72
2. Errors in capitals for titles of persons, usually where
   these are not used as part of a name................. 78
3. Errors in capitals for the main words in the names of
   organizations 71
4. Failure to use commas after introductory clause or phrase,
   when needed 62
5. Failure to set off slightly parenthetical expressions...... 57
6. Failure to use commas around appositives.............. 84
7. Failure to use commas around restrictive clauses........ 64
8. Omission of one or more commas in a series............ 84
9. Failure to use colon for introducing a series............ 89
10. Use of comma for semicolon in compound sentences when
    conjunction is omitted 63
11. Use of comma when a series has only two elements...... 74
12. Use of commas before or around indirect quotations.... 67
13. Confusion of homonyms, such as "there" and "their".... 81
14. Failure of verb to agree with subject, usually because of
    the insertion of a clause or phrase containing nouns of
    a different number 64
15. Confusion of tenses.................................. 84
16. Pronouns in the wrong case after a preposition......... 84
17. Fragments used as sentences......................... 77
18. Stringy sentences 49
19. Lack of parallel construction for parallel ideas......... 44
20. No antecedent or wrong antecedent for pronoun........ 27
21. Omission of small words that are necessary for complet-
    ing the meaning of a sentence...................... 76
22. Misplaced modifier 79

[9] The results given in this section are taken from the various sources listed below: H. M. Clark, "Errors in Freshman Composition," *English Journal* (College Edition), 18: 32–34, 1929; H. E. Potter, "Abilities and Disabilities in the Use of English Found in the Written Compositions of Entering Freshmen at the University of California," Master's Thesis, University of California, December, 1922, 72 pp.; S. L. Pressey, "A Statistical Study of Usage and of Children's Errors in Capitalization," *English Journal,* 13: 727–32, 1924; H. Ruhlen and S. L. Pressey, "A Statistical Study of Current Usage in Punctuation," *English Journal,* 13: 325–31, 1924; J. T. Seaton, "The Errors of College Students in the Mechanics of English Composition," Doctor's Thesis, Ohio State University, 1929, 116 pp.; W. E. Vaughan, "A Survey of Freshman College Composition," *Peabody Journal of Education,* 2: 99–104, 1924; W. S. Guiler, "Difficulties Encountered by High-School Graduates in the Use of Pronouns," *School Review,* 39: 622–26, 1931; and "Difficulties Encountered by High-School Graduates in the Use of Verbs," *School Review,* 40: 455–59, 1932.

TECHNICAL VOCABULARY [10]

Per Cent of Freshmen Recognizing Term [11]		*Per Cent of Freshmen Recognizing Term*	
noun	73	plural:	
adjective	75	of nouns	74
verb	65	of pronouns	64
pronoun	69	of verbs	50
adverb	54	singular:	
conjunction	76	of nouns	73
preposition	47	of pronouns	70
		of verbs	39
first person	71		
second person	67	present participle	58
third person	69	past participle	62
present tense	73	main clause	59
past tense	74	subordinate clause	62
future tense	72		
		subject of main verb	26
phrase	25	object of main verb	23
complex sentence	67		
compound sentence	36	modify	35
simple sentence	74	agree	41
direct quotation	85	antecedent	31
indirect quotation	77	appositive	41
		predicate	9
		possessive	68

[10] W. S. Guiler, "Background Deficiencies," *op. cit.;* R. V. Johnson, "Determination of the Essential Technical Vocabulary for Work in Written English," Doctor's Thesis, Ohio State University, 1927; L. C. Pressey, "The Preparation of Freshmen," *Journal of Higher Education,* 1: 149–53, 1930.

[11] The freshmen were merely asked to tell which word in a sentence was the noun, or which was the subject of the main verb, or which was the antecedent of the pronoun. At no time did they need to give or recognize a definition.

3. FOREIGN LANGUAGE [12]

Per Cent of Freshmen Recognizing Term [13]		*Per Cent of Freshmen Recognizing Term*	
possessive pronouns	67	regular verb	53
possessive adjective	16	irregular verb	46
relative pronoun	38	impersonal verb	22
interrogative pronoun	41	reflexive verb	32
demonstrative pronoun	38	auxiliary verb	14
definite article	55	infinitive	53
indefinite article	42		
		predicate noun or adjective	44
imperfect tense	27	indirect object	62
perfect tense	31	inverted word order	9
pluperfect tense	43	negative sentence	77
active voice	54	prefix	62
passive voice	47	suffix	54
		stem	52
positive degree	13	accent	60
comparative degree	20		
superlative degree	42	conjugation	38
		declension	34
subjunctive mood	19	inflection	6
imperative mood	36		
indicative mood	47		

[12] L. C. Pressey and S. L. Pressey, "Language Concepts Needed by College Freshmen," *Modern Language Journal*, 14: 624–30, 1930, and "The Preparation of Freshmen," *op. cit.;* and W. S. Guiler, "Background Deficiencies," *op. cit.*

[13] The freshmen were merely asked to indicate which word in a sentence was in the imperative mood, or which was a predicate noun, and so on. In no case was it necessary either to give or to recognize a definition.

4. HISTORY [14]

Per Cent of Freshmen Recognizing Term [15]		*Per Cent of Freshmen Recognizing Term*	
abdicate	54	corporation	53
abolish	74	corruption	73
act	73		
aggression	79	decade	69
anarchy	79	decree	79
appropriation	85	denomination	74
arbitrary	58	department	59
arbitration	83	despotism	48
		diplomacy	78
belligerent	56	domestic	75
blockade	83		
bureau	64	embargo	80
		enact	73
campaign	81	era	83
catholicism	67	evacuation	39
caucus	53	executive	64
centralization	71	expansion	83
charter	77	expenditure	82
civil service	81	exploit	20
commission	63		
commodity	79	federal	83
commonwealth	79		
communism	81	graft	73
concede	79		
confiscate	78	heresy	71
conservative	78	homestead	72
conservation	68		
conspiracy	39	imperialism	80
continental	20	indemnity	82
contraband	68	inflation	26
		injunction	69

[14] L. C. Pressey and R. Fischer, "The Geographical Background Necessary for the Study of History," *Educational Research Bulletin,* 11: 234–38, 1932; C. O. Mathews, "Grade Placement of Curriculum Materials in the Social Studies," *Teachers College Contributions to Education,* No. 241, 1926, 152 pp.; L. C. Pressey, "A Study in the Learning of the Fundamental Special Vocabulary of History," pp. 155–218 in *Tests and Measurements in the Social Sciences,* by A. C. Krey and T. L. Kelly, Charles Scribner's Sons, 1934, 635 pp.; "The Needs of College Students in History," *The Historical Outlook,* 21: 218–23, 1930; and "College Students and Reading," *Journal of Higher Education,* 2: 30–34, 1931.

[15] The words were, of course, used in an historical meaning. The exact per cent that recognized the particular definition used depended upon the wording.

GEOGRAPHICAL BACKGROUND

For American History [16]

Per Cent of Freshmen Locating Place on Map		*Per Cent of Freshmen Locating Place on Map*	
Atlanta [17]	76	South Carolina	77
Baltimore	81	South Dakota	74
Buffalo	76	Utah	75
Cincinnati	77	Vermont	81
Cleveland	81	West Virginia	76
		Wisconsin	84
Alabama	82	Wyoming	81
Arizona	69		
Arkansas	78	Chesapeake Bay	56
Florida	80	Columbia River	78
Idaho	76	Erie Canal	65
Iowa	79	Hudson Bay	63
Kansas	82	Lake Erie	73
Kentucky	84	St. Lawrence River	72
Maine	84		
Maryland	81	Belgium	78
Mississippi	80	Hawaii	69
Missouri	79	Holland	71
Nevada	77	Montreal	72
New Mexico	81	Peru	69
North Carolina	78	Philippines	62
North Dakota	71	Portugal	71
Oklahoma	73	Quebec	74
Oregon	81		

[16] Pressey and Fischer, *op. cit.*

[17] The decision to include a place name as preparation rather than as content depended upon whether or not the authors of the text explained where it was (referring definitely to some map) or assumed its location to be known. The names listed above are those that were used frequently, were rated by teachers as important, were known by less than 85 per cent of the freshmen, and were treated by the textbooks as part of the preparation.

For European History [18]

Per Cent of Freshmen Locating Place on Map		*Per Cent of Freshmen Locating Place on Map*	
Adriatic Sea	44	Holland	71
Aegean Sea	41	Hungary	54
Albania	53	Jerusalem	77
Algeria	37	Jugoslavia	57
Athens	48	Leningrad	81
Austria	74	Lithuania	51
Bagdad	43	Madrid	69
Baltic Sea	40	Marseilles	64
Belgium	78	Moscow	71
Berlin	74	Netherlands	61
Black Sea	46	Newfoundland	41
Bordeaux	34	New Zealand	34
Brussels	52	Nile River	77
Budapest	32	Norway	72
Bulgaria	64	Nova Scotia	39
Cairo	49	Palestine	46
Calais	56	Persia	62
Constantinople	52	Poland	69
Crimea	41	Portugal	71
Czechoslovakia	66	Prussia	64
Danube River	49	Pyrenees	72
Dardanelles	31	Rhine River	79
Denmark	69	Rumania	50
Finland	58	Siberia	84
Florence	39	Sicily	75
Frankfort	31	Suez	63
Geneva	78	Syria	53
Genoa	27	Turkey	58
Gibraltar	77	Vienna	76
Greece	72	Warsaw	71
Hamburg	30	West Indies	42

[18] Pressey and Fischer, *op. cit.*

5. READING

The books studied [19] contained a total of approximately 11,000 pages, excluding the space taken up by graphs or pictures. The reading material was classified in a general way according to its nature. The figures below give the per cent of freshmen unable to read typical passages of each type with a comprehension of tenth grade or better.[20]

	Per Cent of Freshmen Able to Read with 10th-Grade-Comprehension
1. Directions for experiments, for writing themes, for carrying out projects, and so on..........	61
2. Descriptions of apparatus, processes, or organisms	57
3. Presentation of theories, rules, or laws, with illustrations	70
4. Discussion of developmental or causal relationships	67
5. Narratives	82
6. All other types	

In the books studied there was a total of 3,250 graphic representations and pictures.[21] Of this number, 1,105 were photographs. Over 90 per cent of others were of the types indicated below:

	Per Cent of Freshmen Able to Read Typical Samples of Each Type
1. Diagrammatic drawings	69
2. Linear graphs	72
3. Cross-section drawings	42
4. Maps	73

About 75 per cent of all the formulae found in the chemistry, physics, and mathematics books were of six types, as shown in the next table. The 1,010 problems were somewhat harder to classify. Of this total, 28 per cent did not involve any numbers. Most of the remaining problems required either two or three steps in their solution.

---

[19] L. C. Pressey, "College Students and Reading," *op. cit.* All the tables in this section are from this article.

[20] From unpublished results of L. C. Pressey.

[21] For further material on the frequency of graphs and on the ability of students to read them, see E. R. Henry, "The Development of Certain Tests on the Basis of the Mathematics Used by College Students," Doctor's Thesis, Ohio State University, 1929, 70 pp.

	Per Cent of Each Type in Original Analysis	Per Cent of Freshmen Able to Read Each Type [22]
Formulas		
1. $x = ab$	25	41
2. $x = \dfrac{a}{b}$ or $\dfrac{ab}{c}$	16	29
3. $x = abc$ or $abcd$	11	43
4. $x = \frac{1}{2}ab^2$	11	22
5. $x = a^2bc$ or ab^2	36	32
6. $x = a + b + c$ or $ab + cd$, etc.....	1	38

	Per Cent of Freshmen Able to Read Each Type
Problems	
1. No numbers	79
2. One operation	81
3. Two operations	72
4. Three operations	53
5. Four operations	40
6. Five operations	18

The above results indicate a general lack of ability to "see through" these special types of reading matter. Less than half the students could read the simplest formula; with any complication, such as a fraction or a square, the per cent declined to something between a fourth and a third. Approximately 20 per cent of the freshmen could not see through a problem without numbers or a single-step problem with figures. As the number of operations increased, the comprehension rapidly declined.

[22] By "reading" a formula is meant the ability to tell in words what x is equal to or what the relation is between any two elements in a formula; by "reading" a problem is meant the ability to tell in words what is to be found and by what steps one would find it. In neither case is there any handling of actual numbers or values.

INDEX

611

maladjustment, amount of, 200–201;
improvement by treatment, 210, 381–
82; types of, 204–5; 208–9
mannerisms, 215, 561–62
manual for preparation, 252
manuals for study, 269
Mark Hopkins, 315
marking systems, 471 ff.
marks, arguments for and against,
463–70; as basis for prediction, 297–
301; attitude of students toward,
464, 468; by department, 475–77;
closed, 464; equalizer, 478–80; first
semester, 300; inaccuracy, 465, 475–
78; individual teachers, 475–78; in
terms of distribution, 471–74; relation to elimination, 90; relation to
other criteria, 304
master teachers, 590–92
mastery of essentials, 243 ff., 597–610;
of subject-matter, 72, 326–27, 332–
33, 423
matching tests, 439–42
mathematics, 46, 243–44, 303, 598 ff.
maturity, emotional, 125–26; intellectual, 394; sexual, 127–28
memorizing, 264–67, 285
mental age, 83, 136
mental development, 136 ff.
mental discipline. See transfer of
training
mental disease, 208–9
mental hygiene, 199 ff.; course in, 103,
218 ff.; development of, 199–200;
improvement as result of treatment,
210; relation of teacher, 202
mental set, 413, 452
methods of study, 378
Mills College, 390
minimum essentials, 240–43, 307
Minnesota, University of, 65 ff., 142,
313, 390
modification of attitudes, 181–85
moodiness, 216–17
motivation. See incentives
Mt. Pleasant College, 26
multiple choice tests, 433–37; values,
435
multiplication of courses. See duplication
Muskingum College, 26

nervousness, 214–15
nonacademic interests, 232, 385–86
nonsense syllables, 222, 282
normal curve, 470–71
North Central Association, 90
note taking, 261–62, 380
number of colleges, 3, 5, 6
number of teachers, 9–11, 534, 539–40

oath of allegiance, 525
objectives, 15 ff.; changes in, 20 ff.;
formulation of, 29 ff.; for a course,

31 ff.; methods for determining,
15–20
objective tests, 427 ff.; effect on study
methods, 449–52; good examples,
443–49; nature, 428–29; relation to
essay tests, 449–50; types, 429 ff.;
use of in colleges, 428
occupational status, 85
occupations, 70, 77
off-campus activities, 344, 518, 522,
531–32
Ohio College Association, 82, 83
Ohio State University, 239
old-age security, 550
open book examination, 196
oral examination, 454 ff.
Oregon, University of, 313
organization, 485 ff.
organizations. See extra-curricular activities
orientation, 103
outlining test, 437–39
overlapping, courses. See duplicating;
high school and college. See articulation

paragraph reading, 379
Pennsylvania survey, 83, 276, 277
pensions, 550
percentile, explanation of, 81
persecution, ideas of, 217–18
personal difficulties. See maladjustment
personality, measurement of, 220;
measurement used in prediction,
301; student types, 213 ff.; teachers',
577 ff.
personnel officers, duties of, 98 ff.;
titles of, 98
personnel movement, reasons for, 94–
98
personnel point of view, 115
personnel work, 93 ff.; records, 99 ff.,
104; teacher's relation to, 101, 104,
106, 114 ff.; values of, 104, 105
Ph.D. degree, 536–37
philosophy of life, 70, 71, 124, 125
physical development, 126 ff.
physics. See chemistry
placement bureau, 102
plant pathology, 338
policies of a college, 494, 497
poor teachers, 561–62, 585–88; characteristics of, 561–62
population. See enrollment
praise versus punishment, 223–24
precollege courses, 69
prediction, aptitude tests, 293–94; college board examinations, 301; decrease in, 297; general level, 292 ff.;
intelligence tests, 292; marks, 297–
98; specific subjects, 302 ff.; use of
scores, 307–8